Greek and Egyptian Mythologies

Greek and Egyptian Mythologies

Compiled by

YVES BONNEFOY

Translated under the direction of
WENDY DONIGER

by Gerald Honigsblum,
Danielle Beauvais, Teresa Lavender Fagan, Dorothy Figuiera,
Barry Friedman, Louise Guiney, John Leavitt,
Louise Root, Michael Sells, Bruce Sullivan, and David White

The University of Chicago Press • *Chicago and London*

Y V E S   B O N N E F O Y,
a scholar and poet of world renown, is
professor of comparative poetics, Collège de France.
Among his many works to have appeared in English, two
have been published by the University of Chicago Press—a
volume of poetry, *In the Shadow's Light* (1991), and a work
of criticism, *The Act and Place of Poetry* (1989), both
translated by John T. Naughton.

W E N D Y   D O N I G E R
is the Mircea Eliade Professor in the
Divinity School, and professor in the Department of South
Asian Languages and Civilizations, the Committee on Social
Thought, and the College, at the University of Chicago.
Under the name of Wendy Doniger O'Flaherty she has written,
among other books, *Women, Androgynes, and Other Mythical
Beasts* (1980), *Dreams, Illusion, and Other Realities* (1984),
and *Tales of Sex and Violence: Folklore, Sacrifice, and
Danger in the Jaiminīya Brāhmaṇa* (1985), all published
by the University of Chicago Press.

The University of Chicago Press, Chicago 60637
The University of Chicago Press, Ltd., London

© 1991, 1992 by The University of Chicago
All rights reserved. Published 1992
Printed in the United States of America

01 00 99 98 97 96 95 94 93 92   5 4 3 2 1

This paperback is drawn from *Mythologies*, compiled by
Yves Bonnefoy, translated under the direction of Wendy Doniger,
and published by the University of Chicago Press in 1991.
That work was originally published as *Dictionnaire
des mythologies et des religions des sociétés traditionnelles et
du monde antique*, sous la direction de Yves Bonnefoy
publié avec le concours du Centre National
des Lettres, © 1981, Flammarion, Paris.

The preparation of the complete English edition was
supported by grants from the French Ministry of Culture,
the Andrew W. Mellon Foundation, and the
National Endowment for the Humanities.

This book is printed on acid-free paper.

Paperback ISBN: 0-226-06454-9

Library of Congress Cataloging-in-Publication Data

Dictionnaire des mythologies et des religions des sociétés
traditionnelles et du monde antique. English. Selections.
    Greek and Egyptian mythologies / compiled by Yves Bonnefoy;
translated under the direction of Wendy Doniger by Gerald Honigsblum
. . . [et al.].
        p. cm.
    Includes bibliographical references and index.
    1. Mythology, Greek—Encyclopedias.   2. Mythology, Egyptian—
Encyclopedias.   I. Bonnefoy, Yves.   II. Title.
BL782.D477 1992
292.1'3—dc20   92-15541
                                                          CIP

Contents

PART 3   EGYPT

Preface to the Paperback Edition

This is one of four paperback volumes drawn from the full, clothbound, two-volume English-language edition of Yves Bonnefoy's *Mythologies*. These paperbacks are not an afterthought, but were part of the publication plan from the very beginning. Indeed, one of the reasons why we restructured the original French edition as we did was in order ultimately to make these separate volumes available. For though there is of course a sweep and majesty in the full editions, both French and English, a breathtaking scope that is the true raison d'être of the work as a whole, there is also, in the English version, a pattern that allows readers to focus on one culture at a time. And it is with such readers in mind that the University of Chicago Press is issuing these paperbacks, which will include (in addition to the present volume) *Roman and European Mythologies*, *Asian Mythologies*, and *African and American Mythologies*. Each book draws from the full work not only the culturally specific material but also the two prefaces and the general introductory essays, which deal with methodological issues pertaining to all the cultures discussed.

Since each culture poses different problems, and each section of essays embodies the work of a different group of French scholars, each has its own methodological flavor and its own contribution to make to the more culturally specific study of mythology. This volume, on Greece and Egypt, is valuable, I think, not because (like some of the other volumes) it presents new data otherwise unavailable, but, on the contrary, because it treats the most basic of all mythologies known to English-speaking readers, the mythologies that most people think of when they think of mythology at all. One might therefore argue that its weakness is in simply providing one more book on a subject that has been done to death already, but such an argument does not apply here. Greek mythology, more than any other, continues to provide the *point d'appui* for European scholars who wish to blaze new paths in new disciplines. It is no accident, after all, that Sigmund Freud used the myth of Oedipus as the focus of his revolutionary theory of psychosexual interactions in the nuclear family, and that Claude Lévi-Strauss, many decades later, took the same myth for his paradigmatic example of a new method of mythological analysis. So, too, the great scholars of the French school whose work is collected here have used the Greek myths to develop their own new disciplines of semiotics and textual criticism, their own new theories of cultural history and human symbolism.

In the nineteenth and early twentieth centuries, it was British scholars that pioneered the study of Greek mythology and, more particularly, the use of Greek mythology to develop their own universalizing theories of culture. The Cambridge school of myth-and-ritual, led by Lord Raglan, Jane Ellen Harrison, and Sir James George Frazer, dominated the scene for decades, supplemented by F. Max Müller's work on comparative Indo-European mythology at Oxford. The innovative translations, commentaries, and analyses by British scholars such as E. R. Dodds and Robert Graves are still part of our legacy, though a legacy that we now use with considerable caution and criticism. But since World War II, it is French scholarship that has made the greatest contribution to the field of classics in both England and America. Some, including myself, would argue that they have entirely dominated it. The works of Vernant, Vidal-Naquet, and Detienne, instead of (or, better yet, in addition to) Frazer and Graves, are what students of the classics cut their teeth on now.

The work of these French scholars is available elsewhere, in French and in English, but for the most part only in the form of long, rather difficult, often rather technical books. The great virtue of the present volume is that it presents a collection of short essays, each of which assumes no specialized knowledge, by scholars who have written whole tomes on many of these subjects. This is therefore the best, indeed the only way to get in a condensed and nontechnical form what each of them has written.

A word about Egypt: We chose to include Egypt in this volume, rather than in a volume about the ancient Near East, for several reasons. Greek mythology, as has been recently argued by Martin Bernal and others, owes a great deal to Egyptian mythology; and the Greeks themselves, from Herodotus on, have always acknowledged this debt. Moreover, Greek mythology in its interaction with Egyptian mythology (as in, for instance, the mythologies of Attis and Osiris) continued to exert an important influence upon Roman and European mythologies. The nature of that influence becomes further apparent in *Roman and European Mythologies*.

Wendy Doniger

Preface to the English Edition
of the Complete Work

Yves Bonnefoy in his preface (which follows this preface) explains why he organized his book—and after all, this is his book—as he did. He had good reasons, and he is eloquent in their defense. But it remains for me to explain the ways in which the English edition differs from the French in more than the language in which it is expressed, since some of what M. Bonnefoy will say does not in fact apply to this edition at all, particularly in what concerns the arrangement of the articles.

M. Bonnefoy graciously if reluctantly allowed me to re-structure his work. As he put it, "Of course I will miss the formula of the dictionary, for the reasons that I indicate in my preface (the rupture with all the apriority of classification, the possibility of surprising juxtapositions, in short, the irony), *but I absolutely do not oppose* your choice, which is in response to very good reasons, and which is better adapted to the English-speaking world in which your edition will appear. I therefore give you carte blanche, with the understanding that you will publish my preface as is. For it is a good idea to point out that the book was originally what I indicate in that preface—this will bring in a supplementary point for reflection."[1] On another occasion,[2] he remarked that there was another consideration (one that, I must confess, had not occurred to me) that had persuaded him to organize his original version of the book in what he termed "the random way," while we might be able to rearrange our version in "the more organized way": French students, he pointed out, have only limited access to open stacks in the French libraries (since there is not enough room to accommodate them) and few of the bookstores are quiet enough to read in. French students therefore have apparently not formed the habit of browsing—except in a dictionary.

Without denying the validity of his arguments, let me state my reasons for the reorganization. And in order to justify the changes, I shall first state my conception of the strengths and weaknesses of the French work itself.

The Strengths and Weaknesses of the French Edition

To begin with, even in its French form, with all the articles arranged alphabetically, it is not a dictionary, nor even an encyclopedia, nor a dispassionate fact-book even for those topics that it covers (and many major items are omitted). It is a quirky and idiosyncratic set of essays, long and short, by a particular group of mythologists, most of whom are French and all of whom participate in the French school of mythology in its broadest sense. The patent omissions and biases have prompted a certain amount of criticism leveled at the French edition,[3] criticism of imbalances, of inconsistencies (in the selection of topics, in the manner of their treatment, in the style, in the methodologies, etc.), and of the choice of illustrations, as well as more substantive criticisms of the interpretations.

Some of these criticisms are just; some are not. The arguments about what *is* there (what is said about the mythologies that are discussed) are interesting; the arguments about what is *not* there are, I think, beside the point. Many of the scholars involved in the project chose not to write about what other people (including certain reviewers) regarded as "central" or "basic" themes of the mythologies they treated; they wrote long essays on the subjects they cared about personally, and gave short shrift to subjects to which other scholars might have given pride of place. The reader who continues perversely to look for ways in which the glass is half empty rather than half full will notice immediately, for instance, that there is almost nothing about Islam or Judaism in the book. This is primarily because Yves Bonnefoy had originally intended to save this material for another volume, on the mythologies of monotheistic religions—a volume that has not yet materialized. It might be argued that this justification is disingenuous, for some of the very best material in the extant volume is on Christianity, which is by most standards monotheistic. But on closer inspection it is quite clear that while the book does treat the appropriation of classical mythology by Christianity, and the incorporation of "pagan mythologies" into what might be called "rural Catholicism," it rightly does not treat main-stream, monotheistic Christianity as a mythology. Moreover, to have dealt with the central traditions of Islam and Judaism in this way would certainly have been tantamount to a betrayal of what the adherents of those religions regard as their basic tenets. Yet this Jewish and Islamic silence is also in part accounted for by the simple fact that the authors who were assembled to prepare this book did not choose to write articles on these subjects. Similarly, the African articles deal almost exclusively (though hardly surprisingly) with Francophone Africa; yet these articles constitute superb paradigms for the study of other African mythologies. So, too, there are only two articles on Buddhism per se, and there is virtually nothing about Buddhism (or Islam, for that matter) in Southeast Asia (though there is a great deal of wonderful material about indigenous Southeast Asian religions, and those two articles on Buddhism are fascinating). On the other hand, there is extensive coverage of the Turks and Mongols, whose mythologies are relatively unknown to Western readers. This sort of imbalance might be regarded as a kind of mythological affirmative action.

This is, therefore, certainly not an encyclopedia. In a famous painting by the surrealist René Magritte, a caption in his neat script, under a painting of what is clearly a pipe, declares, "This is not a pipe." I would have liked to write on the cover of this book, "This is not a dictionary of mythologies." Rather like the ugly duckling that turned out to be a terrific swan, as a dictionary this book leaves much to be desired, but as a book of mythologies it is superb, indeed peerless. If it is not a dictionary, what *is* it, then? It is a most exciting (far more exciting than an encyclopedia ought to be) collection of essays on *some* aspects of *some* mythologies, written by a group of brilliant and philosophically complex French scholars. It is highly opinionated and original, and should inspire hot, not cold, reactions. Like all multiauthored works, it is a mixed bag; there is some jargon, some wild theorizing, some boring surveys, some overclever interpretation, and some of what I would regard as simple errors of fact, but there is also an overwhelming proportion of very sound and/or brilliant articles about mythology in general and about a number of mythologies in particular. This is not primarily a book, for instance, to consult for all the stories about Apollo; one has Robert Graves for that (though this is a far better book with which to begin to formulate some ideas about the meaning of Apollo). It is, however, a book in which to discover the delightful and useful fact that in the ritual celebration of the Brazilian god Omolu, who is of Yoruba origin but came to be syncretized with Saint Lazarus, people dance to a beat called "he kills someone and eats him." I was thrilled to come upon a hauntingly sad and beautiful Inuit myth about the cycle of transmigration of a mistreated woman, a myth that agrees, in astonishing detail, with certain complex myths of transmigration that I know from medieval Sanskrit philosophical texts. Other readers will undoubtedly stumble upon strange stories that are curiously familiar to them—stumble upon them quite by chance, just as Yves Bonnefoy intended them to do.

But if the selection is not as complete as a dictionary should ideally be, neither is it as arbitrary as a nondictionary can be. Most of the great mythological traditions are covered, and within those areas most of the important myths are treated. But this is not the point. What is treated very thoroughly indeed is the problem of *how to understand a mythology,* what questions to ask, what patterns to look for. More precisely, this is a book that demonstrates what happens when a combination of two particular methodologies, those of Georges Dumézil and Claude Lévi-Strauss, is applied to *any* mythology. It is, as its title claims (in English as in French), not so much a book about myths (sacred narratives) as a book about mythologies (whole systems of myths, or even systems of ideas about myths). It is that rare and wonderful fusion, a book about methodology that simultaneously puts the methodology to work and shows you just what it can and cannot do. It is a mythology.

Many of these articles tell the reader how to study mythology in general and, more important, how to study each particular body of mythology, how to solve (or, more often, to approach) the particular problems that each mythology presents. Some tell the reader why it is not possible to write an article about that particular mythology at all (a consideration that does not, however, prevent the author from writing the article in which this assertion is made). The most hilarious example of this (I will leave the reader to decide which article it is) is almost an unconscious satire on the pusillanimity of scholars in certain fields; in it, the author goes on for pages and pages (it is one of the longest articles in the book) telling us, over and over, why there are insufficient data, why the data that we have are skewed, why the extant interpretations of the data are skewed, why all hypotheses and generalizations about the data are worthless, why in fact it is impossible to make any valid statement about the mythology at all. This is in its way a masterpiece, a kind of Zen nonarticle on a nonsubject, a surreal piece of nonscholarship worthy of Samuel Beckett. And yet even this article has its value here as a striking example of one particular methodology, one approach to the subject, that argues in great detail, and rightly, the obstacles that oppose any truly responsible survey of the subject.

But this is the exception, not the rule. The book teems with marvelous primary material, both myths and rituals (with which many myths are inextricably linked), using the materials and the methodological considerations to animate one another, the soul of data within the body of theory, and the soul of theory within the body of data. Sometimes the methodology is in the foreground, sometimes the data; usually they are in a fine balance. In the Greek and European sections, for instance, there are startling reinterpretations of well-known stories, or new emphases on previously overlooked details in well-known stories; many of the articles on the Greeks demonstrate the cutting edge of French structuralism. As Arthur Adkins has remarked, "The dictionary in its French version is a truly remarkable work. The Greek section in particular is quite unlike any other dictionary known to me. [It] for the most part presents the views of the Paris school, and the writers come out fighting. The Paris school is undoubtedly producing the most interesting work in the field at present. . . . [The work] represents more of a *parti pris* than the title 'Dictionary' may suggest."[4] The Vietnamese section, by contrast, abundantly documents a fascinating mythology that is virtually unknown to the English-speaking world, and presents it, moreover, in the context of an enlightened political awareness that is almost unprecedented in scholarly treatments of mythology anywhere (but that is also a notable virtue of the articles in this volume that deal with the Americas and Oceania).

If this is a book as much about method as it is about myths, what is the method? It is a masterpiece of what might be called trifunctional structuralism, a joint festschrift for Claude Lévi-Strauss and Georges Dumézil, a vision of the world of mythology seen through their eyes, la vie en Lévi-Strauss and Dumézil. To combine the methodologies of these two scholars is in itself a most extraordinary and fruitful achievement. If I may oversimplify both approaches for a moment, Lévi-Strauss's basic method, a variant of Hegelian dialectic, is to seek the intellectual or logical framework of the myth in binary oppositions that are mediated by a third term; the Dumézilian approach is to gloss the main figures of a myth in terms of three functions that have social referents: religion and government, defense, and material production. These two theories are in no way contradictory, especially if one resolves the potential conflict between Dumézilian tripartition and Lévi-Straussian bipolarization by taking into account the mediating third term and thus making Lévi-Strauss, too, tripartite. In this sense, both of them operate with triads, though very different triads. Furthermore, they complement rather than contradict one another because they focus on different levels (Lévi-Strauss on abstract intellectual concepts, Dumézil on social functions). Combined as they are in this volume, they are startlingly innovative.

Indeed, the beauty of the book is that it is not doctrinaire in its application of the theories of these two great scholars, but rather creative and imaginative. Dumézil's trifunctional analysis of Indo-European mythology is applied, quite loosely to be sure, even beyond the bounds of the Indo-European world (where it is, properly speaking, no longer trifunctional but tripartite), and a general way of thinking in terms of oppositions and inversions forms the armature of many analyses in which the name of Lévi-Strauss is not actually invoked. The search for tripartitions of both sorts is the driving force behind many of the analyses in this book.

The book is so very French that I thought seriously of putting the word "French" in the title of the English edition: *Mythologies According to the Contemporary French School*, or *The View from France*, or *Essays in the French Style, A French Collection, A Paris Collection, The French Connection*, and so forth. Yves Bonnefoy's remarks, in his preface, explaining why he chose primarily French scholars are delightfully, if unconsciously, Francophile. He has maintained elsewhere that the preponderance of French scholars was simply a natural outcome of choosing to organize the scholarship from the geographical center of the project, Paris, rather than to range over the world at random. But as anyone who has ever had the privilege of working at the Sorbonne will immediately realize, most French scholars think that the only people who know anything are other French scholars. In this instance, at least, they would be right: such is the hegemony of French scholarship in the field of mythology right now that a well-read American or British mythologist would probably draw on precisely these same "French" approaches.

This is one of the great values of the book: it represents, as few other works in any field do, the achievements of the *crème de la crème* of an entire generation of French scholarship in a large and important field. Yves Bonnefoy himself has remarked that he loves the book because it freezes a moment in time, in history, and in space; it is the embodiment of the beauty of the Ecole Pratique.

But in a way, the guiding spirit of the book is not just that of the twin gods, Dumézil and Lévi-Strauss. It is the spirit of Yves Bonnefoy himself. This is, after all, a book put together by a poet, not by a philologist. The editor of this nondictionary is also, let me hasten to say, a scholar of the first rank, but he is at heart a poet. The reader who keeps this in mind is more likely to get from the book what it has to give than the reader who picks it up hoping that it will be a kind of mythological Guinness book of records.

The Restructuring of the English Edition

We decided to restructure the book in order to minimize its weaknesses, emphasize its sometimes hidden strengths, and make it useful to the English-speaking reader in new ways. Its primary weakness is, as I have admitted, that it is not a true encyclopedia. If the English edition were arranged alphabetically, as the French edition is, readers might look for things and not find them and get mad, as some of the French reviewers did; and, on the other hand, readers might

overlook a lot of strange and beautiful essays that no one would ever dream of looking up on purpose at all.

Bonnefoy in his preface explains why he wanted to use a dictionary format: to avoid all prearranged categories, to let the reader find things by chance, to allow accidental juxtapositions to give rise to unexpected ideas. But to some extent this argues for a false naïveté on the part of the reader and even, perhaps, on the part of the editor, for both of them *are looking for something*. In choosing the arbitrariness of alphabetical order, Bonnefoy is indeed shuffling the deck; but he does still have a deck, which, like all decks, is highly structured. The alphabetical shuffle conceals the true order but does not destroy it. Thus, for instance, all the articles on a certain subject are written by a single author, an expert on that subject. Clearly the articles were originally commissioned in this way, and they are still listed this way in the front of the French edition. And each author does have his methodological presuppositions, which the reader encounters every time he or she wanders (arbitrarily, accidentally) into that territory. Bonnefoy chose to conceal the patterns that he saw in the material in order to let readers discover them by chance; I have chosen to set out in the open the patterns that I see, and to let readers decide whether or not they want to follow those patterns. The difference lies in what sort of browsing is encouraged, cross-cultural (through the French edition's physical juxtaposition of the major articles on creation or on sacrifice) or intracultural (through the English edition's grouping of all the Siberian or Celtic articles).

Several of the translators, the Honigsblums in particular, arranged the work according to geographic areas or cultures, which made it easier to check the consistent use of technical terms. Gradually it occurred to us that this arrangement would also be useful to readers. Bonnefoy chose to mix the cultures together to encourage cross-cultural *aperçus*; I chose to separate out each culture to encourage consecutive reading in each tradition. (Another, related advantage of the present arrangement lies in the fact that this arrangement will make it possible in the future to publish sections of the work as individual books, making them available to specialists in particular cultural fields.) For the overall structure I decided to use a kind of geographical swing: beginning with Africa, then traveling up through the Near East, the ancient Mediterranean, the Indo-European world; remaining in place geographically but moving forward in time to later European culture, then back in time to South Asia; on in both space and time to Southeast Asia, East Asia, Inner Asia; across the Bering Strait to North America, South America; and finishing the journey paradisiacally in the South Pacific. Within each category of culture (Greek, Celtic, etc.), I have put the long, meditative, general essays first, and the shorter, more straightforward dictionary entries second. Several pathbreaking essays that are not tied to a particular culture, and that immediately establish the Dumézilian and structuralist stance of the book, form an introductory sequence.

Of course, since both the French and the English editions have detailed indexes, and the French edition has an outline listing the articles according to cultures, it comes down to a matter of emphasis, for in either edition the reader can find materials that are arranged alphabetically (both in the index and in the body of the work in the French edition, and in the index in the English edition) as well as materials that are grouped according to the culture (in the outline of the French edition, and in the body of the work in the English edition). In the restructured English edition, the reader can still use the index as Bonnefoy suggests the French index might be used, to find his or her favorite Naiad or Norse god, and also to find all the articles on, say, creation, or sacrifice, which cut across methodological lines. This is, after all, the same book, and can ultimately be used in all the same ways.

New problems arise out of this rearrangement, however, for some cultures don't really fit into any of the large categories—Turks and Mongols, Armenians and Albanians, Ossets and Georgians, Siberians, Malagasy, Maghreb—and so I had to settle for putting them where they seemed least out of place. Another disadvantage of my rearrangement is the fact that it exposes repetitions, necessary in an encyclopedia (where the author of any one article, who cannot assume that the reader will have read any other article, may therefore have to resupply a certain amount of basic material), but rather jarring in a book such as this (where the reader may well find it annoying to read the same story, or the same theory, almost verbatim in consecutive articles). A good example of this recycling is provided by the very first part, on West Africa, with its recurrent motifs of twinning and sexual mutilation; another occurs in the South Asian section, which pivots around the sacrificial pole and the avatar.

I decided not to cut any of these repetitions, however, for several reasons. First of all, I decided not to abridge or revise (a decision I will attempt to justify below). Second, some readers may only pick up isolated articles and will therefore need the basic information that also appears in other articles. And, finally, these repetitions demonstrate how certain scholars always think in terms of a limited number of particular myths, dragging them into whatever other subject they are supposed to be discussing. For scholars, like their native informants, do just what Lévi-Strauss says they do: they continually rework the same themes in a kind of academic bricolage, and no two variants are ever *quite* alike.

For the most part, I think the rearrangement is a positive move. For one thing, it makes it possible to *read* the book, instead of merely browsing in it or looking things up in it (though, as I have said, readers can still engage in both of these activities in the English edition). For another, it may prove more useful in this form not only to mythophiles and area specialists, but to people interested in French anthropology and philosophy.

The book is therefore *restructured*, because of course it was originally highly structured, ideologically if not organizationally. Its English title, *Mythologies*, to me echoes the wonderful books by Roland Barthes and William Butler Yeats, both with the same title, and further resonates with the French title of the great Lévi-Strauss trilogy, *Mythologiques* (treacherously translated in one English edition as *A Science of Mythology*). *Mythologies* has, finally, the advantage of being simultaneously an English and a French word, a last attempt at bilinguality before the Fall into the English version.

The English Translation

This edition was prepared "under my direction" in not nearly so important a sense as the original was "sous la direction de Yves Bonnefoy." Certain parallel procedures probably exacerbated rather than minimized the inevitable slip twixt French cup and English lip, and one of these was the employment of a team of English scholars to translate the text that was originally composed by a team of French scholars.

Gerald Honigsblum translated the entire second volume of the French edition, with the editorial assistance of Bonnie Birtwistle Honigsblum. The first volume was translated by a group of professional translators (Danielle Beauvais, Teresa Lavender Fagan, Louise Guiney, Louise Root, Michael Sells) and another group consisting of some of my students in the history of religions (Dorothy Figueira, Barry Friedman, Daniel Gold, John Leavitt, and David White). Their initials follow those of the original authors of the French articles. Bruce Sullivan did the bibliographies.

The translated articles were then checked for accuracy (in the transliteration of names, technical terms, and so forth) by specialists in each of the particular fields. Arthur Adkins did by far the most difficult task, working painstakingly and courageously through the enormous and often very tricky articles on the Greeks and Romans. Lawrence Sullivan vetted Africa and the Americas for us; Robert Ritner, Egypt; Walter Farber, Mesopotamia; Dennis Pardee, Semites; Richard Beal, Hittites; Laurie Patton, Celts; Ann Hoffman, Norse; Zbigniew Golab, Slavs; Frank Paul Bowman, Richard Luman, and David Tracy, early Christianity; Anthony Grafton, medieval and renaissance Europe; Françoise Meltzer, modern Europe; Charles Keyes, Southeast Asia; Anthony Yu and Jane Geaney, China; Gary Ebersole, Japan; Bruce Cummings, Korea; Matthew Kapstein and Per Kvaerne, Tibet; Robert Dankoff, Turks and Mongols. I did the South Asian and Indo-Iranian sections.

There are thus several levels at which inconsistencies—in style, in format (citations of texts, abbreviations), in transliteration, in ways of dealing with specific untranslatable concepts—could have slipped in: differences between the technical languages (not to say jargons) and the methodologies employed by the various academic guilds that regard themselves as the proprietors of each culture (anthropologists in Africa, Sanskritists in India, archaeologists in Sumer, and so forth); differences between the approaches of individual French authors, between our several translators, between our experts; and, over the long haul, differences in my own decisions at particular stages of the final supervision, and in the decisions of our copyeditors at the Press. We have tried to minimize the inconsistencies, but we know that many remain.

We left the bibliographies basically in their original form, with the following exceptions: in some cases we have substituted English editions for French editions, or extended the dates of continuing series, and in several cases we have added supplementary bibliographies (clearly designated as such and distinguished from the original French text). But many bibliographies and articles still cite the French editions of texts that have subsequently appeared in English.

We did not follow the usual practice of citing standard English translations of Greek or Latin or Sanskrit works that the French, naturally enough, cited in French. Instead, we translated the French translation of the classical text into English. At first glance this procedure may seem unwise, but we found it necessary because the French version of the classical text (and the subsequent analysis, which depended upon that version) often differed so dramatically from any extant English translation that the sense of the discussion would be totally obscured by the introduction of such a translation. We made an occasional exception, using a standard English translation where there were long quotations not directly analyzed in the French text, or where the available English translation was very close to what the French author had made of the original. (We were also, unfortunately, forced to translate back into English a few citations from English primary and secondary sources that time and other constraints prevented us from obtaining in the original form, and to retranslate several entire French articles that we know were originally written in English, because the English originals were for one reason or another no longer available to us.)

We decided to give Greek and Roman names, wherever possible, in the form used by the *Oxford Classical Dictionary,* which unfortunately is inherently inconsistent. The *OCD* has the advantage of avoiding pedantry by spelling most names in the way that people in English-speaking countries are used to seeing them. This means Latinizing most of the familiar Greek names (not, of course, substituting Roman names: thus we have Heracles, not Herakles, for the Greek god, but Hercules only for the Roman god), but not Latinizing the unfamiliar Greek names, and not Romanizing any of the Greek words when they are not names. All words, including proper names, that are printed in the Greek alphabet in the French edition have here been transliterated. No accents are indicated, and macrons are used not to distinguish long and short *a*, *i*, and *u*, but only on *e* and *o*, to distinguish epsilon from eta and omicron from omega.[5]

We also sought to standardize the transliteration of non-Greek names and terms, such as Gilgameš (vs. Gilgamesh) and Śiva (vs. Shiva), and we used the Pinyin system for most Chinese names.[6] But this general policy was sometimes overruled by the demands of a particular article. We strove for consistency within each article—using English titles for Greek works where the meaning was needed and traditional Latinized titles where it was not, full citations or abbreviations as appropriate, and so forth. Assuming, perhaps snobbishly, that anyone who couldn't read French couldn't read Greek or Latin, I have translated many titles and quotations that my sanguine French colleague, Yves Bonnefoy, had left in their classical splendor. Except for the titles of certain works generally known to English speakers in their original form, and terms that either are familiar to readers or have no English equivalent, I have translated everything, even terms like *polis* (for the most part), and *savoir faire*, and, sometimes, *par excellence*. I fear that this may insult some readers, but I suspect that it will be a welcome (and in any case probably invisible) crutch to *hoi polloi.*

Despite everything, the book remains idiosyncratic, but the idiosyncrasies are in large part a true reflection of the original French edition. In general, we have not *corrected* the original text at all, since, as I noted above, the work is valuable not only for the information and ideas that it contains but for being *what it is*, a moment frozen in time, a fly in amber, an incarnation of the École Pratique as it was in 1981, warts and all. The warts include matters of style and politics, such as sexist and occasionally racist language in the original text. These problems were sometimes ameliorated and sometimes exacerbated by the transition from French to English. Thus, to ameliorate, we often chose to translate *homme* as "human" rather than "man"; but the English "savage" (often more apt than "wild" or "primitive") exacerbates the negative connotations of *sauvage*, which the French often use in a positive sense.

Our respect for the integrity of the French text made us resist the temptation to correct what we regarded as errors in that text. (Of course, we made our own errors, and unfortunately the reader who does not have the French edition will not know, if he or she finds a mistake, which side of the

Atlantic it originated on.) We certainly made no attempt to correct such major problems as wrongheaded (in my opinion) opinions, nor to decipher the impenetrable semioticisms in one or two articles or to excise the unreadable lists in others. At the other end of the spectrum, however, we did correct typographic errors and a few outright howlers (such as a reference to the *Iliad* when the *Odyssey* was clearly intended). It was trickier to decide what to do about the middle ground: infelicities of expression, repetitions, and so forth. Of course we tried to clarify unclear thoughts, though we certainly did not always succeed. But for the most part, we respected our French colleagues' right to live with their own sins.

At first we made no attempt to smooth out the English, striving only to make the French thought accessible in English, leaving it awkward when it was awkward. We did try, however, to say well in English what was well said in French. In the end, however, our collective gorge rising again and again in response to such massive proportions of translatorese and the fatal attraction of the *cliché juste*, we did try to relax the translation a bit.

By and large, I opted for fidelity over beauty. This is rather a shame, for the original French text is, on the whole, very beautiful. Not for the first time I take comfort in Claude Lévi-Strauss's famous dictum that, whereas poetry may be lost in translation, "the mythical value of myth remains preserved through the worst translation."[7] I fear that we have lost much of Yves Bonnefoy's poetry; I can only hope that we have found, for the English reader, most of Yves Bonnefoy's mythology.

Wendy Doniger

NOTES

1. Yves Bonnefoy, personal communication, 28 June 1984.
2. Notes on a meeting with Yves Bonnefoy, 6 June 1988.
3. As, for example, by Robert Turcan, in "Mythologies et religions: Notes Critiques, à propos du *Dictionnaire des Mythologies* . . . ," in *Revue de l'Histoire des Religions* 200, no. 2 (April–June 1983): 189–98.
4. Arthur Adkins, personal communication, 2 March 1988.
5. Our attempt to follow, consistently, the above rule resulted in the following apparent inconsistencies. A distinction is made between the treatment of two forms of the same word when it is used both as a name and as a noun: thus we have Eros (the god) and *erōs* (the emotion), Cyclops (plural: Cyclopes) for the individual and *kuklops* for the class of creature. Exceptions to the general Latinization occur in certain familiar spellings particularly with regard to *clk* (Clytemnestra, following the regular policy, but Kronos, following general usage); to *-osl-us* (Pontus, following the rule, but Helios, following general usage); and to certain plurals (Kronides, but Oceanids and Atreidae; Melissae, but Moirai). In general, upsilon is transliterated as *y* in Latinized names, such as Polyphemus, but as *u* in nouns, such as *polumētis*. And so forth.
6. For the Yoruba names, we chose to follow the French edition in using a simplified transliteration, for the system that is technically, and politically, correct is extremely cumbersome and incompatible with the methods used in other parts of the work.
7. Claude Lévi-Strauss, *Structural Anthropology* (New York 1963), 210.

Preface to the French Edition of the Complete Work

I

A few words of introduction, not in justification of the enterprise, but in order to clarify certain of its intentions and various points of method.

One of our primary convictions was of the need to adopt the dictionary format. Encyclopedias, invariably too lengthy to be read in a single sitting, are usually approached through the index, thereby functioning like dictionaries but with certain disadvantages that dictionaries do not have. For one thing, readers of encyclopedias are deprived of those sudden juxtapositions that alphabetical order can effect between two topics that may have something in common but occur in different contexts: chance encounters from which fresh insights can emerge. And for another thing, an encyclopedia, no matter how rationally intended the order of its contents, cannot but reflect the preconceptions of the time when it was written; it thus rapidly becomes dated and, even, from the very moment of its conception, imposes certain constraints on its readers. We have only to think of the treatises of the not very distant past and their way of drawing distinctions between the Mediterranean world and what is loosely referred to as the Orient, as if western Europeans lived at the center of the world! Progress has been made in this respect, but potentially dangerous prejudices are undeniably still at work in our thinking today. "Any classification of religions . . . will always in some way be factitious or one-sided; none is susceptible to proof," wrote Henri-Charles Puech.[1] Only alphabetical order, arbitrary by definition, can eliminate hidden dogmatism or prevent the consolidation of an error as yet unperceived as such.

Furthermore, and as a corollary to its primary task of rational organization, an encyclopedia also tends toward a kind of unity—if not homogeneity—of discourse; and because any work of this kind attempts to say the most in the least possible number of pages, there will be—in order to achieve coherent exposition of the most important material—an attenuation of what, in a monograph, would remain undiminished or would even be enhanced: diversity of viewpoint, the clash of ideas and methods, to say nothing of the irreconcilability of different scholars' feelings, aspirations, and temperaments. Even when there is consensus on some point, we cannot believe that this disparity, the nutri-ent on which all scholarship thrives, will have lost its seminal value. The advantage of a dictionary, which allows free rein to a greater number of authors, and which facilitates the juxtaposition of both detailed analysis and broad synthesis, is that it can more comfortably, or more immediately, accommodate a living science whose very contradictions and even lapses into confusion serve as a lesson that can inspire, and on which we can reflect. We might say that a dictionary can aspire to a totalization which, because it is still only potential, is less subject to the perils of dogmatic deviation. Within a dictionary's open-ended structure, every aspect of scientific research—classification or comparison, hypothesis or explanation, discovery of a law or conjecture as to its significance—will be allowed to reveal its specificity and find its own level. We may, therefore, regard the dictionary format as the most adequate expression of today's scholarship, which is suspicious of all systems, instinctively realizing the complexity and pluralities inherent in its objects of study as well as the interaction between these objects and its own methods.

There is, in short, a kind of spirit or "genius" in what might simply appear to be the way the subject matter is arranged; and in direct consequence of this conception came the following decision: that in making the choices rendered necessary by the limited space, preference would be given to the process of discovery rather than to what has already been discovered; to new challenges, new departures, and new divergences rather than to the syntheses of the past, even those still found acceptable today. In deciding what to include in the dictionary, our preference has been, in other words, for new problems rather than old (and hence overfamiliar) solutions, even major ones. *Research,* the only endeavor, today, to which we habitually apply the word "pure," has been our true objective. In this book the reader will find what are at this very moment the pivotal points being debated in regard to this or that myth or religious festival, and not a mere enumeration—the comprehensiveness of which would in any case be difficult to establish—of points already settled in the past. And let us remark in passing that, by so doing, we are merely making public, for the sake of a more general reflection, a practice that has already proved itself in certain scientific circles, but only to a privileged few. The introduction to the *Annuaire* of the École des Hautes Études (section V, religions), states that the teaching dispensed by the professors of this institution is a science "in process" and that "those responsible for teaching others will find no better way to exercise their function as the initiating and motivating force behind their students' research than by sharing . . . the results of their own, even if this means admitting to failures." In this dictionary we have not always been quite so radical as these admirable words advise, but we, too, have attempted not to "transmit what is already known, but to demonstrate as concretely as possible how knowledge is acquired, and how it grows."[2]

It should therefore come as no surprise to the reader that some of the assignments normally charged to works on mythology were eliminated from our project at the outset, notably those detailed accounts of demigods, nymphs, demons, genies, and heroes that occupy the forefront of less recent or more conventional studies. Insofar as these figures do not appear prominently among those chosen by contemporary scholars for reevaluation, merely to have listed them and added a few perfunctory remarks about each one—which, as there are thousands of them, is the best we could have done—would have been once again, and once too often, to present only the chaff instead of getting at the grain deep within, to rethrash the oversimplifications of yesteryear with an outward show of scientific objectivity. Apart from a few minor protagonists of Greek myth—retained because of their artistic or literary importance, through centuries of survival or revival or nostalgia for the gods of antiquity—we have chosen to deal, rather, with the innumerable minor characters in the drama of creation and the cosmos within the context of broader-based articles concerned primarily with *structures*: creation, cosmos, sacrifice, the divinity of the waters, divine animals or ancestors, etc.—the structures that modern science has taught us better to discern beneath the apparent disorder of myths. For only through these more active concepts, these more all-encompassing frameworks, can we realize the ultimate meaning of something that has always been only an element in the symbolic totality arising from man's desire to know; only in this way will we be able to perceive the differences, similarities, resonances, and, what is more, the perhaps hidden truth, the quality of mystery, even the power to terrify, that underlies figures who became, in the mirror of classical paintings or in the *Mythologies* of our grandparents, elegant Marsyas or lovable Flora. The reader will, however, be able to find the information that our articles do dispense about many of these tiny sparks from the larger fire, by referring to the index, where many names that he may have regretted not finding more prominently displayed in the columns of the text have been assembled.

We have, on the other hand, been generous in allotting space—and sometimes a great deal of space—to what at first glance might appear to be an excessively specific or technical development on a minor point in a remote religion, or an almost unknown tribe. We have done so because some important aspect of the most recent research in the field is thereby revealed, is therein at work, and the essay is therefore being offered, indirectly, as a concrete example of today's practical methods. In a situation of overwhelming possibility, the guiding principle presiding over the choices we did in fact make was consistently to prefer the illuminating example over the supposedly exhaustive enumeration; except on those occasions when a truly extensive, minutely scrupulous coverage of a field narrow enough to be included in the book in its entirety could also be made to serve as one of our major exemplary cases. This dictionary is in large measure a *network of examples*, each with some bearing on a particular level or category of religious experience or scien-

tific method; if we have included a study of sacrifice in a religion in which sacrifice is especially important, we have deliberately omitted an article on sacrifice for another region of the world in which, by the same token, animals or the presence of the dead have been selected from a mythic narrative in which they are felt to be essential. The advantage of this principle is that it allows us to plumb the depths, which is one way to achieve universality and thus to speak of everything, despite the occasional appearance of superficiality. The reader will note that our articles are seldom very short; allowing for the stylistic terseness characteristic of dictionaries, we strove for an average length that would permit us to publish what are actually brief monographs; I am pleased to note that the present enterprise has served as the occasion for much research, some of it completely new, either in subject matter or in approach. The reader will thus be a witness to the creative process in action.

And if he should be annoyed because he cannot find in our table of contents or even our index some name or subject to which several lines have been devoted in the *Oxford Classical Dictionary* or the *Real-Encyclopädie*, he should also bear in mind the intellectual character of our endeavor, and should listen in the depths of our pages for the stirrings of research in process, that catalyst through which, from the womb of needs as yet unsatisfied, hypotheses as yet unproved, oppositions and even conflicts, are born the research projects, innovations, and ideas that tomorrow will provide the material for new articles in the still open dictionary and, later, for a whole new volume. Any dictionary worthy of the name must affirm, with real fervor, that it will continue thus; that is, that it will turn into a serial appearing twelve times a century, an institution whose past becomes future, a rallying ground that will help keep a discipline alive.

II

What is this discipline, exactly, in our own case? And how did we define or, rather, how were we able to recognize the subjects appropriate to our dictionary?

It is entitled *Dictionary of Mythologies and Religions in Traditional Societies and in the Ancient World*—thus, apparently, introducing two distinct subjects. What really is the subject, and what, in terms of specific content, will the reader find in the book?

Let us state at the outset that what our French publisher wanted was a "Dictionary of Mythologies," explanation enough in itself, because it refers to a specific area and one abundantly rich in problems of great scientific interest today. To quote again from section V of the *Annuaire*: the current tendency for the science of religion to assume a central place in anthropological studies is due to "the increasing importance being accorded to 'myth' for the interpretation and comprehension of the human phenomenon. On this point, the most diametrically opposed schools of contemporary thought are undivided. Religious myths have attained highest priority as objects of study by the most disparate scientific disciplines and schools of philosophy, whether they are regarded as images or projections of a system of communications among men; as manifestations of archetypes of the psyche; or as the special objects of a phenomenology of human consciousness . . ."[3] Certainly we no longer believe, as did the Socrates of Plato's *Phaedrus*, that there is no need to study myth because the important thing is to know ourselves—rather the reverse. Mythology appears to us ever more clearly as one of the great aspects of our relationship with ourselves, as well as being a conception of the world and the terrestrial environment that has been undoubtedly useful; we therefore ought to draw up a balance sheet— however provisional—of the discoveries made by the present century in the various chapters of man's reflection on myth. That there is still not complete agreement among scholars as to how myth should be defined matters little; that the problem of definition may even be premature also matters little, precisely because the plurality inherent in the enterprise of a dictionary as defined above actually makes the juxtaposition of contradictory propositions seem natural and allows them to be compared with one another. Neither in this introduction nor in the body of the book, where the actual choices have been made, will the reader find a definition of myth decreed as law, as if the die were cast. Our only methodological limitation, one that in our view safeguards the rights both of the study of myths as archetypes and of the methods appropriate to myths approached as systems of communication, is to apprehend myth on the level of collective representations, where, as one of our contributors writes, myth is "the form in which the essential truths of a particular society are articulated and communicated." Despite what may be the apparent freedom of the narrative, our task must be to seek within it a body of collective knowledge in contradistinction to the ephemeral creations of the individual consciousness, no matter how impressive these may be in great novels or poems. Apart from a few fleeting insights, included solely that we might better understand and recognize the limitations we have set for ourselves, there are in our dictionary none of the "personal myths" that come from art and the free play of imagination and that perhaps belong to a dialectic entirely different from those that unite human beings under the sign of their communications in the real world, of their confrontation with real necessities, and that are accompanied and made possible by rituals and beliefs. We have similarly omitted from the book what are sometimes referred to as "modern myths," representations that are circulated by popular literature or the media, myths that do indeed touch many spirits but that differ from the great majority of mythic narratives in that they are not so much the expressions of a society as they are the expressions of a yearning for a different society, or of the fear of forces that the structures of our societies have not integrated. In our view, the place for the study of these is, rather, in a dictionary devoted to the basic categories of religious experience as such, in particular, transcendence, eschatology, and salvation.

In short, the myths in this book have been culled only from the mouths of societies or groups. This does not indicate a refusal to study the connection between myth and the deep structures of the human psyche; it merely delimits, in order to avoid any confusion, an object of thought that could then be connected with others, or analyzed in other ways than has been done here. The one form of individual creativity we did consider appropriate to include, at least through a few major examples, is the reflection of those who, although they may have relied on highly subjective spiritual or philosophical preconceptions, nevertheless attempted—as did Plato, for example, or Cicero—to understand myths as society produces them or assumes them. Objective as contemporary scholarship aspires to be, there are a few preconceptions similar to theirs still at work today, perhaps; so who can tell if in these ancient interpretations of myth there is not some lesson that could be of use to future investigations either of myth as the expression of social relationships, or of mythological figures as spearheads cutting through local custom and belief toward more universal spiritual forms?

But assuming nothing about the essence or function of myth except its relationship to a society does not necessarily mean that erecting the boundaries for a dictionary of mythologies presents no further problems. For no myth exists in isolation; none is a narrative drawing only on itself for its terms and its conventions. We still had to decide what, precisely, from a given society or culture, and from among all its conscious or unconscious communal acts, ought to be included in the book so that none of the discussion or information would be elliptical or too allusive. In other words, what complementary studies must be integrated into a dictionary of mythologies to ensure that the overall statement that it makes will not be hobbled, giving only an impoverished and therefore dangerous idea of the field?

Here is where we can justify the ambiguous precision of our title, in which the word "religion" appears next to the word "mythology." Proceeding empirically, at no great philosophical risk, we may hold as evident that in every human society mythical narrative and religious practice are closely related; and thus, that everywhere, or almost everywhere, it is the historian or analyst of religions who also studies mythologies. As a corollary to this, surely we can affirm that it makes little sense to classify and analyze myths without reference to those aspects of religion that have determined them and will certainly clarify them. And, further, if we do so, in order to make room for this additional material we should also be prepared to sacrifice some of the data about myths properly speaking: what is lost in comprehensiveness will largely be regained in the comprehension of the place and the meaning of myth. This book deals with religions as well as with myths; or, rather, it stands at the intersection where the two roads meet—always with the proviso, however, that each of our contributors has been left free to decide for himself how to apportion the two concerns in practice, taking account of the vastly different forms that the same scientific goal can assume in areas as diverse as Indonesia, for example—that huge complex of societies, languages, and religious influences, where current research is still at the stage of amassing data that must subsequently be put in order—or Vedic India, or Greece, which we know plenty about.

We do not mean that all things religious are therefore in a relationship of complicity, or even of continuity, with the production of myths and the sometimes evanescent, sometimes enduring, figures of myth; there is a dividing point at which one must take sides; the consequences are bound to be great and it is important to justify them. It may come as a surprise to the reader that the religions of Sumeria, Egypt, and Persia are included in the book, while Judaism, Christianity, and Islam are not; that the divinities—if that is the right word—of Buddhism are included, but that no reference is made to the spiritual essence of this major religious experience as it occurs in China, Japan, or elsewhere. It may also cause surprise that, more specifically, the studies of the religions which have been included do not mention what has often made them forms of transcendental experience, mysteries, quests for the Absolute, arenas of soteriological ambition for the yearnings or the nostalgia of individuals or of sects. This is because, during such phases in a religion's development, the religious principle—in its essence, perhaps, a contradictory one—turns against the mythic narrative by which it is at other times nourished. When this happens, the spirit is no longer content to rest at the level of the gods but aspires to a transcendence that it senses as amounting to something more than the representations of it provided by myth; it rejects myth or creates in place of it a gnostic system to uncover its secret meaning. And the effort thus made by the religious spirit to reach the divine within mythical manifestations that it regards as paradoxical or imperfect consequently determines that this aspect of the religious experience has no place in a dictionary of myth and of the rituals and beliefs associated with myth. We have not taken into consideration here the aspect of religion that fights the gods, the mediating powers, that holds them to be paganisms; this aspect in itself is so complex and so rich that it would take another book at least the size of this one to do it justice. The reader will therefore not find among the religions introduced in this volume those whose essential vocation is—let us try to be succinct—the direct experience of transcendent divinity; nor those which tend to have a universal message, addressed to all people everywhere, no matter what their culture or where they live; not even those religions whose moorings in the history of a specific society or a specific people have enabled them, through a founder, a theophany, a prophet, or their reform of a previous paganism, to attach to themselves legends or histories closely resembling myths. In practice, we have excluded from this book the great religions of a Word, a Promise; and especially the mystery religions, Judaism, Christianity, Islam, Gnosticism, Taoism, and the legacies of the Buddha. The one exception to this rule consists of certain incursions justified by the "pagan" nature of some of their minor aspects, such as the cult of the saints in our own churches or the gods and demons of Buddhism.

Let us hope that these religions will one day form the subject of another dictionary, one dealing, as it were, with divinity, as opposed to gods; with universal theologies and experiences of unity, in contrast to the rivulets of myths, rituals, and holy places. Upon further reflection, we ought also to reserve for another volume certain problems of boundaries, such as the way in which past and present evangelistic missionaries have regarded the myths of societies they set out to convert, not without repercussions on Christian doctrine; or—to come closer to home—the way in which at certain moments Christianity itself has played the role of a myth: a myth of truth, or progress, even at the price of relinquishing a good part of its aptitude for genuine communion. As one of our authors writes, myths are never recognized for what they are except when they belong to others; it is therefore our duty to apply to our own behavior as people of the Western world the same methods that our science reserved only yesterday for so-called primitive societies. But a great religious experience must first be described before we can go beyond it and begin the task of distinguishing its ambiguities.

And yet certain religions which might be said to represent a quest for the Absolute as obvious as any other—those of India, for instance, and perhaps also of Egypt—have been included; but this is because in their search for unity they involve myth in a very intimate, almost ultimate, manner, if only in an initial stage and as one more form of illusion. We have not used the word "polytheism" to designate the religions whose myths are dealt with in this dictionary, despite its apparent reference to the differentiation, the polymorphy, of the divine. For although there are resolutely polytheistic religions, such as those of ancient Greece or Rome, in other cultures and other lands there are religions based on more complex intuitions, in which the multiplicity of representations at once clear-cut and diffuse exist in a sort of breathing of the spirit that seems to refute our own exaggerated distinctions between entity and nonentity, between the one and the many. Might we not, perhaps, call

these religions "poetic" or "figurative," since an artist knows well the imaginary nature of the figures that, nevertheless, alone can express, in the artist's vision, the essential reality? In any case, such religions belong in this dictionary by virtue of their massive and continuing recourse to the logic of myth.

III

And now for a few words of clarification concerning the geographical and historical area covered by our enterprise. Or rather—since this dictionary by definition covers all terrestrial space and every era of terrestrial history—concerning the relative proportions we decided upon for the various parts of our inquiry.

First, one remark that may be useful: if we have designated and defined myth in the context of an inquiry that by rights extends to the farthermost regions of the globe, this in no way means that we wish to affirm, by emphasizing the most powerful of these mythologies—whose links with the languages in which they are expressed are obviously close—that there is any uniformity on earth in this mode of consciousness. As has frequently been pointed out, the word *myth* itself comes from the Greek, and the concept that we project into this word, although adjusted to accommodate overlappings and overflowings, also has a logic, a coherence, and still bears the mark of its origin; there is therefore no foundation for believing that what some other ethnic group has experienced under the forms that we call myth corresponds to the same laws with which we are familiar. Perhaps there are societies that do not tend to integrate their myths into some meaningful whole but leave them as fragments that flare up and then are extinguished without, in passing, casting any light on what we ourselves are tempted to look for or to find everywhere: the outline, if only a rough one, of the vault of a universe. If in these cases we can often see nothing but an incoherent babble opening the way to higher forms of consciousness, might it not also be possible for us to sense in them an entirely different mode of consciousness, one in which the discontinuous, the partial, the forever incomplete would themselves be perceived as the very being of human meaning? Could we not see them as an ontology of the superficiality of our inscription on the world—an ontology that the planet's recent history would tend rather to confirm than to deny—somewhere beyond the ruin of our own aspirations? The representation of the divine can obey laws as diverse as those of artistic representation, which extends from the controlled irrationality of a Poussin, who was, in fact, an heir to the Greeks, to the fugitive traces on the gray wall of some works of art of our time.

This should remind us if need be that a dictionary like ours, if it is to fulfill its task of describing the variety of mythologies, must supplement its descriptions of the religious data with additional material on the cultures, mental structures, languages, and functionings of the social collectivity. To the extent that myth is one of the forms of asking questions about mystery, it represents a relationship between the human consciousness—in its cognitive functions, its praxis, its historical memory, or its exploration of the outside environment—and the culture as a whole. Recent research has clearly demonstrated that myth's manifest complexity makes it one of the most useful tools for an archaeology of the imagination, of philosophy, or of science. It was therefore essential to the present undertaking that myth appear not only as an act of speech about the divine, but as a text in which the divine is infinitely embedded in signifiers; and it is the task of the ethnologist, the sociologist, and the linguist to decipher and analyze these signifiers. A background in the social sciences is much more than an imperative for this book; it is its natural and inevitable locus, and one from which many of our contributors, either explicitly or implicitly, have strayed but little. But this consideration even further restricts the space available for the purely mythological material within the finite number of pages at our disposal. When the whole world demands to be heard, the time for each part to speak must be allotted sparingly.

How to mitigate this disadvantage? It would have been tempting to reverse ethnocentric custom and to eliminate at a stroke every trace of exclusiveness, every hierarchy; to relinquish forever the specious charm of the old Greco-Roman monopoly, and its belated acceptance of Egypt and the Near East; and thus to have offered to each separate part of the world an equal number of pages. But rational and fair as this was in principle, we knew that in practice it could never be other than a utopian ideal, at least for the foreseeable future. The first and major reason is that the analysis of myths that is most familiar to us is the work of scholars who write or read in French, English, Italian, German, and more rarely in other languages, still mostly Western ones. With all of its virtues and all of its limitations, this linguistic given constitutes an intangible fact that we must first examine before our own consciousness can be raised, before it can be made to apprehend from within how to circumscribe its own difference so as to be more receptive to categories other than its own. If the mythology of Africa or of ancient Japan is an object of study for our language, the myths and divinities of Greece and Rome, not to mention those of the Celtic and Germanic worlds, survive through hidden symbolisms, overt conditionings, artistic or philosophical references, even—and above all—through concepts, in the most intimate being of mythology, that operate on the very level on which our language apprehends and analyzes the object. And these components, all too familiar but never sufficiently explored, never sufficiently distanced, therefore demand an almost excessive attention if we in the West are ever to achieve a valid understanding of the other civilizations of the world.

This invaluable opportunity to psychoanalyze our methods, we felt, should not be sacrificed by unduly abbreviating that portion of the book dealing with our own origins; so, an important place, even though in a most attenuated manner, should once again be given to the cults and mythologies of more or less classical antiquity and to their later effects on the religious, artistic, and intellectual life of Europe, of which we, of course, are a product. And because for other parts of the world we have also had to take into account the very variable degree of progress in the field, so that it would have been unfortunate to weigh each contribution equally, we have resigned ourselves without compunction to being biased in our allocation of space, believing that to define where we stand does not—or at least so we may hope—imply a valorization of what lies nearest to us or any dogmatism. We have reserved almost half the work for the Mediterranean world, the Near and Far East, and for the historical relations between their mythologies and the European consciousness, as demonstrated by such phenomena as the survival of the classical gods or the fascination with Egypt after the Italian Renaissance. The other half of the book is for the rest of the world, here again, however, taking into account the actual importance that one region or another may have today assumed in a field that naturally is not static and that will have fresh insights to contribute to future supplements to the present volume. It is unfortunately only too true that the vast societies of Africa and Asia have in our columns once again been given less space than the tiny population of Greece. But a particular problem concerning a particular, vanishing society in Vietnam has, on the other hand, merited more of our attention than many perhaps expected aspects of our classical world. We can only hope that the reader will not find our distribution of the materials too misinformed.

IV

Here now is some practical information to help the reader find his way through the labyrinth of the dictionary. [The rearrangement of articles in the English-language edition obviates the problems discussed in this paragraph, which we have therefore abridged.] Certain religions or cultures to which, regretfully, we could only allot a few pages are represented by a single article that can easily be found under the name of the country or geographical area, thus, *Albania* or *Crete*. Generally speaking, however, our contributors had more space at their disposal and were able to address various questions that they considered not only basic but exemplary, in articles spread throughout the book. A list of the names of all the authors, in alphabetical order of their initials, allows the reader to go from the initials at the end of each article to the complete name of the author.

This same list also indicates the academic affiliations of the hundred or so scholars who were willing to contribute to the dictionary; it will be noted that most of them teach at the Collège de France, the École Pratique des Hautes Études, or in French universities. Why this preference for the French, in a century when intellectual exchange is so abundant, between some countries at least, and in which we see so many publications—of, for example, papers delivered at colloquia—that mix together in their abstracts the names of professors from Tübingen or Yale with those from Tokyo or Nairobi? It may at once be pointed out that contributions to this type of publication are usually printed in the language in which the original paper was delivered, obviously requiring of the reader that he be made aware of the linguistic and conceptual apparatus presiding at their conception. French scholars know that, in dealing with ideas originally conceived in German, or in English, they must undertake the task of recognizing schools of thought, cultural or religious conditionings or customs, the influence exerted by the words themselves—since every language has its own semantic nodes, as complex as they are uncompromising; and they also know this task may take a long time, demanding further reading or travel abroad. They further understand that it is only in connection with these vast extratextual areas that they will be able to identify and appreciate the meaning of the text itself. It is of course always possible to translate, and to read a translation. But we must not forget that it takes more than a mere rendering of sentences into a new language for these backgrounds to be revealed and for the underlying meaning to be made clear.

This is precisely the risk that prevails when an enterprise such as ours is opened to authors who think and write in different languages—which would have to be many in number for all the major trends in international scholarship to be represented as they deserve. We believed that scholars who thus had to express themselves through translation would find their work deprived of a part of its significance at the very moment when we would seem to be listening to it. Moreover, the converse is also true: problems can best be differentiated, and even antagonistic methods best be revealed, through the widest possible deployment of the unity and diversity—the cluster of potentialities simultaneously contiguous and concurrent—that is embodied in a single language at a precise moment in its history. We therefore deemed it preferable to call primarily on French scholars and, since those responding to our call number among the most eminent and the most representative, thus to offer to the reader, as an adjunct to our panorama of mythologies and religions, a matching panorama of the contemporary French schools of history, sociology, and religious studies, all of which are of the first rank and deserve to be known as such. To sum up: while a few of the original contributions to the *Dictionary of Mythologies* were translated from languages other than French, for the most part the material can be viewed as a whole, produced by a single society—an ever evolving one, to be sure, and one not inattentive to other cultures—at a crucial juncture in the development of a scientific discipline that is still young. This dictionary is French, the expression of a group of scholars all working within reach of one another, as sensitive to their areas of disagreement as they are gratified by their points of convergence. It is our hope that, if it should be translated, the translator will find it vast enough to allow for the emergence, here and there within its mass, of the unstated concept of implied bias not readily discernible in briefer texts; and that these underlying elements will be revealed in a translation offering the reader, and serving as the basis for future debate, an intellectual effort seen whole: not just the visible tip of the iceberg, but its hidden, submerged bulk as well.

V

Such were the guiding principles determining how our work should be organized. It is only proper to add, however, that despite the great trust which it was the present editor's pleasure to encounter in his authors—who sometimes produced material for him equivalent in volume to a small book—the above principles are primarily the expression of his own concept of what scholarship is, and what it is that scholars are attempting to do. Only he can be held directly responsible for them.

I have just used the word "trust." Going back to the source from which all trust springs, however, I should rather have said "generosity," because this word, glossing "trust," better characterizes both the reception that I as editor was given by specialists in their fields who could so easily have refused to credit any but one of their own, and the quality of their contributions, which to me seems patent. I see this now that the enterprise has been achieved. Most of these scholars, all of them with many tasks competing for their time, have been with our project from the beginning, when, responding to my appeal, they consented to represent their respective disciplines in a dictionary that was still just an idea—an idea to which they themselves had to give meaning. Most of them also agreed to oversee the illustration of their articles, thereby enriching the text with a variety of often rare, sometimes previously unpublished, documents directly rel-

evant to the text. Whenever minor vicissitudes befell the project thereafter, decisions were always made in a spirit of mutual understanding and cooperation. I am extremely grateful to all the authors of this book, and to those eminent individuals who were kind enough to advise me when initial decisions had to be made. Indeed, my only great regret is that I am unable to express this gratitude today to two men who are no longer with us, two men who possessed consummate wisdom, foresight, and discipline, and whose example will stand as an enduring one. Historian Eugène Vinaver's masterly command of Arthurian Romance, a borderline topic standing between myth and literature, is well known. So, too, is Pierre Clastres's intense involvement with the Indian civilizations of South America; the articles by him that we are publishing here were the last pages he ever wrote.

I now have the pleasure of thanking Henri Flammarion and Charles-Henri Flammarion, who wanted this dictionary to exist, and who showed such keen interest in the questions with which it deals. My thanks also to those who transformed typescripts, photographs, and graphics into the reality of the present book. First on the list of these is Francis Bouvet, a man attached to the project from the moment of its inception and now, regrettably, only a memory, but a cherished one. My thanks to Adam Biro, who took over the same functions and brought to them the same understanding and the same invaluable support. Thanks to Claire Lagarde, who from start to finish, and with intuitive devotion and unfailing good humor, sent out requests, acknowledged receipts, sent out requests again, read, filed, saved, and expedited contracts, typescripts, documents, and proofs, even at times when her other duties were pressing. And, finally, thanks to Pierre Deligny, who, simply because he was asked, since we had no legitimate claim to his assistance, unhesitatingly accepted in his own name as well as in that of Denise Deligny and Danielle Bornazzini the crushing responsibility for correcting three successive sets of proofs, with their intricate web of unfamiliar names, cross-references, rearrangements, accent marks, and emendations, and who brought the job to a successful conclusion, with Mesdames Deligny and Bornazzini specifically undertaking responsibility for compiling the index. Yes, to these other authors of the *Dictionary of Mythologies,* many thanks, in the name of the authors of the text.

Yves Bonnefoy/l.g.

NOTES

1. Preface, *Histoire des religions,* vol. 1 (Paris 1970) (Encyclopédie de la Pléiade).

2. *Annuaire* of the École des Hautes Études, Paris, vol. 83, no. 1 (1975–76), p. 4.

3. Ibid., p. 3.

Contributors

A.B. Alain BALLABRIGA, attaché de recherche, Centre national de la recherche scientifique.

A.L.-G André LEROI-GOURHAN, professor, Collège de France.

A.S. Alain SCHNAPP, Maître assistant, University of Paris I.

A.S.-G. Annie SCHNAPP-GOURBEILLON, maître assistant, University of Paris VIII.

C.R. Clémence RAMNOUX, professeur honoraire, University of Paris.

E.I. Erik IVERSEN.

F.Fr. Françoise FRONTISI, maître de conférences, Collège de France.

F.L. Françoise LISSARRAGUE, chargé de recherche, Centre national de la recherche scientifique.

F.-R.P. François-René PICON, maître de conférences, University of Paris V.

G.C. Georges CHARACHIDZÉ, professor, University of Paris III and École pratique des hautes études, IVe section (sciences historiques et philologiques).

H.-D.S. Henri-Dominique SAFFREY, directeur de recherche, Centre national de la recherche scientifique.

J.C. Jeannie CARLIER, chef de travaux, École des hautes études en sciences sociales.

J.-L.D. Jean-Louis DURAND, assistant, University of Paris IV.

J.-P.D. Jean-Pierre DARMON, chargé de recherche, Centre national de la recherche scientifique.

J.-P.V. Jean-Pierre VERNANT, professeur honoraire, Collège de France; directeur d'études, Écoles des hautes études en sciences sociales; codirector, Centre de recherches comparées sur les sociétés anciennes.

J.Ru. Jean RUDHARDT, professor, University of Geneva.

L.Br. Luc BRISSON, directeur de recherche, Centre national de la recherche scientifique.

L.K.-L. Laurence KAHN-LYOTARD, ingénieur, École des hautes études en sciences sociales.

M.D. Marcel DETIENNE, directeur d'études, École pratique des hautes études, Ve section (sciences religieuses).

M.El. Mircea ELIADE, professor in the Divinity School, University of Chicago.

M.T. Michel TARDIEU, directeur d'études, École pratique des hautes études, Ve section (sciences religieuses).

N.L. Nicole LORAUX, directeur d'études, École des hautes études en sciences sociales.

P.Bo. Philippe BORGEAUD, professor in the history of religions, University of Geneva.

P.E. Pierre ELLINGER, maître de conférences, University of Paris; member, Centre de recherches comparées sur les sociétés anciennes.

P.F. Paul FAURE, professor emeritus, University of Clermont-Ferrand.

Ph.D. Philippe DERCHAIN, professor, University of Cologne.

P.V.-N. Pierre VIDAL-NAQUET, directeur d'études, École des hautes études en sciences sociales.

S.G. Stella GEORGOUDI, chef de travaux, École pratique des hautes études, Ve section (sciences religieuses).

Introduction:
The Interpretation of Mythology

Toward a Definition of Myth

From Plato and Fontenelle to Schelling and Bultmann, philosophers and theologians have proposed numerous definitions of myth. But all the definitions have one thing in common: they are based on Greek mythology. For a historian of religions, this choice is not the happiest one. It is true that myth, in Greece, inspired epic poetry and theater as well as the plastic arts; yet it was only in Greek culture that myth was subjected to prolonged and penetrating analysis, from which it emerged radically "demythologized." If the word "myth," in all European languages, denotes "fiction," it is because the Greeks declared it to be so twenty-five centuries ago.

An even more serious mistake in the eyes of the historian of religions is that the mythology that Homer, Hesiod, and the tragic poets tell us about is the result of a selective process and represents an interpretation of an archaic subject which has at times become unintelligible. Our best chance of understanding the structure of mythical thought is to study cultures in which myth is a "living thing," constituting the very support of religious life—cultures in which myth, far from portraying *fiction*, expresses the *supreme truth*, since it speaks only of realities.

This is how anthropologists have proceeded for more than half a century, concentrating on "primitive" societies. Reacting, however, against an improper comparative analysis, most authors have neglected to complement their anthropological research with a rigorous study of other mythologies, notably those of the ancient Near East, primarily Mesopotamia and Egypt; those of the Indo-Europeans, especially the grandiose and exuberant mythology of ancient and medieval India; and finally that of the Turco-Mongols, the Tibetans, and the Hinduized or Buddhist peoples of Southeast Asia. In limiting research to primitive mythologies, one risks giving the impression that there is a gap between archaic thought and that of peoples considered "of history." This gap doesn't exist; indeed, by restricting investigation to primitive societies, one is deprived of the means of measuring the role of myth in complex religions, such as those of the ancient Near East or of India. For example, it is impossible to understand the religion and, more generally, the style of Mesopotamian

culture if one ignores the cosmogonic myths and the myths of origin that are preserved in the *Enūma Eliš* or in the epic of Gilgameš. Indeed, at the beginning of each new year, the fabulous events recounted in the *Enūma Eliš* were ritually reenacted; at each new year the world had to be re-created—and this requirement reveals to us a profound dimension of Mesopotamian thought. The myth of the origin of man explains, at least in part, the characteristic vision and pessimism of Mesopotamian culture: Marduk drew man out of the earth, that is, out of the flesh of the primordial monster Tiamat, and out of the blood of the archdemon Kingu. And the text specifies that man was created by Marduk in order to work the land and to ensure the sustenance of the gods. The epic of Gilgameš presents an equally pessimistic vision by explaining why man does not (and must not) have access to immortality.

Historians of religions therefore prefer to work on *all categories* of mythological creations, both those of the "primitives" and those of historic peoples. Nor do the divergences that result from too narrow a documentation constitute the only obstacle to the dialogue between historians of religions and their colleagues in other disciplines. It is the approach itself that separates them from, for example, anthropologists and psychologists. Historians of religions are too conscious of the axiological differences in their documents to put them all on the same level. Attentive to nuances and distinctions, they cannot be unaware that there are important myths and myths of lesser importance, myths that dominate and characterize a religion, and secondary, repetitive, or parasitic myths. The *Enūma Eliš*, for example, could not be placed on the same level as the mythology of the female demon Lamashtu; the Polynesian cosmogonic myth has a completely different weight from the myth of the origin of a plant, since it precedes it and serves as its model. Such differences in value do not necessarily command the attention of the anthropologist or the psychologist. Thus, a sociological study of the nineteenth-century French novel or a psychology of the literary imagination can make equal use of Balzac and Eugène Sue, Stendhal and Jules Sandeau. But for the historian of the French novel or for the literary critic, such mixing is unthinkable, for it destroys their own hermeneutic principles.

In the next generation or two, perhaps earlier, when we have historians of religions born of Australian or Melanesian tribal societies, I have no doubt that they, among other critics, will reproach Western scholars for their indifference to the scales of *indigenous* values. Let us imagine a history of Greek culture in which Homer, the tragic poets, and Plato were passed over in silence, while the *Interpretation of Dreams* by Artemidorus of Ephesus and the novel by Heliodorus of Emesa were laboriously analyzed under the pretext that they better clarified the specific characteristics of the Greek spirit, or helped us understand its destiny. To return to our subject, I do not believe it possible to understand the structure and function of mythic thought in a society in which myth still serves as a foundation without taking into account both the *body of mythology* of that culture and the *scale of values* that it implies or declares.

Indeed, wherever we have access to a still living tradition that is neither strongly acculturated nor in danger of disappearing, one thing immediately strikes us: not only does mythology constitute a kind of "sacred history" of the tribe in question, not only does it explain the totality of reality and justify its contradictions, but it also reveals a hierarchy in the sequence of the fabulous events it relates. Every myth tells how something came into existence—the world, man, an animal species, a social institution, etc. Because the creation of the world precedes all others, cosmogony enjoys particular prestige. As I have tried to show elsewhere (see, for example, *The Myth of the Eternal Return*, New York, 1954; *Aspects du mythe*, Paris 1963), the cosmogonic myth serves as a model for all myths of origin. The creation of animals, plants, or man presupposes the existence of a world.

Of course, the myth of the origin of the world is not always cosmogonic in the technical application of the term, like Indian and Polynesian myths, or the myth told in the *Enūma Eliš*. In a large part of Australia, for example, the cosmogonic myth in a strict sense is unknown. But there is still a central myth which tells of the beginnings of the world, of what happened before the world became as it is today. Thus one always finds a *primordial history*, and this history has a *beginning*—the cosmogonic myth properly so called, or a myth that introduces the first, larval, or germinal state of the world. This beginning is always implicit in the series of myths that tell of fabulous events that took place after the creation or the appearance of the world, myths of the origin of plants, animals, and man, or of death, marriage, and the family. Together these myths of origin form a coherent history, for they reveal how the world has been transformed, how man became what he is today—mortal, sexual, and obliged to work to sustain himself. They also reveal what the Supernatural Beings, the enculturating Heroes, the mythical Ancestors, did and how and why they moved away from the Earth, or disappeared. All the mythology that is accessible to us in a sufficient state of conservation contains not only a beginning but also an end, bounded by the final manifestations of the Supernatural Beings, the Heroes or the Ancestors.

So this primordial sacred history, formed by the body of significant myths, is fundamental, for it explains and justifies at the same time the existence of the world, of man, and of society. This is why myth is considered both a *true story*—because it tells how real things have come to be—and the exemplary model of and justification for the activities of man. One understands what one is—mortal and sexual—and one assumes this condition because myths tell how death and sexuality made their appearance in the world. One engages in a certain type of hunting or agriculture because myths tell how the enculturating Heroes revealed these techniques to one's ancestors.

When the ethnologist Strehlow asked the Australian Arunta why they celebrated certain ceremonies, they invariably replied: "Because the [mythical] Ancestors prescribed it." The Kai of New Guinea refused to modify their way of living and working and explained themselves thus: "This is how the Nemu [the mythical Ancestors] did it, and we do it the same way." Questioned about the reason for a certain ritual detail, a Navajo shaman replied: "Because the Sacred People did it this way the first time." We find exactly the same justification in the prayer that accompanies an ancient Tibetan ritual: "As has been passed down since the beginning of the creation of the earth, thus we must sacrifice. . . . As our ancestors did in ancient times, so we do today" (cf. *Aspects du mythe*, pp 16ff.). This is also the justification invoked by Hindu ritualists: "We must do what the gods did in the beginning" (*Śatapatha Brāhmaṇa*, 8.2.1.4). "Thus did the gods; thus do men" (*Taittirīya Brāhmaṇa*, 1.5.9.4). In sum, the governing function of myth is to reveal exemplary models for all rites and all meaningful human activities: no less for food production and marriage than for work, education, art, or wisdom.

In societies where myth is still living, the natives carefully distinguish myths—"true stories"—from fables or tales, which they call "false stories." This is why myths cannot be told indiscriminately; they are not told in front of women or children, that is, before the uninitiated. Whereas "false stories" may be told anytime and anywhere, myths must be told only *during a span of sacred time* (generally during autumn or winter, and only at night).

The distinction made between "true stories" and "false stories" is significant. For all that is told in myths *concerns the listeners directly*, whereas tales and fables refer to events which, even when they have caused changes in the world (for example, anatomical or physiological peculiarities in certain animals), have not modified the human condition as such. Indeed, myths relate not only the origin of the world and that of animals, plants, and humans, but also all the primordial events that have resulted in humans becoming what they are today, i.e., mortal, sexual, and societal beings, obliged to work for a living, and working according to certain rules. To recall only one example: humans are mortal because something happened in the beginning; if this event hadn't occurred, humans wouldn't be mortal, they could have existed indefinitely, like rocks, or could have changed their skin periodically, like snakes, and consequently would have been able to renew their life, that is, begin it again. But the myth of the origin of death tells what happened *in illo tempore*, and in recounting this incident it explains *why* humans are mortal.

In archaic societies, the knowledge of myths has an existential function. Not only because myths offer people an explanation of the world and of their own way of existing in the world, but above all because in remembering myths, in reenacting them, humans are able to repeat what the Gods, the Heroes, or the Ancestors did *ab origine*. To know myths is to learn not only how things have come into existence, but also where to find them and how to make them reappear when they disappear. One manages to capture certain beasts because one knows the secret of their creation. One is able to hold a red-hot iron in one's hand, or to pick up venomous snakes, provided one knows the origin of fire and of snakes. In Timor, when a rice field is growing, someone goes to the field at night and recites the myth of the origin of rice. This ritual recitation forces the rice to grow beautiful, vigorous, and dense, just as it was when it *appeared for the first time*. It is *magically forced to return to its origins*, to repeat its exemplary creation. Knowing the myth of origin is often not enough; it must be recited; knowledge of it is proclaimed, it is *shown.* By reciting myths, one reintegrates the fabulous time of origins, becomes in a certain way "contemporary" with the events that are evoked, shares in the presence of the Gods or Heroes.

In general one may say:

—that myth, such as it is lived by archaic societies, constitutes the story of the deeds of Supernatural Beings;

—that the story is considered absolutely *true* (because it refers to realities) and *sacred* (because it is the work of Supernatural Beings);

—that myth always concerns a "creation"; it tells how something has come into existence, or how a way of behaving, an institution, a way of working, were established; this is why myths constitute paradigms for every meaningful human act;

—that in knowing the myth one knows the "origin" of things and is thus able to master things and manipulate them at will; this is not an "external," "abstract" knowledge, but a knowledge that one "lives" ritually, either by reciting the myth ceremonially, or by carrying out the ritual for which it serves as justification;

—that in one way or another one "lives" the myth, gripped by the sacred, exalting power of the events one is rememorializing and reactualizing.

To "live" myths thus implies a truly "religious" experience, for it is distinct from the ordinary experience of daily life. This experience is "religious" because it is a reenactment of fabulous, exalting, meaningful events; one is present once again at the creative works of the Supernatural Beings. Mythical events are not commemorated; they are repeated, reiterated. The characters in myth are brought forth and made present; one becomes their contemporary. One no longer lives in chronological time but in primordial Time, the Time when the event *took place for the first time.* This is why we can speak of the "strong time" of myth: it is the prodigious, "sacred" Time, when something *new,* something *strong,* and something *meaningful* was made fully manifest. To relive that time, to reintegrate it as often as possible, to be present once again at the spectacle of divine works, to rediscover the Supernatural Beings and relearn their lesson of creation—such is the desire that can be read implicitly in all ritual repetitions of myths. In sum, myths reveal that the world, man, and life have a supernatural origin and history, and that this history is meaningful, precious, and exemplary.

M.El./t.l.f.

The Interpretation of Myths: Nineteenth- and Twentieth-Century Theories

If we fail to trace its outline clearly at the outset, the subject we discuss here risks either being merely a collection of rather curious interpretations accepted in their own periods, or else getting lost in the underbrush of the most varied hermeneutic enterprises. There are two indispensable points of reference. We must, first of all, distinguish interpretation from exegesis. We will define the latter as a culture's incessant but immediate commentary on its own symbolism and practices, its most familiar stories. There is no living tradition without the accompanying murmur of its exegesis of itself. Interpretation, on the other hand, begins when there is some distance and perspective on the discourse of a tradition based on memory. Its starting point is probably, as Todorov suggests, the inadequacy of the immediate meaning, but there is also the discrepancy between one text and another, from which the strangeness of the first can become evident. For, in the work of interpretation, it is the prefix *inter* of the Latin word *interpretatio* that designates the space of deployment of hermeneutic activity. In the Western tradition, from the Greeks to ourselves by way of the Romans and the Renaissance, the first hermeneutics appears in the gap opened up by what a new form of thought decided to call *muthos,* thus inaugurating a new form of otherness which makes one text the mythologist of the next. But this interpretive path required one more marker to give it its definitive orientation. From Xenophanes and Theagenes in the sixth century B.C. to Philo and Augustine, hermeneutics took as its privileged object the body of histories that a society entrusts to its memory, what today we call a mythology. But the play of allegory often based itself on nothing more than a name, a word, or a fragment of a text, on which it could graft the bourgeoning symbolism whose discourse became all the more triumphant when, with the affirmation of Christian doctrine, the certainty of possessing the truth unleashed the audacities of a hermeneutics like that of the *City of God.* It is only with Spinoza—as Todorov has recently stated—that a theory of interpretation takes shape on which our modern readings still largely depend. It was he who formulated rules whose mere application was enough to uncover the truth of a meaning, inside the text and within the bounds of a work. But before it could become philology in the nineteenth century, this theory of interpretation, which Spinoza applied to Scripture, still needed the presence of a cultural object with a clearly defined shape—mythology—understood as a discourse that is other, with its own distinctive traits.

Within these limits and for both of these reasons, an archaeology of theories of the interpretation of myth can restrict itself to the nineteenth and twentieth centuries. Travel accounts since Jean de Léry have traced an axis of otherness whose two poles are the savage and the civilized, between which the Greeks serve as mediator. It is the exemplary values of Greece that are evoked, in good Renaissance style, and Lafitau (1724)—while orienting it toward a deciphering of the present by the past—was merely to systematize the path already beaten, throughout the seventeenth century, by Yves d'Évreaux, Du Tertre, Lescarbot, and Brébeuf. One of the best understood differences—the importance of which has been shown by Michel de Certeau—is that between nakedness and clothing. The detour via the Greeks allows the naked body, which a purely and simply Christian education leads one to reject as belonging to paganism and noncivilization, to be made an object of pleasure, and it may also allow the surprise of a return to oneself. Savages are so handsome that they can only be virtuous. And men's stature, the proportion of their limbs, their nakedness, in the midst of the forests, in the beauty of a nature not yet offended by civilization, remind most of these voyagers of the lineaments of Greek statues and the natural privilege which distinguished, in their eyes, the heroes of Homer and Plutarch. As a Jesuit father wrote in 1694, "We see in savages the beautiful remains of a human nature that is completely corrupted in civilized peoples." Nothing could be more like an American savage than a Greek of Homeric times. But this splendid animal, whose development has known no obstacles, whose body is not deformed by labor, evokes the citizen of Sparta or the contemporary of the Trojan war only on the moral and physical level. There is no meeting on an intellectual level; all that the travelers of the seventeenth century expected from savages was that they bear witness to a natural religion of which they were the last trustees. Never, it seems, is the mythology of Homer or Plutarch compared with the stories of these first peoples of nature. One reason is probably that classical mythology, thoroughly moralized, had by then been integrated into a culture dominated by belles lettres. Myths would remain masked as long as they were not assigned their own space.

The nineteenth century saw the discovery of language as the object of a comparative grammar and a renewed philology. In this linguistic space, which is to the highest degree that of the sounds of language, mythical discourse suddenly appeared. It did so in the modality of scandal, which would feed the passionate discussions and theories of two rival schools of the second half of the nineteenth century: the school of comparative mythology, and the anthropological school. As the Sanskritist and comparative grammarian Max Müller wrote, "The Greeks attribute to their gods things that would make the most savage of the Redskins shudder." Comparison defines the nature of the scandal. It is as if it were suddenly discovered that the mythology of Homer and Plutarch was full of adultery, incest, murder, cruelty, and even cannibalism. The violence of these stories, which seemed to reveal themselves brutally as "savage and absurd," appeared all the more unbearable since they were being read at the same time as the stories of distant lands, lands that colonial ethnography was both inventorying and beginning to exploit. The scandal was not that the people of nature told savage stories, but rather that the Greeks could have spoken this same savage language. For in the nineteenth century all that was Greek was privileged. The romantics and then Hegel affirmed this enthusiastically. It was in Greece, they said, that Man began to be himself; it was Greek thought that opened up the path leading from natural consciousness to philosophical consciousness; the Greek people were believed to have been the first to have attained "the uttermost limits of civilization," in the words of a contemporary of Max Müller, the anthropologist Andrew Lang. From the moment that the mythology of Greece could resemble the language spoken by "a mind struck temporarily insane" (Lang), neither our reason nor our thought is definitively safe from an unforeseeable return of the irrational element which, the voice of the savages teaches us, is buried at the very heart of those stories that once seemed so familiar.

The mythology that is subjected to the trial of interpretation is, primarily, nothing but an absurd, crazy form of speech which must be gotten rid of as quickly as possible by assigning it an origin or finding an explanation to justify its oddness. On this point, Max Müller and Andrew Lang are in full agreement. Their divergence appears from the time when the presence of those insane statements at the heart of language and in mythic discourse has to be justified. For Max Müller, a contemporary of the discovery of comparative grammar, the only possible explanation was a linguistic one. And his *Science of Language* argues that a stratigraphy of human speech reveals a mythopoeic phase in the history of language. Since 1816, when Franz Bopp published the first comparative grammar, language had been understood as a set of sounds independent of the letters that allow them to be transcribed; a system of sonorities, animated with its own life, endowed with continual activity and traversed by the dynamism of *inflection*. In the history of language, after what is called a thematic stage, in which terms expressing the most necessary ideas are forged, and what is called a dialectal stage, in which grammar definitively receives its specific traits, an age begins that Max Müller designates as mythopoeic, in which myths make their appearance in very specific circumstances.

At the beginning of its history, humanity possessed the faculty of uttering words directly expressing part of the substance of objects perceived by the senses. In other words, things awakened sounds in humans which became roots and engendered phonetic types. Humans "resonated" at the world, and thus had the privilege of "giving articulated expression to the conceptions of reason." As soon as the individual lost the privilege of emitting sounds at the spectacle of the world, a strange disease fell upon language: words like "night, day, morning, evening" produced strange illusions to which the human mind immediately fell victim. For as long as humans remain sensitive to the meanings of words, these first sonic beings are conceived of as powers, endowed with will, and marked by sexual traits, though the physical character of the natural phenomena designated by the words is not forgotten. As soon as the double meaning becomes confused, the names of the forces of nature break free: they become proper names, and from a spontaneous expression like "the sky rains," a myth abruptly emerges based on "Zeus makes the rain fall." There is an excess of meaning at the source of mythopoeic creation, an uncontrolled surplus of signification, which tricks the speaker, prey to the illusions of a language within which the play of these "substantive verbs" produces, in a burgeoning of images, the strange and often scandalous discourse of myths.

To this theory, which based the metaphors of language on natural phenomena and declared that a good mythologist should possess a "deep feeling for nature," without which linguistic knowledge is futile, the anthropological school immediately objected that comparative grammarians seemed to have forgotten somewhere along the way that "the Redskins, the Australians, and the lower races of South America" continued even today, in the forests and savannas, to tell the same savage tales, which can hardly be explained as the unwonted result of a few misunderstood phrases. The road the anthropological school would follow led in the opposite direction from that of the grammarians. It was no longer the past or origins that were to explain the present, but rather the mythology of contemporary savages that could account for the "savage" stories of the past. And Lang attempted to show that what shocks us in the mythology of civilized peoples is the residue of a state of thought once prevailing in all humanity. In contemporary primitives we can see the power of this state of thought as well as its coherence. At the same time, anthropologists began to investigate these gross products of the primitive human mind and to discover that things which to our eyes seem monstrous and irrational were accepted as ordinary events in everyday life. They soon came to the conclusion that whatever seems irrational in civilized mythologies (the Greco-Roman world, or India) forms part of an order of things that is accepted and considered rational by contemporary savages.

This position led to two orientations, which anthropology attempted to explore in parallel. For the first, which leads from Frazer to Lévy-Bruhl, mythology remains the discourse of madness or mental deficiency. In 1909, before he published the thousands of pages of *The Golden Bough*, the prolegomena to a history of the tragic errors of a humanity led astray by magic, James George Frazer wrote a small book (*Psyche's Task*) in which he asked how folly could turn to wisdom, how a false opinion could lead to "good conduct." And at the center of his reflection Frazer places a paradox:

primitive superstitions were the foundation of what now seems desirable to us in society: order, property, family, respect for life. Prejudice and superstition in fact served to strengthen respect for authority and thus contributed to the rule of order, the condition of all social progress. Frazer had given hundreds of examples in his already published works, and in this slim volume he is no less enthusiastic an admirer of the conduct of the son-in-law in a primitive society who avoids speaking to or being alone with his mother-in-law, surrounding her with taboos, as if these people, not yet capable of elaborating a thought-out set of laws, still had a sense that an intimate conversation between these two people could easily degenerate into something worse, and that the best way to prevent this from happening was to raise a solid wall of etiquette between them. Without knowing it, and almost reluctantly, primitive thought, even in its most obstinate errors, prepared the way for the triumphs of morality and civilization.

For Lucien Lévy-Bruhl, who published *Les fonctions mentales dans les sociétés inférieures* in 1910, primitive societies differed from ours in their mental organization: their thought, constituted differently from our own, is mystical in nature; it is ruled by a "law of participation" that makes it indifferent to the logic of noncontradiction on which our own system of thought is based. Lévy-Bruhl finds the characteristics of primitive thought, which surrenders itself to affectivity and to what he calls "mysticism," among both schizophrenics and children, who also think in an affective way and establish commonalities between things and beings whose mutual distinctiveness is obvious to the intelligence of a civilized adult. Lévy-Bruhl would increasingly identify this "prelogical" stage with "mystic experience," and Van der Leeuw, who extended his analysis, would try to show that primitive thought survives in every human mind, that it is a component of all forms of reason, an indispensable element whose symbolic load and image-making power help to balance the conceptual development of our thought. In the *Notebooks,* which were published after his death, Lévy-Bruhl found it necessary to revise his position on the mental and intellectual gap between ourselves and "savages." But his work, in profound accord with that of Frazer, seems to us today to be part of a fencing in of savage thought (*la pensée sauvage*), confining it in the prelogical and thus avoiding any contamination which might threaten our own reason.

At the very moment when these armchair anthropologists were interning primitive thought, others were setting out on voyages of discovery to Africa and Oceania, and so were discovering, alive and functioning, the rationality of a form of thought that operates through and in myth—a rationality different from our own, but no less impressive for that. The great living mythologies of the Pacific or the Sudan fulfill an indispensable function in these simpler cultures. Revealing a distinctive reality, guaranteeing the effectiveness of worship, myths codify the beliefs, found the moral rules, and determine every practice of daily life. When Marcel Griaule brought back the Dogon cosmology, with its astonishing architectures of symbolic correspondences, there could no longer be any doubt that mythology was indeed the keystone of archaic societies, the indispensable horizon of all cultural phenomena and of the whole pattern in which society is organized. Myths not only constitute the spiritual armature of human lives; they are bearers of a real "theoretical metaphysics." For the first time, then, myths came to be studied in their entirety, a study in which every detail, even the most insignificant, found its place in a holistic interpretation, an interpretation so rich, so exhaustive, that the

ethnographer, once introduced into this polysymbolic world, is in serious danger of "having nothing more to say about Dogon society than the Dogon say themselves" (Pierre Smith, 1973).

In 1903, before Frazer and Lévy-Bruhl had begun their investigations, Marcel Mauss, following the French sociological school, set forth in a few pages a program of which Georges Dumézil would one day prove to be the master craftsman. Three points seem essential. 1. To determine the mechanism of the formation of myths means to seek some of the laws of the mental activity of man in society. 2. Mythology can be reduced to a small number of myths, and each type is made up of a certain number of combinations. 3. The apparent illogicality of a mythic narrative is itself the sign of its distinctive logic. For Mauss, Durkheim's nephew and collaborator, myths are social institutions, that is, ways of acting and thinking which individuals find already established and, as it were, ready to hand; they form a fully organized pattern of ideas and behaviors which imposes itself more or less forcefully on the individuals inscribed in a society. Myth is above all *obligatory* in nature; it does not exist unless there is a sort of necessity to reach agreement on the themes that are its raw material and on the way these themes are patterned. But the constraint comes solely from the group itself, which tells the myth because it finds its own total expression in it.

A symbol through which society thinks itself, mythology informs experience, orders ritual and the economy, and gives archaic societies their categories and classificatory frameworks. For the Durkheimian school, myths—which, incidentally, are hardly mentioned in the *Année sociologique*—are of the same order as language, "a property of which the proprietor is unconscious"; and, inseparable from this, just as a language continues to bear centuries-old vocabulary and syntax, mythology implies a certain traditional way of perceiving, analyzing, coordinating. The analogy is even more precise: like language, mythology is tradition itself, it is the symbolic system that permits communication beyond words; it is the historical unconscious of the society. In this perspective, the importance of myths derives from the common nature that links them to the most archaic element of language, in that domain where sociology hoped to discover some of the fundamental laws of the mind's activity in society.

It was Mauss once again who, against Lévy-Bruhl, in 1923 defended the thesis that considerable parts of our own mentality are still identical to those of a large number of societies called primitive. But it was first Marcel Granet, then Louis Gernet, who developed a sociological analysis of religion with its legends and myths. For the Sinologist Granet, attempting to proceed from language to the fundamental frames of thought, the mythology of the Chinese provided material in which the emotions characteristic of ancient festivals were recorded. Behind the legendary and mythic tales were ritual dances and dramas from which imaginative schemas emerged that imposed themselves on the mind and on action. Farther along, social contexts and great technical feats that crystallize the productions of the imaginary order could be glimpsed. For the Hellenist Gernet, in a break with the established positivist history that was content to note the gratuitous play of the imaginary, myths reveal a social unconscious. Just as semantic analysis gives access to the great social fact of language, the study of legends and of certain mythic themes allows one to go back to transparent or explicit social practices. The mythic image thus offers the most convenient means of access, not to a timeless memory, but to archaic behaviors and social actions and—going far beyond the social data that have, as Gernet puts it, "a direct relation to myth"—to fundamental phenomena of mental life, those that determine the most general forms of thought.

The specificity of the Greeks pointed Gernet in yet another direction. Myths, in their fragments, shining splinters, offer not only the prehistoric behaviors that were their reason for being; they are at the same time part of a global way of thinking, whose categories, classifications, preconceptual models exert a major influence on positive thought and its various advances. Thus Gernet, starting from a series of traditions about types of precious objects, attempts to show how money and the economy emerge from a set of behaviors linked to the mythical notion of value—a notion that involves domains which, though separate nowadays, used to overlap or merge together: the religious, the political, the aesthetic, the juridical. Mythology is thus part of a global religious system that is symbolic in character, with a web of multicorrespondences from which law, philosophy, history, and political thought will emerge and become progressively distinct. But since Gernet thought of myths as raw material for the thought that arose with and in the Greek city, in the space of the polis, he examined the mythic element only in terms of what was beyond it, in a break with its own nature and its functioning. By failing to separate mythology either from language or from the institutional system, the sociological model of myth culminated in the paradox of sometimes losing sight of the very object that seemed finally to have been recognized and legitimated.

More serious, certainly, was the misunderstanding between Freudian psychoanalysis and the anthropological problematic, which seems to give access to a form of the unconscious inscribed in myth. In his self-analysis, as recounted in his letter to Fliess of October 15, 1897, Freud discovers that his libido awoke between the ages of two and two and a half, and turned toward *matrem* (confessors' Latin for the name of the mother). Freud refers this desire for the mother to a Greek tragedy, *Oedipus the King*, a reference both cultural and paradigmatic. The first thing that Sophocles' Oedipus gives Freud is a better understanding of himself—but the choice of a Greek paradigm already announces the universal character of Freud's discovery of the heart of the matter. The early hypothesis, that little Sigmund is *like Oedipus*, shifts toward the Freudian thesis that Oedipus marrying his mother *must have been the same as ourselves*. While Freud's enterprise, by showing that there is no essential difference between the mentally ill person and the healthy person, seems to invert the separation marked by Lévy-Bruhl, it does assume, from the beginning, a segregation of Greek myths from those of other peoples. For Freud, *Oedipus the King* still excites us and exerts a profound effect on us because every man, always and everywhere, feels love for his mother and jealousy of his father; and from the day Freud first adopted this view, the Greek myth was invested with a new privilege: that of translating better than any other "an instinctual attraction which everyone recognizes because everyone has experienced it."

It was to Greek mythology that Freud would continue to turn in his quest for successive proofs of the reality of the unconscious, comparing the discourse of dreams and fantasies with the legends of Olympus, which his successors, stubbornly but not without fidelity, were to proclaim as the language in which we can most easily read the drives and works of desire. In asking for an admission of guilt within the Oedipal configuration, psychoanalysis indeed marks a return to myth and the religious; but in seeing both of these as merely the visible tip of the iceberg of the "Unconscious," forgetting that analytical space is that of free association, it has condemned mythology to being nothing but the symbolic and obsessive repetition of a few unconscious representations centered on sexuality.

It was in the direction opened up by Maussian sociology that theoretical work on myth became involved in the first structural analyses. Resuming the project of comparative mythology that had been wrecked by the excesses of Max Müller and his disciples, Georges Dumézil, thanks to a decisive discovery, founded the comparative study of Indo-European religions by ceasing to rely on purely linguistic concordances between divine names and adopting instead the more solid base of articulated sets of concepts. A factual discovery—in Rome, the three *flamines majores* corresponding to the Jupiter-Mars-Quirinus triad; in Iran, the tripartition of social classes—opened the way to structural analysis of the Indo-European world: the tripartite schema was an essential structure in the thought of the Indo-Europeans. Every organized society is based on the collaboration of three distinct but complementary functions: sovereignty, martial power, fecundity. Parallel to this, the gods form a functionally weighted triad, within which the Sovereign, the Warrior, and the group of divinities who preside over fecundity mutually define one another. Since there was never any question of reproducing a definitely Indo-European myth or ritual, Dumézil had to use precise and systematic correspondences to trace a ground plan of the chosen myth or ritual, indicating its articulations, its intentions, its logical significations, and then, on the basis of this schematic figure, projected into prehistory, to try to characterize the divergent evolutions which have led to analogous and diverse results in different places: Indian myth, Roman myth, Scandinavian myth, or Vedic ritual in relation to the Latin rite. For Dumézil, religions are whole patterns in which concepts, images, and actions are articulated and whose interconnections make a sort of net in which, by rights, the entire material of human experience should find its distribution.

By focusing his examination on the concept and on organized patterns, Dumézil radically parts company with a history of religions that thought in terms of genesis and affectivity. For historians like H. J. Rose and H. Wagenvoort, all religion is rooted in the sense of the "numinous" that the human race experiences spontaneously when confronting the phenomena of nature: there is no divine power who was not first one of these *numina*, in which magico-religious force, diffused in the natural world, is concentrated. For Dumézil, by contrast, the observer never reaches isolated facts, and religion is not a form of thought soaked in emotionality. It is in their mutual relations that the various elements can be apprehended, and there always remains, virtually or in action, a representation of the world or of human action that functions on different levels, under a particular type on each level. The religious system of a human group is expressed "first of all in a more or less explicit conceptual structure, which is always present, if sometimes almost unconscious, providing the field of forces upon which everything else comes to be arranged and oriented; then in myths, which represent and dramatize these fundamental intellectual relationships; and then, in turn, in rituals, which actualize, mobilize, and use the same relations." Independently of these gains in the Indo-European domain, Dumézil's method affirmed the virtues of the concept that can equally inform a myth or underlie a ritual. From this point on, "the surest definition of a god is differential, classificatory,'' and the object of analysis becomes the articulations, the balances, the types of oppositions that the god represents. Against the historians of genesis, Dumézil affirms the primacy of structure: the essential problem is not to determine the precise origin of the various elements that have been fitted together but to accept the *fact* of the structure. The important thing, Dumézil declares, is to bring the structure itself to light, with its signification. It would seem to follow that structures are there, that it is enough to be attentive to them, to avoid forcing them, and to show a little skill in disengaging them. Thus it is not necessary to construct structures as one would elaborate a model of the set of properties accounting for a group of objects. In a sense, structuralism is still in the age of hunting and gathering. Myths, for Dumézil, are the privileged theater that makes visible fundamental conceptual relations. But in the spirit of Mauss's sociology, to which he owes a curiosity for "total social facts" that causes him to explore simultaneously all the works produced by the human mind, myths cannot be deciphered until they have been put back into the totality of the religious, social, and philosophical life of the peoples who have practiced them. The mythology posited by the earlier comparativism of Frazerian inspiration as separate from language, as a more or less autonomous object, endowed with permanence and chosen to locate the common themes elaborated by the Indo-Europeans, was referred back to the language of which it formed a part and, through this language, to the ideology that grounds it and runs through it.

The structural analysis developed by Lévi-Strauss was established under the same kind of conditions as the comparative and philological analysis of the nineteenth century. The gratuitous and insane character of mythic discourse was again the point of departure. For Max Müller this was shocking; for Lévi-Strauss it was a challenge. He took up the challenge after he had shown that kinship relations, in appearance contingent and incoherent, can be reduced to a small number of significant propositions. If mythology is the domain in which the mind seems to have the most freedom to abandon itself to its own creative spontaneity, then, says Lévi-Strauss, to prove that, on the contrary, in mythology the mind is fixed and determined in all of its operations is to prove that it must be so everywhere. The structural analysis of myths thus finds its place in a wider project, which aims at an inventory of mental constraints and postulates a structural analogy between various orders of social facts and language.

This whole approach to myth applies to a new domain the methods of analysis and principles of division developed for linguistic materials in the methods theorized by the Prague school and more particularly by Roman Jakobson. But while myth is assimilated to a language from the outset, it is not identical either to the words of a text or to the sentence of communicative discourse. Mythology is a use of language in the second degree; it is not only a narrative with an ordinary linguistic meaning: myth is in language and at the same time beyond natural language. In the first stage of an ongoing investigation ("The Structural Study of Myth," 1955), Lévi-Strauss tries to define the constituent units of myth in relation to those of structural linguistics. Mythemes are both in the sentence and beyond it. In this perspective, the constituent unit is a very short sentence, which summarizes the essential part of a sequence and denotes a relation: "a predicate assigned to a subject." But this sentence is not part of the explicit narrative; it is already on the order of interpretation, the product of an analytical technique. These sentence relations, then, are distributed on two axes: one horizontal, following the thread of the narrative, the other vertical, in columns, grouping together relations belonging to the same "bundle." It is on the level of these bundles of relations that the real mythemes are located. At the same time, structural analysis poses two principles as essential to its practice: there is no authentic version of a myth in relation to others that are false; correlatively, every myth must be defined by the whole set of its versions. There thus takes shape the project of ordering all the known variants of a myth in a series forming a group of permutations.

The next stage of his investigation ("The Story of Asdiwal," 1958) led Lévi-Strauss to propose that myth makes full use of discourse, but at the same time situates its own meaningful oppositions at a higher degree of complexity than that required by natural language. In other words, myth is a metalanguage and, more precisely, a linked sequence of concepts. Attention will be turned, therefore, to registering the various levels on which myth can be distributed. The cutting up of the mythic narrative which in the first phase (1955) seemed to be entrusted to the whim or ingenuity of the model-builder, is now subject to testing—indispensable to all formal analysis—in terms of the *referent*: "the ethnographic context," which the later transformational orientation of the *Mythologiques* would cease to pursue. The surveying of pertinent oppositions in a mythic sequence thus finds the fundamental guarantee of its legitimacy in previous knowledge of an organized semantic context, without which the myth is in principle incomprehensible. Ritual practices, religious beliefs, kinship structures: the whole of social life and social thought is called upon to define the logical relations functioning within a myth, and at the same time to establish the different types of liaison between two or more myths. In the four-volume *Mythologiques* (1964–1971), the progressive analysis continues to show relations between myths, the social life of those who tell them, and the geographical and technological infrastructure, but it does not restrict itself to this back-and-forth between levels of signification and an ethnographic context that reveals the philosophy of a society. The meaning of a myth is no longer inscribed in its structures' reference to a social infrastructure; rather, the position the myth occupies in relation to other myths within a transformation group is henceforth the vector of an analysis that reveals the autonomy of a mythic thought in which every narrative refers back in the first instance to another, picking up and organizing its elements in a different way. Just as each term, itself without intrinsic signification, has no meaning other than a positional one in the context in which it appears to us, in the same way each myth acquires a signifying function through the combinations in which it is called upon both to figure and to be transformed. It is these transformations which, in the last analysis, define the nature of mythic thought.

It has been objected that this practice of mythological analysis makes a choice for syntax against semantics; and, likewise, that while it has been possible to apply the practice successfully to the mythologies of so-called totemic societies, since these are rich in classificatory structures, it excludes Semitic, Hellenic, and Indo-European societies from its field of interest, societies whose mythological thought is marked by renewals of meaning and by a semantic richness that exceeds the powers of structural analysis. One can reply, on the one hand, that for this type of analysis, which gets at the meanings of myths by multiplying the formal operations that allow us to uncover the logical framework of several narratives, the semantics of myths is necessarily enriched through the inventorying of the syntax. On the other hand, the practice of structural analysis is hardly alien to our familiar mythologies, such as that of the Greeks; one may, indeed, be surprised at the remarkable similarities between the way the Greeks themselves thought their mythology and the method used by ethnologists in approaching myths told by nonliterate peoples. More pertinent objections have come from anthropologists such as Dan Sperber, who denounces the semiological illusion of structuralism as well as the distance between the linguistic models invoked and an intuitive practice whose specific procedures, unlimited in number and nature, offer knowledge of the intellectual operations from which the stories we call "myths" are woven.

M.D./j.l.

BIBLIOGRAPHY

The titles listed are in the order and within the limits of the problems formulated by this article.

T. TODOROV, *Symbolisme et interprétation* (Paris 1978). M. DE CERTEAU, "Ethno-graphie: L'oralité, ou l'espace de l'autre," in Léry, *L'écriture de l'histoire* (Paris 1975), 215–48. G. CHINARD, *L'Amérique et le rêve exotique dans la littérature française du XVIIᵉ au XVIIIᵉ siècle* (Paris 1934). M. DETIENNE, "Mito e Linguaggio: Da Max Müller a Claude Lévi-Strauss," in *Il Mito: Guida storica e critica* (2d ed., Bari and Rome 1976), 3–21 and 229–31, with bibliography. H. PINARD DE LA BOULLAYE, *L'étude comparée des religions*, 1 and 2 (Paris 1925). J. DE VRIES, *Forschungsgeschichte der Mythologie*, Orbis Academicus, 1, 7 (Munich 1961). K. KÉRÉNYI, *Die Eröffnung des Zugangs zum Mythos* (Darmstadt 1967). G. VAN DER LEEUW, *L'homme primitif et la religion*, Étude anthropologique (Paris 1940). P. SMITH, "L'analyse des mythes," *Diogène* 82 (1973): 91–108. M. MAUSS, *Œuvres*, V. Karady, ed., 3 vols. (Paris 1968–69). L. GERNET, *Anthropologie de la Grèce antique* (Paris 1968). S. C. HUMPHREYS, "The Work of Louis Gernet," *History and Theory* 10, 2 (1971). J. STAROBINSKI, "Hamlet et Freud," preface to French trans. by E. Jones, *Hamlet et Œdipe* (Paris 1967), IX–XL. S. VIDERMAN, *La construction de l'espace analytique* (Paris 1970). S. FREUD, "Zur Gewinnung des Feuers," in *Gesammelte Werke* (London 1932–39), also in English. G. DELEUZE and F. GUATTARI, *L'anti-Œdipe* (Paris 1972), "Psychanalyse et familiarisme: La sainte famille," 60–162. H. FUGIER, "Quarante ans de recherches dans l'idéologie indo-européenne: La méthode de Georges Dumézil," *Revue d'histoire et de philosophie religieuse* 45 (1965): 358–74. M. MESLIN, *Pour une science des religions* (Paris 1973), "Psychanalyse et religion," 113–38. P. SMITH and D. SPERBER, "Mythologiques de Georges Dumézil," *Annales E.S.C.*, 1971, 559–86. J.-P. VERNANT, "Raisons du mythe," in *Mythe et société en Grèce ancienne* (Paris 1974), 195–250. P. RICŒUR, s.v. "Mythe (3. L'interprétation philosophique)," in *Encyclopædia Universalis* (Paris 1968), 11:530–37. CL. LÉVI-STRAUSS, *Structural Anthropology*, 2 vols. (New York 1963, 1976), originals in French; *Mythologiques*, 4 vols. (Paris 1964–71), = *Introduction to a Science of Mythology*, 4 vols., entitled *The Raw and the Cooked* (New York 1969), *From Honey to Ashes* (London 1973), *The Origin of Table Manners* (New York 1978), and *The Naked Man* (New York 1981).

MYTH AND WRITING: THE MYTHOGRAPHERS

The word *mytho-logy* is but one instance of many in which the proximity of myth and writing inevitably results in a kind of violence, its victim an original word, sacred in nature and condemned to fixity by a profane order. Beyond the words which by their very texture bear witness to this phenomenon (such as *mythography*), Greek privilege has held fast. When strange and unforgettable stories, which sounded very independent and yet bore obvious resemblances to the mythology of antiquity, were brought to us from all continents, early anthropologists turned instinctively to Greece, where a few centuries earlier great minds from Xenophanes to Aristotle had faced the problem of limiting the dominion of myths and had resolved it within their own intellectual activity by drawing a boundary at which mythical thought fades away before the rationality of scientists and philosophers. The split between the land of myth and the kingdom of *logos* served as a precedent for the decision made by Tylor and his disciples to impose a historical limit on the reign of mythology over the human mind. This opposition between two forms of thought and two stages of human intelligence, the latter canceling the former, took the form of a sharp contrast between reason, which used all the resources of the written, and a mythological activity tuned to the fantasy of an incessant babbling.

Henceforth, never the twain shall meet. For those practicing historians who tend to favor written traces, oral discourse has become so totally inaudible that it is quite illegible whenever it manifests itself as writing—a contrived writing, which masks the incoherence of traditions sustained through memory by imposing a factitious order of mythographical classifications. For others, the Greeks so thoroughly ensured the triumph of reason and *logos* that they ruined their former system of thought for good, allowing only frail remains to survive as witnesses of a lost state to which only two possible roads of access still remain: one is the discovery, by an ancient traveler in a forgotten village, of a tale saved from the contamination of writing thanks to a few natives unaware of the progress of culture; the other is the less hazardous road of historical and geographical investigation through which one gains access to a long-deferred vision of a landscape that authenticates the narrative or the myths of which it is the guarantor, the recovered witness.

Within this framework, the truth of the myth is enclosed in a speechlike nature, which writing more or less obliterates, at times by shackling the freedom of a self-expressive memory with the constraints of an interpretation subject to foreign rules; and at other times, more often than not, by reducing the myth's own speech to silence in order to speak on its behalf and to condemn it to an absolute otherness. In an attempt to rectify this division, structural analysis introduced a summary separation between cold and warm societies, the former deprived of a temporal dimension, the latter open to history and to the continual renewals of meaning that writing facilitates. The border thus drawn appeared all the more definite as it seemed to reiterate the distinction between oral and written literature, a distinction reinforced, if not justified, by the decision made by this type of analysis to look for the essential of the "myth" not in the narration but in the story transmitted by memory, a story whose narrative form was left to the discretion and talent of each narrator.

Yet another issue arises, for which the Greek model inspires a formulation that suggests the progressive emergence of writing in a traditional society. Since the time E. A. Havelock first published his studies, the Homeric epic, which Milman Parry had recognized as belonging to oral practice, can no longer be considered an enclave of a living tradition that made room for a culture of the written. The introduction of an alphabetical writing technique caused no immediate changes, nor did it produce any profound up-heaval. Greece experienced not a revolution of writing but, rather, a slow movement with uneven advances depending on the areas of activity; by the turn of the fourth century, writing prevailed mentally and socially. Until the end of the fifth century, Greek culture had been essentially of the oral type. It entrusted to its memory all traditional information and knowledge, as do all societies unacquainted with written archives. And it is here that we must revise the notion of *mythology*, with which the Greeks encumbered us as a consequence of their entanglement with *logos*. For the unified concept "myth," which nowhere seems to be defined as a discrete literary genre, must fade away in favor of a set of intellectual operations fundamental to the memorizing of narratives that together make up a tradition. Claude Lévi-Strauss suggests the term *mythism* for the process by which a story, initially personal and entrusted to the oral tradition, becomes adopted by the collective mode, which will distinguish between the crystal clear parts of the narrative—that is, the levels that are structured and stable because they rest on common foundations—and the conjectural parts—details or episodes amplified or neglected at each telling, before being doomed to oblivion and falling outside the bounds of memory. Every traditional society develops, with varying success, a widely shared creative memory, which is neither the memory of specialists nor that of technicians. The narratives we agree to call myths are the products of an intellectual activity that invents what is memorable.

When writing appears, it neither banishes traditional memory to a state of decay nor sustains an oral practice in imminent danger of becoming extinct. Writing occurs at different levels and in different orders, but always at the encounter between an act of remembering and the works that memory creates. Writing was to introduce a new memory, word-for-word memory, which comes with the book and with education through the study of written texts. Competing ever so slowly with the former kind of memory, mechanical memory alone is capable of engendering the idea, familiar to us, of the *correct* version, a version which must be copied or learned exactly, word for word. In Greece between the sixth and fifth centuries, the first historians, those whom the Greeks call "logographers," selected writing as the instrument of a new kind of memory that would become an integral part of thought and political action. This new way of remembering was constructed on the boundary between a type of oral tradition with its remembrances, spoken narratives, and stories circulating by word of mouth, and, on the other side, the dominant obsession of the new investigators, who respected as knowledge only what had been seen, and who would ultimately condemn, without appeal, those who accepted traditions of the past that were transmitted without precise terminology or rigorous proof. This was the battleground, the wide open space of writing, for the confrontation between variants that became different versions of the same myth, usually examined from within the confines of a city in quest of self-image or political identity.

Elsewhere, other routes were taken that linked writing to the production of myths whose successive variations were inseparable from the hermeneutic activity of scribes and interpreters devoted to textual exegesis. From the moment the traditional narratives of the Bible, the Book of the Hebraic world, were committed to writing, they were swept away by the inner workings of a system of writing which, though initially consonantal, in its hollows called for a vocalic complement to bear its meaning, since one cannot read a consonantal text unless one understands it, that is, unless

one attributes to it a meaning set apart from other possible meanings. In the continuity of interpretation thus opened up, the hermeneutics that was focused on the mythical accounts of Israel claimed a privileged place, which made it more sensitive to the permanence of fundamental themes endlessly revived and reevaluated, but also forced it to be the infinite exegesis, forever interned within its own symbolic wealth.

M.D./g.h.

BIBLIOGRAPHY

R. FINNEGAN, *Oral Poetry: Its Nature, Significance and Social Context* (Cambridge 1977). J. GOODY and J. WATT, "The Consequences of Literacy," *Comparative Studies in Society and History*, 1963, 304–45. J. GOODY, "Mémoire et apprentissage dans les sociétés avec et sans écriture: La transmission du Bagre," *L'homme*, 1977, 29–52. E. A. HAVELOCK, *Preface to Plato* (Cambridge, MA, 1963). R. KOENIG, "L'activité herméneutique des scribes dans la transmission du texte de l'Ancien Testament," *Revue de l'Histoire des Religions*, 1962, 141–74. CL. LÉVI-STRAUSS, *Mythologiques 4* (Paris 1971): 560 (translated as *Introduction to a Science of Mythology*, New York 1969–). L. SEBAG, *L'invention du monde chez les Indiens Pueblos* (Paris 1971), 472–85. J. VANSINA, *De la tradition orale: Essai de méthode historique*, Musée royal de l'Afrique centrale (Tervuren 1961).

Some mythographic texts of ancient Greece: APOLLODORUS, *The Library*, J. G. Frazer, ed. (London 1921). DIODORUS OF SICILY, *The Library*, vol. 4, C. H. Oldfather, ed. (London 1935). ANTONINUS LIBERALIS, *Metamorphoses*. HYGINUS, *Astronomica*, B. Bunte, ed. (Leipzig 1875). HYGINUS, *Fabulae*, H. I. Rose, ed. (Leiden 1933). *Mythographi graeci*, 5 vols.; R. Wagner, Martini, A. Olivier, and N. Festo, eds., Bibl. Script. graec. Teubneriana (Leipzig 1896–1926). *Mythographi Vaticani*, G. H. Bode, ed., vols. 1–2 (1834; reprinted Olms 1968). ACUSILAUS OF ARGOS, PHERECYDES OF ATHENS, and HELLANIKOS OF LESBOS, in *Fragmente der griechischen Historiker*, F. Jacoby, ed., I: *Genealogie und Mythographie* (Leiden 1922; 2d ed., 1957).

PREHISTORIC RELIGION

To speak of "prehistoric religion" without specifying time and place is tantamount to assimilating under modern thought facts and contexts that came to light at very different times and places, tantamount to creating a kind of average image that can only be validated by the judgment of our own way of thinking projected onto some arbitrarily chosen facts. Prehistoric religion no longer occasions a debate in which either pro- or anticlerical convictions are at stake. The science of prehistory has been enriched by much new data and major changes in methodological approaches. Rather than arguing about whether the atheist brute evolved first into the magician and then into the priest, scientists have given priority to inquiries that bring out the deep connections among play, aesthetics, social behavior, economic realities, and practices that rest on a metaphysical framework. The proofs that can be proliferated from a so-called religious approach are largely derived from the realm of the unprecedented, from the presence of peculiar facts found in a context where they are least expected, such as the discovery, on a Mousterian site inhabited by Neanderthal man, of fossil shells, which he collected and brought back to his dwelling place, or the discovery that he gathered red ocher or buried his dead. These diverse elements do not fit in with our vision of Neanderthal man. Yet how could there not be a striking contrast between this primal brute with his bulky brow ridges and the subtle quality of a religiosity polished by two millennia of Christianity and all of ancient philosophy? Neanderthal man was not, in the final analysis, as short of gray matter as was long believed, though the metaphysical level of his cultic activities was certainly very different from ours (at least, as we imagine ours to be).

What matters is the existence of practices within a psychological realm not directly tied to techniques of acquisition, manufacture, or consumption, even if these practices do flow back into material life. Man acquired religious behavior when he developed the whole system of symbolic thought, which cannot be separated from language and gesture as it works out a network of symbols that present a counterimage of the outside world. That Neanderthals had already developed this network of symbols is beyond doubt, but whether one can go on to distinguish evidence of a primordial religion or an extremely diffuse symbolic complex remains questionable. The gathering of magical shells and ocher supports the view that the pump had been primed for the simultaneous evolution of the fields of art, play, and religion, three fields which to this day cannot be separated.

Homo sapiens picked up where Neanderthal man left off, with regard to the gathering of "curios" (shells, fossils, crystals, iron pyrites, stalactite fragments, etc.) sometimes found together in the same pile. Ocher became much more plentiful. The first use of manganese dioxide, a black dye, coincided with the production of a greater number of drawings engraved on bone or stone surfaces. By the Aurignacian period, these drawings took the form of rhythmic incisions and figurative tracings. By 30,000 B.C., figurative art had developed to the point at which subjects could be divided into the following groups: female sexual symbols (sometimes also male), figures of animals, and regularly spaced incisions or punctuations. These themes predominated throughout the development of Paleolithic art, a subject to which we shall return.

Burial Grounds and the Cult of Bone Remains

Neanderthals buried their dead. The practice of inhumation is attested by several obvious tombs and, statistically, by the numerous finds of skeleton fragments. Shanidar in Iraq is the site of the only discovery of a Neanderthal laid out on a bed of flowers, from which a great number of fossilized pollens were found. In Monte Circeo (Italy), in a similarly convincing find, a skull was placed in the center of a cave chamber. In the face of such striking testimony, it is difficult not to ascribe to the immediate predecessors of humankind as we know it today sentiments analogous to our own regarding the afterlife in a parallel universe, a universe which may have been as inexplicit as that of the average subject of any of today's major religions. Difficult as it may be, given the available evidence, to describe Neanderthal man's attitude toward the supernatural, it is even more difficult to demonstrate the meaning of what falls into the category of the "cult of bone remains." Because bone is the only physical element (human or animal) that survives decomposition, any bones found as evidence in an unusual situation could have played a part in a cult. Whether with respect to Neanderthal man or to *Homo sapiens*, we have some evidence that can be explained in terms that are not at variance with an interpretation based on the supernatural. Separated by several scores of millennia, the skulls of Monte Circeo (Mousterian) and the skull from Mas-d'Azil (Magdalenian) attest the special character of the head (the whole head

or merely the skull). Although the idea of "graves" of animals has been advanced repeatedly, it seems that natural phenomena were more often at issue than man himself, especially in the case of the remains of cave bears.

The burial graves of fossil *Homo sapiens* are rare, and hardly a single grave dating from the Upper Paleolithic Age (30,000–9000) has been excavated either with care or with all the technical means that would have assured its documentary value. We do, however, have a certain number of facts at our disposal (graves; bodies, either curled up or stretched out; a head protected by a stone; ocher dusting; and funereal household objects, including, at the least, clothing and ornaments worn by the dead person). In addition, the double children's tomb at Sungir, north of Moscow, where hundreds of ornamental elements adorn the bodies and large spears made of mammoth ivory were found in the grave, bears witness to the development of the concern to equip the dead, a development that occurred at a remote phase of the Upper Paleolithic Age. Obviously, graves do not all reflect identical religious intentions, nor can we be certain what kind of sentiments led to these emotional displays. Mortuary furniture is ordinarily less sumptuous. In several cases we might even speculate that the presence of certain vestiges was connected with accidental conditions surrounding the filling of the grave. But a rather constant factor is the presence of ocher, which varied according to the population's wealth in dyes. Ocher gave the soil and the skeleton that it covered a reddish coloration. This practice, common during the Upper Paleolithic Age, is the indisputable sign of acts whose meaning goes beyond a simple natural emotion. If the use of ocher supports various interpretations according to habitat, the sheer fact of its being brought into a grave where a body had been laid constitutes the most distinct feature of the belief in an afterlife, since the dead person was considered still capable of using what he was offered.

Personal Adornments

Jewelry appeared in the West around 35,000 B.C. Its prior origin is unknown. Throughout Europe, its appearance coincided with the first manifestations of the Upper Paleolithic Age. During the Châtelperronian epoch (35,000–30,000), it appears already quite diversified: at that same time we find annular pendants carved out of bone, as well as teeth from various animal species (fox, wolf, marmot, aurochs, etc.), made so that they could be hung by means of a perforation of the root or a slit. Fossil shells were treated in the same way. It may seem far-fetched to regard ornamental pendants as anything other than purely aesthetic objects, and, in fact, some may have had exclusively decorative functions. However, among the hundreds of pendants acquired from European sites, the majority reveal a preoccupation with magic at one level or another. Those that unambiguously represent male and female sexual organs must surely have had some sort of symbolic value (fig. 1). The cylindrical fragments of stalactite and points of belemnites designed to hang may have a meaning of the same order. This symbolic function of sexual images may have been extended to include fragments of shattered assegai spears that were perforated but otherwise untreated (see the symbolism of the assegai below). The role of teeth designed to hang must have been rather complex, at least in the early stages, for the teeth of some animals, the marmot for example, do not seem to have the characteristics of a trophy or a talisman. This is not true of the atrophied canines of reindeer, which even today are symbols of masculinity and

Pendants with genital designs. Left: series of female symbols; right: phalloid symbol. 7.5 cm. Isturitz (Pyrénées district). (Fig. 1)

works. Between 30,000 and 20,000, certain forms began to appear in engravings. These first forms were executed on blocks and probably on the walls of rock shelters as well. Despite their crudeness, they shed light on the concerns of their creators. The repertoire of these works is very limited; representation of the female genitalia, highly stylized, is the most widespread. A few representations of the male genitalia can be found, but they were apparently replaced quite early by abstract symbolic figures: dotted lines or bar lines that seem to accompany explicitly female figures. There are also highly geometrical figures of animals, parallel to one another and often juxtaposed or superimposed on one another. The Aurignacian-Gravettian bestiary includes the horse, the bison, the ibex, and other imprecise figures indicating that from the very beginning art made use of two clearly defined registers: human figures symbolically rendered, starting with the representation of the entire body and progressing, by way of genital figures and animals, to geometric figures. During the ensuing 20,000 years, the details may have varied but the basic figures, human and animal, remained in the same relationships. These relationships cannot easily be established on the basis of the engraved blocks alone; displacement in the course of time and, especially, following excavations has destroyed the spatial ties that might have guided us to their meaning. But something happened, perhaps by the Gravettian Age but certainly around 15,000: penetration deep into caves and the execution of paintings or engravings, sometimes more than a kilometer from the opening. This boldness on the part of Paleolithic men is of immediate interest to us because the works produced at such locations preserved their positions with respect to one another and with respect to the wall itself. We can therefore raise questions about the possible religious ideology of the creators of these figures. What motives could have inspired the Magdalenians of Niaux or Pech-Merle to their speleological adventure? It is hard to believe that it was just a matter of curiosity, and one is inclined to think that in their eyes the cave must have seemed a mysterious amalgam of female forms. Direct evidence is furnished by the numerous oval cavities or cleft lips painted on the inside in red ocher (Gargas, Font-de-Gaume, Niaux). The execution of numerous genital symbols in deep side passages indirectly reinforces the hypothesis of the woman-cave. To date, explicit male symbols are rare but one may find, on Aurignacian blocks, for instance, signs made up of series of dots or rods accompanying oval or triangular figures depicted with different degrees of realism. All stages of development come together, with regional nuances, from the whole female figure to the pubic triangle rendered as an empty rectangle. This tendency of male and female signs to conceal themselves behind abstract graphics may well have been a response to taboos of a socioreligious character. This hypothesis becomes all the more plausible as other figurative anomalies give evidence of the same meaning. Not only is there no known instance of human or animal mating anywhere in Paleolithic art, but sexual organs are explicitly represented on relatively few figures. At Lascaux (where, however, the bulls have obvious sexual characteristics), two figures appear (fig. 6): the ''jumping cow'' in the Axial Diverticulum and an engraved horse in the Passage, both of which have their hooves turned in such a way that the underbelly on both animals is visible and completely empty. This strange mannerism in figure drawing is not easily explained, but it does show the complexity of Paleolithic thought. Curiously, secondary sexual characteristics (the antlers of the cervidae, the thick withers of the bovidae, and

were imitated in bone or soft stone when pendants first appeared.

The same applies to shells. For the most part they seem to have a purely aesthetic function, but the rather frequent discovery of porcelain (Cyprea), universally attested in prehistoric and historic times as a protective female symbol, makes it highly probable that the collection of shells served as talismans. In short, having gone beyond a strictly decorative function, long and oval pendants encompassed both the aesthetic and the religious realms, and probably the social realm as well, although we still have too little data to clarify the matter.

The Occurrence of Wall Painting

The development of personal adornments does not diminish the importance of the collections of natural curiosities; rather, it was an added feature that prevailed until the end of the Upper Paleolithic Age, ca. 9000. Adornments evolved throughout this period. But in the Aurignacian and the Perigordian Ages, the main event was the spread of pictorial

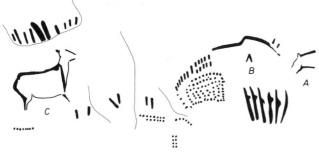

Middle part of the first great panel of the Cave of Pindal (Asturias). Animals A and B (horse and bison) are reduced to the minimal identifiable size: dorsal line and horns for the bison, which also bears a scar from a wound in the shape of an inverted V; central portion of the head and the neck and withers for the horse. Above the bison and the horse, S^2 line of the so-called claviform type (see fig. 5). The photograph includes only the right side of a series of red and black paintings. Between group A-B and the doe (C), there are several groups of S^1 and S^3 signs. The doe is 85 cm long. (Fig. 2)

the horns of the ibex) are rendered very exactly; and, moreover, the animals are frequently depicted in couples, the female in front and the male behind. It is certain that the figures basically connote what might be thought of as a "fertility cult," a generally banal statement that takes on a subtlety in the present instance by virtue of the apparent contradiction of the representation.

Animals

Paleolithic materials yield other peculiar data. The hundreds of figures that cover the walls of caves seem at first glance to defy any kind of order. Even though the idea of a coherent whole emerges from the way the figures are arranged, few prehistorians have used this possible organization to delve further into the ideology of the artists. One rather surprising fact stands out: the fauna that are represented display variations that seem to reflect the environment. In some caves the bison, together with the horse, is the principal subject (Font-de-Gaume, Niaux, Altamira), whereas in others the aurochs plays the main role (Lascaux, Ebbon). But in all the cases cited above, the complementary bovid (bison or aurochs depending on the site) is represented by one or more figures separated from the rest. Another point should also be mentioned: the reindeer that figure in

great numbers among the food wastes of the hunters at the time of these works occupy little space in the iconography of certain grottoes such as Lascaux, Niaux, or Altamira. At Lascaux, rather paradoxically, though the bony remains of reindeer make up almost all the animal wastes, only one figure can be attributed to the reindeer, and even that is somewhat doubtful. Thus the fauna depicted do not always correspond to what Paleolithic man hunted. This fact is important because, if it were confirmed, it would lead us to conclude that at least some of the animals represented played a role unconnected with the food that people then lived on. The number of sites for which it was possible to draw up a list of the animals depicted and a parallel list of the animals consumed as meat is unfortunately too limited to verify this hypothesis.

Groupings

We referred above to groupings of animal figures and signs, starting with the Aurignacian Age (30,000). The most frequent, almost exclusive animal grouping is of horses (100%) and of bison (56%) (or of aurochs, 39%, in other words, 95% for bovidae). This initial dyad, moreover, occupies the center of all surfaces used, and may be repeated several times in the same cave. The groupings in wall paintings have a complexity that derives from the diversity of the caves in which the decorations appear. So, too, geographical location and chronological evolution are reflected in various applications of the initial figurative formula and in the more or less pronounced use of natural forms. In any case, it is likely that the cave or the surface of the shelter wall was the object of a deliberate choice, and that the figures were not piled one on top of another haphazardly.

The horse(A)-bovid(B) twosome appears at all sites (fig. 7.1). Although we must allow for the possibility of caves or shelters that might not fit the basic AB formula, practically speaking the AB group is always present and dominates the groupings both numerically and topographically. But rarely does the AB group appear alone. Another category of animals intervenes, namely, group C (stag, mammoth, and occasionally chamois and reindeer). Among the wall painting groups, the ibex is most often the accompanying animal, but the stag, hind, mammoth, and reindeer also play the same role, most often on the sidelines, on the outer perimeter of the central panel groupings, or in the intermediary sections. The most frequent formula is thus AB + C, making up a triad with one interchangeable element: the ibex at Niaux, the mammoth at Rouffignac, the stag at Las Chimeneas. In the same cave, we can also see "moving" animals, or the following: at Niaux, the stag marks the deepest part of

the large painted surface, the rather numerous ibexes framing the AB figures; at Lascaux, the situation is similar—ibexes appear three or four times immediately to the side of a group of animals, stags being equal in number but farther to the side. In a cave like the Combarelles, in which the figures number into the hundreds, the "third animal" is represented by the reindeer, the ibex, and the mammoth, which are concentrated in the general area of the side panel of each decorated gallery.

Finally, there is also a D category to which fierce animals belong: the rhinoceros, the bear, and the big cats. The bear is a relatively rare animal in Paleolithic iconography and has no clearly defined place, but the rhinoceros and the big cats are marginal animals, most often situated in the deepest or most peripheral parts of the figured group. At Lascaux, Font-de-Gaume, the Combarelles, to cite only a few, the big cats are in this position. In these three places, the rhinoceros occupies an analogous position: at Lascaux, at the bottom of the Well; at Font-de-Gaume, at the end of the main gallery next to the big cat; and at the Combarelles, superimposed over the "lioness" from the end of the second gallery. The complete formula for the grouping is C + AB + C (+ D) in the case of a cave with a single composition, one that forms part of a series. In extreme cases, as in Lascaux or Combarelles, one may encounter a series of groupings with the basic formula repeated time and again.

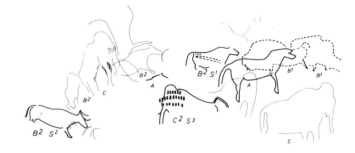

Cave of Pech-Merle (Lot). Middle and left of the great frieze painted in black. Two groups of animals can be seen: the group on the left and the group on the right each include a horse (A) and two bison on the right, two aurochs on the left. The mammoths present in both groupings make up group C. Between the two groupings, there are also three animals marked by signs: (1) a bull (B^2) bearing a sign (S^1) with a male connotation on his side (see fig. 5); (2) a cow (B^2) marked by wounds (S^2); (3) diagonally across from both animals, a mammoth bearing three rows of thick red dashes. The figures are between 60 and 120 cm long. (Fig. 3)

Signs

Signs seem to follow the same general patterns as animal figures. They fall into three categories (fig. 5). The first is made up of male symbols (S^1) ranging from the human body depicted in its entirety to a simple little stick. In between are sometimes very abstract transitions (lines branching out with two extensions at the base, as in Lascaux). The signs of the second group (S^2) correspond to female symbols. Like the signs of the first group, they range from a complete female representation to an empty or partitioned rectangle. The third group (S^3), in comparison with the other two, is homologous to the animals of group C or CD. It is made up of aligned dots or a series of little sticks aligned or clustered. In several cases, the S^3 signs are repeated at the beginning and the end of the figurative series. This phenomenon is quite evident at Lascaux, where the aligned dots are found at the entrance and at the far end of the Axial Diverticulum, between the Passage and the Nave, at the bottom of the Well, and at the end of the Diverticulum of the Big Cats. The signs of the third group, therefore, occupy a position rather set back, most often in the background, as at Font-de-Gaume, Pech-Merle, and El Castillo.

The relationship between signs and animals corresponds to the following broad lines: the S^1S^2 group is found juxtaposed with the animals of groups A and B (fig. 2), as in the case of the Diverticulum of the Big Cats at Lascaux (fig. 6), in which the S^1S^2 signs are in the central panel, right across from an AB group (horse-bison). But the signs may be independent of the animal figures, grouped in a separate diverticulum. Good examples can be found at Niaux (Black Room), at El Castillo, at La Pasiega, and, notably, at Cougnac. The relationship between animals and signs may thus be defined by the following formula:

$$C + AB + C + D$$
$$S^3 + S^1S^2 + S^3$$

or

$$C + AB + C + D/S^1S^2,$$
$$S^3 \qquad S^3$$

Both formulas can even be found in the same cave (La Pasiega).

This complex arrangement must have encompassed an ideology whose elaborate character may be perceived through the arrangement. The situation is further complicated, however, by the role played by the cave itself. Natural caves have many accidental features that evoked, for Paleolithic man, sexual forms, generally female. These natural structures, fissures or stalagmitic formations, sometimes underscored in red (Gargas, Niaux), are also frequently completed with an S^1 sign (little sticks or dots: Gargas, Combel de Pech-Merle, Niaux), proving that the natural phenomenon was considered equivalent to S^2. This is particularly clear in Niaux, where two fissures in the inner gallery were marked at the entrance by a sign of male connotation (branching sign) accompanied in one of the two cases by a horse with its head extended in the direction of the fissure.

In the course of millennia and in a territory as vast as that of Paleolithic cave art, figurative traditions must have undergone numerous variations, and it is remarkable that we should come across an ideographic system that is so well constructed. Yet two rather important questions, concerning the role of wounds on animals and the role of hands, remain largely unresolved.

Cave of Gargas (Hautes-Pyrénées). Panel showing "negative" hands with "mutilated" fingers. Most such hands, colored red or black, are grouped in twos by subject, and appear to have been executed by folding in the fingers or by applying a stencil. (Fig. 4)

Wounds

In art objects as well as mural art, we find animals with wounds. Ever since research on prehistoric religion began, this detail has been thought to reveal the practice of magic spells. This explanation is not altogether impossible, but certain elements lead us to believe that it does not resolve the problem entirely. In fact, 96% of the animal figures on file (between 2,500 and 3,000) show no wounds. We might ask ourselves if the two series, animal and sign, really belong to the same symbolic system, or if two lines of symbols might have existed without any organic ties between them. Signs do seem to have played their role at the same times and in the same places as animals. What is more, both evolved synchronically, and both underwent parallel stylistic transformations. It is very unlikely that signs were slipped in among animals, with no connection to them, in the course of various rituals; too many signs are connected to animals by their position for the relationship not to be a close one, as the Pech-Merle paintings show (fig. 3). This does not preclude the claim that signs are sometimes independent, as at Altamira, where the signs and the animals of the Great Ceiling make up two distinct clusters; or as at El Castillo or La Pasiega, where, for one important portion, the painted

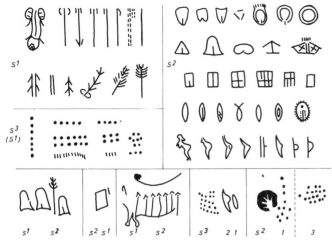

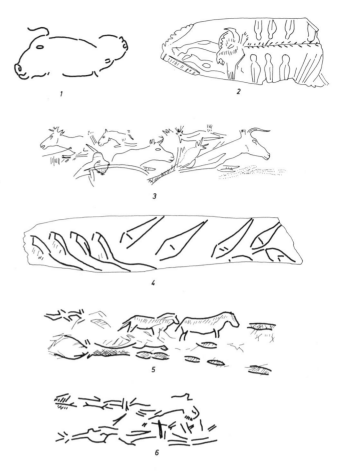

Geometrization of male and female symbols. S[1]: phalloid derivatives. S[2]: principal series of vulvar derivatives. S[3]: rows of punctuation (dotted lines) and barred lines. Below, from left to right: S[1]-S[2] groupings. El Castillo (Santander): triangle derivatives and branching sign. Lascaux (Dordogne): maximal geometrization and abstractions (empty rectangle and bar). Lascaux: crooked bar (S[1]) and seven aligned wounds (S[2]). S[1], S[2], S[3] groupings. Niaux (Ariège): bar (S[1]), claviform (see same S[2] figure), cloud of dots (S[3]). Pech-Merle (Lot): at the entrance of a deep side passage, three figures that appear to correspond in value to S[1]: dotted line with four lateral dots (see same S[3] figure). The negative hand probably corresponds to S[2], and the cloud of dots, farther into the passage, probably corresponds to S[3]. (Fig. 5).

Lascaux (Dordogne): (1) Engraved horse with rump turned such that the perineal region is exposed but devoid of primary sexual characteristics. 60 cm. (2) Paintings from the axial gallery, central part of the righthand wall. Aurochs in the same posture as the horse in front. Secondary sexual characteristics (general profile) are attributable to a cow, but primary characteristics, notably the udder, are invisible. This figure is included in the grouping formula A-B S[1]-S[2] (horse-aurochs, bars, gridlike sign; see fig. 5). 1.70 m. (Fig. 6)

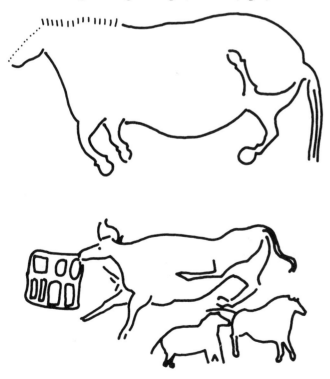

Gourdan (Haute-Garonne). The principle of association of animals A and B may also be applied to portable objects. This engraving on bone plaquette represents the aurochs-horse twosome with the heads of both animals assembled like the faces on playing cards. About 6 cm from nose to nose. (2) Raymonden (Dordogne). Partial pendant (or fish spatula). A scene of a religious nature seems to be unfolding: six or seven persons (perhaps more) are lined up on either side of a line resembling barbed wire at the end of which is the severed head of a bison and two paws with ill-defined hooves. Near the knee, one of these legs bears a "chestnut," a horny growth that is the vestige of the multifingered hoof of the ancestors of the *equidae*. It may indeed be a horse leg, and this grouping with its sacrificial look may refer to the A-B model. (3) Torre (Guipuzcoa). Roll of fine engravings around a bone tube. From left to right: stag, man, horse, chamois, two small ibex with frontal horns, and aurochs. This series of animals referring to A-B model + C is of more than purely artistic interest: between the subjects are abstract tracings (parallel or crossed strokes, beginnings of spherical figures, clouds made of fine dots, etc.) which must have ensured that Magdalenians could "read" this mythogram. (4) Mas-d'Azil (Ariège). Bone plaquette engraved with horses and fish, already strongly geometrized. Mythographic theme born out by several examples. (5) El Valle (Santander). Bone tube with engraved bird. Subject related to preceding one: two horses, one behind the other, a stag facing forward, numerous features with no apparent meaning, perhaps a snake, and some oval figures, probably fish. (6) El Pendo (Santander). Bone tube engravings, like the preceding ones, but virtually uninterpretable. There remains a part of the head and neck of a horse and a herbivore with visible horns (or antlers) and ears borne by a very long neck. Note that these two figures occupy the same situation as those of the El Valle tube. (Fig. 7)

signs are collected in a side passage; or at Cougnac (Lot), where S^1 and S^2 signs are located in a side alcove away from the animal figures, while the S^3 series occurs in the figured panels.

Whether these are two series of symbols executed simultaneously and experienced as forming the frame of a single ideological block, or whether they are two separate series with elements that were to enter one another on synchronic but distinct levels—either case presupposes a highly complex intellectual content, intimately tied to an elaborate social system. Could they be symbols of the propagation of humans and animals, a cosmogony that calls into play the complementary forces of male and female? It is difficult to reach a conclusion without going beyond the available data, but certainly we are in the presence of something quite different from what was long imagined about "the Paleolithic savages."

Of the 4% of animals showing wounds in the thoracic or the neighboring abdominal areas, if we do a percentage count by species, the greatest number goes to the bison (8%), then to the horse (2.5%), with zero or less than 1% for all other species. There is yet another striking fact. Although wounded animals are encountered throughout the Franco-Cantabrian region, most cases occur in the Ariège sector of the Pyrenees, with the greatest number represented at Niaux (25% of figured animals). The value of the wound as a testimony to magic spells for game might be merely an accessory phenomenon, but the hunting symbolism to which it refers is certain. The fact that wounds appear essentially only on the bodies of the basic twosome is perhaps connected with the $AB = S^1S^2$ equation, the wounds being the equivalent of S^2, that is, the female connotation. Three pieces of evidence may be invoked to support this contention: a horse at Lascaux bearing seven wounds on its body and an S^2 sign (fig. 5) on its neck and withers; a bison at Bernifal whose shoulder has an oval wound flanked by two little sticks; and a bison at Niaux engraved on clay, which has three wounds and two little sticks on its side. These parallel sticks belong to the highly varied portion of masculine symbols. One of the best examples of the relationship between signs and animals is that of the great panel of Pech-Merle (fig. 3) made up of two groupings that share the same C animal (C^2 mammoth). One is the aurochs-horse (AB^2), and the other the horse-bison (AB^1). Between the two groupings of figures are three animals: a bull, a cow, and a mammoth. Each bears different signs. The bull bears a double line of dashes with lateral extensions (S^1, of male character). The cow is riddled with wounds that seem to play the role of S^2 signs. The mammoth is covered with red spots aligned to form the equivalent of the S^3 sign. From this evidence we can hypothesize that "wounds" have the value of a female symbol. Establishing this symbolism would open a vast realm of possibilities for the symbolic system of Paleolithic art, one that involves the alternation of symbols of life and death.

Hands

While the problem of wounds allows us to do no more than hint at some kind of metaphysical solution, *positive* hand imprints (in which a hand is smeared with color and pressed flat against the wall) and *negative* hand imprints (in which a hand is laid flat against the wall and outlined in color) raise questions equally resistant to clear answers. Positive hands are substantially rarer than negative hands and show up infrequently in groupings, but the Bayol cave in the Ardèche region has a good example. It shows six positive

hands in a grouping that includes an aurochs, two horses, and one big cat, all treated in a very particular style.

There are several types of negative hands, probably corresponding to several different traditions. The first category is made up of hands integrated in a grouping that includes, notably, dottings; this is the case in Pech-Merle, where in six instances hands are associated with dotted lines in close proximity to the two crisscrossed horses and once with eleven dotted lines above the opening of a very low side passage (fig. 5). The same arrangement of animal figures and dottings is found in El Castillo. In the Périgord, negative hands appear in isolation (one at Font-de-Gaume, one at Combarelles, several grouped at Bernifal, etc.). At Roucadour (Lot), the hands are superposed over the animals, and they have long pointed fingers incised on a black background. The Pech-Merle hands give the impression of being inserted in an arrangement where they play an important role, surely as important as the S^2 signs with their female connotation.

The hands in the cave of Gargas (Hautes-Pyrénées), like those in the neighboring grotto at Tibiran, are very different in nature (fig. 4). Repeated scores of times in different panels and hollows of the cave, they have the special feature of cut-off or, more likely, bent-in fingers. The various combinations of fingers might have been part of a kind of symbolic code of the animals most commonly represented in figurative art (horse, bison, ibex, etc.). The same digital formula appears again in side-by-side hands repeated twice and alternating between red and black (fig. 4). Examples can also be found at the openings of niches or fissures, in the position normally occupied by animals or signs of CD and S^1 groups. As strange as it may seem, the "mutilated hands" of Gargas, which include many children's hands, are not missing all five fingers. They seem to correspond to a fairly rational application of signals involving variably bent fingers, gestures that can still be observed today among certain groups of hunters, notably the Bushmen. Aside from the monumental aspect of the connections between the groups of hands and their natural support, the ideographic aspect is extremely impressive.

Animal and human figures make up the ground on which our tentative explanation of wall painting rests. This explanation calls on data which, in the way they are assembled, suggest a complex ideological construct. To what extent can objects that are found not on walls but on sites of living quarters corroborate this claim?

Objects

Caves contain particularly precious data, if only because the images have preserved their location on walls. A no less precious source of information, however, may be found on the surfaces of Paleolithic floors strewn with objects that bear human and animal figures. Some of these objects are fairly soft fragments of stone or fragments of bone on which figures have been incised or sculpted. No practical function can be attributed to them, and we are struck by their resemblance to the figures on walls. Given their iconographic content, we ask whether they could have played the same role in living quarters as the figures played in the cave, and whether they were used to reproduce the same combinations. These questions are difficult to answer decisively, for the possibilities of iconographic combinations are extremely varied. The figures (statuettes, plaquettes or blocks, weapons or tools, personal adornments) may have been assembled in a meaningful way (according to the C-A-B-C + D model), a configuration that may presuppose, for example, either several plaquettes each bearing one figure, or several plaquettes each bearing several animal figures. Unfortunately rare are the cases where portable objects are found in their functional places, and even rarer are sites where the excavators took the trouble to record the exact position of the relics. Yet we can begin by assuming that, since caves existed only in a limited number of areas while vast territories lent themselves only to open-air settlements, the plaquettes of stone, ivory, or bone or the statuettes which sometimes abound at such sites fulfilled the role that otherwise devolved upon cave walls.

We may also assume that the other decorated objects reflect, in whole or in part, the same ideological scheme that is displayed by the grouping of the figures on the walls.

Statuettes

Statuettes of animals are relatively rare in the Paleolithic art of western Europe. The cave of Isturitz (Basses-Pyrénées) stands out as an exception with its numerous animals (bison, horses, bears) incised in soft rock. The true domain of animal figures in round relief is central and eastern Europe. The pictorial repertory of Europe east of the Rhine is mostly made up of statuettes molded in clay mixed with powdered bone (Moravia), incised in bone or in mammoth ivory; and figurines of mammoth, horse, bison, and big cats. The functions of these statuettes are as yet unclear, but since they must have assumed the same role as that played by the engravings and paintings in the caves, they must have the same symbolic ranges.

One category of figures is made up of female statuettes, inaccurately called ''Venus'' figures, that appear in various forms depending on the stages of the Paleolithic epoch and the regions in which they were executed. The items discovered at Kostienki (on the Don River), on Ukranian sites, at Predmost in Moravia, Willendorf in Austria, and at Brassempouy and Lespugue in southwestern France show in the details of their execution that they belong to the same pictorial traditions. Were the religious traditions that they were supposed to illustrate of the same nature? That is hard to answer, for the good reason that female statuettes can only symbolize a limited number of functions, generally relating to fertility. Based on what we know today, it would be difficult to say any more about them, except perhaps that the statuettes discovered in living quarters may have played an identical role to that of the signs in the groupings of figures on the walls. Male figures by their very scarcity seem to have occupied a much more modest place.

In brief, plaquettes, which are far more numerous in the West than statuettes, and statuettes, which are more numerous than plaquettes in central and eastern Europe, seem to have had the same functions. Given the resemblances between portable art (on plaquettes and statuettes) and mural art, we can ascribe identical functions to them and assimilate them to the same religious process. Unfortunately, this does not entirely clarify the details of the process that we know to have borrowed the same basic symbols throughout all of Europe for twenty thousand years. The formula A-B, C, D + S^1, S^2, S^3 did not necessarily have the same ideological implications in the Urals as it did on the banks of the Vézère. The hundreds of plaquettes of engraved schist from Gönnersdorf (dating from the Magdalenian epoch ca. 10,000) left lying on the ground may not have had the same function as the heavy engraved blocks of the Aurignacian epoch around 30,000.

It seems possible nevertheless to discern in the groupings of art objects and mural art alike the systematic presence of two animals A-B, often associated with one or two animals from group C. Human figures and male and female symbols are also present, as they are in wall paintings. The specialized use of certain objects may have influenced the choice of the figures that were drawn on them. There were relatively few decorated objects during the first millennia; realistic figures, at least, were rare. It is not until the middle and late Magdalenian Age, from 12,000 to 9000, that objects made of reindeer horn and bone begin to be covered with figures. Propelling devices—hooked pieces probably designed to hurl assegais at game—most often depict a single animal, close to the hook. On objects in this category the most eclectic assortment can be found: horse, bison, mammoth, ibex, reindeer, big cat, fish, bird. The propelling devices (their real use is still unknown) thus fall in the same iconographic category as plaquettes and statuettes.

Perforated Sticks

Perforated sticks are a different story. A kind of lever made of reindeer horns, the stick consists of a cylindrical handle with a bifurcation at one end in which a hole three centimeters in diameter has been pierced at the thickest point. Its real use was to straighten out, while hot or cold, the long assegai spears that had kept the curvature of the horns from which they had been made. The class of perforated sticks includes a large number of carefully decorated objects. In a significant proportion of them, the handle is sculpted in the shape of a phallus. Sometimes both extensions of the head of the object have this decoration. There are also many perforated sticks that bear the A-B grouping (horse-bison) or the third animal, in the form of a stag, a reindeer, or an ibex. A whole series of perforated sticks are decorated on their lateral extensions with two heads of bison, highly geometrized and often reduced to two sets of parallel bars. This decorative element can be found from the Asturias to Switzerland. Some perforated sticks feature realistic scenes, such as the one at Dordogne in Laugerie-Basse, which on one side shows a man knocked over by a bison and on the other side a horse; or the one in La Madeleine, which has a man, a snake, and two horses on one side, and two bison on the other. Certainly these animals were not grouped in a fortuitous manner: the H-B + A formula (Human-bison + horse) is the same formula as in the famous scene on the Well at Lascaux (a man knocked over by a bison, with a horse on the opposite wall). The second scene, however, must refer to another mythic content, for its formula, H-A + B (+ S) (Human-horse + bison [and snake]), has no known equivalent, but it does highlight the imperative character of the representation of the complementary animal: in the first case, the horse; in the second, the bison. We should also note that, as at Lascaux, the second animal is on the side opposite to the one with the scene.

Assegais

Assegais make up a category of particularly expressive decorated items. The ornamentation on these spears appears relatively early, around 20,000, and consists of geometric patterns, sometimes of a highly simplified animal figure. These markings may correspond to different hunters in the same group. But as time went by, the animal figures multiplied on some of these assegais. During the late Magdalenian era, some were covered with rows of horses on a raised field, which suggests that they served as instruments for parades or rituals rather than as effective weapons. The ends of assegais are often perforated to make them into pendants. Such pieces may have been part of a particular assegai that was lucky in its hunting and thereby served as a "talisman." The numerous pendants found in the Upper Paleolithic Age are largely inspired by sexual symbolism (cowrie shell, oval pendants, stag canines, etc.). It is thus likely that the assegai played a dual symbolic role. A few indices seem to support this contention, namely, the probable assimilation in mural art of male symbols with the assegai and female symbols with the wound. Many details from the natural relief of walls, such as oval niches painted red and the wounds on certain animals, support such a hypothesis. But it is difficult to consolidate the ideological aspects of this symbolic frame of reference.

Other decorated objects that might shed light on the religious thought of Paleolithic man require an even more sensitive interpretation. Harpoon points with realistic decoration are extremely rare. Conversely, we do have a considerable number of spatulas in the shape of fish, often highly geometrized. They may bear symbolic meaning, but at what level? The scale of values may range from a representation of a primarily aesthetic character to an instrument indispensable for the execution of a ritual. The same may be said of the rings of bone, three or four centimeters in diameter, with a very eclectic range of animal engravings on both sides. The fish spatula with its inevitable iconographic base (usually a species of *Salmonidae*), and the rings of bone on which all species are represented (including the human species) provide us only with a basic assumption and certainly not with evidence for an entire superstructure of beliefs. It is therefore by reference to the figures on walls and plaquettes that the iconography of portable objects can be analyzed. We may also want to view in the same spirit the so-called silhouette outlines, small pendants carved out of a hyoid bone, of which there are many known examples showing heads of horses as well as a group of eighteen ibex heads and one bison head, which may remind us of the triad horse-bison-ibex, the model of wall depiction.

One last category of materials is made up of groupings of figures engraved mostly on cylindrical objects (tubes of bird bone, assegai shafts, etc.), similar to the perforated sticks referred to above. Some of these objects bear explicit figures, like the bone tube of Torre (Spain), which in the space of fifteen centimeters depicts a series of busts including a stag, man, horse, chamois, ibex, and aurochs (fig. 7.1). This grouping, which may also incorporate signs in parallel or converging lines cross-hatched inside with ladders, is not far removed from certain wall groupings, such as the diver of Portel (Ariège), whose middle part is occupied by a horse, a bison, and male and female signs, while the periphery is occupied by the third sign (S^3), an ibex, and a stag. It would be hard not to regard these various assembled animals as the protagonists of a mythical story, a mythogram rather than a catalogue of the presumed victims of a spell of hunting magic. But whatever the figures may designate precisely, we cannot yet afford to go outside the realm of fact to venture an explanation. Thus we have a whole series of groupings on cylinders or plaquettes, graphically explicit but just as mysterious as ever, such as the strange object found in Les Eyzies on which eight hunters carrying assegais on their shoulders

seem to be parading in front of a bison, or another item from Chancelade (fig. 7.2) on which seven human silhouettes appear to surround a bison's head and severed front hooves. These two examples, probably variants of the same theme, show how the discovery of new versions might help us to decipher an increasingly important part of the Paleolithic message.

A significant number of specimens (figs. 7.4, 7.5, 7.6) bear an ornamentation that is very difficult to identify: a row of curves and ovoid figures including a recognizable horse here and there or a highly simplified stag, or sometimes a fish. Given the constancy with which geometric motifs replace explicit figures, we could almost speak of ideograms, though we need not see in these semigeometric figures the elements of "writing." We can assume that the geometrized symbols preserved their meaning, so that a grouping like "chevrons-broken lines" could be equivalent to, for instance, "horse-snake," chevrons being the tail end of a row of horses, and the broken line being the geometrization of the snake's body: both cases exist in an explicit form.

It might seem surprising to hear so little said about "prehistoric religion." As far as practices are concerned, our knowledge consists mainly of gaps. We may imagine that the caves were shrines in which highly elaborate rituals took place, but all we *have* is wall decorations. The fact that the dead were buried with ocher and, at least in some cases, with funerary personal effects, leads us to ascribe to Upper Paleolithic man some notion of an afterlife, but we know nothing about its modalities in any detail. The tablets or engraved blocks tell us about iconographic activities that must have had a religious purpose, but we are far from being able to assert what kind of purpose it was. The same applies to decorated objects (perforated sticks, propelling devices, spatulas, etc.) of which we cannot even claim to know the exact usage. Nevertheless, the wealth of the iconography and the constancy of certain relationships between figures and between figures and the surfaces on which they appear make it possible for us to sketch the bare outlines of a system of religious thought, though its background is still very murky. The complexity and quality of these groupings express feelings (with nuances tied to places and times) that reflect simultaneously the aesthetic and religious life of Paleolithic man.

A.L.-G./g.h.

BIBLIOGRAPHY

H. BREUIL, *Quatre cents siècles d'art pariétal* (Montignac 1952). P. GRAZIOSI, *L'arte dell'antica età della pietra* (Florence 1956). A. LAMING-EMPERAIRE, *La signification de l'art rupestre paléolithique* (Paris 1962). ANDRÉ LEROI-GOURHAN, *Préhistoire de l'art occidental* (Paris 1965); *Les religions de la préhistoire* (Paris 1971); "Les signes pariétaux de Paléolithique supérieur franco-cantabrique," *Simposio intern. de arte rupestre* (Barcelona 1968), 67–77, fig.; "Considérations sur l'organisation spatiale des figures animales dans l'art pariétal paléolithique," *Actes del Symposium intern. de arte prehis.* (Santander 1972), 281–308; "Iconographie et interprétation," *Val Camonica symposium 72* (Capo di Ponte 1975), 49–55. ARLETTE LEROI-GOURHAN, "The Flowers Found with Shanidar IV, a Neanderthal Burial in Iraq," *Science* 190 (1975): 562–64. L. MEROC, "Informations archéologiques, Circonscription de Toulouse, Mas d'Azil," *Gallia Préhistoire* 4 (1961):256–57.

"NOMADIC THOUGHT" AND RELIGIOUS ACTION

When the rainy season comes, the mendicant monk stops wandering and heads back to his monastery.[1]

For some years now, nomadic societies have awakened strong and renewed interest among ethnologists. On an intuitive level, these societies scattered over the globe seem to be mutually comparable, and attempts have been made to construct models of such societies, that is, to go beyond the empirical diversity that science seeks to overcome. These attempts at synthesis, notably the collective work published under the direction of Lee and De Vore[2] on hunter-gatherers, and the works of B. Spooner[3] on pastoral nomads, are evidence of the special position that nomadic societies occupy today in ethnology.

The term "nomadism" covers quite diverse phenomena: hunter-gatherers and pastoral nomads move over greater or lesser distances, more or less frequently; hunter-gatherers make use of wild objects, and pastoral nomads domestic objects, to mediate their relation with the natural environment. Although nomadic societies differ among themselves in their type of economy and in the breadth and frequency of their movements, as a group they contrast with societies that do not move, settled societies, and it is in this light that we shall consider them for the purposes of this study, setting aside the ways in which the group could be subdivided. Dissimilar in many ways, both social and economic, these societies share not only itinerant behavior but also certain characteristics, which we will examine in order to determine whether they are reflected at the level of thought and worldview. Starting with a limited amount of work done on this subject, we can but suggest a direction of study and posit some hypotheses for research. To find pantheons common to nomads, if such a thing were possible, would require far more concerted and exhaustive studies. But it may already be possible to isolate from its various contexts an attitude to the supernatural world and religion that is common to nomads, and to define a framework within which we might study their mythology.

"Free, individualistic, subject to no state nor to any tyranny," such is the "traditional stereotype" of the pastoral nomad.[4] But it is also an objective piece of information to the extent that it is derived from the image that the nomad has of himself. When this self-image comes into close contact with settled societies, it may even be more pronounced, thus affirming in a deliberate way the difference between nomadic and settled ideologies. Pastoral nomads have a realistic vision of the world and a rather meager ceremonial life. They practice a great deal of divination but little witchcraft. Religion is centered on the individual rather than on the group; indeed, a pantheon comprising a great number of divine figures seems to be more common among farmers. If nomads show little interest in religion, and if they refer to manifestations of the supernatural in "stoic terms," this does not mean that they are any more "secular"[5] than any other group. The cosmology of pastoral nomads in the Middle East, for example, tends to be expressed in Islamic terms. Through this filter, as Spooner points out, it should be possible to see those elements of cosmology that antedate Islam or are not integral to it. When these are compared with other cosmologies from nomadic populations in regions lacking such a culturally dominant ideology, it may be possible to isolate the elements that derive from the nomadic adaptation.[6]

The mythology of hunter-gatherer societies presents notable similarities. The myths that retrace the origins of a society are apparently universal and come out of the same mold. In these myths, the culture hero creates mankind and its customs; he domesticates fire, teaches arts and crafts, and shapes the landscape and animals. In the cosmology, spirits are not gods: culture heroes or creator spirits no longer intervene in the affairs of men, and that is why they are not worshiped. They have to do with existential ideology and not with normative ideology. Just as the accent is placed on the person in nomadic society, so the world of spirits is strongly individualized; egalitarianism within the group is reflected in the absence of any hierarchy among the spirits. The individual deals directly with the world of the supernatural. Except for the shaman/doctor, there is no reliable mediation by specialized individuals.[7] The culture hero who offers the world to humans after he has created them is not totally absent from nomadic societies; but probably more characteristic of such societies is the strongly existential aspect of the ideology as well as egalitarianism. The absence of authoritarian chiefs and of a certain type of power excludes certain types of divine figures. Moreover, nomadic hunters pay little attention to what does not involve them directly. Accordingly, the Mbuti are more concerned with the present than with the past or the future. They are practical people. They eschew all speculation about the future or the hereafter on the grounds that not having been there they do not know what it is like and not knowing what it is like they cannot predict what their behavior will be. They say that to try to look into the future is to "walk blindly."[8] Knowledge is considered a way of living rather than a rule. And it is precisely in their behavior in the face of—rather than by the content of—myth or the supernatural that the clear outlines of a way of thinking peculiar to nomads begin to emerge. We see in hunter-gatherers certain features already observed in the pastoral nomads, and profoundly different from the religious attitudes of settled societies. Before we describe nomadic societies as nonreligious or hardly religious, we might first ask whether ethnologists hold too narrow a conception of ritual and symbolic behavior, and whether their analytic tools may be too closely tied to the categories of settled societies, which would hamper their perception of religious phenomena among nomads.

Among the Basseri, pastoral nomads of Iran, the paucity of ritual activity is striking;[9] they are indifferent to metaphysical problems and to religion. But is this really a lack, or are the descriptive categories that are being used incapable of describing the reality of the situation? The central rite of the society is migration itself. For the Basseri, migration is laden with meaning, though not expressed by means of technically unnecessary symbolic acts or exotic paraphernalia. The Basseri respond not to the utilitarian aspects of activities but to movement and its dramatic forms, to the meanings implicit in the sequence of their activities.[10] Is it not rather ethnocentric to assume that an activity that is important from an economic point of view cannot also be important from a ritualistic or symbolic point of view? The migrations of nomads are more than mere business trips; they are also ritually motivated and determined, and our difficulties in observation seem to be due to our conflation of these two domains.

In this discussion of the relationship between religious attitude (taken in a rather broad sense) and nomadism, societies with seasonal variations are both exceptional and typical because they are alternately nomadic and settled. The gathered habitat of the winter season contrasts with the scattered habitat of the summer season, with its mobility and the splintering of the group into families in the narrowest sense of the word. There are two ways of occupying land, but there are also two ways of thinking: "This contrast between life in winter and life in summer is reflected not only in rituals, festivals, and religious ceremonies of all sorts. It also profoundly affects ideas, collective representations, in a word, the whole mentality of the group.[11] . . . In summer, life is somewhat secularized."[12] The ecological constraints to which the group is subject make nomadism necessary, and the group's requirements come to restrict religious thought and practice. But just as we must consider the role of adaptation to the environment, we must also refine our categories of analysis, and when appearances evoke secularization, we must understand that the foundation has yet to be deciphered. The mobility that characterizes nomadic societies is indeed the central feature of their organization, but it is also the main obstacle to our understanding.

"We must beware of any tendency to treat fixed and permanent ties linking together aggregates of people as normal, and loose, impermanent bonds as abnormal and requiring special explanation."[13] The migrations of hunters or pastoral nomads by far exceed those that would be required by the demands of the natural environment and of access to natural resources. The fluidity and the constant coming and going, both of groups and of individuals within the groups, have a political function: they make it possible to ensure order, the resolution of conflicts, and, paradoxically, cohesion, because the lines of fusion and fission of groups and individuals do not necessarily follow the lines of kinship. Among nomads, social relations become activated through changes of place: proximity or distance are not relevant, and space is in a sense negated. Finally—and, in our view, this is an essential point—the changes of place have a religious function: they are highly valued, so highly that Barth sees them as the central rite among the Basseri. It is movement that leads nomads "into closer recognition of the one constant in their lives, the environment and its life-giving qualities. Under such conditions of flux where band and even family relations are often brittle and fragmentary, the environment in general, and one's own hunting territory in particular, become for each individual the one reliable and rewarding focus of his attention, his loyalty, and his devotion."[14] In other words, the nomad "does not have the impression of inhabiting a man-made world. . . . He is controlled by objects, not persons. . . . There is not an anthropomorphic cosmos. Hence there is no call for articulate forms of social intercourse with nonhuman beings and no need for a set of symbols with which to send and receive special communication."[15] The nomad does not seek to improve the environment in which he lives. In this sense, he is controlled by objects and a world that are *wild*, and he is in direct touch with nature. The domestic animals through whose intervention he exploits the wild objects, if he is pastoral, serve only to mediate this relationship with nature. Whether he is a hunter-gatherer or a shepherd, he does not impose his Culture on Nature as do settled peoples. Mobility and fluidity of groups and within groups; decentralized societies, or rather societies with multiple centers; egalitarianism; direct contact with nature—such are the poles that may affect the ideology of nomads and that may be reflected in collective representations and in rituals.

With a few examples, we have sought to come to terms with nomadism and its underlying ideology as a "certain type of behavior,"[16] rather than as a mode of economic production or as a variable determined by environment. This particular attitude, in the face of the supernatural and the symbolic world, is governed by what we might call a nomadic way of thinking that participates in the "primitive/wild/*sauvage*" way of thinking but preserves its own characteristics within it. The analysis of the content of the myths of various nomadic societies may indeed highlight the lines of force around which "nomadic thought" is organized, and will finally allow us to spell out the specificity of a way of thinking in which what is normal is not what is fixed, and the fluid and the moving are order and not chaos.

F.-R.P./g.h.

NOTES

1. M. MAUSS, "Étude de morphologie sociale," in *Sociologie et anthropologie* (Paris 1966), 472.

2. R.-B. LEE and I. DEVORE, eds., *Man the Hunter* (Chicago 1968).

3. B. SPOONER, "Towards a Generative Model of Nomadism," *Anthropological Quarterly* 44, no. 3 (1971): 198–210; "The Cultural Ecology of Pastoral Nomads," in *Addison-Wesley Module in Anthropology*, no. 45 (Reading, MA, 1973).

4. B. SPOONER, "Cultural Ecology of Pastoral Nomads," 35.

5. Ibid., 39.

6. Ibid.

7. E. R. SERVICE, *The Hunters* (Englewood Cliffs, NJ, 1966).

8. C. M. TURNBULL, *Wayward Servants* (Garden City, NY, 1965), 247.

9. F. BARTH, *Nomads of South Persia* (Boston 1961), 135.

10. Ibid.

11. M. MAUSS, "Étude de morphologie sociale," 447–48.

12. Ibid., 444.

13. J. WOODBURN, "Stability and Flexibility in Hadza Residential Groupings," in *Man the Hunter*, Lee and DeVore, eds., 107.

14. C. M. TURNBULL, "The Importance of Flux in Two Hunting Societies," in *Man the Hunter*, Lee and DeVore, eds., 137.

15. M. DOUGLAS, *Natural Symbols* (London 1970), 60–61; cited in Spooner, "Cultural Ecology of Pastoral Nomads," 40.

16. CL. LÉVI-STRAUSS, "Hunting and Human Evolution: Discussion," in *Man the Hunter*, Lee and DeVore, eds., 344.

Greece

GREEK MYTHOLOGY

What is it that we call Greek mythology? In essence, it is a collection of narratives about gods and heroes, the two types of personage to whom the ancient city-states devoted cults. In this sense, mythology touches upon religion: along with rituals, which myths sometimes directly recapitulate, either when they justify in detail the practical procedures of rituals or when they mark out the provinces of rituals and develop their meanings, and along with various sculptural symbols, which give visual form to the gods and thus incarnate their presence at the heart of the human world, mythology constitutes one of the essential modes of expression for the religious thought of the Greeks. The fact that mythology was suppressed is perhaps the facet best fitted to reveal to us the divine universe of polytheism, that society of the Beyond—multiple, complex, altogether burgeoning and altogether ordered—that is disappearing. It does not follow, however, that we can discover in myths the sum of what a Greek had to know and to hold as truth on the subject of the gods, drawn together in narrative form as a kind of creed. Greek religion is not a book religion. Except for a few sectarian and marginal currents, like Orphism, it knows neither sacred text nor holy scriptures in which the truth of faith was defined and laid down once and for all. There is no place in Greek religion for any dogma. Though the beliefs for which myths are a vehicle entail compliance, they have no character of constraint or obligation; they do not constitute a body of doctrines fixing the theoretical bedrocks of piety, assuring the believer a base of indisputable certainties on an intellectual plane.

Myths are something quite different; they are narratives—accepted, understood, and felt as such, beginning with our most ancient documents. In this way they carry, from the very start, one might say, a dimension of the "fictitious," as witnessed by the semantic evolution of the term *muthos*. This term, in contrast to that which is of the order of the real, on the one hand, and to that which is of the order of argued demonstration, on the other, came to designate what is in the domain of pure fiction: the fable. This aspect of narration (and of narration free enough that multiple versions of the same god or the same episode of his deeds can coexist and contradict each other without causing dismay) weds Greek myth as much to what we call religion as to what we today call literature.

Lest I be misunderstood, I do not mean that myths, for the ancients, arose out of gratuitous fantasy, or that of all the works invented by the fancy of an individual or collective imagination they could not claim to be more serious, on the religious plane, or inspire more credence than old wives' tales. On the contrary, if readers wish to enter into Greek mythology, they are invited to leave behind the categories of thought which are habitual to them. Between literature and religion, as between fictional narrative and the truth of what it recounts, between the working out of the plot of a myth and the authenticity of the divine implied in the narrative, there was no rupture for Greeks of the archaic period, no incompatibility such as we are prone to contend. In a religious system without a church, without a sacerdotal body, without specialists in theological questions, without a revealed doctrine or a reference book that could have talked about the gods—setting aside the oral traditions, which are accessible to us only as fixed in one way or another by writing—the divine could only have been formulated in words by people whose function it was to produce the type of discourse through which Greek society is expressed and recognized at different stages of its culture: first the epic song, then the multiple forms of lyric and choral poetry, the hymns, the works of the tragedians, the comedies—in short, all those whom the Greeks, in accord with Plato, rank in the category of poets. For ancient theology is essentially poetry as well: discourse on the gods is mythical narration. It is in the form of narratives relating their legendary adventures, in the thread of dramatic events which mark the career of the gods from their birth, that the Powers of the Beyond are alluded to, expressed, and conceived of in their reciprocal connections, in the zones of action assigned to them, the types of power that characterize them, their oppositions and agreements, their particular modes of intervention on earth and of affinity with man.

In this respect, the mythology of the Greeks is like the allegorical representations of their gods. Both operate in the register we call anthropomorphism. The organization, the equilibrium of divine society—in short, its model of operation—are evoked indirectly by rivalries, conflicts that divide it even to the point of merciless warfare, friendships formed, marriages celebrated, births, relationships that weave bonds of kinship between different divine sectors, contests of power, failures and victories, tests of strength between rivals, and the sharing of honors among allies who are faithful and reliable. Nevertheless, an anthropomorphic statue of Apollo, a naked *kouros,* is not a portrait of the god but a way of making visible in the form of the human body those values that belong to the divine, that are the perquisite of the Immortals and whose reflection illuminates the human body in the prime of life, only to be immediately erased: youth, beauty, balanced force. Nor should the various deeds, the scandals with which poets delight in filling the gazette of Olympus, be taken at face value. Because they transpose into the language of humans what belongs to the domain of the gods, the narratives cannot be taken literally. It is, however, necessary—and entirely necessary—to take them seriously. No matter how free the transposition may be, it obeys rules strict enough to make it possible, in and through the narrative, to point in the direction of the divine powers and to mark their position in relation to one another and their status with regard to humans. We shall select a single example from our most ancient and in many respects least "theological" text, the *Odyssey.* When Homer relates the episode of the adulterous love of Ares and Aphrodite, caught like rats in a trap in the snares of Hephaestus, *in flagrante delicto* before all the assembled gods, the poet establishes enough ironic distance from his own narrative to emphasize the fact that he treats it like a game, even a farce; he would be the first to recognize that there are other ways to tell the fable and vary its plot. But every version, like his own, ought to express, as a joke or as a drama, certain of the characteristics which make the divinities implicated in the scenario into a triad of powers bound by definite relations of opposition and complementarity. Hephaestus, the magician, master of bonds, capable of chaining the living into the immobility of stone and, likewise, of liberating life by animating inert matter; the metallurgist, intimately associated with Aphrodite by that grace, that charm, that *charis* of seduction which the goddess incarnates and whose brilliance the god has the skill to capture, to fix in the fascinating pieces, sparkling with life, that his art succeeds in producing; Ares and Aphrodite, also associated but in another way, just as love and hate, marriage and war combine among men, and as the powers of accord and conflict, of harmony and strife are reconciled in the cosmos; finally, Hephaestus and Ares contrasting as the intelligence, the cunning adroitness of the artisan, and the brutal force, the blind violence of the warrior—Ares with the speed of a racer, the rapidity of a "light-footed" fighter, Hephaestus with the awkward limp of the maimed, of the deformed man with twisted feet. But the god who zigzags as he walks, whose progression is sinuous, is the one who attains his goal directly: it is the invincible racer who finds himself nailed to the ground beside Aphrodite, paralyzed by the crafty tricks of the cripple.

Through the pleasure of a completely human narration, narrative fiction operates according to a code with strict rules for a determined culture. This code controls and guides the game of the mythic imagination; it delimits and organizes the field in which the imagination can produce, can modify the old schemata and elaborate new versions. By taking advantage of the constraints it imposes as well as of the compatibilities it authorizes, by exploring the gamut of directions that are open, the work of narrative invention is accomplished, and by the continuous repetition of tradition it stays alive in a civilization.

Staying alive does not signify merely that the message carried by the narratives continues to be understood, with all its implications and on all its levels. It also means that the field of mythology forever constitutes the place where religious beliefs seek their explanations, where they are perpetuated by being expressed in the mode and form of elaborate narrations. Mythology constitutes the stakes in a debate which goes beyond mythology; it appears imbued with polemics that do not use the weapons of argued discussion or refutation in the manner of the philosophers but operate through an agency different from the material of fable. When we compare, for example, the Orphic theogonies to the traditional Hesiodic schema, or confront various versions of the myth of the foundation of sacrifice, we see that the modifications of the plot can respond to certain fundamental divergences of theological orientation. The digressions in the texture of the narrative, the overturning of the order of sequences, often express contradictory attitudes toward the divine, a different conception of the relationship between man and the gods, the embracing of different religious universes governing cultic practices, or incompatible modes of existence. Mythology thus testifies to the confrontation of opposing religious currents, of groups of believers in competition within the same culture.

Brief as they are, these remarks may, without entirely justifying our approach to the Greek myths, allow us to dispense with a long account of our method, which might have seemed pedantic. The team at the Center for Comparative Research on Ancient Societies—which, thanks to the friendly confidence of Yves Bonnefoy, has taken charge of the category of Greek mythology—has engaged the collaboration of French and foreign scholars, such as Clémence Ramnoux, Philippe Borgeaud, Claude Calame, and Jean Rudhardt, whose competence on certain themes and points was greater. In this enterprise we had no intention of making a catalog of all the Greek myths or all the characters who figured in them. There are, for this purpose, vast and knowledgeable lexicons, indispensable working tools for specialists but reserved for their use. It is impossible to summarize them: their value lies in the exhaustive and precise way in which they detail the assembled documentation. Other dictionaries, more accessible, offer the public, in condensed form, an outline of the principal versions of legends about gods and heroes. We have chosen a different path: from the corpus of Greek myths, we have deliberately taken those groups of myths which, while occupying a central place, have appeared to us to lend themselves to a new reading, a "decoding" based on recent advances in the study of religion and the analysis of myth. Instead of cutting up mythology in thin slices beginning with a multitude of characters listed in alphabetical order, we have, as much as possible, focused on mythological narratives dealing with great fundamental themes: cosmogonies, theogonies and myths of sovereignty, anthropogonies, the origin of men and the subsequent appearance of women, sacrificial myths, animals and the bestiary, divinities of the water, gods and heroes of war, of the hunt, the powers of marriage, gods who are fabricators and artisans, death, the erotic, mythology and philosophy, myth and city-state. Even when we have treated individual characters by reason of their importance or notoriety, heroes such as Heracles, the Amazons, the Argonauts, Odysseus, or such gods as Apollo, Artemis, Demeter, Dionysus, Hermes, or Pan, we have sought not to isolate these figures by envisaging them in themselves and for themselves, but to situate them in the body of the pantheon, to define them by the particular function they assume in it, to emphasize the bonds that attach each heroic deed to the great articulations of mythology—the entire system of legendary creation in which the Greeks sought to inscribe the distinguishing traits of their religious universe, in a continuing effort to translate in terms of narrative the physiognomy of the sacred, the configuration of the beyond, the geography of the supernatural world that belonged to their culture.

J.-P. V./d.f.

BIBLIOGRAPHY FOR ANCIENT GREECE

C. BÉRARD, *Anodoi: Essai sur l'imagerie des passages chthoniens* (Neuchâtel 1974). P. BOYANCÉ, *Le culte des Muses chez les philosophes grecs: Étude d'histoire et de psychologie religieuses* (Paris 1937; 2d ed., 1972). B. BRAVO, *Philologie, histoire, philosophie de l'histoire* (Warsaw 1968). A. BRELICH, *Gli Eroi greci: Un problema storico-religioso* (Rome 1958); *Paides e Parthenoi* (Rome 1969). L. BRISSON, *Le mythe de Tiresias: Essai d'analyse structurale* (Leiden 1976). F. BROMMER, *Herakles: Die zwölf Taten des Helden in antiker Kunst und Literatur* (Münster, Cologne, and Böhlau 1953); *Denkmälerlisten zur griechischen Heldensage*, 4 vols. (Marburg 1971–76); *Vasenlisten zur griechischen Heldensage* (3d ed., Marburg 1973); *Hephaistos: Der Schmiedegott im antiken Kunst* (Mainz 1978). N. O. BROWN, *Hermes the Thief: The Evolution of a Myth* (New York 1947). F. BUFFIÈRE, *Les mythes d'Homère et la pensée grecque* (Paris 1956). W. BURKERT, *Homo Necans: Interpretationen altgriechischer Opferriten und Mythen* (Berlin and New York 1972); *Griechische Religion der archaischen und klassischen Epoche*, Die Religionen der Menschheit, 15 (Stuttgart, Berlin, Cologne, and Mainz 1977). F. CHAPOUTHIER, *Les Dioscures au service d'une déesse: Étude d'iconographie religieuse* (Paris 1935). A. B. COOK, *Zeus, a Study in Ancient Religion*, 5 vols. (Cambridge 1914–40). F. M. CORNFORD, *From Religion to Philosophy: A Study in the Origins of Western Speculation* (London and New York 1912); *Principium Sapientiae: The Origins of Greek Philosophical Thought* (Oxford 1952). P. DECHARME, *Mythologie de la Grèce antique* (3d ed., Paris 1884). M. DELCOURT, *Légendes et cultes de héros en Grèce* (Paris 1942); *Œdipe ou la légende du conquérant* (Liège and Paris 1944); *Héphaistos ou la légende du magicien* (Paris 1957); *Hermaphrodite: Mythes et rites de la bisexualité dans l'Antiquité classique* (Paris 1958). M. DETIENNE, *Les jardins d'Adonis: La mythologie des aromates en Grèce* (Paris 1972); *Dionysos mis à mort* (Paris 1977). M. DETIENNE, ed., *Il mito: Guida storica e critica* (Bari 1974). M. DETIENNE and M.-P. VERNANT, *Les ruses de l'intelligence: La mètis des Grecs* (Paris 1974). J. DE VRIES, *Forschungsgeschichte der Mythologie*, Orbis Academicus 1, 7 (Freiburg and Munich 1961). A. DIETERICH, *Mutter Erde* (3d ed., Leipzig 1925; reprinted 1967). B. C. DIETRICH, *Death, Fate and the Gods: The Development of a Religious Idea in Greek Popular Belief and in Homer* (London 1965). E. R. DODDS, *The Greeks and the Irrational* (Berkeley 1951). CH. DUGAS and R. FLACELIÈRE, *Thésée: Images et récits* (Paris 1958). G. DUMÉZIL, *Le crime des Lemniennes* (Paris 1924); *Le festin d'immortalité: Esquisse d'une étude de mythologie comparée indo-européenne* (Paris 1924); *Le problème des Centaures: Étude de mythologie comparée indo-européenne* (Paris 1929); *Mythe et épopée*, 3 vols. (Paris 1968–73). E. J. and L. EDELSTEIN, *Asclepius: A Collection and Interpretation of the Testimonies*, 2 vols. (Baltimore 1945; reprinted New York 1975). M. ELIADE, *Aspects du mythe* (Paris 1963); *The Myth of the Eternal Return, or Cosmos and History* (Princeton 1954). A. ERMATINGER, *Die attische Autochthonensage* (Berlin 1897). L. R. FARNELL, *The Cults of the Greek States*, 5 vols. (Oxford 1896–1909); *Greek Hero Cults and Ideas of Immortality* (Oxford 1921). A.-J. FESTUGIÈRE, *Études de religion grecque et hellénistique* (Paris 1972). M.-I. FINLEY, "Myth, Memory and History," in *The Use and Abuse of History* (London 1975), 11–33. R. FLACELIÈRE and P. DEVAMBEZ, *Héraclès: Images et récits* (Paris 1966). J. FONTENROSE, *Python: A Study of Delphic Myth and Its Origins* (Berkeley 1959); *The Ritual Theory of Myth* (Berkeley and London 1971). H. FRAENKEL, *Dichtung und Philosophie des frühen Griechentums; English trans. by M. Hadas and J. Willis, *Early Greek Poetry and Philosophy* (Oxford 1975). F. FRONTISI-DUCROUX, *Dédale: Mythologie de l'artisan en Grèce ancienne* (Paris 1975). B. GENTILI and G. PAIONE, eds., *Il mito greco*, Atti del Convegno

Internazionale, Urbino, 1973 (Rome 1977). L. GERNET, *Anthropologie de la Grèce antique*, Preface by J.-P. Vernant (Paris 1968; reprinted 1976). L. GERNET and A. BOULANGER, *Le génie grec dans la religion* (Paris 1932; reprinted with a complementary bibliography 1970). L.-B. GHALIKAHIL, *Les Enlèvements et le retour d'Hélène dans les textes et les documents figurés* (Paris 1955). G. GIANNELLI, *Culti e miti della Magna Grecia* (2d ed., Florence 1963). P. GRIMAL, *Dictionnaire de la mythologie grecque et romaine* (4th ed., Paris 1969). O. GRUPPE, *Griechische Mythologie und Religionsgeschichte*, 2 vols. (Munich 1906); *Geschichte der klassischen Mythologie und Religionsgeschichte während des Mittelalters im Abendland und während der Neuzeit* (Leipzig 1921), in Roscher, *Lexikon d. griech. und röm. Mythologie*, supplement. E. HAHN, *Demeter und Baubo* (Leipzig 1897). J. HARRISON, *Prolegomena to the Study of Greek Religion* (3d ed., Cambridge 1922); *Themis: A Study of the Social Origins of Greek Religion* (2d ed., Cambridge 1927). R. HERBIG, *Pan, der griechische Bocksgott* (Frankfurt-am-Main 1949). W. HIRSCH, *Platons Weg zum Mythos* (Berlin and New York 1971). H. HUNGER, *Lexikon der griechischen und römischen Mythologie* (6th ed., Vienna 1969). H. JEANMAIRE, *Couroi et Courètes* (Lille and Paris 1939); *Dionysos: Histoire du culte de Bacchus* (Paris 1951; reprinted 1970). L. KAHN, *Hermès passe ou les ambiguïtés de la communication* (Paris 1978). K. KERÉNYI, ed., *Die Eröffnung des Zugangs zum Mythos* (Darmstadt 1967); *Dionysos: Archetypal Image of Indestructible Life* (Princeton 1976); *Die Mythologie der Griechen: Die Götter und Menschheitsgeschichten* (Zurich 1951); *Die Heroen der Griechen: Die Heroengeschichten der griechischen Mythologie* (Zurich 1958). G. S. KIRK, *Myth: Its Meaning and Functions in Ancient and Other Cultures* (Berkeley and Cambridge 1970); *The Nature of Greek Myth* (New York 1974). B. KNOX, *Œdipus at Thebes: Sophocles' Tragic Hero and His Time* (New Haven and London 1957; 2d ed., 1966); *The Heroic Temper: Studies in Sophoclean Tragedy* (Berkeley 1964). F. LASSERRE, *La figure d'Éros dans la poésie grecque* (Lausanne 1946). E. LEACH, ed., *The Structural Study of Myth and Totemism* (London and New York 1969). C. LÉVI-STRAUSS, "The Structural Study of Myth," in *Structural Anthropology* (New York 1963); "Mythologie et rituel," in *Anthropologie structurale deux* (Paris 1973), 139–315. N. LORAUX, "Sur la race des femmes et quelques-unes de ses tribus," *Arethusa* 11 (1978): 43–87; "L'Autochtonie: Une topique athénienne. Le mythe dans l'espace civique," *Annales E.S.C.*, 1979, 3–26. R. MARTIN and H. METZGER, *La religion grecque* (Paris 1976). H. METZGER, *Les représentations dans la céramique attique du IVe siècle* (Paris 1951); *Recherches sur l'imagerie athénienne* (Paris 1965). M.-P. NILSSON, *The Mycenaean Origin of Greek Mythology* (Cambridge 1932); *Cults, Myths, Oracles and Politics in Ancient Greece* (Lund 1951; reprinted New York 1972); *Geschichte der griechischen Religion*, 2 vols., Handbuch der Altertumswissenschaft, 5, 2 (3d ed., Munich 1967, 1974). W. F. OTTO, *Die Gestalt und das Sein: Gesammelte Abhandlungen über den Mythos und seine Bedeutung für die Menschheit* (2d ed., Darmstadt 1959); *Dionysos: Myth and Cult* (Bloomington, IN, 1965); *The Homeric Gods* (Boston 1964). J. PERADOTTO, *Classical Mythology: An Annotated Bibliographical Survey* (Urbana 1973). P. PHILIPPSON, *Genealogie als mythische Form: Studien zur Theogonie des Hesiod*, "Symbolae Osloenses," supplement 7 (1936); *Thessalische Mythologie* (Zurich 1944). G. PICCALUGA, *Lycaon, un tema mitico* (Rome 1968). ED. DES PLACES, *La religion grecque: Dieux, cultes, rites et sentiment religieux dans la Grèce antique* (Paris 1969). B. POWELL, *Athenian Mythology: Erichthonius and the Three Daughters of Cecrops* (Ithaca, NY, 1906; reprinted Chicago 1976). L. PRELLER, *Griechische Mythologie*, 3 vols. (4th ed., Berlin 1894–1921; reprinted in 4 vols., Berlin, Zurich, and Dublin 1964–67). L. RADERMACHER, *Mythos und Sage bei den Griechen* (3d ed., Darmstadt 1968). C. RAMNOUX, *La nuit et les enfants de la nuit dans la tradition grecque* (Paris 1959); *Mythologie ou la famille olympienne* (Paris 1962). S. REINACH, *Cultes, mythes et religions*, 5 vols. (Paris 1905–23). W. H. ROSCHER, ed., *Ausführliches Lexikon der griechischen und römischen Mythologie*, 6 vols. (Leipzig 1884–1937). H. J. ROSE, *A Handbook of Greek Mythology Including Its Extension to Rome* (6th ed., London 1958). R. ROUX, *Le problème des Argonautes: Recherches sur les aspects religieux de la légende* (Paris 1949). J. RUDHARDT, *Notions fondamentales de la pensée religieuse et actes constitutifs du culte dans la Grèce classique: Étude préliminaire pour aider à la compréhension de la piété athénienne au IVe siècle* (Geneva 1958); *Le thème de l'eau primordiale dans la mythologie grecque* (Bern 1971). D. SABBATUCCI, *Saggio sul misticismo greco* (Rome 1965). F. SCHACHERMEYR, *Poseidon und die Entstehung des griechischen Götterglaubens* (Munich 1950). K. SCHEFOLD, *Myth and Legend in Early*

Greek Art (London 1966), originally in German. T. A. SEBEOK, ed., *Myth: A Symposium* (Bloomington, IN, 1958). L. SÉCHAN, *Le mythe de Prométhée*, Mythes et religions 28 (Paris 1951); *Sept légendes grecques suivies de l'étude des sources*, Coll. d'études anciennes (Paris 1967). L. SÉCHAN and P. LÉVÊQUE, *Les grandes divinités de la Grèce* (Paris 1966). A. SEVERYNS, *Les dieux d'Homère*, Mythes et religions 57 (Paris 1966). E. SIMON, *Die Götter der Griechen* (Munich 1969). P. E. SLATER, *The Glory of Hera: Greek Mythology and the Greek Family* (Boston 1968). B. SNELL, *The Discovery of the Mind* (Oxford 1953), originally in German. L. A. STELLA, *mitologia greca* (Turin 1956). J.-P. VERNANT, *Mythe et pensée chez les Grecs* (4th ed., Paris 1971); *Mythe et société en Grèce ancienne* (Paris 1974); *Religion grecque, religions antiques* (Paris 1976). J.-P. VERNANT and P. VIDAL-NAQUET, *Mythe et tragédie en Grèce ancienne* (Paris 1972). F. VIAN, *La guerre des Géants: Le mythe avant l'époque hellénistique* (Paris 1952); *Les origines de Thèbes: Cadmos et les Spartes* (Paris 1963). P. VIDAL-NAQUET, "Athènes et l'Atlantide," *Revue des études grecques* 77 (1964): 420–42; "Le chasseur noir et l'origine de l'éphébie athénienne," *Annales E.S.C.*, 1968, 947–64; "Valeurs religieuses et mythiques de la terre et du sacrifice dans l'Odyssée," *Annales E.S.C.*, 1970, 1278–97; "Esclavage et gynécocratie dans la tradition, le mythe, l'utopie," in *Recherches sur les structures sociales dans l'Antiquité* (Paris 1970), 63–80; "Le mythe platonicien du *Politique*; les ambiguïtés de l'âge d'or et de l'histoire," in *Langue, discours, société: Pour Émile Benveniste* (Paris 1975), 374–90. U. VON WILAMOWITZ-MOELLENDORF, *Der Glaube der Hellenen*, 2 vols. (Berlin 1931–32). G. ZUNTZ, *Persephone: Three Essays on Religion and Thought in Magna Graecia* (Oxford 1971).

S.G./d.f.

INTRODUCTION TO ANCIENT MYTHOGRAPHY

Acusilaus of Argos

In *Die Fragmente der griechischen Historiker*, F. Jacoby, ed., vol. 1: *Genealogie und Mythographie*, no. 2 (Leiden 1922; 2d ed., 1957).

Aesop

Fables, E. Chambry, ed. and trans. (Paris 1927).

Antoninus Liberalis

Les métamorphoses, M. Papathomopoulos, ed. and trans. (Paris 1968).

Apollodorus

The Library, J. G. Frazer, trans. (London 1921).

Apollonius of Rhodes

Argonautica, (1) R. C. Seaton, ed. and trans. (London 1912); (2) critical ed. by H. Fraenkel (Oxford 1961); (3) books 1 and 2, F. Vian, ed., E. Delage, trans. (Paris 1974).

Atthidographers

F. Jacoby, *Atthis: The Local Chronicles of Ancient Athens* (Oxford 1949).

Callimachus

(1) *Les origines. Réponse aux Telchines. Élégies. Épigrammes. Iambes et pièces lyriques. Hécalé. Hymnes*, É. Cahen, ed. and trans. (3d ed., Paris 1948); (2) R. Pfeiffer, ed. (Oxford 1949–53), 1: *Fragmenta*, 2: *Hymni et Epigrammata*.

Hecataeus of Miletus

Hecataei Milesii fragmenta, G. Nenci, ed. (Florence 1954).

Hellanicus of Lesbos

In *Die Fragmente der griechischen Historiker*, F. Jacoby, ed., vol. 1: *Genealogie und Mythographie*, no. 4 (Leiden 1922; 2d ed., 1957).

Hesiod

(1) *Théogonie. Les travaux et les jours. Le Bouclier*, P. Mazon, ed. and trans. (Paris 1928); (2) *Hesiod: Theogony*, M. L. West, ed. (Oxford 1966); (3) *Hesiod: Works and Days*, M. L. West, ed. (Oxford 1978); (4) *Esiodo: Le opere e i giorni*, critical ed. by A. Colonna (Milan 1967); (5) *Hesiodi Scutum [Aspis]*, C. F. Russo, ed. and trans. (Florence 1950); (6) *Fragmenta Hesiodea*, R. Merkelbach and M. L. West, eds. (Oxford 1967); (7) *Scholia vetera in Hesiodi opera et dies*, A. Pertusi, ed. (Milan 1955).

Homer

(1) *L'Iliade*, P. Mazon, ed. and trans., 5 vols. (Paris 1937–38); (2) *L'Odyssée*, V. Bérard, ed. and trans., 3 vols. (Paris 1924); (3) *Scholia graeca in Homeri Iliadem*, H. Erbse, ed., 5 vols. (Berlin 1969–77); (4) *Scholia graeca in Homeri Odysseam*, G. Dindorf, ed. (Oxford 1855; reprinted 1962); (5) Eustathius, *Commentarii ad Homeri Iliadem et Odysseam*, G. Stallbaum, ed. (Leipzig 1826–30; reprinted in 4 vols., 1970); Eustathius, *Commentarii ad Homeri Iliadem*, M. van der Valk, ed. (Leiden 1971–79), vol. 1 (A–D); vol. 2 (E–I); vol. 3 (K–M).

Homeric Hymns: (1) *Hymnes homériques*, J. Humbert, ed. and trans. (Paris 1936); (2) *Inni Homerici*, F. Cassola, ed. and trans. (Milan 1975); (3) *The Homeric Hymns*, T. W. Allen, W. R. Halliday, and E. E. Sikes, eds. (2d ed., Oxford 1936; reprinted 1963); (4) *The Homeric Hymn to Demeter*, N. J. Richardson, ed. (Oxford 1974); (5) L. Radermacher, *Der Homerische Hermeshymnus* (Vienna and Leipzig 1931).

Hyginus

Hygini Fabulae, H. I. Rose, ed. (Leiden 1934; reprinted 1963).

Lycophron

Alexandra: (1) E. Scheer, ed., with scholia (Berlin 1881–1908; reprinted 1958); (2) A. W. Mair, trans., in *Callimachus, Lycophron, Aratus* (London 1921).

Nonnus of Panopolis

Dionysiaca: (1) W. H. D. Rouse, ed. and trans., with introduction and notes by H. J. Rose, 3 vols. (London 1940–42); (2) books 1–2, F. Vian, ed. and trans.; books 3–5, P. Chuvin, ed. and trans. (Paris 1976).

[Orpheus]

(1) *Les Argonautiques d'Orphée*, G. Dottin, ed. and trans. (Paris 1930); (2) *Orphei Hymni*, G. Quandt, ed. (Berlin 1955). *Orphicorum Fragmenta*: O. Kern, ed. (Berlin 1922; 2d printing, Dublin and Zurich 1972).

Pausanias

(1) *Description of Greece*, J. G. Frazer, trans., 6 vols. (2d ed., London 1913); (2) W. H. S. Jones, H. A. Ormerod, and R. E. Wycherley, eds. and trans., 5 vols. (London 1918–35); (3) *Pausanias en Corinthie* (book 2: 1–15), G. Roux, ed. and trans. (Paris 1958); (4) *Description de l'Attique*, book 1, trans. and with notes by M. Yon, preface by J. Pouilloux (Montpellier and Paris 1972); (5) ed. trans. into modern Greek with archaeological and topographical commentary by N. Papachatzis, 5 vols. (Athens 1963–74).

Pherecydes of Athens

In *Die Fragmente der griechischen Historiker*, F. Jacoby, ed., vol. 1: *Genealogie und Mythographie*, no. 3 (Leiden 1922; 2d ed., 1957).

Pindar

(1) *Œuvres (et fragments)*, A. Puech, ed. and trans., 4 vols. (Paris 1922–23); (2) *Pindari carmina cum fragmentis*, B. Snell, ed., 2 vols. (3d ed., Leipzig 1959–64).

The History, Geography, and Religion of Greece

A textbook published in 1977, intended for children from eleven to twelve years of age, presents Greek religion in its "natural" arena: "Greek religion, polytheistic, originated in the natural arena in which men lived: a mountainous country composed of small regions dominated by city-states in which the leaders did not have the divine power of a king or a pharaoh." Even very young children have the right not to be told just anything. Between Greece, its religion, its history, its geography, there were bonds that were not a simple matter of cause and effect. First of all, did Greece (the name the Italians borrowed from a group of western Hellenes), or Hellas as it was called in the classical period but not in the time of Homer, really exist? Hellas in the time of Herodotus was a part of Europe corresponding approximately to what we today call Greece. But can we exclude Asian Greece, at that time subject to the Persian empire and, for that same Herodotus, the most stable country in the world? Herodotus is sometimes tempted to use the separation between Europe and Asia as the ideal limit of the Greek world and the world whose allegiance was to the Persian Empire; but that would be to yield Ephesus and Miletus, and Naucratis of Egypt, and Heraclea Pontica, the Megarian colony, to the Great King. The men from the West, from Sicily, Magna Graecia (southern Italy), Gaul, Spain, and Libya (Cyrene), were also Greeks. But is the notion of Greeks, or Hellenes, much clearer? Homer's Danaeans certainly occupied a large portion of "Greek" soil, but, again according to Herodotus, the word *Hellenes* sometimes had a strictly political meaning and designated solely those among the Greeks who had chosen to resist the invader, a designation that excludes old Greek city-states like Thebes.

Greek mythology, history, and geography often developed around the opposition between Hellenes and barbarians, of whom the most ancient example, the Carians, were quite naturally close neighbors; there was, however, no dispute regarding a frontier (a zone or a line) separating two "national" groups, as the Rhine separates France from Germany. On the other hand, a frontier did exist in the interior of Greek land, but it separated the city-states from one another. This was the frontier with which mythology and history were engaged; this was the frontier that defined the geography of the Greek world.

From the archaic period to the Hellenistic period and beyond, the Greek city-state, or rather its ideal type, consisted of a plain planted with cereal grain and bordered by slopes where vines and fig trees grew, sometimes inland, sometimes on the sea. The urban site is settled most often on a hill (acropolis), but this is not always possible (Metapontus is on flat land). Athens and Marseilles are very close to the ideal type; at Syracuse, moreover, the ancient urban center is situated on an island. On the horizon, a mountain is the "natural" frontier—though often humanized—with the neighboring city-state. Thus Cithaeron lies between Athens and Thebes: it was here that the infant Oedipus was exposed.

A double frontier: an ideal line delimited by boundaries set by common agreement, or easily located—the course of a river, for example. The city-state, using a logic of separation and opposition—you are inside or you are outside—knew how to define that separation, as is witnessed still today by a number of inscriptions defining a limit, recording an arbitration between two city-states. But the frontier is also a zone, indefinite and, in the last analysis, undivided between two city-states. Shepherds move their flocks to mountain pastures in this zone and sometimes encounter one another, as in Sophocles' *Oedipus the King*; the Bacchante wandered there, the mythical one, or the city Bacchante that an inscription of Miletus tells of. Bands of young people confronted each other in ritual wars between city-states in Crete, in Thyreatis, between Argos and Sparta. The "black country" between Athens and Thebes is the place where the young Athenian champion Melanthus (the dark) confronted and tricked the Theban champion Xanthus (the fair), under the patronage of Dionysus with the pelt of a black goat, and thus qualified for maturity as a king and as a hoplite.

The Athenian ephebe is the man of the frontier zones, but he takes an oath and at once becomes a hoplite, certifying not only the "boundaries of the fatherland," but also "the grains, the barley, the olive trees, the fig trees," the earth of the civic space that he will have to defend—at least until Pericles, uprooting the Athenians from their demes, enclosing them between "The Long Walls," replaces the defense of the territory with the defense of the city.

From geography, we are thrown into the midst of "history," the moment in the fifth century, at the beginning of the Peloponnesian War (431 B.C.), which to our eyes, as it was to Thucydides, was a turning point. But Greek history as a whole is a succession of disequilibriums and this is precisely what renders it exemplary. The "hot" history of Athens the innovator; the "cold" history of Sparta that kept trying to repeat itself and, moreover, could only diminish after two *akmai* (summits) of glory (the victory over the Persians at Platea under the guidance of Lacedaemon in 479 B.C., and the victory over Athens in 404 B.C.).

Is this in fact Greek history? It is the history of those populations which, integrating the "pre-Hellenics," spoke Greek or, rather, what was to be called Greek. History begins around 2200–2100 B.C. The archaeological picture is that of a massive destruction of most of the very modest settlements which had been previously developed. Twelve hundred B.C.: the world of the Mycenaean "palaces" disappears, never to be born again except in the epic mode. It is this that is referred to, by an improper assimilation with the "great invasions" of the fifth century A.D., as the Dorian invasion. Between these two dates, especially from 1600 B.C. onward, an ancient civilization developed that spoke Greek and wrote Greek (Linear B), the "Mycenaean" civilization of the palaces of Mycenae, Cnossos, Thebes, Tyre, Gla, Pylos, Sparta, the burial mounds, and the golden masks. The deities of these men were called Athena or Dionysus. But what did they bequeath to their descendants of the archaic and classical ages? We hardly know. The Mycenaean world transmitted to us only its walls, its tombs, its accounts, and its names. And then, everywhere except in Cyprus, writing disappeared for three centuries. The Greek city-state—that group of free men who were in opposition to the slave as much as they were to the stranger, to women as much as they were to children, even to artisans—the city-state, that group of warriors, was constructed on the remains of the Mycenaean world, although this process is not clearly definable, nor can we even give it a birth certificate. In the middle of the eighth century, collective authority was strong enough for colonization to begin—that is, the expatriation of groups of men who went into barbarian lands to construct new cities. Greek city-states have innumerable features that distinguish them from one another—from the dialect they used to the nature of the collective magistracy. Yet they have common characteristics too: the collective character of these magistracies (except in Sparta, royalty was hardly more than an annual title), the absence of any opposition between town and country, the progressive predominance of the warrior group—it was the hoplite revolution of the seventh century. Sixth-century Sparta was the mold for certain of the common characteristics of the archaic city-states.

Between Solon (598 B.C.), Clisthenes (507), and Pericles (who died in 429), Athens developed in a completely different direction, opposing the citizen to the slave in a radical way, constituting the *demos* as an organized political group. This group would direct the city-state in the fifth century, theoretically at least, and even a bit more; it would replace hoplites with sailors (four times more numerous), and would receive even non-property owners—artisans, for example—into the citizenry as long as they were born of two Athenian parents (the law of 451). This was the classical age, the age of great sculpture, of tragedy, and of the birth of philosophy. This civilization of political oratory became, little by little, a civilization of the written word. A turning point came at the end of the fifth century in Athens when laws were written and transcribed into a different alphabet. Progressively during the fourth century a chancery style appeared, common to the entire Greek world, which after Alexander would become common to the Mediterranean world and would extend right up to the frontiers of India where Greek cities were still to be found. Hellenistic civilization is defined by its *reproduction* of the classical model, in whatever place—in still independent cities like Rhodes or Athens, urban capitals of new kingdoms like Alexandria and Pergamum, cities form-

ing a Greek network in the heart of the *laoi* (subjugated peoples, barbarians), as in the Seleucid world, exiled cities on the borders, like the city recently discovered in Afghanistan where Delphic maxims on stone have been found. Even further away, in India, King Menander becomes a sage in the Buddhist tradition. There is everywhere a comparable architectural framework, *agora* and porticos, a *paideia* which differentiates the Greek from the barbarian, with its physical education (gymnasium), its intellectual apprenticeship (Homer, Euripides), its outlet for rhetoric or (in a minor way) philosophy. Roman history becomes progressively the history of a capital and then of the capital of the Hellenistic world. The king and then the emperor heads this network of "benefactors" which assures the circulation of a fraction of the riches and maintains the social equilibrium of the cultural group. The local leading citizen depends on the neighboring large property owner, on the "friend" of the king, on the king himself, and finally on the emperor.

It is from this environment that many of our myths have come down to us, the scholarly remains and writings of a mythology that had long been a living one. Its tensions can still be seen in the tragedy and comedy of the classical period; its narratives have been transposed into philosophy. But without this scholarly environment, without the immense effort of Hellenistic repetition, nothing would have survived of that mythology, rewritten in the Middle Ages, nor for that matter anything of Aeschylus, Sophocles, or Homer. We have all been students in the gymnasiums and libraries of Alexandria and Pergamum.

P.V.-N./d.f.

CRETE AND MYCENAE: PROBLEMS OF MYTHOLOGY AND RELIGIOUS HISTORY

The first problem posed by the civilization of Crete of the third and second millennia B.C. and the civilization known as Mycenaean (from Thessaly to the Peloponnesus and the Ionian Islands as far as Cyprus) between 1600 and 1100 B.C. is that of their unity. Their chronologies and the form of their sites and archaeological documents leave room for doubt. Yet, between 1300 and 1220, painted and inscribed texts in the script of Linear B prove that one language was used, with identical administrative structures, at Cnossos in Crete as well as in the palaces of Boeotia, Attica, Argolis, and Messenia. These documents contain similar names of divinities. Thus, at least since the sack of the second Cretan palace (toward 1450 B.C.), a sort of common cultural milieu was created, which united continental Greece with the islands. The name of one people, Achaioi ("the Achaeans"), is found in seven different places, including Rhodes and Crete. Furthermore, several place names, called pre-Hellenic because they do not conform to the laws of formation of Greek words, are scattered all along the shores of the Aegean Sea, from the Dardanelles to Crete. Many of these names refer to sacred mountains (Berecynthus, Dicte, Ida, Apocoronium [or Hippocoronium], Olympus) and sacred rivers (Achelous, Acheron, Amnisus, Inachus, Cephissus, Tartarus). Finally, a great number of cultural terms were borrowed by the Greeks from their predecessors, most notably terms of ritual and mythology as well as proper names; for example *theos*,

divinity; *hieros,* sacred; *laburinthos,* a system of underground tunnels; *triambos,* a kind of hymn; *Kyklops,* the Cyclops; Hermes, the god of shepherds; Hephaestus, the god of smiths; Hyacinthus, the god who preceded Apollo near Sparta and in several cities in Crete. We may thus admit a certain religious continuity between the Old Bronze Age culture of Greece and the so-called Hellenic culture, which ancient historians dated from the installation of the sons of Helen in Thessaly in the sixteenth century B.C. Even though some rites may have changed over a thousand years, and a few names of Indo-European origins, such as Zeus, may have appeared and replaced older ones, the most we can speak of is an evolution rather than a political and religious revolution.

Starting from what we learn about religion from texts written in the thirteenth century B.C., we shall go back to earlier documents, whether or not they contain symbols or images, and from these to the rites and the belief that are implicit in them. We shall not consider it forbidden, while working within such a continuity, to try to interpret images whose legends we only know from several centuries later. Nor shall we hesitate to draw upon votive texts written in Linear A and in hieroglyphics, when such are analogous to the form and the grouping of those written in the more recent Linear B. Hence a second question must be put: to what extent may we speak of a structured religion when the texts are missing? To this we may reply that the analysis of rites and the classification of symbolic images allow us to come to conclusions about certain associations and hierarchies. If we are able to establish, through the study of types of offerings, that the powers which are evoked have their

Central courtyard of the great temple at Phaistos. In the background, the two peaks of Mount Ida. Photo Faure.

Double horns of the south facade of the great sanctuary at Cnossos. In the background, the sacred mountain, Mount Iouktas.

Marble figurine from the harbor of Cnossos (Crete). Ca. 1500 B.C. Cambridge, Fitzwilliam Museum. Museum photo.

Ivory figurine from the acropolis at Mycenae: Demeter, Kore, and the divine child(?). Ca. 1250 B.C. Athens, National Museum. Museum photo.

own domain in the world of nature (the firmament, the winds, the earth, springs, forests, subterranean fire), even in caves of one sort or another, it becomes clear that these powers received the vows and prayers of different social classes and exercised different functions. As a general rule, the gods, whether they have names or not, are not gods of something, but gods of someone.

The most explicit text on the polytheism of the Mycenaean period is written on a clay tablet from the palace of Pylos, Tn

316. Because of the peril which threatens them, the palace sends golden vases and the city assigns some of its personnel to various sanctuaries. Lacking time or memory, the editor enumerates only thirteen divinities, eight female and five male, instead of the twenty-four promised in six paragraphs. We can distinguish a group made up of Zeus, supreme god of the Greeks, Hera his wife, and their son, apparently Dionysus, named on other tablets. These are the protectors of royal dynasties. Four or five appear to be essentially warrior gods: Ares, Peresa, Ipemedeya, Diwya, and perhaps the triple Heros (god of champions?) who receives the same offering as does Ares. Finally, two great divinities of the polis are honored, protectresses of various crafts, who are often associated with the classical epoch. These are Athana Potniya (sovereign goddess) and Posidas (= Poseidon), with their respective companions, on the one hand Manasa (root *men-: cf. Metis, Intelligence?), and, on the other, Posidaeya, as well as the mysterious Dopota ("the Smith"?). Here we have a functional distribution well known in Indo-European pantheons, composed of the gods of priests and kings, the gods of war, and the gods of technical crafts, including those of fire, spinning, and navigation. Was it an intentional act on the part of the scribe to omit, during a time of insurrection, the divinities of the herdsmen and farmers? In any case, we know from other tablets of Pylos and Cnossos that in the thirteenth century B.C. the so-called chthonic divinities (the divinities of the ground and the underground) were the most numerous. We know of the pair of Queens (Wanasoi, in the dual dative) who were the equivalents of the future Demeter-and-Kore; Sitopotiniya "the Lady of Grain"; Erinu (Erinys, which would become one of the surnames of Demeter in Arcadia); the "Gods of the Field" (tablet Fr 1226, concerning the village of Lousoi); the "Thirsty Ones" (Dipisiyoi, mentioned six times). Among the gods who rule over animal breeding, Hermes and Paiawon (Paean, the future Apollo) seem to figure prominently. Pan, the most ancient god of the Arcadian shepherds, does not appear in our texts, and the mention of Artemis under the form of "atemito" remains open to doubt. Diverse local "sovereigns" (Potiniyai) apparently supervised the working of the fields. Their anonymity corresponds to what the historian Herodotus (2.52) tells us about the ancient Pelasgians of central Greece: they offered their sacrifices while invoking the divinities in a general manner, yet they held in particular veneration the god of the herdsmen, Hermes ("he of the pile of rocks or of the erected stone," herma), representing him as an erect penis.

Twelve gods are mentioned simultaneously in Cnossos in Crete: Zeus Dictaeus ("of the Sacred Mountain"), Athana Potniya, Posedaon (= Poseidon), Enyalios (a surname of Ares), Payawon ("the Striker," the future Apollo Paean), Erinys (a surname of the future Demeter), Eleuthyia (= Eileithyia, "she who delivers" pregnant women), Pade (Pandes, Pardes, Phandes, or Païs-Païdos, "the Divine Child"?), Querasiya ("the Huntress"?), the Winds, Pasaya (the goddess of Parsa?), Pipituna (divinity of Gacynthus?), and Malineus. As a rule, offerings are addressed to pasi teoï; that is, to the totality of the gods. The goddess whom tablet Gg 702 designates with the name of "Sovereign Goddess of the Labyrinth," Dapuritoyo Potiniya, may perhaps be confused with one of the six preceding goddesses. Later literary tradition furnishes us with two surnames for the "Huntress" who is mentioned six times in our Mycenaean documents: Britomarpis ("the Sweet Virgin") in eastern Crete, and Dictynna ("She of the Sacred Mountain") in western Crete, who requires that one be barefoot to enter her sanctuary. The so-called daughters of Minos—Phaedra, Ariadne, Acalle (Acacallis), and Xenodice—are nothing more than fallen goddesses. These four names respectively signify the Brilliant One, the Very Pure One, the Flower of Narcissus, and the Right of Guests. They patronize the four classes of Minoan society—the priests, the champions, the farmers, and the craftsmen—which confirms their alliances and lineages in Greek mythology. The Cretan list leaves part of the list of Peloponnesian gods unaccounted for, and anonymity seems to be more frequent. Yet the pantheon is as strongly structured, and serves as a model and guarantor for human activities. We do not find the name of any Titan in the inscriptions, nor that of Demeter, described by literary tradition as being born to and uniting with the Dactyl Iasion in Crete.

This pantheon is served, at least in the cities, by a priesthood which is wealthy, organized, and hierarchized in the image of the gods. We know of numerous priests and priestesses, at Pylos and at Cnossos, who own "foundation" property in the name of the goddess or god, and who also cultivate, or cause to be cultivated, parcels of land allocated by the communes, as well as renting other lots. What remains at our disposal from the cadastral surveys of Crete, Mycenae, and Argolis indicates that the properties of the divinity easily exceeded forty hectares, and that these were also used for raising herds. Along with priests, sacrificers are mentioned, the key bearers of the sacred warehouses or treasuries of bronze and precious metals, the leather bearers (archivists or masked dancers?), the sacred slaves or hierodules (male or female), various servants such as the asitopoqo and the dakoro (sacristan?), and finally the haruspices or diviners, the wetereu, opetereu, and kereta. These also lived on allocations of goods or land, on tributes or offerings, or on sacrificial fees. Anthropomorphism being the general case in the representation of the divine society, the gods were thought to feed themselves like humans, and to adorn themselves, perfume themselves, go for walks, and unite sexually like humans. Fragments of calendars have been found that instruct us that it was customary to offer to the gods—and especially to a demanding clergy—pots of honey, wine, and oil and large quantities of perfume, barley, figs, and high-quality flour. At Cnossos, the following quantities of olive oil were consecrated during the month of Deucios (the month of "the White Lady," Leucothea?) to be used for the lights, ointments, and perhaps the beverage of various divinities: twelve liters to Zeus, twenty-four to Daidaleion (the Great Underground, the work of Daedalus?), twelve to Pade, thirty-six to the All-Gods (of Cnossos), twelve to the "Huntress" (?), twenty-four to the All-Gods of (the port of) Amnisos, six to Erinys, two to the sanctuary of Gadas (galas or gadas designates the Earth in the local dialect), and eight to the priestesses of the Winds, a total of 136 liters. In the course of the month of Lapathos (the Pit of the Hunters), the goddess Pipituna of Gacynthos is satisfied with two liters of oil, but the priestess of the Winds at Aulimos receives thirty-six and that of Utanos eighteen.

In the cities of Crete and the Mycenaean world, in the thirteenth century B.C., the gods had dwellings like those of men. The entire citadel appears, if not as a place of generalized worship, at least as a sacred site and favorite residence of the sovereign powers. The goddess Athana protects the Achaean acropoles of old Greece and the islands. The doors, decorated with heraldic animals, offer or prohibit access into a terrifying space. Several cities are simply called Pylos, or the (Sublime) Door. Thebes is the city of Seven Doors. By simply walking under the lintel of the Door of the Lionesses who protected the solid column of the monarchy at Mycenae, the visitor was introduced to or assailed by a world which was in principle reserved, forbidden. With its double horns crowning the facades of the palace, at Pylos, Gla, or Cnossos, with its sphinxes as guardian angels of the doors of Thebes and of Asine, or with its mobile altars, the royal dwelling presents itself as the most sacred place of all. It is not a temple, but the central square or megaron constitutes the particular sanctuary of the monarchy. It is here that animal victims, covered with their own fat, are sacrificed and burned, completely or partially. Here libations of water, milk, and wine, accompanied by vows and prayers, are offered to the dynastic divinities and to Hestia, the goddess of the hearth. Here honey cakes and the first fruits of the harvest are offered. Every meal is ordered and conceived as a communion with the ancestral gods. The only priest that the domestic gods have is the head of the family.

The palace also housed cults restricted to chapels—small sanctuaries or oratories separated from the megaron. At several places in the upper terraces of the acropolis of Mycenae, fragments of altars and of male and female statuettes have been found; such offerings and idols suggest various rituals. Even though it is uncertain whether an ivory group, representing two women beneath a large embroidered veil with a child between them, along with a male head in painted plaster and two altars, belonged to a chapel situated at the exit of the north stairway of Mycenae, we do know from several texts that there existed throughout Greek history the ceremony of the draping and removal of a multicolored veil on the double goddess who protected the city. The most ancient among these is tablet Fr 1222 of Pylos, where there was also a small sanctuary which opened onto the court to the east of the palace entrance. It bears the inscription "For the two goddess-queens, at the festival of the removal of the veil [tonoeketeriyo, in Greek: thronoelcteriois], two measures of oil perfumed with sage." How are we to conceive of this double goddess, an older and a younger, protecting the divine child, if not according to the schema of the double goddess of Eleusis, where the first sanctuary dates from the Mycenaean period, in which one goddess, who is both virgin and mother, feeds and raises the child she conceived by the supreme god? Once a year, even in the Hellenistic period, the priestesses of the region of Tiryns, a Mycenaean citadel, went with great pomp to immerse the statue of Hera, the goddess who represented the ideal of womanhood, into the Canathos spring at the side of the road which ran from Nauplia to Asine, two Mycenaean ports. The mother goddess was believed to recover her virginity in this bath of living water. In the same way, the priestesses of Aphrodite at Cyprus and at Cytherea ritually bathed the divine idol in the sea, from which she emerged regenerated, reborn. As for the young god, who might well have been named Dionysus in certain places, a name whose literal meaning is "son of Zeus," and whose name in Crete was Kouros (korwos) or Zagreus ("the Hunter"?), he was destined to die (or fall asleep?) in the autumn along with the vegetation, and to be reborn (or to awaken?) with it in the spring. In the classical age the supreme god of the Greeks was believed to have been born in a dozen cities in the Hellenic world, and his tomb was displayed in several places in Crete, near Cnossos and in the cave of Ida. At Athens, on the Acropolis, the virgin Athena was the mother of Erichthonius.

The Mycenaean city also contained local sanctuaries in which various divinities were ritually honored and prayed to. Every group of families, every confraternity, and every guild of artisans possessed its own chapel, celebrated its particular festivals, and addressed itself to one patron god or another, if not to pairs, triads, or colleges of gods. At Keos, Dorion, and Gortyn, archaeological digs have uncovered strange series of rooms, generally of an oblong shape, with side entrances, which bear only a slight resemblance to either the classical temples or the chapels of Pylos or Mycenae. The worshipers placed their painted clay statues on benches or shelves, along with their vases full of delicious liquids, the first fruits of the harvest, bouquets, and branches. The sacrificers slaughtered various animals on the altars, and the priests distributed what had not been burned among the donors, the participants, and themselves. Dogs, black animal victims, and sometimes perhaps—if we are to believe the literary tradition—humans were immolated to the forces of the underworld. The purpose of these festivals was to render the gods propitious. All of the great urban manifestations of the classical age stem from those of the Mycenaean epoch. These include new year's festivals (generally near the fall equinox), festivals of the new wine (toward the beginning of November and January), festivals of the dead (in the autumn and the winter), festivals of navigation (with the morning rising of the Pleiades, at the end of April), and festivals of flowers. One of these festivals, which took place at Pylos, is known to us only through two tablets, Fr 343 and 1217. A bed is erected in honor of Poseidon, who is represented by his statue, painted and perfumed. This is the *lekhestroterion* (Latin *lectisternium*). The god is regarded as participating in a banquet or a wedding festival. The participants, for their part, are regarded as sharing the table or the bed of the god. When they are shown the god and goddess stretched out on the sacred bed, they believe themselves to be in the presence of a union from which their own little world will depart regenerated.

At least three cultic sites are known to us in the southern part of the Mycenaean citadel, inside the last rampart, which was built around 1250 B.C. The first is known as the Tsuntas house. At the end of the last century (1885–1896), an archaeologist called Tsuntas uncovered a hall in which were benches on which idols were probably erected, and a hearth around which liquid offerings were poured. Paintings found in the neighborhood, notably that of the sacred shield, give the impression that a warrior god—probably Enyo, the mother, sister, or daughter of the dread Ares Enyalios—was worshiped behind a salient of the rampart. In the neighboring digs a female head in painted plaster was uncovered, seventeen centimeters in height. This is generally considered to be the head of the sphinx who guarded the sanctuary. A few meters away, the citadel house, or the Wace house, and the complex recently unearthed by G. Mylonas, have been identified as the second and third sacred enclosures. To the east, at the end of a room measuring five by four meters, a stairway goes up to a platform scattered with a dozen large clay idols, seven female and five male, erected on top of hollow cylinders and smeared with black. With or without scepters, they look threatening. By contrast, three idols wearing necklaces and bracelets, discovered in a nearby ruin, have peaceful features. A dozen clay serpents accompanied by small figurines remind one of the offerings made to the divinities of the underworld, to those anonymous beings, the dead perhaps, sometimes designated by texts of the period as "the Thirsty Ones" or, more mysteriously, as "the gods." Ten meters to the west, the Fresco Room resembles a megaron measuring 5.3 by 3.5 meters, with a central hearth, columns, benches, and a pool in the form of a bathtub. A painted image of a seated goddess, holding a bunch of

Mycenaean idols. Photos Lord William Taylour.

crocuses, adorns a niche above the altar. She is accompanied by a leaping animal, a second goddess holding out two handfuls of ears of grain, a god with a lightning bolt, and a retinue of worshipers. Once again we are reminded of the most ancient triad of the Eleusinian mysteries: the mother goddess (Rhea "of the brilliant diadem" from the Homeric Hymn), the goddess her daughter, "Sovereign of Grain" (Sitopotiniya), and the god with the thunderbolt who kidnaps and marries her. This was probably nothing more than an agrarian cult, as indicated by the ears of grain, but one that was connected with the worshipers' hopes for resurrection or a happy life after death, as evinced by the crocuses, plants of eternity.

The divinities who were worshiped in the countryside were not the same as those worshiped in the city in the Mycenaean era. Invisible forces were much closer to men and to the earth in the countryside. They lived in evergreen trees or shrubs such as myrtle, cypress, spruce, lentiscus, laurel, and buckthorn. Everyone remembers the palm tree of Delos at the foot of which the mother goddess Lato (Leto) brought into the world her twins, Sagittarius (the Archer) and Sagittaria (the future Apollo and Artemis); the olive tree of Athens, a gift from the goddess Athena; the plane tree of Sparta; the laurel of Delphi; the oak of Dodona. The union of the god Zeus with Europa is sometimes evoked beneath the evergreen plane tree of Gortyn. If we compare the coins of Gortyn and of Phaestus, we see that the former represent a

young woman, the latter a young man, sitting among the branches of an undetermined tree. A species of plane tree with perennial leaves does exist in Crete. The most remarkable example of this species is found in Gortyn itself, at the place where Theophrastus, Varro, and Pliny located the loves of Zeus and Europa, some eighty meters to the north of the Odeon, in which the famous laws of Gortyn (430 B.C.) are preserved, a tree which even today remains an object of great veneration and mythology: its leaves, when carried between the breasts or placed in the conjugal bed, or when chewed, are believed to make women fertile and to give them sons. It was in the shadow of this tree that the inhabitants of the (Mycenaean) polis founded by the son of Rhadamanthys celebrated the sacred marriage of the local goddess Hellotis (who later became Europa through assimilation) and the god Welkhanos (assimilated to Zeus). The "sacred myrtle" of the monastery of Paliani is still venerated in the village of Apollona (today Venerato, Temenous): its trunk contains an icon of the Virgin which is perceptible only to children. Its leaves are used as inhalants, in concentrates, or as simple talismans. Hyginus (*Fabulae* 139) tells us how Amalthea, the wetnurse of Zeus in Crete, suspended the god's cradle in a tree (in this case a black fruit-bearing poplar) in order that he be discovered neither in the sky, nor on earth, nor in the waters. All these beliefs are vestiges of an epoch in which the deity appeared in a tree, in the form of a human, a bird, or a thunderbolt. These gods of vegetation were named, according to their region, Aphaea, Britomarpis, Daphne, Auxesia, Acacallis, or Hyacinthus, or were designated by very vague titles such as the Mother, the Virgin, the Nymphs.

In limestone regions, running water, springs, lakes, and swamps, which were frequent sources of malaria, were often considered to be the realm of dread powers. We know of the Hydra of the Lernean swamp and the birds of the Stymphalian Lake, against which Heracles had to make use of his superhuman gifts. Boys consecrated their hair, their clothes, and their shoes to the sources of rivers and streams. Infants at the breast were dipped into these places to render their bodies invulnerable. The warriors in the Trojan war knew that if fountains, rivers, and seas demanded worship, it was because their waters were divine. Waters often bore the names of genies or nymphs: Amymone, Arethusa, Triton, and Perseia. It was the Nereids, Naiads, and Oceanids who presided over the education of young warriors and became their spiritual and moral mothers, as the goddess Thetis was for Achilles. Judging from the frequency with which nymphs figure in classical Cretan inscriptions or in stories about the childhood, education, and loves of the gods—Zeus, Apollo, Hyacinthus, Artemis, Hermes, Pan, etc.—we may be sure that these divinities of the waters and forests were worshiped at least from the time of the foundation of the 130 Cretan cities that we know of. One of the most recurrent names on the thirty-odd libation tanks or drinking cups from the fifteenth century B.C., discovered on the hills from which the springs flowed, may be read Nupi or Nopina. Accompanied by the word *wanakana* ("the queen"), it designates, in all likelihood, a nymph of running waters.

In Crete, the popular cults of the Mycenaean period follow the cults of the so-called Minoan era (2200–1450 approximately), and use the same sanctuaries. The proper names of the divinities transmitted to us by the Greco-Roman epigraphic and literary tradition are rare, but quite well developed. Here, in alphabetical order, are the seven gods or genies: (1) Atymnius, who appeared at sunset in the mountains of the Gortyn region; (2) the three Curetes (or Corybantes), educators and advisers of the young supreme god, who are at once magicians, diviners, healers, civilizing heroes, and bronze workers; (3) the ten Dactyls (among whom is Iasion, the lover of Demeter), advisers of the goddess Rhea-Anchiale, who are sometimes confused with the smiths called Cyclopes; (4) Hyacinthus, the young god who dies and is reborn; (5) Kronos, the son of Sky and Earth, the king of the Titans and father of the Olympian gods whom he thought to have devoured at their birth; (6) Talon or Talos, a winged genie who, related to Hephaestus, the god of smiths, is assimilated sometimes to the sun and sometimes to a sort of bronze Minotaur who defended the island from invasion; it is believed that his name reappears in the Hellenistic period in the epithet of Zeus Tallaius and in the Tallaioi mountains; (7) Welkhanos, assimilated sometimes to Zeus and sometimes to Apollo, and sometimes represented as a bull; in the Hellenic period, he was worshiped above the ruins of the Agia Triada palace, in several cities of the east, and it was probably he who gave his name to Canea (Alkhania koma) and to the Pelekania mountains of the province of Selinon (the ancient Pelkin, between Tsaliana and Sklavopoula). We know the names of as many pre-Hellenic goddesses of Crete: (1) Ia, and her derivations, assimilated to a water sprite or a Nereid; (2) Ino-Inachus, who became Leucothea, the White Goddess; (3) Hellotis, at Gortyn, assimilated to Europa; (4) Karme or Karma, the mother of Dictynna, in the White Mountains; (5) Lato Phytia, of Phaes-

tos, who presides over the initiations of youth; (6) a certain number of nymphs (Nupi or Nopina; see above), including those who presided over the education of the young god in the cave of Mount Ida: Adrasteia, Amalthea, Ida, Cynosura, the colleges of the Bees (Mellissae), of the She-goats, and of the She-bears; to these might be added Acacallis, the wife of several gods and the mother of the founders of Cydonia, Elyros, Tarrha, Oaxos, and Milatos; (7) Rhea, the wife of the Titan Kronos, considered in the time of Hesiod (seventh century B.C.) to be the mother of the Olympians; in the classical period, she was worshiped above the ruins of the Minoan "palaces" of Cnossos, Phaestus, Lyktos, and Lebena; her name might well figure among thirty-five seals covered with hieroglyphics dated between 2000 and 1700 B.C. (RE.I.JA), and perhaps even on the disk of Phaestus (1580 B.C.); (8) Thetis, whose name, according to philologists, probably meant "the good mother" or "the great protective sister" in the Cretan dialect, and who was transformed into a marine goddess by the Greeks.

We should note the important place in this list held by the gods of metallurgists—Talon or Talos, the Curetes, and the Cyclopes, who were advisers of the great goddess Rhea-Anchiale. This importance is confirmed (1) by the accounts of classical mythology, in which a group of Cretan smiths hide, raise, and protect the future lord of the Olympian gods (Tan, Zan, or Zen in the Cretan language); (2) by the accounts in which Daedalus (the "Technician" par excellence) is the adviser of King Minos and the builder of the labyrinth in which the Minotaur was enclosed; (3) by the existence of two sacred caves, at Arkhalokhori and Selakano, which are full of bronze objects from the sixteenth and fifteenth centuries B.C.; (4) by the discovery of numerous metal deposits in Crete, and of foundries and slag even in the great sanctuaries of Zakro, Phaestus, and Cnossos. These cults, which were more or less secret, were the object of mysteries and ritual initiations.

We may also glimpse a whole series of myths and rituals connected with the sea. The supreme god of Crete, in the form of a bull that arises from the waters of the sea, seduces the Phoenician Europa (= Hellotis) and engenders Minos, Rhadamanthys, and Sarpedon, the kings of Cnossos, Phaestus, and Milatos. From the Aegean Sea comes another bull, which King Minos refuses to sacrifice and which ravages the coastal regions of Argolis and Attica. The image of a goddess in a boat bringing vegetation with her is depicted on a famous gold ring from the island of Mokhlos and on a seal from Makrygialos. The name of Thetis, a maternal and marine divinity, is often found on hieroglyphic Cretan seals. Ino, an abbreviation of Inachus, is called Leucothea, "the White Goddess," and she protects the sailors of Itanos, Minoa (the port of Aptara), and Inakhorion (the present-day Vathi, near Stomion in the province of Selinon). The myth of the Sirens in the Bay of Suda is attested by Pausanias. Finally, several Minoan sanctuaries, on the edge of the sea, belonged, appropriately, to mariners' cults. Even today, in nearby sites, Saint Nicholas, Saint Pelagia, Saint Galene, and the Virgin Galinusa are the object of a veneration peculiar to the sections of the populations composed mainly of fishermen and navigators.

For the past twenty years, research has paid attention to three kinds of Cretan folk cults rich in offerings, though previously often overlooked because they were addressed to divinities who were usually anonymous. We know of fifty peak sanctuaries, spread over all of the island but concentrated in the Eteocretan lands (Sitia, the Asterusia Moun-

Reclining griffon. Restored painting in the throne room at Cnossos. 1300(?) B.C.

tains, the Ida and Kydonia groups); forty-odd sacred caves that housed a cult during antiquity from Kalamavka in the east to Topolia in the west (as against 250 that later housed Christian chapels); and, finally, twenty-five ground-level sanctuaries in the countryside, including stone enclosures and sacred warehouses and depositories.

Among the most considerable peak sanctuaries, some of which date from about 2000 B.C. in Crete, we must cite those of Mount Petsofas, some five kilometers to the southeast of Palaikastro; Mount Kofinas, two kilometers to the east of Kapetaniana; Mount Iouktas, three kilometers to the west of Ano Arkhanes and six kilometers to the south of Cnossos; Mount Philiorimos, 400 meters to the northwest of Gonies (the geographic center of Crete); and Mount Vrysinas, six kilometers to the south of Rhethymnon. Several sanctuaries are found on a height called Endictis, a name derived from the ancient Dicte, or Sacred Mountain. According to Eteocretan tradition, which was known to the Hellenistic mythographers, the supreme god of their pantheon (Zeus Dictaeus) was born and grew up on the summit of Mount Dicte. The hymn of Palaikastro which is addressed to him calls him Kouros, "Youth." Furthermore, the name of the goddess Dictynna or the Lady of the Sacred Mountain ("Adicitu" on an offering cup from Mount Iouktas, fifteenth century B.C.), and the appellation Mother of the Mountain (Meter Oreia) given by Euripides to the goddess of Mount Ida, both indicate that it was not the young god alone who was worshiped in the peak sanctuaries. These sanctuaries, which are often carefully constructed, appear sometimes as rock enclosures and sometimes as chapels consisting of three adjoining rooms which were used for the the worship of a trinity. The rock constructions and arrangements that we have been able to study are oriented toward the solstice points of the horizon or toward other summits that are

notable for their height or shape, such as the double horn of Mount Ida. All of this leads one to believe that their cult was directed to sidereal divinities, such as the sun, the moon, and perhaps the morning star. On several Minoan seals, the Lady of the Mountain is represented with her two ibexes, lions, advisers, or human characters as yet another image of trinity.

In all such shrines there is a thick layer of ashes, fragments of human or animal figurines, and vases. The use of fire and of sacrifices may be explained by a desire to rekindle the sun's flame at the critical moments of its final approach to the horizon, when it was believed that it would stop and die; or at the moment of its encounter with other sidereal or geographical phenomena (sunrise between the horns of Mount Ida, for example), when it was thought that it was about to be born or to be married, or to move from one dwelling to another. The hanging or the depositing of ex-votos representing deformed or diseased body parts suggests that there was a belief that pilgrims and their herds could be healed at the time the divinity was regenerating itself. In certain cases, these figurines were thrown into the fire of communal resurrection. The annual fire has a cathartic value. In some periods, the offerings were smashed or hidden in crevices in the rocks to make them irretrievable, impossible to use a second time, inalienable. The divinities were thought to protect the health of the worshipers, their herds, their hunting, their fishing or navigation. Thus the offerings include clay fishes, small boats, stones from the shoreline, and seashells, which are sailors' ex-votos. The celestial divinity invoked may also have been regarded as exercising power over the sea.

It was not the highest mountains in any given region that were chosen for the establishment of such sanctuaries, but those most easily accessible—to frail pilgrims, women, children, the sick—as well as those which were the most visible, the most central, with the best exposure. Of all natural phenomena, mountains seemed to offer most of what was considered to be the divine character, not only because of their awesome beauty and inaccessible heights, but because they provided the Cretans with rivers and springs (the sacred Mount Vrysinas, like the Manna of Polyrrhenia, is the "mountain of springs"), with game, edible plants and trees, metals, and living stones, because they were the places where men encountered gods, and because they served as observation posts and shelter in times of peril and as places of training and initiation in times of peace. In classical mythology, Dicte and Ida became nymphs.

If peak cults were reserved for essentially celestial gods, the cave cults in Crete were directed to divinities dwelling and acting beneath the earth. Out of some fifteen examples that we have from the so-called Minoan period, or that of "the palaces," the five most ancient are those of Psykhro, Skotino, Tylissos, Kamares, and Asfendu. These contain all of the offerings common to the region around 2000 B.C. (the end of the Old Bronze Age and the beginning of the Middle Bronze). The criteria for a genuine consecration include numerous, regular offerings (vases, figurines, libation tables, weapons, double-bladed axes); the presence of stagnant or oozing water; traces of soot (often accompanied by piles of ashes); an environment, either in the surrounding area or in the interior of the cave, that allows practice of the cult; the fantastic appearance of the place (rocks or chalk formations resembling humans or animals and a gaping, quite unexpected opening); the existence of an epigraphic or literary tradition, or of one connected with a certain name; the proximity of an ancient city with identifiable roads. In this way, sacred caves are quite easily distinguished from funerary caves, human habitations, refuges, temporary shelters for shepherds, or watering sites. The water of underground sanctuaries is not regarded as a profane liquid to be used for quenching the thirst, washing, or irrigation: it is rather, and especially in limestone regions where its presence seems mysterious, a benediction, the fluid of life itself, comparable to flowing blood or mother's milk. Whether or not it contains mineral salts, whether it is clear or rust-colored, it is always considered to be cathartic, therapeutic, and even fertilizing. We saw how in the Mycenaean era the goddess of pregnant women, Eileithyia, was worshiped in several caves in Crete (Amnisos and Tsousouros), on the islands, and in Attica, because the water that flowed close to the calcite idols seemed to facilitate childbirth.

Different divinities were supposed to correspond to different functions. Just as the shepherds of the classical and Mycenaean periods dedicated a cult to a subterranean Hermes and to Maia his mother, or to Pan and the cave nymphs, the farmers to Demeter and her daughter Persephone who entered and emerged from the shadowy hollows of Greece and Sicily, and the craftsmen and doctors (regarded as craftsmen) to their own gods (Telchines, Dactyls, Hephaestus, Asclepius, Chiron), it is very likely that at the same sites, in the first half of the second millennium B.C., various kinds of worshipers were already addressing themselves to diverse gods. The depositories of bronze objects (tools, weapons, art objects) of the Cretan caves of Selakano and Arkalokhori in no way resemble the wine cups and basins of milk of the caves of Karnari or of Amnisos. The hunting scenes that can be deciphered on the rocky walls of Kato Pervolakia (Seteia) and of Asfendou (Skafion) are addressed to the hunting gods, Dictynna or Britomarpis, both of whom are virgins according to tradition, with no apparent relationship to the

fertile divinities of the farmers. The temporary, if not intermittent, character of the subterranean cults, as much as the sorts of offerings associated with them, assures us of their diversity and functional character.

Out of all of the subterranean mythology of the Minoan era (2000–1300 B.C.) the literary tradition retained only a single pre-Hellenic name, the name of the labyrinth (*dapurito* on the tablets of Cnossos). There, King Minos had the ingenious Daedalus imprison a monster who was half man and half bull, the Minotaur, to whom were delivered in tribute at regular intervals seven boys and seven girls. The hero Theseus, aided by Ariadne's thread, avoided all the traps of the labyrinth, defeated the monster, and saved the children who had been consigned to it. We may recognize in this storytelling an adolescent ordeal ritual, and in the labyrinth an initiatory cave. Certain Cretan caves, being the bowels of the Earth, received the children of the aristocracy and gave birth to them as men who had grown up through their ordeals. A cave of this kind, Skotino (Pediados), may be visited by journeying for four hours (on foot) to the east of Cnossos. With its 120 meters of depth and its four levels, its tortuous tunnels and its dead ends, it offers concretions of travertine marble that resemble monstrous quadrupeds and the faces of a goddess and a god. At the foot of these veritable idols, archaeologists have found piles of offerings that extend from the end of the Old Bronze Age to the third century A.D. Even today, on July 26th of each year, the people of the surrounding regions come to dance at the entrance to this cavern, like the children saved by Theseus according to the legend. At Phaleron, a port of Athens, the rite of the Oschophoria ("carrying of branches"), under the patronage of Ariadne and Dionysus, repeated in the middle of the Hellenistic period the old Cretan ritual of reclusion, ordeals, and necessary rebirth from the labyrinth. Every large Cretan city in the time of "Minos" probably reserved its own initiatory cave for the use of its future warriors. In the gigantic cave of Psykhron—as in the cave of Zeus, between Gortyn and Axos in the seventh century B.C.—there is an abundance of symbolic offerings of weapons. The adventures of the goddess Ariadne (later assimilated to Aphrodite, Athena, or Hera) and those of the young god (later assimilated to Dionysus, Zagreus, or Zeus) served as paradigms and archetypes for the adventures of men.

We know of a dozen sanctuaries in the countryside dating from the "palace" era in Crete. This list is expected to increase in the near future with new discoveries. The four most important of these house-sanctuaries are, from east to west, Katrinia at Piskokephalo (Seteia), Minoikon Hieron at Kato Simi (Viannu), Niru Khani at Kokkini Khani (Pediados), and Kannia at Mitropolis (Kainuriu). Worship took place outdoors, either in small cubic edifices or in groups of adjacent rooms crowned with double horns. Worship was offered to the divinities of the locality, who were certainly very different from one another if we are to judge by their offerings. Thus, at Katrinia, the worshipers, represented by clay statuettes, came to place food in front of a sort of horned beetle, the *oryctes nasicornis*, that was considered to promote maternity in women and vigor in men. At Kannia, five rooms contained altars, offering vessels, and female idols dressed in bell-shaped robes accompanied by snakes, doves, plaques in relief, a statue of a warrior, and a vase in the form of a bull's head. At Kato Simi, two divinities, Hermes and Aphrodite, took the place of the gods of the "Minoan" herdsmen. The earliest cultivators and herdsmen of the Bronze Age venerated gods and goddesses who were apparently associated with and capable of promoting fertility in their fields and in their herds, and health and prosperity in their clan. Annexed to the rooms or sites of the actual cult were large stores of jars filled with provisions. The divinities of the Minoan era must have possessed rural estates and have had revenues just like the divinities of the Mycenaean era and those of the classical and archaic periods. We also know of lands owned by the church in Crete from the Middle Ages down to the present day. The analogy between these rural sanctuaries and the so-called "palaces" of Crete—as much in their orientation and arrangement as in the offerings and symbols discovered in them—may lead one to wonder whether the great "palatial" groupings of Zakro, Malia, Cnossos, and Phaestus were not simply large sanctuaries. In Egypt, Canaan, Syria, and Anatolia at the same period there was an abundance of vast temples including chapels, depositories, workshops, and dwellings for the priests, constituting a good third of every city. Such complexes must surely have existed in Crete, which was part of the same cultural region as the Near East. Furthermore, at Zakro, Malia, etc., *everything* bespeaks consecrations, ritual purifications, idols, symbolic representations, cult objects, and processions. Archaeologists have judged more than thirty rooms of the so-called palace of Cnossos to have been sacred. And next to these groupings in Crete we find "little palaces" and "villas," large secular and civic edifices, which were quite obviously constructed for the rulers. At Cnossos, then, we can assume that Minos (a dynastic title which may have signified "the Happy One") lived in the Little Palace, some 250 meters to the northwest of the actual temple, which was administered by a clergy that was essentially female. In the same fashion, at Jerusalem, the great Temple with its vast courtyard and all of its dependencies was not to be confused with the residence of Solomon.

When the Achaeans took possession of Crete (around 1300 B.C.?), the lords of the cities of Cnossos and Phaestus took over the large, rich sanctuaries as their own possessions, and made them the centers of their civil and military administrations. An important part was nevertheless reserved for cults, old and new. Later, perhaps in the eighth century, their successors constructed temples to the pre-Hellenic goddess Rhe(i)a on the ruins of the antique chapels of Cnossos, Phaestus, Lyctos, and Lebena. This continuity reminds us that the principal divinity of the great "Minoan" sanctuaries of Cnossos, Phaestus, etc., bore the name of the queen of the Titans, the Cyclopes, and the mythic Hundred-Arms—Rhea, a name we often encounter on the hieroglyphic seals of these sanctuaries. We also find what we believe to be the names of Thea, Thetis, Maia (or Ma), and Do(s), which, while they may not necessarily designate other divinities, are epithets or titles of the divine and maternal Rhea ("the Easy," "the Sweet"?) as well. Furthermore, the pictorial or sculptural representation of the bull in these sanctuaries, accompanied by the symbol of the double-bladed ax and a solar symbol— the image of the young "prince" with fleurs de lys accompanied by griffins—in the south corridor of Cnossos suggests that Rhea was not the only one to receive worship there, but that she had a consort—son, lover, husband, or perhaps all three at the same time, following a schema that is well known among Near Eastern religions. His name is unknown to us. Asterion ("He of the Celestial Sphere") could only be a late designation. The myth of Queen Pasiphaë, coupling in the form of a cow with a bull god standing as a guarantor and substitute for King Minos, probably conceals a ritual which we encounter again in the Hellenic period in the Eleusinian mysteries: at the end of a certain period, when it was thought that the solar year coincided with the lunar year, the king, as high priest or incarnation of the god in the city, came to unite

with the high priestess, who was the incarnation of the goddess, and both nature and society were thus regenerated. The author of the *Odyssey,* long before Plato, relates how every eight years—i.e. every hundredth month—Minos went to see his father Zeus and received from him the most just laws in the world. Another sacred marriage or hierogamy is attested in Crete at the source of the river Theren (the present Giophyro Platyperama) by Diodorus of Sicily around 50 B.C. This author adds that in Crete, mysteries are public and performed by everyone.

Next to these divinities of the whole of society, there were probably others of a subordinate rank or active only in a particular domain: at Cnossos, at the bottom of Mavro Spilio (Black Grotto) and in the "Spring Chamber" of the "Caravanserail," a goddess of the spring or a nymph was venerated. At Malia and Gurnia there were neighborhood public chapels which were distinct from the palaces. Monkeys, ibexes, wild goats, eagles, ringed doves, and snakes were at times considered to be incarnations of the divinity. Engravings, paintings, and reliefs represent griffins, sphinxes, and composites of men and various quadrupeds. It is not known whether these are genies, advisers, demons, or simply masked dancers. Snakes are not only portrayed as being curled around the arms of goddesses (or priestesses) or around ritual vases: they seem to have been auspicious

Woman with serpents. Statuette from Cnossos. Heraklion. Archaeological Museum. Photo Xylouris.

Offerings to the heroic dead. Painted sarcophagus from Hagia Triada (Crete). Heraklion, Archaeological Museum. Museum photo.

household spirits in Minoan Crete, protecting the house, just as later, in Athens, the serpent-god Erichthonius, son of Athena, would protect the Acropolis; and as even today, in certain parts of northern Greece, the snake is regarded as a spirit of the family. Large, fine houses had crypts designed for these subterranean divinities. But even in the houses of the poor there was a domestic cult as early as the second phase of the Early Bronze Age, for at Myrto (destroyed by fire around 2170 B.C.) English archaeologists have identified a domestic sanctuary older than any sanctuary of a summit or "palace." Close to a low altar and numerous offering vases, a clay vessel was found that portrayed a clothed goddess carrying a water jug on her left arm. She was conceived to be the supplier of water for a village in which water was particularly scarce.

It might be assumed that similar figurines of the same period found in the necropolises of Kumasa, Malia, Mokhlos, and Tzermiado represented the same divinity. But the differences in their attributes renders such an interpretation doubtful, to say the least. On the other hand, it seems certain that the divinity who presided over the fertility of the earth and the abundance of the harvests also watched over the dead. The use of the same fluted trays to receive grain, the presence of the same idols, the same symbols, and analogous trenches to receive liquids at Kato Khrysolakkos and Malia suggest an identity between the two divinities who were meant to receive these offerings.

It would be misleading to speak of a cult of the dead, unless we were to restrict ourselves to kings, princes, high clergy, and heroicized persons—and these only from the time of the first great sanctuaries. Only exceptional beings who participated in the divine could expect to have a divine power attributed to them. This is what seems to distinguish two clay models from the tomb of Kamilari and on the painted walls of the sarcophagus of Agia Triada. Minos and Rhadamanthys continued to exercise their functions as judges in the beyond. They themselves were the happy

rulers over the souls of their former subjects. The temple-tomb of Cnossos resembles the so-called tomb of Minos in Sicily: at the bottom of the crypt lay the body of the deified ruler, and above the crypt, worship was offered to the goddess to whom Diodorus would apply the name of Aphrodite some 1300 years later.

Given the decorated and written documents currently at our disposal in Crete, it seems possible to conclude that between 2200 and 1200 there were at least two polytheistic religions there, one being that of the islanders who colonized Crete in the Early and Middle Bronze Ages, and the other a religion that added to the preexisting pantheon the divinities of the Achaean peoples, often assimilating them to local divinities. The Mycenaean pantheon was as tightly structured as Mycenaean society itself. The polymorphism and polysymbolism of the Minoan religion allow a glimpse, alongside the strictly geographic cults, of only four kinds of divinities, which apparently correspond to four social classes: the divinities of the priests and priestesses, of craftsmen (particularly metallurgists), of young men expected to fight, and of farmers and herdsmen. The first three cults at least, and probably the fourth as well, gave rise to initiations which were the source of the Greek mysteries. Female divinities played a greater role than male ones, as maternity was more important than any other function. Faced with the constancy and analogy of these schemas, modern historians and sociologists have often been tempted to see a kind of imperfect monotheism in Minoan Crete: one great goddess or one great divine mother was worshiped under various representations and names, and her divine son was nothing other than her hypostasis or simply an emanation of her power. But this is a metaphysics too obviously inspired by Christianity. We should rather pay attention to the fact that, in nearly all of the Cretan cults we have looked at, the divine as well as its symbols appear under two aspects: the god and the goddess, the divinity (male or female) who dies and is reborn (or who appears and disappears), the father and the son, the mother and the child (or the young god), the double goddess, the double-bladed axe, the double horn, the two-lobed shield, and the bipartite sanctuary. In discussing the earliest and most enduring Cretan religion, let us speak, rather, of a deeply rooted dualism.

P.F./d.w.

BIBLIOGRAPHY

(after the deciphering of the Creto-Mycenaean writing)

1. Cretan and Mycenaean Writings
(Published Texts and Interpretation)

a) A. EVANS, *Scripta Minoa*, 1 (Oxford 1909). F. CHAPOUTHIER, *Les écritures minoennes au palais de Mallia* (Paris 1930). G. PUGLIESE CARRATELLI, *Le iscrizioni preelleniche di Haghia Triada in Creta e della Grecia peninsulare*, Monumenti Antichi, 40 (1945), 422–610. W. C. BRICE, *Inscriptions of the Minoan Linear Script of Class A* (Oxford 1961). FR. MATZ, H. BIESANTZ, et al., *Corpus der minoischen und mykenischen Siegel* (Berlin 1946–) = *CMS*. J. RAISON and M. POPE, *Index du Linéaire A* (Rome 1971). J. P. OLIVIER, "Le disque de Phaistos, édition photographique," *Bulletin de Correspondance Hellénique* 99 (1975): 5–34. L. GODART and J. P. OLIVIER, *Recueil des inscriptions en linéaire A* (Paris 1976–).

b) J. CHADWICK, "Linear B Tablets from Thebes," *Minos* 10 (1969): 115–37. J. P. OLIVIER, *The Mycenae Tablets IV: A Revised Transliteration* (Leiden 1969). J. CHADWICK, J. T. KILLEN, and J. P. OLIVIER, *The Knossos Tablets: A Transliteration* (4th ed., Cambridge 1971). E. L. BENNETT, JR., and J. P. OLIVIER, *The Pylos Tablets Transcribed*, 2 vols. (Rome 1973–75). J. P. OLIVIER, L. GODART, C. SEYDEL, and C. SOURVINOU, *Index généraux du linéaire B* (Rome 1973). ANNA SACCONI, *Corpus delle iscrizioni vascolari in lineare B* (Rome 1974). TH. SPYROPOULOS, J. CHADWICK, and J. MELENA, *The Thebes Tablets II* (Salamanca 1975). L. GODART and J. P. OLIVIER, "Nouveaux textes en linéaire B de Tirynthe," in *Tiryns, Forsch. u. Berichte* 8 (1976): 37–53.

c) Interpretations: L. R. PALMER, *The Interpretation of Mycenaean Greek Texts* (Oxford 1963). M. GÉRARD-ROUSSEAU, *Les mentions religieuses dans les tablettes mycéniennes* (Rome 1968). M. VENTRIS and J. CHADWICK, *Documents in Mycenaean Greek*, 2d ed. by John Chadwick (Cambridge 1973). See also articles in the following journals: *Nestor* (Madison, WI), *Minos* (Salamanca), *Kadmos* (Berlin and New York), *La Parola del Passato* (Naples), *Studi Micenei ed Egeo-Anatolici* (Rome), *Linguistique balkanique* (Sofia).

2. Collections of Documents with Illustrations and Commentaries

C. ZERVOS, *L'art de la Crète néolithique et minoenne* (Paris 1956). FR. MATZ, *La Crète et la Grèce primitive* (Paris 1962). A. EVANS, *The Palace of Minos at Cnossos*, 4 vols. (New York 1964). P. DEMARGNE, *Naissance de l'Art grec* (Paris 1964). G. MYLONAS, *Mycenae and the Mycenaean Age* (Princeton 1966); *Archaeologia Homerica*, collected under the direction of Fr. Matz and H. G. Buchholz (Göttingen 1967–). IAKOVIDIS, KARAGEORGIS, SAKELLARIOU, et al., *Historia tou Hellènikou Ethnous*, 1 (Athens 1970). NIK. PLATON, *Zakros: The Discovery of a Lost Palace of Ancient Crete* (New York 1971). SP. MARINATOS and M. HIRMER, *Kreta, Thera und das mykenische Hellas* (Munich 1973). C. W. BLEGEN et al., *The Palace of Nestor at Pylos in Western Messenia*, 3 vols. (Princeton 1966–73).

3. Rites, Myths, Symbols, Beliefs

NIK. PLATON, "Ta minoïka oïkiaka hiera," *Krètika Khronika* (1954), 428–83. M. P. NILSSON, *Geschichte der griechischen Religion*, 1 (2d ed., Munich 1955). FR. MATZ, *Göttererscheinung und Kultbild im minoischen Kreta* (Wiesbaden 1958), 381–450. A. J. B. WACE and FR. H. STUBBINGS, *A Companion to Homer* (London 1962), especially 463ff. on religion. R. F. WILLETTS, *Cretan Cults and Festivals* (London 1962); *Everyday Life in Ancient Crete* (London and New York 1969). P. FAURE, "Cultes de sommets et cultes de cavernes en Crète," *BCH*, 1963, 493–508; *Fonctions des cavernes crétoises* (Paris 1964); "Sur trois sortes de sanctuaires crétois," *BCH*, 1967, 114–50; 1969, 174–213; "Cultes populaires dans la Crète antique," *BCH*, 1972, 389–426; *La Vie Quotidienne et Crète au temps de Minos (1500 av. J.-C.)* (Paris 1973), especially pp. 63–107. ST. ALEXIOU, *Minoïkos Politismos* (Herakleion 1964), especially pp. 63–107, = *Minoan Civilization* (Herakleion 1969). EL. PLATAKIS, *To Idaion Antron* (Herakleion 1965). J.-CL. POURSAT, "Un sanctuaire du MM2 à Mallia," *BCH*, 1966, 514–51. B. C. DIETRICH, "Peak Cults and Their Place in Minoan Religion," *Historia* 18 (1969): 257–75. S. HOOD, *The Minoans: Crete in the Bronze Age* (London 1971), "Religion and Burial Customs," 131ff. B. RUTKOWSKI, *Cult Places in the Aegean World* (Warsaw 1972). EMILY TOWNSEND VERMEULE, "Götterkult," *Archaeologia Homerica*, 3, 5 (Göttingen 1974). C. DAVARAS, *Guide to Cretan Antiquities* (Park Ridge, NJ, 1976).

MYTH IN THE GREEK CITY: THE ATHENIAN POLITICS OF MYTH

Let us construct a fiction: a city has been founded, a group of citizens settled on its territory. What is now the most urgent task for the wise legislator? To set up laws, no doubt? If he takes Plato for a guide, he will start not by creating laws but by forging myths.

He will persuade the citizens "that in reality they were formed and raised in the womb of the earth, they themselves as well as their weapons and the rest of their equipment. And that, when they were entirely formed, the earth, their mother, delivered them, and now they should regard the earth that they inhabit as their mother and their nurse, and they ought to defend her against any attack and regard the other citizens as their brothers, who like them came out of the womb of the earth" (Plato, *The Republic*, 414 d–e).

Forging myths: if we are to believe Plato, this is the first thing to be attended to by the founder of a city (but the Sophist Critias, a "tyrant" of Athens and relative of the philosopher, was saying the same thing when he founded the political order on the fear of the gods, the clever invention of a wise man; Critias, fr. 25 Diels-Kranz). We should take the philosopher in the *Republic* seriously when he hastens, once the foundations of the imaginary city are laid, to submit the mythopoetic activity to the all-powerful authority of an official censor (337 b–c): "bad" myths must immediately be replaced by good ones, "noble lies" destined for the civic body, because all Greek cities, even imaginary ones, live on myths.

Dispensing with the fiction of the first inventor and with the problematical side of the noble lie, let us return to "reality," to truly existing Greek cities, with their own history and political life: myth is there, too; it is always there, an ancient history inscribed in the civic space, repeated in daily practice and in the most circumstantial decisions, retelling the origins of the polis (the Greek city-state) or founding its present. We shall attempt to discern this multiform presence within one city, the prestigious, if not the privileged, exemplar of the Greek politics of myth.

Let there be a city: Athens. A territory (*chōra*) and men (*andres*). At the center of the *chōra*, the urban space, the space of civic life, marked by three high places—the Acropolis, the Agora, and the Ceramicus—the hill of power and of the sacred, the public place, and the national cemetery. A community of citizens, with their wives (who are entitled to the name of Athenians, but not that of citizens) and two categories of noncitizens (metics and slaves). An intense civil life, a dynamic foreign policy, dominated by the imperalist search for power even more than by the desire for expansion.

At Athens, as in other Greek cities, myths speak of necessarily brilliant beginnings, and the legendary deeds of national heroes are recounted as a series of exploits (solitary *erga*) in which the citizens can see a prefiguration of their own collective enterprises.

To begin with, two myths.

I. The Confrontation of Athena and Poseidon: The Myth of Erichthonius

First of all, the quarrel of the gods and what follows (see, for example, Apollodorus 3.14.1; Saint Augustine, *The City of God*, 18.9). The divinity of the polis, Athena, rules over Athens; her temple has stood on the Acropolis since its origins, or, more exactly, since the Athenians chose Athena over Poseidon. This happened in the distant time of the distribution of the *timai* (honors) among the immortals; each god was determined to receive his share of honors from mortals, and the cities of men were the stake of the bitter struggles. It is in Athens, then, that Athena and Poseidon confront one another. Poseidon, the first to arrive in Attica, causes a sea (the Erechtheus) to well up in a hollow of the Acropolis; then, on the order of Athena, the olive tree breaks forth from the sacred rock, and a court of justice, brought together by Zeus, or already established by Athenians, settles the dispute. Cecrops, the native king, half-man, half-serpent, already human but still linked to monstrous creatures from out of the primordial Earth, is present as a witness to the litigation (according to certain versions, it is he who decides). Overruled in his claims, Poseidon is defeated, among the Athenians at Troezen where Athena carries the day, and at Argos and Delphi, where he must retreat before Hera and Apollo. Then the era of civilization begins for the Athenian city. And if, at Athens as elsewhere, civilization and the masculine power of the *andres* are synonymous, the Athenian myths do take account of this equivalence on three occasions. To choose Athena is to choose a warrior goddess, a virgin without a mother, born of a father who is also the all-powerful father of gods and men: Athena, whose "heart is completely given over to men, except for her hymen," and who, during the trial of Orestes, murderer of his mother Clytemnestra, will decide without reservation in favor of the rights of the father (see Aeschylus, *Eumenides* 736–38). Witness or arbitrator, Cecrops is also the inventor of monogamous marriage: he puts an end to the disordered promiscuity of the sexes by instituting patrilineal descent. Finally, and even more clearly, one version of the myth bases the victory of Athena on the political exclusion of women: guilty of unleashing the anger of Poseidon by voting for the daughter of Zeus while the men voted for the god, who was defeated, in fact, by a single vote—there was greater unity on the side of the women!—women are dispossessed forever of all power in the polis. The city of men has come into being: the first truly human ancestor of the Athenians can be born.

The myth of Erichthonius narrates this birth and gives the city its entry into human time. Erichthonius is born of Attic soil, fertilized by the desire of Hephaestus for Athena (see, for example, Apollodorus, 3.14.6); the mythologists of antiquity take pleasure in glossing his name: *Chthonius*, son of the Earth, the product of the bit of wool (*erion*) with which the

pursued virgin wiped the sperm of the god off her leg, unless he is simply the issue of the amorous struggle (*eris*) of the two gods. But this autochthonous creature is from the beginning closely connected with Athena, and with him the ties are bound forever between the polis and the goddess of the polis. The *Iliad* (2.546–551) already distributes roles between Athena and the fertile earth (*zeidōros aroura*): to the earth, childbirth (*teke*); to Athena, the task of raising the child—here named Erectheus—and making her protégé ("then Athena, daughter of Zeus, installed him in Athens in his rich sanctuary"). In the fifth century, Athenian potters often represent Ge giving the newborn child to Athena so that she might bring him up—or, better, that she might acknowledge him (see H. Metzger, "Athéna soulevant de terre le nouveau-né," *Mélanges Paul Collart*, Lausanne, 1976). Erichthonius is indeed descended from Athena, in the way that it is possible to be descended from a virgin who has renounced childbirth forever: through the mediation of the earth. Having become king of Athens, Erichthonius renders to his protectress everything he owes her, instituting the Panathenaea (see Jacoby, *F. Gr. Hist.*, 323a F 2 and 324 F 2) and forever associating the name of the goddess with that of his people (according to Herodotus, 8.44, it was during the reign of Erechtheus that the inhabitants of Attica took the name of Athenians). Thus the autochthonous king inaugurates human time for Athens within mythical history. By his birth, he is of the age beginning with Cecrops; on vases, the man-serpent frequently attends the "birth" of the miraculous child, and his daughters Aglauros, Pandrosos, and Herse are, by the will of Athena, the human nurses of Erichthonius—a difficult task, which they will perform poorly and which will lead to their death (see Apollodorus, 3.14.6, and Pausanias, 1.18.2). The death of Erichthonius—or rather Erechtheus, as tradition seems to reserve this name for the old king—reconciles Athens with Athena's rival. But it is at the cost of two lives. To save the city threatened by the expedition of the Thracian Eumolpus, son of Poseidon, Erechtheus must sacrifice his own daughter before being swallowed up by the earth, struck down by the god's trident; but his death links him forever with the god, and it is under the name of Poseidon-Erichthonius that he will henceforth be honored: a tragic event gives birth to the blessing of a new divine protection for the city. With Erichthonius, or with Erechtheus (whether they are taken separately or not), begins the long-lived theory of the Athenian kings, as shown on the famous vase (Berlin crater; ARV², 1268.2) on which the usual spectators at the birth of Erichthonius (Cecrops and Hephaestus) are joined by Erechtheus, as the adult king, and Aegeus, the father of Theseus (see F. Brommer, "Attische Könige," *Mélanges Langlotz*, Bonn 1957, pp. 152–164).

II. The "Life" of a Hero: Theseus

The history of Theseus comprises all the stages of a heroic saga (see Plutarch *The Life of Theseus*); from childhood to initiatory ordeals, from good fortune to bad, the life of Theseus is a long series of exploits, "condensing all the virtues and all the dangers of human action." Civilizing acts, battle with monsters, transgression of the human condition—Theseus makes all these forms of the heroic exploit his own (concerning the hero, see J. P. Vernant, "Aspects de la personne dans la religion grecque," *Mythe et pensée chez les Grecs*, vol. 2, 4th ed., Paris 1971, p. 90). Son of Aegeus—or, according to some versions, of Poseidon—and of Aethra, daughter of the king of Troezen, Theseus will grow up with his maternal grandfather, already giving many proofs of his bravery. At sixteen, the age

The discovery of the serpent Erichthonius: a daughter of Cecrops, the serpent, and Athena. Attic lecythus. Ca. 450 B.C. Basel, Antiken-museum. Museum photo.

of ephebe-hood, he lifts up the rock under which Aegeus had hidden a sword and sandals and, equipped with these signs of recognition, departs for Athens, taking the most dangerous road. This is the beginning of a long initiation at the end of which he will win the rank of legitimate son of Aegeus: on the way, he will purge the earth of a series of monsters (such as the sow of Crommyon) and fearful brigands, including Sinis, Cercyon, Procrustes (Proc[r]uste); acknowledged by Aegeus, he must still, in order to confirm himself as the worthy son of the king, annihilate the horrible bull of Marathon and triumph over the troop of the fifty Pallantids, his cousins, who are contending for power with Aegeus. But it is the characteristic of a heroic destiny to disdain repose: without delay, Theseus embarks for Crete in order to conquer the Minotaur, to which Athens must periodically deliver up the bloody prey of seven youths and seven maidens. We know that he triumphed over the monster and the Labyrinth thanks to Ariadne, that he abandoned her on Naxos, and that he forgot to raise the white sail as a sign of victory, thus provoking the death of Aegeus

Battle between Greeks and Amazons (detail). Attic lecythus. Ca. 440 B.C. Boston, Museum of Fine Arts. Museum photo.

on his return. This, then, is Theseus, king of Athens. As a political king, he proceeds to carry out the measure of synoecism (from *sunoikismos*, or shared household), uniting the scattered inhabitants of Attica in one city. As a warrior king, he wins glory in an expedition against Thebes and in the war with the Amazons. His adulthood is also an age of immoderation, or at least of the transgression of prohibitions. With his companion Pirithous, he kidnaps Helen, the daughter of Zeus, and descends into Hades to capture Persephone; the adventure turns out badly and results in the hero's long captivity among the dead while waiting for Heracles, who has also come down to Hades, to come and rescue him. Theseus must once again know exile, and violent death at Skyros. This, then, is the career of the most famous of the Athenian heroes, the only one given a complete "Life" and a complex image, the only one not to be subsumed whole into the myth of his birth or death.

Two myths, one heroic legend: identifying their broad outlines has involved a rather rigid classification. But these three narratives have been chosen from the rich Athenian tradition because in them the Athenian city has read (or put) much of itself. They are important narratives, exemplary narratives, and we are trying to discern their stake and their effects at the heart of civic life.

III. The Social Functions of Myth: Athenian Autochthony

As a discourse on the origin and the ordering of the human *cosmos*, myth narrates to the city, and in the name of the city, the coming of culture; in every Athenian it nourishes the representation of Athens that is appropriate both for oneself and for others: that of a polis "beloved of the gods" (*theophilēs*) and by origin doubly anchored in a close relationship with the divine. The quarrel of Athena and Poseidon is evidence of this relationship, and the circumstances which presided over the birth of Erichthonius are evidence that, as "sons of the blessed gods, who came out of a sacred ground and never knew conquest, the descendants of Erechtheus were prosperous at all times" (Euripides, *Medea*, 824–28). The mythic origins of masculine democracy, the legendary war against the Amazons who tried to imitate men and who turned out to be women after all when danger arose (Lysias, *Epitaphios*, 4–5), inaugurate the civic order of the *andres* as opposed to women, the passive "half" of the city. The story of the Amazons is doubly exemplary as it also tells the victory of civilization over barbarity, of the polis over strangers: at the Stoa Poecile (painted portico) where citizens can contemplate the great deeds of Athens painted on the walls, legend and history are neighbors, and "On the middle wall are the Athenians and Theseus fighting with the Amazons, then come the Greeks, masters of Troy . . . and at the end of the painting are those who fought at Marathon" (Pausanias, 1.15.2).

Celebrated in word and image, evoked in official speeches, represented in tragic theater, illustrated many times over on vases and temple pediments, myth runs the great risk, having undergone this treatment, of dwindling away into conventional scenes and rhetorical commonplaces. Its polysemy, reinforced by tragedy, shines forth, by contrast, when it penetrates the prosaic *logos* of politics or when the potters choose to illustrate one sequence from it, and always the same one. In the domain of political representations, however, it does gain by being a necessary mediation between the Athenians and Athens.

To distinguish the multiple functions assumed by myth and the many levels of social experience it takes charge of, one example will suffice: that of Athenian autochthony. It is true that official religion keeps to the strictest orthodoxy as far as the birth of Erichthonius is concerned, and that the story of the prestigious ancestor is an integral part of the *hieros logos* (sacred discourse) of Athena which occupies such a prominent place in the mystical vigil of the Panathenaea (see F. Vian, *La Guerre des Géants*, Paris 1952, p. 250). Between the son of the gods and the native born from the soil of the fatherland, tragedy makes no choice when it evokes the person of Erichthonius, and when they extend the name of Erechtheids to the entirety of the civic body, the tragedians make the Athenians both native sons and divine offshoots. But eloquence goes one step further, and, as though the story of Erichthonius were too well known to be repeated once again, the official orators, those who recite the funeral oration (*epitaphios logos*) to the glory of citizens fallen in combat, in general avoid mentioning the national hero and the divine couple who presided over his birth; instead, they attribute the privilege of autochthony collectively to all *andres Athēnaioi*. It is not surprising that this generalized autochthony becomes an essential element of the ideology of Athenian democracy: not only does it serve to justify Athenian practice in war—champions of right (or considered as such) are what the Athenians are by virtue of their status as legitimate sons of the soil of the fatherland (Lysias, *Epitaphios*, 17)—but the orators go so far as to derive democracy from autochthony or, to use Platonic terminology, to derive political equality (*isonomia*) from the equality of origin (*isogonia*; see Plato *Menexenus*, 239 a). Thus law (*nomos*) finds its basis in nature (*phusis*), and the power of the *dēmos* thereby gains its certificates of nobility: endowed collectively with good birth (*eugeneia*), autochthonous citizens are all equal because they are all noble. One more step and the speeches will contrast Athens with all other cities, anomalous groupings of intruders settling in as metics on foreign soil. Has the myth been lost by the wayside? To answer yes would be to forget that in the time of the religious calendar as in the space of civic life, in daily life as in the festivals of the collectivity, every Athenian is frequently reminded of the myth of Erichthonius: on the Acropolis and in the celebration of the Panathenaea, in the Agora, implicitly illustrated by the presence of Athena beside Hephaestus in the temple of the Artisan (Pausanias 1.14.6), in tragic or comic theater, in the workshop of the potter whose vases, humble containers or objects of beauty, repeat ad infinitum Ge's holding out the child to Athena, in the works of art which embellish their city (see Euripides, *Ion*, 271). And even if a surfeit of eloquence does weaken the myth, it is worth wagering that the Athenian audience took it upon itself to refer the general propositions of discourse to the living context of myth. Unless the Athenians really heard something else in the discourse about autochthony: the *muthos* of Athens.

Myths therefore do not die because they are politicized. How could they, when it is they that tell the city its identity, establishing the origin of the name of Athens or presiding over the *paideia* of the defenders of the territory of the fatherland? Thus it is that the oath of the Athenian ephebes invokes Aglauros, the virgin nurse with her bloody destiny, to begin the list of religious powers taken as witness to the irreversible commitment of the citizens. It is thus that in instituting in 508 the ten tribes which were from thenceforth to constitute the politico-military officers of Athenian life, Clisthenes placed them under the patronage of the ten national heroes, the ten Eponymous Ones, who include, not surprisingly, Cecrops, Erechtheus, and Aegeus, and whose exploits the citizens are invited to repeat in an ever-renewed *mimēsis* (see Demosthenes, *Epitaphios*, 27–31).

Between the gods and the heroes, between the original kinship which unites them collectively to Athena and the classificatory kinship which distributes them into ten tribes, Athenians had no lack of models, inscribed in civic time and space, to encourage them to root their actions in myth.

IV. In the Space and Time of the City, the Myth

Myths are everywhere present, punctuating the space of the city, tracing outlines, and forming constellations, complex knots of tensions and relations.

In the second century of our era, Pausanias the Periegete, an indefatigable traveler and even more indefatigable collector of mythic traditions, visits Athens, inaugurating a series of learned walks through the Greek cities: having entered by the Dipylon gate which, from the cemetery of the Ceramicus, leads to the Agora, he walks around the Agora, goes up to the Acropolis, returns to the Agora, and finally leaves the city by crossing the Ceramicus. This perambulation, both touristic and erudite, allows him to deploy his antiquarian's knowledge (Pausanias, 1.1–29); but already Athens is nothing more than a conservatory of the past. Let us imagine for a moment what an Athenian of the fifth or fourth century would have seen or pictured to himself in following the same itinerary (which has here been deliberately simplified). From the Ceramicus to the Acropolis and from the Agora to the Ceramicus two processions cross one another, processions which the calendar assigned to different times of year but which left their nontemporal mark in space: the procession of the Panathenaea, ascending to the sacred hill where the olive tree of Athena grows, where the goddess receives Erechtheus in her ancient temple, where the virgins, daughters of Cecrops, dance at night, "treading their tracks on the lawns

Surrounding the birth of Erichthonius, some protagonists from Athenian civic mythology. *Above, left to right:* Cecrops, Ge holding Erichthonius up to Athena, Hephaestus, and a daughter of Cecrops. *Below:* a daughter of Cecrops, Erechtheus, a second daugther of Cecrops, Aegeus, and Pallas. Attic cup. Ca. 450 B.C. Berlin, Staatliches Museum. Photo Tletz-Glagon.

facing the temples of Athena" (Euripides, *Ion*, 495–496); and the procession of public funerals which start from the Agora where national heroes stand guard, and go to the official cemetery to bury those citizens dead in combat, worthy imitators of the Eponymous Ones. On the Agora, the center of political life—dominated on the southeast by the Acropolis, to the south by the hill of the Aereopagus on which Athena assembled the first court of justice, to the northwest by the temple of Hephaestus—the twelve Olympian gods stand in close proximity to the Athenian heroes (for the sake of speed, we will mention only the ten Eponymous Ones, whose monument plays an essential role in the political and military life of the city, and Theseus, whose exploits are depicted in the interior frieze of the Hephaestion and in the paintings of the Stoa Poecile—in the Hephaestion, *sub specie aeternitatis*; in the Poecile, for the period of Athenian history, from the war of the Amazons to the battle of Marathon where the hero intervenes in the company of Athena and Heracles). At each step, heroic figures present themselves; in each place, mythic tales are inscribed; in short, this walk is certainly not just civic, for no space is less neutral than that of the city. Anyone wanting to take a walk without everywhere encountering the city presented through its myths would probably have to go out beyond the walls (see Plato, *Lysis*, 203a–203b; *Phaedrus*, 227a). Even that would be a naive hope: it was by the banks of the Ilissos that Boreas kidnapped Oreithyia, the daughter of Erechtheus (*Phaedrus*, 227a); over Marathon hovers the memory of Theseus (Pausanias, 1.32.6), who is also present on the banks of the Cephissus (id. 1.37.4); at Eleusis one can see the tomb of Eumolpus, who was killed by Erechtheus. We can stop counting here: in the country as in the city, myths speak everywhere to citizens of the city.

Let us return to the Agora, or—better yet—to the hill of the Pnyx where the assembly meets, where the political affairs of the Athenians are decided throughout the year: here more than anywhere else, myths speak very precisely of the present and past of the city. Or, rather, orators and politicians strive to make them speak.

It is well known that the historical consciousness of the Greeks is interwoven with myths and heroic legends (see M. P. Nilsson, *Cults, Myths, Oracles and Politics . . .* , pp. 12–15). It will be more useful to investigate further the relationship which, in the very midst of political life, is set up between repetition and event, when the event is part of myth. For this "very ancient history" is a history that is used and reworked. A history, also, that informs the actions of the present.

In the face of other cities, each polis brandishes its own myths and heroes: thus Theseus owes his remarkably good fortune to the fact that the Pisistratids sought to counter the Peloponnesians through their hero Heracles. The history of the hero gives both prefiguration and legitimacy to all territorial expansion: if Theseus chooses to travel from Troezen to Athens by the most dangerous route, via Megara and Eleusis, it will provide him with the opportunity to conquer the enemies of civilization; it is also the case that Athens, after the event or in anticipation, wants to legitimate the conquest of these cities, a conquest that may be insecure or merely desired. If the hero, on his way from Crete to Athens, stops at Delos to dance there, this dance will be a fitting celebration of the victory over the Minotaur, but it also has its function in the city of Pisistratus, for it provides a kind of filigree of justification for his ambitions for the Aegean Sea. As for Ion, eponym of the Ionians and chief of war under Erechtheus (or successor to the king), he takes his place in Athens and in Athenian myths only to make the city of the

Accompanied by Hermes, Heracles brings back Cerberus, the dog of the netherworld. Attic dish. Ca. 510 B.C. Boston, Museum of Fine Arts. Museum photo.

olive tree the metropolis of Ionia—the maritime empire too is in need of myths. What, finally, can be said of autochthony, the cornerstone of intercity rivalry, brandished by the Argives against the Athenians (Pausanias, 1.14.2), by the Athenians against the Tegeans (Herodotus, 9.27)?

More complex, but just as real, is the incidence of myth and heroic legend in internal political life: here, the vacillation between the then and the now is constant. The present remodels the legendary past, and at the beginning of the fifth century, in a city definitively rid of tyrants, the visual representations of Theseus on Attic vases suddenly start to reproduce the attitudes of the Tyrannoctones (murderers of the tyrant), as immortalized by two illustrious sculptors for the edification of the *dēmos*. Likewise, the Periclean law on citizenship, around 450 B.C., may have given a resurgence of authority to the myth of autochthony. Inversely, the present can be made into an imitation of the legendary past: thus, when Cimon repatriates the "ashes of Theseus" from Skyros in order to install them ceremoniously in the heart of the polis, at the foot of the Acropolis and near the Agora, it simply means that Cimon, the politician who wants to be a second Theseus, slips himself adroitly into the figure of the hero.

A strange destiny, that of Theseus in the democratic city. A history with certain eclipses, with vicissitudes and peaks closely wedded to the fluctuations of Athenian politics, from the sixth to the fourth centuries. The tyrants had exalted Theseus, but Clisthenes' reform removed him from view and thus put him at a distance from the Eponymous Ones, of whom, by contrast, his father Aegeus was a member (see P. Lévêque and P. Vidal-Naquet, *Clisthène l'Athénien*, Paris 1964, pp. 118–21). The aristocratic reaction following the Persian wars again made him a dominant figure, the very incarnation of Athenian greatness: did he not fight at Marathon on the side of the Athenians? Also, on the monument to the

45

Eponymous Ones erected by Athens in the pan-Hellenic sanctuary of Delphi to celebrate the victory of Marathon (and the glory of Athens herself), Theseus occupies a substantial place as the aberrant eponym who evicts Ajax (whose principal fault was to have reigned over Salamis); in the civic space of Athens, such a substitution is impossible: he is at least honored everywhere there, in his own sanctuaries or in the friezes of the temples of the Olympian gods. Of course he will be eclipsed again when democracy is strengthened: his connections with Pisistratus and then with Cimon are certainly true enough to make him suspect. From the end of the fifth century, however, he is no longer contested and gradually assumes, in the tragic theater and under the influence of moderate politicians, a new and final shape: that of the democratic king, the ancestor who, back at the time of origin, gave power to the people, or the less compromising figure of the founder of the constitution of the ancestors (*patrios politeia*). Who could any longer disentangle legend and history?

Thus, perpetually reactualized, the telling of far-off *erga* weighs on the actions of the present, whether by inspiring them directly or by playing the role of an interpretive model to be projected onto the action, for the benefit of the actors of history, for their own use or for that of others.

To characterize this overlapping of repetition and event, we may perhaps contend, in parody of Claude Lévi-Strauss ("The Structure of Myths," in *Structural Anthropology*), that nothing more closely resembles ideology than myth, when it becomes political. Perhaps also, refusing to set out on the slippery road of resemblances, we can simply observe that there is no "noble lie" in which the liar is not himself implicated, all the more when the narrator is confounded with the public, when the polis narrates stories to its citizens.

N.L./l.r.

BIBLIOGRAPHY

1. Myth in the City

M. I. FINLEY, "Myth, Memory and History," in *The Use and Abuse of History* (London 1974), 11–33. M. P. NILSSON, *Cults, Myths, Oracles and Politics in Ancient Greece* (Lund 1951). J.-P. VERNANT and P. VIDAL-NAQUET, *Mythe et tragédie en Grèce ancienne* (Paris 1972). P. VIDAL-NAQUET, "Esclavage et gynécocratie dans la tradition, le mythe, l'utopie," in *Recherches sur les structures sociales dans l'Antiquité* (Paris 1970), 63–80.

2. Athenian Myths

M. DETIENNE, "L'olivier: Un mythe politico-religieux," in *Problèmes de la terre en Grèce ancienne* (Paris 1973), 293–306. A. ERMATINGER, *Die attische Autochthonensage* (Berlin 1897). N. LORAUX, *The Invention of Athens*, trans. A. Sheridan (Cambridge, MA, 1986). J. RUDHARDT, "Une approche de la pensée mythique: Le mythe considéré comme un langage," *Studia philosophica* 26 (1966): 208–37.

3. Theseus at Athens

H. HERTER, "Theseus der Athener," *Rheinisches Museum für Philologie*, 1939, 244–86 and 289–326. H. JEANMAIRE, *Couroi et Courètes* (Lille and Paris 1939), 18–21 and chap. 4: "Attika: Les origines rituelles de la geste de Thésée." CH. P. KARDARA, "On Theseus and the Tyrannicides," *American Journal of Archaeology* 55 (1951): 293–300. M. P. NILSSON, "Political Propaganda in Sixth Century Athens," in G. E. Mylonas, ed., *Studies Presented to David Moore Robinson on His Seventieth Birthday* (Saint Louis 1953), 2:743–48. A. J. PODLECKI, "Cimon, Skyros and Theseus' Bones," *Journal of Historical Studies* 71 (1971): 141–43. P. VIDAL-NAQUET, "Une énigme à Delphes: A propos de la base de Marathon (Pausanias, X, 10, 1–2)," *Revue Historique* 238 (1967): 281–302.

PHILOSOPHY AND MYTHOLOGY, FROM HESIOD TO PROCLUS

"Myth" here will designate the legend of the gods of ancient Mediterranean tradition. Even this definition is too broad. During the Roman period, the ancients practiced a Greco-Roman syncretism that had already falsified the pantheons by forcibly superimposing them on one another. Such was the case to an even greater extent with the Greek/Latin/Celtic syncretism that Roman colonization practiced among the Gauls. La Tène culture knew writing, but did not use it for noble tasks; though it had gods and a legend of those gods, not only is the legend lost, but we do not even know if the masters of that tradition had elaborated the equivalent of a pantheon, that is, an ordered totality of the divine world. Greece, by contrast, quite early in its history elaborated an ordered totality which presupposed a serious mental effort. The thought that was crystallized in this endeavor is expressed through "genealogies," of which Greece had several. This mental effort also found expression in debates about the names, seniority, and ranks of the gods. The specialists who took part in these debates were known as "sages."

Sages preserve one or more traditions for other men. These other men—who live in the framework of the extended family, the village, and then the city or confederation of cities—tell or are told stories, "sacred narratives," that remain the heritage of descendants, corporations, cities, or pan-Hellenic shrines. The Greeks told a lot of them, embroidering them with variants that were sometimes highly irrelevant, until they managed to secularize the stories into legends offered as a common resource for artists to rework. The gods, however, each in their own domain, remain the guarantors of the rules practiced in civilized life, civic duty, skilled labor, or war. Ancient myth reigns over sex and violence, trade and farming, navigation and poetry contests. It frames and orders the well-articulated domains of human life, just as it frames and explains the realms of the elements. Polytheism drew man into the battle of the gods, each of whom claimed his own realm and his own honors. That is why one cannot tackle the problem of Greek myth without taking it seriously. It is neither folklore nor the religion of the devil, but a religion experienced by men, endured and sometimes violated for the sake of vengeful immoderation, a religion that is, moreover, thoroughly problematized.

This also explains why we must start with Greek myth, although Europe certainly knew others, such as the Irish and Norse myths, and these too were eventually transmitted in writing. That happened rather late, and in the presence of another learned tradition that transmuted them into poetry, pseudohistory, or fiction; and in the presence of another religious tradition that tried to drive them out as religions of the devil. Philosophy was born of the mental effort provoked by the problematization of Greek myth.

Schelling was the first in Europe—the best informed, at least—to proclaim Greek myth for what it really was: neither poetry, nor the transcription into images of a body of knowledge that had to be deciphered, but a polytheistic religion. He contrasted it, as such, with the monotheistic religion of the Hebrews, not only as the *multiple* in contrast with the *unique*, but as *myth* in contrast with *nonmyth*. It was a matter of the mode of presentation and transmission. Polytheism tells stories: the birth of gods, their childhood, mating, marriages, wars; the decline of the old and the advent of the new; the tripartition of cosmic rule, and the question of knowing if the partitioning applies to everything, absolutely everything, and for all times. From the very start, these stories are *fictitious*. By contrast, the one and only God of the Hebrew tradition speaks to *command*, inscribes his revelation in *writing*, or makes known his *judgment* in the nakedness of the event. Christian tradition, subsequently, welcomes progressive discovery of the hidden meaning of the Book, and even progressive revelation of the hidden things of nature. It possesses what myth never possessed, a moment of exclusion, demanding a choice between the true and the false. If we may venture to speak of the demythologizing of sacred texts, as is done nowadays, two conditions must be met. First, the ideals and the exigence of nonmyth have to have been preserved; second, these have to have been turned against the revelation of the Book. Problematical as it is on this point, our own Christian tradition is all the more suited to come to grips with the ancient problematic of *myth* and *truth*.

I. At the Beginning of a Tradition

From the moment it entered the game, as early as Hesiod, Greek myth viewed itself as *fiction*. It was neither nakedness nor deceit, but a kind of word game version of hide-and-seek. Had the metaphor of the *nonhidden* already given rise to a concept of truth? The man loved by the Muses was aware of his status as gambler in a sacred game, winning some and losing some. Sooner or later, knowledge set to poetry was transmitted by word of mouth, stored in the memory, worked and reworked with the help of competing specialists, and soon was the subject of discussion. This is not to say that these specialists were unaware of writing. They had in their possession the small miracle of a phonetic alphabet that had required the breaking down of syllables into phonemes, which were then fixed by means of nonpictorial signs. The threshold of writing was crossed long ago, if not from time immemorial; also crossed was the first barrier of abstraction. Thus Greek myth held nothing in common with the religion of peoples before the dawn of writing. These specialists were knowledgeable in grammar and music, perfecting their art in contests and their teaching in guilds. They acquired the technician's conscientiousness, which did not lack enthusiasm; indeed, it doubled it by introducing a split. The technician of sacred discourse also knew how to hide his knowledge from other men.

Barely accessible to the historian from the very start, the rivalry of traditions provoked an intellectual effort directed toward problems of a "theological" bent. The Greeks coined the word "theology" to designate the discourse that speaks of divine things. "In the beginning," should one have *one alone*, or *the couple*, or *several*? Male and/or female? A single *mother* of all things, or one for the good things and one for the evil, for falsehood and death? In the sense of a *ruler*, was the first one born all of a sudden in the beginning, or did he have to be engendered, raised, and did he have to win his sovereignty? Was there *one* ruler or were there *several*, joined by a treaty or hopelessly split? Is the present ruler certain to be the ruler forever? Or must one await the coming of another age?

We now find it simple to formulate these problematics (though we still find no solutions to them) through the economics of generations, descents, kinships, and splits. To achieve this we make use of a so-called "conceptual" vocabulary, models of formulas, and models for the concatenation of formulas. But the Greeks had to invent all of that. What made them famous was crossing a new threshold. Others

did the same, of course, but the Greeks remain the celebrated example, and they did it as masters of their own actions. This crucial threshold, as crucial as writing and even more so than printing, was the threshold of conceptual discourse, the threshold of philosophy. We did not have to cross it because the religion of our native culture had received Greek philosophical language as a kind of (dangerous) christening present, and because its priests assumed the (dangerous) mission of transmitting it along with their dogma. That is why we have such difficulty in putting ourselves inside the skin, the diction, and the mental system of the Greeks before philosophy. Afterward the Greeks kept both languages and translated from one to the other. They learned to use myth to say one thing and to hide something else. This is called allegory. Before that, myth was, as Schelling so well put it, "tautegorical": it had nothing to say other than itself. Thereafter, philosophizing often consisted of interpreting.

The threshold was marked by semantic innovation. In the sense of "sacred narrative," *muthos* was an approximate equivalent for *logos* qualified by *hieros*. Families, public bodies, and shrines preserved their "sacred narratives" of ante-historical tradition, before the scattered limbs of Greek myth were gathered together into "theogonies," before a "theology" of twelve great gods was made official in the city. The *muthos* was devalued in the sense of "fiction," itself thought of as something opposed to a *logos* henceforth qualified by *alēthēs* ("truth"; literally, "that which discovers hidden things"). One may say, in Parmenidean style, that truth discovers "nothing except with *logos*." The great ontological fragment of Parmenides completed one evolution and at the same time inaugurated another.

But things are even more complicated than that. Beginning with Hesiod, who himself marked a point of completion for the ante-historical development, heterogeneous languages confronted one another within Greek myth. A genealogy of individuals, called a *theo-gony*, led to a genesis of the parts of the world, called a *cosmo-gony*. The two fit together on the genealogical model of descents. Should we say that fathers and mothers originally inhabited wide open realms with their genesis? That they manifested themselves as the impact of phenomena on our senses? That the rulers of the third or fourth generation were born to rule over domains liberated by the withdrawal of the old regimes? Or should we say that they manifested themselves as an ethical and even a political exigence inseparable from the cosmic order? All of these questions are open to the mediation of the sages. A cosmo-*logy* then completes the cosmo-*gony*, the *logical* describing within its constituted structure what the *gonical* called forth within its constituent structure.

No sooner was it born than the discourse of "the lovers of wisdom" in its turn divided itself into two. At first, *cosmologies* appeared as artfully shaped models that could also be sketched on maps, designed to represent on a small scale what the world must be like on a large scale in order to justify its appearance to the naked eye, with or without any reference to divine inhabitants. Then a statement was verbalized, the subject of which was no longer either the god or the element, but "yet another thing" bearing "yet another name"—the "beginning" of an *archaeo*-logy, the "one" of a *heno*-logy, the "being" of an *onto*-logy, indeed the "god" of a *theo*-logy that became rational. The split between the discourse of the *phusis* and "logies" of another kind was outlined before Parmenides. It ended in favor of contests in which there was a confrontation behind the master, or around him, between his faithful or unfaithful successors, or between both of these together against the "Heraclitean" supporters of an altogether opposed set of principles. Ontology earned the privilege that has remained its own in the European tradition, but earned it only through a controversial evolution that occupied the age of the Sophists until its perfect culmination in Plato's *Parmenides* and *Sophist*. It is a fascinating story, but we do not propose to tell it here. It will be sufficient if we can shed some light on the intention, the motivation that succeeded in making the story dynamic. It was apparently the concern to come even closer to an untargetable goal, to go farther and farther back toward an origin that hid itself away "at the beginning" and "at the command" of everything. The concern was to say it all with a language that was more stripped down than drama or elemental images. The names of the gods did not succeed in saying the real thing, nor did the face of the elements succeed in representing it with images.

The ancients of the Greek tradition searched for this stripping away in the simple words of everyday language. Such was their stroke of genius! They chose words that fit spontaneously in the articulations of drama, preferably verbs, that could not be avoided in telling a drama. For example, a debate among specialists on the important question of knowing whether "in the beginning" there must be "one" (male or female?), or "a couple," or even "one plus a couple," forming a "number"; whether there must be "a couple" with opposing members, such as the "Abyss" and the "Earth," or the parturient cleft of the carrying womb, or "a couple" with separate members joined in copulation; or, rather, a "Mother" who first was torn apart and then, like the "Earth" with the "Sky," copulated, with a third thief set aside in order to bring them closer together in the name of "Love." Instead of designating them with the names and forms of the precipice and the mountain, the night and the light, why not simply name them with words that say the "beginning" (*archē*), the "unity," and the "dual"; with pairs of verbs that say "separate and join," "scatter and gather," "go away and draw near"? If the mental effort suggests that by excluding another thing no name of a thing is adequate to speak of what is wholly at the beginning of everything, even before the beginning, why not speak of it as the "limitless" (*apeiron*), the "inaccessible" (*aporon*), the "altogether apart" (*chōris apantōn*)? Specialists will easily have recognized all these nouns and pairs of verbs as belonging to the composite vocabulary of the archaic forms of philosophy.

Naming counted, but so did *saying* or *telling*, with a formula that assembles a text, and more, with a chain of formulas that form a complete fabric. The more people advanced, the more speech dismissed the primordial concern with "accurately naming" the Divine that was being addressed, in favor of "telling it like it is." Telling was put together with phrases completed by verbs. Not only did the verb complete the telling, but the strength of the telling resided in the verb. Let us take as an example the Parmenidean discourse on being.

Parmenides does not begin by naming "being." He does not begin by positing it as a subject in the place of the god of Xenophanes, his predecessor. Quite the contrary, Parmenides forms a complete sentence with nothing but a verb in the present indicative and without an expressed subject: (it) "is" (*esti*). At the level of the thing already said, the formula can be inverted into: (it) "is not." This is a counter-statement, which the counter-counter-staters invert in turn into "nonbeing is not" through a first use of the double negative, a formulation that should never have been made, since nonbeing cannot possibly be thought or said. Once the formula had been (unfortunately) said, and even written, it gave rise to the scandal of a reinforced contradiction in

"nonbeing is." All that remains to be done is to reinforce the first assertion counter-contradictorily: "being is." Naming it a substantive "being" is done at the level of the "thing said" in the dialectical contests that the master objected to. But "being-thinking-saying" what is here-and-now has the verbal force of a founding act. Once "being" has been named as a god with his own proper name, one subject can easily be substituted for the other in the discourse, "god" for "being," thus opening the way for a rational theology. This was done at the school of Elea, in the presence of the master or after him. His own ontological discourse remained stripped down and pure.

A fortiori, one could apply the same analysis to styles that prefer to use verbs of contrasted movement, preferably as a means: such as, "to draw near and to draw apart," "to gather and to disperse," "to divide and to unite." A fortiori, these styles will condense within the verb the force of the original act. But when one nominalizes, one draws up a table of opposites: "movement and rest," "presence and absence," "assemblage and dispersal," "the one and the other," "the same and the other," like a cold stone tablet on which fixed categories are inscribed. It becomes permissible to "harmonize" divine names with the categories, harmonizing an Eros or a Philia with "to gather," a Neikos or a Polemos with "to divide." How many "abstract" deities were thus begotten! By opening the "parallel roads" of two mutually convertible languages, Greece was henceforth obliged to allegorize. The game of interpretation replaced the dance of the verbs around the *archē*.

The world of culture has remained split ever since. On one side are the preservers of a tradition; on the other are the bold, pushing ahead on new paths. Most people learn to tread on all the paths. Some people reveal their personal dispositions in the choice that engages them in new spheres of knowledge—grammar or cosmology, arithmetic or theology—or in practical politics, with the violent negation of myth. Others are drawn to the pacifism that tolerated parallel tracks, changes of direction, or doubling back. The games of interpretation sanctioned the translation of traditional models of theogonic construction into physics, into ontology, and even into history. The tales of the gods, named according to the articulations of their structures, were made into motifs for drama, poetry, and fiction.

One must not conclude that the interpretation was made, once and for all, in the simple mode of allegory. The transposition has never been quite as rigid as the one that is found later among the Stoics: Zeus = the Ether that thinks and envelops the universe. Nor was the transposition as sophisticated as the one that would later be found, for instance, among the Neoplatonist Orphics: Phanes = the principle of phenomenalization. We are rather inclined to believe that a shaky balance is present between the anti-fiction demand and the imaginative faculty that remained in a Greece seething with inventiveness. The very inventor of pure conceptual discourse, Parmenides, furnishes the example that is most telling because it is least amenable to proof.

Was the anti-fiction demand ever more radical than in the fifty verses of Parmenides' discourse on being? Yet the horses that take off "in proportion to desire" emerge at the beginning of the poem with the vividness of a spoken image. They pull away, even if, after the moment of its appearance, the live metaphor is prolonged with a bit too much affectation for our taste, on the road that symbolizes rhythmic/poetic structure and the model of concatenation that is demonstrative of discourse. The *logos* with which truth is discovered is stabbed three times over by that ancient, stern triad,

Dike-Ananke-Moira. The attributes of the unnamed, its signs, are posited with the hesitation of concepts in formation, dipped in the effervescence of root images: "it is not cut as with a knife," "(it) is all of one mass," "all of a piece," "whole and altogether present." This is not an algebraic abstraction. A great effort at connected utterance progresses through the schematization of a sphere on the path of contraction toward the resting place of thinking. As for the "doxic" poem, we have too little of it available to us to assert that female figures there, as in the poem of Empedocles, came to mirror a table of opposites, lining up in couples in the form of night and day, the attributes of the "cold and silent" corpse in contrast to the attributes of the living. Aphrodite sits enthroned among the alternating crowns of shade and light constituting the cosmic scene in which the goddess has a circle of girls mate with a circle of boys. With Parmenides, the delicate balance between the imaginative and the conceptual is not so different from that of Empedocles. We do have extant from Empedocles a religious poem that mirrors his physics: that is why he is said to have wanted to create the "mystical vehicle" of his wisdom.

Sages and Sophists belonged to an elite: members of families endowed with noble traditions, public bodies endowed with revenues, communities devoted to "works of memory," civic or religious reformers. They stood side by side with the illiterate masses, including women, in a culture that remained largely oral. Greek myth remained bound up with social prestige, mores, and the rites of marriage and death. Hence, those who were violent, pushing the anti-fiction demand to the extreme, were often marginal figures: foreigners, immigrants, exiles, more at ease in the colonial domain than on the home front, exposed to civic proceedings, less likely to govern than to draw up constitutions or to found communities of scholars. As for the more conciliatory, their work of interpretation bridges the gap on the level of discourse, a gap that was quickly and dangerously prolonged on the level of a noble and civic religion consumed by ratiocination, of a myth about to become folklore in the thinking of the majority. Philosophy came of age like a plant of the abyss, cast adrift by a force that had separated the culture of the cities from its native religion. For an imaginative people, it fostered with taste and vigor the foreboding of transcendence that was implicit in the demand for anti-myth.

II. At the End of the Hellenic Tradition: Proclus

By placing ourselves at the beginning of a paradigmatic tradition, we have shown how a new language (archaeo-, heno-, and onto-logical) emerged from sacred texts, scholarly in their own right, and what demand was met by this mutation perceived at the level of the texts. By placing ourselves at the end of the same tradition, we can ask, How did it record the lesson of this long experience? We shall examine Proclus, because: (a) he experienced the articulation of the Greco-Roman and Byzantine periods (the closing of the pagan schools in 529, the fall of Rome in 476); (b) he belonged to the school of Athens that in the course of the fourth and fifth centuries rethought the heritage of Plato in the so-called Neoplatonist schemata; and (c) he was aware of belonging to a tradition that included his forefathers and had to be defended.

In his introduction to *Theologia Platonica*, Proclus distinguishes four modes of exposition that were used by Plato and that coincide with four possible and traditional modes. Ranked from the least noble to the most noble, these modes are (1) exposition "through image," *iconic*; (2) exposition

"through symbol," *symbolic*; (3) exposition "through concepts and demonstration," *dialectic*; and (4) exposition "through inspiration," *enthusiastic* or *apophantic*.

These modes can be regrouped in various ways, for example, two by two:
"unveiling" modes: *dialectic → enthusiastic*
"veiling" modes: *iconic → symbolic*
Read horizontally, within the framework of the major opposition between "unveiling" and "veiling," this diagram depicts the relationship between the superior modes that "unveil" the hidden thing and the inferior modes that "veil" them under a symbol or image. Read vertically, the same diagram depicts another relationship, between the *dialectic* and the *iconic*, modes that seem to be those of scholars; and between the *enthusiastic* and the *symbolic*, modes that seem to be those of theologians.

But the modes can be regrouped in yet another way, by placing them apart from, and above, the *enthusiastic* mode of divine revelation, and apart from, and below, the *iconic* mode of an efficacious knowledge focused on the building of the world. Thus:

$$\textit{enthusiastic}$$
$$\textit{symbolic} \qquad\qquad\qquad \textit{dialectic}$$
$$\textit{iconic}$$

At the middle level, this regrouping brings out a kinship between the *symbolic* and the *dialectic*: both bring about a mediation of divine knowledge, one (the symbolic) through images, by hiding it from other men, the other (the dialectic) through concepts and demonstration, by articulating it for the dianoetic intelligence of scholars.

For example, Proclus illustrated the *iconic* mode through Plato's *Timaeus*. The *Timaeus* constructs the elements of the world by limiting the *limitless* volume of the *chōra* by means of triangular planes, in order to contain the volume within the figures of regular geometric solids. This chapter uses geometry to fashion structures that are applied to the genre of *indefinable being*, which after Aristotle comes to be called "matter." It attributes a physical construction to the demiurgic workings of the gods. Proclus also categorizes political operations under the *iconic* mode when politics functions, as it does in the *Republic*, to establish the city, rank men, and distribute their labors. We should add the operation of the ordinary man, when man functions ordinarily as he does in everyday life in order to measure and harmonize the way he uses his allotted time of life. The *iconic* mode then functions as an operational mode: it operates in man "in the image of" the divine demiurge, and operates in the lesser gods "in the image of" the operation of the first god, the one that Plato calls "the Demiurge," constructing the framework of the cosmos according to the arithmetic of those who are mediated.

We must be careful to distinguish between the "image" (*eikōn*) and the expression "in the image of." Through the illustration of the *number* and the *figure*, the image designates the operational scheme of a physical and political architectonics. The expression "in the image of" applies to a *praxis*. Among the gods of the tradition and among men, *praxis* works to produce what we see all around us, in the city and the world-at-large. Man has a right to depart from his working *praxis* in order to formulate an idea of the divine operation "in the image of" which his own *praxis* operates. Then he makes another use of it, "for remembrance."

The same observation results from the illustration given by Proclus for an extra-Platonic, traditional *iconic* mode: the numbers and figures of the Pythagoreans. It is expressly stated that the Pythagoreans used numbers and figures "for remembrance." In this context, therefore, there are two possible uses for the *iconic* mode, a practical use, in the sense of a physical or political construction, which is the sense of a descent, and a use in the sense of an ascent, which is *mnemonic*, "for remembrance." The image itself (*eikōn*) is located at the point where the descending practical movement joins the ascending *mnemonic* movement. The image, like the number and the figure, had to be constructed, the number based on a law of a series, the figure based on a rule of construction. At the head of the laws and operational rules are the *principles of the dialectic*. This rooting of the *iconic* within the *dialectic* justifies their being grouped together. We are dealing with science in the dual aspects that we call speculative and practical.

The Platonic illustration given for the *symbolic* refers us back, by contrast, to myths: those of the *Gorgias*, the *Symposium*, and the *Protagoras*. The traditional extra-Platonic illustration refers back to the "Orphic series." With the "Orphic series," we are dealing with one or more models of cosmotheogonies of a later period that are reconstituted by derivation from the archaic models of a tradition on the fringe of the Hesiodic tradition. The "Orphic series" is characterized by the promotion of one Mother, named *Night,* who gives birth to a god named Firstborn, Protogonos, or Phanes. The allegorizing hermeneutics of the later period translated Phanes as "principle of phenomenalization," emerging from an unimaginable, unthinkable, unrepresentable foundation, which the emergence of the principle had covered as soon as it had uncovered it.

The *symbolic* mode refers back to myth. The symbolic mode requires that the myth be translated into the language of principles. It is the process that Schelling denounced in the Neoplatonists as resulting from allegory, that is, as actually exposing something other than what it professes to tell about, invoking a translation into the language of concepts. To this *allegorical* myth Schelling opposes the *tautegorical* myth, which actually exposes nothing but itself. The gods of polytheism dispense with conceptual translation. They are just what they profess to be.

The late period of Greco-Roman civilization, when it was contaminated with Orientalism and used to establish equivalences between one pantheon and another, was certainly not at a loss to translate the pantheons into philosophy. Yet Proclus's thesis is not so easily reduced to the game of allegory. It is singularly subtle and complex. A few observations are in order.

1. Among the works of Plato, Proclus gives a special place to the *Phaedrus*—more precisely, the second discourse of Socrates in the *Phaedrus*—as based upon the very first mode of exposition, the one we have called *enthusiastic*. This genuinely inspired discourse, spoken in enthusiasm, amounts to revelation.

2. In the same Platonic literature, Proclus also gives a special place to the myths of transparent artifice, lessons on morality or political ethics that are easy to read beneath their outer garb of drama—for example, the myth that Plato puts into the mouth of Protagoras in the dialogue of the same name. He teaches that human genius, aided by Promethean fire, is probably sufficient to invent the arts, language, and ritual, but not sufficient to bring about peace in the city. For this, two additional virtues are needed: justice, which dictates law, and a sense of decency, which respects prohibitions.

3. In the *symbolic* genre, Proclus distinguishes between series and drama. Series on the Orphic model refers to the genealogical framework of a theogony. The twelve great gods of the official theologies provide another example. Drama refers to the stories of birth, childhood, marriage, and war that clothe the framework—stories to tell or to play. To "tell" and to "play" already have a literary meaning, but to "tell" and to "play" also preserve a strictly ritualistic meaning. We are indeed dealing with religion. We should note that the essential of *symbol,* which requires its *dialectic* counterpart, is not drama itself but its framework. The dialectic counterpart articulates the concatenation of its demonstration upon the genealogical framework.

4. Proclus praises Plato for having expurgated his myth by removing the scandalous drama of traditional myth. But this praise is not without ambiguity. Elsewhere, he praises traditional drama for the impact it makes on man's soul; by contrast, he criticizes the severe mode of dialectical demonstration for the violence it visits on man's soul.

We should therefore distinguish among various kinds of myth; above all, we should separate the artificial kind from the traditional religious kind that could almost be called natural. As found in literature, artifice consciously invents a moral or political lesson that is easy to read. As found in theology, artifice composes or recomposes the outer trappings of a framework that is inherited from ancient sources and is then itself reshaped into a system, or that is "received" through enthusiasm. As for the kind of myth inherited from an immemorial past and attributed to those holy men, the ancient poets with amazing names, it puts forth the enigma of its fascinating and scandalous drama. This myth exerts its power on man for better or for worse. It is the type of myth of which Proclus wrote:

> It is ancient, this mode of expression of mythology that consists in revealing divine principles by means of obscure references, of drawing a number of veils over the face of truth, and of imitating that nature that offers sensory products in place of intelligible beings, material and divisible products instead of immaterial and indivisible beings, and out of true beings fabricates images and false beings. (*Theologia Platonica*)

We should note that the term *images* here is a translation not of *eikōnes* (icons) but of *eidōla* (idols). Those holy men, the ancient poets who, according to tradition, are said to have fashioned myth, labored "in the image of" the demiurgy of *Physis*, a kind of Hellenistic or Byzantine Maia who, like the Weaver who weaves her own veils, herself fashions the fascinating and deceiving beauty of the world.

We could go on to say that fable requires no interpretation at all, only an illustration through example, taken from life and from a particular event. The artificial myth of the philosopher or theologian requires translation because it means something other than what it seems to be saying: the translation of divine names into the names of principles, or the transposition of genealogical frameworks into an architecture of systems. Only the natural myth (the inspired myth, if there is such a thing) requires a hermeneutics. It separates the framework from the drama, and from the framework itself it draws the *apophansis*, or "pronouncement," of an inspired core (if such exists). It reconstitutes a dialectical chain of reasons by articulating a parallel speculative system. All this requires fuller explication.

To illustrate the dialectical genre of Plato, Proclus cites the second part of the *Parmenides*. He himself confesses that he would rather practice this kind of "clear and distinct" discourse, which he values above all others except inspiration or enthusiasm, before which modesty compels him to disqualify himself.

Platonic dialogue makes use of an interplay of concepts that bear the simple names that the evolution of philosophical discourse has distinguished since its origin: the One and the Being, the Whole and the Part, the Same and the Other, and so forth. It has chosen the One for the subject of a proposition stated in the positive or in the negative for the verb "to be." The One is split into two as the One-One and the One-Being. We can then draw certain inferences about the One and the Others, under the titles of the series of concepts. Such are the rules of a game that we shall not reconstitute here. The initial propositions, positing the One-One and the One-Being, assume them "to be" and "not to be," with a formula based on "if." From there, propositions are drawn that affirm or deny, or affirm and deny at the same time, the other concepts taken as attributes, each time with an argument, a "logism," in the form of a demonstration. Hence we have a chain, the "logisms" forming its links, with "repetitions" of the initial propositions that various traditions have variously enumerated.

Proclus's reading of this dialectic first proves that the nonveiled mode of exposition is a blinding mode. The reading consists in superimposing, like the stages of an ontology, the "repetitions" called "hypotheses," and, within those same "repetitions," arranging the derived propositions and their "logisms" in tiers. The argumentation counts for less than the actual order of the links in the chain. Upon the framework of the order, the ontotheological reading builds the series of its processions.

It is not our purpose here to analyze further. Suffice it to have shown that Proclus's reading dispenses entirely with any recourse to myth. It practices ontology, archaeology, if you will, a science of principles rather than of symbolic mythology. Reciprocally, natural myth dispenses with any recourse to dialectics. We can believe in the gods of a polytheistic religion, recite their series, and enact their rituals, without practicing dialectics. But we cannot dispense with it entirely. For one thing, the veils of the myth, such as the image of the world, create illusions. For another, the enigma and scandal of drama persist. Hence the renewed demand among the best of them to unveil in order to possess the naked truth, and to resolve the enigma proposed by drama. Hence the move back toward the origin of an initial "enthusiasm."

At the lower levels of physical demiurgy and political architecture, Proclus has expressly and energetically rejected allegorical interpretations, both the Stoic interpretations of myth as a physical phenomenon and the Euhemeristic interpretations of myth as history. The *iconic* mode of sciences that are focused on their operative accomplishment, the constructions of a geometrical or architectonic physics of the city, dispenses with interpretation. These clear and efficient sciences are self-sufficient. Their storytelling is just a game.

At the upper levels, hermeneutics distinguishes structures. It extracts their inspired core (if one exists). With *dialectics* on the one hand, and myth and ritual on the other, we are likely to be dealing with parallel developments stemming from a common inspirational root or from intertwined roots sinking to the same foundation: two heterogeneous modes of exposition, one "veiling" from the very beginning and repeatedly veiling until an illusion is created; the other impelled from the outset by a will to "unveil" at the risk of blinding. Does this dialectic succeed in doing anything but envelop the originating gift in a shroud of concepts borrowed from a cleverly simple language? Does it hope to

evoke remembrance through this dance of words? Is it better for the sage to practice the oscillation from speculation to myth, and vice versa? Will he then manage to close up the two shells of symbol? Does Pythagoreanism achieve remembrance more easily through the symbolic use of numbers and figures? Or must we believe that myth and dialectic deny one another in order to create within thought the emptiness receptive to the gift? And if the gift occurs, what is the expressive mode appropriate for its *apophansis*?

The illustration given by Proclus's text is perplexing. It is the second discourse delivered by Socrates under the inspiration of the nymphs in the *Phaedrus*. We take this passage to be unquestionably a myth fully developed in images. It tells a story of falls and recoveries, a whole odyssey of the soul through its reincarnations. It meshes with comparable narratives in other dialogues, the *Gorgias*, the *Phaedrus*, the *Republic*, in such a way as to create a coherent whole: a myth of the soul and its destiny. To look at it more closely, the mythical entity of the *Phaedrus* possesses an *archaeo-logical* core: it proposes and places at the very start an *archē kinēseōs*, a principle at the beginning and at the command of movement, in all the Greek and Platonic meanings of movement, implying birth, growth, change, and their opposites. This *archē* is the principle forever at the beginning and at the command of all that lives and dies. It itself has neither beginning nor end, neither birth nor death, since it is sufficient unto itself to begin anew in perpetuity and is sufficient for all that lives and dies and that would have long since died without it. This principle having been proposed and deductions having been made, it is finally identified with what is called soul, its equivalent in common language. The *Phaedrus* as a whole also contains a "series" of the gods walking at the head of processions of souls and of the hierarchical grades of ways of life suitable to ensure the ascent of souls, like the clothed framework of an *Odyssey*.

This is, then, a complex entity with pieces that have been ground up in different ways. One would wager that the core of inspiration appears here with a name and with an image, the name of the principle *archē kinēseōs*, the "living metaphor" of the chariot, as it had already emerged at the beginning of old Parmenides' poem, and now reemerges with the same impulse. The prolongation of the living metaphor comes from the poetic demiurgy that creates myth. Its explication comes from the dialectics. Metaphor is made into symbol and is exposed to allegory. Under the name and under the image, as they rise to the surface of consciousness and of the poem, a demand and an impulse still live in their immanence, the same at the end and at the beginning of the tradition. What has just been said is interpretive.

What can be so easily read in Proclus's text is that his lucid modesty has made him disqualify himself from the "enthusiastic" or *apophantic* mode of revelation. He has chosen for himself the mode of clear and distinct exposition, through concepts and demonstration. Having chosen this speculative mode, his task as a philosopher consists in developing the abrupt, assertive formulas of an *apophansis*, in making explicit the concatenation of demonstrations, in shedding light on the enigmatic use of symbol, and in referring the political lesson to actual experience.

Conclusion

What lesson is to be learned from the synthesis of Proclus?

1. Proclus lived during an age and in a world in which the traditions of the eastern Mediterranean basin intersected with one another and with others still, and also with a

flowering of new movements. He was not eclectic. He chose to remain faithful to one tradition, his own, and within it to a perfectly defined lineage. He knew his forefathers.

2. He succeeded in building a framework within which the varieties of Greek experience could take place: the experience of the mysteries, of theology, of philosophy, the experience of the sciences that depend on measurement and numbers, and the experience of poetry and even of ethical and political praxis.

3. Myth, as it is viewed here, arises as the product of a poetical demiurgy functioning "in the image of" the divine demiurgy that created the beauty of the world, with its fascination and its power of illusion. Its return toward its origin, and beyond toward the foundation common to its veiled wisdom and its clear wisdom, passes through an architectonic. The structuring movement of this framework, or of this structure, respects the hidden laws that are also found in numerical "series" and in figures.

We too live in an age in which all the religions of the world meet, not only the religions of today with their movements of renewal but, thanks to archaeology and history, the religious past of our forefathers, back to our remote ancestors of the Cro-Magnon age. We live in an age in which scientific knowledge has broken through the roof, has gone so far as to unveil the structure of the very nucleus of matter, the structure of genes, and the mechanisms of procreation. As long as our collective wisdoms fail to build a framework within which to arrange these treasures, each in its own place and according to its own rank, too much knowledge exposes us to too much danger. Is it not wiser to remain faithful to the tradition that we know best, by asking its forefathers to rediscover their exigence and their impulse? As for the enigma posed by the mythology of all peoples, exposed for display in the showcase of our imaginary museums, the task clearly imposed upon us is to build this "transcendental fantasy" that a number of people have already called for. No phenomenology of religion will ever succeed without penetrating deeper into the infraphenomenal processes of the imagination.

C.R./g.h.

BIBLIOGRAPHY

M. DETIENNE, *Les maîtres de vérité dans la Grèce archaïque* (Paris 1967). J. PEPIN, *Mythe et allégorie* (Paris 1958). PROCLUS, *La théologie platonicienne*, trans. H. D. Saffrey (Paris 1968). C. RAMNOUX, "Les modes du penser philosophique d'après Proclus," in *Faire, croire, espérer* (Brussels 1976); *La nuit et les enfants de la nuit dans la tradition grecque* (Paris 1958). F. W. SCHELLING, *Introduction à la philosophie de la mythologie*, trans. Jankelevitch (Paris 1945). L. TARAN, *Parmenides*, text, trans., and commentary (Princeton 1965). J.-P. VERNANT, *Les origines de la pensée grecque* (Paris 1962); *Mythe et pensée chez les Grecs* (Paris 1965).

PLATO'S MYTHOLOGY AND PHILOSOPHY

Mythology may be defined as a system of narrative representations playing both explanatory and normative roles with respect to the gods, the world, and humankind. Every theogony that extends itself into a cosmogony and an anthropogony offers a primarily genetic explanation of reality. But this explanation presents a clearly normative character because it situates the beings who constitute this reality in a well-defined place, and in so doing inscribes each of these beings within a network of relationships with other beings who are located at the same level or at a higher or lower level.

I. Mythology and Philosophy in Ancient Greece

In ancient Greece, as early as the eighth century B.C., Hesiod collected and put in writing a certain number of myths that had been until then transmitted orally. Writings attributed to "Orpheus" have a historical origin that is very difficult to determine with any certainty, but they develop a mythology substantially different from the one found in Hesiod, which constitutes the definitive version of the traditional mythology of ancient Greece. All of the poets, Homer the greatest among them, refer to a more or less significant number of myths in their works.

In this frame of reference, therefore, mythology, which in ancient Greece constituted the explanatory and normative system—with respect to the gods, the world, and humankind—around which the world revolves, proved to be inseparable from poetry, the literary form in which it was expressed. That is why traditionally intellectual education, which complemented physical education with gymnastics, rested essentially on music, which in a large sense covered the domain of the Muses, and then in a more limited sense the domain of poetry, wherein mythology lies.

But from the last third of the seventh century B.C., a totally new type of speculation arose in Greece, one which would later be called "philosophy." This new type of speculation could not help but develop against mythology to the extent that philosophy too claimed to play an explanatory and normative role with respect to the gods, the world, and humankind, and that, in so doing, it claimed for itself the first place in education. But whereas for mythology the point of incidence was situated at the level of the gods, for the nascent philosophy it was situated at the level of the world. Moreover, philosophy subjects mythology to a radical criticism based on much stricter requirements both on the explanatory and the normative level.

On the explanatory level, philosophy aspires to universality, a requirement that mythology cannot meet. To the extent that it is sullied by that anthropomorphism which Xenophanes objected to (ca. 570–475 B.C.), mythology can found only a false universality. On the one hand, such universality does not recognize the fundamental differences that distinguish beings of different levels (a case in point being gods and humans): "But mortals consider that the gods were born, and that they have clothes, a language, and bodies like their own" (DK 21 B 14 = Clement of Alexandria *Stromateis* 5.109.2). On the other hand, this same universality does not work out the abstraction of accidental differences between beings of the same level (in this case, humans). And this abstraction alone can make for a true generality: "Ethiopians say [of their gods] that they are pugnosed and black; the Thracians say that they have blue eyes and red hair" (DK 21 B 16 = ibid. 7.22.1). By pushing the argument to its extreme, that is, by conjoining these two difficulties, one arrives at situations as droll as this: "But if bulls and horses and lions had hands like men, and, like men, were able to paint and produce works, horses would paint figures of gods in the likeness of horses, and bulls in the likeness of bulls" (DK 21 B 5 = ibid. 5.109.3). In this perspective, philosophy focuses its criticism of anthropomorphism, proper to mythology, on the search for explanations endowed with true universality, which it will progressively despair of ever finding in the realm of the sensory: a universality that would both respect the essential differences that distinguish beings at different levels, and abstract the accidental differences that affect beings of the same level.

To this demand at the explanatory level another far more restrictive demand came to be added at the normative level. Indeed, Xenophanes denounced Homer and Hesiod as follows: "All the things that the gods have been charged with by Homer and Hesiod are matters of abuse and blame among men: theft, adultery, mutual deception" (DK 21 B 11 = Sextus Empiricus *Adversus mathematicos* 9.193). This second argument against mythology was to be the one most often explicitly invoked by pagan and Christian philosophers alike.

Having said this, we must not conclude that mythology and philosophy never coexisted in ancient Greece. On the contrary, both among the philosophers labeled "pre-Socratic," notably among the Pythagoreans, and among those of the classical period, mythology, in which philosophical thought is rooted, not only survived but even revived up to a certain point, within the framework of philosophical thought. This statement presents no paradox if we consider the status of mythology with respect to the philosophy of which it became an integral part. It is useful to draw a parallel between the status of mythology within tragedy on the one hand and within philosophy on the other. To be sure, philosophy and tragedy represent at first glance two domains seemingly difficult to compare. However, during the classical period, mythology experienced significant transformation simultaneously within the framework of philosophy and within that of tragedy. And the similarities and differences that the transformation brought out in the one case and in the other are pertinent on more grounds than one.

In tragedy, myths are reinterpreted in terms of the political and ethical demands of the Athenian city, where democracy instills and establishes its power. Similarly, in philosophy during the same period myths are reinterpreted in terms of the epistemological and ethical demands of individuals who elevate reason to the supreme principle. Thus, in each case the status of mythology is modified. Having lost the privilege of being in first place, mythology, which does not die as a consequence of this loss, finds itself in a position of dependency on principles that are imposed on it from outside, and that dictate the major lines of this process of reinterpretation to which mythology is subjected.

II. Mythology and Philosophy in Plato

From this point of view, Plato seems to be the best example of the integration of mythology into philosophy, a process inextricably connected with a profound reinterpretation. For the philosophers who came before Plato, the distance between mythology and philosophy was not yet great enough to be defined in a clear and conscious fashion. Conversely, for the philosophers who came after him, that distance was so considerable that any integration of mythology into phi-

losophy introduced an artificial and forced character, which limited its use to the literary domain, notably to allegory. But Plato seems to have found a means of bringing about this integration in a way that was both conscious and somehow natural, a fact which cannot fail to surprise us. We may compare this fact with another, equally interesting and surprising. The dialogue in Plato's works constitutes a thoroughly harmonious expression of a philosophical doctrine in which dialectics played an increasingly important role; but after Plato it falls, like mythological references, to the level of artificial and forced literary processes.

In order to describe the integration of mythology into philosophy in Plato as pertinently as possible, we should determine precisely the *status, referent,* and *function* of mythology in the philosophy of Plato.

A. The Status of Mythology in Plato's Philosophy

From the onset of play, it is plain that the status of mythology in Plato's philosophy can only be inferior to the status of the realm of intelligible forms. Indeed, for Plato intelligible forms play the primordial explanatory and normative role with respect to the gods, the world, and humankind.

Intelligible forms meet all the requirements of universality and morality that myths cannot satisfy. On the ontological level, the forms supply the universality that makes it possible to save phenomena, that is, to explain the transitory existence of a plurality of perceptible things by taking into account their participation in the same intelligible form. On the epistemological level, this universality makes possible the distinction between truth and error, not only at the level of intelligible knowledge but also at the level of sensory knowledge. Moreover, the hypothesis of intelligible forms seems to have been imposed above all by Socrates' and, later, Plato's insistence on immutable values, that is, values that were never actually established and consequently cannot be destroyed—the values upon which an incontestably ethical and political system might be founded.

These demands of universality and of morality cannot be met by myths. For Plato, perceptible things are only images of the intelligible forms of which they are part and which play the role of models for them. But poets and imitators of all sorts make images of those images that are perceptible things. Thus, on the ontological level these creations are thrice removed from the intelligible forms, and on the epistemological level the knowledge derived from them and the discourse held about them present even less verisimilitude than the knowledge that can be derived from perceptible things and the discourse that is brought to bear upon them (Plato *Republic* 595a–608b; Plato *Sophist* 264b–268b). Hence myths, which are nothing but images of particular images, cannot claim to constitute explanations presenting any value of universality whatsoever, either from an ontological standpoint or from an epistemological standpoint. As one might expect, however, Plato takes particular issue with the immorality of myths, especially in the long passage in the *Republic* (376e–398b) in which he reviews a series of examples drawn from the works of various poets. On this point, Plato's arguments present no real originality, since they are much akin to the arguments of Xenophanes in particular and of many other of his predecessors.

By virtue of his criticism of mythology, it might be thought that Plato refuses to take myths into account. That is not the case, and for two reasons. First, Plato proves to be highly innovative in several areas, notably in metaphysics, where he develops a new system; in physics, where he elaborates

Antrum Platonicum. Print by Jean Saenredam (1565–1607). Paris, Bibliothèque nationale, Cabinet des Estampes. Photo BN.

an original cosmology; and even in mathematics, where he takes into account the most recent discoveries; yet he turns out to be rather conservative regarding anything that touches on religion, closely or distantly (Plato *Republic* 427b–c; Plato *Laws* 738b–d). Second—and more important—in Plato's system myth has a real referent and is endowed with a precise function.

To be sure, as a poetic product myth is but an image of the images of intelligible forms that are perceptible things. Nonetheless, mythical discourse, which ranks even lower than discourse about perceptible things, proves to be the only kind of discourse capable of speaking about certain things.

B. The Referent of Mythology in Plato's Philosophy

For Plato, true being inheres in intelligible forms, which are outside the limits of space and time, in a state of absolute immutability. And it is only about true being that one can have true knowledge and discourse. Conversely, perceptible things are subject, in time and space, to generation and corruption, and have no being except by participating in intelligible forms, so that there can be only probable knowledge and discourse about them (Plato *Timaeus* 51d–e). Having said this, we must recognize that these two types of knowledge and discourse fail to encompass a certain number of facts situated at the fringes of time and space, facts that can be experienced. And so, to mitigate this shortcoming, Plato calls on myth.

Thus we can understand why, up to a certain point, Plato regards the *Timaeus* as a myth (Pl. *Ti.* 59cb, 68d2, 69b1). In this dialogue, which describes the origin of the world and, by extension, the origins of gods and humans, the plausible discourse, namely, Plato's, goes beyond its own limits (Pl. *Ti.* 30b7, 34c3–4, 44d1, 48c1, 48d2, 49b6, 5325, 55d5, 56a1, 56d1, 57d6, 59c6, 68d2, 72d7, 90e8). Not only must he describe the constitution of time and take into account the totally formless spatial environment, but he must also explain the appearance of the group of beings which experience apprehends only in their ultimate state. Because of this, Plato oscillates in the *Timaeus* between plausible discourse and myth.

Having examined the extreme case which the *Timaeus* represents, we must return to consider more directly the subject at hand, that is, the actual myths found in Plato's work. From all accounts, these myths transgress the usual limits of time and space. In the first place, the myths about the individual describe the human soul before (Plato *Phaedrus* 246a–248e) or after its stay in a body (*Gorgias* 523a–527a; *Phaedo* 107d–114c; *Republic* 614a–621b; *Phaedrus* 248e–249b). Moreover, myths about the city show approximately the same features. The myth of the golden age that is mentioned in the *Gorgias* (523a–527a), developed in the *Politics* (268d–274e), and taken up again in the *Laws* (713a–714b), a myth which should apparently be associated with the myth of autochthony (Pl. *Rep.* 414d–e) and the myth of the classes (ibid. 415a–d), describes an age that Plato considered to be radically different from ours. He places this age in the reign of Kronos, whereas the myth of Atlantis (Pl. *Ti.* 20e–26d; Plato *Critias*) refers to a fabulous past when Zeus was already king of gods and takes place in an equally fabulous geographical setting. Yet another example is the myth of Gyges (Pl. *Rep.* 359d–360b), which tells of the extraordinary origin of the Mermnad dynasty in Lydia.

This anchoring in a fabulous time and space is precisely what makes possible a better definition of the true meaning of the myth of Atlantis. For in order to criticize the Athens of the fifth and fourth centuries, when good and evil were inextricably intermingled, and in order to criticize this Athens according to the absolute criterion constituted by the ideal city described in the *Republic*, Plato sets up what amounts to a contest between the good city (i.e., primitive Athens, which, because it more closely resembled his earlier model than the Athens in which he lived, was an exclusively land-based city) and the bad city (i.e., Atlantis, which was primarily a maritime city). Thereby Plato judged the Athens in which he lived in terms of a past considered to be better, and in so doing he was able to denounce its present faults by projecting them onto a city that was then thought to be on the fringes of the world, namely, Atlantis, whose excesses caused its demise.

Primitive Athens was ruled by kings intimately tied to Athena and Hephaestus, its two tutelary deities. Its boundaries varied little, and it remained more or less as it is today. To be sure, primitive Athens was richer than today's Athens, but no metal, least of all gold or silver, was anywhere to be found. Its flora and fauna, which included no species of wild animals, were abundant, though not excessive. They were abundant enough to feed the 20,000 men and women who constituted the upper level of the guardian class. These people lived on the slopes of the Acropolis, on top of which was the common sanctuary of Athena and Hephaestus and, most likely, the residences of the kings. On the plain extending from the foot of this Acropolis into the countryside lived the producers, peasants and craftsmen, responsible for meeting the needs of the guardians.

Atlantis, by contrast, whose tutelary divinity was Poseidon, had as its kings five pairs of twins, who were the descendants of Poseidon and Clito, the only daughter of Evenor and Leucippe. Its territory with its ever increasing boundaries abounded in metals of all sorts, notably silver and gold. Its flora and fauna, which included the elephant, were indescribably profuse. As far as population was concerned, the same superabundance prevailed. In addition, Atlantis was covered with a network of canals, rectangular in the countryside and circular in the city. On the central island of the three that made up the city, the kings lived near the shrine of Poseidon. On the inner island stood the barracks housing the warriors guarding the kings and various other installations. On the outer island was a huge hippodrome. The three islands were connected to one another by a canal that led to the outer harbor toward which everything converged.

Atlantis, which was the sea god Poseidon's share of the world, was thereby essentially a maritime power primarily devoted to trade. While this accounted for all its merchants and its fleet, which primitive Athens entirely lacked, it also accounted for the decline of Atlantis, according to Plato. In fact, the kings of Atlantis, who assembled alternately every five and six years, performed a ceremony that allowed them to renew and tighten their bonds with their father Poseidon. But little by little their godly nature ceased to dominate, and the kings launched an imperialist war, which ancient Athens alone resisted victoriously. Zeus, the god of gods, punished Atlantis by sinking it into the sea, that is, into what was the origin and cause of its excesses, whereas primitive Athens sank into the earth from which it originally sprang.

Thus these two opposing cities disappeared, cities that cannot be situated in a definite time and space, since from the very start they belonged to a mythical time and space located beyond the perceptible and this side of the intelligible.

The myth of the cicadas (Pl. *Phdr.* 259b–d) and the myth of Theuth (Thoth) (ibid. 274c–275b) also belong to a past so remote that it no longer has anything to do with the present time. Although the action of the myth of Theuth takes place in the region of Naucratis in Egypt, while the myth of the cicadas makes no reference to any precise place, the temporal remoteness that characterizes them both tends to neutralize even that geographical localization.

Finally, both the myth of the cave in the *Republic* (514a–517a) and the myth of Eros, for which Diotima is Plato's spokesman in the *Symposium* (201d–212c), imply a passage from the perceptible world, which is *inside* time and space, to the intelligible world, which is *outside* time and space.

Consequently, in Plato, for whom the status of mythology is inferior not only to discourse on intelligible forms but also to discourse on perceptible things, mythology seems to take on a precise referent, one that is not to be found in the realm of the intelligible, but is situated on this side and the other side of time and space where perceptible objects are manifested.

C. The Function of Mythology in Plato

Having thus defined myth in Plato and described its referent, we now turn to the function of myth in Plato's philosophy. At this level, however, matters get complicated. Although its status and referent remain the same, the function of myth is modified according to Plato's conception of the human soul and especially of the city.

On both of these points, and particularly on the latter, two dialogues, the *Republic* and *Laws*, offer two doctrines which, if not altogether opposed to each other, are at least very different. We shall therefore examine the function of myth in these two dialogues.

1. The Function of Mythology in the Republic

In the *Republic* (427d–444a), Plato first divides the human soul into three parts, taking as a model the division of the city into three classes.

The human soul is fundamentally divided into two species: a rational species and an irrational species. The latter is subdivided into two subspecies: the irascible subspecies (*thumos*) and the lustful subspecies (*epithumia*).

Only the rational species is truly immortal. Before its incarnation into a body, the human soul sees itself reduced to its rational species, a residue of the substance of the soul of the world, the substance fashioned by the demiurge (Pl. *Ti.* 41d4–7); high up on the star to which it is allied (ibid. 41e1–2), it contemplates the world of intelligible forms (ibid. 41e1–3). For a reason difficult to determine, this human soul falls at a given moment into a body (ibid. 42a3–4; Pl. *Phdr.* 248c–e). This fall into a body implies significant changes for the human soul. To the immortal species to which it was previously reduced is added a mortal species fashioned by the aids of the demiurge (Pl. *Ti.* 69c8, d5, 70e5). This mortal species itself is subdivided into two subspecies: an irascible subspecies (ibid. 70b3, c2), which has the task of defending man against all the dangers that come from within and from without; and a lustful subspecies (ibid. 90b1–2, 70b5), which ensures the functions of nutrition (ibid. 70d7–8) and reproduction (ibid. 91c7–d1), functions that became indispensable as a result of the soul's incarnation into a body, which is subject to generation and corruption.

Man, who is born of the union of this soul and a body, will be able to live a good life only if he maintains a just proportion, that is, a harmony, between his body and his soul under the sway of the rational and immortal species of this soul (Pl. *Rep.* 436a–445e; Pl. *Ti.* 42b2). And he will be able to obtain and maintain this harmony only by means of education, which allows him to learn and practice philosophy, mathematics, music, and gymnastics.

But education is inseparable from city life. According to Plato, the city should be divided into three classes, each assigned to a different function: royal, military, and productive. The third class, largely made up of craftsmen and farmers, would have no duties—over and above the basic reproduction of its own effective forces—other than supplying food and equipment to the other two classes (Pl. *Rep.* 4l6d–417b). The guardian class would in turn be educated in music and gymnastics, that is, traditionally educated, and would devote itself exclusively to soldiering, maintaining law and order within the city, and warding off attacks against it from without (ibid. 415d–e). Deprived of all wealth (ibid. 416a–417b), the guardians would not have wives of their own (ibid. 456b–460b). From among them, a select group representing the best would be chosen. These would be given an education based on the study of mathematics and the mastery of dialectics, and would become capable of contemplating the intelligible forms unified by the good (ibid. 521c–541d). Having thus become true philosophers, they would be dragged away from that contemplation and forced to return to the perceptible world, to govern the city (ibid. 514a–521b).

A city constituted in this way would be able to live with justice, if there were a true harmony between the three classes that composed it, that is, if the philosophers proved to be men of wisdom and the guardians men of courage, and if all the classes practiced temperance (ibid. 427d–444e).

Following this dual development, it is possible to determine with certainty the extent to which the tripartition of the human soul effectively models itself on the division of the city into three classes. The most remarkable difference between these two tripartitions appears at the level of the bipartition on which they respectively rest. In the human soul, the rational species, which alone is immortal, is seen as separated from the other two subspecies, the irascible and the lustful, which constitute the irrational species, which is mortal. Conversely, in the city the class of philosophers and the class of guardians seem to constitute a whole clearly distinct from the class of producers. On the one hand, those who are to become philosophers would be selected from among the guardians. And on the other hand, whereas wisdom belongs to philosophers and courage to guardians, temperance is common to all classes in the city.

But this difference at the level of the bipartition of the human soul and of the city brings about no important changes on the level of education or, more specifically, on the level of education through music.

Because myths are only images of images, as are all the other productions of poets and imitators of every kind, it stands to reason that education through music cannot be the only or even the prime form of education as tradition would have it. In addition, to become an object of education, myths

Diotima, Eros, and Socrates. Bronze plate found in Pompeii. Naples, National Museum. Photo Soprintendenza.

have to be transformed in terms of very strict moral requirements. Plato, who in the *Republic* (595a–608b) banishes the poets from the city, claims that only hymns to the gods and poetic tributes to honorable people, forms of poetry that already exist, must be admitted into the city (ibid. 607a). Thus, only when they are reinterpreted in terms of these requirements can myths become objects of education within the framework of music.

On the level of the individual, it would seem that education through music and gymnastics addresses not only the irascible subspecies of the human soul, but also the rational species, for which education through mathematics and philosophy is reserved, to the extent that music and gymnastics, which also develop the body, should ensure harmony between the rational species and the irascible subspecies (ibid. 411e–412a, 441e–442a). As for the lustful subspecies, which is too far removed from the rational species of the human soul to be subjected to any form of education whatsoever, either it submits to the influence of the irascible subspecies, which transmits to it the orders of the rational species, or else it confronts a direct action of the rational species in dreams (Pl. *Ti.* 71d–e).

At the level of the city, education through music and gymnastics would be reserved for the guardians. And as the best among them would be selected to receive an education through mathematics and training in dialectics so as to become philosophers who would govern the city, we are bound to conclude that education through music and gymnastics would be reserved first for the warrior class and then for the philosopher class. The third class, the producers, at least officially would have no access to any form of education.

This stance may seem surprising. One objection immediately comes to mind. What about the two myths, that of autochthony (Pl. *Rep.* 414d–e) and that of the classes (ibid. 415a–d), which Plato designated for the citizenry as a whole? This objection, however, is valid only to a certain point.

First, even if Plato very explicitly designates these myths for the philosopher kings, the guardians, and the other citizens, we have to recognize that Plato in these two cases attenuates the full implication of this injunction. He begins by asking: "How can we go about making the leaders themselves believe this beautiful lie, and *if we can*, the other citizens?" (Pl. *Rep.* 414b–c; italics mine). He then continues: "I shall *first* try to persuade the leaders themselves and the guardians, *and then* all the other citizens" (ibid. 414d; italics mine). This attenuation can easily be explained by the fact that only the class of guardians and, by extension, the class of philosophers have, institutionally speaking, access to education through music, the area where myth is generally situated. It follows then that any teaching that is about myths and is aimed at the third class (the producers), since it is not institutionalized, can function only to a limited extent, insofar as it ranks behind the priority education reserved for the philosopher and guardian classes.

We should also note that the only two myths that could have been intended for the producers concern not only producers but also guardians and philosophers. We can see here a parallel between the situation of these two myths and that of the virtue of temperance, which the producers must practice but which is not particular to them in the way that courage is particular to guardians and wisdom to philosophers, since guardians and philosophers must also practice temperance (Pl. *Rep.* 427d–434d, esp. 430d–432b). In this context, it is not surprising that Plato tells no myth about technical knowledge or about agriculture, which would primarily concern the producers. In fact, it is Protagoras, the Sophist whom Plato respects most even though he opposes him irreconcilably, who develops the only myth in the entire work of Plato that really does concern technical knowledge (Plato *Protagoras* 320c–322d).

We must therefore conclude that myth cannot address through habit or priority either the class of producers, at the level of the city, or the lustful species of the soul, at the level of the individual. Consequently, any intervention of myth at these levels either in the city or in the individual can only be exceptional and secondary.

The accompanying chart represents this argument schematically.

Partition		Education	Virtues
City	Individual		
Philosophers	Reason	Philosophy / Mathematics	Wisdom
Guardians	Irascible	Music (General mythology) / Gymnastics	Courage
Producers	Lustful	Selected mythology	Temperance

We can now draw certain conclusions about the function of myth in Plato.

At the level of the individual, myth has the function of mitigating, however imperfectly, the fundamental problem raised by a Platonic ethics founded exclusively on reason, since the notions of will and freedom were not to appear until several centuries later. For Plato, the reign of the good must therefore necessarily coincide with that of truth (Pl. *Ti.* 44b–d), whereas the reign of evil must coincide with that of error, whether error be the outcome of madness or of ignorance (ibid. 86b2–4). Consequently, reason being natu-

rally oriented toward the world of intelligible forms united by the good, man should always be good. This is not the case, however, to the extent that the preeminence of reason can be contested; and since this preeminence depends essentially on the action and reaction of the irascible subspecies of the human soul, the weak point in Platonic ethics is located at the juncture of the rational species of the human soul and the irascible subspecies. This is precisely the level at which the effects of education through music and gymnastics should be felt. And it is also at this level that myths can have a certain influence.

This function of myth within the Platonic ethical system shows why myths about the individual in Plato have a bearing on two themes which, in effect, constitute two moments of the same story. These two themes are the state of the human soul before its incarnation (Pl. *Phdr.* 246a–248e), and, above all, its fate after death (Pl. *Grg.* 523a–527a; Pl. *Phd.* 107d–114c; *Rep.* 614a–621b; Pl. *Phdr.* 248e–249b). In both cases the function of myth is the same: to justify the preeminence of the rational species of the human soul and to indicate the consequences of respecting and not respecting this preeminence. Since such preeminence can only be established if there is harmony between the rational species of the human soul and its irascible subspecies, it is evident that the function of myth is to ensure the realization of this harmony.

On the level of the city, things are somewhat different. Myths can address neither philosophers nor producers, since philosophers directly contemplate the intelligible forms that are unified by the good, and producers receive no education. Myths therefore seem to be reserved for the guardians per se and, by extension, for the philosophers (before they are selected as the best of the guardians). These are the ones for whom, in the *Republic*, Plato intends his noble lies, among which are the myth of autochthony (Pl. *Rep.* 414d–e) and the myth of the classes (ibid. 415a–d).

This function of myth in the economy of the Platonic political system shows why, in Plato, the myths about the city are divided into two groups. In the first group is the myth of Atlantis told at the beginning of the *Timaeus* (20c–26d) and in the *Critias*, describing the armed struggle that Athens waged against the invasion organized by the kings of Atlantis. In the second group is the myth of the golden age—mentioned in the *Gorgias* (523a–527a), developed in the *Politics* (268d–274e), and taken up again in the *Laws* (713a–714b)—in which Plato defines the type of monarchy appropriate for the present era, and justifies, by extension, the type of monarchy that he wishes to impose. The myth of Gyges, playing a negative role in this respect (Pl. *Rep.* 359d–360b), describes the founding of a royal dynasty based on injustice.

Finally, the central myth in Plato's work, that of the cave in the *Republic* (514a–517a), synthesizes these two levels, that of the individual and that of the city. It can in fact be read both as a description of the movement of the human soul from the world of perceptible things to that of the intelligible forms unified by the good and as a description of the making of philosopher-kings.

This leaves three Platonic myths that do not fall into either one of these two groups. But the three myths are hardly strangers to this typology. Quite the contrary, they reinforce it and justify it by a kind of ricochet reaction.

Two of these myths reflect on the origins of both aspects of what was known as music in ancient Greece. We refer first of all to the myth of the cicadas (Pl. *Phdr.* 259b–d). According to this myth, the origin of the cicadas can be traced back to individuals who died of starvation and thirst because they were fascinated by the newborn Muses and did nothing but sing. The *Phaedrus* (274c–275b) also refers to the myth of Theuth (Thoth), the Egyptian god who invented writing. Ever since the eighth century B.C. in ancient Greece, this god has sustained all the poets, including Hesiod, "Orpheus," and Homer.

The myth that Plato puts in the mouth of Diotima in the *Symposium* (201d–212c) embodies a veritable synthesis of all that has just been said. First, because Eros is an intermediary daemon between gods and humans, between the perceptible and the intelligible, and between the rational and the irrational, this myth is related to the myth of the cave in the *Republic* (514a–517a), to which it bears a striking resemblance on several points. Second, because Eros has as his object the beautiful as well as the good, he sides both with music and with philosophy.

Having said this, we should mention two other great myths found in Plato's work which illustrate positions diametrically opposite to his own. We refer to the myth of Protagoras in the *Protagoras* (320c–322d) and to the myth of Aristophanes in the *Symposium* (189a–193d).

The first is a myth about the origin of the city, developed by Protagoras to justify both the advent and the maintenance of democracy, and the existence and role of the Sophists as masters of that speech in which all power in the democracy resides. This myth constitutes the most complete and coherent objection to the political doctrine developed by Plato, notably in the *Republic*, a doctrine that finds its most elaborate mythical expression in the myth of the cave (Pl. *Rep.* 514a–517a). The second myth, the myth of Aristophanes, appears in the *Symposium* as the polar opposite to the myth that Plato puts in the mouth of Diotima (Plato *Symposium* 201d–212c). In fact, for Aristophanes the action of Eros is carried out in the perceptible world only as a force of attraction between one male and another, between a male and a female, and between one female and another. All of them seek to unite in order to reconstitute the double being that they once formed and for which they still feel nostalgia.

Finally, if we assume the perspective adopted by Plato in the *Republic*, myth has a double function. In the individual it must ensure harmony between the rational species of the human soul and its irascible subspecies by justifying the preeminence of the rational species and by describing the consequences of respecting or not respecting this preeminence. In the city, it must ensure harmony between the class of philosophers and the class of guardians by justifying both their joint membership in the same city and their hierarchical distinction, by making it possible to define clearly the true nature of the royal function, and by giving examples that exalt the combat implicit in the warrior function. This frame of reference also shows how Plato devotes two myths to music—one to music itself and the other to music as conveyed by writing—and one myth to Eros, the intermediary daemon par excellence, whose ties with music are obvious.

2. The Function of Mythology in the *Laws*

These conclusions, such as they are, apply, mutatis mutandis, to Plato's work as a whole, with the exception of the *Laws*. In this dialogue, they must be reconsidered in terms of the important ways in which Plato alters the political doctrine that he had first explicitly and exhaustively developed in the *Republic* and apparently maintained ever since with very few modifications.

The citizens of the city described in the *Laws*, whose number is set at 5040 (Plato *Laws* 771a–b), are primarily peasants, each of whom owns a plot of land (ibid. 739e–740a; 744d–745b). Since they are denied all craftsmanship, these citizens coexist among aliens (ibid. 846d–850d) and slaves (ibid. 916a–c), who may be freed under certain conditions (ibid. 881c, 941a, 932d). For the citizens, the age of majority is set at twenty years (ibid. 785b) and involves political rights and military service, including the defense of the city in case of danger.

In the city of the *Laws*, there are no longer any philosophers or guardians for whom education is reserved and who form two classes radically separate from the class of producers. Gone are the kings who ruled the city with the help of armed forces, ruling as a function of their contemplation of the world of intelligible forms, in an illegality situated not on this side but on the far side of legality. Hence the need for laws enacted by real legislators.

To ensure that these laws are respected, Plato envisages several colleges of magistrates who are either elected or chosen by lot. Among these magistrates are the following: a director of education (ibid. 765d–766c); *correctors* who supervise the other magistrates (ibid. 945b–948b); and guardians of the laws, whose function remains ill-defined but who seem to preside over all of political life and also legislate bylaws (ibid. 770b, 772c–d, 867e). Sitting on another level is the Nocturnal Council (ibid. 961a ff.). It is made up of those *correctors* who have obtained the highest office, ten guardians of the laws currently serving, and the director of education; in addition, each member chooses an aide younger than himself. This Nocturnal Council will judge all information and proposals likely to improve the laws, as well as the honors and penalties earned by informers who have returned from missions abroad.

The power of deliberation is represented by the council and the assembly. Accessible by right to all citizens, the assembly meets when convened by the council, either in regular session or in extraordinary session if so warranted (ibid. 758d). The 360 members of the council, who are appointed for one year (ibid. 756b–e), are divided into twelve sections, each sitting for a month at a time (ibid. 755e, 758b–c, 766b).

Finally, the judiciary in the *Laws* involves three steps. The first is a sort of arbitration exercised by parents and by friends that both sides have chosen for themselves (ibid. 766e). If this arbitration is not accepted, the case goes before a first court of appeal, made up of judges selected by lot (ibid. 767d, 768b). From this court, parties can appeal to another, whose members are appointed annually by the assembly of magistrates, at the rate of one per magistrature (ibid. 767c–d). In criminal cases this court has primary and final authority, and in the most serious cases it will be joined by the guardians of the laws.

In the city of the *Laws*, *education is compulsory for all citizens* (ibid. 804d–e). As far as formal education is concerned, a director of education (ibid. 765d–766c) supervises the activities of the principals of the schools and gymnasiums (ibid. 764c–d), for this education is based on gymnastics, which must develop the body, and on music, which must form the soul (ibid. 795d).

Gymnastic exercises have as their exclusive goal the preparation for war (ibid. 795d–796c).

As far as music is concerned, Plato proves to be somewhat less severe than he is in the *Republic*. Poets regain their place in the city, but on very strict conditions. New compositions are to be approved by judges especially appointed for that purpose and by the guardians of the laws (ibid. 801b–e), basing their judgments on the following three criteria: that

Illustration of the androgyne in the myth of Aristophanes. Reverse side of a medallion of Marcantonio Passeri (1491–1565). Paris, Bibliothèque nationale, Cabinet des Médailles. Photo BN.

the compositions be auspicious, that they be accompanied by prayers to the gods, and that the prayers be appropriate for the gods they address. As for old compositions, they will be selected by men at least fifty years old who have been elected for that purpose and who have surrounded themselves with specialists to help determine if these compositions are to be accepted, rejected outright, or reworked (ibid. 802a–803c). Plato also offers examples of criticisms that can be addressed to ancient myths: whatever the poets may have to say about it, Hermes is not a thief (ibid. 941b); the myth that tells of Zeus's passion for Ganymede was totally fabricated by the Cretans, in order to justify their vice (ibid. 636c–d); and yet another myth—which recounts that Hera had driven Dionysus insane and that Dionysus sought revenge by introducing the Bacchic frenzy and making a gift of wine (ibid. 672b–c)—constitutes an affront to those two deities. But whatever the case may be, no educator has the right to use a work which has not been officially approved (ibid. 811d–e, 957c–e).

This education, completed by the study of mathematics (ibid. 817d–822d) and perhaps even by philosophy (ibid. 964e ff.), is continued well beyond the school years, primarily by means of contests in gymnastics or in music. For these contests, the judges who are named operate under the jurisdiction of the director of education (ibid. 764c–766b).

The contests take place during festivals that are carefully organized and regulated by the guardians of the laws and the magistrates in charge of religious matters. Only those gymnastic contests able to serve in preparing for war are accepted for the gymnastic competitions, which is why the only speed races that are held are those in which the athlete is fully armed and equipped as a soldier (ibid. 832e–833d). For tests of strength, Plato is partial to wrestling, boxing, pancratium (a combination of wrestling and boxing) (ibid. 833d, 834a; cf. 796a), fencing, and armed combat (ibid. 833d–834a). Horse

racing is a contest between armed men on horseback (ibid. 834b–d). In addition, music competitions first have to abide by all the rules in effect concerning dancing (ibid. 814d–816d), singing (ibid. 799a–d, 700b, 801e, 800d, 947b–c, 960c), comedy (ibid. 816d–e), and tragedy (ibid. 817a–e).

Two more institutions extend the education of the citizens. One consists of taking meals in common (ibid. 780d–781e), about which Plato is not very explicit, and which seems to be a kind of military institution. Then, Plato says, there ought to be three kinds of choruses (ibid. 664b–667b). The first, the chorus of Muses, made up of young boys and girls, would come forward to sing maxims in public. The second, the chorus of Apollo, made up of citizens under thirty years of age, would invoke Apollo Paean and would call on him to witness the truth of these principles. The third, the chorus of men between the ages of thirty and sixty, dedicated to Dionysus, would not actually make up a chorus in the strict sense of the term, because men over fifty could not be expected to sing and dance in public. Therefore, they would perform for themselves in the privacy of their company and not before strangers. And to help them cope with the withering effects of old age, they would be allowed to drink wine. Finally, those who passed the age of sixty would be excused from singing and allowed to content themselves with telling myths (ibid. 664d). The institution of the third chorus is primarily related to the symposium (drinking together) of which Plato left us a celebrated example in the famous dialogue by the same name.

These three choruses essentially aim at producing the kind of enchantment needed to dispose the soul, either through joy or through sadness, to accept more readily the persuasion that the legislator strives to impose on the soul of the citizens (ibid. 659c–660a). The term "delight" (epōidē in Greek) recurs rather frequently in the *Laws* (ibid. 659d–e, 665c, 666c, 671a, 773d, 812c, 837e, 887d, 903b, 944b). It designates above all a state of the soul, marked by joy or sadness, which is provoked by "song" (ōidē in Greek), a term which otherwise designates a large collection of musical compositions (ibid. 700b). We are led to conclude that for Plato in the *Laws*, education through music and thereby through myth, even if strictly regulated, constitutes a basic element of government to the extent to which it aims to elicit the delight that will facilitate the persuasion the legislator must bring into play in order to make sure that the laws he has enacted will be respected.

Between the *Laws* and the *Republic*, the differences in the function of myth prove in the end to be less profound than might first have been thought. The general definition of this function remains fundamentally the same: to create within the soul that state, marked by joy or sadness, that helps reason to persuade the irrational element, which is susceptible to its influence. They differ only in the psychological and especially the socio-political coordinates in connection with which this function operates with great precision.

L.Br./g.h.

BIBLIOGRAPHY

Three French translations of the complete works of Plato are useful: that of the Association Guillaume Budé, 14 vols. (Paris 1920–64), with many reprints; that of É. CHAMBRY and R. BACCOU, 8 vols. (Paris 1936–46), recently reissued; and that of L. ROBIN, with J. MOREAU for *Parménide* and *Timée* (Paris 1940–42), with many reprints.

On the myths found in Plato, there is no single general work in French which surpasses that of P. FRUTIGER, *Les mythes de Platon* (Paris

1930), reprinted in *History of Ideas in Ancient Greece* (New York 1976). And for certain details, see P. M. SCHUHL, *Études sur la fabulation platonicienne* (Paris 1947; 2d ed., 1968), and *Le merveilleux, la pensée et l'action* (Paris 1952; 2d ed., 1969).

Otherwise, on such myths in particular, see: (1) On the myth of Atlantis: P. VIDAL-NAQUET, "Athènes et l'Atlantide," *Revue des études grecques* 77 (1964): 420–42. LUC BRISSON, "De la philosophie politique à l'épopée: Le *Critias* de Platon," *Revue de métaphysique et de morale* 75 (1970): 402–38. (2) On the myth of *Politicus*: LUC BRISSON, *Le même et l'autre dans la structure ontologique du "Timée" de Platon* (Paris 1974), 478–96. P. VIDAL-NAQUET, "Le mythe platonicien du *Politique*, les ambiguïtés de l'âge d'or et de l'histoire," in *Langue, discours, société: Pour Émile Benveniste* (Paris 1975), 374–90. (3) On the myth of Theuth in *Phaedrus*: JACQUES DERRIDA, "Plato's Pharmacy," *Dissemination*, trans. Barbara Johnson (Chicago 1981), 61–171. (4) On the myth of Aristophanes in *Symposium*: L. BRISSON, "Bisexualité et médiation en Grèce

ancienne," *Nouvelle revue de psychanalyse* 7 (1973): 27–48. (5) On the myth of Protagoras: L. BRISSON, "Le mythe de Protagoras: Essai d'analyse structurale," *Quaderni Urbinati di cultura classica* 20 (1975): 7–37.

On the history of education in antiquity, see the great work by H. I. MARROU, *Histoire de l'éducation dans l'Antiquité* (Paris 1948; 6th ed., 1965).

In other languages, two general works on the myths found in Plato deserve to be mentioned: J. A. STEWART, *The Myths of Plato* (London 1905), edited and newly introduced by G. R. Levy (London 1960; New York 1970). W. HIRSCH, *Platons Weg zum Mythos* (Berlin and New York 1971) (bibliography, pp. 395–99).

Abbreviation

DK: *Die Fragmente der Vorsokratiker*, griechisch und deutsch, H. DIELS, 10. Ed. W. KRANZ, 3 vols. (Berlin 1960–61).

THE NEOPLATONISTS AND GREEK MYTHS

According to one of the most knowledgeable scholars in the field, A.-J. Festugière, "what characterizes a Greek god above all is the legend that is attached to him and the visible form given him by art."[1] Greek legends or myths are stories about gods and heroes. Like the lives of the saints in Christianity, these stories generally tell of the births of gods, their lives, their exploits, and their sufferings. They catalogue their "virtues" and the "miracles" that they performed, and they circulate the various traditions surrounding their cult in order to give them wide exposure. Legends and myths, therefore, supplied a kind of raw material for the prayers and rituals of worship, and for theology. In this double capacity, they were held in high esteem by the Neoplatonists, since it was a characteristic of Neoplatonism to have elaborated philosophy as a theological science.[2]

A contemporary of Iamblichus, the philosopher Theodorus of Asine (fourth century), pronounced the following formula: "All things pray, except the First."[3] This means that for the Neoplatonists prayer was the movement of conversion that brought all things back toward their own cause, and closer and closer to the first cause, the One, the Highest Good. It is with the Neoplatonists that systematic treatises on prayer first appear: by Iamblichus in his *De Mysteriis* 5.26; by Proclus, who wrote commentaries on Plato's *Timaeus* (206.26–214.12 Diehl), in which we also find summaries of the doctrines of Porphyry (ibid. 207.23–209.1), Iamblichus (ibid. 209.1–9), and Proclus himself (ibid. 209.9–214.12).[4] Iamblichus pointed out that prayer is principally the act of "beings able to be saved by those who save the universe," understood to be the gods and their providence. With Plotinus, prayer remained essentially the effort of the intellect, which rises rationally toward the divine. But, starting with Iamblichus, prayers accompany rituals in order to express their meaning; they "bring worship to perfection and entwine us indissolubly in holy communion with the gods."

In a society becoming politically and administratively Christian, a little at a time and with varying speed in different regions, as was the Roman Empire in the fourth, fifth, and sixth centuries, the pagan cult had become more or less clandestine and was for this very reason practiced with great piety by its last adepts. Under the pressure of this slow transformation, the cult became more and more spiritual. "Sacrifices of incense" replaced bloody sacrifices; private

daily worship, consisting principally of the recitation or singing of hymns, took the place of processions and public contests.[5] In Porphyry's *Vita Plotini*, Eunapius's *Vitae Sophistarum*, Marinus's life of Proclus, and Damascius's *Vita Isidori* we can see the implacable progression of the new mentality.[6] The moment had arrived when the noun "Hellene" became synonymous with "pagan." Just about every great Neoplatonist philosopher composed hymns for the cult.

Inspired by the immediate disciples of Iamblichus, the emperor Julian undertook the work of restoring the pagan cult. In 363, he wrote: "One must learn by heart the hymns in honor of the gods. There are a great number of very beautiful ones composed by the Ancients and by the Moderns. Let us see to it that we know at least those that are sung in the temples. Most of them are a gift given by the gods themselves in answer to our supplications. Only a few are the work of men who, thanks to divine inspiration and a soul inaccessible to evil, composed them in honor of the gods. . . . We must pray to the gods often, in private and in public, preferably three times a day and, at the very least, in the morning and in the evening."[7] In Egyptian Alexandria, Julian ordered the commissioner to organize a choir of young men to sing sacred hymns.[8] These measures probably reflect at least in part the practices transmitted to Julian by the philosopher Maximus of Ephesus, his personal adviser, who had been trained by Iamblichus.

Along with the corpus of Homeric hymns and the hymns of Callimachus, two large collections of philosophic/religious liturgical hymns have been preserved—the Orphic hymns and the hymns of Proclus. We should also mention the hymns of Synesius, but, as we know, their inspiration is not purely pagan, and we find more of the Chaldean oracles in them than traditional mythology.[9]

Orphic hymns, which are Orphic only by name, seem to have been the "choir book" of a religious community in Asia Minor[10] (perhaps at Pergamum). Preceding each hymn in this collection is the name of the god or goddess to whom it was to be addressed and an identification of the kind of incense that was to be offered while the hymn was sung. The collection is knowledgeably composed, opening with two hymns to the goddesses Hecate and Artemis Prothyraia, then continuing with hymns dedicated to the cosmic gods— Night, Heaven, the Stars, the Moon, and Nature—and finally hymns to the gods of mythology and of Olympus: Pan, Heracles, Kronos, Zeus, Dionysus. All of these gods are meticulously invoked by their names and by their cult

Bust of Plotinus. Rome, Vatican Museum. Museum photo.

epithets, which are derived from the myths concerning them, or signify the favors that they bestow.

We may legitimately wonder how this choir book belonging to a community of devotees of Dionysus in Asia Minor could have been saved. The proximity of all the manuscripts in this collection of Orphic hymns to the hymns of Proclus may put us on the right track. For we know from Marinus that Proclus had to go into exile in Asia for an entire year, and that, according to what he said, "It was the divinity that gave him the opportunity for this journey, so that he might not miss being initiated into the most ancient rituals that are still practiced among the people there. In fact, he taught himself all of their practices. The people in turn were instructed by him if, with the passage of time, they had come to neglect one of their ceremonies; the philosopher would explain to them in a more comprehensive manner what concerned the divine cult."[11] We are tempted to believe that Proclus retrieved this collection in order to augment it with his own hymns.

Traditionally, the hymns of Proclus are seven in number, to which we now must add the hymn to Ares from the Homeric Hymns[12] (the eighth in the collection), and as we know of fragments from two hymns that have been lost, this brings to ten the number of known Proclean hymns. But there must have been many more, since Marinus says that Proclus only slept for a very short period of time and therefore beguiled the long waking hours of the night by composing hymns. Marinus also reports that even after the age of seventy, when his health was declining, Proclus nevertheless continued to pray and to compose hymns. He tells us that Proclus celebrated feast days assiduously, not only those of the Greek gods but also those of many barbarian gods, and that he often turned them into occasions for night vigils and the singing of hymns.[13] Similarly,

Joannes Lydus refers to the "hymn book" of Proclus (*ta humnaria*).[14]

Thus we have in their entirety eight hymns of Proclus dedicated to Helios, Aphrodite (conceived as the mother of spiritual and physical love), the Muses, the Gods, Aphrodite the Lycian (Proclus was originally from Xanthus in Lycia), Hecate and Janus (Hecate is the great goddess of the Chaldean oracles), Athena of the good counsel, and Ares. These hymns were all composed in the same way, and they were made up of two parts: first, an invocation of the god or the goddess by his or her names and traditional attributes, which always came from the best-informed mythology; then a prayer characterized by a style of personal sincerity that was particularly striking and expressed the tender devotion of its author. For example, Aphrodite is "born of sea foam"; she is the one who gave birth "to Winged Loves." Aphrodite the Lycian is the "queen of the Lycians"; the union of the "heavenly Aphrodite" with the "fiery Hephaestus" is the symbol of the spiritual wedding of the intellectual life. Ares is the "rampart of Olympus" and the "father of victory in successful wars." The commentators on these texts, E. Vogt and M. L. West, have cited all the parallels with the mythological literature. As for prayer, Proclus beseeches Athena: "Hear me, you who cast forth so pure a light from your face. Grant me, as I wander on earth, safe harbor. Grant my soul pure light, wisdom, and love, as a reward for my holy hymns in your honor. Through love imbue my soul with sufficient force and with the ability to draw it out of the depths of the earth and bring it back up to Olympus toward the dwelling of its Father. . . . Have pity on me, Goddess of gentle counsel, savior queen of mortals. Keep me from lying helpless on the ground, falling into the hands of the chastising women who send chills down my spine because I delight in being yours."[15] To Ares, he addresses the following supplication: "O benevolent god, grant me a resolute heart that I may dwell under the inviolate laws of peace, by escaping the warfare of my enemies and violent death."[16] And we know that this prayer was granted!

We should note, moreover, that these two sets of hymns are in no way isolated phenomena. Even in Porphyry's *Life of Plotinus* we find a very long hymn in the form of an oracle to Apollo in response to Amelius. This cannot actually be a Delphic oracle, but it is a hymn in which we can easily recognize Porphyry's hand.[17] Moreover, if it was carefully preserved in this place, we can assume that it was used as a prayer by other members of the school in honor of their founder. Written in the same sophisticated style, it ends with an invocation to the Muses that celebrates the feast of Plotinus with Apollo, who is supposed to have composed the hymn.[18] Here it may be appropriate to recall the words of Proclus himself on this subject: "It is possible to reveal divine realities in several ways. Poets inspired by Phoebus (Apollo) do it by means of mythical expressions and with rich, strong elocution; those poets who adopt the tragic mode for their mythical subjects, especially those who make the gods speak, do so by means of religious and holy expressions and in a form of composition that lifts one upward to the sublime."[19] But after Proclus and until the end of paganism, we learn that there were composers of new hymns. For example, we know that a student of Proclus named Isidore had composed several hymns, and we are told that another of his students, Asclepiodotus, had "augmented the corpus of hymns," thus supplying specific evidence to prove the existence of such a collection of hymns in the school of Athens. Furthermore, we are told that in the next generation a student of Isidore's, Asclepiades, composed other hymns especially in honor of Egyptian gods.[20] Who can say that the two acrostic hymns to Dionysus and to Apollo preserved in the *Anthologia Palatina* (9.524–5), in which the litanies of epithets are organized in alphabetical order, are not a part of this corpus? No one has ever remarked on the fact that we still have a verse preserved in Proclus's commentary on the *Cratylus*,[21] and probably taken from another hymn to the goddess Hestia: "Young men, praise Hestia, the most ancient of goddesses." This fact is of utmost significance because of the importance of the worship of Hestia in the cities, where she played the role of tutelary goddess in the prytaneum, the city hall, at Ephesus among other places.[22] It is also significant because of an extraordinary tapestry that was found in Egypt and is preserved in the United States, which distinctly represents "Hestia, full of grace," and which may already be called the icon of the goddess and of her gifts, light and fire, along with wealth, joy, good reputation, the celebration of official banquets, virtue, and progress[23]— in short, everything a well-educated citizen could ask for. Hestia had always been the goddess of the hearth, at first the family hearth but also, with the passing of time, the communal hearth of the whole city on which the immortal, i.e. eternal, flame burned.

Not only did traditional mythology clearly contribute the wealth of its vocabulary and the profusion of its images to the prayers of the philosophical hymns; more important, it was to enter in its entirety into the construction of the theological system of the Neoplatonists.

Two related movements characterized the advent of theology as a science. The first was syncretism, "symphonies," an attempt to make all human traditions converge to build the theological edifice. Literature, mythology, and philosophy, in their diverse modes of expression, yield the same doctrines regarding the same gods. Theological science was systematically built by comparing and combining the contributions of these three traditions. These combinations made it possible for the scholar to exhaust the lists in order to assign an exact place to each deity, along with his or her particular

properties and attributes, within the pantheon as a whole. Mythology was, therefore, a major theological locus.

Already in Plotinus we find expression of the fundamental principles of the theological interpretation of myths. It is no longer a matter of establishing more or less artificial correspondences between mythological images and the realities of nature or the rules of ethics, as in ancient exegesis. What is here revealed is the structure of the world that encompasses the gods and the visible universe. The text reads: "Myths, if they are truly myths, must separate the circumstances of the narrative in time, and often must distinguish between beings who may be mistaken for one another and are differentiated only in their rank or their powers" (*Enneades* 3.5[50], 9, 24–26). Myths, therefore, lay bare in a temporal and spatial narrative the eternal and immutable structure of the divine world by multiplying characters and plots. Consequently, an interpretation has to backtrack from the chronological to the hierarchical, to rediscover the theology in the history, and to highlight what Plotinus here calls "the rank and powers of Beings." An echo of this fundamental principle can also be heard in chapter 4 of Sallust's treatise *Of Gods and of the World,* when in speaking of the content of myths he writes: "These things did not occur at a determined moment; they always exist: the intellect sees the whole at a single glance; it is the discourse [of the myth] that establishes a succession of primary and secondary events." In an extremely forceful manner, Proclus expresses this approach with a slogan in the form of a play on words borrowed from Plato himself in the *Gorgias* (523a 1–2), saying that "myth is not only a myth (*muthos*), but also a philosophical argument (*logos*)," that is to say, a religious truth, a theological reason.[24] Myth is no longer simply fiction, it is pure truth, pure truth that several generations of exegetes will strive to discover and reveal through scholarly analyses, comparisons, etymologies, and explanations, a good number of which prefigure the "wax nose" of the medieval theologians, which is twisted in every direction.

From these fundamental principles emerges a classification of myths that easily brings them all back to theology. Once again it is Sallust who tells us that there are four kinds of myths: *theological myths,* which are about the very nature of gods; *physical myths,* which are about nature insofar as it is filled with the effects of the gods' providence, and thereby reveals the gifts of their goodness and their action within the universe; *psychological myths,* which show us the actions of the soul in its quest for the divine; and *material myths,* which were evidently the least interesting for a theologian. Later Neoplatonists found a means of interpreting *material myths* theologically as well, for if it was absurd to identify the gods with the material elements of the world, it was nonetheless very instructive to look in plants, stones, and animals for the laws of their affinity to the gods, and for the mysterious traces that made them kindred with the divine, for through them one might ascend, by means of magic, to the gods themselves.

At this point, Sallust uses an example. He analyzes the myth of Attis by giving it a theological interpretation:

> The mother of the gods fell in love with Attis, whom she had seen lying beside the river Gallus; taking a star-studded bonnet, she put it on his head and henceforth kept him at her side. But he became infatuated with a nymph, abandoned the mother of the gods, and lived with the nymph. At this, the mother of the gods caused Attis to go mad. He cut off his genitals, left them beside the nymph, and returned to live with the mother of the

Hestia Polyolbos (full of grace) and her attributes. Wool tapestry. Egypt, fourth century. Washington, Dumbarton Oaks Collection. Museum photo.

Bust of Homer. Munich, Staatliche Antikensammlungen und Glyptothek. Photo Koppermann.

Since there is a very close tie between the myth and the world, we who imitate the order of the world celebrate a festival in order to conform to that world order. First of all, since we too fell from heaven and since we united with the nymph, we suffer affliction and abstain from bread and all other heavy and unrefined food. Next come the felling of a tree and the fast, as if we too were cutting back all future progeneration. After that our nourishment is milk, as if we had participated in a second birth. These, then, are the manifestations of joy, of rewards, and something of a return upward toward the gods.

In the first generation of Neoplatonists, we find in Plotinus the allegorical interpretation of the myth of the birth of Aphrodite in Plato's *Symposium* (*Enn.* 3.5), but the most striking example of a systematic exegesis of a myth is given by Porphyry, the disciple of Plotinus, in his explanation of the cave of the Naiads (*De antro nympharum*) described in Homer's *Odyssey* (13.102–112). As Jean Pépin remarked, following Karl Praechter,[26] Porphyry's allegorical interpretation lacks unity. The author, for one thing, does not restrict himself to a single type of allegory. The beginning and the largest part of the tract show the application of an essentially metaphysical allegory, that is to say, theological and only subordinately physical. But toward the end, moral allegory abruptly appears: once inside the cave, we are called upon to cast aside all worldly goods and to see to it that our passions are obliterated. Furthermore, within the metaphysical allegory itself, a single term may assume several different symbolic values. These polyvalences underscore the wealth of the process by which our authors take pains not only to give us an account of the realities of the divine world but also to direct our souls toward those realities by purifying them. Faithful to the most ancient tradition of Greek philosophy, for them the practice of philosophy implies a better way of life.

Nothing could stop the exegetes in quest of the allegories behind the divine myths, since they considered their very absurdity to be a stimulant in the search for hidden meanings. Sallust is always the one who posits this principle: "But why is there talk in myths of adultery, rape, fathers bound in chains, and all those other strange things? Could there not be a wonderful design here, intended to make the soul, thanks to these apparently strange things, *immediately* regard these accounts as veils and the truth as an ineffable thing?"[27] Besides, Plato himself may have felt something of the sort when he had Critias say in the *Timaeus* (20d7–8), apropos of Solon's account of the myth of Atlantis: "A very strange account and yet absolutely true." Commenting on this passage, Proclus transmits forthwith the opinion of his master, Syrianus, according to whom

it is necessary to detach this opposition [between the Athenians and the inhabitants of Atlantis] from the realm of human things in order to extend it to cover the entire field of the cosmos, and so that we may thus apply its coextensive meaning to all that is real, by observing in what way the real participates in the opposition by virtue of the diversity of forces. Since all things indeed derive both from the One and from the Dyad subsequent to the One, and are in some way mutually linked to one another while also having an antithetical nature, as there is a sort of antithesis between the Same and the Other, Movement and Rest, and since all the realities in the world participate in these categories, we would be well advised to consider the opposition that penetrates all that is real.[28]

gods. [And now for the theological interpretation.] The mother of the gods is a life-giving goddess, which is why she is called mother. Attis is the artisan who makes whatever is born and dies, and that is why it is said that he was found near the river Gallus, for Gallus suggests the galaxy, or the Milky Way, which is the outer limit of matter subject to change. Just as the primary gods perfect the secondary gods, the mother becomes enamored of Attis and gives him heavenly powers [this is what is symbolized by the star-studded bonnet]. But Attis in turn becomes enamored of the nymph: nymphs preside over progeneration, for all that is engendered vanishes. However, since progeneration had to have an end, for fear that what was already evil might produce something even worse, the artisan who produced it all cast his generative powers into the world of things to come and once again united with the gods.[25]

We can see that this interpretation signifies the fate of the soul, its fall into matter, and its ascension toward the gods by means of fasting and rituals. The strangest and most repugnant accounts can thus assume spiritual value by conveying the loftiest truths of the doctrine of salvation.

This theological interpretation is in fact extended through the justification of a ritual or a festival. The text goes on to say:

War only illustrates the opposition that pervades all of nature.

Proclus immediately goes on to say that this is the way war must be understood, even among the gods.

> Among the very gods themselves the divine Homer (*Iliad* 20.67 ff.) sets up antitheses, opposing Apollo to Poseidon, Ares to Athena, the River [Xanthus] to Hephaestus, Hermes to Leto, Hera to Artemis. We must indeed consider what is to happen among bodies and among incorporeal beings and among beings who belong to both states. We must understand that Poseidon, in a way that is total, and Apollo, in a way that is partial, create a world in the process of becoming; that Hera and Artemis make possible the production of life, one the life of the mind and the other the life of the body; that Athena and Ares cause the opposition that permeates two things together, being and life, one responsible for the opposition that is determined by understanding and the other responsible for a more material opposition inspired by passion; that Hermes and Leto preside over the double perfection of souls, one over the perfection due to cognitive powers and to the projection of reasoning, and the other over the perfection due to the free-flowing, voluntary, and freely accepted production of vital powers; that Hephaestus and Xanthus are the authors of all physical composition and of the forces that dwell in the body, one attending to the active forces and the other to those that are passive, like matter. Homer, however, puts Aphrodite in a place of her own, separate from the others, so that she may cast on all things the shining light of unification and accord, and so that she may come to the rescue of weaker realities, because unity for these realities is not as strong as multiplicity.[29]

But it is not only war among the gods that Proclus justifies in this way. All the other passages that in Homer, Hesiod, and the Orphics had always scandalized ancient readers are given an acceptable theological explanation. When Socrates in the *Republic* outlines his program of education for young Athenians, he forbids them to read the poets because of the immorality of the myths. This line of argument, relentlessly adopted after Socrates by pagan and Christian authors alike, was refuted at length by Proclus in one of the numerous dissertations that make up his commentary on Plato's *Republic*. We refer to the sixth dissertation, entitled "On Plato's Objections in the *Republic* to Homer and the Art of Poetry." This is a veritable defense of Homer and the poets, meant to show their profound agreement with the loftiest theological doctrines developed by Plato. Simply enumerating the questions raised by our author gives an idea of the theses discussed in philosophical and religious circles: "How can one argue in defense of myths about the gods that seem to make them responsible for evils?"(an explanation of the "two vases" of Homer *Il.* 24.527–528). "How poetry [Homer] seems to attribute to the gods the breaking of oaths: rules to identify the truth on this point." Why Zeus involves the gods in taking part in the Trojan War (Hom. *Il.* 20.4 ff.). What is the meaning of the judgment of the three goddesses by Paris (Hom. *Il.* 24.28–30 and Cyprian chants)? What is the meaning of the metamorphoses of the gods? "How we must, while showing that the Divine is incapable of lying, defend the act of sending down a dream to Agamemnon, an act that seems to involve the gods in lying" (Hom. *Il.* 2.1 ff.). The defense of myths about Hades (a justification of the eschatological myths of Homer and Plato against the Epicureans). On the tears shed by the gods and heroes (tears shed by Zeus over Hector [Hom. *Il.* 22.168 ff.], and over his son Sarpedon [ibid. 16.433 ff.]). On the laughter of the gods (the famous "Homeric laugh" at Hephaestus, *Il.* 1.599 ff.). Does Homer encourage people to despise temperance? A detailed allegorical exegesis of the union of Zeus and Hera (Hom. *Il.* 14.153–351). Yet another case of divine union, that of Aphrodite and Ares (Hom. *Od.* 8.266 ff.). On the love of wealth among heroes. On the apparent scorn of the gods by heroes [Achilles] in Homer. On the apparent cruelty of heroes in Homer. The chapters in this long dissertation all seem to come to the same conclusion: not only does Homer teach us nothing immoral about the gods, as long as he is correctly interpreted, but he is a theological authority without equal. To be precise, in the second book of this dissertation Proclus takes up the subject in a positive way by showing first how Plato always admired Homer; why, nonetheless, in the *Republic* he rejected poetry as being inappropriate for the ears of young men; and why, despite all this, he appears everywhere to be emulating Homer, both in his style and in his ideas. Proclus then returns to pleading in defense of Homer against the accusations in the *Phaedrus* and, more particularly, those in book 10 of the *Republic*.[30]

Although he need not defend Plato's myths as he does Homer's, Proclus takes pains to interpret them, using the same methods to the same end. A perfect example of this exegesis of Platonic myths is found in the sixteenth dissertation of the commentary on the *Republic*, entirely devoted to the myth of Er.[31]

Unlike his predecessors, Proclus was not content to be a more or less inspired interpreter of divine myths that were supplied to him by the poetic, religious, or philosophical tradition; he went farther, giving mythology its true status

Bust of a Neoplatonist, perhaps Plutarch of Athens. Athens, American School of Classical Studies. Photo Alison Frantz.

within the science of theology. Not only did Proclus give myths a theologically acceptable meaning, but in legends about the gods he found valuable confirmations of his own views on theology. With Proclus especially, and for the first time, mythology ceased to be the principal source of theology but merely confirmed or illustrated theology. The main event that caused mythology to lose its privileged rank was the discovery by Proclus's teacher Syrianus of the correct interpretation of the hypotheses in Plato's *Parmenides*. For the school of Athens, the *Parmenides* was the principal, indeed the only, source of theology as a science. It is therefore to this text that all other theological passages in Plato's dialogues and all other theological sources, among them mythology, must be subordinated.[32] In the eyes of Proclus, the first two hypotheses in the *Parmenides* are the revelation of the First God, that is to say the One, by means of negations and the revelation of the entire hierarchy of all divine classes, designated in the second hypothesis by their Platonic units and their characteristic attributes. These include the gods called Intelligible, Intelligible-Intellective, Intellective, Hypercosmic, and Encosmic; the universal souls; angels; demons; and heroes.[33]

On this point, Proclus said:

> If we absolutely must have under our eyes in a single dialogue of Plato the totality and integrality of theology and also its continuity, which corresponds to the numerical order of the gods from first to last, this will perhaps be a paradox, and undoubtedly what I am going to say will appear obvious only to those who belong to our spiritual family. But despite everything, we must be daring precisely because we have entered into these kinds of arguments, and we must say to those who object, it is the *Parmenides* that you want. . . . In fact, within these pages all the divine classes not only proceed in good order from the very first cause, but they even show the cohesion that ties them together. . . . Briefly, all the principles of the science of theology appear in a perfectly clear manner in this dialogue, all divine worlds can be found in it in the continuity of their coming into existence, and it contains nothing other than the song of the generation of the gods and of all that exists, in whatever form this may be, starting with the ineffable cause of the universe. . . . Yes, we must add the total number of dialogues to those to which we have referred, and those in turn must be included in the unique and perfect theory of the *Parmenides*.[34]

This fervent page is the real manifesto of Proclus's theology. It is quite clear that in this framework mythology and its interpretation can only intervene in support of scientific conclusions drawn from the *Parmenides*. This is what we might call "Proclus's demythologization."[35]

It has rightly been said, as we can now see, that for Homer's Olympians—the most anthropomorphic creations of the human spirit—to have ended their careers inside this museum of metaphysical abstractions was one of the greatest ironies in the history of ideas.[36] We should understand how it can be argued that the place reserved for traditional mythology by Syrianus and Proclus (the last of Plato's successors in Athens) in their theological system bestowed on mythology a poetic and mystical dimension that did much to attract admirers and disciples from century to century— Pseudo-Dionysius and all those who claim kinship with him, the Platonists of the Renaissance, and all that is called in the broad sense of the term the Platonic tradition. Let us hope that the future will add new links to this golden chain.

H.-D.S./g.h.

NOTES

1. A. J. Festugière, "La religion des Romains d'après un ouvrage récent," *Revue biblique* 65 (1958): 78–100, reproduced in *Études de religion grecque et hellénistique* (Paris 1972), 226–48; the text cited, pp. 86 and 234.

2. H. D. Saffrey and L. G. Westerink, *Proclus, Théologie platonicienne* (Paris 1968), I:clxxxviii–cxcii.

3. Proclus, *In Platonis Timaeum commentarii*, ibid. I:213, 1–2; W. Deuse, *Theodoros von Asine, Sammlung der Testimonien und Kommentar* (Wiesbaden 1973), Test. 7, pp. 35 and 96–97.

4. These texts have been translated by Ed. des Places, *Jamblique, Les mystères d'Égypte* (Paris 1966), 181–83, and by A. J. Festugière, *Proclus, Commentaire sur le Timée* (Paris 1967), 3:27–36. On these texts, see H. P. Esser, *Untersuchungen zu Gebet und Gottesverehrung der Neuplatoniker* (diss. Cologne 1967).

5. M. P. Nilsson, "Pagan Divine Service in Late Antiquity," *Harvard Theol. Rev.* 38 (1945): 60–69, and R. Harder, "Inschriften von Didyma," no. 217, in *Navicula Chiloniensis*, Festschrift F. Jacoby (Leiden 1956), 88–97, reproduced in *Kleine Schriften* (Munich 1960), 137–47.

6. For a good account, see P. Brown, *The World of Late Antiquity* (London 1971), 49–112, and A. Cameron, "The End of the Ancient Universities," *Cahiers d'histoire mondiale* 10 (1967): 653–73.

7. Julien, *Lettre* 89, pp. 169–70, Bidez-Cumont.

8. Julien, *Lettre* 109, pp. 186–87, Bidez-Cumont.

9. The hymns of Synesius have been edited by N. Terzaghi (Rome 1939), translated into French by M. Meunier (Paris 1947), studied by U. von Wilamowitz-Moellendorff, *Die Hymnen des Proklos und Synesios* (Berlin 1907), reproduced in *Kleine Schriften* (Berlin 1971), 2:163–91, and W. Theiler, *Die Chaldäischen Orakel und die Hymnen des Synesios* (Königsberg 1942), reproduced in *Forschungen zum Neuplatonismus* (Berlin 1966), 252–301. On the link between Synesius and the philosophical schools, see H. I. Marrou, "Synesius of Cyrene and Alexandrian Neoplatonism," in *The Conflict between Paganism and Christianity in the Fourth Century* (Oxford 1963), 126–50, reproduced in *Patristique et Humanisme* (Paris 1976), 295–319.

10. A. Dieterich, *De hymnis Orphicis* (Marburg 1891), reproduced in *Kleine Schriften* (Leipzig-Berlin, 1911), 69–110; O. Kern, "Die Herkunft des orphischen Hymnenbuches," in *Genethliakon für Carl Robert* (Berlin 1910), 87–102; R. Keydell, *Orphische Dichtung* (I. Hymnen), in Pauly-Wissowa, vol. 18 (1942), cols. 1321–33; and M. P. Nilsson, *Geschichte der Griechischen Religion* (Munich 1961), 2:430. The *Orphei Hymni* have been edited by G. Quandt (Berlin 1955).

11. Marinus, *Vita Procli*, chap. 14.

12. M. L. West, "The Eighth Homeric Hymn and Proclus," *Classical Quarterly* 20 (1970): 300–304. The *Procli Hymni* have been edited by E. Vogt (Wiesbaden 1957).

13. Marinus, *Vita Procli*, chap. 24, 6, 19; and for a lost hymn to Theandrites, H. D. Saffrey, "Un lien objectif entre le Pseudo-Denys et Proclus," *Studia Patristica* 9 (1966): 98–105.

14. J. Lydus, *De mensibus*, p. 23, 10 Wuensch.

15. Translated by A. J. Festugière in "Proclus et la religion traditionnelle," in *Mélanges André Piganiol* (Paris 1966), 1581–90, reproduced in *Études de philosophie grecque* (Paris 1971), 575–84 (the text cited, p. 1587 = p. 581).

16. See the context in H. D. Saffrey, "Allusions antichrétiennes chez Proclus, le diadoque platonicien," *Revue des sciences phil. et théol.* 59 (1975): 553–63.

17. On the poetic gifts of Porphyry, one should recall the words of Plotinus about a poem which Porphyry had read at the celebration of the festival of Plato: "You reveal yourself to be not only a poet, but also a philosopher and, moreover, a hierophant!" (*Vita Plotini*, 15.5). On the oracle of Apollo on the subject of Plotinus, see H. W. Parke and D. E. W. Wormell, *The Delphic Oracle* (Oxford 1956), 2:473.

18. Porphyry, *Vita Plotini*, 22, and the French translation in J. Bidez, *Vie de Porphyre, le philosophe Néo-platonicien* (Gand-Leipzig 1913), 122–26.

19. Proclus, *In Parmenidem* I, col. 646, pp. 21–29, Cousin.

20. Damascius, *Vita Isidori Reliquiae*, ed. C. Zintzen (Hildesheim 1967), § 61, for Isidore; § 209, for Asclepiodotus; § 164, for Asclepiades.

21. Proclus, *In Cratylum*, § 138, p. 79, 3–4, Pasquali.

22. J. Keil, "Kulte im Prytaneion von Ephesos," in *Anatolian Studies Buckler* (Manchester 1939), 119–28, and F. Miltner, *Jahreshefte des Oesterreichischen Archäologischen Institutes,* 44 (1959): col. 291, n. 66.

23. P. Friedländer, *Documents of Dying Paganism* I: *The Hestia Tapestry* (Berkeley–Los Angeles 1945), 1–26, reproduced in *Studien zur antiken Literatur und Kunst* (Berlin 1969), 488–510. My interpretation of the document, however, is not that of Friedländer.

24. *Proclus, Théol. plat.* I, 4, p. 18, 26–27; *In Tim.* I, p. 80, 20–22, and *In Rep.* I, p. 156, 25.

25. The version given here is based on A. J. Festugière, *Trois Dévots païens,* III *Sallustius, Des dieux et du monde* (Paris 1944), 24–25.

26. K. Praechter, "Richtungen und Schulen im Neuplatonismus," in *Genethliakon für Carl Robert* (Berlin 1910), 122–28, reproduced in *Kleine Schriften* (Hildesheim 1973), 182–88, and J. Pépin, "Porphyre, exégète d'Homère," in *Porphyre* (Vandœuvres-Geneva 1966), 241.

27. Sallustius, ibid., p. 22, A. J. Festugière, trans. On the history of the principle, see J. Pépin, *art. cit.,* 251–58.

28. Proclus, *In Timaeum* I, p. 78, 1–11 (A. J. Festugière, trans.).

29. Proclus, ibid., p. 78, 27–79, 19 (A. J. Festugière, trans.).

30. All of this dissertation has been translated by A. J. Festugière, *Proclus, Commentaire sur la République* (Paris 1970), 1:86–221. It is noteworthy that Proclus owed most of his arguments to his master Syrianus, as he himself said many times, and that Syrianus in turn depended on a long tradition of exegesis. On this subject, see A. J. Friedl, *Die Homer-Interpretation des Neuplatonikers Proklos* (diss. Würzburg 1936), 59–65.

31. This dissertation is the longest of the dissertations in the commentary. One may thereby judge the importance that Proclus attributed to this myth.

32. *Proclus, Théol. plat.* I, chaps. 4–12, pp. 17–58; Saffrey and Westerink, "Introduction," I:lx–lxxxix.

33. From the class of Intellective gods and *a fortiori* those of the Hypercosmic and Encosmic gods, Proclus proposed correspondences between the gods philosophically defined by properties drawn from the *Parmenides* and the classic gods of the Olympian pantheon. There is a table of these correspondences in Saffrey and Westerink, *Proclus, Théol. plat.,* "Introduction," I:lxvi–lxvii.

34. *Proclus, Théol. plat.* I, 7, pp. 31–32.

35. For what we call "Proclus's demythologization" and its connection with the theory of the Platonic units, see *Théol. plat.* (Paris 1977), III:lxvi–lxxii.

36. E. R. Dodds, *Proclus, the Elements of Theology* (2d ed., Oxford 1963), 260.

BIBLIOGRAPHY

1. General Studies

C. A. LOBECK, *Aglaophamus sive de Theologiae mysticae Graecorum causis,* 2 vols. (Königsberg 1829). K. PRAECHTER, "Richtungen und Schulen im Neuplatonismus," in *Genethliakon für Carl Robert* (Berlin 1910), 105–56, reproduced in *Kleine Schriften* (Hildesheim 1973), 165–216. A. BIELMEIER, *Die Neuplatonische Phaidrosinterpretation: Ihr Werdegang und ihre Eigenart* (Paderborn 1930). J. TATE, "On the History of Allegorism," *Classical Quarterly* 28 (1934): 105–14. F. BUFFIÈRE, *Les mythes d'Homère et la pensée grecque* (Paris 1956). J. PÉPIN, "A propos de l'histoire de l'exégèse allégorique: L'absurdité, signe de l'allégorie," *Studia Patristica* 1 (1957): 395–413; *Mythe et allégorie* (1st ed., Paris 1958; 2d ed., Paris 1976). E. WIND, *Pagan Mysteries in the Renaissance* (London 1958). E. KAISER, "Odyssee Szenen als topoi," *Museum Helveticum* 21 (1964): 109–36 and 197–224. H. DÖRRIE, "Spätantike Symbolik und Allegorese," *Frühmittelalterliche Studien* 3 (1969): 1–12. P. CROME, *Symbol und Unzulänglichkeit der Sprache* (Munich 1970). R. T. WALLIS, *Neoplatonism* (London 1972). H. DÖRRIE, "Zur Methodik antiker Exegese," *Zeitschrift für die NT. Wissenschaft* 65 (1974): 121–38. J. PÉPIN, "L'herméneutique ancienne," *Poétique* 23 (1975): 291–300. J. A. COULTER, *The Literary Microcosm: Theories of Interpretation of the Later Neoplatonists* (Leiden 1976). J. PÉPIN, "Aspects théoriques du symbolisme dans la tradition dionysienne: Antécédents et nouveautés," in *Simboli e Simbologia nell'Alto Medioevo* (Spoleto 1976), 33–79. J. DILLON, "Image, Symbol and Analogy: Three Basic Concepts of Neoplatonic Allegorical Exegesis," in *Significance of Neoplatonism* (Norfolk, Va., 1976), 247–62.

2. Plotinus

R. ARNOU, *Le désir de Dieu dans la philosophie de Plotin* (Paris 1921), appendix A, "Quelques remarques sur l'emploi de la mythologie dans les Enéades," 296–300. J. PÉPIN, "Plotin et les mythes," *Revue phil. de Louvain* 53 (1955): 5–27, reproduced in *Mythe et allégorie* (Paris 1958; 2d ed., 1976), 190–209. V. CILENTO, "Mito e poesia nelle Enneadi di Plotino," in *Les sources de Plotin* (Vandœuvres-Geneva 1960), 243–323. J. PÉPIN, "Le temps et le mythe," *Les études philosophiques* 17 (1962): 55–68, reproduced in *Mythe et allégorie* (2d ed., Paris 1976), 503–16. W. THEILER, "Diotima neuplatonisch," *Archiv für Geschichte der Philosophie* 50 (1968): 29–47. J. PÉPIN, "Plotin et le miroir de Dionysos (Enn. 4.3[27].12.1–2), *Revue intern. de philosophie* 24 (1970): 304–20; "Héraklès et son reflet dans le néoplatonisme," in *Le néoplatonisme* (Paris 1971), 167–92. P. HADOT, "Le mythe de Narcisse et son interprétation par Plotin," *Nouvelle revue de psychanalyse* 13 (1976): 81–108.

3. Porphyry

J. PÉPIN, "Porphyre, exégète d'Homère," in *Porphyre* (Vandœuvres-Geneva 1966), 229–72. A. R. SODANO, "Porfirio commentatore di Platone," in *Porphyre* (Vandœuvres-Geneva 1966), 193–228.

4. Imablichus

J. PÉPIN, "Merikôteron-Epoptikôteron (Proclus, *In Tim.* I, 204, pp. 24–27): Deux attitudes exégétiques dans le néoplatonisme," in *Mélanges d'histoire des religions offerts à Henri-Charles Puech* (Paris 1974), 323–30.

5. Sallust

E. PASSAMONTI, "La dottrina dei miti di Sallustio filosofo neoplatonico," *Rendiconti della Reale Accademia dei Lincei, Cl. di Sc. morali, storiche e filologiche,* S. V 1 (1982): 643–64 and 712–27. A. D. NOCK, *Sallustius, Concerning the Gods and the Universe* (Cambridge 1926), xliii–lv (commentary on chaps. 3 and 4).

6. Proclus

A. J. FRIEDL, *Die Homer-Interpretation des Neuplatonikers Proklos* (diss. Würzburg 1936). E. ZELLER and R. MONDOLFO, *La Filosofia dei Greci nel suo sviluppo storico* (Florence 1961), 6:185–88. J. PÉPIN, "Le merveilleux dans la vie et la pensée de Proclos," *Revue philosophique* 173 (1973): 439–52. A. D. R. SHEPPARD, *Studies on the 5th and 6th Essays of Proclus' Commentary on the Republic* (Göttingen 1980). J. TROUILLARD, "Les fondements du mythe selon Proclos," in *Le mythe et le symbole* (Paris 1977), 11–37.

GREEK COSMOGONIC MYTHS

From early antiquity the Greeks must have known multiple and divergent traditions of cosmogonic myths. We find traces of some of these in Homer. In two places in the *Iliad,* the poet gives Oceanus and Tethys titles which make them appear as the primordial divine couple. Oceanus is first called the origin (or generating father) of the gods, *theōn genesis,* and Tethys their mother (14.200; cf. 302); later the same expression is repeated and expanded: Oceanus is the original father (14.246) of all things or all beings (*pantessi*). Even Plato and Aristotle accorded these passages a cosmogonic import: long before Thales, who would make water the principle from which all things arose, Homer placed the liquid element at the origin of the gods as well as of the world (*Theatetus* 152e; *Metaphysics* A 3 983 b 27). One might conclude that in Greece, as in many other cultures, this "primary" value accorded to aquatic powers derives from the twofold nature of fresh waters: first, their fluidity and absence of form predispose them to represent that original state of the world in which everything is uniformly submerged and confused into a single homogeneous mass; and, second, their vivifying and generating virtue—life and love evoke the wet element for the Greeks—implies that they hold in their womb the principle of successive engenderings. In the epic, however, Oceanus and Tethys do not merely define the initial state of the world or the power that presides over its generation. They continue to exist in the organized universe, but are relegated to its borders, driven back to its extreme limits. Moreover, the couple has split up: Oceanus and Tethys no longer sleep together (14.304–6 and 205–7), which is another way of saying that their activity of engendering has now halted and that the cosmos, in the form of a divine society organized under the reign of Zeus, has attained its definitive form and stability. Are we to understand by this that the primordial divine couple no longer has anything to do, that its presence on the borders of the world serves only to evoke the memory of a bygone time? It would seem, on the contrary, that the role assigned to them at the beginning of the genesis determines their place and function at its end, in the differentiated and ordered universe of the Olympian gods. Oceanus is that living stream of water which flows around the world, girdling the world in an incessant flux, just as the waters of a river, after a long trajectory, are brought back to the springs from which they arose, feeding them in an eternal cycle. At the extremities of the cosmos, Oceanus constitutes the *peirata gaiēs* (14.200, 301), the limits of the earth, which are conceived as bonds holding the universe in. This image of a circular river that encloses the world as if in a knot operates not only on the horizontal plane, on which the sun and the stars are seen to emerge from Oceanus when they rise and to plunge back into him when they set, deriving from this daily bath in the primordial waters a vigor and a youth that are ever renewed. Mythic indications, although admittedly fragmentary, also show how springs, fountains, wells, and rivers which carry life up to the surface of the earth are themselves fed by the flow of Oceanus, which presupposes that his waters, or at least a part of them, circulate underground while the others encircle the world (*Iliad* 8.478; *Odyssey* 4.563, 10.511, 11.13f.; Hesiod, *Theogony* 788). Furthermore, we may wonder whether the celestial waters are not in turn connected with the course of Oceanus (Aristotle, *Meteorologica* 347a10; *Etymologicum Magnum* 821.8), which would thus hem in the whole of the cosmos, upwards and downwards as well as toward the east and west, in the liquid netting of his flux. The temporal unfolding of a genesis that has the world emerge progressively from the primordial waters would thus also articulate itself in exactly the same way in the spatial schema of a universe closed in on all sides by the same waters that gave rise to it, with their channels serving as markers for its limits even as they constitute the inexhaustible source of its vitality.

This model, both a cosmogonic and a cosmological whole, though well attested elsewhere, is nowhere presented in the Greek tradition in the form of a systematic explanation. We grasp its scattered elements as if concurrent and parallel traditions had left nothing behind but debris. In Homer himself, another passage seems clearly to confer upon Nyx, the night, an authority and a power that Zeus, even as lord over all, must recognize as being a primordial Power anterior to his reign (*Il.* 14.258). Thus in the Orphic cosmogonies, Night, as the original entity, takes the place of Oceanus and

Tethys, and the theme of darkness, in which all things remain confused before emerging into light, takes the place of the theme of flowing waters. These two themes, moreover, are not mutually exclusive; there are enough affinities between them for them sometimes to reinforce one another. It is nocturnal darkness that reigns in the depths of the waters, while the night is composed, for the Greeks, of a mist of wetness, a dark, opaque fog.

The publication in 1957 of a papyrus of commentaries on a cosmogonic poem written by Alcman confirms that, beginning with the seventh century B.C., poetry could be inspired by mythical traditions which were already quite sophisticated, in which the primordial waters were closely connected with the original night. Alcman places at the beginning of the world the Nereid Thetis, who is a marine divinity like Tethys, the wife of Oceanus, and is generally presented as the grandmother of Oceanus. Thetis has at her disposal the same power to take any form and the same crafty intelligence as the Oceanid Metis, who is promoted to the rank of great primordial divinity in the Orphic cosmogonies. In many regards, these two divine powers are doubles of one another. Dark goddess of the oceanic depths, Thetis the somber, *Kuanea*, is associated by Alcman with three entities: Obscurity (*Skotos*), who reigned alone in the beginning when all was unformed and undiscernible in her; then, closely tied to one another, Poros and Tecmor, who emerged, flanking Thetis as soon as she appeared in the womb of the night of the primordial waters—waters she represents as marine goddess but which, because of her intelligent capacity to manipulate the future, she can get the better of. Poros—the way, the trajectory, the outcome—and Tecmor—the sign, the index, the reference point—act as intelligent principles of differentiation: in the obscurity of the sky and the waters which were originally commingled, they cause precise and diversified directions to appear. They trace the paths for the sun to follow in order to bring the light of day and for the stars to follow in order to draw in the nocturnal sky the luminous highways of the constellations. The world gradually becomes organized through the visible trail of the celestial movements and the clear demarcation of diverse parts of the horizon, so that the confused obscurity of a liquid mass gives way to an organized, delimited, and well-oriented space in which man, instead of losing himself, finds a framework and points of reference that he may observe, conjecture, prognosticate, foresee—in short, situate himself in the place which best suits him.

But in comparison with these somewhat secondary, marginal, or splintered traditions, the theogonic poem of Hesiod presents itself, such as it has been transmitted to us in the form of a complete and systematic work, as the central testimony, the major document we have at our disposal for understanding Greek mythic thought and its main orientations in the sphere of cosmogony.

The first problem is to discover on exactly which level to situate any reading of this text. We might treat it simply as a literary fantasy, even if it fits into the pattern of a literature which writing had already begun to standardize, and even if we find in it an entire series of formulaic elements borrowed from Homeric tradition. We may nevertheless show, even in those places in which borrowings are most directly attested, that the values of the formulas—fragments of lines, whole lines, or groups of lines—are modified by slight changes so as to produce, distinct from the original model, the effect of a new meaning demanded by the poet's project, a project no longer epic but theogonic. Neither should we read Hesiod by

The Moirai. Fragment of the large frieze from the Altar of Pergamum. Ca. 180 B.C. Berlin, Pergamum Museum. Photo Boudot-Lamotte.

referring to later philosophical systems, as these presuppose the development of a conceptual vocabulary and ways of thinking which differed from those of the Boeotian poet. It is not that his discourse does not indicate a powerful effort of abstraction and systematization; it is rather that he operates on a different level and follows a different logic from that of philosophy. We are thus in the presence of a way of thinking that is foreign to the categories to which we are accustomed: it is at once mythic and scholarly, poetic and abstract, narrative and systematic, and traditional and personal. It is this peculiarity that constitutes the difficulty and the interest of the Hesiodic *Theogony.*

It is a theogony because it is of the venerable race of the gods that Hesiod sings, under the inspiration of the Muses who, while he drove his sheep by the foot of the Helicon, revealed the "truth" to him and taught him "all that was and all that will be" (22 and 32). His account faithfully reproduces the song of the Muses, the song with which they charm the ears of the lord of the gods by celebrating his glory, that is, by ceaselessly reactualizing through words his genealogy, his birth, his battles, his exploits, and his triumph. The Hesiodic

narration is thus indisputably a theogony, an exposition of the series of divine generations, and a vast myth of sovereignty that relates in what way, through which battles, against which enemies, through what means, and with which allies Zeus succeeded in establishing over all the universe a royal supremacy that would provide a foundation to the present order of the world and guarantee its permanence.

But this encomium, to be wholly effective, must trace the divine act from its beginnings, by going back to its first origin, *ex archēs* (45); it is thus rooted in a time in which neither Zeus nor the other Olympian gods, the objects of worship, yet existed. The account opens with the evocation of the divine Powers whose names, place, and role indicate their cosmogonic signification. These "primordial" gods are still enough a part of the physical realities which they evoke that we cannot separate them from what today we would call forces or elements "of nature." Before the universe may become the theater for the battles for sovereignty between the gods proper, the setting in which these battles are to unfold must be set up and the props put in place. It is this part of Hesiod's text, the prelude to the entrance of the Titans onto the scene as the first "royal" gods, that constitutes the truly cosmogonic stratum at the heart of the *Theogony*.

"Thus before all else, there came into being the Gaping Chasm (Chaos)," writes Hesiod, "but there followed the broad-chested Earth (*Gaia eurusternos*), the forever-secure seat of the immortals who occupy the summits of snowy Olympus and of the Tartars of the dark mist, in the depths of the underground of broad ways—and also Love (Eros), the most beautiful of the immortal gods, he who breaks limbs" (116–121). Chaos, Earth, and Love thus constitute the triad of Powers whose genesis precedes and introduces the entire process of cosmogonic organization.

How are we to understand this Chaos whose birth Hesiod places before everything? Chaos has been interpreted— starting with the ancients—in philosophical terms: people have seen it/him either as the void, space as a pure vessel, the abstraction of the private place of the body (Aristotle, *Physica* 208b26–33 and H. Fränkel), or, as the Stoics saw it, as a state of confusion, a mass in which all the constituent elements of the universe are mixed together without distinction, a *sugchusis stoicheiōn*, connecting Chaos with the verbal form *cheesthai*: to pour, spread. But these two interpretations are flawed by anachronism. If indeed Chaos defined the void, a pure negativity, how could one admit that this *nothing* might be born (*geneto*)? A related point of view makes Chaos the equivalent of what the epic calls *aēr*, that is, a mist that is wet, dark, and lacking in density. The fact that these elements may be present in Chaos presents no problem. But to identify Chaos with the *aēr* as an element, in the sense given to the term by Anaximander in the Ionian cosmogonies, is to create problems in every way. First of all, Hesiod himself distinguishes *aēr* from Chaos (697–700); and, besides, Erebus and Nyx, who have more in common with *aēr*, are born of Chaos, who is thus logically as well as chronologically anterior to them.

One might also attempt a "mythic" interpretation—and from numerous perspectives. According to F. M. Cornford and G. S. Kirk, Chaos designates the space between the sky and earth; in naming it to begin with, Hesiod was anticipating what would follow in his account when, mutilated by the castrating blow of the knife wielded by his son Kronos, Ouranos-Sky would forever separate himself from Gaea-Earth. The atmospheric space is thus evoked twice in the course of the text: first in the beginning, even before Gaea appears; then after Gaea and Ouranos have been set in place, disunited from each other, as the space which opens up between the two. But what could this space between sky and earth have been at a time when neither sky nor earth yet existed?

Should we not, then, represent Chaos as a bottomless pit, a space of indefinite wandering, an uninterrupted fall similar to the immense abyss, the *mega chasma* of line 740, in the description of Tartarus? It is said of this gaping chasm that its bottom may never be reached, not even after a full year, but that while falling through it one is blown from one side to the other, in every direction, by great gusts buffeting all the directions of space into confusion.

To understand how Chaos came into being, we must situate it/him in its/his oppositional and complementary relationship to Gaea, expressed in the formula: "*prōtista . . . autar epeita*, first (was Chaos) . . . but next (Earth)." The term Chaos is etymologically connected with *chaskō, chandanō,* to gape, to yawn, to open. The Gaping Chasm which is born before anything else is without bottom and without top: it is

the absence of stability, the absence of form, the absence of density, the absence of fullness. As a "cavity," it is less an abstract region—the void—than an abyss, a vertiginous whirlpool that swirls ever deeper, without direction or orientation. Yet, as an "opening," it opens into that which, while being connected to it, is also its opposite. Gaea is a solid base that can be walked on, a firm support that can be leaned on; she has full, dense forms, mountain heights, and subterranean depths. She is not only the floor upon which the edifice of the world is to be constructed; she is the mother, the ancestor who brought to birth all that exists, in every form and in every place—with the sole exception of Chaos himself and his descendants, who constitute a family of Powers entirely separate from all others.

The stabilizing, generating, and organizing role of Gaea becomes translated into qualities which are attributed to her from the beginning: she is an ever-solid seat for the immortals, first by virtue of the mountains that rise up toward the sky (the seat of the Olympians); and then by virtue of the depths which extend her downwards (the seat of the Titans, the subterranean gods, *hupochthonioi*). Stable and secure on her vast surface, extending vertically in two directions, Gaea is not only the opposite, the positive replica of somber Chaos; she is also his counterpart. On her celestial side, she is crowned by the white luminosity of the snows; down below, the Earth roots herself deep in the darkness of Tartarus, which represents, at its base and on a spatial plane, the same original yawning, the same vertiginous abyss, beginning from which and against which Earth has constituted herself since the beginning of time. As soon as she is named, Gaea presents herself, in her function as seat of the gods, as stretched between the two poles of above and beneath, extended between her clear snowy peaks and her dark subterranean base. In the same way, Chaos, as soon as he appears, gives birth to two pairs of contrary entities. Infernal darkness (Erebus) and black night (Nyx) first; then their children, ether (Aithēr) and daylight (Hēmerē). The ordering of this group of four is not done by chance. In each of the two pairs, the relationship between the first-named and the second is the same: Erebus is to Nyx as Aithēr is to Hēmerē. On the one hand we have a dark and a light, with each isolated in the absoluteness of its nature; on the other, a dark and a light brought together in their mutual relativity. In fact, night and day are inseparable; they are joined in their opposition, with each implying the existence of the other, which follows it in a regular alternation. In contrast to the relative clarity and obscurity of a day and night that combine to form the weaving of time on the surface of the earth, infernal darkness and ether correspond to the extreme and exclusive forms of a Black and a White with no common characteristics, which reign over the highest and lowest levels. Ether is the brilliance of a constantly illumined sky, as ignorant of the shadows of clouds as it is of those of the night, the abode of those blessed gods for whom the nocturnal has no place. Erebus is total and permanent darkness, the total night that is never pierced by the rays of the sun, the radical blackness beyond the abode of night (744), to which the fallen gods are doomed in their cosmic prison. It is precisely in front of this abode that day and night meet, confer, and exchange their positions, adjusting to one another to balance their cycles exactly (748–57).

Since from Chaos are born, along with Erebus, which is like a direct prolongation of Chaos, a night that already touches on diurnal light and, especially, the pure luminosity of the ether and the more mixed luminosity of day, Chaos cannot be reduced, as H. Fränkel reduces it, to Nonbeing as

Athena, crowned by Nike, struggles with Alcyone. At right, Gaea, mother of the giants. Fragment of the large frieze from the Altar of Pergamum. Berlin, Pergamum Museum. Photo Boudot-Lamotte.

opposed to Being, or to the Other as opposed to the Same, or, as Paula Philippson does, to Nonform, in short to pure negativity. Admittedly, if we wish to translate into philosophical terms the problem that is thought to underlie the Hesiodic cosmogonic discourse, we should formulate it, as does H. Fränkel, in the following manner: ''All that is exists by the fact that spatially, temporally, and logically it lies against a nonbeing void. And it is determined to be that which it is by defining itself against that which it is not: the void. Thus it is that the whole world, and everything in the world, each according to its rank, has limits at which it collides with the void'' (*Dichtung . . .* , pp. 148–49). But to express oneself in this way is to bias and force the Hesiodic text by illuminating it in the light of concepts. To say that the question is not posed in these terms in the *Theogony* is not enough, for the question is not posed there at all. Hesiod is not responding to a preexisting difficult theoretical problem; he is inviting us to relive a birth; he is recounting the process of a genesis (*geneto*). That which comes into being is first the Gaping Chasm and then Earth. These two Powers are joined, not only as the two successive aspects of a single process of genesis, but also because the relationship of tension that unites them and sets them against one another from the start never ceases to keep them attached to one another. In the differentiated and organized universe, Gaea still ''holds'' to Chaos, who remains present in her deepest place, in the center of herself, as that reality *against* which she had to and still has to establish herself. Here the word *against* is given

two meanings: first, in opposition to a Gaping Chasm which is separated, isolated, sealed off by an entire apparatus of doors, walls, ramparts, floors, sealed platforms, thresholds of unassailable bronze; but also in the sense of using a Gaping Chasm as a support without which the Earth could neither have been born nor continue to exist.

The dependence of Gaea upon a connection with Chaos is thus complex in a different way from the relationship between being and nonbeing. Chaos is not simply the negative of Gaea. Chaos produces that light without which no form would be visible. Inversely, Gaea, who engenders all that has density and shape, is herself called *dnophera* (736), which is an epithet of Nyx (101): dark earth, black earth. Between these two primordial entities there are mergings, passages, and intersections that become acknowledged to the extent that each of them develops the dynamic of genesis that they carry in themselves by virtue of their power of engendering. They are connected, but they do not unite. No child descended from Chaos will ever sleep with any of Gaea's offspring. These are two strata that envelop one another and prop one another up, without ever mixing together. And if it happens that the same entities find themselves in two different lines (like Apate, deception, and Philotes, amorous tenderness), this is never the fruit of a mixture of races but a proof that, in spite of their contrast, there can be certain effects of resonance and something akin to an oscillation between one primordial Power and another.

The presence of Eros, alongside Chaos and Gaea in the

primary triad, also presents problems. Eros cannot represent the force of attraction which brings opposites together, which unites the male and the female in the procreation of a new being different from those who engendered it; for Chaos and Gaea do not unite with one another, and the parturitions that each of them accomplishes at the beginning of genesis are effected without sexual union. Chaos and Gaea bring forth from themselves the children that they cause to come into being. Furthermore, when Hesiod specifies that a divinity gives birth after having been sexually united with another or outside of such a union, he tells us not whether the offspring was conceived with or without the help of Eros but, rather, whether it was with or without *philotēs* (125, 132). It is the birth of Aphrodite that marks the moment when the generative process becomes subject to strict rules: henceforth it will function by the momentary union of two opposite principles, masculine and feminine, brought together by desire, but without confusion or excesses and kept apart by the opposition of their natures. Once Aphrodite is born, Himeros (desire) and Eros become aspects of this goddess, who will thenceforth preside over sexual union, which is given as the necessary condition for all normal procreation. Older than Aphrodite, to whom he adapts and associates himself when the time comes, Eros represents a generative power which precedes the division of the sexes and the opposition of contraries. This is a primordial Eros like that of the Orphics—in the sense that he expresses the power of renewal that is at work in the process of genesis itself, in the movement that first incites Chaos and Gaea to emerge successively into being and then, as soon as they are born, to produce from themselves something other than themselves which, though an extension of them, places itself in opposition to them—something that is at once their reflection and their opposite. Thus a world comes into being in which there exist, associated and in confrontation, partners who will endow genesis, as it develops, with a dramatic course composed of marriages, procreation, rivalries between successive generations, alliances and hostilities, battles, defeats, and victories.

But before the cosmogonic poem opens into the account of the great divine deed, it is necessary for Gaea, through her power of childbirth, to complete the production of all that is still lacking in the world in order to make it truly a universe. Gaea first gives birth to the starry Sky (*Ouranos asteroeis*); she makes him "equal to herself" so that he may cover and envelop her on all sides (126–27). This doubling of Gaea places before her a masculine partner who in turn appears, like Earth herself and like Chaos, stretched between the dark and the bright: he is the dark sky of night, but one which is constellated with stars. This double aspect answers to the role Sky will be led to play when he becomes definitively separated from Gaea: to reflect, in a light or dark form, the alternation between day and night which follow one another in the space between earth and sky. Because he is the equal of Gaea-Earth, Ouranos-Sky covers her exactly when he stretches himself over her; perhaps this equality should be understood in the sense of his enveloping her even into her depths as he extends himself around her. Whatever the case, the primitive tension between Gaping Chasm and Earth gives way to an equilibrium between Earth and Sky, whose complete symmetry makes the world an organized whole, closed in upon itself: a cosmos. The blessed gods can dwell there as in a palace in complete security (128), each in the place reserved for him. Gaea then gives birth to the high mountains, which show her affinity with the offspring Sky she has just produced. But mountains imply valleys (there

are no mountains without valleys, in the same way that there can be no chaos without earth, no earth without sky, nor darkness without light). These valleys will serve as the abode of a particular category of divinities: the Nymphs. Just as she produced the starry Sky, Gaea ends by giving birth, from herself, to her double and her liquid opposite, Pontus, the oceanic flood, whose waters are sometimes of a limpid clarity (*atrugetos*), and sometimes darkened by chaotic tempests.

Thus ends the first part of the cosmogony. Until this point the Powers which have come into being present themselves as forces or fundamental elements of nature (cf. 106–10). The theater of the world has now been set up for the entrance upon the scene of divine actors of a different sort. Gaea no longer produces them by drawing them out of herself. She unites, for love, with a masculine partner in order to create them. The change from one form of procreation to the other is comparable to the change by which Gaea is born after Chaos: in both cases, the same formula is used to express this mutation: *autar epeita*, "but next . . ." (116 and 132).

From the embrace of Ouranos, Gaea engenders three series of children: the twelve male and female Titans, the three Cyclopes, and the three Hundred-Handeds (Hecatoncheires). The Titans are made up of six boys and six girls. Kronos, the youngest and the direct rival of Zeus in the battle for the kingdom of the sky, is named separately, as the last. All the rest are as if framed on one end by Oceanus, cited as the first (immediately after the evocation of Pontus, to whom he is opposed by his double origin, celestial as well as terrestrial), on the other by Tethys, mentioned at the end of the list, just before Kronos. The first generation of the divine sons of Earth and Sky, to the extent that they already represent the whole of the cosmos, are seemingly encompassed by Oceanus and Tethys. Associated with Phoebe, the Brilliant, Coeus is undoubtedly related to the vault of the sky, as his sister and companion Phoebe is related to celestial light. Crius, who evokes superiority and supremacy, will marry a daughter of Pontus, Eurubia (375–77), Extensive Violence, and their son Pallas will beget in Styx, the Oceanid, the two Powers who, attached to the person of Zeus, will ensure his sovereignty: Kratos (Power) and Bia (Violent Strength) (385–88). Hyperion, he who goes on high, unites with his sister Thea, the Luminous or Visible One, who brings into the world the sun, the moon, and the dawn (Eos), who is the mother of the celestial bodies, the morning star, and regular winds. In certain respects, Hyperion and Thea remind one of Poros and Tecmor, in the cosmogony of Alcman. Like them, Hyperion and Thea express, in the sky, aspects of regular rotation, luminous trails, and well-defined astral configurations, which make the celestial vault a differentiated and oriented space. Iapetus uniting with Clymene, the daughter of Oceanus, is the father of a line of rebels—Atlas, Menoetius, Prometheus, and Epimetheus—all of whom are excessive in their ambition, strength, subtlety, and unpredictability. All of them act on the periphery of an order against which they revolt. The last two bring hardships to mankind in their encounters with Zeus. Themis and Mnemosyne have a greater affinity with the earth than with the sky. Themis represents that which is fixed and settled; she is an oracular power who tells the future as an already established fact. Mnemosyne, memory, the mother of the Muses (54), knows and sings the past as if it were still there. Through their marriage to Zeus, both of them bring him the total vision of time—the co-presence in his spirit of what has been and will be—that he needs to rule. Rhea, the companion of Kronos, is very close to Gaea. She is a mother, attached to her children and ready to defend them even against the

Zeus struggles with three giants. Fragment of the large frieze from the Altar of Pergamum. Berlin, Pergamum Museum. Photo Boudot-Lamotte.

father who engendered them. She is a crafty power who has, like Gaea, a sort of primordial knowledge.

The Titans are thus divided up between the earth and the sky, sometimes more to one side, sometimes more to the other. None of them is a simple physical power in the way that Ouranos and Gaea are. Yet their characters as gods are not wholly disengaged from the elementary forces. They retain certain primordial aspects, but they respond to a universe that is more complex and better organized. The Coeus-Phoebe and Hyperion-Thea pairs are more particularized and better delimited than the starry sky; Themis, Mnemosyne, and Rhea represent specific and precise aspects of Gaea. Not all the male and female Titans were to fight Zeus. Some remained neutral; others took his side to support him with the primordial powers and knowledge which he could not do without. But considered collectively as the group of divinities engendered by Ouranos and Gaea, they constitute the first generation of gods who are masters of the sky, the first gods to play a royal role. Under the guidance of Kronos, who represents and leads them, they play the role of direct adversaries of the second-generation gods, the Olympians, against whom they engage in a battle whose stake, along with sovereignty over the world, is the distribution of the rights and honors due to each divine power, that is, the definitive ordering of the universe.

Brothers of the Titans, the Cyclopes and the Hecatoncheires (Hundred-Handeds) have in common, along with their monstrous features, the brutality and violence of en-

tirely primitive beings. Quite different from the wild herdsmen of the *Odyssey*, the Cyclopes of Hesiod, with their single eye in the middle of their forehead, combine with their unparalleled strength the crafty savoir-faire and ingenious manual dexterity of skillful metallurgists (*mēchanai*, 146). Taking the raw iron that Gaea hides in her depths, they work the metal and make a useful instrument, the absolute weapon of victory: lightning. In their names, Brontes (Thundering), Steropes (Flashing), Arges (Brightening), we can hear the roar and see the brilliance of the weapon they give Zeus, which is related to the magic power of a threatening gaze.

Just as the Cyclopes confer upon Zeus in his hour of need the privilege of a supreme gaze with the flaming of his lightning eye, the Hecatoncheires lend him in decisive moments extreme strength in his arm and hand. By virtue of their prodigiously multiplying limbs, which shoot out of their shoulders with amazing suppleness, Cottus, Briareos, and Gyges (or Gyes) are invincible fighters, warriors who possess the secret of an irresistible grip and are capable of seizing any enemy in their terrible hands.

With the triple lineage of Ouranos and of Gaea, the actors who will play out the last episode of the cosmogonic process are in place. Ouranos, in the simplicity of his primitive power, knows of no activity other than that of sexuality. Sprawled over Gaea, he covers her with his whole body and pours himself into her ceaselessly, in an eternal night. This constant amorous overflow makes Ouranos the one who "hides"; he hides Gaea, spreading himself over her; he hides his children in the very place he engendered them, in Gaea's lap, as she wails, encumbered in her depths by the burden of her progeniture. Ouranos, the parent, blocks the course of the generations by impeding his children from acceding to light, just as he hinders the day from alternating with the night. Distraught with love, pressed against Gaea, and full of hatred toward his own children who might interpose themselves between her and him if they grow, he throws those he has engendered back into the darkness of the time before birth, into Gaea's very womb. The excessiveness of his disorderly sexual power immobilizes the process of genesis. No new "generation" may appear as long as this incessant engendering continues to be accomplished by Ouranos, who remains united to Gaea without pause. He leaves no room, neither a space between himself and Gaea nor a period of time in which the lineages of new divinities might be born, one after the other. The world would have remained frozen in this state if Gaea, indignant at her cramped existence, had not thought up a treacherous trick which would change the order of things. She creates steel, the white metal, makes a billhook of it, and exhorts her children to punish their father. All hesitate, trembling, except the youngest, Kronos, the Titan of audacious heart and cunning astuteness. Gaea hides him, places him in ambush; when Ouranos stretches over her in the night, Kronos cuts off his sexual organs with a stroke of the blade. This act of violence was to have decisive cosmic consequences. It forever separated the Sky from the Earth, placing it at the summit of the world as the roof of the cosmic edifice. Ouranos would no longer unite with Gaea to produce primordial beings. Space opened up, allowing the diversity of beings to take shape and find their place in the expanse of space and in time. Genesis was unblocked, and the world became peopled and organized.

Nevertheless, this liberating act is at the same time a terrible infamy, a rebellion against the Sky-Father. It is as if the cosmic order, with its hierarchies of power and the differentiations of competence among the gods, could only be instituted by means of a guilty act of violence, a treacherous trick for which a price would have to be paid. The mutilated, rejected, and impotent Ouranos brings down a curse upon his sons that institutes for all time the *lex talionis* from which Kronos, who has become the lord of the sky by virtue of his cunning audacity, will be the first to suffer. War, violence, and deception all enter onto the scene of the world with the slash of Kronos's blade. Not even Zeus will be able to suppress them, any more than Gaea could do without Chaos: the best he can do is to keep them away from the gods, relegating them to mankind when necessary.

Before the curtain falls upon this cosmogonic part of Hesiod's poem and the stage is set for the great divine battles for world sovereignty, two final sequences illustrate the necessary entrance of war, trickery, vengeance, punishment, and evil powers in general into the very foundation of the organized universe: the birth of Aphrodite and the children of Night.

We will begin with the birth of Aphrodite. In his left hand Kronos holds Ouranos's sexual organ, which he has sliced off with the blade he holds in his right hand. He gets rid of these immediately, throwing the bloody remains over his shoulder, without looking, so as to avert an evil fate. His effort is in vain. The drops of celestial blood fall upon Gaea, the dark earth, who receives them into her womb. The sexual organ, thrown further, falls into the liquid waves of Pontus, who carries it out to sea. Ouranos, emasculated, can no

longer reproduce; but by inseminating the Earth and the Ocean, his generative organ will fulfill the curse he brought down upon his children: that the future would avenge their infamous deed (210). On Earth, the drops of blood will bring about the birth of three groups of divine powers: those that take charge over the pursuit of vengeance, the punishment of crimes committed against one's parents (the Erinyes); and the two groups who patronize warlike enterprises, activities of combat, proofs of strength (the Giants and the Nymphs of the ash trees, Meliai). After a long gestation in the womb of Gaea (184), these Powers, in the course of a thenceforth unimpeded time, will mature; they will deploy themselves over the world on the day when Zeus becomes capable of avenging Ouranos (493) by forcing Kronos to pay "the debt due to the Erinyes for his father" (472); at this time a merciless battle will be unleashed upon the divine world, a test of power that will divide it against itself.

Carried for a long time on the moving waves of the Ocean, the amputated sexual organ of Ouranos mixes the foam of the sperm that sprang from his flesh with the foam of the surrounding sea. From this foam (*aphros*) is born a girl whom gods and men call Aphrodite. From the moment she sets foot upon Cyprus, where she first touches land, love and desire (Eros, Himeros) make up her retinue. Her share among mortals and immortals lies in the prattle of young girls, smiles, deceptions (*exapatai*), pleasure, and amorous union (*philotēs*).

The castration of Ouranos thus engenders, on Earth and in the Ocean, two sets of consequences which are inseparable in their opposition. On the one hand, violence, hatred, war; on the other, sweetness, harmony, love. This necessary complementarity of the powers of conflict and the powers of unity, both issued from the sexual organ of Ouranos, first makes its mark in the system of the procreations inaugurated by the mutilation of the god. When Ouranos united with Gaea in an indefinitely repeated embrace, the act of love—due to a lack of distance between the partners—resulted in a kind of confusion or identification between them which left no room for any of their progeniture. Henceforth, with Aphrodite, love is accomplished by the union of principles which, even in their coming together, remain distinct and opposed to each other. The opposites adjust and fit themselves to one another; but they do not fuse. As if quartered, the primordial power of Eros now operates through the differentiation of the sexes. Eros becomes associated with Eris, strife—the same Eris whom Hesiod, in *Works and Days*, would place "at the roots of the earth" (19).

The world will thus organize itself through a mixing of contrary principles, a mediation between opposites. But in this universe of mixed beings in which powers of conflict and powers of agreement are balanced, the dividing line is not placed between the good and the evil, positive and negative. The forces of war and of love both have their bright and dark aspects, their beneficial and harmful sides. The relationship of tension that holds them apart from one another is also manifested in each one of them, under the form of a polarity, of an ambiguity inherent within their own nature.

Terrifying and implacable, the Erinyes are also the indispensable auxiliaries of justice, once justice has been violated. The combative ardor of the Meliai and the Giants "of sparkling weapons and long javelins" is the same as the ardor that the Hundred-Handeds dedicate to the service of Zeus so that he will cause order to triumph. As for Aphrodite, even if she is unschooled in the violence of vengeance or the brutality of war, the cunning goddess makes use of

Birth of Aphrodite. Fragment of a three-sided relief known as the Throne of Ludovisi. Central panel. Ca. 480 B.C. Rome, Museum of the Thermae. Photo Brogi.

weapons no less effective or dangerous: the charm of smiles, the cheating chatter of women, the perilous attraction of pleasure, and all the deceptions of seduction.

We thus understand why the sequence of the children of Night immediately follows the episode of the castration of Ouranos, with the birth of the marine Aphrodite set against the terrestrial Erinyes, Giants, and Meliai—an episode which is completed with the sky god's cursing his children.

The daughter of Chaos, Night, without uniting with anyone gives birth to emanations of herself, which she draws out of her own depths—all the forces of darkness, of unhappiness, of disorder, and of privation that come to operate in the world. These entities bear witness, by their existence, to the necessary inclusion of "chaotic" elements in the very womb of the organized universe. These are the inverse of order, the price which must be paid for the emergence of a differentiated cosmos, for the precise individualization of beings and of their forms.

Without going into the details of this series of Powers which are essentially concerned with the world of men—that mixed world in which every good has its opposite, in which life and death, like day and night, are linked—we might note that, apart from Death, who, under a triple name, heads the list and is associated with Sleep and the race of Dreams, most of these entities may be sorted into two groups, which, under the heading of the dark and the chaotic, parallel the two categories of divinities that arise, through the Earth and the Ocean, from the amputated genitals of Ouranos. The

Erinyes correspond exactly to Nemesis and the Keres, implacable avenging spirits who pursue those who commit faults against gods or men, goddesses whose wrath ceases only when the guilty have been punished. The Giants and the Nymphs of the ashes are echoed, in an entirely sinister key, in odious Strife, *Eris stugerē*, along with his retinue of Skirmishes, Battles, Murders, and Massacres. Aphrodite herself, the golden Aphrodite (but there also exists a black Aphrodite, Melainis) finds, among the children of Night, the Powers that incarnate her abilities, her means of action, her divine privileges. The prattle of young girls (*parthenioi oaroi*), the deceptions (*exapatai*), the amorous union (*philotēs*) that are hers to bestow are reproduced by Night, who tailors out of the fabric of darkness the somber sorceresses named Lying Words (Pseudea), Deception (Apate), and Amorous Union (Philotes).

At the end of the cosmogonic process, the act of violence that pushed Ouranos away, opened the space between sky and earth, unblocked the passage of time, and balanced the contrary principles in procreation is also that in which the obscure primordial power of Chaos converges and apparently becomes confounded with those young gods whose birth marks the advent of a new order of the world. Through Kronos's transgression—a transgression that places rebellion and disorder at the foundation of order—the children of Night spread even into the divine world; responding to a need for vengeance, they deliver that world, still in gestation, to war and combat, trickery and deception. It will be the task of Zeus to expel this nocturnal race from the ethereal regions, exiling it from the light-filled abode of the Olympian gods, exiling it into the distance, relegating it to the world of men; just as it will be necessary for him, by ordering Poseidon to seal the Titans behind doors of bronze, to separate and isolate forever from the Cosmos the gaping and chaotic abyss of Tartarus.

J.-P.V./d.w.

BIBLIOGRAPHY

The principal texts or fragments concerning the Greek cosmogonic myths are gathered and discussed in: G. S. KIRK and J. E. RAVEN, *The Presocratic Philosophers* (Cambridge 1960), in chap. 1: "The Forerunners of Philosophical Cosmogony," pp. 8–73. See Hesiod, *Theogony,* text established and translated by P. Mazon (Paris 1947). See the commentary in Hesiod, *Theogony,* edited with Prolegomena and Commentary, by M. L. West (Oxford 1966). The scholia to this text have been published by H. FLACH, *Glossen und Scholien zu Hesiodos Theogonie* (Leipzig 1876). On aquatic cosmogonies: J. RUDHARDT, *Le thème de l'eau primordiale dans la mythologie grecque* (Bern 1971). On Hesiod's cosmogony: F. M. CORNFORD, *Principium Sapientiae: The Origins of Greek Philosophical Thought* (Oxford 1952). M. DETIENNE and J.-P. VERNANT, *Les ruses de l'intelligence: La mètis des Grecs* (Paris 1975). H. FRÄNKEL, *Dichtung und Philosophie des frühen Griechentums* (New York 1951; 2d ed., Munich 1960) = *Early Greek Poetry and Philosophy* (Oxford 1975). O. GIGON, *Der Ursprung der griechischen Philosophie von Hesiod bis Parmenides* (Basel 1945; 2d ed., 1968). G. S. KIRK, *The Nature of Greek Myths* (Harmondsworth, Great Britain, 1974), especially 113–44. P. PHILIPSSON, "Genealogie als mythische Form," *Symbolae Osloenses,* supplement 7 (1936). C. RAMNOUX, *La nuit et les enfants de la nuit* (Paris 1959). H. SCHWABL, *Hesiods Theogonie: Eine unitarische Analyse* (Vienna 1966). FR. SCHWENN, *Die Theogonie des Hesiodos* (Heidelberg 1934). M. C. STOKES, "Hesiodic and Milesian cosmogonies," *Phronesis,* 7, part 1 (1962): 1–37; 8, part 1 (1963): 1–34. J.-P. VERNANT, *Mythe et pensée chez les Grecs* (Paris 1965, 5th ed., 1974), 2:95ff.

THEOGONY AND MYTHS OF SOVEREIGNTY IN GREECE

The cosmogonic phase of Hesiod's *Theogony* ends with Kronos's mutilation of Ouranos and its consequences: the separation of sky and earth, the dawn of the new generation of the Titan gods, the appearance of the powers of conflict, vengeance, and war, and in counterpoint, the birth of Aphrodite, the mistress of amorous unions.

At this juncture, the deities who make up the universe are, first, Gaea with her lofty mountains, her underground depths, and her ultimate abyss, a Tartarian site that, like an umbilical cord, joins the cosmic edifice as a whole to the primordial chaos from which it arose. Then comes Ouranos, now immobilized at the ethereal summit of the world; from its heights, the new gods and masters of the sky can survey all that happens throughout their empire. Finally comes Pontus, the Salt Sea, an inexhaustible liquid mass in perpetual motion, defying all attempts to seize it or to impose any form on it. Pontus begets Nereus, the Old Man of the Sea, in whom dwell all the beneficial virtues and all the fluid subtlety of the waters of the seas. To her husband Nereus, Doris the Oceanid gives fifty daughters, the Nereids, who, in the image of their begetter, express such aspects of the sea as navigation, intelligent knowledge, loyalty, and justice. By contrast, in his union with Gaea, Pontus shows the reverse side of the sea, namely, its absence of form. From this union springs a line of monstrous hybrids, half men, half serpents, bird-women, elusive, swift, and violent as the winds.

Henceforth, the children of Ouranos and Gaea occupy center stage, especially the youngest, boldest, and wiliest among them, the shrewd and cunning Kronos. By withdrawing from Gaea, Ouranos leaves the field free for them. They are no longer stuck in the entrails of the earth. Each finds his place, pairs with one of his sisters, or chooses a mate from among cousins and nieces, thus establishing between the lineages of Gaea, Ouranos, and Pontus a series of alliances that weave a tightly knit network of connections joining one cosmic realm to another. Oceanus and Tethys produce all the nourishing, life-giving waters in the form of rivers, spring-heads, and underground streams. Hyperion and Thea beget Helios (Sun), Selene (Moon), Eos (Dawn), all three heavenly, luminous, and regular powers. Coeus and Phoebe have two daughters: the first, the gentle Leto, will give Apollo and Artemis to Zeus; the second, Asteria, is the mother of Hecate, who in Hesiod's eyes occupies a place apart in the divine scheme of things. She exerts power over land and sea as well as in the sky. Her honors and privileges, unanimously recognized by the gods, will never be questioned by either camp in the course of the great war in which the children of Ouranos will confront the children of Kronos. Hecate takes her place on the sidelines and above the fray in the conflict between the Titans and the Olympians. To these three initial brother-sister couples we must add two Titans: Iapetus, whose union with the Oceanid Clymene results in the birth of a line of rebels; and Crius, who mates with Pontus's daughter, Eurubia, and begets sons endowed with superior strength and uprightness in action—Astraeus, the father of the regular winds, through his union with Eos; Perses, husband of Asteria and father of Hecate; Pallas, to whom the Oceanid Styx gives Kratos and Bia, Power and Force, both of whom will someday take their places at Zeus's side. Two female Titans in turn marry males other than their own brothers—Themis and Mnemosyne. Lying with Zeus, Themis gives birth to the Horai (Seasons) and the Moirai (Fates), while Mnemosyne begets the *Mousai* (Muses). The last Titan couple is that of Kronos and his sister Rhea. On the instigation of his mother Gaea, Kronos alone among all his brothers has the courage to castrate Ouranos. He thus not only conquers freedom, but with the consent and support of the other Titans he becomes master of a universe at long last duly constituted, the ruler of the world, and the king of the gods. According to the Hesiodic tradition, Kronos is the first monarch, and as such quite different from his father, Ouranos. The problems he has to confront are quite different, too. Ouranos indulged his carnal appetites recklessly and could see no farther than Gaea's pudenda. Kronos is not a power overflowing with excessive vitality like his father. He is a violent, underhanded, and suspicious prince, always on the alert, constantly on guard. Ruling over a diverse, hierarchical empire, he is concerned and anxious about his supremacy. The exploit—born of daring and treachery—that opened the

Zeus and Kronos. Pediment of the Temple of Artemis at Corfu. Detail. Late seventh century B.C. Photo D.A.I. Athens.

If establishing supremacy by a show of force involves an injustice toward another and a constraint imposed by a mixture of brutality and ruse, the struggle for domination is likely to be repeated and to reemerge with each new generation, so that sovereign power will forever be caught in the cogwheels of crime and punishment that Kronos set in motion when he seized power for himself by mutilating Ouranos. This being the case, the order of the world established by each ruler of the gods upon his accession to power is in constant jeopardy. Such is the problem addressed by the account of the war of the gods and the victory of Zeus.

Rhea has six children by Kronos: Hestia, Demeter, Hera, Hades, Poseidon, and the youngest, Zeus *mētioeis*, Zeus the cunning. No sooner has she delivered a child than Kronos, who stands watch over her, seizes the baby and devours it. Ouranos forced his offspring back into Gaea's womb. Forewarned by his parents that he would someday meet his fate by succumbing to his own son, Kronos shuts his own descendants inside himself for greater security. Violent and cunning as he is, however, the First Ruler meets his match in someone stronger and shrewder than he. In concert with Gaea and Ouranos, Rhea hatches a clever plot, a *mētis*, to let Zeus, the last of her offspring, escape the fate of his predecessors. Rhea's secret maneuvers escape her husband's watchful eye. She gives birth clandestinely, hides her son in Crete, and wraps a stone in swaddling clothes. She offers what looks like a newborn child to the voracious but unsuspecting Kronos. The shrewd, clever First Ruler is thus tricked by his own wife and her parents, making it possible for the last-born to stay alive, unbeknownst to his father, and soon to force him off the throne and to rule over the immortals in his place (ibid. 489–91).

Wily intelligence and alert shrewdness (*mētis*) are necessary weapons for a god who seeks to ensure for himself victory and control over others, whatever the prevailing circumstances or conditions of the struggle and whatever the power of his adversary. This theme winds like a red thread all through the complex fabric of the Greek myths of sovereignty. It would seem that only superior *mētis* can bestow on a supremacy the two features that can make it a true sovereign power, namely, universality and permanence. The king of heaven must have available to him, over and beyond sheer brute force, a nimble intelligence to anticipate as far ahead as possible, to lay the ground for future action, prudently to contrive the means and ends in such minute detail that when it is time to act there are no risks. Thus the future holds no surprises, as no one and nothing can catch the god off guard or come upon him when he is unarmed.

The competition between Kronos and Zeus, between Titans and Olympians, is enacted on the battleground in a show of force, but the secret of success lies elsewhere. As Aeschylus states in *Prometheus*, victory was to go "to him who would win not by force and violence but by ruse" (*Prometheus Bound* 212–13). Within the perspective of tragedy, Prometheus, the *aiolomētis*, the prodigious schemer, "capable of finding his way out of even the most inextricable predicaments," the resourceful disentangler, is the one who employs against Zeus the very stratagem that his side needs. In Hesiod's version, Zeus's rise to power from the very beginning comes under the rubric of shrewdness, skill, and deceit. His triumph is ensured by his first marriage to the Oceanid Metis, the changeable and wily goddess, patroness of good advice.

In the *Bibliotheca* of Pseudo-Apollodorus, Metis is the one who serves Kronos the potion (*pharmakon*) that forces him to vomit up the stone that he had swallowed thinking it was

path to power for him also inaugurated among the gods the history of the avatars of sovereignty. The question at the core of the cosmogonic myths is that of the connections between disorder and order. With the establishment of the first king of heaven and the ensuing struggles for divine hegemony, the problem is displaced. Henceforth, the stress is on the connections between order and power.

The sexual excesses of Ouranos block the course of genesis by obstructing the birth of his children. Kronos's behavior toward his children, though no more tender, is motivated by strictly "political" considerations: he tries to prevent one of his sons from taking over from him "the royal honor among the immortals" (Hesiod, *Theogony* 461–62). A myth of succession to power is substituted for the narrative of a genesis. Even if he is divine, the monarch may not be able to avoid the gradual erosion and aging of his authority as the years go by. Kronos hoists himself onto the throne by attacking his father. Because the sovereign rule that he founds is based on an act of violence, an act of treason against his "elder" who hated him, will he not have to suffer at the hands of his son the same treatment that he inflicted upon his father?

Zeus, and with it all the rest of Zeus's brothers and sisters, who would support the Olympian in his struggle against the Titans. In Hesiod, Metis is not referred to by name. There is merely a plot hatched at the instigation of Gaea and designed to make Kronos regurgitate his entire progeny.

Freed from their father's stomach, the junior line of the Kronides marshals its forces on Mount Olympus facing the Titans perched on top of Mount Orthrys. War breaks out and continues indecisively for ten years. Gaea finally reveals to Zeus how he can achieve victory. He must avail himself of the thundering weapon in the possession of the skillful Cyclopes and engage the terrible Hundred-Handeds, with their unparalleled strength, as allies in the battle. In other words, the defeat of the Titans is achieved by rallying to the cause of the new gods certain deities who are related to the old gods through their parentage, nature, and age. Zeus has no hope of winning unless he gets the support of Powers that embody the same original vitality, the same primordial cosmic vigor that he takes pains to control as he subdues the Titans. To establish order, one needs a power capable of imposing itself on the forces of disorder. But if it is to prevail, what sources of energy can this regulatory power feed on other than the very same sources that originally nourished the dynamic powers of disorder?

The Cyclopes and the Hundred-handeds, brothers of the Titans, thus play the part of renegades and come over to the Olympian camp. They are sorely needed. Since they possess the absolute weapon, the thunderbolt, and have an attack that cannot be parried, as well as bonds that cannot be broken, they are indispensable allies in the maintaining of sovereignty. To justify their rallying around Zeus, the myth tells us that after they are separated from their jailer and father, Ouranos, Kronos leaves them, or places them once

more, in a state of servitude from which Zeus alone is able to free them. No sooner does he free them from their chains than the Olympians offer the Hundred-handeds nectar and ambrosia, thus assuring their full accession to the honors of divine status. In recognition of these benefits, the Cyclopes and the Hundred-handeds place at the disposition of Zeus a skill and strength akin to those of the two cosmic entities from which they are descended. Henceforth, they no longer play the role of primordial monsters, but of the faithful guards of Zeus. Similarly, Kratos and Bia, Power and Violent Force, children of the Styx, on the advice of the elder Oceanus, their ancestor, are the first to rush to Mount Olympus with their mother to enter into the service of Zeus, whom they will never again leave for a single moment (ibid. 385ff.).

Everything is now going to be played out rapidly. The Titans are struck by Zeus's thunderbolt and buried under stones by the Hundred-handeds, who usher them off in chains to the misty Tartarus; there Poseidon locks them up behind bronze doors in front of which the three Hundred-handeds stand guard in the name of Zeus.

This time matters seem settled. But Gaea couples with Tartarus and gives birth to the last of her offspring, Typhon or Typheus, a monster with powerful arms, tireless legs, and a hundred serpent heads with eyes flashing fire. This monster, whose highly modulated voice sounds at times like the gods, at times like wild animals, and at times like the forces of nature, embodies the elemental power of disorder. The last of the children of Gaea, he represents within the organized world a return to the primordial chaos to which all things would revert if he were to triumph. But the victory of the chaotic monster does not come to pass. His many eyes of fire can do nothing against the vigilant gaze of Zeus, who

Zeus and Typhon in combat. Ca. 530 B.C. Chalcidian hydria. Munich, Staatliche Antikensammlungen. Photo Koppermann.

does not get caught by surprise, notices him first, and strikes him with a thunderbolt. The Olympian hurls Typhon to Tartarus. His sloughed skin emits storm winds, impetuous and unpredictable, which, unlike the regular gusts born of Aurora and Astraeus, burst out in squalls from one side and the other, exposing human living space to the arbitrariness of pure disorder.

In Hesiod, the defeat of Typhon marks the end of the struggles for sovereignty. The Olympians urge Zeus to take the power and throne of the Immortals. The new king of the gods, their second sovereign, then distributes honors and privileges among them. His rule follows that of the deposed Kronos, but does not duplicate it; rather, it redresses it. Zeus combines in his person the highest power and a scrupulous respect for justice. His sovereignty reconciles superiority of strength and the precise distribution of honors, the violence of war and the honoring of binding agreements, physical vigor and all the forms of intellectual shrewdness. Order and power, associated in his reign, are henceforth inseparable.

Another tradition, which has a particularly strong echo in Pseudo-Apollodorus, added a chapter to the history of the battles for the sovereignty of the sky. The Olympians must still brave an assault by the Giants, who represent an order, that of fighters; an age group, that of young men in the flower of their virility; and a function, war. At the start of the battle, the status of the Giants seems equivocal. Will defeat deliver them to death or will success make them attain divine immortality? Zeus is warned that to triumph over them he will need a lesser being: the Giants will have to die at the hands of a mortal. Heracles, who has not yet been deified, is elected. In the meantime, Earth, the mother of the Giants, prepares a countermeasure. She seeks out an herb of immortality that will preserve her sons. Here again, Zeus's foresight thwarts his adversary's schemes. Using tricks to keep one step ahead of Earth, he himself picks the herb of nondeath. No force can ever again prevent the Giants from perishing and the warrior function from submitting to a sovereignty that it has the duty to support unconditionally.

The account of the struggle against Typhon was itself embellished to dramatize the perils of sovereignty and to underscore the role of cunning in the exercise of sovereignty. In Pseudo-Apollodorus, Typhon takes the advantage in his first fight with his royal adversary; he disarms him, cuts the sinews in his arms and legs, and delivers him paralyzed into the custody of a serpent-woman known as Delphyne. The day is saved by two crafty accomplices, the shrewd Hermes assisted by Aegipan. Unseen by anyone, they spirit away Zeus's sinews and put them back in place. The combat is resumed. It would have remained undecided were it not for a second deceit, worked by the Moirai, which got the better of the monster's strength. The daughters of Zeus persuade Typhon to swallow what they claim to be a drug of invincibility. Far from bringing him a fresh surge of energy, however, this *pharmakon* is an ''ephemeral'' food that one cannot taste without experiencing, as men do, fatigue, the exhaustion of strength, and death.

In the *Dionysiaca* of Nonnus, Typhon, a candidate for the sovereignty of disorder, succeeds in laying his hands on Zeus's thunderbolts and sinews. Bewildered, the gods abandon heaven. Zeus and Eros then devise a crafty plan for the ingenious Cadmus to carry out with the help of Pan. In order to fool the powerful brute, Cadmus puts Typhon's violence

to sleep with the sound of his flute. Typhon is beguiled and wants to make the young man the official singer of his realm. Cadmus asks for the sinews taken from Zeus to string his lyre. The music lulls the monster into a deep sleep, allowing Zeus to retrieve his sinews and his thunderbolt. When Typhon wakes up, it is too late. Zeus envelops his enemy in the burning glow of his thunderbolt.

These late developments of the myth are not gratuitous. With a rather baroque fantasy, they illustrate a theme already prominent in Hesiod, the marriage of Zeus and Metis. In the *Theogony*, no sooner is Zeus promoted to the rank of king of the gods than he takes as his first wife Metis, the daughter of Oceanus, a goddess "who knows more than any god or mortal." This union merely recognizes the service that has been rendered him by the wily intelligence that brought him to the throne. It illustrates the need for Metis in the founding of a sovereign rule which can be neither overcome nor exercised nor preserved without her. Since they inherit from their mother the same kind of cunning that characterizes her, the sons of the goddess could not fail to be invincible and to overthrow their father. Thus, through the very marriage that consecrated him as king of the gods, Zeus sees himself threatened by the same fate that befell the previous ruler, namely, to succumb to his own son. But Zeus is not like other rulers. When Kronos swallowed his children, he left untouched, outside of himself, powers of cunning superior to his own. Zeus goes to the root of the danger. He fights Metis with her own weapons: cunning, deceit, and surprise. Fooling her with tender words, he swallows her before she has a chance to give birth to Athena so as to prevent her from going on to bear a son who might be fated to become the ruler of men and gods. By marrying, subduing, and swallowing Metis, Zeus becomes more than a mere monarch. He is now sovereignty itself. Because the goddess, deep within his entrails, warns him of everything that is to happen to him, Zeus is no longer simply a crafty god like Kronos; he is the *mētieta*, the all-wily god. Nothing can now surprise him, escape his vigilance, thwart his designs. He no longer experiences the distance between a project and its fulfillment that subjects other gods to the ambushes of the unexpected. Sovereignty ceases to be the stake of an ever renewed contest. In the person of Zeus, it has become stable and permanent. Order is not merely founded by the supreme power that distributes honors. It is established once and for all.

The dark powers of vengeance, war, and fraud, widespread in the divine world through the transgression of Kronos, no longer have their place. If an occasional quarrel should arise between deities, and one of them, transgressing in his turn, should perjure himself with a false oath, that deity is immediately expelled from the company of the gods through the quasi-juridical process that Zeus instituted with the waters of the Styx, is banished from the gods' councils and banquets, and is deprived of nectar and ambrosia. Under the reign of Zeus, any god guilty of mixing with one of the Children of Night, even for a moment, is immediately exiled—a punishment similar to that of the Titans, who were cast to the ends of the world, to the borders of the Gaping Chasm, where the cosmos accommodates itself to Chaos and secures itself firmly against it.

J.-P. V./g.h.

DEITIES OF WATER IN GREEK MYTHOLOGY

Numerous divinities in Greece were associated with fresh water and the sea. Of diverse natures and unequal importance, these gods were undoubtedly of different prehistoric origins, and many of them continue to be connected with local traditions. Whatever their origin, mythology nonetheless establishes certain bonds of kinship between them, connecting them with other gods and integrating them within the systems in which all divine and cosmic entities find their place.

I. Oceanus, Father of the Gods, and Tethys

The *Iliad* preserves traces of one of these gods; though fragmentary and sporadic, numerous texts show his importance in Greek thought and his persistence in the literature until the imperial era. Even though he underwent several variations, his principal characteristics can be outlined as follows.

Oceanus, the father of the gods, the generating force of all beings, is connected with Tethys, their mother. This ancestral couple symbolizes both the state of things before the first events of the cosmogony and the drive or principle of the long process which will take place within the cosmogony.

Oceanus is a powerful river, with a tumultuous course, which is still unconfined, in an amorphous space in which there is neither sky nor earth; he is also a male being, endowed with life, feelings, and moral qualities that several of his daughters will also exhibit. Tethys is a mass of water that cannot be distinguished from the course of Oceanus itself, but she is female, equally animated and personal. United to one another, they give birth to innumerable children. The complex character of the primordial substance is thus evoked through heterogeneous images. Fluid and without precise boundaries, yet dynamic and moving, this substance carries life within it; as a flowing mass, poorly defined but animated, it includes, together with the duality of masculine and feminine, an inexhaustible fecundity and, in a potential way, all the plurality that will spread throughout the universe. Though precosmic, it is already divine.

Just as these disparate images symbolize primordial reality, the development of the cosmogonic process is evoked in two complementary ways: through anthropomorphic or biological images and through physical or material images.

Oceanus and Tethys unite; they have children, then countless descendants. The cosmogony thus reveals one aspect of a genealogy. Scattered hints in the fourteenth book of the *Iliad* and the evidence of later authors allow us to reconstruct the broad outlines of this genealogy with some plausibility. Oceanus and Tethys give birth to Ouranos and Gaea, who in turn give birth to the Titans, and two of the Titans give birth to the Kronides, according to the theogonic plan most current in Greece. But Ouranos and Gaea were not the only children of the ancestral couple; they also produced springs and rivers, all the waters which irrigate the Earth, as well as those which circulate in the underworld; among the Oceanids are Europa and Asia; there are also divinities of wealth or abundance and, according to certain traditions, goddesses who influence destinies.

Several texts concerning the location of Oceanus in the completed world suggest another view of the cosmogonic event. Sky and Earth came from the primordial waters; water therefore exists outside the newly formed universe, sur-

Heracles fighting Achelous. Attic stamnos. Ca. 500 B.C. London, British Museum. Museum photo.

rounding it and forming its boundary. Despite this distance, Oceanus feeds all the springs and rivers through subterranean routes; the rivers flow into the sea, whose waves finally rejoin his own. With the vast expanses of water, he therefore produces the very regions they define—he is truly the father of the continents.

The remoteness of Oceanus and Tethys is signified by the flowing image just described. Oceanus rolls his tumultuous waves to the ends of the earth and the limit of nothingness. His course is circular, so that his waters constantly pass over the same bed. A particular place does exist, however, where the oceanic waters undergo a transition between their point of arrival and the point at which they take on a new spirit. Several texts call this mysterious region "the springs of Oceanus" and situate it in the east, where the sun rises.

The same remoteness is evoked in other language. Oceanus and Tethys are a very old couple; they live at the ends of the earth, in a distant palace where their ardor has cooled; they have long since ceased to couple; their generative role is finished. We must note that Oceanus thus keeps himself apart from the great conflicts which pit the gods against one another; he does not participate in the overthrow of Ouranos or in the war of the Olympians against the Titans, though several of his daughters do take Zeus's side, perhaps on his advice.

The same being from whom all things take their existence thus also constitutes their limit; the universe is not plunged into pure nothingness; it bathes, so to speak, in its own principle. This original principle developed all its potentialities in the production of the world; however, though it may no longer exercise the same cosmogonic function it once had, it retains its ancient virtues, indispensable to the life of the cosmos.

At the ends of the world, the oceanic waters have a cathartic and regenerative power. With the exception of the Great Bear, forbidden as a punishment, the sun and all the stars dive into these waters at their setting; later they reemerge (the sun after purifying itself at the eastern springs), endowed with new vigor and sparkle. Two marvelous islands bathe in these waters. One is inhabited by the blessed who escape ordinary death; they are constantly given life by the ocean breezes. On the other island is the nuptial chamber of Zeus and Hera, closely connected with the source of ambrosia. The divine marriage is an act of fecundity, and ambrosia, which comes from a spring on this oceanic island, regenerates to the point of bestowing immortality itself.

By the springs that he feeds, and by the rivers, his sons, the waters of Oceanus penetrate to the interior of the lands that they water and fertilize; they make life there possible. They are also responsible for abundance; the ancestral god is clearly the father of the gift-givers Eurynome, Polydora, and Eudora, as well as the father of the rich Pluto.

Finally, beneath the earth, the tenth part of his waters flows into the river Styx, the most prestigious of his children. The waves of the Styx retain their oceanic qualities more than any other river. Their regenerative powers are such that Thetis immerses Achilles in them to make him immortal; they exert an effect similar to that of ambrosia. In addition they are the instrument of the greatest oaths sworn by the gods. In invoking Styx to witness their commitments, the gods stake the bond that unites them to the original principle from which they draw their existence and vitality. If he breaks this bond, the lying god no longer receives ambrosia; he remains inert for nine years; separated from his source, he is deprived of the vigor which makes possible his very divinity.

Though all gods are descendants of Oceanus, the youngest find themselves separated from him by many generations. Some, however, among those most active in the current world and those most present in worship become closer to him by marrying one of his daughters. Such is the case with Zeus, who unites with Dione, Eurynome, and especially Metis. Metis, "who knows more than any of the gods or mortal men," makes explicit certain components of the ancient ancestor's wisdom, as do her sisters Idyia and Peitho. She retains a part of her generative power; she will in fact be able to give birth to a son more powerful than Zeus. For this reason, Zeus the son of Kronos swallows her, integrating the powers of the Oceanid into his own being.

II. The System of Hesiod: Gaea, Pontus

The system just outlined is clearly not the only one into which the Greeks attempted to integrate all of their myths. As early as the eighth century, the Hesiodic theogony presented a different system. The principal divinities that Hesiod treats are those we have already met; he attributes to them the characteristics and acts by which they are commonly known throughout the tradition, but he arranges them in an original way. Hesiod makes the earth the primary substance, in accordance no doubt with an ancient teaching, concurrent with the one which attributes this original function to water.

As a primordial entity, the Earth (Gaea) exists before all things in the gaping chasm of Chaos, along with Eros, the immanent principle of desire and generation and the future operating force of the cosmogony, who nevertheless will have no descendants. Gaea draws out of herself Ouranos, the sky, and Pontus, the expanse of ocean, and these will hereafter form her boundaries.

The word *pontos* is a common noun designating the sea; it is applied to a god in the Hesiodic works, although this god does not play an important part in the myths, except at this level of the cosmogony. Even during this decisive phase, he is a masculine principle with no clearly defined personality; he is the vast ocean where nothing grows. Gaea unites with him, as she did with Ouranos, and all beings come from these two primordial couples: Ouranos-Gaea, Pontus-Gaea; but there is a strange dissymmetry between the two lines.

The first is innumerable, and includes the sovereign gods as well as most of the gods who will influence the lives of men and be the objects of their worship; the second, less rich, includes minor gods and monsters.

In attributing the principal place to Gaea, Hesiod must make Oceanus and Tethys appear at a later stage in the theogony. He does not situate them in the line of Pontus—for these are river gods and not sea gods, and their excessive fertility would probably be misplaced—but in the line of Ouranos, among the Titans. Other traditions, however, have so clearly molded the shape of these two gods that they do not fit well into the group of the first Ouranides. They have a better-defined personality than their brothers and sisters, a cosmic reality more easily grasped and a more numerous progeny. Furthermore, Oceanus does not appear to participate in the battle of the Titans, for he is not thrown into the Tartarus with the conquered gods but continues to roll his waves around the earth.

There are several marine creatures among the immediate descendants of Pontus. We will here mention only Ceto and the powerful Phorcys. Their personalities are not clearly drawn in the *Theogony*, but in other texts Phorcys is an old man of the sea. He therefore resembles his brother Nereus, one of the most famous children of Pontus in the Hesiodic genealogy. Several traits distinguish Nereus from his father. He is not conflated with the sea itself as Pontus is, but lives in its depths and moves within it; he also possesses a more clearly defined personality as an old man filled with wisdom. In retrospect, although he is a marine god rather than a river god, he somewhat resembles Oceanus, whose daughter, Doris, he marries. Like Oceanus, he is old and respected; like him, he has many daughters. Certainly the progeny of Oceanus are more varied and extensive, but many of his daughters are so close to those of Nereus that Greek traditions sometimes consider them Oceanids, sometimes Nereids. In both families, there are gods whose names refer to the knowledge or wisdom of their father and a great number of goddesses who are difficult to distinguish from one another, all closely linked with the life of the waters. Young and gracious, these goddesses play in the sea, bounding among the waves; poetry and monuments depict them in association with the Tritons and with the Hippocampi.

III. Poseidon

Followed by Hesiod and Homer, a general tradition in Greece attributes the function of god of the seas to Poseidon, although he is a god of many powers, wider-ranging than a simple marine deity. The origin of this complexity has been sought in prehistoric times, and it has been shown that the attributes of several ancient divinities were probably based upon his personality. Here we shall merely indicate how his different characteristics were coordinated in Greek thought during the historic era.

Poseidon is a son of Kronos, a grandson of Ouranos; but the progeny of Ouranos also belong to Gaea. Though the attributes and powers of Gaea are most evident in her female descendants, notably in Rhea and Demeter, they are also partially transmitted through her male descendants. Kronos himself retains certain affinities with the maternal earth; these continue to survive in other forms in Rhea's son, Poseidon.

Many epithets link Poseidon closely with the earth; a plausible etymology would make him the lord or husband of the earth. Certainly the authority he exerts on earth is not unlimited; his powers are clearly defined, as befits a god of his generation. He manifests himself most often as the "earth shaker"; he is the author of earthquakes and their rumblings, just as, in the sky, Zeus is the source of lightning and thunder: the adjective *baruktupos* applies to both of them. Perhaps the myths which make him a builder of walls signify the protective action expected of someone whose anger destroys human constructions by earthquakes. But Poseidon has other links with the earth as well; though he is not exactly a god of vegetation, he is no stranger to the fertility of the soil. Sometimes called Phytalmius, he is associated with several agricultural festivals.

He is also closely associated with horses; he fathers several horselike creatures, and is invoked as Hippius, the protector of horsemen. The horse and the earth are related—Earth gave birth to Sciphius, the very first horse, when she was impregnated by the seed of Poseidon. According to the ancient myths, the god Hippius fell in love with the earthly Demeter; in order to escape him, she metamorphosed herself into a mare. He in turn took the form of a stallion, coupled with her, and gave her two children—the horse Areion and a daughter whose true name may not be spoken. This daughter is honored with her mother in several mystery cults in Arcadia. The union of Poseidon and Demeter thus mirrors the union of Zeus and Demeter; the Arcadian daughter of Poseidon resembles the Eleusinian Persephone, and is called Despoina, "Mistress" or "Young Lady," just as Persephone's common name is Kore, "Young Woman."

These different characteristics are coherent. They fit one of the Kronides, the brother of Zeus, to whom Poseidon bears a certain resemblance. According to minor traditions, Poseidon escapes the voracity of his father thanks to a substitute that Kronos swallowed; the well-known substitute for Zeus was a swaddled stone; for Poseidon it was a colt. According to other, later traditions, he was raised by the Telchines, as Zeus was raised by the Curetes. As an adult he brandishes a trident, while Zeus has a thunderbolt. Poseidon retains certain virtues inherited from his ancestor Gaea, while Ouranian virtues predominate in Zeus, but the two brothers have many characteristics in common: notably, their father's ambition and his will to dominate. This is why conflicts can put the two brothers on opposite sides; Poseidon has difficulty in accepting the authority of Zeus; he is often hostile to him; once he even tries to put him in chains.

How is it, then, that Zeus predominates and that the earthly Poseidon also becomes a sea god?

The heritage of Kronos included sovereignty. Although his role in the battle of the Titans may have prepared Zeus to rule among the gods, the transmission of this heritage posed a problem. The great division of the earth mentioned in the *Iliad* and several other texts resolved it. Three different domains were assigned to the sons of Kronos: the sky to Zeus, the infernal world to Hades, and the sea to Poseidon; the earth and Olympus, however, remained common to the gods. One must not misunderstand the significance of this division: it does not define all the powers of the three gods, nor does it put them at the same level. The Kronides and the other gods had distinct personalities and traits before it took place. We know which affinities united Poseidon with the earth; those that connected Zeus to the sky were especially attested by the thunderbolt that he received from the Cyclopes, at the beginning of the battle with the Titans. The division of space between the three Kronides did not alter the qualities and functions which already defined them; it was simply a distribution of the sovereign power previously held by Kronos, or, more precisely, a delimitation of the areas where each god would exercise that sovereign power in an immediate way. In addition, contrary to what Poseidon insinuates in a moment of revolt according to the *Iliad*, the division was not equal. There is a strong link between the sky and sovereignty, which is transmitted in the lineage of Ouranos; celestial lightning is a symbol and the instrument of power. He who receives sovereignty over the sky receives by that very fact an authority superior to that of all the other gods. Zeus took the initiative in the revolt against Kronos and received the definitive weapon in the form of lightning; after their victory, the gods recognized his preeminence. Though Hades and Poseidon are masters of their own domains, they nonetheless owe Zeus their obedience. Olympus remains common to the gods, as they participate in the Olympian assembly, but Zeus presides. In addition, on earth, which is also held in common, many of them also exercise particular functions, in accordance with their respective natures as defined throughout the theogony; this was particularly the case with Demeter and Poseidon.

Not everything was arranged, however. On earth, the cities of men would create privileged relationships with certain gods to whom they would consecrate their principal cults. The gods fought among themselves to obtain such prerogatives. Poseidon was most often disappointed in these contests. Two famous examples: Argos prefers Hera to him, by the judgment of Phoroneus; by the judgment of Cecrops, Athens prefers Athena. Thus he fails to gain first place in the worship of the cities of his choice; nonetheless, by virtue of that choice he retains an important role and influence in them, as some of his descendants, such as Theseus in Athens, can confirm.

In brief, the function that Poseidon exercises in the domain of the sea is based on the divisions of the heritage that devolved upon the three sons of Kronos. Without losing the competences and virtues he already possesses, Poseidon thus becomes king of the seas. Though many gods live in the ocean and act there freely, as we have seen, they do not hold power: this is transmitted solely through the line of Ouranos, royalty belonging more precisely to Kronos and then to his sons. The sea world is thus organized as follows. All the seas are in communication with the distant course of Oceanus, who feeds the springs and the rivers by means of subterranean channels. Their salt expanse is invoked in the name of Pontus. Powerful creatures, like Phorcys or Ceto, live in their depths, as well as the wise old man, Nereus. Oceanids and Nereids move about, sometimes on the crest of the rolling waves or, near the shore, in the surf. The existence of all these divinities, the life of the sea, and the destiny of the men who cross it are subject to the authority of Poseidon—whose trident symbolizes his power. Husband of the Oceanid or the Nereid Amphitrite, he lives with her in a palace at the bottom of the sea. When he arrives in his chariot, the sea creatures welcome him as their master.

Unhappy rival of Zeus, kept out of first place in the worship of many cities, Poseidon is an irritable god. In the sea world over which he reigns, his wrath unleashes tempests; thus he diverts Odysseus from the route to Ithaca by stirring up waves. Navigators pray for his goodwill and make efforts to appease him. In the same way, fishermen of the high seas, in particular the tuna fishermen, consecrate offerings to him.

His violence can also be seen in the effect he has on the creatures that he sometimes causes to arise out of the waves. A monster that he incites in this way is responsible for ravaging the Troad. The bulls that he causes to come out from the waves cause many catastrophes and dramas, like the bull who causes the death of Hippolytus or the one who engenders the Minotaur and terrorizes Crete before being captured by Heracles. When associated with Zeus and with Ouranian virtues, the power of the bull is positive; but it seems negative when connected with the sea and Poseidon. By contrast, the generative power of Poseidon is manifested in equine form in his relationship with the earth.

As an antagonist of Athena, Poseidon caused salt water to appear on the Acropolis in Athens by striking the rock with his trident. He thus manifested his dual role as earthshaker and ruler of the seas; but it is probably by virtue of his earthly functions rather than his maritime sovereignty that he used his trident similarly to cause springs to flow in other places. The maker of earthquakes creates openings in the ground through which fresh water may flow from its depths. His power is communicated to certain of his equine sons, whose hooves produce the same effect. The god of earthquakes is also capable of closing these openings; he dried up the springs of Argolis and caused a drought in order to punish Argos for preferring Hera to him. Between the earthshaker and the waters there is thus a closeness which may explain why Poseidon was said to have sovereignty over the seas; in an analogous fashion, the Ouranian virtues of Zeus were preparing him to receive sovereignty over the heavens.

According to Hesiod's *Theogony*, Poseidon's son by Amphitrite was the great and powerful Triton, but Greek traditions also attribute other children to him. We know of those that Demeter gave him, according to Arcadian myths. Like other Olympians, Zeus in particular, he couples with minor deities, nymphs, and mortals, thus engendering heroes who are often eponymic of peoples or regions or figure in the royal genealogies of Greek cities; he was, for example, the father of Boeotus, Rhodus, Eumolpe, and Theseus. His descendants also include formidable and disquieting characters who manifest the sometimes destructive violence of Poseidon and his inclination to revolt; like certain monsters spawned by Pontus, they seem to reveal obscure affinities with both the son of Kronos and the ancient god of the salt waters over which he reigns. He begets the giants Antaeus and Polyphemus, such evil creatures as Cercyon, Sciron, and Lamos, as well as the Aloadae who undertake to battle with the gods. Better yet, he unites with one of the granddaughters of Pontus, the Gorgon Medusa, with whom he engenders Pegasus and Chrysaor; Chrysaor in turn will become the father of Geryon, the three-headed monster, and of the terrible Echidna.

While the distribution of regions between the three sons of Kronos delimits the domains in which each exercises his part of the paternal sovereignty, there are several indications that lead us to believe that this distribution was not arbitrary; it seems to have been made in consideration of the qualities which these gods respectively acquired in the genealogical development and in the great conflicts of the theogony. Although sovereignty over the seas was certainly given to Poseidon in this great distribution, it was directly suited to the earthly and equine god, master of earthquakes, whom we first evoked.

IV. Other Systems: Thetis, Proteus

The two systems just described resemble one another in more than one respect. They are opposed principally in the way they represent the situation at the beginning of the cosmogony: the original entity in the first is water, while in the second it is earth. The prestige of the Hesiodic *Theogony* confers on the second system a predominant place in Hellenic thought, though the image of primordial water continues to inhabit it. It is notably responsible for a new interpretation of Chaos. In accordance with its etymology, Chaos in the *Theogony* is a gaping hole; it is the still amorphous space in which the cosmogonic event will take place. From the fourth century at the latest, exegetes connecting its name with the verb *chein*, "to pour," would regard it as a fluid element, which some would not hesitate to identify with water. According to this interpretation of the Hesiodic teaching, two substantial entities, earth and water, thus existed before all others. The idea of Chaos evolved, however, in another direction. By virtue of the connection with the verb *chein*, it can be seen as a fluid mixture in which all the elements are mingled: a *sugchusis stoicheiōn*. This was to become Ovid's conception.

The idea that water or its divinities played a decisive role at the beginning of the cosmogony is also expressed in Greece in several mythic systems, but they have disappeared; we can find only a few traces of them.

A papyrus of Oxyrhynchus preserves the partially destroyed commentary of a poem by Alcman. It attributes to Thetis an essential function in the very first phases of the cosmogony, if not at the origin of all things. The nature of her intervention remains enigmatic for us, but the existence of a myth which gave her a more important role and situated her more closely to the original entities than did the *Theogony* helps us to understand two things. Thetis has a more detailed personality, and takes part in richer adventures, than the other Nereids to whom Hesiod assimilated her. In addition, like the Oceanid Metis, daughter of the primordial gods, she is destined to give birth to a son more powerful than his father.

Later texts make Proteus the firstborn god or the initial substance from which the rest of the universe emerged. It may have been his name that suggested such ideas to later authors. Proteus occupies a marginal position, fulfilling very episodic functions in Greek mythology, and his cults are local. One observation might, however, suggest other hypotheses to us.

Several traits connect Proteus with the marine gods who belong to the ancient ranks of Greek tradition. He is called "Old Man of the Sea," as were Nereus, Phorcys, Glaucus, and perhaps Triton. Like them, he haunts the depths of the ocean or approaches the coasts. He shares with Nereus the power to metamorphose himself in order to escape his adversaries. The image of an old and very wise god, closely linked with the sea in which he resides, capable of clothing himself in several forms and thus symbolizing the fluidity of the water with which he is interconnected, appears to have remained in the Hellenic mind and received different names in different places. We can see the resemblance which unites these old men with Oceanus, an old man like them and, like them, the father of gods whose names evoke wisdom, lucidity, destiny, or the knowledge of destiny. We might therefore suppose that the Old Man of the Sea, under whatever name, had at one time played a cosmogonic role comparable to that of Oceanus in the system first described here, and that later texts about Proteus still preserved the memory of this figure. It should be noted that this ancient myth differed from the myth of Oceanus on one major point: while the primordial entity is river water in the Oceanus myth, it was sea water in the other. Such hypotheses are not confirmed in the documents which have survived to our times.

Heracles wrestling with Triton. The triple Nereus. Pediment from the first Hecatompedon of Athens (sixth century B.C.). Athens, Acropolis Museum. Photo Alinari-Giraudon.

Right: Poseidon. Mid-fifth century B.C. Athens, National Museum. Photo Boudot-Lamotte.

V. Local Gods and Poorly Integrated Myths: Nymphs and River Gods

We have devoted our attention to the clearly organized mythic collections within which the deities of the waters are situated and are systematically connected with one another and with other entities; they help us to understand the different functions served by these gods in the eyes of the Greeks. Still, though mythic thought tends to organize all the figures in such groups in order to express the Hellenic understanding of the solidarity between men and things in a coherent world in which the divine is manifest, this tendency is not developed everywhere in the same way. In the presence of waters that trickled, streamed, or flowed in a region they both eroded and fertilized, the Greeks seem to have experienced their encounters with the divine power in rather precise ways; these experiences inspired the cults of local gods and were sometimes expressed in curious myths which were not at first integrated into a universal myth. Springs and brooks are frequently connected in spirit with the nymphs, just as the rivers are connected with the gods that bear their names.

Young and gracious, the water nymphs resemble the Nereids but are also associated with other nymphs who represent the valleys or groves where their waters flow, and, like them, they keep company with Hermes, Pan, or Artemis. Amorous or genealogical relationships unite them with the river gods, with the great gods, with the ancestral and eponymic heroes of certain peoples.

The river gods also have their own myths, which evoke their strength, their loves, or their angers, the bonds that unite them to the countries bathed by their waves. Local genealogies make some of the river gods the sons of Zeus or of Poseidon, but they do not abolish the universal myth which shows them all deriving from Oceanus. These gods are sometimes said to have an Oceanid for their mother, or appear to be metamorphosed heroes whose name replaces the original name of the river and who either replace the ancient gods or are superimposed upon them. Aside from such stories, the river gods show great affinities with Oceanus. They take on the appearance of bulls, like the

ancestral god whom Euripides calls Taurokranos and whom we see depicted with the neck of a bull on the François vase. Very fertile, the principal river gods engender numerous offspring, as Taurokranos did. Among their descendants we find mortals who occupy an important place in the genealogy of the Greek peoples. It should also be noted that many of the river gods are able to take several forms in succession, as do Nereus and Proteus.

Thus the deities of the waters seem naturally capable of changing their shapes; it is a common ability that many of them share. This is no doubt why myths can depict several of them born of a single metamorphosis. Such is the case with certain springs or rivers, as we have already said; it is also the case with Ino, the daughter of Cadmus, who, after throwing herself into the sea, becomes similar to the Nereids, under the name of Leucothea; it is also true of Glaucus. Several stories, differing in certain details, agree that he was a mortal who became a god and lived in the waters as an old man of the sea.

J.Ru./d.b.

BIBLIOGRAPHY

1. Articles devoted, under their proper names, to various divinities of water in the two large dictionaries: *Lexikon der griechischen und römischen Mythologie*, by w. h. roscher (Leipzig 1884–1921); *Paulys Realencyclopädie der classischen Altertumswissenschaft* (abbreviated as *R.E.*), by g. wissowa (Munich 1894–).
2. Other studies: m. ninck, *Die Bedeutung des Wassers im Kulte und Leben der Alten* (Leipzig 1921). n. fischer, *Nereiden und Okeaniden in der hesiodischen Theogonie* (Halle 1934). p. philippson, *Der Kosmos des Okeanos* (Basel 1940). e. buscher, "Meermänner," *Sitzungsberichte des Bayerischen Akademie der Wissenschaften* (Munich 1941). a. s. pease, "The Son of Neptune," *Harvard Studies in Classical Philology* 54 (1943): 99ff. a. lesky, *Thalatta: Der Weg der Griechen zum Meer* (Vienna 1947). f. sachermeyr, *Poseidon und die Entstehung des griechischen Götterglaubens* (Munich 1950). l. séchan, "Légendes grecques de la mer," *Lettres d'humanité* 14 (1955): 3ff. a. d. nock, "Nymphs and Nereids," in *Mélanges Université Saint-Joseph* (Beirut 1961), 37; reprinted in *Essays on Religion and the Ancient World* (Oxford 1972), 2:919ff. h. schwabl, s.v. "Weltschöpfung," in *RE Suppl.*, Bd. 9, col. 1433ff. j.-p. vernant, "Thétis et le poème cosmogonique d'Alcman," in *Hommage à Marie Delcourt* (Brussels 1970), 38ff. j. rudhardt, *Le thème de l'eau primordiale dans la mythologie grecque* (Bern 1971).

Gods and Artisans: Hephaestus, Athena, Daedalus

In the economic and social history of ancient Greece, the artisan class was not considered an autonomous category. There was no term exactly corresponding to what we understand by "artisan." The term *dēmiourgos* offers far too broad a range and covers very diverse functions. In the *Odyssey*, for example, Eumaeus asks, "What guests are sent to fetch the stranger? Those who can serve as craftsmen, diviners and doctors and carpenters, or bards, who are beloved by heaven . . . ! It is those who are sought from the ends of the earth!" (*Od.* 17.382ff.). Later (*Od.* 19.135), Homer includes in this group the heralds, whose functions are also very diverse; used as ambassadors, heralds direct assemblies, fill the office of assistant during sacrifices and even serve at table during meals. The artisan is therefore only a particular aspect of the *dēmiourgos*. As elsewhere, the term *technē* covers the categories of art and craftsmanship, which are distinct in our eyes.

I. Hephaestus

In Greek mythology, a certain number of gods and men can be considered artisans. Among the gods, the figure who primarily takes this role is, incontestably, Hephaestus. In the *Iliad*, Hephaestus first appears as a cupbearer for the gods (*Il.* 1.596ff.); then as a master of metals and talismans (*Il.* 2.101; 18.369ff., 410ff.); and finally as a master of fire, an element with which he is almost identified (*Il.* 21.330ff.).

Certainly, Hephaestus is master of fire, but not just any fire. His is essentially the technical fire, the fire that is used to accomplish the tasks of artisans, not the hearth fire, which is the domain of Hestia, nor the celestial fire, the lightning of Zeus. What is more, Hephaestus is not the master of just any technical fire, but essentially of the fire that is used in metalwork. The fire that burns the earth is reserved mainly for Prometheus, probably because he is a Titan, a name deriving from the term *titanos*, the quicklime formed from an earthy element and from fire (Aristotle, *Meteorologica* 4.11.389a28).

Moreover, Hephaestus works only noble metals: gold, silver, bronze, brass, etc. The working of iron, which is used to fabricate the tools of daily life, belongs to the Dactyls (the Fingers) who also have proper names: Acmon (Anvil), Damnameneus (the Subjugator, that is, the Hammer), and Celmis (perhaps the Casting). The invention of the metallurgy of iron, too, is attributed to the Dactyls of Ida in Phrygia, where ironwork goes back to ancient times (Phoronis, frag. 2 Kinkel E.G.F.). And for the Dactyls (Schol. Apollonius Rhodius, *Argonautica* 1.1129), as for Hephaestus, metallurgy proves to be inseparable from magic.

Hephaestus, in fact, appears as the preeminent binding god. Certainly, as metallurgist he can fashion and unfashion material bonds. But his action is especially magical, and it is with immaterial bonds that he usually binds his victims; notably Hera, whom he immobilizes on a throne (Plato, *Republic*, 2.378d: cf. Libanius, *Narrationes* 7 [8, pp. 38–39 Foerster]); and especially Ares and Aphrodite: having caught these adulterers *in flagrante delicto*, he snares them in an invisible net (*Od.* 8.266–366).

If he has the power of binding, Hephaestus also has the power of unbinding. It is Hephaestus himself who releases his mother, an act which permits her to return to Olympus. But Hephaestus is especially famous for mobilizing and therefore, in a sense, unchaining beings who are by nature immobile. Hephaestus has at his disposal two servants made of gold, who work in his workshop like living beings; the bellows in his forge move without his having to work them, and he fashions automatic tripods (*Il.* 18.369ff.).

The science of metallurgy and magic appears inseparable, in the case of Hephaestus, from the crippling of his lower limbs, which has been represented in several ways. This infirmity, which was no longer represented in classical art, appears sometimes as a debility of his legs, sometimes as a deformity of his feet, so that they turn backwards. In the latter case, the god could move about not only forwards but also backwards, somewhat like the double creatures described by Aristophanes in the *Symposium* (190a4–5). This

The return of Hephaestus to Olympus. Attic krater. Ca. 490 B.C. Paris, Musée du Louvre. Photo Hirmer.

lameness is explained in various ways. It can be seen as the price of his extraordinary knowledge. This crippling of the only god who devotes himself to technical craftsmanship can also be recognized as a sign of the public contempt with which work was regarded in ancient Greece. Plutarch essentially affirms this: "There is no young man of good birth who, having seen the Zeus of Pisa [that is, the chryselephantine statue of Phidias at Olympia] or the Hera of Argos, would wish, for all that, to become a Phidias or a Polycletus, or to become an Anacreon, a Philemon or an Archilochus when he has been pleased by their poems. For a work can seduce us with its charm without constraining us to take its worker as a model" (*Pericles* 2.1). In this double gait we can distinguish the ambiguity that characterizes Hephaestus and manifests itself not only in his actions but also in his adventures.

There are several versions of the birth and infancy of Hephaestus. We will mention only those reported by Homer and Hesiod. According to Hesiod, Hera gave birth to Hephaestus "without union of love, through anger at her husband" (*Theogony* 928). According to Homer, at the moment of Hephaestus's birth, Hera threw him from the sky into the sea, because he was crippled and she was ashamed of him; but Hephaestus was taken in by Eurynome and Thetis, who raised him in an underwater grotto, where he learned the art of metallurgy (*Il.* 18.394ff.). However, still according to Homer's *Iliad*, it was Zeus who threw Hephaestus from the sky into the sea one day when Hephaestus took his mother's side. Then Hephaestus fell onto the island of Lemnos, where the Sintians took him in (*Il.* 1.586ff.).

The main interest of all these versions rests in the fact that they allow us to establish the relations between Hephaestus, on the one hand, and Ouranos (the Sky) and various marine powers on the other.

Like Ouranos (Hesiod *Theog.* 123–132), Hephaestus (*Theog.* 928) is conceived without the intervention of love. Moreover, Hephaestus is the only god other than Ouranos who is not endowed with physical perfection. As an effect of the mutilation inflicted upon him by Kronos, Ouranos is castrated, while Hephaestus suffers a deformity of his lower limbs. In order to pursue this comparison, it is relevant to note that Hephaestus is thrown from the sky into the sea like the testicles of Ouranos, whose sperm makes possible the

birth of Aphrodite—often considered the wife of Hephaestus. In the *Iliad*, Homer describes the workshop of Hephaestus thus: "Silver-footed Thetis arrived in the dwelling of Hephaestus, the imperishable and starry dwelling, radiant among all in the eyes of the immortals, all in bronze and constructed by the bandy-legged one himself" (*Il.* 18.369–371). Now, this description inevitably makes one think of the starry vault of the sky, which the Greeks considered to be made of metal: the poets also say that the sky is made of bronze (*chalkeos* or *poluchalkeos*) or of iron (*sidēreos*). That is why, in an Orphic context, Proclus can write: "Let us add to our traditions the convictions that we have received from the very first from the (Orphic) theologians concerning Hephaestus. . . . They say that he is a smith, because he is a worker and also because, since the sky is made of bronze in its function as the symbol of the intelligible, he who made the sky is a smith" (Proclus, *In Platonis Timaeum* [23d–e], 1.142.18ff. Diehl). The comparison is reinforced by the fact that on certain illustrated documents Hephaestus's hair is arranged in a *pilos*, an egg-shaped cap, of dark blue, which Eusebius of Caesarea compares to the celestial vault (*Praeparatio Evangelica* 3.2.23).

Hephaestus also had clear connections with numerous marine powers. It was into the sea that Hephaestus fell when he was thrown from the celestial heights. According to Homer, he was taken in and raised by Eurynome, one of the daughters of Oceanus and Tethys, and by Thetis, one of the daughters of Nereus, the old man of the sea, and Doris. According to another version, also found in Homer, the Sintians took him in at Lemnos. According to a third version, Hera, having conceived Hephaestus as a result of premarital sexual relations with Zeus, delivered Hephaestus to the Naxian Cedalion, who taught the young man to work metal (*Schol. Il.* 14.296ff.).

Whatever the case, Hephaestus spends a part of his life either in the sea or on an island in the middle of the sea. During this time he is initiated into the arts that he practices, metallurgy and magic. This is significant, as demonstrated by two types of mythical characters.

Of one type are the Telchines, demons of Rhodes, associated with seals (Suetonius, *On Terms of Abuse in Greek, On Greek Games*, ed. Taillardat, Paris: Les Belle-Lettres, 1967, p. 54 [text] and pp. 133–36 [commentary]). Like seals, the Telchines are ambiguous characters, halfway between fish and men, toward whom they have mixed sentiments of neighborliness and hostility, and between the sea and the earth, that is, between the wet and the dry. The Telchines are both magicians and metallurgists. As magicians, they have the evil eye: their glance alters all things (Callimachus, frag. 9 Pfeiffer. Hesychius s.v. *Telgines, Telchines*). As metallurgists, they are credited with a number of works of art, notably the sickle of Kronos (Strabo 14.2.7) and the trident of Poseidon (Callimachus, *Hymn to Delos* 31).

The Cabiri, whose native land was Lemnos and whose principal sanctuary was in Samothrace, are said to have had Hephaestus for a father, or at least for a divine ancestor (Strabo, *Geo.* 10.3.21; Stephanus of Byzantium, s.v. *Kabeiria*). Marine powers, they are explicitly identified as crabs by Hesychius: "The Cabiri are crabs (*karkinoi*), animals particularly honored in Lemnos, where they are held to be gods. It is also said that they are the sons of Hephaestus" (Hesychius, s.v. *Kabeiroi*). This crustacean has several points in common with Hephaestus. The crab is an amphibious animal that lives in the sea and on the earth. But its extremities are what make it particularly interesting. The crab's way of walking inevitably reminds us of the double gait of Hephaestus, and its two claws remind us of the pincers of the metallurgist (in ancient Greek, *karkinoi*). Like Hephaestus, whose descendants they are, the Cabiri are metallurgists.

As a metallurgist and smith, Hephaestus participates above all in that *mētis* with which Athena is endowed. Hephaestus is said to be *klutomētis* (*Homeric Hymn to Hephaestus* 1) and *polumētis* (*Il.* 21.355). We can thus understand why it was he who, with a one-two punch, delivered Athena when she was trapped in the head of Zeus. Zeus had swallowed Metis upon the advice of Ouranos and Gaea, who had revealed that, if Metis had a daughter by him, she would then give him a son who would dethrone him, as Zeus himself had dethroned Kronos.

These close mythical relations uniting Hephaestus to Athena find their material manifestations at Athens in their common temples and cults. Thus, the small cult of the Erechtheum could be the oldest Athenian cult of Hephaestus, guest of Athena of the Polis. This sanctuary sheltered Erichthonius, the Phidian hero, who was thought to be their child. It is related that Hephaestus received Athena in his workshop when she came to ask him for weapons. He was overwhelmed by a strong desire for the goddess; she fled, but Hephaestus caught her. Athena defended herself, and in the fray the god's sperm spilled on her leg. The goddess dried herself with some wool and threw the sperm onto the earth. Thus impregnated, Gaea (the Earth) produced a child, Erichthonius, who was one of the first kings of Athens (Apollodorus, *Bibliotheca* 3.14.6ff.)—a type of conception comparable to that which follows the castration of Ouranos by Kronos (Hesiod, *Theog.* 178–206).

The personal temple of Hephaestus, the Hephaesteum, which he shared with Athena, is located beyond the Ceramicus, the potters' area, near the Temple of Aphrodite. During the peace of Nicias (421 B.C.), an artist was commissioned to erect bronze statues of Athena and Hephaestus on the same pedestal. Nearby, at Colonus of the Agora, Hephaestus is found in the proximity of Prometheus and Athena.

Two festivals of unequal importance were celebrated in honor of Hephaestus. The Chalcheia, which took place in the beginning of November, became a festival of artisans who worked with metal; this festival was also called the Athenaea, indicating that the goddess also played a role in it (Sophocles, frag. 844 Pearson). On the other hand, the Hephaesteia, from which Athena was absent, was a more important event than the Chalcheia, though less well known.

Be that as it may, it is Plato, notably in the *Critias*, who relates the myth of Atlantis, where Athena and Hephaestus are found most closely united: "Hephaestus and Athena have the same nature, first, because, as brother and sister, they have the same father, and second, because their double love for knowledge and art leads them to the same end. The two of them received this region (Athens) in a common and unique lot. It should properly belong to them, being naturally suited for virtue and thought. Having placed respectable people there as autochthons, they organized the city according to their taste" (Plato, *Critias* 109c–d). In this same dialogue, Plato situates the common temple of Athena and Hephaestus at the top of the Acropolis, near the dwellings of the kings. On the slopes, warriors live, charged with protecting the kings. Finally, on the plain that extends from the foot of the Acropolis the craftsmen and farmers are settled. In this perspective, the temple of Athena and Hephaestus on the Acropolis is reminiscent primarily of the linked presence of Athena of the Polis and Hephaestus in the Erechtheum; secondly, of Athena Parthenos, the warrior; and thirdly, of

Athena Ergana (the Worker) of the plain, who shared a temple with Hephaestus at Colonus, an outlying part of Athens inhabited by artisans and shopkeepers.

L.Br./d.f.

II. Athena

Whether alone or associated with Hephaestus, Athena occupies, like him, a fundamental place among divinities of the crafts. Throughout the multiplicity of her aspects—warrior goddess armed with the lance and the aegis, protectress of carpenters, mistress of harnesses and pilot of ships, patroness of weavers and potters, inventor of the swing plow—whatever the domain into which she enters, Athena sets in motion the same qualities of manual skill and practical intelligence. This intelligence she gets directly from her mother Metis, the wife swallowed by Zeus when he wanted to incorporate her substance into himself.

The warrior Athena, who sprang armed from the head of her father, has remained a virgin; by renouncing femininity and its fulfillment within marriage, the virgin rejoins the male camp and by this inversion incarnates the warrior values with their maximum intensity. She bears Metis's nickname, the Spartan name of *Chalkioikos*, "she of the bronze dwelling," the goddess as dazzling as the armor with which she is girded. In the battle against the giants as in the battles of the *Iliad*, she carries out or inspires the ruses of war, surprise attacks, ambushes, and other tactical maneuvers which constitute the technique of war. But her action calls on more mysterious means. Like the art of Hephaestus, the

Athena making a horse of clay. Attic oenochoe. Ca. 440 B.C. Berlin, Antikenmuseum. Photo Geske.

warrior *technē* of the bronze Athena is greatly influenced by magic. Concealed by the aegis—a large shawl of finely woven metal, with long fringes, decorated with the masks of Confusion, Quarrel, and the terrifying head of the Gorgon— she paralyzes her adversaries or renders invincible the heroes she protects. In the fray, she raises her voice, as piercing as a trumpet, and her flashing eyes make even the most courageous lose their heads. Conceived by her mother, Metis, at the same time as her armor, like a metallurgical product, she came into the world uttering a war cry. Athena possesses and deploys in battle the magical courage that looks and sounds like bronze, the warrior metal that is worked and animated by the craftsman's fire.

The Athena who protects and instructs artisans appears in general with the characteristics of a more serene and familiar divinity. Her modes of action seem more accessible, except when they involve a technique that uses fire. This applies to little but pottery, since the domain of metallurgy belongs entirely to Hephaestus. During the firing, the potter addresses his prayers to Athena, asking her to "spread her hand over the kiln." The goddess will indicate to him the right moment when the vessels are properly baked, when the varnish will be shiny enough. She also intervenes by ridding the kiln of a troop of demons with evocative names: the Breaker, the Cracker, the Inextinguishable, the Burster. A Corinthian tablet represents her in the form of a large owl perched on top of a potter's kiln, facing a phallic dwarf, the bearer of the evil eye. The protectress of potters is a divinity who is the mistress of fire, of its alarming powers, its benefits, and its evil spells.

Athena presides especially over woodworking. Woodcutters, carpenters, chariot builders, and shipbuilders benefit from her attentive protection. She cherishes in particular the carpenter Tekton, son of Harmon, the Adjuster, who knew how to make masterpieces of all sorts and constructed for Paris the ship which brought Helen to Troy (*Il.* 5.59–60). She assists Danaus, the inventor of the first ship, with her advice and her aid (Apollodorus, *Mythographus* 2.1.4; Hyginus, *Fabulae* 272). According to one tradition, it was she and not Demeter who invented the swing plow (Servius, in Virgil, *Aeneid* 4.402). The *Works and Days* of Hesiod attributes to the "servant of Athena" alone the capacity of attaching a piece of curved wood to the stock and fitting it to the shaft of a plow to make the plowman's tool (Hes. *Op.* 430ff.). In the construction of these various works, Athena intervenes at all stages of woodworking, beginning with the felling, because "it is *mētis* and not force that makes a good woodcutter" (*Il.* 15.412). When Athena directs the construction of the ship of the Argonauts, she herself goes to Mount Pelion to select the trees, which she fells with a hatchet (Ap. Rhod., *Argon.* 2.1187–89). She teaches the carpenter, Argos, the art of measuring lengths of wood with a ruler (*ibid.* 1.724). She watches over the assembling and adjusting of different pieces with the help of dowels. She is seen planing and polishing the wood of Pelias's lance herself (*Cypria* frag. 3), and her protégé Odysseus, the *polumētis*, is an expert in all these operations when he has to build a ship to leave Calypso's island (*Od.* 5.234–257).

In the domain of chariots and ships, Athena's competence does not stop at building. The art of driving chariots and piloting ships also belongs to her. In both cases, her functions are clearly distinct from those of Poseidon, master of the horse and of the sea.

A Corinthian tradition attributes to Athena Chalinitis the invention of the bridle. According to Pausanias (2.4.1) and Pindar (*Olympian Odes* 13.63–87), it is she who procures for

Bellerophon the instrument necessary to tame Pegasus. But the episode occurs in a different context. It implies that technical intelligence doubled by magic that we have seen at work on the battlefield and at the potter's kiln. On the one hand, the bit is a metallic object, produced by the *mētis* of the blacksmith and endowed with the mysterious values of the metal that comes out of the fire. On the other hand, it has an effect like a magic hold on the wild horse, a restless animal driven by a demonic and savage force, which is subdued for the uses of war.

Concerning mastery of the chariot, the qualities and expertise that the charioteer demonstrates when inspired by Athena Hippia come from a more humane *technē*, from a *mētis* quite close to that of the carpenter. The goddess teaches the charioteer to plot his course, to foresee obstacles, to use the peculiarities of the course, to exploit the weakness of his adversary by a questionable maneuver, in short, to make a slower and less vigorous team win by means of trickery (2.23; Nonnus, *Dionysiaca* 37).

But the major preoccupation of the charioteer is to drive his chariot straight, without deviating from his route, exactly "like a carpenter who hews beams and boards in a straight line." The comparison between the two domains occurs frequently, especially in the *Iliad*: constructing and driving a chariot demand the same aptitudes. It is the same with navigation. Foresight, vigilance, and straightness are the fundamental rules for navigating on the sea. Athena guides the pilot as she inspires the charioteer. It is she who prepares and directs—in the character of Mentor—the voyage of Telemachus. When she has presided over the making of the ship, the Argo, the goddess herself chooses the helmsman, Tiphys. After the passage between the Clashing Rocks, he thanks the goddess, not for having propelled the ship beyond the dangerous pass before it could be shattered, but for having fit the parts of the ship firmly together (Ap. Rhod., *Argon.* 2.598ff.).

Athena the Constructor and Athena the Driver—on earth and on the sea—operate according to the same modalities of action. The same technical intelligence makes, and then uses, these works of trimmed wood—chariots and ships. Odysseus shows his dexterity when he builds his ship, felling and hewing the trees, shaping the beams on a straightedge, fitting the planking, setting up the mast, and fastening the sails. He is equally dexterous when, at the helm, he sets a straight course as a vigilant pilot, his eyes fixed on the constellations (*Od.* 5.234–274).

Another group of artisans who depend upon the patronage of Athena are those who work in wool and in fabrics. The goddess presides over and excels in spinning, in weaving, in making sumptuously decorated cloths by the methods of tapestry (embroidery is unknown in the Homeric world). Athena makes her own beautiful cloak and that of Hera. Although she teaches her art to Pandora (Hes., *Op.* 64), and bestows upon the women of Phaeacia the skills to become the finest of all weavers (*Od.* 7.110), Athena does not tolerate being surpassed by a rival. The imprudent Arachne sees her all too perfect work torn apart by the goddess, and she herself is transformed into a spider (Ovid, *Met.* 6).

There is no hiatus in Greek thought between this branch of Athena's craftsmanlike activities and the preceding branch. Between the two domains there are numerous analogies in vocabulary. The work of the weaver seems to be apprehended according to the same mental scheme as that of the carpenter. Both artisans in wood and workers in textiles proceed in two successive operations: cutting and assembling. The spinner who fashions into a thread the lock of wool she has isolated from the mass of shearings works in the same way as the carpenter who shapes and planes the boards and the beams cut by the woodcutter from the tree trunk. The carpenter and the weaver then construct a new whole by associating separate elements, by the juxtaposition of beams or the interlacing of threads. The protection the goddess gives Penelope is exactly symmetrical to the concern she has for Odysseus.

The same technical intelligence is expressed, therefore, in different categories of artisans. The technique is of the same substance as Athena's intelligence, such that the vocabulary of *technē* furnishes images to express that technique even when it is concerned only with mental operations. The verbs "to spin" (*huphainein*) and "to construct" (*tektainesthai*) often accompany the noun *mētis*: thus Athena and her protégés sometimes *spin* their tricks and *weave* their plans, sometimes *arrange* their projects and *construct* their subtle traps.

III. Daedalus

Besides the two great technical divinities of its pantheon, Greek mythology knew a series of heroes remarkable for their dexterity, like Odysseus, and sometimes endowed with the title of "first inventor," such as Epeus, Palamedes, Daedalus, etc. All of these mortals are celebrated at least as much for their intellectual qualities as for their practical skill. This is certainly true of Daedalus, the prototype of the artist and of the artisan; his genealogy illuminates both sides of the paradigmatic personality of the artisan.

Among his direct ancestors are Eupalamus, "skillful hand," and Palamaon, "manual," two names which denote the dexterity and creative skill of the hand. But Daedalus's father is most often said to be Metion, "the man of *mētis*," and his mother is sometimes Metiadousa, "she who delights in *mētis*," sometimes Iphinoe, "she of the vigorous spirit," and even Phrasimede, "she who conceives of a plan."

The series of fabulous adventures which are spun into the thread of his legend give his character a marvelous dimension. "Daedalus was famous throughout the whole world for his talent, but also for his wanderings and his misfortunes," Pausanias reports (7.4.5). This hero is an Athenian. He belongs to the line of the Metionidae, the younger branch of the royal family of Athens, and is descended, through Erichthonius, from Hephaestus and—almost—from Athena. He begins by creating statuary or, according to another tradition, inspires great progress in this art. The statues which come from his hands are almost alive. He also invents several implements indispensable for the work of the carpenter and the architect: the hatchet, the plumb line, the gimlet, and glue. But he has a nephew, his sister's son, who, while still a young apprentice, threatens to surpass his uncle's genius: the lad devises the lathe, the carpenter's compass, and, by imitating a snake's jaw, the first saw made of metal. Such ingenuity provokes Daedalus's jealousy, and he throws the child down from the top of the Acropolis. Pursued, or condemned to exile, the artisan seeks refuge in Crete, at the court of King Minos. There he fashions statues, a place for Ariadne to dance, and an ingenious machine for Pasiphaë: a cow of leather-covered wood which permits the queen, hidden inside, to unite with a bull. She gives birth to the Minotaur. At the request of Minos, Daedalus constructs the labyrinth in which the monster is imprisoned. Young Athenians are regularly handed over to him as fodder. Theseus—a cousin of Daedalus—arrives, and to please Ariadne, who is in love with the hero, the artisan gives her the ball of string which will help Theseus to emerge victoriously from the

trial. But Minos finds out, and, as a punishment, shuts Daedalus and his son Icarus in the labyrinth. The artisan then fashions wings and the two fly away. Icarus imprudently climbs too high in the sky, the heat of the sun melts the wax which holds the feathers together, and the young man plunges to his death before his father's eyes. Daedalus reaches Sicily and places himself at the service of King Cocalus. He builds a dam, fortifies a citadel to shelter the king's treasure, lays the foundation of a temple to Aphrodite on the peak of a crag, installs a heating system. But Minos pursues him in hatred, seeking him with tenacity and cunning: he offers a reward to anyone who knows how to thread a snail's shell. King Cocalus assigns the task to Daedalus, who has taken refuge with him. Daedalus attaches the thread to an ant's body and puts it into the shell through a hole pierced in the top. When the ant comes out again, the problem is solved. Minos thus detects Daedalus's presence and demands to have him back. But in order to keep Daedalus, the king of Sicily's daughters help him to scald Minos in his bath. In this way the artisan triumphs over the sovereign.

This romantic story displays a certain number of themes—or *mythemes*—which are also found in mythologies of the artisan in other cultures: living statues, headlong flights, flying men, labyrinths, murders, etc. But their organization in the Greek context takes on specific qualities and depends on a coherent group of representations and a system of special values—values that structure the characters of the technician divinities, Hephaestus and Athena.

This legendary narrative is packed with traditions about a series of precious objects produced by a group of artisans of luxury, objects called *daidala* (Daedalian). Analysis of this narrative allows us to distinguish the framework of thought that governed the way the Greeks perceived art and technique.

The artisan-artist is defined as an ambiguous and disconcerting person. The ambivalence of *technē* is expressed in a series of oppositions, also characteristic of mythical logic.

There is an opposition between the notions of "to show" and "to hide." The inventor of the statue is a creator of a spectacle, of an object meant to be seen. Daedalus was the first to "reveal the appearance of the gods." In showing the divinity, the sculptor renders the invisible visible. When tradition makes Daedalus the author of decisive progress in Greek plastic arts, and not their inventor, he is given credit for "having opened the eyes of statues." In the one case, he creates an image to be seen; in the other, he gives this image sight. The two traditions are complementary. Their duality expresses the reversibility of the Greek conception of vision: "to see" and "to be seen" are equivalent. Sight is both the organ and faculty of vision and its object. When applied to the divine image, this principle of reciprocity is applied to a background of religious representations: it is just as dangerous to see the face of the god as it is to fall under his gaze. Blindness and madness are the punishments inflicted on rash humans. The inventor of art seems to make a game of this danger.

But Daedalus is also the one who hides, who renders the visible invisible—hiding Pasiphaë in the wooden cow, shutting up the Minotaur in the meanderings of the labyrinth (only to reveal him to Theseus later), fortifying the hiding place of the royal treasure of Cocalus—and Daedalus himself hides to escape the vengeance of Minos.

The giver of sight is also the creator of life. Certainly art imitates life; and the works of Daedalus have a striking realism: "they seem to look and walk" because "he unglued

Bronze-smith's atelier. Polishing a statue. Attic cup. Ca. 490 B.C. Berlin, Antikenmuseum. Photo Geske.

the arms from the bodies of statues" and "separated their legs." But the life of Daedalus's statues is not simply a metaphor. He breathes real life into them. Their mobility is so great that they have to be tied up to prevent them from running away (Plato, *Meno* 97d). They escape, and are endowed with sight and even with speech. This mysterious life is of the same order as that of the magical works the secret of which Athena taught the inhabitants of Rhodes, whose "streets bear figures that resemble walking, living beings" (Pindar, *Ol.* 7.52); to this same order belong Hephaestus's automatons, self-moving tripods, and golden servants, and the gold and silver guard dogs from the palace of Alcinous. By creating objects that mirror life, the ingenuity of the artisan can also produce a monster against nature: by permitting an impossible union, Pasiphaë's machine causes the birth of the Minotaur.

Though he is the master of animation and of life, the craftsman is also the one who kills, helps kill, or makes others kill: he is the passionate killer of his pupil and disciple; the murderer (through his imprudence) of his son Icarus; the accomplice in Theseus's killing of the Minotaur, his "creature"; and the instigator, finally, of the assassination of Minos, his sovereign.

This second opposition, "to create" versus "to kill," is closely linked to the first, for to produce is to bring to light, and to kill is to make disappear, to send to Hades (*a-vidēs*, the Invisible).

The ambiguity of art also appears in a series of antitheses which oppose form to illusion, beauty to evil, truth to falsehood. The creator of form is the maker of illusion. There is a story that Heracles, finding himself face to face with a statue of himself made by Daedalus, believed he was facing an adversary and struck him. Beauty that fascinates can hide the worst of evils, like Pandora—the creation of Hephaestus and Athena—who was sent to earth, adorned with jewels made by Daedalus, to sow misfortune among men; like the Trojan Horse, which amazed the Trojans and brought them disaster. The *technē* that imitates the true is nothing but a lying artifice. The cow of wood and leather is unnatural and holds a real woman. It acts as a lure for the bull, which gets caught in the trap. It is a trap just like the labyrinth, from which one cannot extricate oneself. In one anecdote, Daedalus spreads nets to capture thieves who have stolen a treasure. The entire legend puts art and ruse in constant correlation. *Technē* both embellishes and falsifies. The artisan is the master of forgery and subterfuge.

In the specific domain of technique and invention, the dominating opposition is between the notions of straightness and circularity or sinuosity. Like every good carpenter, Daedalus guides his plane straight. When he begins the first flight, he adheres strictly to the rules of navigation: he flies with his eyes fixed on the constellations—Boötes, Ursa Major, Orion's Sword—which are the reference points of the sailor. The essential rule he sets down for Icarus is that of the straight route, halfway between the high and the low. The failure and drowning of Icarus, a bad pilot, comes from ignoring this rule. The parallelism between the two types of navigation, aerial and maritime, is further underlined by a more prosaic and rationalist version of Daedalus's adventure: he escapes aboard a small boat furnished by Pasiphaë, and Icarus drowns while approaching the island which, henceforth, bears his name.

But the carpenter-pilot who has mastery over straightness also knows how to weave undulating nets and draw curves. The Labyrinth at Cnossos is, in fact, described only in terms of its sinuous form and its intertwinings. This figure, to which the artisan left his name, is notably redundant in the legend. It is immediately taken up again in the sequence of the ball of string that Daedalus gives Ariadne so that Theseus can retrace his steps: the solution is a redoubling of the problem. The following episode, in certain versions, tells how, at Delos, Daedalus teaches Theseus and the surviving young Athenians a dance "of which the figures imitate the turns and detours of the labyrinth, with a rhythm marked by alternating and circulating movements" (Plutarch, *Theseus* 21.1; *Schol. Venet. ad Il.* 18.590). And the anecdote of the thread that follows the spiral of a snail shell is, of course, a last redoubling of this theme. The polymorphous thread is a perfect symbol of the ambivalence of the artisan: Daedalus invents two antithetical aspects of it, the thread as a rigid plumb line and the soft, round ball of Ariadne.

Mastery and excess form the next paradox in the character of Daedalus. At times, as a vigilant technician he knows how to follow the middle path, respecting the equilibrium between the extreme dryness of the sun's heat and the humidity of the sea; he knows the precise dosage needed to temper the boiling vapor emerging from a grotto at Selinus, so that he can build a heating system there; but at other times he gives way to murderous transports of jealousy and kills his nephew, or uses his competence in hydraulic engineering to commit an assassination: by scalding Minos, he is in effect doing something that is an inversion of what he did at Selinus, where the vapor, once under control, was put to the service of those taking the cure. The valuable servant of kings is transformed into a formidable adversary. *Technē* always conjoins two sides, one beneficial, the other harmful.

The last antithesis is already present in Daedalus's genealogy: the one who has manual dexterity is characterized essentially by his intellectual qualities. The narration of the adventures of the artisan puts the accent on the form of mentality that he must prove: an inventive subtlety rich in ruses and stratagems. The most famous realization of his talent as an architect, the labyrinth, is not presented as an edifice. An enigmatic place, scarcely material, it is an inescapable course, the spatial representation of the notion of *aporia*, a problem that is unsolvable or that contains its solution within itself. The Daedalian labyrinth is the very image of the mind that conceived it, tortuous, sinuous, and infinite in its changes of direction, just as the genius of its author is inexhaustible in its resources. If the intelligence of Athena is technical, the *technē* of Daedalus is conceptual. Indeed, to make the artisan betray his own presence, Minos

89

proposes not an ordeal of the manual kind, but a test of intellectual ingenuity.

This may be how Greek culture resolves one of its major contradictions. It is an artisan's culture, since most of its creations are the work of those Homer called "craftsmen" (*dēmiourgoi*), yet this culture assigns the artisan to a subordinate place in society, and it depreciates the manual laborer on the plane of theoretical reflection. But by becoming a legendary hero, the artisan is rehabilitated by his *mētis*.

F.Fr./d.f.

BIBLIOGRAPHY

Concerning the historic figure of the artisan in ancient Greece, see K. MURAKAWA, "Demiurgos," *Historia* 6 (1957): 385–415.

On Hephaestus and the mythic figures that are related to him, see M. DELCOURT, *Héphaistos ou la légende du magicien* (Paris 1957). More precisely, on the connections between Hephaestus and Athena and the artisan class, see M. DETIENNE and J.-P. VERNANT, *Les ruses de l'intelligence: La mètis des Grecs* (Paris 1974), 165–258, "Les savoirs divins: Athéna, Héphaistos." On Daedalus, see F. FRONTISI-DUCROUX, *Dédale: Mythologie de l'artisan en Grèce ancienne* (Paris 1975).

THE ORIGINS OF MANKIND IN GREEK MYTHS: BORN TO DIE

The Greeks did not have a *Genesis* to assign to them once and for all their Creator and the day of their birth, and no poem written in Greece on the origins of the human race has ever had the authority of the *Theogony*, Hesiod's poem on the birth of the gods. Fortunately, however, in their attempts to speak of the first men or to think about the origin of the human condition, the Greeks never lacked myths, stories of times gone by when the Earth Mother relieved humanity of its persistent concern about the reproduction of the species, when the eternal spring of the Golden Age disguised death as sleep and promised mortals the life of the gods.

Man originated from the earth. Poets and philosophers agree on this point, which is the zero degree of myth, rarely developed for itself alone, but more often evoked in an allusion or as a mere innuendo. The concept was also a part of the national tradition of the city-states and the stories about the origins of the Greek race. But there were at least two ways for humanity to come forth from the earth. In certain myths, such as the Platonic myth of the *gēgeneis* (born [the root *gen-] of the earth [*gē*]: see Plato *Politics* 270e–271c), and likewise in the Athenian or Theban myths of autochthony (from *autochthōn*, born of the soil [*chthōn*] itself [*autos*] of the homeland), man—humanity, one man, or men—arises from the ground as a plant comes out of the soil or a child out of the womb. According to other myths, such as the Hesiodic account of the creation of woman (and we shall see that the opposition of the sexes is not without meaning), the human creature, made of earth and molded by an artisan god, is the product of craftsmanship: earth-as-field is to earth-as-matter as soil is to clay. Since, on the level of social practice, sowing (or, more generally, agriculture) and pottery making (or, more generally, craftsmanship) are contrasted as nature is contrasted to artifice (see J.-P. Vernant, *Mythe et pensée chez les Grecs*, 2:16–36), it is not surprising that there are more differences than resemblances between these two versions of the origin.

On the one hand, earth-as-field spontaneously fertilizes or is fertilized by "seeds," the products of men who are seen as a primitive race spontaneously springing from *gē*, like the Platonic *gēgeneis*, or arising from a natural environment into a "mediated chthonic birth" (Cl. Bérard, *Anodoi*, Neuchâtel 1974, p. 32)—men "born of the oak tree and of the stone," Hesiod's bronze race born of ash trees (Hesiod *Works and Days* 145). Autochthones born of the soil of the homeland—among them the Theban Spartans, born as adults and ready for combat—are, as their name indicates (*spartoi*, the sown

ones), the product of strange seeds, since they arise out of the plain on which Cadmus cast the teeth of a dragon. As for Erichthonius or Erechtheus, the mythical ancestor of the Athenians, although his family history is somewhat complex, he was also the fruit of the soil. As the virgin Athena was fleeing from the pressing and precise advances of the artisan god Hephaestus, the earth, which had gathered the sperm of the rejected lover, brought into the world the miraculous child who would be the king of Athens.

On the other hand, the earth turns itself into docile matter fashioned by a divine artisan, sculptor, or potter. In Hesiod, this artisan is called Hephaestus, and woman is his artificial masterpiece. According to a later tradition, however, all of humanity was hatched inside the workshop of the mediator Prometheus; this may be a late invention or perhaps the invention of a philosopher or comic poet. But the point essential to Greek mythic thought is that man is the result of a technical feat.

Man has at his disposal two concurrent mythical discourses about his own origin. Either he is born of Earth (the primordial *gē* of the cosmogonies; the anthropomorphized *gē* of the visual representations of the birth of Erichthonius; *gē* the one and only female power of childbirth; a fertile and nurturing *gē*, the universal producer of life, out of whom men grow like vegetables; *gē patris*, the civic earth, which its autochthones will defend as a mother and father) or he is made of earth (or, more exactly, in certain versions, of earth and water, like woman in Hesiod, or like the frightened Achaeans whom Menelaus will henceforth only call Achaean women [*Iliad* 7.99]).

By and large, myths of fertility seem to prevail over myths of artifice. The earth is mother rather than matter in Greek thought as in the Greek language, where there is an inescapable interference between the semantic fields of sexualized reproduction and plant growth. Without trying too hard to decide whether earth imitates woman or vice versa—an essentially Greek question raised by Plato (*Menexenus* 238a) and discussed again and again by the moderns (among them Dieterich in his celebrated work *Mutter Erde*², Leipzig and Berlin 1913)—in marriage rituals as on the tragic stage, woman is a field to plow, a furrow to sow.

Yet we must go one step beyond the opposition between these two models, because the Greeks themselves sometimes blurred the distinction between earth and clay (this applies to Pandora, the first woman, as we shall see). The concepts merged mainly because these two mythical versions of the origin tended with a single impulse to replace the question of the beginning with the question of what follows.

To clarify: humankind exists because the "first men" came along; yet assigning them a birth is not as difficult as granting them a posterity. In other words, if the Greeks readily

Birth of Erichthonius. Attic hydria. Ca. 450 B.C. London, British Museum. Museum photo.

believed that "the people of the preceding age were born of the earth instead of begetting one another" (Plato *Republic* 269b), it was still necessary one day to open up the endless cycle of reproduction to which humankind is tied in order to perpetuate itself on this earth. Of course this process does not simply function of itself without delays or failures, for in their attempts to characterize the beginnings of humankind, myths multiply their repetitions, duplications, and discontinuities. At times men are born of primordial beings, themselves arisen from the earth, who by way of a kind of dress rehearsal ensure the transition between man's origin and man's time in history. Thus the "parents" of Phoroneus, the "first man" and mythical ancestor of the Argives, are the river Inachus and the nymph Melia (Pausanias 2.15.5; Apollodorus *Bibliotheca* 2.1.1), herself the daughter of the Ocean (according to Apollodorus) or the sister of the Meliai, the nymphs of the ash tree, born of Gaea and fertilized by the blood of Ouranos (Hesiod *Theogony* 187). Similarly, in the Orphic myths humankind rises from the ashes of the Titans, whose fate dramatically foreshadowed that of the human race (M. Detienne, "Dionysos mis à mort . . . ," *Annali della Scuola Normale Superiore di Pisa* 4 (1974): 1213–16). At other times, duplication and discontinuity dominate, and myth is fond of annihilating a first humanity the better to ensure a new beginning for humans. Thus the flood wipes man off the surface of the earth, but by throwing stones on the ground Deucalion and Pyrrha give rise to a new humanity that is about to engage in the process of its reproduction with no further delay.

For the man who is truly man is born of men and not of the unknown.

"Tell me your race and your homeland, for you did not come out of the legendary oak tree nor of the stone" (Homer *Odyssey* 19.167). To this Homeric question, Socrates gave the answer several centuries later: "I too have kin, for, as Homer said, I was not 'born of an oak tree nor of a stone,' but of human beings, and so I have parents" (Plato *Apology* 34d). To rigidify the origin in a proverb in this way is what we might call an elegant way of dodging the issue. Greek myths do not make this choice openly, and for a good reason, namely, that there are no myths other than myths of origin. But it is as if these myths were less interested in origin for its own sake than in that separation from the origin which has definitively shaped the human condition.

Hence the delays and constant new beginnings, as if the cycle of generations were unable to find its autonomous rhythm straight off. So between the historical time of men and the time of the origins, myth readily inserts several humanities that have appeared successively and then disappeared forever. This is the case with the first four races of the Hesiodic myth—the golden, silver, bronze, and heroic races (*Works and Days* 106–201); the fifth, the iron race, our own, is not, strictly speaking, *descended* from the first four (as observed by P. Vidal-Naquet, "Le mythe platonicien du *Politique*," p. 377). Rather, it is descended only from itself. But to exist it needed a narrative, that strange temporal web full of false starts and true endings. The gods "made" (*poiēsan, poiēse:* Hes. *Works and Days* 110, 128, 144, 158) the first four races. To the fifth, Hesiod gives neither a creator nor an origin; it exists, and that is what is important. But it lives out its existence in the mode of exclusion, which is what the myth leads us to understand.

Genesis thus rushes to the rescue of structure, and in speaking of the origin we come to understand the human condition *hic et nunc*.

Man is born, and dies. Everything in myth, including its language, underscores mankind's mortality. Men are *mortals* (*brotoi, thnētoi anthrōpoi*) before they are designated as earthlings. And they are earthlings only as they are "those who live on the earth," *epichthonioi* (for example: Hesiod *Theogony* 372, 564, 755; from *epi* [upon] and *chthōn* [earth]). *Chthōn* is not the primordial earth (*gē*) but the soil solidly rooted between the sky of the Olympian gods and the depths of Hades, the soil upon which the dwellings and cities of men are built. At the very most, the word *chamaigeneis* (Hes. *Th.* 879; *Homeric Hymn to Ceres* 352) refers to the origin. But this rare and obscure term surely designates nothing but "men who are born *on* the earth." G. Dumézil (*Le festin d'immortalité*, pp. xv–xvi) observes that for the majority of Indo-European languages man is "the earthling" (thus in Latin: *homo* from *humus*) before he is "the mortal," making the Greek choice of mortality more than a linguistic preference: it is a quiet affirmation free of euphemism. The problem with men in the final analysis is not that they exist—in a manner of speaking, man is what is there—but that they die; to put it another way, they are constituted by death.

A later tradition tells that humanity, created by Prometheus and Athena, is made of clay and wind (*Etymologicum Magnum*, s.v. "Ikonion"), just as Babylonian man is made of clay mixed with the blood of a god, or as Hebrew man is dust to which the Creator gave the breath of life. But, more generally, Greek mythology does not care to construct a duality of the mortal body and the immortal soul. It leaves the question to philosophers, who associate the body with earth and the soul with ether (see Euripides *Suppliants* 531–6) or who use fire to give life to the mixture of earth and water that makes the human being (Empedocles frag. 454 Bollack; Plato *Protagoras* 320d). Greek myths read death into life and prefer to tell of the irremediable separation that has excluded men from the company of the gods.

To generalize from what J.-P. Vernant writes about the myth of Prometheus in Hesiod, "in a certain way the narrative [of this separation] accounts for the creation of man" ("Prométhée," pp. 6–7).

For while men were close to the gods during the golden age of origins, they are no longer so. Hesiod and Pindar go as far as to say that men and gods have a common origin (Hes. *Works and Days* 108; Pindar *Nemean Odes* 6.1ff.). Clearly, they were all born of Gē, but some fault broke the happy time of conviviality to which certain texts allude (Hesiod frag. 1 Merkelbach-West), and in the *Iliad* 5.440, Apollo brutally reminds the hero Diomedes that "there will always be two distinct races, that of the immortal gods and that of the humans who walk on earth."

In the myth of Prometheus in the *Theogony* 535–616, Hesiod also gives an account of this separation. Before the assembly of gods and men, the Titan Prometheus proceeded with the first sacrificial distribution, giving an advantage to men at the expense of the gods by means of a clever trick; ever since, human generations (*phula anthrōpōn*: Hes. *Th.* 556—and it is no accident that men were henceforth so designated) offer sacrifice to the immortals in an attempt to reestablish the broken link. But the break is made permanent when Prometheus repeats the offense by stealing for the human race the fire that Zeus denied them in his wrath. With fire for cooking, man comes into his own as a social being who cooks his food. Though the days of nectar and ambrosia are gone forever for him, at least he will not have to eat everything raw as animals do. But Zeus is not a god to admit defeat, and his wrath is hardly appeased by seeing "the dazzling glow of fire shine among men." Therefore, "in place of the fire he creates an evil destined for humans" (ibid. 567–70), and this evil is called woman (*gunē*).

He makes woman beautiful and evil, a costly luxury, a poisoned gift for humanity.

But if there were humans before woman was created, how is this added piece to become part of humanity? Formulating this abrupt question, we notice immediately that the humanity of woman is by definition ambiguous (J.-P. Vernant, "Le mythe prométhéen," pp. 192–93). If extending the word humanity is at stake, things are played out between two words that are distinguished in Greek but translated indiscriminately in French and English (languages even more radical than Greek) as "men": *anthrōpoi*, humans as opposed to gods; and *andres*, males as opposed to females. Greek social and political practices allowed only the *andres* to speak, and in the far reaches of their mythical thinking one can guess how sorry they were when women came along, and how they dreamed of living and reproducing themselves without passing through women (see Euripides *Medea* 573–75; Euripides *Hippolytus* 618ff.). Woman is the other, and the text of the Hesiodic myth designates her as long as possible in the neuter gender, as if it were necessary to delay the appearance of the feminine even in the signifying noun. The consequences, to be sure, are not minor: from the moment that this beautiful evil receives a name (591), "men" cease to be designated as *anthrōpoi* (588–89), and receive instead a new name, *andres* (592). If the creation of woman is the ultimate consequence of the separation of men and gods, the paradox consists in the fact that "men" are really born into the human condition only by becoming *andres,* or one half of humanity.

Two halves make a whole; that should have made (will have to make) them into one. But the two halves were originally alien to one another, since the creation of woman,

carefully distinguished from that of *andres*, comes out of an independent account. This is a specifically Greek trait: in *Genesis* the creation of woman is inseparable from that of man, even in the midst of a process in two time frames, and in the Babylonian myth of the creation of humanity seven couples of primordial ancestors emerge from the mold. Better yet, woman is not born, but made by an act of craftsmanship, that of Hephaestus carrying out the will of Zeus. She is therefore an artifice, a living *daidalon* (F. Frontisi-Ducroux, *Dédale*, Paris 1975, pp. 73, 102). "The famous lame smith modeled out of earth a being just like a chaste virgin" (Hes. *Works and Days* 71). In this semblance lies all the truth about woman: woman resembles a virgin; woman resembles a woman; it is the same as saying that she is entirely and essentially *a simulacrum*. Woman is indeed the "deceiving female form" of the Indo-European myths studied by Georges Dumézil, with this essential difference, that for the Greeks the "false woman" is not a man disguised but woman herself. Unlike the golden servants of Hephaestus, animated artifices in which the automaton resembles a living creature (Homer *Iliad* 18.417–20), woman lives by being an artifice.

In her and through her, therefore, duality is reintroduced into humanity. Not only does the addition of this surplus to the human species have the effect of cutting it in two. But if we are to believe the account of *Works and Days* 54–105, which echoes that of the *Theogony* without saying quite the same thing, woman is made of both earth and water, joining within herself "the voice and vigor of a human and . . . the beautiful, obliging body of a virgin, in the image of the immortal goddesses" (ibid. 61–63) and "the mind of a bitch" (ibid. 67). Until, later in the poem, Hesiod makes a womb for her. But, henceforth, the function of this womb is to reproduce humanity.

Here again, further aggravated, is the tension between the origin and human time. If it is difficult to go from the birth of the *gēgeneis* to the human cycle of generation, how could a living artifice assume the function of fertility? Hesiod resolves the difficulty nominally: the woman receives the name of Pandora, and it is not immaterial, even though the poet covers his tracks by inventing a new etymology for this word ("she who is the gift of them all": ibid. 81–82), that it is also

Pandora as mannequin; Aphrodite to the left, Ares to the right. London, British Museum. Museum photo.

one of the names for the earth ("she who gives all"). But it would be drawing a hasty conclusion simply to say that "the mortal Pandora is but a transposition of the maternal Earth into the human order" (L. Séchan, "Pandora, l'Ève grecque," *BAGB*, April 1929, p. 5). It would, for example, mean forgetting that in the Greek mythical tradition, at least the one preserved by the texts, we look in vain for even *one* autochthonous woman. And yet woman will indeed have to assume what used to be a function of the earth. Reflecting in their own way upon the strange relationship established between fertility and artifice in Pandora, Athenian potters eventually succumbed to the desire to conflate the Earth Mother and clay earth in her person. A cup in the British Museum shows Athena and Hephaestus busying themselves with a female figure, a statue or an automaton, a stiff doll to which the sculptor has curiously given the name of Anesidora—another ritual name for the Earth Mother; on the other hand, on a bowl at Oxford a splendid Kore named Pandora comes up out of the ground, betrothed and ready for marriage (see M. Guarducci, "Origine dell'Umanità," pp. 436ff.). Do we finally have her, this autochthonous woman? Those who hold the naturistic thesis, who claim to recognize in any female figure a hypostasis of the Earth Mother, are probably delighted. Others are surprised or attribute this contamination between Pandora and Pandora to the double nature of woman.

If everything is in order on the level of image, things are a bit more complicated in the narrative. For in the *Theogony*, the conclusion of the myth holds out one last ambiguity. "From her came the female breed of women" (Hes. *Th.* 590). Thus, far from designating the first woman as the mother of humanity—something we have a right to expect, after all!—the text makes the original woman the mother of a self-contained group, the female *genos*, the race of women, as if the same thing could only give birth to the same thing, as if the female sex could reproduce in a closed circuit. As in the myth of Aristophanes that is reexamined by Plato (*Symposium* 190b), the male is born of the sun—masculine—and the female of the earth—feminine. To complicate matters even more, a third sex, the androgyne, is born of the moon (see L. Brisson, "Bisexualité et médiation en Grèce ancienne," *Nouvelle Revue de Psychanalyse* 7 [1973]: 27–48).

The ambiguity of the word *genos* in Hesiod and Plato alike makes it as well suited to designate a sexual gender as to characterize humanity as a whole. But this is more than a simple question of words. "Are we born of one or of two?" "Is the same born of the same or of the other?" Under the rubric of these two variants formulated by Lévi-Strauss ("La structure des mythes," p. 239), the Greeks themselves raised the problem. Apparently, it was not an easy matter to admit the mixing of the sexes. How can men who are truly men and women who are indeed women be born of sexual union? Must we admit that there are male seeds and female seeds? And how can the one come out of the mixed? These questions were raised repeatedly by philosophers and physicians, tragic and comic poets, and also, perhaps, legislators. But it was myths that first raised them.

Pandora has forced us to make a significant detour—no doubt a female trick of hers!

One final word, however, before consigning this "artificial heart" to silence. The myth of Pandora is perhaps the only myth of origin that established itself in Greek tradition without any rival or challenger (see for example Aristophanes *Thesmophoriazusae* 786ff.), so that the *genos* of women is in Greece the bearer of the misfortune and death of men, in a word, the bearer of the tragic (see Aeschylus *Seven against Thebes* 182–201).

Returning to the topic of *andres* and taking the term this time in its civic sense, the *andres* are the adults, the citizen-soldiers. A Greek adage asserts that their assembly constitutes the city (*polis*). The national tradition of each city gives it as ancestor a "first man," a founding father and a civilizing or political hero, born of the earth like Erichthonius of Athens; born of a nurturing river like Phoroneus of Argos; born of a swamp like Alalcomeneus of Boeotia, or born of the union of a god and a mortal woman (or nymph)—thus Arcas, eponymous ancestor of the Arcadians, is a son of Zeus and the nymph Callisto, and Pelasgus is a son of Zeus and the mortal Niobe. The cases of contamination between these different origins are many. Erichthonius the autochthon may also rightly be called "the son of the gods," and Athenian tradition is fond of this glorious title, which it extends collectively to all *andres Athēnaioi*. Similarly Pelasgus, the son of Zeus, in another version of the myth is "similar to a god, he whom the black earth brought into the world in the mountains with the long-haired summit, so that there might be a race of mortals" (Pausanias 8.1.4). Phoroneus, sometimes the son of the river Inachus alone, and sometimes son of Inachus and Melia, is the "first human," the "father of mortal men."

Nineteenth-century German scholarship (e.g., L. Preller in *Philologus* 7 [1852]: 1–60) attempted to reduce these multiple legends to a single myth, a myth of the origin of humanity, that was common to all Greeks and of which each city presented merely a local form: men born of the earth or of the union of the earth and the sky (Zeus representing the sky and each of his female companions a barely individualized hypostasis of the Earth Mother). These tiresome reductions to a single and everlasting history usually forget the specific traits of each tradition or figure, divine or human—Zeus is not the sky; Deucalion will not be reduced to Zeus nor Pyrrha to the red earth; the fire of Phoroneus, a fire of heavenly origin like the one Zeus sometimes lit on the top of ash trees (Hes. *Th.* 563), could not possibly be confused with the fire that Prometheus stole for men, nor with the fire that burns in the forge of Hephaestus, the "father" of the Athenians (Aeschylus *Eumenides* 13). Besides, it is poor method to keep trying to reconstitute a unity, as if a primitive *logos*, unique and lost forever, could still find expression through fragments of discourse, through the contingent vestiges of a paradigm that has disappeared.

It is not that each city yearns to narrate the birth of the first man in its own way, but that any national tradition is less interested in giving a version of the beginnings of humanity than in postulating the nobility of the stock from which it originated. The Erechtheides, the Athenian autochthons, liked to recall that the Erechtheum was also the temple of Athena (see Homer *Iliad* 2.549); as descendants of Pelasgus, the Pelasgi are the true inhabitants of the Peloponnese. To be sure, such traditions tend to raise the problem of the passage to humanity. If Erichthonius or Phoroneus open up the time of human history for the *polis*, be it Athenian or Argive, what is there that is closely related to Athena that makes the first of the *andres Athēnaioi*? How can the son of Inachus put an end to the primordial time when the first inhabitants of Argos were the rivers? Zeus is the most frequent "father" of national heroes, which leads certain people to take literally the Homeric expression "Zeus, father of gods and men," which they may see only as a kinship term. Be that as it may, the problem persists: What makes a son of gods the first of

Pandora is born of the soil. Attic krater. Ca. 450 B.C. Oxford, Ashmolean Museum. Museum photo.

the humans? This question was really of little concern to cities. What mattered was that the eponymous ancestor was both fully human and yet prestigious by virtue of his birth. Thus the present finds its justification in the genealogy that ties it back to the farthest reaches of the past. From the archaic period onward, poets, the first logographers (and the magistrates of the cities?), determined these "ancient histories," quasi-histories of the cities or even of the Greek people, tracing the Pelasgian race back to Phoroneus or Pelasgus, and the race of the Hellenes back to Deucalion.

Between each of these "first men" of miraculous birth or divine origin and the races of the first men who came out of the earth or were created by the gods, a gap widened, the same gap that separated the individual from the species, the name from anonymity. To put it simply, no generic ancestor of humanity received a name in the Greek myths—not even the name of Man, as Adam does in *Genesis.* Conversely, every ancestor of a heroic stock or of a civic community was characterized by the name that he bore and handed down to his descendants in one way or another. (Thus for the tragic poets the Athenians are all Erechtheides, and one of the ten tribes that make up the civic corps of Athens is called Erechtheis. Likewise the Argives commemorate the memory of the first city founded by Phoroneus, *astu Phoronikon: Paus.* 2.15.5.)

Certain texts refer to Pelasgus or to Phoroneus as the "first man" (*prōtos anthrōpos*). Must we conclude that by assigning themselves a primordial ancestor all the cities claimed, each

for itself, the honor of having given birth to humanity, like those peoples who call themselves "men, thereby showing that in their eyes the essential attribute of humanity disappears when one steps outside the limits of the group" (see Claude Lévi-Strauss, *Les structures élémentaires de la parenté,*[2] Paris 1968, pp. 53–54)? To be sure, the insularity of the Greek cities fostered this point of view, while the competition for prestige set one against the other. Thus, Argos makes Phoroneus the civilizing hero who, by gathering his men in one city, became the first to put an end to their dispersion and solitude (Paus. 2.15.5); the Argives went so far as to assert that it was Phoroneus and not Prometheus who had given fire to humanity (ibid., 2.19.5). But another model took precedence in Athens, where the citizens attributed the autochthony of Erichthonius to themselves collectively and thought of themselves primarily as exemplary *andres,* born of the civic soil which was not only a mother but the land of their fathers. So too the desire to have witnessed the birth of the first human (*anthrōpos*) waned once the exemplary status of the autochthons had been proclaimed, and it is not altogether certain (despite Plato *Menexenus* 237d 7) that it ever played an important role in the national tradition of Athens.

Faced with the myths of the Athenians and the myths of the Argives—the two chief contenders (according to Pausanias 1.14.2) for the grand prize in the contest of antiquity which pitted Greek cities against each other by their interposed mythical ancestors—we would again suggest that there can be no single discourse on the origin but, quite to the contrary, a proliferation of rival and parallel statements.

By way of conclusion, let us take one last myth, that of Deucalion and Pyrrha.

The son of Prometheus and of an Oceanid—or of Pandora herself—Deucalion married his sister or cousin Pyrrha, the daughter of Epimetheus and Pandora. When Zeus in his wrath unleashed the flood to destroy humanity (or the bronze race, according to certain versions), Deucalion and Pyrrha owed their survival to the *larnax* (chest) in which they took refuge and escaped the cataclysm by floating on the waves for nine days. When they finally landed on dry ground, Zeus, to whom Deucalion had offered a sacrifice, granted him a wish. Because Deucalion wished that there be men again, a new humanity was born of stones, which the primitive couple threw over their shoulders. As they made contact with the earth, Deucalion's stones became men and those of Pyrrha, women. Later, Deucalion and Pyrrha would have children, among whom would be Hellen, the ancestor of all Greeks.

This myth is told by Apollodorus (1.7.2) but is not the late invention of a mythographer, as is confirmed by very ancient witnesses (Hesiod frag. 2, 4, 6, and 234 Merkelbach-West; Acusilaos of Argos, *F. Gr. Hist.,* 2. frag. 34–35; Pindar *Olympian Odes* 9.41ff.). It will serve as an example because in it the origin keeps splitting in two, ad infinitum (the origin of humanity and the origin of the Greek people; the "hard" race, born of the stone, and the heroic stock of Hellen, born of a man and a woman). In any case, all (or almost all) the cities adopted this myth to explain the common origin of mankind, and at the same time each claimed for itself the honor of having one day welcomed in its midst Deucalion, survivor of the flood and civilizing hero, founder of cities and temples (see Apollonius Rhodius *Argonautica* 3.1085–86).

How can this inextricable tangle of origins be unraveled? By beginning at the beginning, which is not really the beginning but, again, a new beginning: once there were men, and then there were none (or not enough). So humanity is born (or reborn). It is born of death (the *larnax*, the Greek ark, serves as a coffin at the birth as well as at the death of men) or of stone, which is the same thing if we accept the equivalence of petrification and death (e.g., Homer *Iliad* 2.308ff.). Only then will the cycle of generation be able to (re-)commence, with Hellen, the heroic founder of an illustrious race. On the one hand, we have men of stone: a play on words connects *laoi*, the people, with *lāes*, stones. On the other hand, at a later indeterminate time we have men who are children of men, but men whose ancestors are the mediator Prometheus and the first woman. Here the tangle of overlapping origins bears witness to the fact that myth is always an overdetermination of discourse.

By falling on the ground, stones become men. By mutation or by fertilization? If we are to believe the Latin version of the story (Ovid *Metamorphoses* 1.393–94), stones are the bones of the Earth, the great universal Mother, and the Earth is thus fertilized by herself, as the same by the same. But it is just as true that the same engenders the same: Deucalion produces *andres* and Pyrrha women, without sexual union (Pindar *Ol.* 9.44); separate and parallel sexes reproduce themselves, each for itself, without mixing. However, Deucalion and Pyrrha had parents: the cycle of generation had therefore been well under way. But we are led to believe that the fragile cogs of this process had quickly jammed. Certainly, the mother of Pyrrha is called Pandora, and in her the relationship between woman and earth is not simple. Encouraged not to recognize anyone but the Earth as their mother, Deucalion and Pyrrha seem to bear witness to the fact that the appearance of woman was for naught. But the creation of Pandora had its use, if only its delayed effect. For from that time forth the existence of woman was irreversibly established, and at the conclusion of this series of false starts, men and women were to unite and procreate, just as Deucalion and Pyrrha united

in order to have descendants. Here the myth stops: everything begins, there is nothing more to say about it.

By condensing within itself many Greek questions about the origin, the myth of Deucalion serves as an example. In no way does this mean that we have shown the Greek myth of origins *in extremis*. In most Greek cities, Deucalion is only a guest and not the first man.

For each city, everything has already begun.

N.L./g.h.

BIBLIOGRAPHY

1. Variations on the Myth of Origins

F. DUPONT, "Se reproduire ou se métamorphoser," *Topiques* 9–10 (1972): 139–60. M. GUARDUCCI, "Leggende dell'antica Grecia relative all'origine dell'umanitá e analoghe tradizioni di altri paesi," *Atti della Reale Accademia Nazionale dei Lincei*, 1927, 379–458. CL. LÉVI-STRAUSS, "La structure des mythes," *Anthropologie structurale* (Paris 1958), 1:227–55. P. VIDAL-NAQUET, "Le mythe platonicien du *Politique*, les ambiguïtés de l'âge d'or et de l'histoire," *Langue, discours, société: Pour Émile Benveniste* (Paris 1975), 374–90.

2. Man in His Exclusion: Myths of the Races, of Prometheus, and of Pandora

G. DUMÉZIL, *Le festin d'immortalité*, esquisse d'une étude de mythologie comparée indo-européenne (Paris 1924). E. SIMON, "Pandora," *E A A* 5:930–33. J.-P. VERNANT, "Le mythe hésiodique des races: Essai d'analyse structurale"; "Le mythe hésiodique des races: Sur un essai de mise au point," *Mythe et pensée chez les Grecs* (2d ed., Paris 1971), 1:13–41 and 42–79; "Prométhée et la fonction technique," ibid. 2:5–36; "Le mythe prométhéen chez Hésiode," *Mythe et société* (Paris 1974), 177–94. P. VIDAL-NAQUET, "Valeurs religieuses et mythiques de la terre et du sacrifice dans l'*Odyssée*," *Annales ESC* 25 (1970): 1278–97.

The Powers of Marriage in Greece

I. Hera, Artemis, and Aphrodite

Like bread made of ground wheat and wine distilled from the "savage mother" (Aeschylus *Persians* 651), or meat made edible by the flame of the hearth, the bride takes her place among the inventions convoked to launch what Greek men referred to as the cultivated life, the life that turned them away from savagery and made them sink roots in a state intermediate between animals, which eat plants or raw meat, and gods, who never feel the need for wine or bread. Without the grace of such divine powers as Demeter and Dionysus, closer than others to the earth of mortals, men would never have eaten anything but acorns or have drunk anything but water. The intervention of the gods was therefore decisive, even if they handed over their gift without hidden motives only to devoted heroes like Triptolemus or inventive heroes like the king of Eleutherae, proportioning pure water to be mixed with wine in order to temper its violence, which was too strong for anyone not of divine nature.

But the gods seem to have been less active when it came to establishing a monogamous relationship between man and woman. Of the two principal myths that tell of the form of

association that we call marriage (a word without an exact equivalent in the Greek language), one focuses on the character of the legislating king and gives a privative version of marriage, while the other, dominated by the collective and almost anonymous image of extraordinarily industrious women, traces an outline of marriage consisting of triumphant virtues and mastery. Cecrops, the first semilegendary king of an Athens that questioned its own origins, brought to an end the era when haphazard unions were the only rule, when any man could mate freely with any woman by chance encounter, so that the father could never recognize his offspring. Cecrops put an end to sexual promiscuity: henceforth, one woman was joined to one man. Human sexuality began where coitus in the manner of animals ended. This male law of Cecrops was built both on the absence and on the sole identity of the father. The other myth tells the story of Bee-Women. In the olden days, men ate each other like animals; this was the era of allelophagia ("eating one another"). One day in the middle of the forest a woman discovered honeycombs. She tasted them and learned that they could be eaten as well as drunk after being mixed with water. From this fruit of the tree, half dry, half humid, the woman named Melissa, the Bee, drew nourishment, which she taught men to consume, thus tearing them away from their diet of red meat. Thanks to her and her female companions, henceforth known as Bees, mortals entered a new phase of life marked by respect for the gods as well as

Nuptial procession. Attic lecythus, ca. 550 B.C. New York, Metropolitan Museum of Art (Baker). Museum photo.

Nuptial procession. Lecythus by the "painter of Amasis." New York, Metropolitan Museum of Art (Baker). Museum photo.

respect for oneself and others. Modesty (*aidōs*) went hand in hand with chastity, and the first act of weaving soon covered the body with veils. That is why, according to the myth, no marriage has ever been celebrated since then without according the nymphs and Demeter the first sacrificial honors. Indeed, the relations between Demeter and the Bee-Women were secured at the level of the ritual of the Thesmophoria, where legitimate spouses bore the name of *melissai*, while the nymphs, familiar with modesty, occupied the place of the *nymphē*, a term that extended from the betrothed girl to the young bride. The Demeter of honey ranked second, and the Bee-Women opened the nuptial proceedings with the help of powers that their long lives situated at a spot equidistant between the Immortals and short-lived men.

But the gods' discretion at the inception of marriage found its counterpart in the multiplicity of their interventions all along the path from little girl to married woman. The marriage ritual bore witness to this fact when it prescribed, as Plutarch notes (*Quaestiones romanae* 264b), the offering of sacrifices to at least five deities: Zeus Teleios, Hera Teleia, Aphrodite, Peitho, and Artemis. To be complete, one should also add, besides the nymphs and Demeter, the Charites, Hermes, and the Moirai. In mythical and ritualistic terms, the configuration of powers summoned around the bride is arranged according to lines of force that are neither the exact copy of nor the model for institutional realities but that introduce at random, in their effort to delimit certain roles of woman, the variety of relationships, both of affinity and of antagonism, among the gods who share the conjugal territory.

Among the three female powers that occupy a strategic position in the marital arena, Hera incontestably holds first place, but the ritual insists on her necessary complicity with Artemis and Aphrodite alike. During the sacrifice that took place before the marriage, in the Proteleia, Hera was associated with Artemis and with the Moirai. Together they received the gift of the first cuttings of hair that young girls sacrificed to them before the nuptials. On the day of the wedding, Aphrodite joined them, bringing along with her Hermes, Peitho, and the Charites. But on another of the paths leading up to marriage, on the occasion of the sacrifice known as the Gamelia, Artemis seems to have been absent, and in this context her disappearance is undoubtedly signif-

icant. The Gamelia designates a type of sacrifice somewhat reminiscent of marriage, though it took place at a different time. It was the sacrificial banquet offered to members of the phratry by a young Athenian desirous of establishing official ties between his closest fellow citizens and the woman just introduced into his house. But the young bride had already left the domain of Artemis. She had made her way into the nuptial chamber, to which Hera possesses the keys, and she had slept in the bed prepared by the Charites, under whose sign the bride offered herself to her groom, while Aphrodite watched over their mutual pleasure in lovemaking. Woe to anyone who neglected to sacrifice to each of them; for having forgotten Artemis, who had further allowed him to harness a lion and a boar to the same chariot, Admetus entered a nuptial chamber filled with snakes. After his victory over Atalanta, Hippomenes performed the ritual sacrifices of marriage in honor of all the gods but Aphrodite; both he and his bride were transformed into wild animals. Equally indispensable, Artemis and Aphrodite held distinct positions in the marital territory. As the fourth-century A.D. rhetorician Libanius noted, girls proceeded from one to the other, from Artemis to Aphrodite.

Marriage was one of the frontiers of the domain reserved to Artemis, for along with the hunt, wild animals, and the wilds, virginity was her concern. No woman could become a bride unless she first dwelled in the kingdom of Artemis and paid the required tribute upon leaving: dolls, toys, hair, or, better still, as in Attica, playing the little "she-bear" in the service of the goddess. But the domain of Artemis is a place merely to pass through. It is a place of transition. No one can dwell in it, or attempt to return to it with impunity. The adventures of Atalanta bear witness to this fact. The female counterpart of Hippolytus, she devoted herself to the hunt because of her hatred of marriage. To escape the "gifts of Aphrodite," and to guard her virginity, she had to arm herself and wage war up to the very territory of Aphrodite in order to subvert marriage. In place of the close race of suitors, in which the desired body was promised to the fastest, she substituted the pursuit of an unarmed man fleeing before the huntress like desperate prey, his death inevitable if he is not the faster of the two. But virginity remained no more tenable in the middle of the forests or on the mountaintops than it was in her father's house. Trapped

Nuptial procession. Lecythus with black figures by the "painter of Amasis." New York, Metropolitan Museum of Art (Baker). Museum photo.

Young bride bearing a *lebēs gamikos*. Attic *lebēs gamikos*, ca. 440 B.C. Copenhagen, Nationalmuseet. Museum photo.

by Aphrodite, Atalanta was transformed into a frigid lioness, having failed to hold fast within the domain of Artemis. So too, Polyphonte wished to play the she-bear in defiance of Aphrodite, but was soon possessed by an irresistible desire to make love with a bear while the chaste Artemis looked on.

From Artemis to Aphrodite, the road is not from a wilderness to a richly cultivated land. In a manner of speaking, it is the Demeter of bread and grain who stands at the opposite end of the field, facing the borders of Artemis. Aphrodite's place is elsewhere, wherever desire is at work (*himeroenta erga gamoio:* Homer *Iliad* 5.429), as the Orphic commentary expresses it: "when a man and a woman couple, they are said to enjoy the pleasures of Aphrodite" (on the *Papyri Derveni* 17.12 [ca. 350 B.C.]). Without Aphrodite, without physical desire, the union of man and woman is destined to be sterile. But pleasure dwells in marriage like a disturbing force. Two models may encompass the bride's ambiguity, two animal figures, the bee and the mare. The bee is the female emblem of domestic virtues, more a nurse than a mother, with aspects of Artemisian purity, beyond desire and totally preoccupied, in her home, with producing abundant honey. The mare, by contrast, symbolizes the woman who must be reined in, like a horse not yet disciplined to the bit, because of the untamable violence of her desire. In Thessaly, land of horsemen, it was the custom on the wedding day to bring in a bridled war-horse and offer it to the new bride, holding it by the bit (Aelianus *De Natura Animalium* 12.34). "She who does not bear a yoke" is one of the names for a virgin, the wild filly whose master leads her by the bridle on the day of the wedding; she is covered with a nuptial veil and wears the circle of gold, the *ampux,* a word meaning both the horse's headstall and the bride's narrow diadem. On the level of vocabulary and through a series of images, the mare betrays the wild power that must be tamed in the young bride. The symbolism of the horse is marked by socioreligious values in accordance with the worth ascribed to this animal by a martial and aristocratic civilization; by exposing the bestial side of female sexuality, this symbolism provided an orientation for much of the tradition. The mare, says Aristotle, is the model of the female in her folly (Aristotle *History of Animals* 6.18.578a 8ff.). Passionately eager to make love, greedy to taste pleasure, mares in heat discharge from their genital organ a liquid that resembles

semen but is, as Aristotle specifies, much clearer than male sperm. It is the *hippomanēs*, a humor that resembles the mucosity of sows and is said to be particularly sought after by women who know the secret of love potions. Mare is the derogatory name reserved for women who indulge excessively in the pleasures of love. An old exegesis of the myth of Diomedes could transpose the monstrous character of his mares, which devoured passing strangers, by assigning this character to his own daughters, who were so wild in their lustfulness that no one compelled to make love to them could come out of it alive (schol. ad Aristophanes *Lysistrata* 1029).

The wildness of Artemis is something that a woman rids herself of as soon as she stops being the innocent little girl of the woods, while the unbridled madness of Aphrodite is something that each bride brings with her into her house. Each domestic hearth (*hestia*) bears within it the threat of a devouring fire, just as the opposite of the Bee-Woman, ever since Hesiod, is a voracious hornet that gorges herself on honey and knows no rules but those that satisfy her excessive desires. It may well be the Plato of the *Laws* who spoke in the most discursive mode of this inner enemy. To abandon women to their disorder, he said, is not only to neglect half the city, it is to run the risk of seeing them take on a role twice as important. That is why in the depths of his citadel the lawmaker entrusted selected women with the task of spying on young married couples all the time that procreation was increasing in abundance. Each day for ten years they met in the temple of Eilithyia, and indicated to one another those men and women the right age to procreate who were preoccupied with concerns other than those assigned to them by sacrifices and nuptial rituals (Plato *Laws* 783d–3).

Hera cannot do without Aphrodite, who is herself subject to her own law as much as she authorizes its enforcement. On the pediment of marriage is inscribed the figure of Hera Teleia, or Hera the Perfected One, a stern, sovereign figure. Her perfection comes not from her status as wife of Zeus, the first among gods and their king, but from her exclusive competence in all that the word *telos* implies for woman. Just as the body, in its prime, cannot keep its flower from blooming and cannot help knowing the sweetness of its fruits, so the female species is bound by nature to become a legitimate spouse or at least to be consecrated to that state by the marriage ritual. During the festival of the Theogamia,

Amymone and the satyr. Mosaic from Neapolis (Nabeul). Fourth century A.D. Photo Jean Marc Vène.

celebrated in Attica during the month of Gamelion (January–February), the season most propitious for fertility in human marriages (Aristotle *Politics* 1335a), Hera was associated with Zeus, for it was their union, celebrated by all the gods, that the ritual recalled. The drawing power belonged not to the husband but to the bride. The Attic calendar of the deme of Erchia specified that the victims chosen for the Theogamia were offered in sacrifice in Hera's shrine, and another regulation of the cult goes so far as to call the Zeus of marriage "Hera's Zeus" (Zeus Heraios: *IG*, I², 840, 11.20–21). The indications given by the cultic practice are confirmed at the level of myth when, in confronting Paris, who has been talked into choosing the fairest, Hera invokes her power as the sovereign of Zeus's royal bed in order to oppose Aphrodite's desires (Euripides *Iphigenia in Aulis* 900ff.). From Hera's perspective, the bride could know of no more certain accomplishment than to see herself identified by the ritual vows with the childbed in which her legitimate children would be born and in which the seed of a house of men would take root.

To understand clearly Hera's royal status, we must see it in the context of the legal impotence of a marriageable woman in a world of men. All the transactions were made between

males. They did not marry women; rather, women were given to them in marriage according to a spatial model that informed the rituals and the ceremonies. One of the powers of the father was to put his daughter at the disposal of another man; the contract, or *enguē,* by which the son-in-law and the father-in-law made a public agreement had as its objective the transfer of the woman from her paternal home to the house of the husband. In Greece, marriage was patrilocal, and the woman was a "stranger" (*othneios*) in her husband's family. As far as the pious tradition was concerned, she was the suppliant whom the groom led forth by the right hand. And the journey took place under the double patronage of Hermes and Aphrodite, both riding on a chariot whose symbolism extended, on a whole series of vases, to the classical chariot harnessed to mules and flanked by a train of attendants. It was on a chariot that Pelops carried away Hippodamia in her long veils, and the Boeotians preserved the practice of burning the axle of the marriage chariot in front of the house (Plutarch *Moralia* 271c–d). Master of the open spaces, Hermes was skillful in tracing a path leading the stranger, the bride, from one *hestia* to another; but through his association with Aphrodite, and in his function as a persuader, he sometimes whispered to the young bride the words that would lure her spouse; at other times, standing at attention in the bridal chamber, he placed his agility at the service of the pleasures of love. A terra-cotta plaque found in the sanctuary of Persephone at Locri shows Hermes mounted on the chariot of Aphrodite drawn by two conjoined figures of Eros: one male, carrying a dove; the other female, carrying a flask of perfume. The complicity between Hermes and Aphrodite was, furthermore, explicitly established through the beliefs about Hermaphroditus, the power that brings about in a single body the synthesis of both sexual powers and that receives the homage of his devotees on the fourth day of the month. This day is specifically devoted to Hermes and Aphrodite, and the *Works and Days,* attributed to Hesiod, recommends it as one on which to bring home your wife (schol. ad Hesiod *Works and Days* 800). But Hera takes great care to avoid being confused with the shapely and smiling Aphrodite. Tiresias learned by sad experience: called upon to settle the question of which one of the royal couple had more pleasure in love, the soothsayer provoked the wrath of Hera by revealing that the woman's body experiences nine times as much pleasure as that of the man during intercourse. In Hera, the Greeks conceived an image of marriage as a refusal of what is called *aphrodisia*—desire and pleasure—in the name of a contract and commitments that assure woman the status of legitimate wife. The distance is all the more marked in that Greek society made a distinction between the woman for pleasure and the mother of legitimate children; concubines and het-aerae on the one hand and, on the other, the woman whose children are introduced into the phratry by a citizen who can swear that their mother is a wife bound by contract to a man of the city.

On an Attic vase with red figures in the Louvre Museum, Hera carrying the royal scepter assists in the bride's marriage preparations. She herself wears the cecryphalis, the lotus flower diadem, and a large black mantle, while Zeus stands at her side also holding a scepter. But the sovereignty of woman, here represented in the glory of the wedding ceremony, also recognizes its counterpart in this very place where the undivided autonomy of the legitimate wife seemed to be affirmed. For a series of mythical accounts surrounding Hera and her conflicts with Zeus explore the powers of the female body. The most detailed story is played out in the garden of Flora. Hera has set out for the ends of the world, the home of Oceanus and Tethys, traveling toward a wide river of sweet water in which the first couple dwells, brother and sister born of the same mother, and in which the nuptial chamber from which Hera derives her power and her rights over marriage is also established. She is angry; Zeus, after devouring Metis, has found himself pregnant with a daughter that he begot by himself with his own body, thus becoming a father without the help of his wife and dispossessing Hera of her essential power, the legitimacy of the conjugal bed, which coincides with her sovereignty over the royal bed. She therefore comes to this primordial place looking for ways to avenge herself. As she confesses to Flora, she is ready to try every potion, explore the seas, descend into the abyss of Tartarus. But ever since the West Wind carried her off, Flora, formerly known by the name of Chloris, the Verdant, has reigned over a garden of a thousand colors, for everything in flower is hers, from wheat, the vine, and wine aging in the cellar, to youth in bloom, when bodies are vigorous and full of fire. Strange seeds come from her garden: some are flowers born of the blood of handsome young men who have been mortally wounded, like Hyacinthus or Adonis. And on the side,

unique and anonymous, is a flower from the land of Olen, which makes those who touch it fertile and cannot be resisted by sterility, a flower that engenders life and new blood, as opposed to the anemone, whose stem is formed of shed blood.

In the corner of Flora's garden Hera discovers the seed that allows her to conceive without contact with any other body. From the flower of Olen, Ares, the god of war, will be born. Three other narratives are part of the same series. The first two deal with monstrous children, of whom one is far more terrifying than the other: Typhon and Hephaestus. The blacksmith, who bears in his deformed feet and twisted legs the marks of his dominion over fire and wind, is born of a mother who conceives without "uniting in love," by defying the one she haughtily calls "her bedfellow." As for Typhon, also master of wind and fire, he emerges either from Gaea, the earth, when she is invoked by Hera, at the same time as heaven and the Titan gods, or from two eggs covered with the semen of Kronos and entrusted to the earth by Hera, who once again leaves for the ends of the world to avenge herself against the despotic power exerted by Zeus.

But between the two sons, who were conceived in order to confront the sovereignty of the king of gods, a more subtle relationship develops. The double egg covered with semen that engenders Typhon has its counterpart in the birth of Hephaestus, himself born of a clear, unfertilized egg, which the Greeks say is "carried by the wind" and which certain domestic birds are thought to conceive when the female of the species emits semen without the intervention of the male. These eggs are sometimes referred to as clear eggs and at other times as Zephyrian eggs, from the name given to the fertilizing West Wind—the same wind that carried off Flora and gave her the gift of her marvelous garden. They are at the center of the controversy over the female body, its powers, and its limits. For Aristotle, who insists on the futility of the female's autonomous progeny, the eggs of Zephyr are decisive proof that, left to itself, the female species is naturally marked by an inadequacy and is incapable of producing a seed that is sufficiently "cooked." A female is never anything but a mutilated and sterile male. Conversely, in a pre-Socratic tradition represented by Anaxagoras, Empedocles, and various other biologists, the same phenomenon clearly demonstrates that the female body is not at all inferior to that of the male, that the female provides a part of the sperm, and that she can spontaneously produce life from herself.

The monstrous children of Hera, whom she begets without uniting in love with her husband, are part of the tradition of the autonomous female body. Hera wants to bring proof that she can be both mother and father. But the claim made by the power known as *teleia* is expressed in the conjugal framework within the limits of the matrimonial realm upon which the sovereignty of Zeus's wife is exercised. The fourth narrative, which corresponds to the story of Ares, adds an essential act to Hera's plot: It is the birth of Hebe, or Adolescent Youth, whom her mother produces after eating a head of lettuce. The sister of the god of war—who in the masculine mode embodies the virtue of youth—bears a name that in Greek means the age of sexual maturity, when the pubis is first covered with hair. Now Hebe, who is the female version of the handsome Ganymede at Phlius, for example, is born of a plant whose virtues are clearly defined in Greek tradition: a cold and damp plant, the lettuce has a well-established reputation for being a food for cadavers and for making those who eat it impotent. The death of Adonis, the seducer, is closely connected with it. Thus lettuce is marked by symbolic values that appear contradictory: by swallowing it, the austere Hera, deity of marriage, conceives a daughter, Hebe (Youth), the nubile body in all its splendor; whereas the all too beautiful Adonis sees himself bereft of his sexual power upon contact with the same vegetable. The paradox of lettuce would be insurmountable but for two other elements that serve to clarify the ambivalence of this vegetable. On the one hand, lettuce has the virtue of promoting lactation and menstrual flow, that is, the humors of the female body which are the signs of fertility; on the other hand, women are forbidden to eat the heart of the lettuce, that is, the part of the plant containing the milky juice that most closely resembles male semen. What the plant associated with Youth provides for Hera is thus the dual promise of an autonomous fertility and, at the same time, of the death of male sexual power. Woman alone occupies the space of legitimacy, but she is no more than a body without pleasure, tied by unbreakable bonds to the conjugal bed, trapped in her wifely status, which deprives her of all association with *aphrodisia*.

M.D./g.h.

II. Other Myths: The Danaids, Cyrene, Bellerophon

A number of situations and exemplary mythical figures seem to play a significant role in connection with marriage as defined in the Greek.

This is particularly clear in the case of the Danaids, whose entire fate seems to be wrapped up in the institution and rituals of marriage. They follow their father to Greece and set foot on the plain of Argolis "of a thousand thirsts" (*Etymologicum Magnum*, s.v. "Polydipsion Argos"), a land stricken with drought as a result of the quarrel between Hera and Poseidon. Repulsing the advances of the fifty sons of Aegyptus who are pursuing them, they flee. This refusal of marriage in its normal process, a process that includes a final exchange and the surrender of the authority of the father in favor of the authority of the husband, seals the fate of forty-eight among them: Aeschylus depicts them as rebelling against the idea of being led away by the sons of Aegyptus like so many bridled mares (Aeschylus *Suppliants* 430–32; see also 8–11, 141–43, 287–89, 392–96, 787–99); they are ready to hang themselves rather than accept marriage. They later seem to consent to concluding a matrimonial contract, but when their father gives each a dagger and orders each to put her husband to death in the course of the wedding night, it is again their father that they obey, and it is the blood of their husbands and not that of their virginity that will flow during the nuptial night. Later in their earthly story they are handed over by their father to men of no means, whom he excuses from the obligation of offering presents, thereby once again fostering a scandalous relationship in that it is deprived of the *exchange* characteristic of true marriage. The Danaids are finally massacred by the surviving son of Aegyptus, who thus avenges his brothers; and, beyond death, they are condemned to pour water forever into a bottomless receptacle in Tartarus—in other words, to perform *eternally* the *loutrophoria*, the essential ritual of marriage, which they refused to perform *once* on earth on the occasion of a completely regular, legitimate wedding.

Against this tragic and negative background, the fate of the two other Danaids, Hypermestra and Amymone, unfolds in the opposite direction. Hypermestra was the one who, during the fatal night, disobeyed her father's orders, thus agreeing to surrender her status as a maiden and to take up that of a wife in submission to the authority of her husband. Henceforth she sides entirely with the *genos* of Aegyptus, and it is thanks to her that vengeance against her sisters will be carried out at the hands of Lynceus, the spared husband. Amymone, whose myth is very rich, is, by contrast with her forty-eight misguided sisters, one of the leading models of womanhood as defined by Greek thought, illustrating the normal female condition in which fully accepted marriage occupies a central place. At first a compliant *parthenos*, she obeys her father when he asks her to fetch water in the arid Argolis. During this errand, two versions of her myth (Apollodorus 2.1.4 and Hyginus *Fabulae* 169) depict her as engaged in hunting—normally a male activity. Inversion is a characteristic of rites of passage. She is then accosted by a satyr and refuses to be possessed *without something in exchange*, which would amount to rape. Meanwhile, Poseidon intervenes and drives the satyr away; since he offers Amymone a union freely consented to, complete with *the exchange of a present* (which turns out to be the very water that her father asked for), she is able to accept the terms of the exchange, which in effect constitutes a marriage contract. The trident stuck into the ground symbolically seals the union (Nonnus *Dionysiaca* 8.241 refers to it as *sē gamōn*); water bursts forth (to become the springs of Lerna), ending the thirst of Argos. Amymone, who assumes the status of *nymphē* (young bride), becomes at the same time the *nymphē* (nymph) of the newborn spring. This is the same spring to which the young women of Argos responsible for weaving Hera's veil will henceforth go first to be purified (Callimachus *Aetia* frag. 66). Not only is Amymone the heroine of a perfectly accomplished nuptial *loutrophoria*, but she also becomes a source of future *loutrophoriai* for the young girls of Argos. As such, Amymone, just like Hypermestra, escapes the punishment of the other Danaids (Lucian *Dialogi Mortuorum* 8), in whose crime she had no part (although mythographers say that she killed Enceladus, the son of Aegyptus. Already united with Poseidon, she did not have to suffer yet another husband). The celebration of Amymone's marriage to Poseidon is described explicitly by Nonnus (*Dionysiaca* 43.383–93), but the nuptial character of their relationship is implicitly marked, in most texts of the myth, by the use of the words *gamos*, *gamein*, and *gameisthai* (Aeschylus *Amymone* frag. 13, Nauck; Philostratus *Imagines* 1.8). The evidence of visual representations is no less eloquent. The *hydria*, which occupies a central place in the symbolism of Amymone, stands out as the archetypal *loutrophoria*. In the fourth century B.C. there are definitely nuptial representations of the couple, and E. Simon, who has catalogued these representations, attributes a nuptial use to many of the vases that evoke this myth. Finally let us note that a late mosaic discovered by J. Ch. Balty at Apameia represents Amymone enthroned next to Poseidon in her capacity as legitimate wife. In the face of the other Danaids, Amymone constitutes the mythological model for the successful passage from maidenly to wifely status through acceptance of the nuptial exchange and accomplishment of the ritual of *loutrophoria*, in terms of which, as we have seen, all narratives about the Danaids are organized.

Beside this particularly rich and coherent corpus, Greek myth includes other exemplary figures in the domain of marriage, notably Cyrene in her connection with Apollo (Pindar *Pythian Odes* 9.5–70). Like Amymone at the beginning of her myth, Cyrene is at first a young virgin occupied with hunting. Apollo notices her when she indulges in the eminently male activity of fighting a lion with her bare hands. (The lion is conquered in all versions of the myth.) Taken with her, Apollo knows that he must *delay* the satisfaction of his desire. He first carries her away to Libya, to the "marvelous garden of Zeus and Hera." There the nuptial chariot is welcomed by Aphrodite, who is full of "amiable modesty" and blesses the "marriage between the god and the daughter of the powerful Hypseus." It is not until after he has given her the *gift* of sovereignty over Libya, where she is awarded a *legitimate domain,* that Apollo unites with her in her golden palace. The fountain of Kure is named after her. In its water, which feeds the grotto of Artemis, young women of the city of Cyrene were to come to purify themselves before their nuptial union (Sokolowsky, *Lois sacrées,* 115: *lex cathartica* of Cyrene, 7). Like Amymone, Cyrene assumes the condition of a nymph in its entirety by being both a nymph of the spring water and a young bride (*pēgē kai hē neogamos gunē:* Photius, s.v. *numphē*).

We rarely see the adolescent god Apollo engaged in a matrimonial relationship, and this aspect of his myth must be plumbed more deeply. There is, however, no doubt that the couple that he forms with Cyrene exemplifies a solemn marriage based on *exchange* and on the observance of all the rituals. This is further confirmed by the personality of Aristaeus, the hero born of this union, who is, as M. Detienne has shown, the model of the accomplished man (his very name demonstrates this). A young man with a first-class education, abiding by all the social rules, the perfect host, the perfect son-in-law, he is the irreproachable husband—until the moment of his fateful meeting with Eurydice, who diverts him for a moment from the straight path only to the extent that, as mistress of the honeymoon, she signifies the threat of excess in the marital relationship itself.

Along with Aristaeus, Bellerophon is a figure whose fate seems to be organized entirely as a function of the problematics of marriage seen from the male point of view. His mythic course vacillates almost entirely between one marriage missed and another consummated. The first sequence of his myth finds him in Troezen, where he is a Corinthian suitor for the hand of Aethra, the daughter of the wise old king Pittheus, and is forced to renounce her because of his exile from Corinth (Pausanias 2.31.9); and one of the last sequences, if not perhaps the very last, is the celebration of his wedding with Philonoë, the daughter of Iobates, king of Lycia. Deprived of all rights to the aristocratic status of head of the *genos* because of an original exile, the cause of which remains mysterious (mythographers, basing their theory on a fanciful etymology of his name, have claimed that the cause was the murder of a certain Belleros), Bellerophon covers an itinerary that leads him to regain this status after a series of trials over which he triumphs successively.

The first is the most difficult, and his success in this guarantees success in all the others. This first task is the taming of Pegasus (Pindar *Olympian Odes* 13), the archetypal horse, son of Poseidon and of the Gorgon and hence a half-brother of Bellerophon, who is a descendant of the same god. Despite all his efforts, the hero cannot master Pegasus without Athena's intervention. She teaches him the necessary ritual and gives him the gift of a "bit, that golden diadem." Obeying the goddess scrupulously, Bellerophon immediately gains mastery over the animal and makes him execute dance steps. Pegasus is a very rich figure semantically: his taming implies mastery over the unchained natural forces that emanate from Poseidon and also dwell within

Poseidon and Amymone. Mosaic from Nea-Paphos. Third century A.D. Cyprus Museum. Museum photo.

Wedding of Bellerophon and Philonoë. Mosaic from Neapolis (Nabeul). Fourth century A.D. Photo Jean-Marc Vène.

Bellerophon, his own brother. But given the relations that mythical thought establishes between the tamed and harnessed horse and the young bride, this initial success metaphorically foreshadows the hero's triumphant wedding: the henceforth constant presence of Pegasus harnessed and bridled at the side of Bellerophon confirms the thesis that the theme of taming/marriage is at the very core of the myth. The evidence of visual depictions illustrates this parallelism explicitly by having Bellerophon flanked, symmetrically, by Pegasus, held by the bit, and the young woman in a bridal gown. (It is undoubtedly the same symbolism that explains how young adults coming of age at Cyrene are offered, upon leaving the banquet of the Artamitia, a horse harnessed and bridled with gold; see Athenaeus 550a.)

The second task is that of illicit seduction. As in the case of Amymone, for whom he is the male counterpart (Homer calls him *amumōn*, irreproachable; Homer *Iliad* 6.155, 190), Bellerophon must first show that he is capable of rejecting seduction in order to be able to accede to marriage; and that is what he does when he resists the advances of Stheneboea, the shameless wife of Proetus, the king of Argos, who is his host and is giving him shelter. Falsely accused by Stheneboea (sometimes known as Anteia) of having attempted to violate her, Bellerophon is sent off by Proetus (who cannot put him to death because he is his host) to visit his father-in-law Iobates, king of Lycia, bearing a letter which demands his

execution. Iobates, who grants Bellerophon hospitality for nine days before breaking the seal of the letter, and who, like Proetus (and Bellerophon), scrupulously respects rules, cannot put Bellerophon to death either, but exposes him to a series of combats, the canonical succession of which thoroughly underscores the hero's progress toward his glorious final status and can hardly be the result of pure chance. First there is the exemplary hunt for the Chimera, a monstrous embodiment of wildness compounded of goat, lion, and serpent. Then comes the victory over the Solymi, a tribe of wild men. Although more than a hunt, it is not yet war. The fight with the Amazons is a real war but a war against a monstrous (if civilized) people consisting exclusively of warrior women. Finally comes the confrontation with the best of the Lycian warriors. Bellerophon, who from the beginning has been armed with a spear (as a hoplite), here finally encounters his true peers, and his victory marks his reentry into the very heart of the city. A seventh and last trial still awaits him, however, once again challenging his relationship with woman and constituting his ultimate victory over himself. Having conquered the Lycian soldiers, Bellerophon is furious with Iobates for ceaselessly exposing him to new perils; intent on destroying the city, he invokes the help of his father, Poseidon. He advances, and behind him advances a giant wave, which covers everything and threatens to swallow up the city. The Lycian women then come forward and offer themselves to him, imploring him to spare the city in exchange for their favors. But his *modesty* prevails, and he who has vanquished warriors withdraws, *hup'aischunēs*, before the women. The wave withdraws, the city is saved (Plutarch *On the Virtues of Women* 9; Homer's narrative, *Iliad* 6.155–205, does not refer to this final trial). The happy fate of Bellerophon is finally sealed. As a token of their admiration and esteem, the people offer him a *temenos*, which this time puts him in a position to assume the terms of marital exchange, while Iobates offers him his daughter Philonoë and presents him with half of his royal privileges. The banished man, the fugitive, henceforth shares the prerogatives of kingship. Victory over wild forces without and within, victory in the hunt and in war, as well as the acquisition of a patrimony—Bellerophon has to go through these necessary steps in order to achieve at the end of his career the major social act, marriage, an enterprise of which the inexperienced adolescent, devoid of patrimony and virtue at the start of the myth, was incapable and unworthy. His fate is symmetrical to that of Amymone, and their myths define the respective positions of man and woman in the institution of marriage. The woman must be willing to accept marriage in order to attain fulfillment of her femininity, whereas the man must first and foremost realize the fulfillment of his virility before he can accede to marriage and to the founding of a *genos*. By means of piety, modesty, and virtues (the list of Bellerophon's moral qualities as it can be reconstructed from the texts is quite impressive), both he and she finally succeed in "fleeing from evil and finding the best," to quote the terms of the ritual formula of marriage in ancient Greece.

J.-P.D./g.h.

BIBLIOGRAPHY

A. BRUECKNER, "Athenische Hochzeitsgeschenke," *Mitteilungen des deutschen archäologischen Instituts, Athen. Abt.* 32 (1907): 79–122. J.-P. DARMON, *Nymfarum Domus. Étude des pavements de la Maison des Nymphes à Néapolis—Nabeul, Tunisie* (Leiden 1980). M. DETIENNE, "La panthère parfumée," in *Dionysos mis à mort* (Paris 1977); "Orphée au miel," in *Faire de l'histoire*, J. Le Goff and P. Nora, eds. (Paris 1974), 3:56–75. L. DEUBNER, "Hochzeit und Opferkorb," *Jahrbücher des deutschen archäologischen Instituts* 40 (1925): 211–23; "Eine Hochzeitsvase in Bonn," *JDAI*, 1936, 175–79. S. EITREM, "Les Thesmophoria, les Skirophoria et les Arrétophoria," *Symbolae Osloenses* 23–25 (1944–47): 32–45. F. HARL-SCHALLER, "Zur Entstehung und Bedeutung des attischen Lebes gamikos," *Jahreshefte des österreichischen archäologischen Instituts in Wien* 50 (1972–75), c. 151–70. A. R. W. HARRISON, *The Law of Athens 1: The Family and Property* (Oxford 1968). K. KÉRÉNYI, *Zeus und Hera: Urbild des Vaters, des Gatten und der Frau* (Leiden 1972). R. MUTH, "Hymenaios und Epithalamion," *Wiener Studien* 47 (1954): 5–45. F. SALVIAT, "Les théogamies attiques, Zeus Télios et l'*Agamemnon* d'Eschyle," *BCH*, 1964, 647–54. E. SIMON, "Amymonè," in *Lexicon Iconographicum mythologiae classicae* (Zurich and Munich 1981). P. E. SLATER, *The Glory of Hera: Greek Mythology and the Greek Family* (Boston 1968). J.-P. VERNANT, "Le mariage," in *Mythe et société en Grèce ancienne* (Paris 1974). H. J. WOLFF, "Marriage Law and Family Organization in Ancient Athens," *Traditio* 2 (1944): 43–95.

KINSHIP STRUCTURES IN GREEK HEROIC DYNASTIES: THE HOUSE OF ATREUS AND THE HOUSE OF LABDACUS

The history of the two principal heroic dynasties of Greek mythology demonstrates that both were concerned from beginning to end with the dominant problem of establishing the fundamental structures of society. The essential function of the dynasty may well have been to frame and resolve this problem, explicitly or implicitly.

I. The House of Atreus

Behind the myth of the house of Atreus lies the problem of the devolution of power (or of an inheritance) and of the mode of accession to sovereignty, with the risks that sovereignty presupposes by virtue of the proximity this privilege establishes between a mortal and the gods.

Tantalus was the son of Zeus and Pluto (Wealth). A king in Asia Minor, he established a relationship of commensality with the gods. Invited to their table, he consumed nectar and ambrosia, superhuman nourishment, and, in exchange, offered them a monstrous meal (his son Pelops cooked as a stew), all the while stealing nectar and ambrosia to feed to mortals. This behavior, so tainted with excess, earned Tantalus an eternity of punishment in Tartarus (having consumed ambrosia, he was immortal), where he would experience never sated hunger and never quenched thirst.

Such were the origins that foredoomed Pelops to his royal function. Reconstituted by the horrified gods (one shoulder, devoured by a famished Demeter, was to be replaced with an ivory prosthesis), Pelops was at first the cupbearer of the gods and then became king in Elis through his marriage to the daughter of Oenomaus. His intrinsic courage, along with his protection by the gods and his cunning and treachery, enabled him to fake a disloyal course of action that saved the princess Hippodamia from an abusive father/king, whom he managed to eliminate. Pelops then brought to Greece the fabulous riches of Asia, which he obtained from his father and from his mother, Euryanassa, the daughter of Pactolus, River of Golden Sands.

Among the many sons of Pelops, we find first Pittheus, the wise king of Troezen, the father-in-law of Aegeus, the mentor of Theseus, and consequently the ancestor and model of Athenian monarchy, the perfect monarchy. Last of the sons is Chrysippus, who was loved by Laius and was thus the cause of the first homosexual love among humans as well as the misfortunes of the monarchy of Labdacus in Thebes, the accursed monarchy. In the middle of the dynastic line, we find the twins Atreus and Thyestes, who with their descendants played the leading roles in the tragedy of the devolution of power in Mycenae, the city "rich in gold," where the throne was an endlessly recurring object of dispute.

There the origin of royal power resided in a wish of the people: bereft of a king (Eurystheus had been killed by the Heraclidae and left no child), Mycenae decided, on the advice of the oracle, to call one of the sons of Pelops to the throne. Both Atreus and Thyestes had long ago taken refuge in Mycenae. Which should be king? Atreus was the *older* of the two (though twinhood is precisely intended to weaken and contest the privileges of primogeniture), the *legitimate possessor* of the Golden Fleece (though this legitimacy is sullied as a result of disrespect toward the goddess Artemis), and the *husband* of Aërope, who was the granddaughter of Minos, the archetypal founder of monarchical power in Crete. Thyestes was the *younger*, the *thief* of the Golden Fleece, and the *lover* of the same Aërope. The people first chose Thyestes. Zeus himself produced a miracle on behalf of Atreus: the sun and the stars moved back in their course and set in the east. Thyestes abdicated and went into exile, and Atreus became king. But his excesses immediately compromised his legitimacy: Thyestes was recalled to Mycenae on the pretext of sharing power, but in reality he was fed a stew consisting of his sons, who had been massacred by Atreus despite the fact that they had sought shelter at the very altar of Zeus. *After having eaten of them*, Thyestes beheld the severed heads of his sons and took flight, cursing.

Thyestes needed an avenger, that is, a son. On the treacherous advice of the oracle, he united with his own daughter Pelopia without allowing her to recognize him (a triple sin because Pelopia was also a priestess and the rape took place during a sacred ceremony). Aegisthus was born of this union. Pelopia, armed with the sword she had taken from her unknown assailant, then returned to Mycenae, where Atreus, in a second marriage, took her as his wife and adopted Aegisthus as his son. The question of the devolution of power was thus raised in the following terms: Who should inherit the throne of Mycenae—Agamemnon, *elder son* from the first marriage, born of the *older* branch, fruit of the *legitimate* union and great-grandson of Minos; or Aegisthus, son of the *second* wife, *adopted* son, born of the *younger* branch, and fruit of a union that was not only *illegitimate* but also *monstrous*?

The second fit of excess perpetrated by Atreus favored the younger branch in a decisive way. Agamemnon and his brother Menelaus were sent abroad to seize Thyestes, who was imprisoned. Aegisthus was charged with the execution. He brandished a sword which Thyestes immediately recognized as his own, stolen by Pelopia during the rape. Aegisthus then killed Atreus and put Thyestes back on the throne of Mycenae.

Thereupon Agamemnon rose up against King Thyestes, the *younger son*, the *cannibal*, the *incestuous* partner, the *murderer* of his brother. Agamemnon took up arms, and with support from Tyndareos, king of Sparta, whose daughter Clytemnestra he married, he regained the throne of Mycenae and exiled Thyestes definitively. The *elder of the elder branch, legitimate son by the first marriage, innocent of all crime*, seemed to be solidly in power. But his excesses compromised everything. Full of pride in being the king of kings, chief of the expedition against Troy, he sacrificed his eldest daughter Iphigenia to obtain favorable winds, and thus aroused against himself the inexpiable hatred of Clytemnestra, who, Agamemnon barely on his way, took Aegisthus to bed. Mycenae now belonged to the *younger son, the son of the concubine, born of incest, the murderer*, who soon added to the murder of Atreus that of Agamemnon, who was ambushed on his return from Troy and slaughtered.

The pendulum of power swinging between the two families now returned the older branch to the throne in the person of Orestes, Agamemnon's son, who had been brought up abroad. On coming of age, Orestes returned to Mycenae and killed Aegisthus. But immediately after this vengeance his legitimacy was compromised by his excesses, which led him also to assassinate his own mother, who had been an accomplice in Agamemnon's murder. This time Orestes incurred the wrath of the powers of vengeance, the Erinyes, and was forced to flee from them. The throne of Mycenae was once again empty.

Order, as it was willed by the Olympians, was finally established. Orestes was ritualistically purified and then tried. The trial ended in his acquittal and established the supremacy of the father over the mother and the exclusively patrilineal character of descent. It guaranteed to the male, that is, the legitimate son of the older branch, the devolution of inheritance and power. Implicitly, this judgment placed an evil mark forever upon all the characteristics (increasingly monstrous with the passing of time) assumed by the younger branch.

II. The House of Labdacus

The history of the Theban dynasty of Labdacus is mainly concerned with the problem of setting in order the structures of kinship, a succession of generations that permits a linear evolution of time, something *it fails to establish* to the extent that it fails to grant woman her rightful place either as mother or as spouse.

The anomaly regarding the woman's position can be seen in various forms from one end of the story to the other. Cadmus, the founder of Thebes, by sowing the teeth of the dragon of Ares, caused a harvest of Spartans, whose survivors were the original Theban noblemen: he gave his son Polydorus to Nycteis (Night), the daughter of the Spartan Chthonius (Born of the Earth); and he gave his daughter Agave to the Spartan Echion. From these two Spartans were born the various families among whom the throne of Thebes incessantly alternated. Thus, in their origin, these motherless heroes were at the same time sons of the earth, the omnipresent mother.

When the female members of the dynasty played a notable role, it was that of the excessive mother. Agave in her Bacchic fury tore her son Pentheus apart with her bare hands; Nycteis deprived her son Labdacus of power in favor of his maternal uncles Nycteus and Lycus; Iocasta, the great-granddaughter of Pentheus, married her own son, Oedipus. On the other hand, wives were often passed over in silence. The wife of Pentheus and those of his son Oelasus and his grandson Menoeceus played no roles and left no names; on Polydorus's side, the same applied to his son Labdacus and his great-grandson Eteocles. If Laius, the great-grandson of Cadmus, had a grand passion, it was for a young man, Chrysippus, the son of Pelops; it was Laius who introduced homosexual love among humans, which was the origin of the curse placed on him and on his descendants. Pentheus in Euripides' *Bacchae* and Eteocles in Aeschylus' *Seven against Thebes* begin by reviling women and boast of wanting to make Thebes an exclusively male city.

The anomaly in the relationship between the sexes is mirrored by a chronic anomaly affecting the transfer of power in Thebes. Each ruler had kinship ties with the preceding king, of various kinds: son (Polydorus succeeds Cadmus), nephew on the sister's side (Pentheus), cousin on the maternal uncle's side (Labdacus), maternal grandfather (Nycteus), brother (Lycus), grandsons born of the daughter (Amphion and Zethus), distant cousin on the wife's side (Laius), brother-in-law (Creon), both brother-in-law and nephew (Oedipus), both brother-in-law and uncle (Creon), both nephew and grandnephew on the sister's side (Eteocles and Polynices), both uncle and maternal great-uncle (Creon), and both grandnephew and great-grandnephew (Laodamas). In this incoherent succession, the transfer of power through women plays an exorbitant and tangled role, fostering in effect three lineages of which only two have a lineal descent from Cadmus. Except for Polydorus, no son directly succeeds his father; and after Oedipus, words fail to describe the kinships. Oedipus was simultaneously both son and husband to Iocasta, father and brother to Eteocles and Polynices, uncle and grandfather to Laodamas, and nephew and brother-in-law to Creon.

As a result of the impossibility of putting the generations in order, *time slides*. Creon is always there to insure the interregnum, whether after the death of Laius, the departure of Oedipus, or the death of Eteocles. Better yet, Tiresias the soothsayer, who is a contemporary of Cadmus, reappears in just about all the mythical sequences that touch upon the Theban family; he is present as well at the death of the final scion, Laodamas, when he helps the people flee. Succession

to the throne could take place, as we have seen, equally well by climbing up or down the genealogical tree.

The fruits of so much confusion were sterility and death. Lycus died without descendants; Amphion saw all his children by Niobe die one after the other, as did Zethus, who lost the children that he had had by Thebe; Creon saw his son Haemon die. The only one to ensure a line of descendants was Laius; but Laius was cursed for having loved Chrysippus, and his race was doomed: Oedipus committed incest; Eteocles and Polynices killed each other. The last sequence of the myth shows Laodamas dead, the people in exile, and the city dismantled and sacked by the Epigoni.

J.-P.D./g.h.

DEATH IN GREEK MYTHS

I. Thanatos (Death), Son of Nyx (Night), and Trickery

To the Greeks, death was first of all the daughter of Night. According to Hesiod (*Theogony* 212), she belonged to the primordial period of solitary childbirths and of separations, in which Eros played no part. Alone and without sleeping with anyone, herself born of Chaos, Nyx gave birth to odious Death, gloomy Keres, and Decease. Thanatos, brother of Sleep (Hypnos) and Dreams, is thus inserted in a somber genealogy that includes the Moirai (the Fates), Nemesis (vengeance), Apate (deceit), Philotes (pleasure of love), and finally Eris (the discord springing from a violent heart) (see Cl. Ramnoux, *La Nuit et les enfants de la Nuit*, Paris 1959).

But this is not the only way the Greeks represented death. Side by side with this view, other deities came to refract the various aspects of death. First among them was Hades, who came by chance to be king of the dead. "We are three brothers sprung from Kronos, born of Rhea," says Poseidon; "Zeus and I and a third, Hades. . . . The world was divided into three parts, and each one had its lot. The lot I drew was to live forever in the white sea; Hades had for his lot the dark mist, and Zeus the vast sky, in the bright air and in the cloud" (Homer *Iliad* 15.187ff.) This tripartition of the world may be a natural split of the elements that surround the earth, the living space of men, but it is also a cultural tripartition of a mental universe. When the immortal gods reign and govern from the top of their Mount Olympus, and when the sea unfurls the uncertain motley of its powers, Hades is there, below. Zeus Katachthonios, "Zeus of the Underworld" (Homer *Il.* 9.457), marks the finiteness of mortals. Despised by everyone, even by the gods (Homer *Il.* 20.65), he rules over a moldering world (Hesiod *Works and Days* 153), its doors shut tight (Homer *Il.* 8.367), in an immobility disturbed only by his rape of Persephone (and then by his marriage to her). Inflexible (*ameilichos*) and indomitable (*adamastos*), he is ineluctable fate.

Next to Hades, another deity has a place in representations of death, Hermes of the Night, the chthonic psychopomp. His intervention in the underworld, however Olympian he may be, is justified on several counts. First, death involves a crossing over, a passage, for which Hermes serves as a guide. He thus appears at the head of the troop of suitors massacred by Odysseus: "Responding to the call of Hermes of Cyllene, the souls of the suitors hastened to him; the god

held in his hands the beautiful golden wand with which he charms the eyes of men or wakens them, as he pleases" (Homer *Odyssey* 24.1ff.). It is therefore he who leads men into the realm of the shades. His mobility qualifies him particularly well for this role. Guide, messenger, traveler, he will be all of these both among men on earth and among the chthonic shadows. As Diaktoros, he ensures the passage from one space to another. Death is a threshold, and Hermes helps to cross it. The coupling of Sleep and Death, "the one quiet and kind to mortals," but "the other with a heart of iron, and a brazen soul" (Hes. *Th.* 762–66), lends an ambiguity to the position of Hermes as master of dreams, as he appears when Ajax, preparing himself for death, invokes Hermes of the underworld: "May he put me to sleep gently and may it be a quick and easy leap when I tear my flank with this sword" (Sophocles *Ajax* 831ff.).

It is, however, not in terms of this passage that Hermes Nychios and Chthonios intervenes in Aeschylus's trilogy. The context is that of vengeance for the murder of Agamemnon, in which contrivance, trickery, and double meaning are of prime importance. Death, whether it is suffered or dealt, is an act of violence inscribed within the equivocal limits of an initial seduction; this seduction, nocturnal and disastrous (*talaina peithō*), never ceases to inspire traps, stratagems, and machinations. Death thus becomes an ambush from which there is no escape, a snare that will be specifically materialized by the ambiguous words of Clytemnestra and Orestes.

Thus primordial death, death as passage, and death as a trick—we must derive from these systems of representation what their confluence meant for the Greek vision of death.

But before embarking upon this line of inquiry, we should mention an axis of interpretation summarized rather clearly by E. Rohde in his book *Psyche:* "Dwelling under the earth, [the chthonic gods] see to it that the inhabitants of this land who revere them enjoy a double advantage: they bless the cultivation of the fields and ensure good crops for the living; they welcome the souls of the living into their deep dwelling place." Even when Wilamowitz (*Glaube der Hellenen*, 1:202ff.; cf. M. P. Nilsson, *Geschichte der Griechischen Religion*,[3] 1967, 1:456ff.) distinguishes between *gē* and *chthōn*, the former meaning wife and mother, the latter the cold depth of the ground, it is nonetheless their synonymy that forms the basis of an image of death in which the Earth, both the earth mother and the earth of fertility, is in the foreground. This theme underlies the happy return to the womb of an ever fertile soil and at the same time the beneficent circularity of a death transforming itself into fertility. Around this theme a whole series of signs intersect so as to become so many pieces of evidence. The wife who reigns over the realm of the dead, the formidable Persephone, is none other than the daughter of Demeter, Kore, who was abducted by Hades. But Hades in the context of the Eleusinian myth bears the name of death less than that of Pluton (which seems to be related to Plutus, son of Demeter and Iasion [Hes. *Th.* 969], who dispenses wealth). If Hades-Pluton may be recognized as the wealthy hoarder of corpses, he becomes through this arrangement the daimon of a fertility that is closely tied to Gē-Chthōn. Herein probably lies the explanation of Hesiod's advice: "Make your prayers to Zeus of the underworld and to Demeter the pure, to make the sacred grain of Demeter heavy in its ripeness" (Hesiod *Works and Days* 465).

But how do we then explain the intervention of a chthonic Hermes? Within the same quest for the original state of beliefs, we find at the sources of Hermes the psychopomp the marks of an archaic representation of fertility. On the one hand, given this sign of virility associated with the god of the phallic herms, we can understand that he would be the multiplier of herds, invoked at the same time as Hecate (Hes. *Th.* 444ff.): Hermes *polugios* (Pausanias 2.31.13) is therefore also a figure of fertility. On the other hand, the herm was initially probably a cairn, a simple stone marker placed on a mound. S. Eitrem (*Hermes und die Toten*, Christiania 1909) suggests that the custom of placing the herm in front of doors or on roadways can be traced back to an older practice: the dead used to be buried at these spots. If Hermes is the spirit of the stone, the spirit of the stone is a dead ancestor. Thus from the interpretation of a chthonic origin and from the phallic aspect there arises a Hermes who is inscribed in a universe where death is already fertility and the source of life, and where the spirit of the dead is protection for the living. P. Raingeard writes: "What can one expect, in practical terms, from the chthonic angel? Good tidings, namely, that the lord of the land does not hold a grudge against us. The earth will not open up, there will be water in the fountains, women will have children, ewes will have lambs, the crops will grow" (*Hermès psychagogue*, Paris 1934).

But the vocabulary and the situations described in the few myths dealing with Thanatos take us in a different direction. Death gets us through trickery, and it is through trickery that we may be able to escape him. Cerberus, the watchdog of Hades, is an irresistible monster (*amēchanos*: Hes. *Th.* 310) who guards his master's realm by playing a nasty trick (Hes. *Th.* 769: *technē kakē*): he fawns on the new arrivals with his tail and his ears, but once they have crossed the threshold, he forbids them to return. Conversely, Admetus was able to escape death because Apollo resorted to a subterfuge (*doliē technē*) in order to deceive the Moirai (Euripides *Alcestis* 33–34). Sisyphus's struggles against death are exemplary in this regard: according to one version of the myth (schol. ad *Iliad* 6.153 = F. Jacoby, *F.Gr.H.*, 3 F 119), in order to punish him for denouncing Zeus as the abductor of Aegina, the daughter of Aesopus, Zeus sends Thanatos to Sisyphus, who, instead of simply giving in, takes Death by surprise and chains him hand and foot. As a consequence, nobody dies anymore. Zeus (or Ares, according to some variants) is forced to intervene directly and to unbind Death so that he can get back to his business, whereupon Sisyphus dies. But, and here is the second trick, Sisyphus manages to convince his wife not to give him any funeral honors; thus, when he arrives in front of Hades, he can complain of his wife's impiety and ask Hades to let him cross the threshold in the opposite direction so that he can return to earth and punish the disloyal woman. Thus he manages to live happily to a ripe old age. But when he finally dies, the gods of hell, who

have not forgotten the crafty workings of his mind, condemn him in turn to a relentless task: he must eternally roll an enormous rock to the top of a slope, the rock keeps rolling back, and Sisyphus must keep starting up the hill with it again.

The trickery of Sisyphus is double, duping first Thanatos and then Hades. In words and action, Sisyphus makes use of a trap and a lie. In the binding trick, the chain proves impossible for Thanatos to loosen, and its circularity requires the intervention of Zeus. The trick then takes the form of a verbal dodge by which Hades is compelled to fulfill his own requirement that funeral rites be performed. The double reversal of the situation is that the victims of Sisyphus are trapped in the snare of their own laws. These are the very rules that govern the shifting universe of *mētis*, wily intelligence (see M. Detienne and J.-P. Vernant, *Les ruses de l'intelligence*, Paris 1974, passim, in particular "Le cercle et le lien," pp. 261–304); for if Sisyphus's refusal to die, coupled with his doubling-back subterfuge, characterizes his action as an *amēchania*, this very action is the mirror-image of death. In principle, no stratagem, no *mēchanē*, can allow escape from the snare cast by the brother of Hypnos, like a hunter, on his victim. Death is *aporia*, difficult for anyone to deal with except for Sisyphus, the cleverest man of all (*kerdistos*: Homer *Il.* 6.153), who resembles a god in the subtlety of his foresight (Pindar *Olympian Odes* 13.72). Death is confinement; it is circularity. And when Sisyphus, now an old man, must face the hour of ending his sojourn on earth, the gods, who have not forgotten the trickery and craftiness of his mind, weigh him down with a penalty that in its very characteristics harkens back to his past action by duplicating the circular chain of death itself. With neither beginning nor end, the movement of Sisyphus follows no trajectory but is rather a perpetual beginning again, in which the apparent mobility of the man forever pushing a rock to the top finally ends in the repetition of a paralyzing gesture: a mobility that engenders immobility, such is the infernal circle.

The wily intelligence of Zeus devised a full-scale representation of this phenomenon, reserved for his divine rivals: Tartarus. (According to one tradition, Thanatos was born of Gē and Tartarus; Sophocles *Oedipus at Colonus* 1573ff.) A space that can be neither measured nor defined, Tartarus is above all a place of the confusion of directions, caught in the unintelligible crosscurrents of winds blowing from every side, where the overturning of orientation neutralizes the trickery of the shrewdest people (Hes. *Th.* 869ff.). A universe without points of reference, "a triple row of shadow seals its narrow mouth" (ibid. 726–35). But if by virtue of its contour it is a place of irremediable enclosure—separated from everything, a kind of island set on the outer edges of the world, "in which the sources and the extremities of everything lie side by side" (ibid. 738)—this enclosure is inverted into a spatial infinity, an "immense abyss, whose depths one cannot reach even after an entire year has elapsed since one passed through its gates" (ibid. 740–41). It is not so much the enclosure itself as the interior whirlwind that overcomes the victim. Here too an excess of motion immobilizes the adversary. Not far from here lies "the frightful dwelling of infernal Night" (ibid. 744) and the dwelling place of her terrible children, Sleep and Decease (ibid. 756).

Death therefore has two frames of reference. As inscribed in the chaos of Night—chaos that has no representations since it has no orientation by any cardinal points—death is indefinable, measureless, defying all images. But in many instances, the vocabulary that describes death belongs to the semantic field of trickery. Its connections with sleep help to

Persephone and Hades. Apulian krater. Detail. Ca. 330 B.C. Munich, Bayerische Staatsgemäldesammlungen. Photo Koppermann.

The three Kronides: Zeus, Poseidon, Hades. An Attic cup of Xenocles. Ca. 550 B.C. London, British Museum. Museum photo.

Thanatos and Hypnos carry a dead warrior to his tomb. Attic lecythus. London, British Museum. Museum photo.

reinforce this aspect, an aspect that can at any moment become the instrument of subterfuge. Whether it be a deceiving sleep such as that with which Hypnos, bribed by Hera, envelops Zeus (*Dios apatē*: Homer *Il.* 14.233ff.), or the brutal and unrefreshing sleep with which Hermes strikes the guards of the Achaeans' camp in order to let Priam pass (Homer *Il.* 24.445), in all cases Hypnos, who is specifically referred to as the brother of Thanatos and who always carries around with him a certain taste of death, envelops his victims and deprives them simultaneously of vigilance and sight. It can be no accident that the only characteristic of Hades is a helmet of invisibility (*Haidou kunē*), a helmet "which contains the darkness of night" (Hesiod *Shield* 216ff.). In the context of a combat that is always unfair and necessarily wily, certain heroes or deities make use of this helmet to mete out death to individuals who are formidable or invincible—in a word, *amēchanoi*. This happens when Perseus confronts Medusa, or when Hermes kills Hippolytus in the Battle of the Giants (Apollodorus *Mythographus Bibliotheca* 1.6.2). Similarly, we may note that the ancients proposed etymologies connecting the name of Hades with the verb "to see" preceded by the privative alpha (*a-idein*): the Invisible. To see without being seen is one of the tricks of Hades, who does the final tally and whose "soul sees all, and keeps the imprint of all the faithful" (Aeschylus *Eumenides* 273ff.).

Trickery and death: from their intersection is born the dramatics of Aeschylus's trilogy, in which encounters with Thanatos are expressed in terms of hunting (see J.-P. Vernant and P. Vidal-Naquet, *Mythe et tragédie*, Paris 1972, pp. 135ff.). The net of Hades (*Haidou diktuon*: Aeschylus *Agamemnon* 1126–27), into which Agamemnon falls at Clytemnestra's hands, is the disguised snare (*mēchanēma*) that the king has just stumbled into: a limitless network (*apeiron*), a real fishnet (ibid. 1382). The fisherman's trickery duplicates the trickery of the ambiguous words with which Clytemnestra promises a way out, exceeding all hopes, as she rolls out the purple carpet. This *poros* is none other than Hades, the aporia. The death that strikes Agamemnon is a treacherous death (*dolios moros*: ibid. 1495, 1520), in which guile is a function both of the femininity of the avenger and of her power of seduction, *peithō* (ibid. 956–57, 1115, 1636).

Yet this fraudulent death also contains a component of truth. Out of the lie comes the light (Aeschylus *The Libation Bearers* 806, 961), in a story of death in which Dike takes her place next to Eris. Death is also a function of memory, and just as Hades is a scrupulous bookkeeper, the avenging wrath that guides Clytemnestra is a treacherous housekeeper (*oikonomos dolia*: Aeschylus *Agamemnon* 1555), the guardian of the palace of Argos. The death that is a chain of trickeries raises the question of its origin; and its origin goes back to a *talaina peithō*, a disastrous but seductive persuasion which, by turns, suggested to Atreus the idea of preparing for his brother Thyestes the sinister banquet consisting of the flesh of his children, to Paris the idea of abducting Helen, and to Agamemnon the idea of sacrificing Iphigenia. Henceforth, death is no longer a maneuver but a loss of one's way or a form of distress, which tips everything onto the side of Night and her dark, painful, and implacable progeny.

Thus the representation of death can be distinguished on two levels—one articulated in terms of trickery, the other in terms of the night—which join together around an original, malevolent, and nocturnal *peithō*. Through these two levels the double aspect of death is expressed, and upon them man could always work out the twofold contradictions of its power: there is one kind of death that man conceives of, imagines, and represents for himself, a death of which he will certainly be the victim but which conversely he may be able to provoke, a death he can manipulate and in certain respects control; this is the *mēchanē* death, the one that Sisyphus faces. But this death contains within it the second dimension, which radically dispossesses mortals even while they themselves lay the trap of their vengeance. The chorus in *Agamemnon* cries out: *amēchanō* (1530). The *amēchania* referred to here emerges less from the succession of plots hatched by the heroes than from the ultimate and absolute encirclement that is the very space of death and in the end subdues protagonists and spectators alike.

These two figures are also depicted in *The Libation Bearers*, in which the *dolia peithō* is revealed in its intimate connection with the darkness that envelops the house and is set beside the aspect of the mastery of death called righteous punishment, the reciprocity of trickery and murder (Aesch. *LB* 93–95). In this context, Hermes Chthonios is invoked as the ally who is indispensable to the conception of such an overturning of the *mēchanē* (ibid. 1 and 24ff.).

The nocturnal and turbid *peithō* (ibid. 726ff.) has, moreover, for its promoter Hermes Nychios who "with one dark word spreads the shadows of Night over the eyes" (ibid. 812ff.). This invisible speech—*askopon epos*, discourse bereft of representation, akin to Thanatos, the swooping shadow that "day will never be able to dispel"—contrasts with the vengeance that is invoked as the palace dwellers await "the return of light" (ibid. 806, 961). Echoing this *askopon epos* is the final madness of Orestes, the wordless vision (ibid. 1061) of the avenging Furies, who have tied together their chain of dancers and their chant of horror (Aesch. *Eumenides* 387ff.). They are the daughters of Night, and for their victim their hymn sung without a lyre spells vertigo and the chaining of the soul (ibid. 365ff.). *Eumēchanoi* (ibid. 381), full of skill and tenacity, they preserve a faithful memory of crimes, and their hearts remain insensitive to human tears. Crossing the dark mire of a night shut off from the sun, with a single stroke they affirm their ancient privileges and reveal the indelible mark of a unanimously ratified law: justice and death. They have a share in darkness and Tartarus, and their irruption now breaks the ground for a human ordinance which henceforth will exclude any justification for a genealogy of murder. When Apollo has to face them, he designates Hermes as the guide for the suppliant Orestes.

From the multiple descriptions of the trap set by Clytemnestra, the treacherous side of death (Aesch. *LB* 247, 492, 498, 624, 980–82, 997–1001), to this final losing of the way, whereby Orestes founders on the reverse side of death, the nocturnal side, we perceive the weaving of a drama in which Hermes moves about freely, "hiding his deceit in the shadow" (Sophocles *Electra* 396). Mobile as death, through successive dissections Hermes will be able to change his role from Chthonios to Nychios and finally to become Pompaios.

He is situated at the crossroads of the plotted stratagem and the deadly delirium, a spot marked by the malevolent *peithō*. Hermes is particularly designated to ensure that death be traced back to an initial seduction (Aesch. *LB* 726–29), for like *peithō* he moves along an axis that goes from the best to the worst. In this case it is indeed a malevolent *peithō*, for the good *peithō* keeps its distance from Hades (Aeschylus frag. 161 Nauck[2]). Should this *peithō* be defined as a function of woman (Aesch. *Agamemnon* 1636), Hermes would only be more at ease with it. "Trickery clearly reverts back to woman," and Clytemnestra with her sweet words and sorceries certainly had that soul of a bitch which Pandora received as her share from Hermes.

This woman, the first woman—who appears with the characteristics of a marriageable young girl—is herself a deep and inescapable trap (Hes. *Th.* 588ff.), from which "their damned breed" emerged, "a horrible plague established in the midst of mortal men." The unfathomable workings of her desire mingle with the dark treachery of her seduction: Thanatos lies in wait at the outcome (*erōs* and *dolos*, see Soph. *El.* 197–200). "The union that joins couples is treacherously defeated by the unbridled desire that overpowers the female among humans as well as among beasts" (Aesch. *LB* 599ff.). Pandora appears when man falls from the paradise of the Golden Age.

Here we touch upon an elective affinity between woman and death. All of its themes are captured in the harmonious song of the Sirens (Homer *Odyssey* 12.40ff.), whose irresistible voices promise praise. But it is a song of death that rises from their shore, its evidence sketched on the sand by the *amēchania*: human remains, skin, bones, all belonging to the wretches who let themselves be entrapped by the spell. For what else do Sirens do but seduce people until they die? Nothing comes between their outward appearance as young girls and this death, nothing but a sound, the sound of their voices. It is not Night; it is not the darkness of the mire of the Keres. But here, in the luminous clarity of their rising chant, we do nevertheless stumble upon something both primordial and unspoken, something that hatched in Greece around the enigma of the representations of death in conjunction with woman.

II. Persephone: The Young Woman and Death

We can give this enigma the name of Persephone, the silent sovereign of the silent world of the dead. This is how she appears in the *Odyssey*; and when Odysseus dares to penetrate the dwelling place of Hades, it is not Hades whom he finds there—how can he, a mortal who has lost his way among the dead, see the Invisible?—but the all-pervasive authority of his spouse, Persephone, the Noble (*agauē*: Homer *Od.* 11.226, 635), the Terrible (*epainē*: ibid. 10.491, 11.47; cf. Homer *Il.* 9.457), the pure (*hagnē*: Homer *Od.* 11.386). Among these ambiguous titles in which respect barely conceals dread, in which praise speaks the language of terror (how could the Greeks, accustomed to wordplay, ever resist the etymologically reprehensible but tempting desire to associate *epainē* and *epainos*, praise?), there is one title above all that speaks of the ambiguity of Persephone. *Hagnē*, in both texts and cult—since she is honored with this name in Messenia (Paus. 4.33.4)—she bears within her the *agos*, the prohibition that belongs to the divine and that most particularly characterizes the powers of death, untouchable, in themselves utterly pure but fearsome, even loathsome to the mortal who dares to cross over into the forbidden territory. *Hagnē Persephoneia*: Persephone the pure, Persephone the loathsome.

The all-powerful daughter of Zeus (Homer *Od.* 11.217), she rules over a people of pale ghosts, souls without memories, forever deprived of feeling; she alone left wisdom to Tiresias alone—or rather to the shade of the blind prophet (ibid. 10.494–95). She alone raises up and repels the cohorts of the shades (ibid. 10.214, 226, 385), and Odysseus was overcome with "the green horror . . . that the superb Persephone might cast upon him from hell the head of the Gorgon, that frightful monster" (Homer *Od.* 11.633–35). Over the centuries, anecdotes and various scenes came to adorn Hades, which became peopled by a steadily increasing number of inhabitants—personnel in the service of the sovereigns of death, notorious condemned criminals or heroes who had violated their charge. The motionless figure of Persephone is never affected by any of this; she remains powerful, august, and formidable.

We know nothing more about her, or very little, for what story could come to pass in hell, where time is abolished? Even the great tragedians, usually eager to clothe each deity richly in layers of meaning, exhaust the subject of Persephone with the sole evocation of her name. The dominant tradition gives her no posterity and bestows upon her only one passion, a frenzied and doubly impotent passion for Adonis, the effeminate seducer and most beloved lover of

Aphrodite (see M. Detienne, *Les jardins d'Adonis*, pp. 124–38, 187–226, and passim).

But there is another name for Persephone, which furnishes the goddess of the dead with both a venerable *muthos* and a rich background of representations. Persephone is also called Kore, the young girl, and it is under this name that she is officially worshiped by many cities. By this she adds beauty to her power (*Homeric Hymn to Demeter* 405.495: *perikallēs*, the very beautiful) and also acquires a history, with a before and an after, a space, a high and a low. The myth tells the story of the abduction of the young girl Persephone by Hades: the introduction of a queen into hell and, for the lord of the dead, the conquest of a wife. A major event in his dreary career as a solitary despot, this abduction is the only myth in which Hades actively intervenes and perhaps also his only incursion into the land of the living. For Persephone, it means a separation from her mother, Demeter.

The abduction might be called simply a rite of passage: the girl passed from her mother's hands to her husband's, remaining passive during this operation, of which she was the stake. This is how Hesiod, in the *Theogony* 912–14, briefly presents the issue: "Zeus slept with Demeter, the nourisher, who bore him the white-armed Persephone. Aidoneus [Pluton] abducted her from her mother, and Zeus, the wise, gave her to him." Zeus, the father; Hades; and Demeter: these are also the principal parties to this crisis in the *Homeric Hymn to Demeter*. Brutally wrenched away from her girlish games and dragged into the womb of the earth, Persephone is completely powerless: neither her shrieks of terror (HHD 38–39), quickly stifled in the weighty silence of hell, nor her mother's loneliness (*pothos*: ibid. 344), nor the plans for vengeance and revolt that she plots (*mētiseto*: ibid. 345) without so much as a word to her husband and master at her side are of any avail to her. How could she withstand the profound *mētis* of Zeus (*Kronidēo pukinēn dia mētin*: ibid. 414)? For as he is both the father of gods and men and the father of this girl, he has a double title to make a decision that cannot be appealed. And when at last a compromise was reached to end the crisis— that Persephone would spend one-third of the year with Hades and the rest of the year with her mother and the Olympian gods (ibid. 398–400, 463–65)—it was because the will of Zeus was swayed by the savage grief of Demeter.

Kore: the name makes clear the close and privileged relationship that unites mother and daughter, Demeter and Persephone. This relationship excludes men from the cult (during the Thesmophoria) and dominates the myth in which Persephone, caught between Demeter of the splendid harvests (*aglaokarpos*: ibid. 4) and the infernal Host (ibid. 9, 17, 31), goes from mother to husband as one goes from life to death (see Kerényi, *La jeune fille divine*, p. 133). If, in the final settlement, it is Demeter who gets the advantage by being allowed to see her daughter for two-thirds of the year, the Kore is but the brilliant paradigm of the figure of "the young girl with the delicate skin," whom Hesiod imagines "staying indoors, by the side of her tender mother, still ignorant of the work of golden Aphrodite" (Hes. *Works and Days* 519–20). Her mother's only daughter, she is, like Hecate, *mounogenēs ek mētros* (Hes. *Th.* 448, 426): the *genos gunaikōn*, it is true, tends to reproduce itself in a closed circuit, at least according to the obsessive and thoroughly masculine fantasy that spans Greek mythical tradition.

And yet, though she may be all Kore, Persephone remains the wife of Hades.

Shall we then invoke the affinities that connect marriage, like all "rites of passage," with death? The departure for Hades is thus a metaphor for marriage as on the terra-cotta tablets (*pinakes*) of Locri on which the young groom tirelessly repeats the exploit of Hades carrying off Persephone in his chariot (cf. Souvinon-Inwood, *The Young Abductor . . .*); but, conversely, marriage for a virgin is a metaphor for death: dream of marriage, dream of death, says Artemidorus; and long is the cohort of "the brides of Hades," who exchanged the wedding song for the funeral dirge, and their nuptials for a funereal wedding with the god of hell (see Artemidorus *Oneirokritika* 2.65; Sophocles *Antigone* 810ff.; *Anthologia Palatina* 7.13.183, 186, 476; P. Roussel, "Les fiançailles d'Haimon et d'Antigone," *REG*, 35 [1922], pp. 63–81; and H. J. Rose, "The Bride of Hades," *Cahiers Philosophiques*, 20 [1925], pp. 238–42). Death that is like marriage, marriage that is like death: they are equivalent and always interchangeable metaphors. The trouble is that there is nothing metaphorical in the status of Persephone: the girl really becomes the wife of Hades, and she does not die. An immortal goddess, she is able to cross over the threshold of Erebus, fatal to humans (cf. Homer *Od.* 12.21–22). Better still: wife and queen, Persephone remains a Kore. "She who lives underground" is also "the beautiful child sovereign of the dead" (*kallipais anassa*: Euripides *Orestes* 963–64).

Such is the paradox of Kore for us, that she remains the Young Girl in the deepest reaches of hell, as if she never completed the rite of passage. Whether it is made of language (see L. Gernet, "Frairies antiques," *Anthropologie de la Grèce antique*, Paris 1968, p. 41: *korē, numphē,* and *parthenos* oscillate indecisively between the young girl and the young woman) or made of thought, this permanent state itself must be questioned. It is true that in the *Homeric Hymn to Demeter* the movement that leads from earth to Hades is periodically reversed, a two-way street that, each year, brings Persephone back to her mother and Kore back to her husband. But this is an Eleusinian and eschatological perspective, fit to nourish the hopes of the *mystai*, and there are many versions of the myth—certainly in Homer, perhaps at Locri, and in still other cities—in which Persephone does not go back to Demeter. Rather, by remaining motionless at her husband's side, she does not attain the full status of *gunē*. She attains the status of "blossoming wife" (*thalarē akoitis*: HHD 79) of Hades through her floral beauty but not through the fertility that characterizes the *gunē*, and in the far reaches of the world of the dead, the willows that bear dead fruit in the grove of Persephone symbolize her sterility (Homer *Od.* 509–10).

So Persephone does not move; it is as if the luminous Nysaean plain (HHD 17) had opened itself upon the darkness of Hades without a break, as if the girl had already necessarily made her peace with death.

On the Nysaean plain there is a sweet meadow (*leimōn malakos*) where flowers grow: roses, crocuses, violets, irises, hyacinths, and, especially, the narcissus, unique among flowers, "a trap (*dolos*) for the young girl with the face of a flower, a trap that Gaea made grow." The whole universe is known to have smiled before the marvelous narcissus; how could this child have resisted the temptation? She takes hold of it, and the earth opens up before the chariot of Hades (HHD 5–18; cf. Paus. 9.31.9). Thus, like Europa, Oreithuia, Creusa, and Helen, Persephone is carried away in a meadow while she is picking flowers (as a prelude to marriage? or to death? cf. L. Gernet, "Frairies antiques," p. 43, and A. Motte, *Prairies et jardins*, pp. 38–47). Among the flowers, the girl is a flower (HHD 8.66; see also 108, 176–78, and Milton: "That fair field / Of Enna where Proserpine, gathering flowers, / Herself a fairer flower, by gloomy Dis was gathered"). But the desirable flowers (*anthea eroenta*: HHD 425) are flowers of

death, and especially the narcissus, the flower of Demeter and of Kore (Soph. *O.C.* 681), the bearer of *narkē* (torpor). The cold and humid narcissus that is planted on tombs; the narcissus that grows where the underworld breaks out onto the earth; the narcissus whose miraculous appearance arouses in gods and mortals the same kind of awe and admiration that was aroused, Hesiod tells us, by the appearance of the first woman, that other trap (HHD 10–11; Hes. *Th.* 588–89). Persephone looks too much like a flower. Some resemblances are dangerous.

As for the *leimōn*, what about its ambiguity? Captivating and sweet (HHD 7 and 417: *himertos, malakos*; cf. *Homeric Hymn to Mercury* 72), it is the place where young girls go and nymphs stay, like Calypso (Homer *Od.* 5.72), but it is also the place of those dangerous *parthenoi*, the sirens (Homer *Od.* 12.159). But meadows are often inviolable and forbidden, like the sexual organ of a woman or girl, for which *leimōn* is one name among others (see Euripides *Cyclops* 171 and Empedocles frag. 610 Bollack: *schistous leimōnas Aphroditēs*, the cloven meadow of Aphrodite). Desire and prohibition: it is not surprising that meadows serve as shelters for the love affairs of the gods, sometimes legitimate, often violent, always furtive (Zeus and Hera: Homer *Il.* 14.346ff.; Poseidon and Medusa: Hes. *Th.* 279; Zeus and Io: Aeschylus *Prometheus Bound* 653ff., Aeschylus *Suppliants* 540–58). But the *leimōn* is preeminently a deadly place. The green grass on which the daughters of Cecrops tread, dead yet dancing (Euripides *Io* 495–98), the deadly *leimōn* of the madness and death of Ajax (Sophocles *Ajax* 143–44, 654–55), the inviolate *leimōn* of Oeta, where the funeral pyre of Heracles is raised (Sophocles *Trachiniae* 200), the meadow of lotuses where the sons of Oedipus slaughter each other (Euripides *Phoenician Women* 1571), and—the model for all the others—the Meadow of the World Below, the Asphodel Plain of the Dead (Homer *Od.* 11.538–39).

A flat meadow, sweet-smelling and covered with flowers, surrounded by steep precipices: such is the site of Henna in Sicily, which claims to have witnessed the abduction of Kore (Diodorus Siculus 5.3). But there is no need for visible precipices. The abysses that one does not see are the most formidable, and there is no *leimōn* that does not dissimulate "obscure depths under its verdant surface" (A. Motte, *Prairies et jardins*, p. 243). Both here and, always, elsewhere, the whole meadow is a trap. Undoubtedly Persephone was unaware of this.

Undoubtedly. And neither the beautiful young Oceanids, whom the goddess Persephone obligingly counts among her companions, nor Athena and Artemis, divine virgins associated in other texts with the abducted Kore (HHD 417–28; cf. Euripides *Helen* 1315–16, Paus. 8.31.2; Diod. 5.4), could come to her rescue. Because Hades burst forth suddenly like a bolt of lightning on his chariot drawn by immortal horses; or because Demeter was absent; or because Zeus willed it. But also because, in Greek mythical thought, the young girl, the untamed virgin, is a carrier of death—for herself and for others.

There are girls on whom death closes in cunningly (as, in Hesiod, winter closes in on the girl: *Works and Days* 504ff.): those who kill themselves or who are killed, "tender virgins carrying their first mourning in their hearts" (Homer *Od.* 11.38), the cohort of the followers of Artemis, the cohort of the imitators of Athens—Iodama turned to stone for having seen the Gorgon; Pallas, also turned to stone for having wanted to play with the goddess (cf. F. Vian, *La guerre des Géants*, Paris 1952, pp. 270–71) and all the girls of the Acropolis, for whom suicide or patriotic sacrifice lay in wait

(Aglauros and her sisters, the daughters of Erechtheus, and many more).

There are virgins who bring about death. The sirens (*parthenikoi korai*: Eur. *Hel.* 168); the Sphinx (*kora*: Sophocles *Oedipus Rex* 508; *parthenos kora*: Euripides *Phoenician Women* 1730); Artemis the archer (*HHD* 424), whose arrows send one straight to Hades; Athena with her flashing eye, she who is covered by the shield on which the head of the Gorgon is enthroned (cf. M. Detienne and J.-P. Vernant, *Les ruses de l'intelligence*, pp. 173–74), Athena who is not good luck for her rivals; and, first and foremost, Pandora, with her body of a *parthenos aidoiē*, forbidden and respectable (but *aidoios* as a neuter noun designates shame itself: the pudendum, the sexual organ), Pandora from whom the female race has sprung: the artifice named woman.

Kore-Persephone is their sister.

The girl resembled the narcissus too closely: she had to be repatriated immediately into the womb of the earth (*HHD* 415).

At first she is ill at ease. Seated next to her husband, she thinks about her mother. While she ruminates upon her sorrows and her vengeance, Hermes the messenger arrives, sent to Hades by Zeus in order to bring Persephone back to the Olympian gods. "The lord of the people of the underworld, Aidoneus, laughs with his eyebrows but dares not disobey the injunctions of Zeus the king" (*HHD* 358–59). He addresses Persephone with kind and clever words, reminding her of his qualities as a divine husband and promising her a *timē* of absolute power (*desposseis pantōn*—"You shall reign over all" [*HHD* 365]; and it may be recalled that the cultic name of the Young Girl in more than one city is *Despoina*, the Mistress). But exactly where and over whom will this power be exerted? Down below, over the dead? Above, over the living? The speech of Hades is ambiguous— hence that laughter in his eyes, so surprising in someone who ordinarily "darts his glance from under his somber eyebrows" (Euripides *Alcestis* 261–62)—but perfectly clear to anyone who wishes to understand him (Would Hades send back to Demeter forever the wife he himself snatched from her play?). Persephone leaps for joy. Whereupon, surreptitiously, escaping the vigilance of Hermes, he gives her a pomegranate seed to eat (accepting food in hell ties one irrevocably to the infernal world, and the pomegranate has a lot to do with marriage), and Hermes brings Persephone back to her mother on Hades' chariot. To Demeter's urgent questions, she answers: "Oh Mother dear, I will tell you the whole truth. When kindly Hermes, the swift messenger, came in the name of Zeus the father, son of Kronos, and all the Ouranians, to rescue me from dark Erebus, . . . I leapt for joy; but cunningly he placed in my hand a sweet and fragrant food—a pomegranate seed—and though I resisted, he forced me to eat it" (*HHD* 406–13).

Like Odysseus or Hermes (Homer *Od.* 14.192, *HHD* 368– 69), who tell the truth only to lie better, Persephone multiplies her protestations of truth, but invents a story: the text does not say that she was forced against her will. As a matter of fact, the text says nothing about it. But this deafening silence on Persephone's reaction to the cunning offer of Hades suggests that in her joy she accepted—in her joy at leaving hell, in her joy of attaining a *timē*. To be sure, Hades' speech was ambiguous; but he knew that in Persephone he was dealing with a wise and prudent woman (*daïphrōn, periphrōn*: *HHD* 359, 370), in a sense already the queen of hell, whose wisdom is underscored in the etymologies found in the *Cratylus* (Plato *Cratylus* 404d). Did Persephone understand the speech? Again, the text does not say what she

Hades and Persephone. Locri tablet 470–60 B.C. Naples Museum. Museum photo.

understood. In any case, she begins to speak—for the first time in the *Hymn* after the screams of rape and the silence of hell—only to mask herself, shifting the entire responsibility for her anchorage among the dead from herself to Him whom she does not name. For it may be impossible to tell the truth about what goes on in the underworld; and Persephone had entered into a compact with Hades without which there would have been a need for constraint. Unlike the Virgilian Proserpina, deaf to the repeated calls of her mother (Virgil *Georgics* 1.39), Persephone is effusively reunited with Demeter, but it is important to point out that, contrary to later versions, which devote a third of their efforts to denouncing her, she herself makes the confession that henceforth ties her to the darkness of the underworld.

Between Demeter and Hades; between young girl and wife—an admirable compromise between before and after, between motionless virginity and womanhood, henceforth acquired yet impossible.

Lest we lose ourselves in the silence of Persephone, let us take stock of the Greek tricks that account for death.

The snare of vengeance echoes the snare of a death that may be accessible; set down for more or for less in the accounts of the living, death may become involved in an exchange and may set out the stakes by which mortals can return the blows received by the dead (Aesch. *Libation Bearers* 93–95: *antidounai*).

The disorienting circularity of Tartarus echoes the inexorable *amēchania* that is Hades. Faceless, death bears the name of the nocturnal and remains in the realm of the invisible.

From one extreme to the other, Hermes equivocates between the two, rather like a hinge. Allied to secrecy and scheming, Hermes guides Orestes, while at the same time he whispers to him the *askopon epos*.

Epos: the Sirens' song is such that those who listen to it cannot understand it, so entranced are they by the voice that dominates the hymn. The charm of this voice, which Hermes will bestow on Pandora as well, is the carrier of a death without funeral or display, blind as the *talaina peithō* that pervades the *Oresteia*.

Opposite the death that is masculine, the death borne by eulogy or by the civic voice of the funeral oration, the feminine face of death emerges, which in the heart of the Greek community can find its place only in an inverted form—that of the prophetess Cassandra, whose words, lacking the gift of the persuasive power (*peithō*) and the essential enchantment (*thelxis*), are powerless to express death.

Obedient Persephone, the beautiful child, has eaten the pomegranate. The "truthful word" speaks of constraint, but silence acquiesces to the pact of death, sweet as honey.

How can we describe the disturbing transparency of Kore? Like the pupil of an eye, the young girl-mirror in the center, well protected by its moist covering (see Plato *Alcibiades* 133; Empedocles frag. 415 Bollack), Persephone, standing by the side of Hades the Invisible, is the very ambiguity of brilliance in the depths of black light (*melamphaeis muchous*: Diod. 5.5). The strange mirror of Despoina, in which mortals cannot see their reflection (Paus. 8.27.8), the petrifying fascination of the Gorgon's head, the threat that Persephone brandishes against the intruder, the living lost among the dead: death in the form of a young girl reflects only itself. The *Arrhētos Korē*, she does not speak of herself, she does not see herself. She remains impenetrable.

L.K.-L. and N.L./g.h.

BIBLIOGRAPHY

1. General Articles

A. LESKY, "Thanatos," in Pauly/Wissowa, *Real-Encyclopädie* (1934), cols. 1245ff. PRELLER-ROBERT, *Griechische Mythologie* (4th ed., Berlin 1894); see "Schlaf und Tod," 1:842–48. C. ROBERT, *Thanatos* (Berlin 1879). K. HEINEMANN, "Thanatos in Poesie und Kunst der Griechen" (diss., Munich 1913). E. ROHDE, *Psyché* (London and New York 1925), original ed. in German.

2. Nyx and Thanatos

CL. RAMNOUX, *La nuit et les enfants de la Nuit* (Paris 1959).

3. The Metaphors of the Hunt in the Trilogy of Aeschylus

P. VIDAL-NAQUET, "Chasse et sacrifice dans l'Orestie d'Eschyle," in J.-P. VERNANT and P. VIDAL-NAQUET, *Mythe et tragédie en Grèce ancienne* (Paris 1974).

4. Tartarus

M. DETIENNE and J.-P. VERNANT, *Les ruses de l'intelligence: La métis des Grecs* (Paris 1975).

5. Homeric Death

B. MOREUX, "La nuit, l'ombre et la mort chez Homère," *Phoenix* 21 (1967): 237–72.

6. Persephone

The Rape

R. FÖRSTER, *Der Raub und die Rückkehr der Persephone* (Stuttgart 1874). A. MOTTE, *Prairies et jardins de la Grèce antique* (Brussels 1973). G. PICCALUGA, "Ta Pherephattês anthologia," *Maia* 18 (1966): 232–53.

Narcissus

S. EITREM, "Narkissos," in Pauly/Wissowa, *Real-Encyclopädie* (1933–35), vol. 16.

Mother and Daughter

M. DETIENNE, *Les jardins d'Adonis* (Paris 1972).

Persephone-Kore

CH. KERÉNYI, "La jeune fille divine," in C. G. JUNG and CH. KERÉNYI, *Introduction à l'essence de la mythologie* (Paris 1953), 127–87. G. ZUNTZ, *Persephone* (Oxford 1971), 158–68, Locri; 400–402, "Persephone not returning to the Upper World."

Agos

P. CHANTRAINE and O. MASSON, "Sur quelques termes du vocabulaire religieux des Grecs: La valeur du mot *agos* et de ses dérivés," *Mélanges Debrunner* (Bern 1954), 83–107. J.-P. VERNANT, "Le pur et l'impur," *Mythe et société* (Paris 1974), 121–40.

Locri

H. PRÜCKNER, *Die lokrische Tonreliefs* (Mainz 1968), on Persephone, 68–74. CH. R. SOURVINOU-INWOOD, "The Young Abductor of the Locrian Pinakes," *BICS* 20 (1973): 12–21. P. ZANCANI-MONTUORO, "Locri Epizefiri," in *EAA*.

THE TOPOGRAPHY OF HELL IN ARCHAIC AND CLASSICAL GREEK LITERATURE

I. The Cosmic Site and General Portrayal of Hell

a) Hell and the West

Like the peoples of the East, the ancient Greeks situated the Kingdom of the Dead, or Hades, in a "beyond," which was sometimes subterranean, sometimes at the furthest limits of the sea, where the river Ocean flowed. The first description appears in the *Iliad* (20.6l; 22.482; 23.50) and the second in the *Odyssey* (10.508; 11.13; 24.11). In *Oedipus the King* (179), Sophocles states that the souls of the dead Thebans, like winged birds, flock toward "the coast where rules the god of the West." Within a framework of universal polarity, in which light and shadow are like the right and left of the world (*Iliad* 12.239–240), the East and the Dawn (*eos*) on the right are in opposition to the *sinister* character of the cosmic left, where the shadows (*zophos*) of the West lie. This opposition of "dawn light/shadows" (*eos/zophos*), which includes other opposing pairs—east/west, north/south, high/low—established the West as a low, shadowy region of the world, but there are certain inconsistencies in the locations of Hades.

b) Hell and Tartarus

Whereas the *Iliad* (8.13–16) situates Tartarus, the prison of the Titans, at the very lowest level of the universe, "as far below Hades as the Sky is above the Earth," the description of Tartarus in the *Theogony* (767–773) suggests an overlapping of Hades and Tartarus—which, moreover, appears as a primordial cosmological site. In Plato's *Phaedo*, there is an analogous duality: Tartarus, cosmic center and origin of the waters (112a), is also the place of punishment for the greatest sinners (113e).

c) General Representation

The general representation of the bowels of the earth includes several characteristics, which are occasionally combined in the same passage. The most unstructured is that of the underground hiding place (*keuthos, keuthmōn*) of the dead (*Il.*, 20.482; *Od.*, 24.204), or of the Titans (*Theog.*, 158; Aeschylus, *Prometheus* 220), or of the cavern (*speos*) of Echidna (*Theog.* 301). On the other hand, the whole infernal world of Tartarus in the *Theogony* (726 ff.) seems to be represented as a gigantic jar. But most often, Hell is presented as the abode of Hades (*Il.* 22.52; *Od.* 9.524; 24.204), an enclosed space with doors that must be passed through (*Il.* 5.646; 9.312; 23.71; *Od.* 14.156). In the description in the *Theogony* (749, 811), these doors (*pulai*) have a bronze threshold.

II. Shadow and Light in Hell

Hades, like Tartarus, is the realm of pure Shadow, of Erebus (*Il.* 16.327; *Od.* 10.528; *Theog.* 515), of misty shadow (*zophon ēeroenta: Il.* 15.191; 21.56; 23.51), which already prevails at the entrance to Hell, in the land of the Cimmerians (*Od.* 11.13–19), as befits a dreadful place that must remain sealed and invisible to mortals as well as to immortals (*Il.* 20.61–65). However, whereas the epic usually refers briefly to the rising of the sun out of the Ocean or its setting into the flow of this same river, without including the underground journey of this star, the *Odyssey* (10.191) expresses the idea that the sun may go "underground," while the *Hymn to Hermes* (68–69) has him plunge "beneath the earth into the Ocean, with his horses and his chariot." The *Odyssey* (24.12) also mentions the "Doors of the Sun," at the entrance to Hell, near the course of the Ocean, the White Rock, the country of Dreams, and "the Meadow of Asphodels where souls, phantoms, and the deceased dwell." These various passages do seem to imply the presence of both shadow and sun in the underworld. So, too, in the *Theogony* Day and Night alternate in the abode of Night, within Tartarus itself (748–757). Hades proper remains nocturnal and misty, whereas the land of the Blessed is a country of nocturnal sun, according to one fragment of Pindar (*Threnois* 1, ed. Aimé Puech, Belles Lettres, col. 4, p. 195).

III. Infernal Landscapes

a) The Meadow and the Mire

Even though Hell, in the epic, is the domain of humidity and mold (*eurōeis: Od.* 10.512; *Theog.* 731, 739, 810; *Works* 153), the Meadow of Asphodels in the *Odyssey* refers, although somewhat obscurely, to a split in the representation of the beyond. As a humid place, fertile and flowered, the meadow has certain affinities with the 'Elysian Field' (4.563–569), with the Isle of the Blessed in *Works* (170–173), and with the land made up of these very meadows, described by Pindar in the fragment cited above. In the *Republic* (10.614e, 616b), Plato mentions a meadow of judgment, and in Aristophanes' *Frogs* (326, 333, 374) the meadow is a place reserved for the initiated, which implies a separation between the blessed and the damned, while the epic simply opposes the mass of insubstantial souls in Hades with the chosen ones, the rare heroes (Rhadamanthys, Menelaus). The theme of the meadow is contrasted with that of the mire, a region reserved for the uninitiated and the damned (Aristophanes, *Frogs*, 145.273; Plat. *Phaedo*, 69c, *Rep.* 2.363 d–e).

b) Trees and Rocks

The theme of the forest of Hell can be described in terms either morose (*Od.* 10.509–510) or merry (*Frogs* 441). Conversely, the frequent references to rivers of Hell in a steep and rocky landscape leave the impression of an essentially chaotic universe (*Il.* 8.369; *Theog.* 778.786–7; Aeschylus, *Agamemnon* 1161; Arist., *Frogs* 470s). The White Rock (*leukas pētrē*) of the *Odyssey* (24.11), near the Doors of the Sun, marks the place where the sun sinks into the night and also forms a boundary between the conscious and the unconscious.

IV. The Infernal Waters

a) The Primordial Waters: Ocean and Styx

Ocean, "the current which turns in on itself" (*Theog.* 776), the "perfect" river (*Theog.* 242), encircles the earth and the sea with nine rings (*Theog.* 816). Because it constitutes the chaotic periphery of the world, it can also appear as a subterranean river (*Hymn to Hermes,* 68–69), the first of the great currents of water which separate the living and the dead (*Od.* 11. 156–159). This duality in representation between the peripheral river and the infernal river is analogous to the duality mentioned earlier in regard to Hades. Plato still makes the Ocean figure prominent in his system of underground waters (*Phaedo* 112e).

The Styx was both an Arcadian river near the village of Nonacris (Herodotus 6.74; Pausanius 8.17.6–8.18.6) and a primordial figure—Styx, the daughter of Ocean (*Theog.* 361.776; *H. to Demeter* 423). It appears in the cosmographic map as a branch of Ocean (*Theog.* 789), of which it constitutes a tenth ring. This final whorl of primordial water, forming the outer boundary (*herkos*) of the universe, is used as an oath (*horkos*) of the gods (*Il.* 2.755; 13.271 ff; 15.36–38 = *Od.* 5.184–186 = *H. to Apollo,* 84–86; *to Demeter,* 259; *to Hermes,* 519) because the cosmic and underworld limit, proceeding from Ocean, like the gods' food of immortality (Euripides, *Hippolytus* 748), is by nature qualified to separate the perjured god from the sources of life and cosmic order (*Theog.* 793–804), just as the waters of oblivion cause whoever drinks of them to lose his memory of the beyond. Here we have an example of the ambivalence of the primordial water, which can be both the water of death, plunging even the immortal into a sort of coma, and the water of life, as when Thetis plunges her son Achilles into the water of the Styx to make him invulnerable.

b) The Tributary Rivers: Cocytus, Pyriphlegethon, Acheron

The Cocytus, a branch of the Styx, joins with the river of fire, the Pyriphlegethon, to form the Acheron (*Od.* 10.513–515), described as a river or a marsh (*Frogs* 137), which traditionally constitutes the expanse of water that souls must cross on the ferryman Charon's boat (*Frogs* 182–183; Eur., *Alcestis* 440; Plat., *Phaedo* 113d). Unlike its inland homonym (Herodotus 5.92.7; Pausanias 1.17.5) and the swamp of Aristophanes, which may be influenced by the theme of the mire of Hell, the Acheron of the *Odyssey* appears as a chaotic mixture of fire and Stygian water, glacial like Hell itself (*Works* 153). From this theme of a cosmic mixture, which reappears in the description of the Planctae (*Od.* 12.67) and the double source of the Scamander (*Il.* 22.147), the *Phaedo* organizes a grandiose underground system of rivers of fire and mud in conjunction with volcanic phenomena (111 d–e), and makes Tartarus the center of a spherical universe in which all the rivers converge in order to redistribute the central water in balance (*aiōra*, 111e–112a). This action is assimilated to a cosmic respiration (112b), recalling the description of Charybdis (*Od.* 12.235–245), as well as the punishments of Tantalus and Sisyphus (*Od.* 11.582–600), since in Plato certain sinners are left for a time to the buffeting of the waters of Tartarus (114a–b). We note finally that the four rivers of the Platonic Hell—Ocean, Acheron, Pyriphlegethon, and Cocytus—were conceived as corresponding to the four elements and the four directions of the sky in the Orphic interpretation mentioned by Olympiodorus in his commentary on the *Phaedo* (p. 202 of the William Norvin ed., Teubner 1913).

c) The Waters of Memory and Oblivion

The earliest reference to the "Plain of Oblivion" (*Lēthēs pedion*) in the *Frogs* (186) seems to refer to the notion of Hades as a place where terrestrial life is forgotten, without necessarily placing at the entrance to Hell a fountain of oblivion at which the dead must drink. Only in a much later mystic tradition, attested especially in texts written on strips of gold carried by certain corpses to guide them on their journey into the beyond (see Diels-Kranz, 1B, 17–17a, 14th ed. 1969, pp. 15–16), do we find the notion of a crossroads, with the water of Memory (*Mnemosyne*) on the right and on the left a spring that, though anonymous, could be identified with the water of Oblivion. This type of eschatology inverts the notion of oblivion in the underworld: the water of Memory permits the soul to rejoin divine and celestial realities, while the water of Oblivion separates him from realities that have now ceased to be earthly. In Plato's *Republic* (10.621a–b), the soul must drink the water of the river Ameles, in the plain of Lethe, in order to erase his memory of the beyond before his reincarnation.

A.B./d.b.

BIBLIOGRAPHY

Dictionaries and General Works

D. WACHSMUTH, "Unterwelt," in *Der Kleine Pauly*, 5, cols. 1053–56. O. GRUPPE and PFISTER, "Unterwelt," in *Lexikon der griechischen und römischen Mythologie*, 6, cols. 66–70. WUESST, "Unterwelt," in Pauly-Wissowa, *Real-Encyclopädie*, vol. 9, part 1, cols. 672–82. P. GRIMAL, "Topographie des Enfers," in *Dictionnaire de la mythologie grecque et romaine* (5th ed., Paris 1976): 5a (Achéron), 89a (Charon), 93a (Cimmériens), 98a (Cocyte), 370a (Phlégéthon), 431b (Styx), 437b (Tartare). A. DIETERICH, *Nekyia* (Leipzig 1893). E. ROHDE, *Psyche: The Cult of Souls and Belief in Immortality among the Greeks* (London 1925).

Specialized Works

I a: N. AUSTIN, "The One and Many in the Homeric Cosmos," *Arion* 1 (1973): 219–74.

II: L. GERNET, "La cité future et le pays des morts," in *Anthropologie de la Grèce antique* (Paris 1976), 139–53.

III a: G. SOURY, "La vie de l'au-delà: Prairies et gouffres," *Revue des études anciennes* 46 (1944): 169–78. A. MOTTE, *Prairies et jardins de la Grèce antique* (Brussels 1973).

III b: G. NAGY, "Phaethon, Sappho's Phaon and the White Rock of Leukas," *Harvard Studies of Classical Philology* 77 (1973): 137–78.

IV a: J. BOLLACK, "Styx et serments," *Revue des études grecques* 71 (1958): 1–35. J. RUDHARDT, *Le thème de l'eau primordiale dans la mythologie grecque* (Bern 1971).

IV c: J.-P. VERNANT, "Aspects mythiques de la mémoire," in *Mythe et pensée chez les Grecs* (Paris 1969), 51–78. G. ZUNTZ, *Persephone* (Oxford 1971).

THE POWERS OF WAR: ARES AND ATHENA IN GREEK MYTHOLOGY

Ares and Athena are the two divine powers in Greece who have the monopoly on matters of war (*Iliad*, 5.430). Their positions are rigorously antithetical. Ares, the male power, is the son of Hera alone, who conceived him without recourse to the male seed. Athena, the female power, is the daughter of Zeus alone, who, after swallowing Metis, and without recourse to any womb, conceived the infant in his head, from which she sprang forth fully armed after a blow from the liberating ax of Hephaestus. Athena is the supreme virgin goddess, the Parthenos. Ares rapes and impregnates, is credited in mythology with numerous amorous adventures (with Erinys, Chryse, Althaea) and, notably, with an adulterous union with Aphrodite, the ultimate power of romantic seduction. Athena is abundantly endowed with *mētis*; Ares, of all the gods, is the most lacking in it, incapable even, in the murderous folly of combat, of distinguishing between the two camps (*Il.*, 5.761 and 831–834). Ares is hated by all the gods, Athena respected universally. The antinomy is symbolized explicitly, at the mythic level, by the physical confrontation between the two gods at the heart of the Trojan melee; Ares always loses: Athena wins and imposes her will each time (*Il.*, 5.765 and 824–864; 15.121–142; 21. 391–415).

Ares is the god of warrior fury that runs riot. The forces in his retinue are Phobus (Fear), Deimos (Rout), Eris (Discord); his children, among others, number Diomedes, the barbarian king of Thrace with his man-eating horses; the brigand Cycnus; the impious Phlegyas; Oenomaus and Evenus, fathers who murdered their daughters' suitors; Molos (Combat); the hunter Meleager, himself related to Tydeus, the terrible warrior of the war of Thebes (Aeschylus, *Six against Thebes*, 377–397, and Euripides, *Phoenician Women*, 134). Ares is excess and lack of control; dedicated to the warrior function, he is the dominant force of the Bronze race (Hesiod, *Works and Days*, 144–146); and all that comes from him bears the exclusive mark of war. In Colchis, the Gegeneis were born in Ares' fallow field, from the teeth of Ares' dragon which Jason had sown there; the Spartans, heroes of the warrior function, were born near Ares' fountain in Thebes; and the Amazons, monstrous women who were murderers, warriors, and enemies of men and marriage, were his daughters. The furious force that Ares incarnates is necessary to the city for it to survive and conquer, but it contains elements that can shatter the city if not controlled by a higher order of measure and reason. Thus, myth establishes the submission of Ares, the raw force of war, to a divinity closely associated with the function of sovereignty.

This divinity of course is Athena, great goddess of the polis, both political and industrious, who masters Ares, substituting the ordered combat of hoplites for the wild melees of heroes. She rules over war to the extent that war is a function of the city as a whole. She puts the technical skill of blacksmiths at the disposal of the hoplitic war: Athena Promachos is clothed from head to foot in hoplitic gear (helmet, cuirass, shield, lance). As befits a ruling power, however, she draws her major strength from a magical object, the Aegis, which is the very symbol of her mastery over excessive natural forces. At the center of this shield, which is a weapon both defensive and offensive, the hideous head of the dead Gorgon will petrify for all eternity anyone who dares to look upon it. Possession of the Aegis allows Athena to guarantee Zeus's victory over the rebellious giants

Athena Parthenos. First century B.C. Athens, National Museum. Photo Alinari-Giraudon.

and decisively to strengthen the threatened Olympian order. Through Athena, war is domesticated, subjugated to the ruling power, and made available both to the macrocosmic order of the City of the Gods and to the microcosmic order of the city of men. To the city's benefit, Athena tames the forces deriving from Ares as well as Ares himself, just as in other realms she subdues the savage energies in the orbit of Poseidon.

J.-P.D./d.b.

BIBLIOGRAPHY

J.-P. VERNANT, ed., *Les problèmes de la guerre en Grèce ancienne* (Paris and The Hague 1970).

HEROES AND GODS OF WAR IN THE GREEK EPIC

The Trojan War is undoubtedly one of the fundamental elements of Greek, and indeed, Greco-Roman, cultural tradition. Especially through Homer's *Iliad*, the Trojan cycle has, over the course of the centuries, served as an inexhaustible reservoir of ideas, themes for reflection, mythical illustrations, etc. Greek tragedy of the fifth century as well as children's reading lessons, poetry, and even philosophy all refer to its more famous heroes; and when Rome in turn celebrates her origins in the epic mode, it is once again the city of Troy which appears on the backdrop. The Homeric texts also provide for historians, whose information on these remote eras would otherwise be quite meager. Thucydides first analyzed the Trojan war in the fifth century as the first recorded instance of a Greek coalition against a common enemy, reasoning as follows: "It is even, in my opinion, because Agamemnon had superior strength, and not so much because he led Helen's suitors, bound by oaths made to Tyndareos (Helen's foster father), that he was able to put together the expeditionary force" (*Archeology*, book I.9). Since that time, there has been a succession of studies, and each writer has been able to reconstruct the Troy of his dreams, since the historical data, indirect and chronologically heterogeneous, leave much latitude for interpretation. The Homeric poems (the *Iliad* and the *Odyssey*) are less the story of a war, however real in the beginning, than the illustration of a social ideology. The epic marks a particular moment in history. It restores for Greece a code of aristocratic and resolutely individualistic values, as well as a vision of an anthropocentric universe, where the world of the gods and the world of men coexist and resemble one another. The poet is above all the spokesman of the society which produced him, a brilliant artisan who models the behaviors and norms imposed by the society by means of a knowingly artificial language. Yet the epic is not just a manual of aristocratic savoir-vivre, any more than it can be reduced to its mere poetic value. The richness of expression, the plasticity of the language are the very essence of Homer and constitute his individual and irreplaceable contribution. But the epic interests us above all as a globalizing enterprise, which integrates within a conventional linear development (the "history" of the Trojan War) the totality of elements by which it defines the ideal society. To this end, the poet uses an essentially mythical heritage for goals that are no longer those of the myth; he offers an organized, complete vision of the world, a vision that leaves cosmogonies in the shadows. He scatters the myth in fragments which balance the construction of the poem, and subordinates them to the ends of the genre he is creating.

War in the epic is the perfect expression of social relations; it is a way of life. The hero is defined by the war he wages as much as he is determined by his origins. The forms of war shown in the *Iliad* are thus strongly hierarchized, as a function both of the hero and of the particular role that he plays in the course of the epic action.

I. The Forms of War

The apparent confusion of a number of battle descriptions is belied by the almost immediate identification of repetitive *topoi*. To say that, despite the size of the forces confronted, individual encounters always take center stage is a commonplace. Homer has no interest in the main body of troops and offers little in the way of descriptions of the whole. The hero is primarily the one with a name, and he fights an enemy designated by a name, which distinguishes him radically from the mass. He is always *promachos*, ahead of the lines, which does not necessarily mean that he fights alone. The most frequent scenes describe a small martial elite who have descended from their chariots (symbols of social rank rather than instruments of war) and who face the enemy—paradoxically perhaps—one on one, shoulder to shoulder. These melees are found throughout the *Iliad*—the exploits of Achilles excepted—and may turn to the advantage of the Achaeans as well as the Trojans. The heroic honors are thus shared by the restricted collectivity of the dominant social group.

A hierarchical threshold is crossed with the description of the individual exploits of a particular hero. The action takes place in an autonomous fashion, following a well-established pattern: the hero fights a great number of adversaries single-handedly and causes real carnage among the enemy ranks; he is most often inspired by a god. This is referred to as an *aristeia*. A superior form of heroic action, the *aristeia* assumes variable importance depending on the hero it is describing and the place he occupies within the poem. Some, like Odysseus, are never distinguished in this way. The *aristeiai* of Diomedes, Patroclus, Hector, and above all Achilles, on the other hand, are choice passages in the poem. It would be worthwhile at another time to examine the function of these different heroes to determine the significance of their *aristeias*. Heroic honors culminate in the duel, the last stage of the hierarchic structure. Two prestigious warriors, of similar strengths, face one another alone. The duel is codified in a precise manner, usually preceded by a verbal exchange between the adversaries (a recital of genealogies, description of previous exploits, eventually imprecations and curses). It consists of throwing the javelin or lance, followed if necessary by recourse to various weapons (stones, swords, etc.). If a hero like Tlepolemus appears in no other context but the duel (a tie, against Sarpedon, in book 5), his case is exceptional, because the duel is the crowning of a warrior's exploits. By way of corollary, it is the main province of epic action. Unlike the *aristeia*, which involves ebb and flow in the advance of the armies, but never a short-term denouement, the duel is always presented as the decisive moment in a situation. In the game of epic construction, each duel seems to be the ultimate step; the fact that it is nothing of the kind, in all cases but the final one (Achilles-Hector), causes a spectacular new development in the narrative but in the end changes nothing. In book 2, the fate of the war was to be settled once and for all by the confrontation between the two principals, Menelaus and Paris-Alexander. The two armies, sitting across from each other, calmly await the results; but the gods have decided otherwise and rescue Paris. Without this outside intervention, the duel would have provided an economic and satisfactory solution for all. This situation is repeated in book 7 in the fight between Ajax and Hector; the tied score once again indicates the will of the gods: Troy will be destroyed. In the same way, Diomedes sees Aeneas carried off by Aphrodite (book 5). The duel, a superior form of action, clearly shows the opposition between human desires and divine will. Unlike these aborted examples, the connected confrontations between Sarpedon and Patroclus and between Patroclus and Hector are integrated in an episodic construction that culminates in the final duel, the conclusion of all battles, the meeting of Achilles and Hector. The success of the duel is confirmed in each case, contrary to the preceding examples, by the death of a prestigious hero.

As the ultimate demonstration of heroic honor, the driving force of the epic narration, the duel expresses the individualistic and elitist vision of the Homeric ideology at its peak.

II. The Hero in the War

War defines the hero, and the hero is defined by the type of war he wages, or does not wage. The poem leaves little to chance, and the positions of the various heroes are never interchangeable. It is significant that Agamemnon, whose warrior skill is exalted by his companions, is almost never shown in battle. The poet describes with delight his magnificent armor before according him an *aristeia* that is as prestigious as it is brief (book 11); an opportune wound keeps the hero from appearing on the field of battle. Agamemnon does not meet a single notable adversary in the course of his exploits, and does not take part in a single duel. We see here the mechanism of a contradiction which the poet does not resolve: Agamemnon symbolizes the royal function, he commands all the Achaean forces uncontested, and he is in principle the strongest of the warriors. Yet the murderer of Hector and destroyer of Troy is Achilles, whose position among the Achaeans might be described as marginal. Even though he is a king, Agamemnon, in depriving Achilles of his booty, appears as a violent character whose hubris, for the Greeks, is laden with terrible consequences. For all of these reasons his warrior exploits bear the stamp of impossibility. He who holds the royal scepter would not yield in combat before anyone, but the presence in the same

Bronze chariot from Monteleone. 550–540 B.C. New York, Metropolitan Museum of Art (Fund). Museum photo.

camp of a more valorous warrior implies a transfer of Agamemnon's activities from the battlefield to the assembly, where his authority and his hubris function together. At the level of the epic plot, Agamemnon sets the Iliadic adventure in motion; he is, one might say, the one through whom the scandal happens. But throughout the poem he retains the sacred aura of the royal function of which he is the living symbol.

Ajax, curiously, appears as a defensive hero, except in his hopeless duel with Hector. In book 11, during the Achaean rout, it is enough for him to keep his head; later, overcome by fear, he abandons the field. In book 17, he defends the body of Patroclus and manages to retrieve it from the Trojans, vaguely aided by Menelaus, who never appears in battles. Ajax's role in the *Iliad* is not that of a hero of the first rank in war, even though he is renowned as one of the greatest Achaean heroes. The post-Iliadic tradition (especially the legend of his suicide) does much to embellish the dimensions of his character.

Achilles, Patroclus, and Hector are in one sense inseparable. Their three destinies lead to a glorious death (even though the death of Achilles is only suggested in the *Iliad*), and their unavoidable interactions seal the ruin of Troy. But their bond is more than circumstantial; the triangle that they form leads to a game of mirrors in which each in turn reflects the other. Patroclus is a doublet of Achilles; his death inaugurates the true tragedy of the *Iliad*, and his funeral rites, marked by excess, are also those that Achilles celebrates for himself. Hector's end marks the end of Achilles as a warrior, for the war ends with the disappearance of the Trojan leader. Hector and Achilles are the richest characters in the *Iliad*. Hector, the sole Trojan warrior whose valor is truly equal to that of the best Achaeans, destined for the royal function but above all destined to be the great conquered warrior of the epic, is hence a polymorphous hero who combines in himself most of the qualities and attributes of the Greek heroes. When we recall that he alone is involved in a fabric of family relations on the site of Troy, that he appears simultaneously as leader, father, husband, and son of the king, we perceive the singularity of his position in the poem. But he shares with Achilles the psychological dimension, the richness of behaviors and attitudes, that make them living, human, and autonomous characters, not stereotypes. Hector is at the center of the adversarial world, a world of tragic separation, the progressive cutting of the bonds that tie it to its environment. As James Redfield clearly demonstrates, he travels a path that makes him symmetrical with Achilles, whose origins, anger, and intransigent concept of honor relegate him to the periphery of heroic society. Both find themselves alone at the moment of the final duel, and the death of one foreshadows the death of the other.

There remains another character, however, who appears in total contradiction to Achilles in the poem—Diomedes, son of Tydeus. The following brief study refers to one more aspect of war in the epic—the temporality of the action.

III. Epic Dimension and Mythic Time

The war is strictly delimited; each character has his function. But in briefly examining the role played by Diomedes, a character who is fundamentally ambiguous to begin with, we note certain peculiarities in the actual practice of the war. Diomedes, whose *aristeia* appears in book 5 of the *Iliad*, is, in the opinion of the Achaeans themselves, the greatest warrior among them after Achilles. His character is symbolized by the lion; he is a "savage" (*agrios*) warrior throughout his exploits. In contrast to Achilles, he fights without hubris. He is nevertheless the instrument of the gods, the weapon that Athena uses to settle her accounts in the divine world. The only mortal whose eyes have been opened to the vision of divinity, he fights and wounds Ares and Aphrodite, and attempts to oppose Apollo. The war he wages seems to have more to do with the conflicts of the gods than with the realm of men. In book 5 we find this strange formulation: "But you could not have told which camp the son of Tydeus was fighting for, whether he was on the Trojans' or the Achaeans' side. He went storming forth . . ." (5.85–87). Set in motion by Athena, Diomedes is stopped by Zeus, who in book 8 throws his thunderbolt in front of the wheels of the chariot that is carrying Diomedes into the Trojan ranks. His designation as the son of Tydeus, the brute, the eater of human flesh, is constantly emphasized, far more frequently than the epithets applied to other heroes. Athena, Tydeus to whom she refused immortality because of his bestiality, and Diomedes the socialized savage form a permanent triangle in the epic. Another proof of this exceptional bond is furnished by Dolon in book 10. There we see Diomedes, accompanied by Odysseus and under the protection of Athena, engage in a sort of nonheroic war, nocturnal, combining the aspects of a manhunt and a ritual murder. The pursuit of Dolon the Wolf by Diomedes the Lion (the animal skins are expressly indicated), the cutting of the throat of Rhesus, the king of Thrace, in his sleep, which so strongly resembles a human sacrifice, the theft of the horses—the bond between Diomedes and horses is constant in the *Iliad* and his name is linked with equine cults in later tradition—this entire curious episode is situated in a sort of inversion of the heroic tradition, in a world of darkness and trickery from which the hero is bound to be excluded. The figure of Diomedes is ambiguous because it is always split, carrying within it both the right side and the dark reverse side, and because it appears in a place and a time that are not exactly those of the epic. The place is an intermediate space between the world of the gods and the world of men; the time can be deduced by analyzing the forms of war that Diomedes uses.

At the level of the epic plot, it is evident that nothing decisive can happen before the death of Patroclus convinces Achilles to emerge from his superb isolation. The poem thus divides, from the point of view of the advancement of the "story," into a static part and an evolving part. The acceleration of the narrative, centered directly on the final crisis and its denouement, the confrontation of Achilles and Hector, the death of Hector and its consequences, corresponds to a first, indecisive phase, in which the advantage is held first by one side and then by the other, a sort of non-time in the epic action. But this non-time is relative, diversified into several sectors of different importance and different levels. The *aristeia* of Diomedes, despite its great prestige, leads to a tie insofar as the course of the war is concerned. Indeed, it seems only to lead to the Achaean rout and to result exclusively in the episode of Dolon the Wolf. Diomedes is wounded in book 11 and then disappears from the scene of battle. He is never compared with Achilles, and their paths cross only in exceptional circumstances (during the funeral games, where Diomedes again plays an equivocal role: does he not fail to kill Ajax in a simple wrestling match?). The double and fixed structure of Diomedes' character—which integrates the mythic figure of Tydeus, the "berserk" side identified by M. Delcourt, the temporality on the margin of the narrative in which he moves, the close connection with the divine world and with one goddess in particular—belongs to a realm more mythic than epic. The mythic narrative as such rarely intervenes in the *Iliad*. It emerges, as though from a far-distant past, in two specific instances, in the figures of Bellerophon (*Il.* 6.154 ff.) and Meleager (*Il.* 9.531 ff.). But this is precisely a fable, about ancient things, used as an argument within an oratorical construction. The adventures of Diomedes are quite different; the poet seems to insert into a moving plot a series of fixed scenes whose goal is to add a missing dimension to the epic. The epic narration never tries to explain the world; it furnishes a display of social values. The character of Diomedes, by means of a particular aspect of the warrior function, may make it possible to return to the genesis of the genre, to indicate how and why the epic uses myth.

A.S.-G./d.b.

BIBLIOGRAPHY

A. W. H. ADKINS, "Threatening, Abusing and Feeling Angry in the Homeric Poems," *Journal of Hellenic Studies* 85 (1969): 7–21; *Merit and Responsibility* (Oxford 1960). C. M. BOWRA, *Tradition and Design in the Iliad* (Oxford 1930). M. DELCOURT, "Tydée et Mélanippe," *Studi e materiali di storia delle religioni*, 37 (1966), fac. 2: 139–88. B. FENIK, "Typical Battle Scenes in the Iliad," *Hermes Einzelschriften*, 21 (1968). J. S. KIRK, *The Songs of Homer* (Cambridge 1953). A. A. LONG, "Morals and Values in Homer," *JHS*, 90 (1970). D. L. PAGE, *History and the Homeric Iliad* (Berkeley 1955). J. REDFIELD, *Nature and Culture in the Iliad* (Chicago 1976). CH. SEGAL, "The Theme of the Mutilation of the Corpse in the Iliad," *Suppl. à Mnemosyne*, 1971. G. STRASBURGER, *Die kleinen kämpfer der Ilias* (diss., Frankfurt 1964). C. H. WHITMAN, *Homer and the Heroic Tradition* (Cambridge, MA, 1958).

DOLON THE WOLF: A GREEK MYTH OF TRICKERY, BETWEEN WAR AND HUNTING

Inserted into a context of war but presenting all of the aspects of a hunt, the myth of Dolon furnishes useful material, for it brings into play several reversals and ambiguities that have been defined with regard to cynegetic myths, myths about hunting.

Dolon, a Trojan hero, goes out at night, at the request of Hector, to spy on the Greek camp. In order to pass unnoticed, he covers himself with the skin of a wolf. Thus he is transformed from warrior into animal. In parallel, Diomedes volunteers for a similar spying mission, and asks to be accompanied by Odysseus. These two equip themselves with light arms (bows, javelins) which are hunting weapons, not fighting weapons, and leave the Greek camp in the night. A favorable presage from Athena, the cry of a heron, encourages them at the moment of their departure. Odysseus and Diomedes see Dolon, the wolf, pass them in the dark. They allow him to advance, and surprise him from the rear. He can no longer go back to the Trojan camp; the two Greek heroes pursue him, capture him, and force him to talk; then they execute him and sacrifice his remains to Athena in thanksgiving. Their expedition then continues. Once in the Trojan camp, Odysseus and Diomedes massacre the Thracian king Rhesus and twelve of his men. On the way back to their camp, they pick up Dolon's remains and attach them to the prow of Odysseus's ship.

Such is the account given both in the *Iliad* (book 10: the Doloneia) and in a tragedy, the *Rhesus*, of Pseudo-Euripides.

This episode of a night battle and raid is in fact a hunting episode and contains none of the heroism of battles. The time and space of normal combat are abolished here: this is a night chase that takes place away from the plain, among the tamarisks, bushes that grow on shorelines, at the periphery of cultivated lands. The warrior values themselves have disappeared: Dolon is no longer a warrior, for he makes use of a trick and renounces the weapons of a fighter. His name underlines this aspect of the hero (*dolos* = trickery). By disguising himself as a wolf, he presents himself as something that he is not: an animal.

Moreover—and this is characteristic of the ambiguity of the trick—Dolon collides with someone craftier than he.

Odysseus and Diomedes take him for what he pretends to be, an animal, and make him their game. The spy is surprised, the voyeur is seen, the hunter becomes the hunted. Thus, following a schema frequently encountered in hunting myths, the roles are reversed. Dolon's trick is countered by a supertrick, that of Odysseus; the blindness of the Trojan is countered by the clairvoyance of the Greek.

Finally, Dolon is not only pursued and trapped, but he is also sacrificed to Athena by Odysseus and Diomedes, who cut his throat as one would an animal's, and then sacrifice the best part of his remains to the goddess. Dolon, who shows his own pride and excess—his hubris—by asking Hector for Achilles' horses as a reward, is abandoned by the gods. Odysseus and Diomedes, accompanied by a favorable omen and able to place themselves under the protection of Athena, prove their piety by the sacrifice. The Trojan-animal, right up to the end, plays the role of the animal in the sacrifice, the intermediary between men and gods.

Thus this myth in which, beyond war, hunting and sacrifice are associated, underlines the parallelism of these two activities, a parallelism which has been analyzed elsewhere.

The various aspects of the myth, such as we have presented them, are also found in the iconography of a few ceramic pieces. The theme did not inspire many works and hence was never stereotyped. Each of the images that have reached us is like a new reading of the myth.

The vase reproduced here—an Attic oil flask with red figures, from the middle of the fifth century—places great emphasis on the animal aspect of Dolon's character: on top of his short tunic, the wolf skin is carefully adjusted; he moves on all fours, thus abandoning any semblance of being a warrior; unarmed, he is hidden by a tamarisk, which is sketched schematically.

An earlier Corinthian cup shows Dolon alone, excluded from the hoplitic combat scenes that cover the rest of the vase.

The episode of Dolon's capture is found on several Attic vases, with Dolon always represented between Odysseus and Diomedes, who bar his path in both directions. In these we find the same wolf disguise, rather precisely drawn, and a curious distribution of weapons which clearly contrasts the Trojans to the Greeks. Where Dolon has the weapons of a hunter (bow, javelin), the Greeks are armed with swords; and where Dolon has a sword—which occurs in one case—

Dolon the wolf. Attic lecythus. Ca. 460 B.C. Paris, Musée du Louvre. Museum photo.

HEROES AND MYTHS OF HUNTING IN ANCIENT GREECE

For the Greeks, the hunt is an alien world. The search for edible flesh entails dangers and risks that render the hunter a marginal and threatened character. The hunt is a troubling domain, entered at one's peril. The fundamental instability of the world of the hunt is marked by its reversibility: the hunter becomes prey, the hunted is transformed into a savage beast. This fundamental ambiguity of hunting is inscribed in a precise configuration centered on the status of meat as food.

Man may obtain meat in two ways: by hunting and by breeding animals. According to their proximity, animals are attainable by one or the other of these two techniques. Woe to him who attempts to use the wrong one! Odysseus and his companions treat the goats of the Cyclopes as game (*Od.*, 12.155–60) and sacrifice the cattle of the Sun (*Od.*, 12.351–55). The price paid for this confusion between domestic and wild animals, between sacred and domestic animals, is the disappearance of Odysseus's companions.

Within the city, sacrifice regulates the relations between men and the gods in the preparation of meat. Outside, the hunt organizes the relations between men and savage nature. The chase, the stalk, and the trap are codified moments of a cynegetic ritual imposed upon hunters. Which game may be lawfully pursued, the method of pursuit, and the age of the hunter or hunters are all subject to social rules dictated by the city (Plato, *Laws*, 823b). The world of the hunt is also an expression of ideological tensions. Praised for its civic merits, the hunt is at the same time a place of perdition. It may often turn into a passion which expels the hunter from the social group. The young woman who would venture to pursue wild game exiles herself from female society; the hunter lacking in skill or too highly skilled is equally threatened. On the narrow track leading to meat, false steps may be lethal. Most of the Greek heroes are heroes who hunt. To this we might add that hunting is one of the signs of the hero's threatened condition. For Actaeon as for Meleager, for Orion as for Atalanta, the hunt is fraught with conflict, with danger: the very qualities of the hunter are the causes of his difficulties.

Even before being defined as a biological necessity, hunting symbolizes the ability of the human group to resist nature: "The greatest and most necessary of wars is that of men as a group against the savagery of beasts. Then follow those wars waged by the Greeks against the barbarians and those who are their natural enemies" (Isocrates, *Panathenaikes*, 163). Hunting is the primary technique that differentiates men from beasts. It is at the same time a body of practices, an institution, and a form of training codified by the social group. While a model for war, it does not require political mediation, as war does. It does not have to be justified to appear natural. In the triangle of relationships that unite hunting, war, and sacrifice, hunting partakes of war in the training it demands, but it also participates in the sacrifice because, like the sacrifice, it is a means of obtaining food. Thus the mythic image of hunting oscillates constantly between two poles: the hunt undertaken as a productive necessity, and the hunt conceived as the self-affirmation of the human group in the world of savage nature.

The earliest images of the hunt connect it with the fight against monsters, with resistance to the overflowing of a

the Greeks have a bow. The two parties in this hunt are not wholly equivalent, though their roles may be inverted.

As for the sacrifice, it is most clearly portrayed on an Italiote vase of the fourth century, a time when ceramics were increasingly accentuating the tragic aspects of the episodes they illustrated. Dolon is on his knees, being struck not by Odysseus but by Diomedes, the fiercest of the Achaeans, under the gaze of Athena.

Thus the Attic painters of the fifth century, like the author of the *Rhesus*, focused on Dolon's animal disguise. Artistic representations of such transformations are rare in Attic ceramics. The only iconographic parallel that might be drawn is that of Actaeon the hunter, who, transformed into a stag by Artemis, also becomes the victim of his own hunt.

The story of Dolon, the night soldier, is also the story of a failure.

F.L./d.w.

BIBLIOGRAPHY

L. GERNET, *Anthropologie de la Grèce Antique* (2d ed., Paris 1976), 154–71. F. LISSARRAGUE, "Iconographie de Dolon le Loup," *R.A.*, 1980.

Above: Youths hunting on horseback. Attic black-figure amphora. Ca. 510 B.C. Paris, Musée du Louvre. Photo Chuzeville.

Below: "Heroic" deer hunt. Detail from an Attic red-figure krater. Ca. 440 B.C. Paris, Musée du Louvre. Photo Chuzeville.

natural world contained only with difficulty. Each of the great heroic cycles of Heracles or Theseus is connected with the purgative action of heroes who deliver men from a monster. The Nemean Lion, the Erymanthean Boar represent so many constellations that shine in the universe of the hunt. At the same time, in their exemplary nature itself, these great purgative hunts are not hunts in the proper sense of the word. Theseus and Heracles do not use traps, nor do they beat the bushes for their game. They face their prey with their bare hands or with strange or ambiguous weapons like the club or the bow. Their heroic action drives the monsters out of the city, and the hunter returns marked by his confrontation. Like the savage warrior, the solitary hunter who has succeeded in his exploit is a dangerous being who is best kept under surveillance. Heracles, dressed in a lion skin, club in hand, symbolizes, in the middle of the city, the foreignness of savage nature. He is the defender of a civic order to which his very character presents a threat; his integration is possible only through his divinization.

In the same way, Orion and Cephalus illustrate the dangers of the hunt. Both are exceptional mythical hunters who rid the earth of wild beasts. Both hunt with too much abandon, too much success, and both are pursued by Artemis. This tragic destiny connects them with Actaeon, who is devoured by his own dogs. Competitors of Artemis in their skill, these three heroes also symbolize the connections

Erotic scene: homosexual lovers, one active and the other passive, in interfemoral coitus; the passive lover is holding a hunting staff (*lagobolon*). The other figures represent a dog chasing a hare. Medallion from an Attic black-figure cup. Late sixth century B.C. Paris, Musée du Louvre. Photo Chuzeville.

between the hunt and the erotic. They are victims as much of their prowess as hunters as of the erotic attractions of the hunt: the nymphs of Artemis or Artemis herself incite in them an illicit amorous desire. The heroes thus unleash the wrath of the divinity. Orion and Actaeon perish as the result of the vengeance of Artemis, and Cephalus slays his friend Procris in a hunting accident. The cycle of love and the hunt lies at the root of the various adventures of Melanion, Hippolytus, Meleager, and Atalanta. Throughout the accounts of their adventures the rival powers of Artemis and Aphrodite confront one another. Outside the rules of conduct of the city, in the wild locales of the hunt, an erotic quest casts its nets between hunter and huntress. This quest involves two overflowings: the excess of the hunter who refuses Aphrodite (Melanion, Hippolytus), and the presumption of the woman who refuses to marry (Atalanta). The interplay of love and the hunt reflects a mythic drama that assigns to men and women a place and a determined role they may not transgress. The hunt and the erotic lend themselves all the better to this mythological game in that both are situations in which roles are reversible. In the amorous hunt as in the plain hunt, the relations of the pursuer and the pursued may be reversed at any time.

Tragedy is the best witness to this transparent reversibility. In Aeschylus's trilogy, each character is in turn hunter and prey. The black eagle Agamemnon who devours his daughter is killed by the lioness Clytemnestra and the wolf Aegisthus, while the serpent Orestes, his mother's assassin, is tracked by relentless huntresses.

The tragedies of Sophocles make use of the same system of symbols, under different forms. Philoctetes, who, thanks to his bow, is a miraculous hunter, becomes the prey of wild beasts when he is divested of it. Ajax treats domestic animals like human beings and hunts cattle that he takes for Greeks: his madness for revenge causes him to confuse the three domains of hunting, war, and sacrifice. The tragic interference that reverses the relationship between hunter and prey culminates in *Oedipus the King*: throughout the whole of this drama, Oedipus tracks a prey that is none other than himself. The interaction of these metaphors attains a kind of tragic paroxysm in the *Bacchae* of Euripides. The huntresses of Dionysus, led by Agave, hunt Pentheus and devour him. The price they pay for this act of cannibalism is the loss of their status as wives and mothers. When Agave declares, "Having left behind shuttle and loom, (I have) set my sights on higher things, and hunted wild beasts with my own hands" (*Bacchae*, 1236–37), she assumes Atalanta's course of action and, like her, cuts herself off from the city forever.

At the same time, the adventures of Atalanta and Meleager are incarnations of something more than a hunting exploit. The pursuit of the boar is, among other things, linked to the purgative tradition of the hunting of the monster. Rather than expressing the hero's solitude, it symbolizes the collective values of the hunt. Led by the best among them, young nobles would go in pursuit of monstrous game. By slaying the game, they proved their aptitude for hunting as well as their moral worth. In this sense, the collective hunt has certain initiative aspects. To be fully noble or the son of the king, it was necessary to have participated in one of these great collective acts of beating the bushes and slaughtering game. It is to this cycle of initiation hunts that the hunt of Autolycus in the *Odyssey* (19.429) belongs. Accompanied by his uncles, Odysseus goes off in pursuit of a gigantic boar, which he must confront alone: the wound he receives on this occasion illustrates his courage and valor. So, too, when Herodotus (1.36) describes the boar hunt undertaken by the son of Croesus, he establishes an equivalence between the royal function and the hunt: "O king, there appeared in our land a boar of enormous size, which ravaged our fields; in spite of our efforts we cannot vanquish it; we thus beseech you to send us your son, accompanied by choice young men and dogs, so that we may rid the land of it."

Hunting is an aspect of the royal function. The king must protect his subjects from dangerous beasts by delegating his son, accompanied by young nobles. The success of this undertaking is by no means assured. A hunting accident caused the death of Croesus's son, who was killed by the same Adrastus that his father had sent to protect him.

The territory of the hunt is riddled with ambushes: offending the goddess, having an accident, or being pursued by the game one is hunting are the daily lot of the heroic hunter. Throughout the images of the hunt one may distinguish stakes that go well beyond the pursuit of game. The mythical dimension of the hunt is not solely anthropological. Hunting adventures reflect much more than the definition of the relationship between man and nature; they also symbolize the pulse of social life. In the place such adventures accord to the erotic, through the opposing powers of Aphrodite and of Artemis, we may perceive part of a code which strictly defines the place of each sex in society.

Thus emerges the double function of the hunt. In relation to sacrifice, it helps define the position assigned to men in their search for meat; through its ties with the world of eroticism, it expresses the tensions between licit and illicit sexuality. To this double role must be added the hunt's ambiguous position with regard to war. Hunting is regarded as the best training for war, and the heroic tradition bears witness to the confederacy of war and the hunt in the exaltation of manly virtues. Friendships made in the primary and secondary levels of Athenian education as well as in collective expeditions sealed a pact between young men that bound them together in war as it did in the hunt. But war and hunting are not separated by a precise and impassable boundary. It is always possible to pass from one to the other. Furthermore, in the fourth century the hunt would lend war certain of its tactical models. In the *Cyropedia*, the new strategy of ambush and surprise attack is introduced in the form of hunting techniques. Lure the game, lie in wait, encircle it: these are the rules offered to the young Cyrus as models of combat (*Cyropedia*, 2.4.24–25).

From sacrifice to the erotic and thence to war, the hunting triangle is complete: the hunt in its various aspects reflects the city and man in the city. The hunting adventure, with its unforeseen developments, its reversals, the role of the marvelous and the strange, lends itself admirably to the tangled webs of meaning that run through the myth. The language of the hunt and the itinerary of the hunt form a group of ordered images that allow us to glimpse, through the multiplicity of narratives, the message of the myth.

A.S./d.w.

BIBLIOGRAPHY

A. BRELICH, *Gli Eroi Greci* (Rome 1958). W. BURKERT, *Homo necans* (Berlin and New York 1972). K. SCHAUENBURG, *Jagddarstellungen auf griechischen Vasen* (Hamburg and Berlin 1969), which includes a bibliography.

Sacrifice in Greek Myths

I. Prometheus

In Hesiod's *Theogony* (535–616), at the end of the passage devoted to the descendants of the Titan Iapetus, the father of a line of rebels, we find the account of the first blood sacrifice as instituted by Prometheus. The document is of great importance for its portrayal of the figure of Prometheus, both for the context of the victim's slaughter and the apportionment of the victim's parts between men and gods, and for the immediate and far-reaching consequences of Prometheus's act, first in terms of the modalities of the ritual process itself and then, more generally, in terms of the human condition. This myth could be said to constitute a frame of reference for understanding the place, the function, and the meanings of blood sacrifice in the religious life of the Greeks.

The scene takes place in Mecone, in a plain of wealth and abundance that evokes the golden age. It unfolds in a time before gods and men had separated, when they lived together, sitting at the same table, eating the same food at common banquets. But the moment of dividing and apportioning arrived. The allotment of honors between Titans and Olympians was achieved by war, force, and brutal violence. Among the Olympians, it was decided by mutual consent and agreement. But how was the distribution to be arranged between Olympians and men, and who would do it? The task fell to Prometheus, the son of Iapetus. In the world of the divine, he occupied a position that was ambiguous in every respect. He was neither an enemy of Zeus nor a sure and faithful ally. He was a rival, but did not aspire to be ruler of the sky, as did Kronos. Without Kronos's ambition, he nonetheless stood for a principle of protest in the very midst of the society of the Olympian gods. He instinctively sympathized and conspired with all those whom Zeus's established order rejected from its scope and doomed to constraint and suffering: the shadows in the picture of divine justice. Whenever this spirit of rebellion questioned Zeus's sovereignty from within, it leaned heavily on the type of wily intelligence peculiar to Prometheus. The Titan was characterized by the same inventive shrewdness, the same *mētis*, that assured the king of the gods his supremacy. The method of distribution employed by Iapetus's son as he carried out his charge was no less ambiguous than his character, nor any less equivocal than his status among the Olympians. Based neither on open warfare nor on any sense of binding agreement, it was an evasive, rigged, and fraudulent process, a contest of cunning between Zeus and Prometheus. Beneath the surface goodwill and fake mutual respect in this duel lurked the fighting will to corner the opponent quietly by catching him at his own game.

In its singularity, this mode of distribution accords with the particularity of human nature, which is also contrastive and vacillating. Like animals, whose mortal condition they share, humans are strangers to the divine sphere. But among all creatures subject to death, and unlike animals, they alone have a mode of existence that is conceived only in relation to the supernatural powers. No human city existed that did not foster an organized cult to establish some sort of community with the divine. Sacrifice expresses this hesitant and ambiguous status of humans in their relationship with the divine. It unites men and gods, but at the very moment when it draws them closer, it underscores and consecrates the insuperable distance that separates them. Between the character of Prometheus, his status in the divine world, the distribution over which he presided, sacrifice, and man's position between animals and gods, there is a close connection from the very outset.

The drama narrated in the *Theogony* and continued in *Works and Days* (42–105) unfolds in three acts.

1. To manage the distribution, Prometheus brought a large ox before men and gods, slaughtered it, and cut it in pieces. Out of all the pieces together, he made exactly two shares. The boundary that was to separate men from gods followed the dividing line between what parts of the sacrificial animal went to men and what went to the gods. Thus, when the sacrifice was performed for the first time, it appeared as the act that consecrated the segregation of divine status from human status. Each of the two portions prepared by the Titan was a lure and a trick. The first portion (the god's share) disguised under the more appetizing appearance the bones of the animal entirely stripped of its meat; the second portion (men's share) disguised all the edible pieces under the cover of a repulsive-looking skin and stomach (*gastēr*). Zeus, of course, had to make the choice. By pretending to play the Titan's game, Zeus, who "understood cunning tricks and knew how to recognize them" (Hes. *Th.* 551), turned the tables on humans by taking advantage of the very trap that Prometheus had set for him. He chose the portion that looked alluring on the outside, the one that hid the inedible bones under a thin layer of fat; this is why men burn the white bones of an animal for the benefit of the gods on the fragrant altars of sacrifice, while they themselves eat the animal's flesh. In other words, they keep for themselves the portion that Zeus opted against: the meat. But in this underhanded contest, the reversals between appearances and reality still held some surprises for Prometheus. The choice portion in Prometheus's eyes, that is, the edible portion that he intended to keep for men by giving it the false appearance of being inedible, turned out to be the bad portion. The bones burned to ashes on the altar constituted the only authentically good portion. For by eating the meat, men behaved like gluttons or "bellies" (*gasteres oion*) (ibid. 26). If they took pleasure in feeding on the flesh of a dead animal, if they had a pressing need for such nourishment, it was because their constantly recurring hunger involved exhaustion, fatigue, aging, and death. By contenting themselves with the smoke from the bones, by living off smells and fragrances, the gods revealed themselves to be of an altogether different nature. They were the Immortals who live forever, eternally young, whose existence involved no perishable element, nor any contact with the realm of the corruptible.

2. Zeus wanted to make men pay for the fraud for which Prometheus was clearly to blame, having rigged the portions to favor men at the expense of Zeus. He proceeded to hide fire, his heavenly fire; in other words, he stopped making it available to men, who until that time were able to use it freely. Deprived of fire, they were unable to cook and eat the meat that they had received as their share. The king of the gods also hid from men their life, *bios* (Hesiod *Works and Days* 42–47), in other words, cereal food, the grain that until that time the earth had given them to their heart's content without their having to work for it. Corn and wheat had grown spontaneously and in plentiful quantities, just as fire from heaven came forth of itself whenever they wanted it.

The grain being hidden, men had to bury it in the womb of the earth by plowing furrows if they hoped to harvest it. Henceforth there was no more abundance to assuage hunger without hard labor.

The heavenly fire being hidden, Prometheus secretly stole a seed of it, a spark, which he disguised and brought down to earth in the hollow of a fennel stalk. Buried deep inside its hiding place, the stolen fire escaped the notice of the vigilant Zeus until it was already burning in the hearths of kitchens on earth. Prometheus's fire is an ingenious fire, a technical fire, but it is also precarious, perishable, and hungry. It does not subsist of its own accord; it must be engendered with a seed, fed constantly, and conserved in embers under the ashes when it is extinguished.

Of all the animals, man alone shares with the gods the possession of fire, and fire also unites him with the divine by rising to the sky from the sacrificial altars where it is kindled. However, like those who domesticated it, fire is ambiguous: heavenly in origin and in destination, it is also mortal, like men, because of its consuming ardor.

The boundary between the gods and men was therefore simultaneously crossed by the sacrificial fire that united them to one another and reinforced by the difference between the celestial fire that belonged to Zeus and the fire that rose from the earth after Prometheus had brought it back to men. The function of the sacrificial fire is, moreover, to distinguish in the sacrificed animal the gods' portion, entirely burned, from that of men, cooked just enough not to be consumed raw.

In this regard, the ambiguous relationship between men and gods in the edible sacrifice is mirrored in the equivocal relationship between men and animals, in that both men and animals need to eat in order to survive, whether their food is vegetable or meat. They are also both mortal. But men alone cook what they eat, and do so according to certain rules. To the Greeks, cereals, a specifically human food, were "cultivated" plants, thrice cooked—by an internal cooking, by the action of the sun, and by the hands of man. Similar to sacrificial animals, and therefore suitable for consumption, were domestic animals, whose flesh was ritually roasted or boiled before it was eaten.

3. Furious at seeing, among men, the fire that he had determined to withhold from them, Zeus concocted a gift tailor-made for men. All the gods contributed to the design of the gift, which was the counterpart, the reverse, of the stolen fire: it would burn men, make them pine away, and do so not with flames but with strain, trouble, and anxiety. This gift was Woman, named Pandora, "gift of all the gods." She appears in the myth as the first woman and the ancestor of the female species. Until that moment, men lived without women. They arose directly out of the earth, which produced them all by herself, like crops. They knew nothing of birth by begetting nor of the old age and death that went along with it. They disappeared into a state of peace similar to sleep, still just as young as they were in the first days of their lives. The Woman was man's double and his opposite. The male was going to have to plow her to hide his seed within her womb if he wanted to have children, just as he had to till the earth to hide the grain within it if he wanted to have wheat, and just as he had to hide the seed of fire in the hollow of a fennel stalk if he wanted to kindle it on the altar. So Zeus molded this Woman as a lure, a deep trap from which there was no escape (ibid. 589). On the outside, she looked like an immortal goddess; irresistible grace and charm radiated from her beauty. On the inside, along with lying and deceit, Hermes inserted the soul of a bitch and the temperament of a thief. Divine in looks, human in speech and in her role as legitimate wife and mother, bestial in her insatiable appetites for sex and food, the appetites of a bitch, Woman summed up in her person all the contrasting elements of what it means to be human. She was evil, but a likable evil clothed in stirring beauty, a *kakon kalon*, the kind of evil one can neither do without nor endure. If you marry her, her belly eats you out of house and home and lands you in poverty in your own lifetime. But if you do not marry and lack a female belly to receive your seed and nurture the embryo, you have no children to carry on your line, and as you cross the threshold of death, you are all alone. With Woman, good and evil, like the divine and the bestial, are merged and confused.

The very incarnation of this relentlessly split and ambiguous form of existence that awaited the human race once it was separated from the gods, Pandora in all her beguiling charm was sent by Zeus to Epimetheus, the brother of Prometheus, his double and opposite. Prometheus is the "forethinker," who guesses in advance, while his brother is the "after-thinker," who understands too late, after the fact. Man resembles both Prometheus and Epimetheus; in his intelligence and his blindness, he embodies both aspects of the Titans. Even though Epimetheus was warned by his brother, he welcomed Pandora into his house and took her as his wife. So, along with marriage, Woman was ushered into the world of mankind. Men had lived without knowing fatigue, labor, pains and sorrows, or illness and old age. All the ills were still sealed up in a jar, which Pandora opened on Zeus's order. All of its evil contents spread over the earth and mingled with the good, so that they could be neither foreseen nor recognized. Some evils roved about the world, hidden and invisible. Others, lurking about the home like the "beautiful evil" that Pandora was, hid under the deceitful guise of seduction.

In the myth of Prometheus, sacrifice and all of its consequences appear as the result of the rebellion of the Titan who sought to thwart the designs of Zeus at the time when men and gods had to separate and determine their respective shares. The moral of the story is that no one can fool Zeus. Prometheus, the most subtle of the gods, gave it a try, and men had to pay the price of his failure.

To perform the sacrificial ritual by making contact with the deity is therefore to commemorate the Titan's adventure and to accept its lesson. It means recognizing that through sacrifice and all that it entails (Promethean fire, the cultivation of cereal grains with the attendant labor, women and marriage, misfortune and death), Zeus placed men in what would henceforth be their own place, between animals and gods. By offering sacrifice, men submit to the will of Zeus, who made mortals and Immortals into two clearly distinct races. Communication with the divine is established in the course of a ceremonial banquet, a meal that reminds us that the ancient commensality is over. Gods and men are now apart; they no longer live together or eat at the same table. It is impossible both to sacrifice in the Promethean mode and to claim, through whatever ritual, to be the equal of the gods. By trying to compete with Zeus in trickery in order to give men the better share, the Titan doomed his protégés to the sorry fate that is theirs today. Ever since the Promethean fraud instituted the first sacrificial meal, everything in human life has its dark shadow and its wrong side. There can no longer be any contact with the gods that does not also involve, through sacrifice, the consecration of an insuperable

Bulls being led to sacrifice. Frieze from the Parthenon. Ca. 440 B.C. Athens, Museum of the Acropolis. Photo Alinari-Giraudon.

barrier between the human and the divine. There can no longer be happiness without unhappiness, birth without death, abundance without toil, knowledge without ignorance, man without woman, Prometheus without Epimetheus.

J.-P.V./g.h.

II. The Myths of Argos and Athens

Hesiod's story of Prometheus is not unanimously recognized by the Greeks. The people of Argos, whose traditions were collected by Pausanias (2.19.5), deny that the Titan son of Iapetus had any role whatsoever in giving fire to humans. They attribute the discovery of fire, primordial to men, to a certain Phoroneus, king of their land at the time of origins and, according to some, the very first to have exercised power as a king. The invention of fire and that of sacrifice go hand in hand with royal power in these stories, and no place is made for tensions or conflicts between men and gods. As the first human master over the Argive land, Phoroneus paid its divine mistress, Hera, the homage that was her due. He also invented for her places of worship and even martial weapons. Nothing on the mythical horizon of Argos seems to have any real connection with sacrifice. The fire of Phoroneus, which appeared on earth without provoking any contest or any distribution of prerogatives, has its place within the total fabric of connections between the world of the gods and that of men. Around Phoroneus, men who were formerly dispersed unite in a community, a *koinon*, the first of its kind.

The truth about Argos, however, lies elsewhere. Before Phoroneus's men arrived, the land was occupied only by rivers. Inachus, the father of Phoroneus, was one of the primordial occupants of the part of the Argive domain that was committed to the element of water. Hera was not the uncontested mistress of this land. Poseidon, the master of the waters, once contested her right to possess it. The rivers,

Inachus foremost among them, decided in favor of the goddess. The god reacted immediately, either by submerging the land under the flood of sea waters or else by causing the river waters to disappear. Inachus and his fellow Argive rivers thus became mere riverbeds, dependent on the rain waters without which they would be condemned to dry up. At this moment, Phoroneus arrived with humans to occupy the space abandoned by his father and the rivers, the original inhabitants. The time of Phoroneus corresponds to the receding of the waters from Argive soil. It was to this space, henceforth condemned to drought, that Danaus and his daughters came from Egypt. To offer sacrifice, there has to be water, as exemplified by Amymone's quest for water. She intervenes several times in an effort to obtain the water needed for the sacrifice. The hidden truth about Argos was the secret of the distribution of the waters. Having disappeared in the time of Phoroneus, the waters were to reappear as a result of the hydraulic activities of the daughters of Danaus in connection with their marriage. Amymone succeeded in procuring water from Poseidon as a return for his union with her. The sacrifice made it possible for water to return to Argos through the circuitous route of the marriage of one of Danaus's man-killing daughters.

The lack of water when it was withheld by Poseidon parallels the lack of fire when it was withheld by Zeus in the story of Prometheus. On the positive side, the result of this lack is matrimonial union; on the negative side, the king of the gods gives men the treacherous gift of Pandora. In Argos, the lack of water blocks the sacrifice just as the lack of fire blocks the sacrifice in Mecone. The fire stolen for the sacrifice brings men to reproduction by birth and death. The vanished water is restored by its divine master, Poseidon, through the medium of matrimonial union. Amymone, who goes in search of sacrificial water on the parched land of Argos, reintroduces the liquid element through marriage, to which water is equally indispensable, into a mythical landscape profoundly marked by a cosmogony in which the primordial waters occupy a key place. The Argive stories about sacrifice reveal the deeply rooted Greek homology between sacrifice and marriage, which are linked by the element of water in the traditions surrounding Inachus, Phoroneus, and the daughters of Danaus. In exchange for royal power, Phoroneus, the first human ruler on earth, invented sacrifice for Hera and a certain form of community life for men, who assembled in a *koinon* in a space reserved and built for that purpose and bearing Hera's name. But the king who was born of a river did not found a city, the requisite political framework of Greek life with its strict set of rules and laws.

In the exemplary city of Athens, sacrifice was the city itself, the polis, even the democratic city, an egalitarian self-governing community that had power over what happened to it. As in Argos, Poseidon competed for dominion over Attic soil with the goddess Athena, the daughter of Zeus. By means of a vote, the people of Athens showed their preference for the goddess over the god. But the city where men exercised power collectively had to pass through the master of power, Zeus himself, the father of gods and men, who then became Polieus, protector of cities. Similarly, Athena Polias, protectress of the new institution, instituted the first sacrifice in which an animal victim was immolated by the civic community. She thus became the patron goddess of the community, having given it the olive tree along with the gift of a life that was both cultured and urban. The olive tree, the official tree of the city, "lives forever," as Plutarch put it. Thus Athens, too, experienced a version of the origin of the death of animals in homage to the gods, a version that presents no major difficulties. In a system of three terms, whereby animals are killed and then eaten in honor of the gods, who in turn do not eat, sacrifice makes good sense. Since it was an immortal goddess who was credited with the invention of the practice of sacrifice, there can be no doubt about the pious nature of this practice among men. But in Athens as in Argos, a less serene, submerged reality marked the city with an undeniable sign—a sacrificial ritual, the *Bouphonia*. The stories that explain the origin of this shocking act of slaughter in homage to the gods revolve around one paradoxical but certain detail of this rite. The officiating priest who slaughtered the beast would flee, and, in the course of a trial, the instrument of death was found guilty and cast into the sea (Pausanias 1.24.4; 1.28.10). Thus, an ordinary sacrifice, the pious obligation of humans, officially performed every day and in normal times by the entire city, was linked to a serious incident. Its implications were brought to light by an exegetical commentary that explains in the fashion of a myth how it all happened for the first time. The traditions are not uniform and their divergences are surely significant. We shall limit ourselves here to the lengthy account in Theophrastus's lost work, *On Piety,* which is quoted at great length by the philosopher Porphyry (*De Abstinentia* 2.29–31).

The situation appears akin to that of Argos at the time of Phoroneus. Gathered together in a sort of community, men who had been separated from the gods knew about sacrifice, but there is no indication of organization in this *koinon* of primordial Attica, not even the presence of a king and his authority. In this fully humanized space, work existed as a given from distant times, but it was not exclusive to the human race. Farming, a human activity, was also an activity of a group of animals that was associated with men—namely, oxen. In a space still totally devoid of any organization, where no place was yet fixed or assigned for anything, somewhere a sacrifice of the *koinon* took place. On a table, offerings of grain awaited consecration, and oxen returning from their work found themselves in the midst of the preparations for the celebration. Not far away, an ax was being sharpened, adding still more to the strangeness of the scene. In this space, thought of as solely agricultural, even though activities of one sort or another had hardly been organized, a two-edged ax, the *pelekus*, was probably the instrument used to clear land. It tamed the wild, open space of the bush for men and turned it into cultivated land, a place of cultivation and of civilization. To use the Greek term, it was a *chōra*, a zone of fields, but still without a place reserved for men, a *chōra* in the process of being established out of the bush with the aid of oxen.

Animals, strangely close to men in this civilizing enterprise, nevertheless remained ambiguous and, through a complete reversion, capable of great savagery. In the confused realm of origins, anything was possible, and the ox devoured the offerings that someone named Sopatros had prepared to pay homage to the gods. Himself an ambiguous figure, Sopatros shared in everyone's activity in the farming *koinon,* although he was not locally born. Because he tilled the land, he participated by right in the oblations of the fruits of the earth, the *karpoi,* which is what sacrifice consisted of in those primordial times, the times without meat. The story of Sopatros begins "before" that of Prometheus, for the animal here is still on its legs. "After" the story of Phoroneus, the *koinon* already existed. Therein lies the problem: the sacrifice was bloodless, and animals were totally uninvolved. But Sopatros's ox, which could not tell the difference, started to eat the share reserved for the gods. Beside himself at this

unspeakable act, the infuriated Sopatros picked up the civilizing ax and slaughtered the animal, which seemed to have reverted to wildness. When he regained his composure, the man found himself standing beside the dead body of the workmate he had just murdered. After piously giving it the last rites that are due to humans, Sopatros felt he was in a state of impurity because of the blood shed by the dead creature. He left the country and crossed the sea to Crete, thus placing all the distance of the seas between himself and the land of Attica.

From then on, Attica was dead; nothing else could happen there. As dead as Sopatros's ox, the land was doomed to a total drought, which condemned men and beasts to starvation and ruin. The second episode of the story takes place outside this space altogether. The men of the *koinon* gathered to appeal to the god of Delphi as a last resort. Human knowledge was incapable of ending the catastrophic process that had overtaken the Attic *chōra.* Only outside intervention could assess the situation and give men the power of intervening in their blocked world. No available knowledge could give them the means to change anything. The powerlessness of men stemmed first from the fact that they could not name events. The first episode was a silent one, while the second is made up of anguished questions and barely perceptible answers. In her reply, the Pythia at least set aside a place for Sopatros's deeds. He was in effect a murderer and as such was going to suffer punishment, but a punishment that would have to reconstruct all the events that had occurred in the original *koinon,* on condition that the men would eat all the meat of the dead animal, rejecting none of it. A new form of solidarity thus came into being: the action of one person could have consequences suffered by all. To kill, even if only an ox, concerned the group as a whole. Before this group solidarity could be expressed in a meal of meat, Sopratos had to be found and an agreement had to be made with him: the anxiety of the group was not yet appeased. To know that a solution was possible did not mean that the solution would be found. The group was in fact unable to respond to the Pythia's demands all by itself. They wondered how to put the animal to death again without bringing on the primordial catastrophe once more. Sopatros, already a murderer, could easily repeat the very deed that would land the group in serious trouble. Pointing that out, he joined with the group in a kind of contract that set up a new reality in which he demanded an equal share. He became a citizen, *politēs,* within the structure of the city, the polis.

At that moment, Sopatros blended into the newborn social body that, in the third episode of the series, was organized around a sacrificial practice of a previously unknown genre. The death of the ox was assumed to have taken place: all that was left to do was to prepare it for eating. In doing this, the citizens introduced into the city all that the *koinon* had lacked since the death of the first animal. First, water, which had disappeared along with the animal's corpse after the burial, revealing that the burial was impure, had to be brought back, as Amymone had brought it back during the drought in Argos. Here the group of young girls designated for that purpose did not take the detour of marriage. The water was the water of sacrifice, a water revealing the very meaning of the sacrificial waters that bring death. Cereal crops had disappeared, buried in the ox's stomach. In the rite, they concealed the mortal weapon of the sacrificer. Touched by the water, the land-clearing ax of the first episode split into two, giving rise to the new instrument of political solidarity whereby meals are taken in common. The slaughtering knife that thenceforth accompanied the ax was also the instrument for carving meat, at once a murderer and an apportioner, the *machaira*. The ax itself soon lost its place in the narrative. Its land-clearing action and its primordial violence had no place in the polis, where all was perfectly regulated and there was no room for the unexpected. The deeds of the first episode were carefully organized into an unbroken ritual chain leading from the instruments dipped into the recovered water to the actual introduction of meat into the world of humans. Corresponding to the impotence of the second episode was the delegation here of powers that characterized the new political order: the actions of one may affect all. The violent act of the reckless Sopatros here became the calm endpoint of a series aiming in a single direction, in which each person had a role to play and all benefited by the final meal of meat. At the final link in the chain, there was even someone to offer, with a restrained gesture, the instruments of slaughter that Sopatros had seized and used with such bestial violence in the first episode. The demands of the Pythia were finally met, point by point. One and all, men ate a small part of the meat and put an end to the famine. They brought food back to their region, which was now saved from death. By the same stroke, they had become totally and definitively separated from the oxen they now consumed.

But things did not stop there. A detour, which was made through marriage in Argos, was made through labor in Attica. Meat was not to become the exclusive diet of man. When the ox was eaten, cereal grains did not reappear, but were on the verge of disappearing altogether along with the ox that had swallowed them on that first occasion. The ritual then continued and made a double of the ox in the same way that it had made a double of the instrument of death. Buried in the earth with the grains hidden in its stomach, the ox was emptied of its own meat. Fed on cereals, it became, in turn, food for men. Filled with hay, the food for animals, it became thenceforth man's helper in the production of cereal crops. The ox buried the seeds in the soil with the mediating help of the plow. Cereal crops again became available to humans. In this sense, the intervention of the ox was a double one: itself a source of food and also a producer of food, it demonstrated the homology between diets of grain and of meat. The two foods were connected for good in the new ritual framework. The ox rose to a new level of dignity by working as a farmhand in collaboration with man, and contributed to the organization of the *chōra* in which farmland and political values were henceforth connected, as agriculture and the polis now shared the same level of reality. But the murderer was still unpunished, and in the background of sacrificial practice another form of solidarity asserted itself, different from the one offered by the commensality of men sharing meat. The chain of actions that led the group to eat together was once more examined. Retrospectively, they recognized the succession of deeds that led to death. Little by little, the cause was identified, namely, the *machaira*, the slaughtering and carving instrument that had actually caused the bloodshed. The ax and the person who struck the blow disappeared from the story—like Sopatros. From within the ranks of this group, however, a pole of organization emerged whereby the power of speech became the decisive power for one and all.

The lawsuit had just been born. Men called on one another to participate in a collective action, this time defined as judgment on a murder. From a group consisting of juxtaposed people of ambiguous status in the first episode, we have moved to a group in which each person could express himself concerning the place he occupied in a succession of

events. A single person, like Sopatros, could no longer judge himself without saying anything about it. Others no longer had as their only solutions anxiety and questions without answers in a situation with no hope of resolution except for some recourse outside the community. The group was endowed with a voice that could compel any one of its members to respond. The obstacle presented by the first episode, whereby the Pythia and Sopatros were supposed to respond from without to the questions asked, was no longer possible. Henceforth, questions and answers were exchanged from within in a functional system of communication. Anyone unable to answer, having no voice, was thereby excluded and cast out. In the framework of the city, sacrifice had law on its side along with agriculture. The ritual was organized around individual acts and their chain of succession. At its limit, it was completely silent, speechless. Law was a matter of speech, and speech shaped its power.

Thus, quite logically, since it could not answer because it had no voice, just as an abashed defendant stands speechless before a jury, the slaughter weapon, the *machaira*, was the last to be accused. Unable to shift the blame, it was convicted of murder. Appearing in contractual form in the second episode, the group's relationship with the individual had been impossible in the first episode, in which speech had no outlet for expression and allowed for no communication among the members of the *koinon*. From then on, it was the function of the new entity, with all its plans of solidarity, to pronounce, with words of executory power, the rights of each person. Everyone submitted to its decrees, even if it meant shifting by its own words the imputation of causes, with which legal action really began. The chain of ritual acts

Celebrant carrying a libation jar and a grain basket. Attic cantharus. Detail. Ca. 440 B.C. Altenburg, Lindenau-Museum. Museum photo.

will thus be examined no longer religiously but legally—
"Who causes what?"—when there is no incontestable support for the final action in a series which demonstrates the
solidarity of all. Sacrifice, which first took the detour from
agriculture to the harnessed plow, then moved on to the
establishment of law. But sacrificial practice was still the
pivotal point of the whole life of the political group, or polis.
A final disposition of the groups of sacrificial agents in the
model city of Athens ends Theophrastus's exegetic commentary on the *Bouphonia*. From Sopatros and other primordial
men of action, the groups evolved that organized the sacrificing city. The blood of the animal disappeared entirely in
favor of the sharing of meat, required for the feast. Among
the sacrificing groups there were no slaughterers, only
distributors, *daitroi*. The city kept only the egalitarian commensality, as if the animal's death were a difficult act to
integrate. The account ends with the ultimate expulsion from
the civic domain of the object that remained the murderer
even though it served on the side of redress, the *machaira*.
Wrenched once and for all out of the arable realm of men, it
was cast into what for the Greeks was the opposite domain,
the depths of the open seas.

Sacrifice was tormented from within by a secret evil, the
killing of animals. When Prometheus distributed between
men and gods the doubly unequal shares whereby their
respective statuses would be fixed, the ox was already a dead
animal. When its death was recounted, a story as complex as
that of Sopatros was required to give a full account of it, or,
rather, to confess that animals are rather bothersome creatures or that they consent to the treatment that they get. That
is what was related in the brief Athenian stories included by
Porphyry, who sometimes quotes Theophrastus, in his treatise on vegetarianism (*De Abstinentia* 2.9–10). Icarius's goat
was as wicked as can be, and for browsing on the holy vine
of Dionysus it had to be offered in sacrifice. As for the pig,
Delphi supplied a sufficiently vague response to men's
questions for them to continue to kill the animal. The sheep
accepted its fate, according to the usual custom of sacrificial
ritual. As far as the ox is concerned, we know how it
undermined vegetable offerings. Close to men and sharing
their domain, animals became the objects of sacrifice without
major difficulty. Too close to men, they raised problems such
that only the prodigious casuistic scheme that structures the
Bouphonia could take account of them. In any event, the city
that could not do without the sacred sharing of meats
adhered strictly to Promethean orthodoxy.

Those who revealed the secret evil of sacrifice and refused
to accept the violence inflicted on animals or the food that
resulted from their slaughter were not just ordinary vegetar-
ians. They questioned the very social order, taking a position
outside the city and refusing to live in a world marked by the
original evil of sacrifice. The disciples of Orpheus wanted
nothing to do with an institution that condoned murder as a
pious act. In total renunciation of earthly values, they sought
to draw closer to the gods by means of food restrictions.
Nothing corruptible could be part of their nourishment.
Nothing in their sacrifices maintained the separation between men and gods. No meat, no smoke coming from
grease and bones, as in the practice (repulsive to them) of
those who followed the Promethean path. In their accounts

(*Orphica Fragmenta* 34–36, 209–14 Kern), the only sacrifice
that involved the slaughter, distribution, and cooking of a
victim was the sacrifice of a god. The primordial evil powers,
the man-eating Titans, were punished by Zeus, who struck
them with his thunderbolt. Their ashes are the basis of the
men of today who are drowning in the misery of the human
condition, separated from the primordial unity with the
divine. To refuse to perpetuate Promethean deeds is to
attempt to put an end to this intolerable situation. The
disciples of Pythagoras thought likewise: their position with
respect to sacrifices allowed them to define their attitude
before the human polis. Some, of strict observance, renounced the world, followed the path of asceticism, and
refused any kind of blood sacrifice. Others, actively participating in the city that they intended to reform from within,
worked out an elaborate and subtle theology by which they
distinguished the meat of the plowing ox and wool-yielding
sheep from the nonmeat of goats and pigs.

To do as the gods do is one way of refusing to do as men
do. A third alternative was open to anyone who refused the
Promethean deeds and the use of fire to treat the meat of a
sacrificed animal, namely, to follow the values set forth by
Dionysus, values of the wilderness that made it possible to
recognize the presence of irrational forces within each man:
to do this was to do what animals do, and eat raw foods. In
the *Bacchae*, Euripides tells how dangerous it is to resist the
power of a god capable of leading his worshipers up a
mountain to tear the flesh of a hunted animal in pieces. To
eat raw food with Dionysus is to become wild in order to
enter into contact with a form of the divine of which he alone
is the guarantor, namely, madness, *mania*, which surpasses
human forces.

Myths of the origin of sacrifice—speculative commentaries
on the practices of men united by the ritual act of eating
cooked meat, shocking stories that express the horror of
bloodshed or the mad attraction of raw meat—were ways for
the Greeks to test or to deny human limits, to tell how they
no longer were, no longer could be, or had tried to be in the
lost past or at a special moment, like the gods.

J.-L.D./g.h.

BIBLIOGRAPHY

On the general practices of blood sacrifice: J. RUDHARDT, *Notions
fondamentales et actes constitutifs de culte dans la Grèce classique* (Geneva
1958), 249–300. J. CASABONA, *Recherches sur le vocabulaire des sacrifices en
grec, des origines à la fin de l'époque classique* (Aix-en-Provence 1966).

On the thesis proposed here: D. SABBATUCCI, *Saggio sul misticismo
greco* (Rome 1965). M. DETIENNE, "Ronger la tête de ses parents" and
"Dionysos orphique et le rôti bouilli," in *Dionysos mis à mort* (Paris
1977), 135–60 and 161–217. J.-P. VERNANT, "Sacrifice et alimentation
humaine," *Annali della Scuola normale superiore di Pisa* 7 (1977):
905–40. J.-L. DURAND, "Le corps du délit," *Communications* 26 (1977):
46–61.

On other proposals: W. BURKERT, *Homo necans* (Berlin and New York
1972). J. RUDHARDT, "Les mythes grecs relatifs à l'instauration du
sacrifice: Les rôles corrélatifs de Prométhée et de son fils Deucalion,"
Museum Helveticum 27 (1970): 1–15.

THE SEMANTIC VALUE OF ANIMALS IN GREEK MYTHOLOGY

Animals certainly had semantic value in the mythological discourse of the Greeks. The use of certain species as attributes of various gods constitutes the most obvious example of the symbolic function of the bestiary. The owl is consecrated to Athena: its representation evokes the presence of Athena, and its actual appearance in the midst of reality makes her manifest. The dove of Aphrodite, the peacock of Hera, the doe of Artemis, and the eagle of Zeus function in the same way, although the nature of these attributions, as well as the reasons for them, still need to be stated precisely. A great number of animals are closely associated with various divine powers or mythical figures, and careful study of the place of animals in myths reveals that much of the bestiary functions according to a system closely allied, in its principles, to heraldry. To stop at this point, however, would be superficial. To the degree that animals function as symbols and not just as signs, they have a semantic value of their own, sometimes very rich, that can be discovered by tracing the appearances of each animal, both in mythical sequences (which often include etiological narratives about the different species, generally telling how they resulted from the metamorphoses of characters who, upon analysis, prove to be significant themselves) and in innumerable pictorial representations. Animals' semantic value may also be found in other modes of discourse, whether the systematic reports of a scholar with scientific pretensions (treatises on animals, medicine, natural history) or the spontaneous expressions of popular folk wisdom—accessible mainly in collections of proverbs—or, finally, poetic usage, which draws heavily on the animal kingdom for its metaphors.

It is understandable that a global study of this kind, leading to a totally new concept of research, should barely have been broached; very few species have been subjected to systematic study in these different aspects. Only here and there, in an attempt either to interpret the mythology or to decipher the iconography, has new light been shed on this little-explored area. After a discussion of the original results of research on the role of the animal in Homer, we shall merely indicate some recently obtained data regarding the semantic position of certain animals in the symbolic system of the Greeks of the classical period. This division is of course illusory: everything valid for Homer remains valid for the classical period, for which Homer remains to the end an essential reference.

J.-P.D./d.b.

I. The Heroic Bestiary

Homeric epic is filled with all sorts of animals which, thanks to extensive zoological research, could be identified and classified very early. It would be wrong, however, to ascribe to Homer "scientific" interests in describing various animal species, at times very precisely. Homer is no more a zoologist than he is a sociologist or a historian, and epic poetry cannot be read as a veterinary treatise. Moreover, the use of the animal figure in the anthropocentric world of the *Iliad* and the *Odyssey* in no way implies an autonomy of information or even the perception of a radical otherness. The animal world is never presented as a partner to the world of men. At the level of analogy (there are at least a hundred animal similes in the *Iliad* alone), through a complex game of mirrors, it offers a reflection of the highest values of the heroic world. Simultaneously symbol and model, the animal image expresses the recognition of an essential identity between its subject and the hero it describes. And when an animal intervenes as an active agent in the narrative, it is often perceived as a mediator between men and gods. Livestock functions in this way, mediated by sacrifice and the consumption of meat. Evidence of personal wealth, livestock is also one of the instruments for putting the universe in order, and its economic value is inseparable from its religious function. The animal is occasionally a companion, like the dog or the horse, but the specific values attached to it in these cases shatter the simple framework of domesticity. The animal also expresses, as exemplified by the bird, the dimension of the ineffable, the limits set on the irresistible progression of human knowledge. By turns a means of social definition, a guarantor for man in relation to the gods, a mediator, the Homeric animal is never itself.

1. The Animal as Reflection

The analogy of a man with an animal can be read at several levels. As the description of a movement, of a rapid action at a given moment, the complex illustration of a situation or even of a state of being, it expresses permanent characteristics, an essential bond, an ideological connection between the symbolic nature of the animal and the status of the man. "It seems," writes G. E. R. Lloyd, "that the early Greeks held that animals not only symbolized certain characteristics, but *permanently manifested them*." The animals chosen to describe the warrior mettle of the hero are both few in number and strictly hierarchized; at first sight, they all belong to the world of animals called "wild" in our Western definition, which sets them against the "domestic" sphere (we will see later how mechanistical this scheme is when applied to Homer). The usual hierarchy puts the lion first, then the wild boar, and then birds of prey.

The lion, a central character, represents in epic the attitude of the warrior in combat. The preeminent heroic symbol, his image is obligatory in descriptions of the highest exploits, though it appears more frequently in connection with certain individuals (like Diomedes). At the highest level, the lion expresses the aristocratic values of courage, nobility, disdain for death in favor of an intransigent code of honor; he exalts the prowess of the lone individual in the face of a collective enemy. Far more than a model of behavior, however, the lion becomes the hero's doublet. Here is an example of the most frequent type of comparison with the lion:

> But Hector fell on their ranks like a ferocious lion that attacks a great herd of cattle grazing in the wet grass of a vast swamp—the herdsman with them is one who has never learned exactly how to fight a wild beast, how to keep him from killing a cow with curved horns. He always walks either at the head or at the rear of the herd, but the beast leaps in right at the middle and devours a cow, stampeding all the others. (*Il.*, 15.630–36)

The behavior of the wild beast is thus wholly conceived as a direct confrontation with the human community. Far from being a model of the wild predator, the lion fights with man, on his own territory, for the food which most aptly defines him socially and religiously: livestock. In the midst of the herd, the lion is still careful to choose the best animal, the one that could as well be consumed in the course of a sacrifice. And the lion's method of operation is related to a model that is clearly described in the Homeric texts: the raid

Lion and siren. Corinthian aryballos. Mid-sixth century B.C. Paris, Musée du Louvre. Photo Chuzeville.

Horse's head. Attic amphora. Ca. 560 B.C. Paris, Musée du Louvre. Photo Chuzeville.

Armed owl. Attic cup. Ca. 440–430 B.C. Paris. Musée du Louvre. Photo Chuzeville.

Hunt for the Calydon boar. Corinthian aryballos. Late fourth century B.C. Paris, Musée du Louvre. Photo Chuzeville.

on the herds, carried out against a neighbor by whom one thinks one has been injured, or even in enemy territory, far from home. The vocabulary further accentuates the lion's proximity to the hero: the meat eaten by the lion is called *krea*, just like the meat that nourishes men, meat obtained after a sacrifice. The lion also has the warrior virtue (*alkē*) and the mettle of the hero, or the warrior spirit (*menos*). Occasionally (though less often) the lion is found in his natural habitat. There he hunts wild game and, remarkably, pits himself anew against the men in pursuit of the same animal. The confrontation is transferred to the world of the hunt, but remains essentially the same. There is no trace, and for good reason, of a lion hunt in the *Iliad;* can one hunt oneself? The

lion is simultaneously a symbolic model and a complete doublet; the hero is like the lion because the lion is considered to be like the hero. We are far from the notion of the wild animal here: the Homeric lion is a pure ideological construction, a cultural archetype which has broken its ties with the naturalistic universe.

Much more than the lion, for whom the place of confrontation with men matters less than the confrontation itself, the boar is determined by his territory. Hunters track him to the heart of the "wooded mountains," the area furthest from inhabited land.

The boar is on the defensive, while the lion is an attacker. The heroic values attached to the two therefore will not be exactly the same. While remaining a prestigious model of behavior (valor, tenacity, lust for battle, disdain for danger and death), the boar no longer corresponds directly to the hero in a pattern of identification and total reversibility. Unlike the lion, the boar has admirable qualities which are also those of a wild animal insofar as they are radically opposed to the human race as a whole. Outside the realm of analogy, the Calydonian boar (*Il.,* 9.539ff.) clearly illustrates this aspect: the monster sent by the gods to ravage the vineyards—which are the epitome of the "civilized" place—

129

is experienced as the eruption of savagery into the human world, as the manifestation of a natural disorder encroaching relentlessly on the social order. Thus the boar is a heroic symbol, but also the expression of a distance, an insurmountable difference. The image of the boar combines the two planes of war and hunting, by inscribing itself in the space of savage nature. His position in the hierarchy of symbols is therefore somewhat lower than that of the lion.

The bird of prey plays still another role. At first sight, the analogy functions in a more purely descriptive way: the speed and infallible accuracy of the eagle or the kite are brought into play by their affinity to comparable warrior traits. The model is that of a purely animal hunt, without intervention, at this level, from the human community. The bird, moreover, does not challenge his adversary; he is content to attack defenseless prey. The absence of the human element, the absence of equal combat—the image takes on a quite different meaning from those previously considered; it is on a lower level than the symbolic. But identification with the bird is not insignificant, since it refers to an animal outside all classification, as will be demonstrated later.

Whether a confused reflection of cultural values projected upon the mirror of animality, or the expression of a savagery implicit in man's domination of his environment, the essential function of the analogical representation is to situate the hero in the world that encompasses him, to define him socially in relation to other individuals like him, and, more generally, to place him within an anthropocentric vision of the universe.

2. The Animal as Agent

Along with his warlike activities, the Homeric hero spent much time at his meals. Sacrifices followed by banquets are common in the *Iliad* and, to a lesser extent, in the *Odyssey*. Livestock thus appear constantly in the narrative. The animals involved (oxen and cows, sheep, goats, pigs) are entirely passive; witnesses rather than actors, they are counted among the objects possessed by men. The wealth of an individual, the price of his equipment, the amount of a ransom are all determined in heads of cattle, which played a true pre-monetary role. Homeric poetry emphasizes cattle-breeding, which alone determines the rank and social prestige of the individual, as if the heroic condition were incompatible with being a farmer. The ideological distortion introduced by Homer (it seems likely, to judge from realia, that archaic Greece was agricultural rather than warlike by vocation) reveals the close link between social hierarchy and the status of meat. The hero is one who feeds on roast beef after he has sacrificed the animal to the gods (there are no meals without sacrifice in the *Iliad*). Bread and wine are also necessary for the definition of a man, but the consumption of beef is above all the act of a hero. In this light, it is easier to understand the stakes involved in the sacrilege committed by Odysseus's men in sacrificing the oxen of the Sun: in order to brave such a fearful taboo, they must have had at least the hope, in that illusory world, of thereby restoring their heroic status. A study of the values attributed to each category of livestock reveals, not surprisingly, a strict hierarchy. At the top are the bovines, closely followed by "fat sheep," then, considerably lower, pigs, and finally goats. The ox (or the cow; the term is the same for either, in contrast to the uncastrated male) is the victim of choice for the best sacrifices, the food for solemn occasions. The sheep (always a castrated male or a ewe) is most often associated with the ox. Sacrifices of pigs and goats, on the other hand, were rare,

reserved for particular gods (goat kids for Apollo, for example), and generally were much less prized. The male animal was reserved for special sacrifices, very infrequent, except in the case of the bull. The boar and the ram sometimes had their throats cut, but were not eaten afterward. The young, untrained animal, closest to his natural state, also had a special sacrificial vocation. The goat merits special attention. Halfway between wild and domestic, the goat is constantly ambiguous; references to him, especially in the story of Odysseus, are never without significance (the fact that he is hunted like wild game on the island of goats—*Od.* 9.156ff.—returns the goat to his wild status and makes him food unfit for heroes; the traitor Melantheus at the palace of Odysseus is, as if by chance, the goatherd; etc.).

The dog and the horse, both of whom we would classify as domestic animals in our contemporary vocabulary, appear in the narrative in very different ways. The dog is a minor companion (despite the touching story of Argos, Odysseus's dog, in the *Odyssey*), valued only for his use in hunting. The hero always has a number of hunting dogs, which live close to him and serve as prestigious goods. The negative side of the dog is depicted more often, however: he is a scavenger, devouring unburied corpses; he barely recognizes his masters when left as a guard dog (cf. the dogs of Eumaeus, in *Od.* 14.29ff., who almost devour Odysseus and obey only when beaten). The aspect of bestiality and latent or avowed savagery that can be derived from the image of the dog is reinforced by his very position vis-à-vis man. When Priam, in book 22 of the *Iliad*, laments his approaching death, he refers to the "carnivorous dogs" that will tear him to pieces in his own house, "the dogs that I fed *at my table*," he adds, "*in my palace*, to guard *my doors*, and that, *after lapping up my blood*, their hearts in fury, will lie down in *my vestibule*" (*Il.* 22.66–71; our italics). The horror of this scene culminates in the brutal inversion of the categories of the domestic and the wild; from a table companion, the dog becomes a man-eater, switching without transition from the closest proximity to the most radical estrangement. The ambiguous aspect of the dog in the poems is drawn essentially from this symbolic ability to reverse order and disorder, the world of the living and the world of the dead.

The image of the horse, on the other hand, has an entirely different connotation; there is nothing negative in his presentation. The horse is the warrior's indispensable companion; like his weapons, he is an integral part of the warrior's being. Possession of the horse is a necessary luxury, and the animal's value is not solely economical. Defined as "*agalma*" in the fourth book of the *Odyssey* (602), the horse, like other unusual and priceless objects, is part of the honorific cycle of the exchange of gifts. The warhorse is an animal that is harnessed (to a chariot) and not mounted, which makes his bond with the hero still closer and more compelling. He is totally subject to human will; and even "divine" horses have no autonomy. Divine horses are numerous in the *Iliad*, which indicates that they were valued far above other animals, yet even these are merely, so to speak, normal models pushed to the point of perfection. The horses of Achilles are superior to their counterparts only in that they do not suffer the ills of mortals. They remain totally incapable of escaping their destiny, and the power of speech which was granted to them is idle speech. Connected to human sacrifice (see the funeral of Patroclus), the horse appears as a sort of substitute for the hero, simultaneously his extension and his double, while embodying all the human dreams of lightness and speed and fleeting grace, like the wind and the water with which he is often associated in worship.

The bird is the final subject of this brief analysis. The image of the bird appears linked to that of the horse by virtue of his rapid movement. The horse, for example, is often "as swift as a bird." The gods journey by harnessing horses to a bronze chariot or by taking the form of birds to travel from sky to earth or from sky to water. Unlike other animal species, both the horse and the bird have a particular relationship with the world of the gods. But these relationships are quite different from each other. The divine horse has no shadow side for man, for despite his connection with the sphere of the gods, he remains part of the known order. The bird, however, rejects the double nature that conferred domestication upon the horse. Less "wild" than radically "other," the bird is above all a manifestation of the unforeseeable, a witness of the beyond. The appearance of a bird is never gratuitous; sign or portent, he always indicates a message from the gods to men. Woe to those who, like the suitors in the *Odyssey*, or Hector in the *Iliad*, doubt the infallibility of the messenger bird (*Od.* 2.180–88, or *Il.* 12.237–40); their end is near! The bird is an absolute stranger, both in his role as scavenger (in which he embodies the worst of curses, barring the dead warrior's access to rest in Hades) and when the gods choose his form alone for their epiphanies. The transformation of the god into a bird, an actual transformation (the vocabulary used is the same as that which describes the momentary transformation of gods into men in certain episodes of the narrative), is the only flaw in a resolutely anthropomorphic conception of the world of the gods. In Homer, the bird is not really an animal, so powerful and mysterious are his connections with the world of the gods. Capable only of "animal behavior," the bird is a marginal figure, unrestricted by the opposition between "wild" and "tame"; his essential role is that of a mediator between the visible world and the realm of the gods.

The study of Homer's bestiary raises the question of the animal's position in the cosmogony. Boundaries seem not to be at issue here; beasts and gods are not the two opposite poles of a relationship, with man exactly in the middle. The animal, as mirror and mediator, helps to situate man in relation to the gods and in relation to himself; he has no existence of his own, no special world. In a society that undoubtedly celebrated man's complete triumph over nature, even manifestations of wildness appear to be somehow integrated, neutralized, and occasionally utilized. Order reigns, among men as among gods; the dangers which might threaten that order are combatted in the same way on both sides, so similar are the two worlds. The presence of the animal reinforces and affirms their complete solidarity.

A.S.-G./d.b.

II. The Classical Greek Bestiary

Since the symbolism of animals in classical Greek thought has not yet been studied as a whole, we will have to depend on certain notations, relying heavily on a few species whose semantic value has been examined in the course of specialized studies.

Often the animal remains enigmatic. Why, on a certain Etruscan mirror, and on a mosaic from Cyprus, is Bellerophon accompanied by a little dog? What does the iconography mean? This is one of the questions that remain unanswered. Sometimes the meaning can be deduced from proverbial allusions or from the explicit meaning of the images: thus the hare, often depicted as a lover's gift on vases, and supposed to be constantly engaged in the games of Eros, is certainly an animal with marked erotic and aphrodisiac connotations; but why does he often appear on the back of a mosaic, eating a bunch of grapes? A connection with the Dionysian realm is suggested, but only a systematic study of texts, myths, and proverbial expressions as well as images will allow a more precise determination of the hare's meaning here. In other cases, however, clearer allusions can be discerned.

Among the insects—even though the significance of the cricket, which appears so frequently on vases and carved mirrors, remains unclear, and even though we must limit ourselves to an instinctive deduction, based on the shape of Psyche's wings, that the butterfly has some connection with the soul—at least the symbolism of the bee has been clearly explicated, largely due to the observations of Marcel Detienne. The bee's frequent connection with Demeter was known, but today it is apparent that this sober and industrious insect, producer yet nonconsumer of honey, proverbial enemy of profligates and their perfumes, is the very picture of the ideal wife, chaste mother, and diligent mistress of the household, celebrated at the festival of the Thesmophoria as the faithful devotee of Demeter.

As for birds, the role of certain species in the mythology of spices depicts them as indispensable intermediaries between high and low, that which rots and that which is burned, that which is within and that which is beyond the human realm. This is, at all events, the privileged role of the vulture, a bird of prey that nests on inaccessible heights but loves putrified flesh, a bird whose intervention is regarded as essential to the harvesting of certain essences. It is also the vocation of the phoenix, the mythical bird of spices, sometimes on this side of the vulture, crawling like a worm or fluttering painfully near the ground, sometimes, without transition, beyond the eagle, reaching ethereal heights, sustained for hundreds of years by its incorruptible feathers.

Another bird whose semantic value has recently been studied is the rooster. Iconographic studies on cockfights by Ph. Bruneau and, later, H. Hoffmann have revealed on the one hand that the rooster was a symbol of victory (painters of Panathenaic jars freely used the symbol of the rooster in place of Victory, on either side of the magnified hero) and, on the other hand, that this bird's heroic significance was matched by his erotic significance, since the rooster often denoted amorous conquest. This second connotation is confirmed by a whole series of observations which clearly place the rooster in the realm of Aphrodite. Fighting cocks are often depicted on vases, paintings, and mosaics as being encouraged by *Erotes*, and on a certain mosaic from Lixus they bear the names of *Paphius* and *Cytherius*, which are also two of the epithets of Aphrodite; on a bronze mirror from Corinth (cf. for example, Daremberg, *Dictionary*, fig. 181), Eros is holding a rooster in front of his genitals, in such a way that the animal is given an explicit phallic meaning. On many vase paintings, the *eromenos*, or active male homosexual lover, holds a rooster, symbol of his victory over the *erastos*, or passive lover (for example, in *Corpus Vasorum*, Vienna, Kunsthist. Mus. [2], 3, 1, pl. 59.1); the same is true of Ganymede being carried off by Zeus in the famous terracotta of the Museum of Olympia, and of Persephone carried off by Hades on several plaques from the Locri Epizephyrii; Priapus (or at least an ithyphallic character apparently closely related to him) is sometimes depicted as a rooster, or with a rooster's head, or holding a rooster (cf. H. Herter, *De Priapo*, p. 162, s.v. *Priapus gallinaceus*). The coins of Himera bore the image of a rooster: one wonders if it was not a sort of rebus (analogous to those used on the coins of Selinus or Leontini, etc.) and if the rooster is not, more precisely, a symbol of

Woman on a bull, holding a panther. Attic amphora. Ca. 510 B.C. London, British Museum. Museum photo.

Himeros, the personification of passionate desire, more particularly amorous desire, often associated with the cortège of Aphrodite; the ambiguity of the rare word *alektōr*, which simultaneously means "rooster" and "husband," is further confirmation of the rooster's connection with the world of Eros and with that of Aphrodite—the mandatory patron of marriage—along with Hera. The double kinship of the rooster with heroic combat and amorous combat is confirmed in exemplary fashion by the only noteworthy appearance of the rooster in a myth: Alectryon (*alektruōn*, "cock"), the character who was destined to be changed into a cock, and with whom the species originated, appears as a companion to Ares at the precise moment in the myth when the god of war begins his furtive union with Aphrodite (Lucian, *The Cock*, 3). This divided loyalty is perfectly suited to Himeros, whose name may be derived from Eris, "Rivalry," as well as from Eros, and who, moreover, is found at the intersection of the two areas, the erotic and the heroic.

With respect to wild animals, L. Kahil, a student of the Brauron ceramics, has recently clarified the connections between Artemis and the bear, or, more specifically, the she-bear. Artemis changed Callisto into a she-bear when her pregnancy revealed the fact that she had rejected the virginity of the companions of the Huntress; and, following her example, the young women who serve Artemis at Brauron, but are destined to leave her service to take the normal course of marrying and having children, ritually become bears. As for the panther, Detienne has shown that he is closely linked to the realm of perfumes and seduction, which would explain one aspect of his relationship to Dionysus and his association with Adonis, the son of Myrrha: this animal hunts by means of the scent he emits, which is irresistible to his prey.

Turning to domestic animals, studies on sacrifice, notably the work of J.-L. Durand on the Bouphonia, demonstrate the role of the ox as a close companion to man and, in a way, as

his substitute—hence the need for reparation for the blood spilled when an ox was sacrificed. Associated with man's work, with the cultivation of the earth, the ox is so close to man that the consumption of his flesh can ultimately be assimilated to cannibalism, which would explain the absolute prohibitions established in Pythagorean circles. The horse is quite another matter: inhabited by forces from the wild, this animal belongs to Poseidon, from whom he receives irresistible strength; his *gorgon* eyes, with their petrifying glare, connect him with the Gorgon (who, in the myth, is the mother of Pegasus, the archetypal horse she conceived by Poseidon). Through the invention of the bit, however, this turbulent animal was subdued by Athena, and symbolizes the domestication of wild forces that man achieved through the intervention of the goddess of technical skills, mistress of the helm and of all government. Nonetheless, the champing of the bit in the foaming mouth of horses is a fearful sight in battle, alarming to the enemy but also to the masters of the horses themselves, for the animals, once out of control, could at any moment send their own chariot flying into splinters, as happened to the unfortunate Hippolytus. Theirs is a disturbing and necessary power, destined to be domesticated by man for the greater benefit of civilization; in this, the horse may symbolize woman, as is also suggested by the oft-noted resemblance between the bit or headband of the horse and the diadem that is forced upon the young wife. The multiple metaphors of poetry, especially tragic poetry, that describe woman as a mare, a horse, an obstinate filly, etc., as well as the myths of Bellerophon and Hippolytus, make full use of this symbolism and can only be understood in terms of it.

The donkey, a humbler animal, forever sullied with a poor reputation, rarely attracts much attention. Mythology, folklore, iconography, and literature are nevertheless full of facts about the donkey. Certain aspects of the animal have piqued the curiosity of the best authors, from S. Reinach to W. Deonna, though no one has ever treated this rich subject as a whole. The most immediately apparent fact is that the donkey is almost always present in Dionysian scenes, particularly in the mythical processions of the votaries of Dionysus. Classical representations on Thiasic vases almost always include the donkey, bending under the weight of Silenus, proudly carrying Dionysus, or following along without a rider, always enormously ithyphallic (to the point of carrying baskets hung accordingly), ears lowered, or attentive, or perky, or trembling before the threat of imminent attack by a satyr. The donkey is found on reliefs on Dionysian sarcophagi, where Roman modesty modifies the animal's ithyphallism while maintaining its eminently comic character, stumbling, collapsing, always ridiculous, but always present. The donkey also appears in mosaics as Silenus's mount. His connection with Dionysus—and with the comic genre—is again confirmed by his presence in Aristophanes' *Frogs,* a comedy in which the main character is Dionysus himself, accompanied by a grotesque servant who identifies himself with the beast of burden upon whom he travels, clarifying his status with the famous line *onos emi agōn mustēria* ("I'm the donkey in the Mysteries," 159). Elsewhere, myths tell of numerous services performed by the donkey for Dionysus: it was the donkey who, by browsing moderately in the vineyard (unlike the goat, who destroyed the whole plant), taught men how vines should be trimmed, thus helping them to take better advantage of this gift of the god (Pausanias 2.2–3); the donkey took Dionysus to Dodona on his back (Hyginus *Poetica Astronomica* 2.23); in exchange for this service, the myth adds, the god changed the donkey into a star and gave him a human voice. In fact, in his dealings with Dionysus the donkey appears to be a symbol of the worshiper who has been, or is being, initiated: coarse, lewd, lazy, stubborn, ridiculous, but loyal, hardened to work, and obstinate, the donkey ends up, through the grace of the god, exchanging his dreadful braying for a harmonious voice, just as the initiate is freed from bestiality and ignorance through a mystical operation. It has been suggested that identification with the donkey is so closely associated with Dionysian initiation that initiates bear the title "donkey" (*onos*), in the same way that women of the Thesmophoria were called bees (*melissai*), and the young women of Brauron were she-bears (*arktoi*). The symbolism of the donkey is older than its strictly classical Dionysian framework and goes back to the most distant past; a Mycenaean vase shows a procession of characters parodying donkeys, which leads us to believe that since that time there has been a ritual identification or mythological meaning for the donkey which was already moving in the direction of a possible transformation between men and donkeys.

This symbolism also extends toward the future and to other religions, for the donkey is the hero of two important ancient works of fiction, Lucian's *Lucius* and Apuleius's *Golden Ass* (both of which, it is said, were based on a Greek model from the fourth century B.C.). Apuleius's narrative is explicitly connected with the cult of Isis: the first degree of the initiation into the mysteries of Isis is what allows Lucius to abandon his animal condition and assume human form again. These two stories are based on the theme of reversibility between man and donkey: they are the story of a fall and a redemption, and the analysis of this story reveals that it is structured with precision: the donkey is a symbol of man, who, fallen into bestiality, finally achieves salvation, through the grace of Isis in Apuleius and without explicit divine intervention in Lucian (though there may well be some implicit intervention which escapes us—the liberating rose, for example, certainly has some symbolic value). In the iconography as well, many of the portrayals of the donkey appear significant, though they cannot definitely be attributed to the cult of Dionysus: the painting at Pompeii in which a donkey, acclaimed by a palm-bearing Victory, asserts sexual domination over a lion, reduced to its final extremity; or the famous mosaics of Djemila where, in two places, the image of a donkey is accompanied by the phrase *Asinus Nica*, "Victory of the Donkey," in a strange Latinate Greek. The donkey always seems to be a bearer of the hope of victory and salvation, and his discordant braying may carry triumphant announcements of good news (*evangelion*), as in Lucian. This animal seems to have been a comic and optimistic symbol of man himself, full of animal clumsiness but also of goodwill, and promised, in spite of everything, a happy end.

J.-P.D./d.b.

BIBLIOGRAPHY

PH. BRUNEAU, "Le motif des coqs affrontés dans l'imagerie antique," *BCH*, 1965, 90–121. W. DEONNA, "Laus asini," *R. B. Phil.* 34 (1956): 5–46, 337–64, 623–58. M. DETIENNE, "La panthère parfumée," in *Dionysos mis à mort* (Paris 1977). M. DÉTIENNE and J.-P. VERNANT, *Les ruses de l'intelligence* (Paris 1974). H. FRÄNKEL, *Die homerische Gleichnisse* (Göttingen 1921). H. HOFFMANN, "Hahnenkampf in Athen: Zur Ikonologie einer attischen Bildformel," *RA*, 1974, 195–220. O. KÖRNER, *Die homerische Tierwelt* (Munich 1930). B. LAUM, *Heiliges Geld* (Tübingen 1924). G. E. R. LLOYD, *Polarity and Analogy* (Cambridge 1966). H. RAHN, "Das Tier in der homerische Dichtung," *Stud. Gen.* 20 (1967): 90–105; "Tier und Mensch in der homerischen Auffassung der Wirklichkeit," *Paideuma* 5 (1953): 277–97 and 431–80. A. SCHNAPP-GOURBEILLON, *Monde animal et monde des hommes dans l'Iliade et l'Odyssée* (diss., Caen 1975). B. SNELL, *The Discovery of the Mind* (Oxford 1953). W. THOMPSON D'ARCY, *A Glossary of Greek Birds* (Oxford 1936). M. TIERNEY, "Onos agōn mustēpia," *Mélanges Octave Navarre* (Toulouse 1935), 195–220.

ACTAEON

A Greek hero, the son of Aristaeus the beekeeper and Autonoë of Thebes, Actaeon was a hunter in the realm of Artemis, his protector. But imprudence led him to compete with the goddess and to claim that he was the better hunter. He may even have had the audacity to propose marriage to Artemis. Some say he tried to rape her, or that he surprised her at her bath, where she was surrounded by her nymphs. As punishment, Artemis unleashed the fury of Actaeon's fifty hunting dogs, who turned against their master, and, when Actaeon changed into a stag, tore him apart.

J.C./d.b.

Actaeon being devoured by Artemis's dogs. Metope from the Temple of Hera at Selinunte. Ca. 460 B.C. Palermo, National Museum. Photo Alinari-Giraudon.

ADONIS AND THE ADONIA

The beautiful lover separated from Aphrodite by a wild boar, or the youthful god buried among the fruits of the earth before being reborn, Adonis in his long travels is difficult to recognize by any single label. His history is paradoxical. Semitic, since his name means Lord, as Ba'al means Master, this Phoenician, they say, must have been seen in Sumer long before arriving in the Greek ports of Athens and Alexandria, which gave him a great reputation in the tradition of classical antiquity. But all the information available on Adonis the Phoenician, whose very name has been Hellenized, is Greek—written and thought up by Greeks. Exegesis and interpretation have never left him. Origen, in the second century A.D., collected his traits as they were delineated by the "theologians of myth" who would so vividly impress James G. Frazer: "The god that the Greeks call Adonis is called Thammuz among the Jews and Syrians. It appears that certain sacred ceremonies are held each year; first he is mourned as if he had ceased to live, and then he is a cause for rejoicing, as if he had been brought back to life. But those who pride themselves on the interpretation of Greek mythology and what is called mythical theology say that Adonis is the symbol of the fruits of the earth, which are mourned when they are planted but through their growth bring joy to the farmers."

The kinship with Thammuz, the resurrection from the dead, the great seasonal rhythms that regulate the cycle of vegetation—thus Origen summarized a Greek interpretation from the second century A.D., which belongs incontestably, as much as any others, in the dossier of Adonis. But Origen did not suspect that eighteen centuries after the polemics of the apologists the quarrel between pagan mysteries and the Christian mystery would be raised again by Modernism, when the Abbé Loisy would declare that the lover of Aphrodite-Astarte was the model for the risen Christ, whereas in the 1960s—just yesterday—the reverend father K. Prümm (see "Mystères," in the *Dictionnaire de la Bible*, Suppl. VI, 1960) would refer ironically to the pitiful "triumph of death" of a minor hero of vegetation, incapable of breaking out of the cyclical course of nature.

Even if we were well versed in the background of Thammuz—something no Assyriologist can claim today—we could not accurately trace the Greek traditions about Adonis, so vigorous that they appear to have eclipsed any Phoenician memory of his character, even in Byblus, his country of origin. We can assume, of course, that the exegesis recorded by Origen and presented as the opinion of "interpreters of mythical theology" is the most economical system of interpretation and the one which best accounts for the various elements of Adonis. But in arguing for this view we still could not conjure away the differences between the Adonia of Byblus and those of Alexandria or Athens, nor could we ascribe every difference to some nebulous "god of renewal," "spirit of vegetation," or "eternal return," as is the tendency of many Orientalists (R. Dussaud, Ch. Virolleaud, B. Soyez, etc.).

I. The Adonia of Athens

Of the three main versions of the festival of the Adonia—in Athens, Alexandria, and Byblus—the first, which is also the oldest, clearly puts the Phoenician in the context of an agricultural type, whose ritual emblem can be seen in the famous gardens of Adonis. By every indication, however, the Adonis of the Athenians could not have been a god of vegetation but the very opposite. The miniature gardens, planted in fragile earthenware containers or in plain baskets, grew in eight days in the heat of the summer sun. The Adonia were celebrated during the dog days, at the high noon of the solar year. The young shoots barely turned green before they withered and dried up in the heat of the sun. Indeed, these premature crops were put as close as possible to the sun: women climbed up ladders with them and left them on roofs, midway between earth and sky. As imitation crops, the gardens of Adonis are diametrically opposed to the crops of Demeter, the plowed earth, the fields in which the fruitful seeds ripened slowly according to the cycle of the seasons, in which men grew and harvested the grains—barley and wheat—that make bread for mortals and are the very marrow of living creatures.

The gardens of Adonis, where new growth withered, were conceived by the Greeks themselves as the negation of the cultivation of grain and the order of Demeter. From Plato to Simplicius, an entire tradition has viewed the gardens of Adonis as crops without fruit, essentially barren. They are the image of all that is light, superficial, immature, rootless—a garden of stone, cold and opaque as death.

This negation of true cultivation is further confirmed by the mythological tradition of the Greeks which focuses on the seductive aspect of Adonis and, at the same time, on his connection with spices. Born of Myrrha, who was transformed into myrrh following an incestuous incident with her father, Adonis, irresistibly seductive, awakens the desire of Persephone as well as that of Aphrodite. As the seducer of deities of opposing reigns, Adonis is for the Greeks neither a husband nor even a virile being: he is nothing but a lover and an effeminate, whose followers, Plutarch noted, were confined to women and androgynes. This young man of abundant seed, precocious lover of beautiful mistresses, is the antithesis of marriage and fertile sexual union. His excessive sexual power is simply the other side of immaturity, of under-age sexual union, which goes with sterile insemination. Destined to fall in a garden of stones, the seed of Adonis could never take root like good, legitimate seed. The itinerary of the precocious seducer follows the same course as his gardens: deprived of offspring and condemned to perish in the flower of his youth, Adonis moves suddenly from the realm of spices to that of lettuce; from the myrrh tree that gives him his powers of seduction to the cold, moist garden vegetable that receives the dying Adonis after his hunting failure and establishes him in the place of impotence, for which lettuce is a recognized symbol.

The Athenian festival of the Adonia plays on the theme of seduction. It has two phases. The first seems to indicate the sterility of seeds thrown into spring water or into the sea, while the second appears to use the "gathering of spices" to celebrate the pleasure of perfumes and the promises of seduction. These two phases are so discretely set down in the constraining time of a single ritual that they appear to be two concurrent ways of describing Adonis: from the point of view of the city, by failure and the reversal of the serious order of Demeter; and from the inside, for his followers and their lovers who celebrate the virtues of pleasure outside of marriage but in the intimacy of home, beyond the reach of the pervasive politico-religious regime. This is why in Athenian memory the lamentations of the women, which seemed to imitate funeral rites, over figurines and miniature gardens have alone remained associated with the departure of the expedition for Sicily, which ended so tragically for the city of

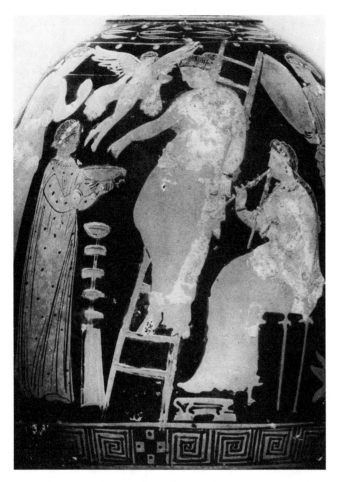

Feast of the Adonia. Aryballoid lecythus. Berlin, Staatliches Museum. Museum photo.

Athens (Plutarch, *Life of Nicias*, 13.10–11; *Life of Alcibiades*, 18.5). The Athenian Adonis, adopted by women and celebrated in the home, suggests a crisis in the city marked by the intrusion of private values, rather than a cosmic drama occasioned by the death of a god who is supposed to be the symbol of the agricultural cycle.

II. The Adonia of Byblus

In Byblus, the native land of this Phoenician hidden under a Greek name, the first representation we know of Adonis is already doubly distorted; it is a version of the myth from Cyprus but was undoubtedly told by the Greeks. The Cypriot Adonis was called Gauas, and the Muses plotted his downfall; the boar killed him and Aphrodite mourned him. This is a completely Greek narrative about the problems of a hunter who is treated as an antihero but whose place in the ritual and festivals seems almost totally eclipsed by a great bisexual Aphrodite with many sanctuaries. In Aphrodite's mysteries the initiates received a phallus and a little salt, symbols of the birth of a goddess born of the sea and the foam. Absent from royal inscriptions in Byblus between 1000 and 800 B.C., the Adonis of Byblus was only brought out of the shadows by Lucian's ethnographic research in the *De dea Syria* (6–9) in the second century A.D. This time, unlike other cultic sites, the whole of Byblus appears to have been given

over to Adonis and the festival in his honor. Two sanctuaries of Aphrodite delimit the country of Byblus: one on the Acropolis, the other on the mountain, at Aphaca, where the river of Adonis, the Nahr Ibrahim, has its source, and where the waters are tinted with blood each year in memory of the mortal wound inflicted on Adonis by the boar in this very region. The ceremony mobilized the entire country, men and women alike. There was a public feast, almost national, marked by two strong rhythms: a great wake, with lamentations and a funeral sacrifice, "befitting a corpse"; then a procession to escort the living Adonis to the open air. Specifically Phoenician traits of Adonis are even harder to determine since the exegeses of the people of Byblus tend to relate him to the Egyptian Osiris, for whom their Adonis is merely a mask and a local figurehead.

In this exegetical account, not mentioned in the *Treatise on Isis and Osiris*—while in the "Alexandrian" version the quest of Isis makes an unpublished detour by way of Byblus—the "Osirisized" Adonis is again lost, but this time in the middle of his own country, and he disappears in the form of another divine power. He is swallowed up by Osiris, who ranks not only as a cosmic god but as a great king of the dead, whose burial by Isis gave him sovereignty over life in the other world, beyond the alternating exchange that Greek tradition reserved for Adonis, shared between two mistresses as if between two identical dwelling places.

In the festival of Byblus, which includes no reference to gardens or other agricultural practices, a curious sexual custom caught the attention of Lucian. During the period of the wake, women who refused to have their hair cut were required to prostitute themselves for a day, but only with strangers, and to offer to the sanctuary of Aphrodite the money they received from this business. It was a constrained prostitution, which sanctioned a violation but punished the offenders—a funereal prostitution, the apparent antithesis of the erotic exchanges of the Athenian festival. The traditions of Cyprus confirm this distance in recounting the story of the daughters of Cinyras, king of Paphos and father of Adonis. These women were condemned to prostitute themselves with strangers, or to be exiled, or to be changed into rough stone by Aphrodite because they had denied her power (Apollodorus, *Library*, 3.14.3; Ovid, *Metamorphoses*, 10.220–42). Prostitution here again is a punishment whose final form is transformation into cold and insensitive stone.

In Cyprus, under his native name of *Aoös*, Adonis has no place in any rituals except in a festival of Aphrodite, where all we know is that cut trees were offered to the goddess. Neither in Cyprus, where he is associated with local demons, nor in Byblus, where he fluctuates between a figure of Osiris and a Greek mask, does Adonis appear as a Semitic god. It is nonetheless Adonis who is called for in a story in which the reference to the Near East appears to indicate a destiny that the Greeks certainly did not delineate arbitrarily, even if their Adonis takes his essential characteristics from the exegesis that integrated him into the Athenian and Alexandrian world.

Byblus received the signal for the Adonia from the capital of the Ptolemies. Sometimes it came in the form of the omen of a "head" of papyrus carried by sea from Alexandria to the port of Byblus, where Lucian claimed to have seen it during his stay. Sometimes it was in the form of a letter sent from the women of Alexandria to the women of Byblus—a message placed in a sealed vase and thrown into the sea to announce that Adonis had returned. Each year at the same time, the followers of Aphrodite stopped their lamentations on learning that their mistress was no longer separated from her Adonis.

III. The Adonia of Alexandria

In the Alexandria of the Ptolemies, this festival seems first of all to have been a spectacle, a play with chorus and actors. When Aphrodite mourns the death of Adonis, the choir groans and laments; and when she returns from hell and says she has found the one she was searching for, they all rejoice with her and begin to dance. This scene was performed in the sanctuaries (Cyril of Alexandria, in *Greek Patrology*, 70.440–41). According to Cyril of Alexandria, during the fifth century A.D. the spectacle ended with the joy of the reunions. According to Theocritus, however, the festival-spectacle given in the palace of Queen Arsinoë, wife of Ptolemy Philadelphus, began with songs about the union of the two lovers, who were placed under a bower of fennel stalks close to a collection of the fruits of all trees, delicate gardens in baskets of silver, unguent boxes made of alabaster and gold filled with Syrian perfume, and all sorts of cakes in the shape of animals flying or walking (Theocritus, 15.111–18). The second part of the play, which began the next day, opened with a funeral procession: the women, in a group, carried a figurine of Adonis out of the city to a place where waves were breaking on the shore (132–35). Tearing their hair, their breasts bared, they intoned a mournful song. This procession inverts the *pompē* of Byblus, in which the living Adonis is paraded in the open air. But Theocritus's poem ends with the evocation of the demigod Adonis, the only one among the heroes of ancient Greece (Agamemnon, Hector, the Pelopidae, the Pelasgi, and the Lapithes) who alternately appears on earth and returns to hell (136–44).

Even in Alexandria, some centuries later, the double love life of Adonis can be interpreted in either of these two ways. But each year brings the time of the Adonia, with the alternation between mourning and joy, rejoicing and lamentation. It is a small theatrical ritual in which, as in Athens, women again play a principal role, but in another city, open and cosmopolitan, where neither seduction nor horticulture appears to have the same meaning or even to occupy a similar position. The miniature gardens, placed among fruits and pastries, have become the symbol of happy lovers, and the same recumbent Adonis may be seen simultaneously as a corpse to be mourned and as a guest at a banquet of pleasure.

M.D./d.b.

BIBLIOGRAPHY

W. ATTALAH, *Adonis dans la littérature et l'art grec* (Paris 1966). C. COLPE, "Zur mythologischen Struktur der Adonis-Attis und Osiris-Ueberlieferungen," *Festschrift Von Soden*, 1969, 23–44. M. DETIENNE, *Dionysos mis à mort* (Paris 1977); *Les jardins d'Adonis* (2d ed., Paris 1979). A. S. F. GOW, "The Adoniazusae of Theocritus," *Journal of Hellenic Studies*, 1938, 180–204. S. RIBICHINI, "Per una riconsiderazione di Adonis," *Rivista di Studi Renici*, 1979, 12–23. B. SOYEZ, *Byblos et la fête des adonies* (Leiden 1977). N. WEILL, "Adôniazousai ou les femmes sur le toit," *Bulletin de correspondance hellénique* 60 (1966): 664–98. E. WILL, "Le rituel des Adonies," *Syria* 52 (1975): 93–105.

THE AMAZONS

The Greeks have never quite stopped believing in the actual existence of the Amazons. They placed this race of warrior women at the boundary of the inhabited world and/or in a distant era, at the border of mythical times. Plutarch, for example (*Life of Pompey*, 35), does not hesitate to remark that during Pompey's campaign against Mithridates, after a battle with the Caucasian mountain men, the Romans found "the boots and buckles of Amazons" on the battlefield. Moreover, Plutarch seriously studied the possible itineraries of the Amazons' raid on Attica during the time of Theseus (*Life of Theseus*, 26–28). Even today, some people think along these lines when they trace historic events in Herodotus's narratives about the Amazons, the ancestors of the Sauromatae.

The myth of the Amazons allowed the Greeks to vary and combine in different ways the characteristics of a triple otherness: the Amazons are barbarians; they are women, with all that that included, for a Greek, regarding their animal nature; above all, beginning with Homer, they are the men-women, *antianeirai* (*Iliad*, 6.186), which involved, as was explained very early, a play on the two meanings of *anti*, both "equal to males" and "enemies of males," formidable warriors since an expedition led against them was considered an exploit through which a young male warrior could prove himself.

As barbarians, the Amazons knew nothing about navigation (Herodotus, 4.110); they did not cultivate grain (Diodorus, 3.53), they were "flesh eaters" (*kreobororoi*, Aeschylus, *Suppliants*, 287); they fought on horseback and not from chariots; they were considered more outrageous than the Scythians, those ultimate barbarians. As women, they forced a particular sort of behavior on the warriors who fought them, as is clear in the following account by Herodotus (4.110ff.): The Greeks, having taken them prisoner, took them onto their boat; the women killed them all, justifying their name "killers of men" (*androktonoi*); the Scythians, among whom they landed, began by fighting them, "taking them for men"; but as soon as the mistake was recognized, war was abandoned in favor of seduction. It would perhaps be more accurate to use the term "domestication" here: the word used by Herodotus means literally "to tame." The youngest of the male warriors moved toward them, a little at a time, as one does toward a wild animal, and finally united with them: seduction succeeding where war failed. For these "enemies of men" were also "women who liked men" (*philandroi*, Plutarch, *Life of Theseus*, 26), and their union with the young Scythians in the open air under the midday sun struck them as a bit of luck too good to pass up. The Scythians, however, were only partly successful: their intention in taming the Amazons, Herodotus tells us, was to have children by them—boys, no doubt, who would make good Scythian warriors. If, as the story goes, the Amazons agreed to marriage, it was according to their own terms. They imposed on their husbands their own way of life and led them far from their country, beyond the Tanaïs (Don), where together they produced the race of the Sauromatae, among whom the women were also warriors. In contrast to the classical tradition, it was the women who carried off their husbands.

Among the various models that the Greeks developed to describe the society of the Amazons and their relations with

Battle of the Amazons. Volute krater by Euphronius. Arrezo, Museo archeologico. Photo Tavanti.

men, Herodotus's account represents the minimum departure from the ordinary. For Amazons usually rejected marriage. It is significant that in the exploits of Heracles (Apollodorus, 2.5.9) he was to steal from the queen of the Amazons that belt (*zōster*) which was, for her, the symbol (*sumbolon*) of her excellence as a warrior but which, for a young bride, marked the fulfillment (*telos*) of her life as a woman when it was untied on her wedding night by her husband. Situated outside the matrimonial field, the relations between Amazons and men were imagined to entail either the submission or the segregation of men. According to Diodorus (3.52ff.), Amazon society formed the exact counterpart of Greek society: the women made war and were judges, the men spun wool and cared for the children. Sometimes, submission was more radical (ibid., 2.45): boys were maimed to make them unfit for war; likewise, little girls had their right breasts burned, so they would not be hampered in throwing the javelin. This mutilation of the Amazons, which is purely a product of the language (the Greeks analyzed *a-mazōn* to mean *without-breast*) without any pictorial representation, appeared from the fifth century in a text by Hippocrates, where physiological logic admirably serves ideology: the right breast (of the Sauromatae women) was burned "in order to channel all the strength and growth into the shoulder and arm" (*On the airs, waters, and places*, 17). Others present the society of the Amazons as radically without men: in order to perpetuate the race, the Amazons united once a year with the men of neighboring tribes; of the children born of this union, they kept only the girls (Strabo, 11.5.1). This union took place "at random and at night" under conditions which prevented them from knowing the identity of their partners. The union with the young Scythians took place—another transgression—in the open air at midday. These are two symmetrical ways of showing that, situated outside of marriage, the relations between Amazons and men could only be deviant. While "real women" bring to men their earth-wombs in order to be given seed and to grow the male plant that will continue the race after their death, the Amazons—another masculine dream—steal the man's seed and use it for their own purposes: to raise girls who will continue to threaten the male order, on its borders.

J.C./d.b.

BIBLIOGRAPHY

"Amazones," in ROSCHER, *Ausführliches Lexicon . . .* , 1, part 1, cols. 268–80. F.-M. BENNET, *Religious Cults Associated with the Amazons* (diss., Columbia University 1912). F. G. BERGMANN, *Les Amazones dans l'histoire et la fable* (Colmar). VON BOTHMER, *Amazons in Greek Art* (Oxford 1957). F. IMHOOF-BLUMER, "Amazons on Greek Coins," *Nomisma* 2 (1909).

APOLLO

For an entire tradition, beginning with the rediscovery of the Greek world through Winckelmann's archaeological work, Apollo was the symbol of spirit dominating matter, the god that Hegel called the "most Greek of all the gods," and that Walter Otto regarded as the Idea of the distant and the transcendent. Today, though we have not forgotten this component of the Apollonian figure, we can see that this line of interpreters was influenced by an exegesis of the myth widely deployed by Pindar, one which favored the brilliant and luminous image of Apollo over his more frightening and even nocturnal side.

The Greeks were fond of enumerating the many aspects and attributes of the son of Leto: "No one has as many arts in his hand as Apollo; he has as his share both the archer and the poet—for the bow is his possession, and also the song. To him belong prophetesses and diviners; and doctors, too, derive from Phoebus the science of deferring death. Phoebus we invoke as shepherd, too. . . . It is in the steps of Phoebus that the fortifying walls of cities are laid out; Phoebus delights in establishing them, and his hand builds their foundations" (Callimachus, *Hymn to Apollo*, 40–55). To this list, let us add that he is also, and par excellence, eternally young, the *kouros* (adolescent), model and protector of human *kouroi*; he not only champions cities but furnishes them with the nonmaterial foundations of a harmonious constitution; finally, he is Phoebos, both the Pure—Purifier and Purified—and the Brilliant, whose epiphany terrifies and stupefies his protégés.

Among all these diverse, even disparate, characteristics the Greeks continued to weave close connections, using indirect means—metaphor, etymologies that were not just meaningless games. As a result, Plato could justify the great functions of the god—physician-purifier, honest oracle, archer, master of earthly and celestial harmony—under the single name of Apollo, so that the figure of the god, from the archaic period, seems to us rich indeed, but well structured and possessed of an organic coherence. It matters little if in some inaccessible period of prehistory this particular divinity

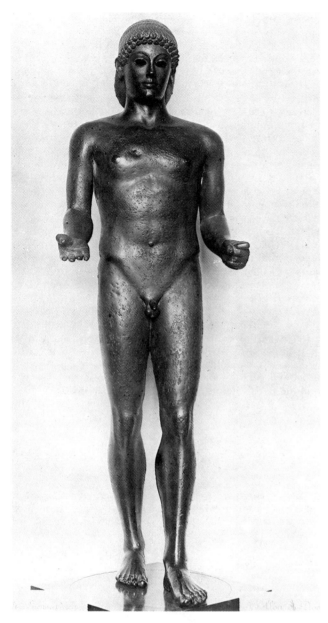

Apollo from Piombino. Bronze. Ca. 475–450 B.C. Paris, Musée du Louvre. Photo Giraudon.

sitting. She leads Apollo to take his place on a throne. The father gives his son nectar in a golden cup, and welcomes him. At that moment, the other gods sit down. And the noble Leto is happy to have given birth to a son who is strong and who knows how to wield a bow.

The bard of the *Hymn to Apollo* chose to begin his poem not with the birth of the god but with this story of Apollo's terrifying advent, bow drawn, in the midst of the assembly of the gods. Like his little brother Hermes, but in completely different ways, Apollo conquers Olympus, which was not given to him at birth. This son of the king of gods was born "where seals and sea monsters are born, on the lost rocks" (Callimachus, *Hymn to Delos,* 241–43): no land was willing to welcome Leto when she was about to give birth, so dangerous was the wrath of Hera. Asteria, a small, arid island, floating and without roots, finally accepted Leto, who gave birth to Artemis and then to Apollo. The island was immediately covered with gold and received its reward: it became rooted in the middle of the Greek sea, and took the name of Delos, the Shining; and the riches of the hecatombs from all the Greek lands were promised to it.

As a true child-god, however, Apollo was no sooner born than he threw off his swaddling clothes, claimed his lyre and his bow, and proclaimed himself the herald of Zeus's infallible purposes. Before becoming the master of oracles, however, he had to wander for a long time, to kill the Beast that guarded the entrance to Delphi, and to succeed in a competition against the Dreams for the role of a chthonic oracle: Zeus intervenes in favor of his son, and "frees men from shadowy prophecy" (Euripides, *Iphigenia in Tauris,* 1278–79).

It was as a *kouros* (young man) that Apollo performed these feats and was received in Olympus. Poets are fond of describing the signs that make him the god of perpetually renewed youth, in whom youthfulness is a positive quality, with its reserves of energy, even of violence, rather than a form of immaturity: ". . . with the appearance of a man robust and strong, in the first years of his youth; his hair covered his broad shoulders" (*Homeric Hymn to Apollo,* 449–50); "A god always beautiful, always young; no trace of down ever grew on his tender cheeks" (Callimachus, *Hymn to Apollo,* 36–37); "Never, Lord, will your hair be cut, never damaged: such is the law" (Apollonius of Rhodes, *Argonautica,* 2.708–9). Cutting the hair is precisely the ritual which marks the passage of boys to adulthood in many traditions.

The eviction of the old chthonic oracle is not the last test of Apollo, however. In order to cleanse himself of the impurity caused by the blood of the Beast, "to become truly Phoebus, or Pure," he is obliged to go and purify himself in Thessaly, in the vale of Tempe. Subsequently, on two different occasions, each time for rebelling against Zeus, Apollo is banished from Olympus and condemned to temporary servitude (*latreia*)—first with Laomedon, king of Sparta, for whom he constructs the ramparts and/or guards the flocks; later, again as a shepherd, with Admetus, whose livestock flourish because of him. Every winter, the god retires from his Greek sanctuaries. During these "retreats" (*apodēmiai*), he lives, according to one tradition, in a sort of Paradise "beyond the North Wind," among the perfectly pure Hyperboreans, where he enjoys their perpetual banquets.

II. Proximity and Distance

A whole group of mythical stories about Apollo can be explained in terms of proximity and distance. Proximity to men: as the model for the *kouroi*—ancient statuary, which

was created from various borrowed elements. In following the trail left by the Greek poets and philosophers themselves concerning their myths, we shall attempt to explore first the stories and then the domains of Apollo.

I. The Advent of Apollo

I will speak of him, I will not forget him, Apollo who strikes from afar, he whose steps in the house of Zeus make the gods tremble. They all rise from their seats when he comes in, when he draws his shining bow. Only Leto remains beside Zeus, who loves thunder. She unstrings the bow and closes the quiver. Then she lifts the bow from the powerful shoulders of the god and hangs it on a gold hook, against the column where his father is used exactly the same image for human *kouroi* as for the divine *kouros,* mirrored in its way the discourse of the poets—Apollo was also their patron. Hesiod's *Theogony* named Apollo, along with the Rivers and Oceanids, as a divinity that protected young people. In the *Odyssey,* it is under his patronage that Telemachus reaches manhood, and he is also the one who protects the Argonauts, those young sons of kings in quest of exploits which will test their manhood. It was to Apollo, together with Heracles, another juvenile hero, that young men dedicated the first locks cut from their hair. The wanderings, the late entry into Olympus, the banishment, the servitude which the myth attributes to this god: all these things, according to sociologists, reflect a vanished custom which imposed on young men a time of exile and wandering, outside the space of the city, before being formally accepted into it. Whether this is a reflection of an actual custom or a purely mythological construction, it is certain that the god-model, like the *kouroi* of the heroic legends, was required to pass qualifying tests before being admitted to the assembly of his peers, the Olympians.

Wandering and banishment, which bring him close to men because he shares their condition and because, in two cases, he finds himself closely bound in servitude to a man, also distance Apollo temporarily from the gods. Yet it is he who, in the *Iliad,* emphasizes so forcefully the irreparable distancing which has developed between gods and men: "Earth-shaker, you would say that I had lost my mind if I should do battle with you for the sake of poor mortals who are like leaves, who live for a while full of brilliance, eating the fruit of the earth, then are consumed and fall into nothingness" (*Il.* 21.462–66). He does not guide his protégés by the hand, as does his sister Athena, who takes pleasure in discreet disguises; the Argonauts, for example, trembled and were struck dumb when he appeared, resplendent in the dawn, to encourage them. By the time they dared to raise their eyes, he was already "far away," soaring "toward the immense people of the Hyperboreans"; he never even spoke to them (Ap. Rhod. *Argon.,* 2.680ff.). If he attempts a closer relationship with men, he seems even less able than other gods to breach the distance between them. His human love affairs often end badly. Two of his female lovers reject him for a human male—one, explicitly, because she is not interested in a companion who will remain eternally young. Even more significant perhaps is the rejection of his love for the young Hyacinthus. While playing with him at throwing the discus, the god—elsewhere so skillful—kills him by accident; and in this context of a friendly game the thrown discus offers a pertinent substitute for mortal arrows.

Distant even to his protégés, formidable even to those whom he loves, the god experiences an even more radical distancing when he withdraws to his Hyperborean paradise, far from men and gods. And when the Greeks begin to elaborate on the notion of divine transcendence, it is not surprising that they often use Apollo as its symbol.

III. Apollonian Fire

When, at the beginning of the *Iliad,* Apollo descends from Olympus, with the arrows in his quiver which will kill the Achaeans, he is, the poet tells us, "like the night." If, however, there is one attribute which seems essential to him (and the German scholarship of the nineteenth century would add: original), it is certainly his solar and luminous quality. The assimilation of Apollo to the Sun is not found in our sources before Aeschylus; but in the Homeric poems the

epithet for Phoebus is the Luminous. The myths often pit him against nocturnal and chthonic forces: against Gaea, mistress of nocturnal Dreams, in *Iphigenia in Tauris,* and especially against the Erinyes (Furies), those daughters of Night, in Aeschylus's *Oresteia.* The unclean creature that he pierces with his arrows at Delphi is an inhabitant of dark caves, and the giant Tityus, whom he kills to defend Leto, came from the earth at his birth. One of the most famous depictions of Apollo shows him as a *sauroktonos,* killer of lizards. But to have a preference for battling a certain category of adversaries is still to have a special relationship with them; and the relationships between Apollo and crawling animals, chthonians, *gēgeneis* (born of the earth), are curiously ambivalent. He is himself, from the very first time we see him, a god "of the Rat" (Smintheus); it is precisely this nocturnal Apollo, master of epidemics, whom the priest invokes by this name at the beginning of the *Iliad* (1.39). To later authors, Apollo Smintheus is both the god who saves people from a plague of rats, and the friend of the rats (or mice) that were placed, either alive or depicted in art, around his statue. The rats themselves, called *gēgeneis,* appear in this same context, sometimes as destroyers, sometimes as saviors: they eat through the strings of the bows of the enemy (Clement of Alexandria, *Protrepticus,* 2.39.7; Aelianus, *De natura animalium,* 22.5). In addition, the myth gives Apollo sons who are similar to himself, such as Aristaeus, physician-purifier and killer of serpents, but also children who are very different from him: Asclepius and Trophonius, hero-serpents, soothsayers marked by their complicity with the earth and its mantic powers, form a dark side to the luminous and celestial Apollo.

The Apollonian fire is nothing like the small artisan's fire that Hermes sparked, with patience and skill, from two sticks rubbed together; neither is it, or is it only, the peaceful and supernatural light with which Pythagorean mysticism likes to surround Apollo. Here, for example, is his entrance into Delphi: "Then the lord Apollo, the archer, jumped from the ship, like a star at midday. Innumerable sparks flew off him, and their light reached the sky. Passing the tripods of great price, he entered his shrine, and there he made a fire, revealing his lightning arrows (*kēla*), and the brightness filled all of Crisa. And the wives and daughters of the Crisans, with their fine sashes, gave a long cry at this blast (*ripē*) of Phoebus, for he put great fear in all of them" (HHA, 440–47). Blast, immediacy, possession, terror, cry: the Apollonian light has been described since the *Homeric Hymns* in terms that evoke the violent nature of the bow (*kēla,* arrows, *ripē,* cast or throw)—the bow being the characteristic weapon of the god, which gains him access to Olympus.

IV. The Archer

Like his sister Artemis, like Zeus with his thunderbolt, Apollo is a god "who strikes from afar" (*hekēbolos*). To men and animals, his arrows bring illness and death. His name may easily be explained by the word *apollunai:* to cause to perish. Terrible is the sound which springs from his bow when he is angry with the Greeks and strikes them with his arrows (*Il.,* I.48ff.). But this same bow which inspires terror may also fend off evil: Apollo is the *Hekaergos,* who sends away, and the *Alexikakos,* who turns away evil. The bow that killed the Beast of Delphi purified the region of a monster that killed both men and beasts. Recounting this victory, Callimachus makes a close connection between the savior god and the archer god when he interprets the traditional cry "Iēpaiēon" in honor of Apollo as "send forth (*hiei*), Paean,

Apollo and Artemis massacre the children of Niobe. Attic krater. Ca. 460 B.C. Paris, Musée du Louvre. Photo Giraudon.

yes, send forth your arrow, you who were the Savior from the moment your mother gave birth to you'' (Callimachus *Hymn to Apollo*, 103–4). Significantly, when the Greeks look for etymologies for this ''Iēpaiēon,'' which is both a chant and an epithet of the god, they explore the two themes at once: ''to heal'' and ''to throw,'' connecting the ''iē-'' now with healing (*iaomai*), now with throwing (*hiēmi*), while explaining the second part of the word either by *paiō*, to strike, or by the proper name Paean—and Paean, before becoming a mere epithet of Apollo, was the physician of the gods, according to Homer.

If Apollo's beneficial influence on livestock (under his care, the females bear twice as many young) cannot be explained according to this model, the protection he extends to men, as a physician, and to planting and harvesting is certainly that of the archer Alexikakos. He keeps rats, grasshoppers, and blight from the crops. As a physician he is less a ''healer,'' like his son Asclepius, than a power capable of staving off illness and death. *Anablēsin thanatoio*, ''delaying,'' literally ''rejecting,'' death is the way Callimachus (Callim. *Ap.*, 46) defines his medical technique, borrowing once again the root of the verb *ballō*, to throw. In Euripides' *Alcestis*, Death, coming to get Alcestis, explodes in anger against the god: ''Why are you hanging about here, Phoebus? . . . And now, with bow in hand, you are guarding this woman well'' (29–35). In this case, however, the god departs, and it is Heracles, the champion of hand-to-hand combat, who triumphs over Death, girdling him with his arms (847). Many centuries after Euripides, during the imperial era, an effigy of Apollo the Archer was placed in front of the gates of a city to ward off a plague or an epidemic, on the advice of the oracles.

For the Greeks of the archaic era, all healing was also a purification; illness could be the result of pollution, sacrilege, murder: pollution both material and moral, which contaminated not only the guilty man, even if he was ignorant of his crime, but the entire city. Phoebus was the grand master of purifications. He himself was exiled to Thessaly—some say to another world—to cleanse himself of a murder; the other gods, however, killed monsters without polluting themselves. Apollo purified Orestes, after ordering him to pollute himself by killing his mother. In each case, the god unfail-

ingly knows the exact rites which will erase the stain. But quite often the fault is quite unknown, secret, and ancient. Then, in myth as in reality, in order to know both the cause of the trouble and the remedy for it, men inquire of the god who knows everything, ''the number of grains of sand and the dimensions of the sea'' (Herodotus, 1.47).

V. Oracular Speech and Poetic Speech

Apollo is the preeminent oracular god. At Delphi, his prophetess, the Pythia, after performing the rites which were intended to put her in the proper mood to receive the god, gave out oracles in verse or in prose, and the god said ''I'' through her mouth. From all parts of the Greek world, as well as from among the barbarians, private individuals and official ambassadors came to ask her questions. It is generally agreed that the oracles with double meanings, which Loxias ''the Oblique'' gave out so generously in Herodotus, were never uttered; simply the means of a good story, they nevertheless underline the blindness of man and the clairvoyance of the gods. True oracles formulated above all—and in a totally unambiguous manner—the required rituals, the purifying ceremonies. Master of purifications, Apollo is therefore entitled to three titles: he is Phoebus the Brilliant but also the Pure; he is the physician who wards off evil; he is the oracle who knows the cause and the remedy for evil. This solidarity between physician and oracle—''Physician-prophet,'' *iatromantis*, is what Aeschylus calls him—is emphasized in another way by Plato when he affirms that by using the same procedures as a physician or as a prophet (fumigations, sprinkling of lustral water) the god produces the same effects: cure—or purification—of bodies and of souls (*Cratylus*, 405 a–c). The soul, a new idea at that time and foreign to the archaic problematics of the pure and the impure, offers the philosopher a clever solution to the problem of the unity of a divine figure.

This omniscience of the oracular god was constructed by Pindar on the model of an immediate and just design coming from afar. In the *Third Pythian* (25ff.), the poet tells how Coronis of Thessaly, ''who carried in her womb the pure seed of the god,'' two-timed him with a stranger from Arcadia. Apollo was at that time far away, at Delphi. Here, traditional legend places a mediator: a crow, who announced to the god the infidelity of his beloved. According to Pindar, however, the god could see everywhere, negating the distance, needing no intermediary: nothing escapes the perfectly straight and direct spirit (*euthutatos*) of Loxias the Oblique (the two words appear next to each other in the same line)—neither the thoughts nor the deeds of anyone, god or man. This work on the myth attempts to accomplish two things: first to contest the mythic tradition that sees Apollo the Oblique as the god of ambiguous oracles—in this same sense, Plato explains the word *Apollon* as *Haploun*, the Simple—and second, even more important, to read the divine omniscience in terms that evoke the distant purpose of the god with the silver bow.

''The lyre and the bent bow are mine, and I will reveal to mankind the infallible designs of Zeus'' (HHA, 131–32), cries Apollo when he has barely emerged from the womb of his mother, Leto. The Greeks saw a clear connection between the lyre (or zither) and the bow. After the futile attempts of the suitors, Odysseus seizes his bow: ''As a singer who knows how to play the lyre easily stretches the new string on the key and attaches the well-twisted gut at both ends, Odysseus bent the great bow without effort. Then, with his right hand, he vibrated the string, which sang well and clearly, like the cry of a swallow'' (*Odyssey*, 21.405–11). But if the bow resembles a lyre, the song of the lyric poet inspired by Apollo resembles an arrow sent from afar that reaches its target: ''Armed with the bow of the Muses, with the bow that-strikes-from-afar (*hekatabolōn*), cover with the arrows that they give . . . the august promontory of Elis . . . Send one of these sweet arrows toward Pytho! There is no danger that your words will fall to earth in vain'' (Pindar, *Ninth Olympian*, 5–12); and it is the ''arrows'' (*kēla, ripai*) of the lyre that lull to sleep the thunderbolt of Zeus or the impetuous Ares (Pindar, *First Pythian*, 5–12).

Thus a common metaphor, that of aiming directly at a distant goal and always reaching that goal, is the means of articulating between poetic speech and oracular speech. But here the metaphor refers to an essential relationship: for archaic Greece, poetic speech was not simply the object of aesthetic enjoyment; like the oracle, it was the aim and the achievement of Truth. Poets and soothsayers, two categories inspired by Apollo, both claimed the title of ''Masters of Truth.'' The essential identity between these two fields of knowledge and power, as they were conceived in ancient Greece, fully justifies this single patronage.

But if poetry is an achievement of truth, it is also, with the music that accompanies it, a way of forgetting trouble, a harmony, and an invitation to the dance. The archer Apollo makes the gods dance. As a counterpart to his frightening advent at the beginning of the *Homeric Hymn*, there appears in the second part, as if to emphasize the ambiguity of this divine figure—an ambiguity that opens up rich and prolonged reflection, that of Apollonian mysticism, among the Pythagoreans, the Orphics, and even modern scholars—the

singer with the lyre, resplendent with light: ''Then the Immortals think of nothing but the lyre and song . . . The Graces with their beautiful hair and the happy Hours, Harmony, Youth, and Aphrodite . . . dance, holding each other by the wrist . . . Ares, and Argeiphontes with his sharp eyes, dance with them; Phoebus Apollo . . . is surrounded with light; brilliance flashes from his feet and his fine tunic'' (*HHA*, 188–203). Apollo's lyre calms and appeases all that is wild, filled with disorder and strife. Guarded by Apollo, the herds of Admetus graze with lynxes, lions, and does, and they dance, charmed, at the sound of his lyre (Euripides, *Alcestis*, 575–87). Even Zeus's thunderbolt, even impetuous Ares, were ''put to sleep,'' ''possessed'' or ''enchanted'' by the lyre. Apollo's dance is not one of passion and disorder but a dance of ordering, adjustment, harmony. The Athenian of Plato's *Laws* (653ff.) makes a contrast between natural movements, common to men and animals, and the sense of rhythm and harmony that is the gift of the Muses and of Apollo.

''If all men learned music, would that not be a way to come to some agreement and to see universal peace in the world?'' This jest of Molière's would have been seriously affirmed by the Pythagoreans. All the Greeks considered Apollo the guarantor of good legislation and cities founded on sound constitutions. The Pythagoreans knew why: it was good rhythm and harmony, that is, the correct relationships between all parts of society, that produced concord and peace between the citizens, and this could be created from the same arithmetical relationships that create good music. Naturally, Apollo would sponsor both endeavors. But Apollo, that ''founder'' (*archēgetēs*) of Greek colonization, was sponsoring them long before the theologians discovered and explained—or invented—the connections which they wove between music and good government.

Order reigned also—and especially—in the heavens. Plato affirmed it thus: the third meaning of the word Apollo is ''he who causes [the heavenly bodies] to move (*polōn*) together (*a-*)'' and in harmony, something altogether natural for a musician god. And when later poets imagine that the god maintains the universe in the harmony of its movement by the sounds of his lyre, using the sun's rays as a bow for his lyre, they are only transposing to the cosmic level the image of a ''well-tempered society'' that the Pythagoreans had constructed before them, under the patronage of the divinity who makes the worlds dance as he makes the gods dance.

J.C./d.b.

Apollo crossing the sea on his winged tripod. Attic hydria. Ca. 490 B.C. Rome, Vatican Museum. Photo Alinari-Giraudon.

BIBLIOGRAPHY

The Ancients

CALLIMACHUS, *Hymn to Delos; Hymn to Apollo*. [HOMER], *Hymn to Apollo*. PLUTARCH, *Moralia 6*.

The Moderns

P. AMANDRY, *La mantique apollinienne à Delphes* (Paris 1950). M. DELCOURT, *L'oracle de Delphes* (Paris 1955). E. R. DODDS, *The Greeks and the Irrational* (Berkeley 1951). H. GRÉGOIRE, R. GOOSSENS, and M. MATHIEU, *Asklèpios, Apollon Smintheus et Rudra* (Brussels 1949). K. KÉRÉNYI, *Apollon* (Vienna 1937). W. OTTO, *Les dieux de la Grèce* (Paris). H. W. PARKE and D. E. W. WORMELL, *The Delphic Oracle*, 2 vols. (Oxford 1956). W. H. ROSCHER, s.v. ''Apollon,'' in *Ausführliches Lexicon der griechischen und römischen Mythologie*, vol. 1, cols. 422–29. G. ROUX, *Delphes, son oracle et les dieux* (Paris 1976).

Heracles and Argos. Attic wine-pouring vessel. Ca. 460 B.C. Naples. Photo D.A.I.

ARGOS

Argos had eyes in the back of his head; according to other sources, his body was entirely covered with eyes. This vigilant figure (for his eyes were never all closed at the same time) killed the Echidna—the woman with a serpent's tail, who was both a monster and the mother of monsters—when she was asleep. Hera then made him responsible for guarding the cow Io, whom Zeus loved. But Argos of the hundred eyes was killed by one even more vigilant than he—the god Hermes, who succeeded in putting Argos to sleep. The peacock, consecrated to Hera, carries on his plumage the many eyes of Argos, faithful servant of the goddess.

J.C./d.b.

THE ARGONAUTS

King Aeolus had seven sons. One of these, Athamas, ruled over Boeotia; Cloud (Nephele), his wife, bore him two children named Phrixus and Helle. When Athamas repudiated Cloud and married Ino, the new stepmother decided to destroy the children of his first marriage. She persuaded the Boeotian women to parch all of the seed grain, unbeknownst to the men, and nothing grew that year. Ino then bribed the servant sent to Delphi to return with a false oracle: in order to end the famine, Phrixus, or Phrixus and Helle, should be sacrificed. But Zeus, or Cloud, their mother, provided the children with a means of escape: a marvelous talking ram,

the son of Poseidon, for whom Hermes had made a fleece of gold. On his back, the children fled.

The gods were angry, however, and drove Athamas mad as punishment for the attempted infanticide: with his own arrows he killed Learchus, one of his sons by Ino, and in hatred pursued Ino herself and his other son, Melicertes, both of whom escaped by throwing themselves into the sea, where Ino became the White Goddess, Leucothea. Athamas, banished and left to wander, again consulted the oracle: he was, he learned, to settle where wild beasts would show him hospitality, which came to pass among the wolves in Thessaly.

In the meantime, Phrixus and Helle fled toward Colchis, the land of the rising sun. Helle, however, fell into the sea which would thereafter bear her name: the Hellespont. Phrixus arrived safely in Colchis. According to legend, upon the advice of the animal himself, Phrixus immediately sacrificed the ram to the Zeus of "fugitives" and hung the golden fleece in a grove sacred to Ares, where it was guarded by a dragon who never slept. Aeëtes, the king of Colchis, received Phrixus kindly and gave him one of his daughters in marriage. Some say that he eventually had Phrixus assassinated, however, having been warned by an oracle to beware of an Aeolean stranger. Aeëtes was the son of the Sun; he had married one of the daughters of Oceanus, Eiduia, She-who-knows; or, according to other accounts, he had married a terrible sorceress, huntress, and killer of men, Hecate, who tried out her poisons on passing strangers. The daughter of this union was Medea.

Cretheus, a second son of Aeolus, was king of Iolcus in Thessaly. His son Aeson was driven out by the usurper Pelias, a cousin or second cousin, son of Poseidon and descendant of Aeolus through his mother. To save his newborn son from the wrath of Pelias, Aeson gave him over into the care of the centaur Chiron, who raised the child in his mountains and named him Jason.

Much later, Pelias, the uncontested king of Iolcus, called all of his subjects together for an important sacrifice to Poseidon. Jason hurried to attend. But while crossing a river—or, in other versions, while carrying an old woman who was actually Hera—he lost a sandal. Seeing him, Pelias remembered the words of the oracle: his downfall would come through a *monosandalos* stranger. In order to rid himself of his rival, he gave Jason an impossible task: to bring back the Golden Fleece from Colchis, and with it the unhappy soul of Phrixus.

The most valiant men of Greece responded to Jason's call, hurrying to Thessaly to sail on the ship Argo. Along their route, they would have to overcome a hundred obstacles and engage in much combat. They crossed the terrible Symplegades, the floating rocks that separated merely to crash back together with the movement of the sea. When the Argo managed to escape them, they became fixed in place forever. The Argonauts finally arrived in Colchis, and asked Aeëtes to give them the Fleece. He promised it to Jason if he could succeed in harnessing his bronze-footed, fire-breathing bulls and could use them to sow the teeth of a dragon, from which armies of giants would be born. But Hera intervened, and Medea fell in love with Jason. With the help of her spells, he was able to perform the required tasks. Aeëtes then refused to keep his promise, so Jason stole the Fleece, while Medea's spell put the guardian dragon to sleep. When the Argonauts fled, they took with them both the Golden Fleece and the king's daughter.

Some say they also took Apsyrtus, the young son of Aeëtes. Medea cut her brother's throat, dismembered him, and threw the pieces overboard one by one. While Aeëtes lost valuable time recovering these pieces and burying them, the Argonauts sailed out of his reach.

It was again Medea who became Jason's instrument of revenge in Iolcus. She persuaded the daughters of Pelias that by killing their father, dismembering him, and boiling the pieces according to her directions, they would make him young again. Had she herself not just made an old ram into a young lamb using this same method? Hence, Pelias perished at the hands of his daughters.

Jason therefore became king of Iolcus, thanks to Medea. But he left Thessaly (or was forced to leave) and settled in Corinth, where he lived happily with Medea and had many children. Unfortunately, he fell in love with Creusa, daughter of the king of Corinth, and repudiated his former wife. Medea responded by sending the new bride a poisoned wedding gift—a dress which burst into flames, consuming the princess, the king, and the royal palace. To complete her revenge, Medea killed the children she had had by Jason and fled in a chariot drawn by flying dragons, which her grandfather the Sun had sent to her.

The story of the Argonauts wavers between a quest for the Holy Grail and a set of nautical instructions; or, at least, it confuses the two in the interweaving of overly scholarly accounts, as we follow the adventures of Jason through the epics of Apollonius of Rhodes or Valerius Flaccus. Stratigraphic analysis disputes the number of layers from the time of the commercial routes of pre-Hellenic times, between the Pontus and the Baltic, marked out by archaeologists, until the chronicles of the last colonizations undertaken by the Greek cities toward the limits of the Tanaïs (Don), "the greatest market of the barbarians beyond the Panticapeum" (Strabo, 7.4.5). The voyages of Odysseus were obviously influenced by "the great sea-going vessel Argo, known to everyone" (*Odyssey* 12.70), and when Circe the sorceress described to Odysseus's companions the long route home,

Athena, Jason, and the Dragon. Attic cup from Doris. Ca. 490 B.C. Vatican Museum. Photo Hirmer.

the problem of the Moving Rocks, the Planctae, was already known to Jason's band. With the help of Hera, they had already made it through the tortuous passage and across the uncrossable route where fire and water meet, making sea and sky indistinguishable. But the geography in the myth of the Argonauts is not a level of signification that should be expanded upon: the quest for the Golden Fleece is best described as a periplus, a course in space whereby the return voyage structures the outward passage and calls upon the memory to assign each exploit its place and its position in an organized space.

According to Herodotus (7.197), while Xerxes was crossing Achaea, the land of the Aeolians, with his troops, his guides told him a local story concerning the sanctuary of Zeus Laphystius, the Devourer: "how Athamas, the son of Aeolus, joined with Ino, and plotted to kill Phrixus; how the Achaeans, obeying an oracle, then created the following tests for his descendants: the eldest son in the family was refused access to the *lēiton* (this is what the Achaeans called the prytaneum, or council chamber) and the Achaeans themselves kept close watch; if the son entered, he would not be able to leave it until the moment of his sacrifice; they added that many, while waiting to be sacrificed, had taken fright and fled to other countries, and that if they returned after a period of time, they were taken by surprise before entering the prytaneum . . . (lacuna), and they explained how the victim was led to the altar, covered with garlands and ribbons, in procession." Xerxes was not in the least interested in a story of royal hubris, where violence begat violence. It is said that he simply refrained from entering the disturbing sanctuary. Was it not there, as Herodotus goes on to remark, that the Achaeans, in obedience to an oracle, had wanted to sacrifice Athamas, the son of Aeolus, in order to purify the country?

Thus the story of the quest begins with a monstrous sacrifice, a sin which must be atoned for, but one in which the original sacrifice leads to others, each more monstrous than the last. The ambiguity of Zeus is at the heart of this periplus: in the land of Aia, in Colchis, Zeus is the protector of fugitives, Phuxios, and it is to him that Phrixus sacrifices the ram and offers the Fleece (Apollonius of Rhodes 2.1140–1150). In Aeolis, however, Zeus is represented as a bestial power, a god who enjoys devouring men, like the impious Busiris, who had a reputation for sacrificing strangers, or Lycaon, who offered his guest Zeus the well-prepared flesh of one of his children.

A drought lays waste the kingdom of Athamas. Already at work is the magic of a woman—Ino, who hates the children of Cloud (Nephele), the repudiated wife. Does Cloud's withdrawal proclaim the drying up of the water from the sky? Ino precipitates the course of events: the stepmother persuades the women of the country, whose job it is to dry the harvested barley and grains at their hearths, to roast all of the seed grain as well. The cycle of nature is interrupted and the oracle demands the blood of Phrixus. In Herodotus's version (7.197), it is Athamas himself who is led to the altar, like a steer decked out in ribbons and garlands, an expiatory victim who will purify the land. The descendants of Cytissorus, son of Phrixus, continue to bear the burden of this sacrifice, because Phrixus, returning from Colchis, had rescued his father, Athamas, thus provoking the divine anger, the wrath of Zeus the Devourer, turned this time onto the one who had created an obstacle to the monstrous sacrifice. Two other details again underline the theme of the strangeness of what the descendant is allowed to eat. In Achaea, the descendants of Athamas are forbidden to enter the pryta-

143

neum, the former royal quarters, and the banquet hall, lest they be used as sacrificial offerings. Elsewhere, in the version of Apollodorus (*Bibliotheca*, 1.9.2), Athamas, driven by the wrath of Hera to kill Learchus and pursue Melicertes, then banished and left to wander, is instructed to settle "where the wild beasts offer him hospitality." His solitary wandering throughout the countryside comes to an end on the day he happens upon a pack of wolves dividing the sheep they have slaughtered. At the sight of him, the ferocious beasts disperse, abandoning to him what they had been about to share among themselves. This is where Athamas settles and builds a city, after marrying Themisto, the daughter of Hypseus. A wolf to men, having slaughtered his own children, Athamas returns to the city and to the territory of men by way of a detour through a city of wolves, assembled for the formal distribution of what can be viewed as both the spoils of their kill and a sacrificial offering. Theirs is an ephemeral city that disappears as soon as it takes shape, but its dissolution seems to also imply a kind of invitation to this man who is more wolf than they: to sit at their table and take the place that is no longer their own. By eating the portions of victims abandoned to him by wolves, Athamas regains his humanity. He is redeemed by way of a detour through a sacrifice by wolves—the other side of the killing that had condemned him to exile and to the solitary life of a "lone wolf."

When Jason appears, as Athamas's closest relative, he is charged with removing his pollution and bringing back the Fleece. Jason comes down from the mountains, covered in animal skins; but Chiron has educated him, and if he seems at once a stranger and a native, the shoe missing from his left foot is enough to qualify him, in the eyes of Pelias, as the one who will take back the throne that has been usurped. What Pelias does not know is that the man marked by this sign is thereby qualified to perform the impossible task which Pelias immediately assigns to him. Hera protects her hero: he alone consented to help her when she was testing men at the river's edge, and it was during this crossing, according to one version (Hyginus, *Fabulae*, 13; Valerius Flaccus, *Argonautica*, 1.83–85), that Jason lost his sandal. The expedition, which will take place under the sign of Hera, is first of all the crossing of an uncrossable space, the sea, the high seas, an immense expanse whose only borders are the sky and the water. Tossed and furrowed by the winds, ceaselessly whipped by the rolling waves, the sea that the Argo must cross is a path constantly erased, a passage never charted, a route that closes as fast as it seems to open. Aporia achieves its highest form in the Symplegades, or Wandering Rocks, the Dismal Ones: no exit seems to present itself, no means of escape from this space where all directions are abolished, unless a divine power should intervene to clear the way and open the passage. In the *Argonautica*, attributed to Orpheus, a bird sent by Athena (whose familiar is the sea rook) flies ahead of the ship to wait for the proper moment to pass between the two rocks, which keep moving apart and back together again. As he takes off, the moving rocks are already closing up, not fast enough to block his way but enough to sever the tip of his tailfeathers. In his wake follow the Argonauts, their ship's course now foreshadowed by the flight of the bird. The importance of this flight in the myth echoes ancient techniques of navigation, where, lacking a compass, sailors released birds into the air when they needed to know the direction of land. But the parallels between the bird and the ship are reinforced by one detail: in crossing the pass, the ship escapes the deadly embrace of the Rocks, but leaves behind several pieces of the stern, just as

Jason, while fording the stream, left one of his sandals in the water and found himself subsequently marked, in the same way and in the same place as the bird, by what we can easily argue as being an "initiatory" test.

Hera's protection is expressed indirectly through Medea, without whom Jason would never have succeeded at the "labors" assigned to him by the king of Colchis. The daughter of Aeëtes, who combines within her the power of the Sun and the forces of night, Medea belongs to the family of women who are expert in magic and in occult knowledge. Like Agamedes, Hecamedes, and Perimedes, she is full of ideas, and has that disturbing intelligence which Pindar defines as *mētis* in his eulogy of Bellerophon (*Thirteenth Olympian*, 18–22). Strength, no matter how powerful, is conquered by this cunning intelligence, but without feints, tricks, or other resourcefulness: Medea aims at a practical efficacy, making use of magic, herbs, and potions, mobilizing the powers of the night. Medea is a woman of *mētis*, but her alliance with Jason is not the marriage of Zeus with Metis, his first wife, who gave him his sovereignty. For Jason, the spells of Medea clear the path to the Golden Fleece—a talisman whose loss will signal to Aeëtes the end of his reign (Diodorus, 4.47), but which does not automatically give Jason access to the kingdom usurped by Pelias. Without the sorceress, Jason would not have regained the throne of the son of Aeolus. And the wife and ally can become an enemy, all the more fearful since matrimony is against her nature.

In certain traditions (Diodorus, 4.45ff.), Medea's mother is Hecate, the daughter of Perses, who was born in the mountains of Taurus and lived in the desert regions, hunting men and collecting the thousand poisons that the earth produces, far from cultivated fields. Like her mother, who was also the mother of Circe, Medea can only rule over deserts, mountains, and wild forests. Uncultivated lands furnish her with the instruments of her power: poisons and remedies. Medea is the sorceress and has the sorceress's disquieting violence, burning passions, wild reversals of mood, melancholia, and the culpable duplicity that she uses against those she loves the most.

One of the important traits of this magician is her interest in disquieting culinary operations. Her instrument, her weapon, is not the skewer but the cauldron and the pot, the same utensils used to prepare the meat from the victim of a sacrifice. But the distortion here is twofold: first, in Greece, the preparation of meat is not a job for women; only men may become cooks, butchers, sacrificers; and the kettle belongs to him who also holds the skewer and the knife. Medea thus appropriates a male privilege. As for her cuisine, it has the appearance of a sacrifice but she indulges in an inverted form of the killing of a living creature: it is life that is supposed to come out of her cauldron, as from the belly of the woman, renewed life, such as Medea promised to Pelias, showing him the brand-new lamb taken from the cauldron in which she had put the dismembered ram. But the cauldron becomes the means of putting Pelias to death, hiding him in the belly of the Earth.

Just as the sorceress can only be a disquieting cook, she does not seem to be able to reproduce. Medea, in Corinth, is the Wanderer, the woman who allows herself to be carried off, though she herself ravishes and kidnaps, as if coming from the wild world prevents her from putting down any roots or developing any affinity with the cultivated fields and the hearthside. Medea's children are accursed: their mother hides them in the sanctuary of Hera, or they are all stillborn, or each time Medea brings a child into the world, she ends by burying it. And the slaughter of her sons, in the Corinthian version, is connected with the monstrous sacrifices of Athamas or of Apsyrtus, the brother dismembered by his sister, Medea.

J.C./d.b.

BIBLIOGRAPHY

1. The Ancients

APOLLONIUS OF RHODES, *Argonautica* (books 1 and 2). *Apollonii Rhodii Argonautica,* H. Fränkel, ed. (Oxford 1961). *Scholia in Apollonium Rhodium Vetera,* C. Wendel, ed. (3d ed., Berlin 1974). EURIPIDES, *Medea.* PINDAR, *Pythia* 4. [ORPHEUS], *Argonautica.* VALERIUS FLACCUS, *Argonautica.*

2. The Moderns

Articles ''Argô, Argonautensage'' (1, 1: cols. 502–37); ''Athamas'' (1, 1:669–75); ''Iason'' (2, 1:63–88); ''Medeia'' (2, 2:2482–2515); ''Pelias'' (3, 2:1847–61); ''Phrixos'' (3, 2:2458–67), in ROSCHER, *Ausführliches Lexicon der griechischen und römischen Mythologie.* G. DUMÉZIL, *Le crime des Lemniennes* (Paris 1924). E. DELAGE, *La géographie dans les Argonautiques d'Apollonius de Rhodes* (Bordeaux and Paris 1930). A. HURST, *Apollonios de Rhodes, manière et cohérence* (Geneva 1967). R. ROUX, *Le problème des Argonautes* (Paris 1949).

ARTEMIS

''I sing of the brilliant Artemis with her golden arrows, the venerated virgin, the Archeress who strikes deer with her arrows, the sister of Apollo with his golden sword, she who, in the shadows of mountains and on the mountaintops whipped by the winds, stretches her bow of pure gold, and, for the joy of the hunt, shoots the arrows that make her victims groan. The peaks of great mountains tremble. The forest in its darkness screams with the frightened clamor of the animals of the woods. The earth trembles, as does the fish-filled sea. The goddess of valiant heart runs and leaps, appearing everywhere, sowing death among the race of wild animals'' (*Homeric Hymn to Artemis,* 2.1–10). The Archeress also descends toward the ocean, toward the mouths of rivers thick with rushes, through lagoons and swamps. At night, accompanied by her Nymphs, she dances on the prairie covered with flowering thickets. From mountaintops to the bottom of the sea, as Huntress (Agrotera) or Goddess of the Marsh (Limnatis), Artemis constantly roams the wild space which surrounds the territories of men.

''To the cities, Artemis does not often come down'' (Callimachus, *Hymn to Artemis,* 19). It is left to humans to go out to meet her, traveling to the mountains or to the sea. The young women of Sparta went to Caryae (the Walnut Trees), at the edge of the dark forests of oaks which covered the mountains between their country and neighboring Arcadia. Their choruses danced there in the open air, around the statue of Artemis Caryatis, Mistress of the Walnut and of all wild trees that bear fruit. Or, under the protection of the king, they crossed the passes of the Taygetus to the sanctuary of Artemis Limnatis, Goddess of the Marsh, on the steep slopes overlooking wet ravines. Their neighbors from the other side of the mountain, the Messenians, had climbed the mountain from their side for the festival. Tragedy erupted—

young women were raped, committed suicide; the king was killed defending them—from which there arose an inexpiable war.

The sanctuary of Brauron in Attica is situated at the extreme edge of the territory, above the rich plain of the Mesogaea, this time by the sea, on the shore of the Euboean narrows. In the midst of swamps and humid meadows surrounded by wooded hills, the sanctuary is bathed by the Erasinos river, whose slow waters spread into a broad harbor as they reach the sea. The little girls of Athens would go to this sanctuary to ''play the She-bear.'' For a she-bear had once entered the sacred area and had been tamed. But a very naughty little girl would not stop tormenting it, and finally the exasperated bear scratched her. The brothers of the little girl were furious and killed the bear. Artemis avenged the crime by sending a plague that devastated the city. Since that time, in expiation for the killing, little girls from Athens came to ''play the She-bear,'' running and dancing with torches in their hands, for Artemis—and to learn to behave themselves. It was again to the sea, to the temple of the goddess on the high point of the Rhoccan promontory, that the Cretans of Rhithymna carried victims of snakebite. Rabid dogs ran at them; from the top of the cliff, they threw themselves into the water (Aelianus, *De natura animalium,* 12.22; 14.20).

Sometimes, it is true, the short distance covered made the voyage more symbolic than real, as at Agrae (the Hunting Preserves), just outside Athens, where Artemis hunted for the first time, or at Limnae (the Marshes), near Sparta, at the entrance to the marsh of Eurotas: here, young Spartans underwent the ordeal of the whip under the statue of Artemis Orthia. The meaning, however, remains the same: one had to go to the edge of the cultivated territory and into the wild area beyond, the *''agros,''* the hunting grounds of the goddess; into pasturelands, forests, and mountains separating the territories of the cities and surrounding them, often running to the sea; into barren headlands, swamps, and meadows of the lowlands or, further inland, lakeshores and riverbanks. The sanctuaries of Artemis are generally at the end of cultivated territory. Already wild, adjoining the mountains or a part of them, bordering the sea, these regions bear the Greek name of *eschatiai:* the extremities, the limits, the land ''at the end.'' This boundary between cultivated territory and wild country is neatly demarcated when the mountains rise directly from the cultivated fields on the plain, but it is just as often confused, disconnected, and varying according to the inclination of the intermittent clearings. It may even be mobile, as on the plains of Arcadia, constantly menaced from within by the waters of the lakes and marshes that flood the plains, which are hemmed in by mountains on all sides. The villages took refuge on the slopes and fervently sought the protection of the goddess—as at Stymphale—in the wake of a catastrophic flood which buried all cultivable land, for she punished the slightest departure from the rituals and returned their world to wilderness. As transitional lands, the *eschatiai* expressed the complex relations between civilization and wilderness, between nature and cultivation, that were expounded by the mythology of Artemis.

In a Greek city, civic and political territory was identified with cultivated territory. Its periphery formed a border, the Limits of the City. The wild space was considered ''outside the city.'' Cultivated land was the space of adults, citizens, their work, their conflicts, and the wars they waged to defend this land. Massive phalanxes of hoplites met there in broad daylight to do loyal and unified battle. The *''eschatia,''*

Artemis "Ptonia thēron." Ajax carrying the body of Achilles. Attic krater, detail of handle. Ca. 570 B.C. Florence, Archaeological Museum. Photo Soprintendenza.

on the other hand, was a "marginal" area, a passageway from cultivation to the completely wild space, which was both symbol and site of another passage—from childhood and adolescence to maturity, from the wild and "thorny" life to the "milled wheat" of the cultivated life, through which young men achieve the status of soldier, citizen, and husband. On the *eschatiai*, where male initiation rites were sponsored by the goddess, young men guarded small border forts, waged—at least in myths—an artful, nocturnal, solitary war, braved the wild beasts, and proved their ability to integrate themselves into the city. The *eschatiai* were also the site of female initiation rites: the She-bears of Brauron, the dances and choirs on the mountain and in the prairies, rituals which prepared the *parthenoi* for marriage. Earlier, the girls would have dedicated their waistbands and their toys to Artemis. Then the goddess would enter human cities to aid young married women in the pain of childbirth, through which, by becoming mothers of citizens, they achieved the definitive status of womanhood, later confirmed by other births. Finally, Artemis Kourotrophe ("she who made the young boys grow") extended her protection to newborn children and their nurses so that the children would thrive. Thus, from nursing infant to *ephebus* (young man) and young woman, from birth to the age of reproduction, Artemis presided over the wild time of life. Eternally virginal herself, she would never reach the cultivated territory of adulthood.

Woe to him who tried either to force or to impede this passage. In the city of Patras, there were once two young people who loved one another equally: Melanippus (Black Horse) and Comaitho (Long Hair), the priestess of Artemis; both were wondrously beautiful. Their parents, unfortunately, were opposed to their marriage. In defiance of the laws of men and the gods, Melanippus and Comaitho dared to give vent to their passion in Artemis's own sanctuary, using it as their nuptial chamber. Artemis made her wrath felt by the entire city: the ground bore no more fruit and the people died of strange illnesses. According to the poet Callimachus, "the plague ravaged their flocks and the frost their fields; the old men cut their hair to mourn their sons; and the women died in childbirth, suddenly, or, if they survived, brought forth progeny who were not straight and strong" (*Hymn to Artemis,* 124–28). The oracle of Delphi was consulted and revealed the crime of Melanippus and Comaitho; he ordered that they be sacrificed to Artemis and that each year the most beautiful young man and woman of the country should be sacrificed to the goddess. Later, according to the myth, the introduction of the cult of Dionysus put an end to this bloody practice. A ritual celebrated by the youth of Patras commemorates the sacrifice, as a reminder of the standards of good conduct (Pausanias, 7.19–20).

In establishing the rules of life in society according to the Justice of Zeus, men left the animal world and entered the world of Culture, the life of Cities. Artemis punished all returns to the wild state, all attempts to blur the distinctions between the two realms at every level of human activity: hunting, war, politics, and sex. Transgressions call out and reply to one another from one level to the next, leading the guilty to their inevitable doom.

Thus the hunt, a human activity in the wild or savage world, may not itself be wild or savage or cause unlimited destruction. The young of animals, as well as of humans, were under the protection of Artemis and were to be spared. Orion was a savage hunter who exterminated animals without observing any limit; likewise, he pursued the Nymphs to violate them. He died making an attempt upon the virginity of Artemis. According to Aeschylus, the Achaeans, assembled for the Trojan War, see a terrible omen: two eagles, kings of birds, appear to the "kings of the ships"; one is black, the other white. Perched well in sight, on the side of the arm which brandishes the lance, they are devouring a pregnant female hare. The soothsayer Calchas recognizes the eagles as the Atreidae, Agamemnon and Menelaus; in the crime of hunting, the hare eaten along with her young in her womb, he prophesies the crime of war, the total ruin of Troy. This ruin, Agamemnon, the black eagle and cursed hunter, will be able to buy only at the price of his progeny, by the sacrifice of his daughter Iphigenia, on the marine *eschatia* at Aulis where Artemis holds back the fleet by unfavorable winds. He himself, returning victorious, will fall into the trap set for him by his wife Clytemnestra, to avenge the murder of her daughter. He becomes, in his turn, the game, tracked by the lioness that his wife becomes for him.

The war with Messenia, historic but also mythic, in the seventh century B.C., saw the destruction and subjugation of one Greek people by another; it could only have been started by a shocking transgression, which alone could justify its horror: the violation of young Spartan women at the sanctuary of Artemis Limnatis. Struck at its very power of reproduction, Sparta could only survive and restore itself by annihilating the guilty city. Spartan warriors swore never to return to their country, nor to reunite with their women, until Messenia was destroyed. The war would last twenty years, exactly a generation. An oracle had promised salvation to the Messenians, on condition that one of their princes sacrifice his virgin daughter. Aristodemus offered his daughter for this purpose. In order to save her, her fiancé claimed that she was pregnant. In a rage, her father disemboweled the girl; the allegation was proved false. Aristodemus had killed his child, not sacrificed her. As king, and model king, he could not save his people. The omens of the end were clear. Aristodemus dreamed that his dead daughter scattered the sacrifice before the battle: she threw away the entrails of the victims and, uncovering her own wound, gave him her own entrails to examine; then she took away his weapons and covered him with the winding-sheet of the royal family. A plant called *agrōstis*, "the wild" (dog's-tooth grass), grew in the center of his palace all around the hearth, the royal Hestia, symbol of the permanence of his race. Each night, the dogs of the Messenians came together and howled like wolves, and then left as a group to go over to the enemy. Finally, the statue of Artemis, who protected the country, dropped her shield. In despair, Aristodemus committed suicide on the tomb of his daughter. The wilderness had reclaimed the city. Artemis had taken her revenge (Pausanias, 4.13; Plutarch, *Moralia*, 168f.).

In wars such as this, without *dikē* (Justice), men become like fish, wild beasts, and winged birds, which devour each other (Hesiod, *Works and Days*, 275–77) and are sought in the same way, like game, by the arrows of the goddess. It is surely for this reason—so that the ordered confrontation of troops and the test of power according to the ideals of hoplite warfare should not degenerate into blind carnage, into the annihilation of the youth of the city—that the Spartans, at the very moment when they engaged in battle, sacrificed a goat to Artemis Agrotera. On the eve of the disaster of Leuctra, from which Sparta would never recover, wolves devoured all the sacrificial goats. The battle itself took place around the tomb of two young countrywomen who, many

years before, had killed themselves after being raped by two young Spartans who had just come back from consulting the oracle of Apollo at Delphi.

A city dominated by a tyrant and no longer governed by laws is another image of a world gone wild. Sometimes the tyrant is a man of the woods who seldom appears in the city, like an *ephebus* who never finishes his liminal period. At Melitaea in Phthiotis, the tyrant in the myth bore the name of Tartarus, a predestined sign of his exclusion from the city. He took young women before their marriage. Aspalis, a young woman of noble birth, learning of the arrival of his guards, anticipated them and hanged herself. Her young brother, still a beardless youth, discovered her body. He dressed in the clothing of his dead sister, went to the tyrant thus disguised, in her place, and killed him. The cursed body of Tartarus was thrown outside the city limits into a river which would thenceforth carry his infernal name. Meantime, Aspalis's body had disappeared, and in its place a statue appeared next to the idol of Artemis. It was called by the young girl's name. "Each year the virgins of the country hung a young female goat that had never known a male goat onto the statue, in memory of Aspalis, who was a virgin when she hanged herself" (Antoninus Liberalis, 13). In other myths, Artemis appears in person to order the death of the tyrant, or she incites a lioness to hunt him down and devour him. Believing himself above laws and men, the tyrant is worse than a beast and suffers the same fate. His failure in the hunt with dogs shows his fundamental inability to integrate himself into the city—just the opposite of the young man disguised as a girl who destroys him like a fierce wild animal.

But a return to the wild state is not the only way to blur the distinction between Nature and Culture, or to fail to recognize the integrity of the Universe. There is another way: to try to limit the world to the confines of its cultivated areas, as if the city stood alone rather than at the heart of the wilderness. This was the sin of Oeneus. In the world that was reborn after the Flood, the new race of men—born of the stones thrown by Deucalion, the Greek Noah—came down from the mountains and relearned the arts of civilization: Deucalion's son was Orestheus, "the Mountainman," who in turn had a son named Phytius, "the Planter," who then became the father of Oeneus, "the Man of the Vineyard." According to this genealogy, which went from wild nature to the cultivated land, Oeneus was the inventor of arboriculture. As king of Calydon, at the heart of the Aetolian forests, he cultivated a magnificent garden of vines and olive trees on the plain. He had a son named Meleager. But on the seventh day after his birth, the Moirai came to determine the child's future: he would live as long as the piece of wood which burned on the hearth of the king. His mother Althaea heard them; immediately she seized the half-burned log and shut it up in a chest in the deepest reaches of the palace. In another version, Meleager's exterior soul is that of an olive plant which his mother ate while she was pregnant and to which she gave birth at the same time as her son. Meleager's destiny becomes intertwined with that of the olive tree, the royal and millenary tree which is reborn from itself, avoiding sexual generation. "The young Meleager is the promise of an olive tree destined to cover all the land of Calydon with its foliage" (M. Detienne); it is the most beautiful tree in the garden of Oeneus.

On the day of the harvest, Oeneus offered the first fruits to the gods; but to Artemis alone among the Immortals he made no offering, "either because he forgot her completely, or because he thought he had done what he had not" (*Iliad*, 9.537). This is a curious lapse of memory for a man who

Artemis as huntress. Attic pelike. Ca. 380 B.C. London, British Museum. Museum photo.

named his son Meleager ("he who gives all his attention to the Hunt"). In her anger, the Power of the Forests of Calydon aroused an enormous boar, alone, with great white tusks: "Ceaselessly he ravaged the vineyards of Oeneus and brought down from their heights the great trees together with their roots and their shining fruits" (*Il.*, 9.540–42). Oeneus quickly sent his son and the elite of the young Greeks against the monster, the new Flood. Among them was a young woman named Atalanta. A virgin, hunting with bow and arrow, she wandered in the mountains, shunning men. Her hand was the prize in a race: her suitor had a head start, but if she overtook him, she would put him to death. The hunters started the monster, who killed several of them; Atalanta was the first to strike him with her arrow; finally, Meleager, immortal as long as the olive tree or the half-burned log remained intact, killed the boar. Artemis immediately provoked a violent quarrel between Atalanta and Meleager. Who was to have the remains of the animal? Meleager, who fell in love with Atalanta despite the fact that he was newly married, made her a present of the beast, refusing to give it to his maternal uncles, the Curetes. The situation came to blows. Meleager killed his uncles. From this point, there are many versions of Meleager's death, as there are of his birth. In the most famous, in order to avenge the death of her brothers, Althaea threw the half-burned log, the double of her son, onto the fire. In another version, she had cursed her son; out of spite, Meleager refused to defend the city of his father against the Curetes and withdrew to his wife's private apartments. Deaf to the supplications of his fellow citizens, he did not enter into battle until the city had been taken, and then only to defend his own house. The moment he annihilated the enemy, his mother burned the log. Finally, in the version of the olive tree, Oeneus himself, after demanding in vain the remains of the monster, tore up the olive tree and, in killing his son, completed the destruction of his garden.

The paradox of the hunt at Calydon is that it supplied the Greeks with the heroic model for the collective hunt, but it was a hunt that was cursed, impious, the story of an impossible initiation. It is the myth that is exemplary, not the heroes. The sin of Oeneus and the destiny of Meleager are parallel, identical in nature: the strange forgetfulness of Oeneus, the Man of Culture, is already contained in Meleager's birth. The illusion of conquering Death corresponds to a denial of Nature. The prophecy of the Moirai is interpreted by Meleager's mother not as the prediction of a life as fleeting as that of a burning ember, but as the artificial possibility of warding off death from her child forever. In the olive tree version, Meleager swings to the side of Culture: he is the epitome of the cultivated tree, a tree which is quasi-immortal, which renews itself by sending out new shoots, remaining always the same being, totally avoiding sexual generation, the succession of generations, and the difference of the sexes. But in escaping Nature so completely, Meleager is also completely dispossessed of himself. An ember kept in his mother's coffer, an olive tree in his father's garden—his fate is entirely in their hands, never in his own. Thus, when he reaches maturity, Meleager loses his destiny as a warrior and the son of a king. Instead, he becomes the impious hunter, murderer of the boar of Artemis, refusing to divide the spoils equally with his companions. Married, he dishonors his wife's relatives out of an impossible desire for a virgin who hates men. As a warrior, he kills only his allies in a disorganized struggle, and when true civil war breaks out as a result of his actions, and he must defend the walls of his

Artemis killing Actaeon. Attic krater. Ca. 480 B.C. Boston, Museum of Fine Arts. Museum photo.

city, he hides among the women in his wife's apartments. He comes out only to defend his own house, not his country.

We know that the ritual of Artemis of Calydon consisted of a holocaust in which live animals, especially wild animals such as stags, wolves, and bear cubs, as well as the fruit of cultivated trees, were burned over a huge fire. For having refused the goddess "the share of the fire," Oeneus loses all of his double harvest at the very moment when it comes to maturity, both his garden and his son, burned not on a sacrificial pyre but on the Hestia of the Palace, at the hearth of his own father.

Oeneus the Father wanted to recognize only Culture. For the gods, this is a crime equal to honoring only Artemis, which would imply lack of respect for another god. It is a young man's mistake, the mistake of Hippolytus, as described by Euripides. The son of Theseus devotes himself single-mindedly to the hunt; ceaselessly, with his pack of hounds, he prowls the mountain and the meadows still untouched by human works, except when he is training mares along the shore. He avoids women and scorns Aphrodite. But if Artemis is meant never to submit to gentle love, a mortal man cannot do the same with impunity. The rest of the story is well known: the passion of Phaedra, the wife of Theseus, for her stepson, Hippolytus's haughty refusal, the suicide of the young woman who accuses him of raping her. Cursed by his father, on his way to the place of exile along a deserted stretch of coast, Hippolytus sees a monstrous bull rise from the waves, aroused by Poseidon in answer to Theseus's appeal. Stampeded like mares in heat, the virgin fillies that Hippolytus has trained with his own hands overturn the chariot and crush its driver to pieces. Aphrodite has returned them to their natural wildness, and Artemis does not intervene to save her devotee.

The sin of Hippolytus, like that of Oeneus, is to reduce the world to only one of its aspects. It reminds us that the gods are part of an interdependent and cohesive pantheon in which none may be ignored. A knowledge of the system of the Greek gods must include a study of their reciprocal relations. Our analyses, which were limited to considering Artemis as a Power of wild Nature in its relation to Culture, have thus reached their boundary.

P.E./d.b.

BIBLIOGRAPHY

References: TH. SCHREIBER, "Artemis," in W. H. Roscher, *Ausführliches Lexikon der griechischen und römischen Mythologie* (Leipzig 1884), vol. 1, cols. 558–608. K. WERNICKE, "Artemis," in Pauly/Wissowa, *Real-Encyclopädie*, vol. 2 (1895), cols. 1336–1440.

General studies on Artemis: L. R. FARNELL, *The Cults of the Greek States* (Oxford 1896), 2:425–607. K. HOENN, *Artemis: Gestaltwandel einer Göttin* (Zurich 1946). L. PRELLER, *Griechische Mythologie*, 1: *Theogonie und Götter* (4th ed., Berlin 1894): 296–335. L. SÉCHAN and P. LÉVÊQUE, *Les grandes divinités de la Grèce* (Paris 1966), 353–65. ERIKA SIMON, *Die Götter der Griechen* (Munich 1969), 147–78.

Festivals, rituals: M. P. NILSSON, *Griechische Feste von religiöser Bedeutung mit Ausschluss der Attischen* (Leipzig 1906), 179–256.

Some major cults and sanctuaries: R. M. DAWKINS, ed., *The Sanctuary of Artemis Orthia at Sparta* (London 1929). J. HERBILLON, *Les cultes de Patras avec une prosopographie patréenne* (Baltimore 1929), 38–74. LILLY G. KAHIL, "Autour de l'Artémis attique," *Antike Kunst*, 1964, 20–33. I. D. KONTIS, "Artemis Braurōnia," *Archaiologikon Deltion* 22 (1967): 156–206 (with summary in French). CH. PICARD, *Éphèse et Claros: Recherches sur les sanctuaires et les cultes de l'Ionie du Nord* (Paris 1922).

Iconography: LILLY KAHIL, "Artemis," in *Lexicon Iconographicum Mythologiae Classicae* (Zurich 1981), abbrev. *LIMC*.

On Iphigenia: W. SALE, "The Temple-Legends of the Arkteia," *Rheinisches Museum* 118 (1975): 265–84. P. VIDAL-NAQUET, "Chasse et sacrifice dans l'*Orestie* d'Eschyle," in J. P. Vernant and P. Vidal-Naquet, *Mythe et tragédie en Grèce ancienne* (Paris 1972), 135–58.

On Meleager: M. DETIENNE, "L'olivier: Un mythe politico-religieux," in M. I. Finley, ed., *Problèmes de la terre en Grèce ancienne* (Paris and The Hague 1973), 293–306. J. TH. KAKRIDIS, *Homeric Researches* (Lund 1949), 11–42.

On the idea of *eschatiai*: L. ROBERT, "Recherches épigraphiques," 5: "Inscriptions de Lesbos," *Revue des Études Anciennes* 62 (1960): 304–6, reprinted in *Opera Minora Selecta*, 2 (Amsterdam 1969): 820–22.

Finally, no reader should miss P. KLOSSOWSKI, *Le bain de Diane* (Paris 1956, 1972).

ASCLEPIUS

A healer and hero, the object of an ardent devotion that made him a durable rival of Christianity, rich in all the marvelous tales of the healings that he produced in his temples, Asclepius nevertheless presents a surprisingly meager "mythological history."

According to almost unanimous tradition, he is the son of Apollo. Thessaly, Messenia, and Epidaurus in Argolis contend for the honor of having witnessed his birth; the debate was even brought before Apollo at Delphi, who decided in favor of Epidaurus. Homer, however, makes him a Thessalian hero, father of Machaon and Podalirius, skilled physicians of the Achaean army (*Il.* 2.731). Pindar, in the beautiful poem dedicated to Asclepius (the *Third Pythian*), relates his miraculous birth and tragic death as follows: Apollo's unfaithful mistress Coronis, daughter of the Thessalian king Phlegyas, perished under the arrows that Artemis used to avenge the insult to her brother, Apollo. But when her parents had placed the body of the young woman on the pyre and the "impetuous flames of Hephaestus" had surrounded her, Apollo rushed to save his son. He "stole him from the corpse; the flames parted before him." Thus, Asclepius passes victoriously through the trial by fire, which myths so often made a test of immortality; he is born of a corpse and springs forth from a funerary fire, which will reverse the paths of life and death for him. Apollo meanwhile entrusts the child to Chiron, the good Centaur, educator of so many young Thessalian noblemen, one destined by his double nature—man and wild beast, *thēr*—to communicate to men a useful sphere of knowledge about wild nature, beasts, and plants—namely, the arts of hunting and medicine. His name *Cheirōn* makes him, for a Greek, "the one who has hands" (*cheir*), the one who knows how to use his hands. So it is the medicine of an artisan, very different from Apollonian medicine, that Asclepius learned from the Centaur "with profound *mētis*" (*eurumedōn, bathumēta*): this *mētis* is efficacious knowledge about things, an accurate glance, a quick appreciation of the propitious moment. At Chiron's school, Asclepius studies magic incantations, potions and unguents, and skillful surgery that straightens distorted limbs. He is henceforth "the gentle artisan of robust health," and the word *hameros* or *himeros*, "gentle," chosen by Pindar, connotes also the quality of what is tamed, domesticated, not wild.

The most widespread tradition relates that Asclepius, placing his knowledge at the service of men, went so far as to resuscitate the dead. For he had received from Athena, Apollodorus tells us (*Bibliotheca* 3.10.3), a magic potion, the blood of the Gorgon: drawn from her left side, it destroys the patient; drawn from her right side, it saves. A strange, ambivalent medicine about which Pindar does not deign to speak. Hades is indignant: his prey is being stolen from him; and "the Rich" (*Ploutōn*) is growing poor: since Asclepius is attending to men, the dead are becoming scarce in Hades. With such a helpful hero, might men not become immortal? But, as always, Zeus is watching: his thunderbolt annihilates the proud hero. From this punishment, Pindar makes every moral lesson explicit. While traditional versions tend to make Asclepius a hero who, out of benevolence, has chosen the side of men against the gods—thus, in a late story, he is struck with lightning for having cured a blindness that was a divine punishment—Pindar alone attributes the transgression of Asclepius to a self-interested motive: love of gold. In this way the Olympians do not appear jealous and vindictive but merely the just guardians of an equitable division between men and gods: "O my soul, do not aspire to the immortal life, but exhaust the range of the possible" (60–61).

Thus Asclepius's career, which opens in the fire of Hephaestus, is completed in the fire of Zeus, the thunderbolt that punishes but also consecrates and immortalizes. Indeed, Asclepius does not join those great criminals in hell who are guilty of divine *lèse-majesté*. He loved men even to the point of displeasing Zeus: in the fifth century there was certainly a pardon for that fault. Without recounting his apotheosis, as was done for Heracles, it was acknowledged, in the fifth century and even before, that Asclepius was a hero; he was soon to become fully a god. A wholly beneficent god, *charma brotois hapāsi*, the delight of mankind, people kept saying, indulgent of the faults of men, compassionate for their sufferings. He inspired in the poet Isyllus (fourth century) verses that, mediocre though they are, bear witness to the intimate and confident devotion that would surround, until the end of antiquity, "the one who, of all the gods, loved men most."

The grandson of Phlegyas the Blazing, son of Phoebus the Brilliant, born from fire and returning to fire, Asclepius is nevertheless, in several of his aspects, a chthonic god, allied with dark powers that oppose his father Apollo. His favorite animal, almost always represented at his side, coiled about his staff, is the snake. The god even assumes, on occasion, the appearance of a snake, as when he is brought from Epidaurus to Sicyon, on a chariot drawn by mules (Pausanias 2.10.3). But the decisive trait that makes Asclepius a divinity in close participation with the earth, with its divinatory and salutary powers, is incubation, practiced in all the great sanctuaries of Asclepius until the end of antiquity. For at Epidaurus the patient was not cured exactly as at Lourdes: the cure was received through the medium of a dreamlike revelation. After accomplishing certain prescriptions aimed at placing them in a state of ritual purity (sexual abstention, fasting, abstinence from certain foods), suppliants who had come to request the curing of their ills were admitted into the *abaton*, the "forbidden place," a dormitory adorned with a statue of the god and traversed by "snakes with bulging jaws" that were peculiar to Epidaurus and entirely inoffensive. There the sick lay down on the ground, in contact with the earth, the bearer of dreams, and fell asleep. The god then visited them during their sleep, cured them in a dream—and in the morning they were indeed cured—or prescribed a medical treatment for them in the dream. The inscriptions at Epidaurus, the testimony of Aelius Aristides (second century A.D.), an eternal invalid and devotee of Asclepius, clearly inform us of these two modes of operation of the god: the miraculous cure, often strictly incredible, such as the cure of the one-eyed man who had no more than a hole instead of an eye, or the deliverance of the woman pregnant for five years (Herzog, *Wunderheilungen . . .*, 9 and 1); and the extended cure, punctuated by numerous dreams distributed over several nights, full of reasonable directions such as "the god ordered me not to fly into a rage so often." The variety and abundance of ex-votos discovered at Epidaurus clearly testify to the scope of the god's powers. But he exercises these powers through the intermediary of that "dark mantic" from which Apollo, we are told, freed men by supplanting the oracle of Gaea at Delphi.

As master of incubation, the son of the solar god was perhaps connected, in former times, with the mole—an animal even more chthonic than the snake since it lives underground and myths place it in direct conflict with the sun. The compilation of indices assembled by Grégoire and Goossens, the parallelism of certain Vedic facts, might support such a conviction. First there is the very name of the god: Asclepius, or, under its Thessalian form, *Askalapios*, might be an adjective formed from *skalops*, which is a dialectal form of the name of the mole. Just as there is a well-attested Apollo "of the Rat" (Smintheus), so the healer god might be none other than an Apollo Askalapios, "of the Mole," who acquired his independence and became an autonomous divine figure, though always closely connected to Apollo. Moreover, the excavations of the sanctuary of Asclepius at Epidaurus have revealed, under the *tholos* of the classical period, the foundations of a strange subterranean labyrinth made of concentric rings, which bears a striking resemblance, we are told, to the underground galleries of a molehill. To support this argument further, one might emphasize the particular characteristics of the mole, a divinatory animal, benevolent-malevolent, used in Greece and elsewhere in numerous prescriptions on the borderline between medicine and magic.

Although the mole may belong to the animal prehistory of Asclepius, it should be noted that if he actually was once a mole god, or a god of the mole, the Greeks completely forgot this fact, or, to put it better, they refused, for reasons that escape us, to remember it. In the substantial dossier compiled by Grégoire and Goossens, not a single direct testimony to the connection has come from Greece. If they were ingenious in their etymologies, which were all the more significant because they were never burdened by any linguistic consideration, the Greeks never dreamed of exploiting what was offered by the resemblance between Asclepius and *skalops*. Their etymologies move in a quite different direction. Lycophron simply calls him *Ēpios*, the gentle, the benevolent; and his wife is *Epionē*. An interpretation for the beginning of the word was also devised: *aiglē*, brightness. Brilliant and benevolent—that is Asclepius.

How could a god like Apollo, the declared enemy of all crawling and subterranean creatures, the victorious rival of the oracle of incubation, have produced and protected a son so marked by his complicities with the earth, the producer of dreams? Asclepius is not an isolated case. Trophonius is sometimes counted among the sons of Apollo: a snake hero, swallowed by the earth, a prophet operating in a subterranean lair; and, among the god's protégés, another prophet, Amphiaraus, who is consulted through incubation and continues to live underground, since Zeus, with his thunderbolt, opened up the earth and banished him beneath it with his followers. The resemblances between these three prophetic heroes have been emphasized, all three chthonic in varying degrees; but the myth makes them sons or protégés of Apollo. It is rather as if, through the subterfuge of lineages and patronages, the irreducible part that returns to the earth in any oracle is restored, re-allied to Apollo but kept at a good distance. Aeschylus and Euripides recount the eviction, at Delphi, of the oracle of incubation, following a process of succession. By restoring the chthonic prophets to Apollo, the myth comes to a different distribution; it may also suggest that coexistence is possible between the two oracles. In this distribution, Asclepius, the more closely attached to Apollo, is also the one in whom the chthonic character is less marked; he has in some way aspired to the Apollonian light and brilliance: struck by lightning but not swallowed up; a snake but not a mole.

J.C./b.f.

BIBLIOGRAPHY

E. J. EDELSTEIN and L. EDELSTEIN, *Asclepius: A Collection and Interpretation of the Testimonies*, 2 vols. (Baltimore 1945). H. GRÉGOIRE, R. GOOSSENS, and M. MATHIEU, *Asklépios, Apollon Smintheus et Rudra* (Brussels 1949). R. HERZOG, *Die Wunderheilungen von Epidauros* (Leipzig 1931), = *Philologus*, supplement, 22, 3. A. TAFFIN, "Comment on rêvait dans les temples d'Esculape," *Bull. de l'Ass. G. Budé* (October 1960), 325ff. L. SÉCHAN and P. LÉVÊQUE, *Les grandes divinités de la Grèce* (Paris 1966), 227–42. THRAEME, "Asklepios," in Roscher, *Ausführliches Lexicon der griechischen und römischen Mythologie*, 1, cols. 615–41.

CENTAURS

In Greece, when one leaves the city and the cultivated fields, one always runs the risk of strange encounters. Among the mythic figures that haunt nature, the centaurs hold a special position. Half man and half horse, they live on the fringes, in the forests and mountains, off the beaten tracks of men. In these spaces, which they share with various spirits of the woods and forests, the only humans that they meet are hunters: rather special hunters, since their names are Heracles or Atalanta. While searching for the boar of Erymanthus in the Pholoan mountains, Heracles is the guest of the centaur Pholus. This hospitable centaur offers the hero cooked meat and wine—although, according to the tradition of Apollodorus, Pholus himself never consumes anything but raw meat. But the fragrance of roasted meat, like the fragrance of wine, gives rise to an unexpected phenomenon: centaurs from every corner of the forest flock to that place to take advantage of the windfall. Heracles is forced to drive them away through combat, from which arises the conflict in the relations between men and centaurs.

Strange characters: "savages, without social organization, of unpredictable behavior" (Apollodorus), they are nevertheless capable of offering men roasted meat and wine. "A savage breed," yet masters of herbs and salves. "Natural" hunters who use no weapons other than stones or branches, they are no match for the bow of Heracles any more than for that of Atalanta. For although the centaurs are fond of meat and wine, they are not indifferent to women either. Woe to the huntress who frequents by herself the forests in which they dwell: she awakens their sexual potency, more animal than human, and can save herself only with her infallible bow.

Theseus is one of the actors in the conflicts between men and centaurs. At the marriage of Pirithous, the king of the Lapiths, to Hippodamia, the centaurs attempt to carry off the bride. Leading the guests, Theseus kills the centaurs. The battle is a rout, as the warriors armed with their swords oppose the centaurs, who defend themselves with rocks and sticks. These are savages, incapable of resisting their natural impulses, who throw themselves at wine and women.

Yet they are strange savages, since they are the inventors of hunting and of medicine. Thus the centaur Chiron is the preeminent civilizing hero: his complicity with the world of nature confers upon him, along with the art of hunting, the art of cultivating plants. Asclepius is his pupil in medicine, and Actaeon, Peleus, and Achilles are his pupils in hunting. Thus, even these barbarian monsters are educators: the "childhoods" of Achilles pass in the company of the centaur

Centaurs present as Heracles opens a jar of wine. Attic lecythus. Ca. 480 B.C. Paris, Musée du Louvre. Photo Chuzeville.

Chiron. The infant Achilles is brought to the centaur Chiron by his father Peleus, in order to receive from him an initiation into hunting. Why does Peleus, the hunter par excellence, feel the need to seek the aid of someone like the centaur? It is because Achilles, the fruit of the union of a mortal and a goddess, is in the greatest danger from his mother: for did she not kill her first children by plunging them into a fire in an attempt to ensure their immortality? Neither the world of gods nor the world of men is without danger for the young Achilles. That is the reason for his princely initiation in the world of centaurs. In the abode of Chiron, the young man learns to master boars and bears without weapons; he is also initiated into music and medicine. The centaur is the master of the liberal arts, but also—and especially—the master of ethics. Chiron is, according to Homer, "the most just among the centaurs," the model of moral conduct.

Another experience of Peleus, the father of Achilles, illustrates the ambivalence of centaurs. During the hunt of Calydon, Peleus accidentally kills his father-in-law, Eurytion. Taking shelter at Iolcus in the house of King Acastus, Peleus arouses the desire of the king's wife. When he refuses to respond to her advances, she denounces him to Acastus. The king, who does not wish to lay hands on a man whom he has purified of a crime by offering him asylum, devises a stratagem of hunting to get rid of Peleus. After a hunting expedition in the mountains, he takes advantage of Peleus's sleep to abandon him, after hiding the hero's *machaira* (the

Peleus brings the child Achilles to Chiron. Attic wine-pouring vessel. Ca. 490 B.C. London, British Museum. Museum photo.

they exist only through the play of this tension. On the periphery of the inhabited world one can only expect to meet extraordinary beings, who are beyond good and evil. In this sense, the centaurs symbolize the opposing principles that organized the Greek city: on the one hand, the world of culture, of arts and techniques, and on the other, the natural world. In short, the centaurs are the natural state of culture. To appropriate for oneself the arts which they possess, it is necessary simultaneously to measure oneself against them and to win their goodwill. The techniques of which they are masters are of no use to them, but become meaningful only when heroes reveal them to men. Ambiguous and reversible, the centaurs bear the mark of a hunting territory in which anything is possible.

The representations of centaurs on archaic vases express their double nature. While the centaurs are represented naked, with human forequarters and four equine hooves, Chiron (and sometimes Pholus) is represented in a double aspect, with a human body and human legs in a drapery or tunic in front, and a horse's body behind. Thus the representation itself bears the mark of the centaur's ambiguity: the division between humanity and animality takes place, not between the top and the bottom, but between the front and the back. The depiction of the centaur partakes of its symbolic condition.

There is another dimension to the centaurs which complements their physiognomy. In an early comparative investigation, Georges Dumézil attempted to show how, in the most diverse Indo-European traditions, horse-men played a role in initiation and in festivals marking the end of winter. Disguised as horse-men, young boys file through the village streets, indulging in various jests which mix wine with women. Although the Greek texts are practically silent about these rites, we may allow the conclusion that Henri Jeanmaire came to: "The ritual disguise and the mask, in initiation scenarios, are not only for the initiates. They also belong to the masters of the initiation and to the directors of the rituals that are connected with it. Of these disguises, which were generally animal disguises, ancient Greece knew, among other varieties, two principal kinds: that of the horse-men and that of the wolf-men" (*Couroi et Courètes*, Paris 1939, pp. 370–71).

A.S./d.w.

BIBLIOGRAPHY

G. DUMÉZIL, *Le problème des centaures* (Paris 1929). H. JEANMAIRE, *Mélanges H. Grégoire, Chiron* (Brussels 1949), 256–65. B. SCHIFFLER, *Die Typologie des Kentauren in der antiken Kunst* (Frankfurt am Main 1976).

DEMETER

From Hegel to Walter F. Otto, in the perspective of aesthetic religion, which turns away from mysteries, from the powers of the earth, and from the laughter of Dionysus, the Olympian in whom "the ideal of the ideal" is incarnate is the god of light and knowledge, Apollo, whom distance and an extended gaze qualify to enjoy the greatest spiritual freedom. In the *Iliad*, it is he who recalls, for those who might be tempted to forget, the insurmountable gulf between the gods

sacrificial instrument that is also a weapon of battle) in the manure of his cattle. Threatened by centaurs—or by wild animals—Peleus owes his life to the intervention of Chiron, who gives him back his weapon.

Thus the centaurs are systematically construed as double beings. Barbaric and coarse, they are also educators; the rivals of men, they are often the heroes' best friends. It is not surprising that an attempt was made to divide them by placing the "good centaurs," Chiron and Pholus, in opposition to the "bad centaurs," Nessus and the undefined band that attacked Heracles or Peleus. But to consider them in this way is to miss precisely the point of their true nature. Occupying the two extremes of the nature-culture spectrum, and men who walk upon the earth: "There will always be two distinct races" (*Iliad* 5.440–42). And how could the immortal powers dispute among themselves for the sake of poor humans, "like leaves that now live, full of luster, by eating the fruit of the earth, and soon decay and fall to nothing" (*Il.* 21.462–66)? To eat in order to live and to die is the lot of men, who tread the paths of the broad-sided earth, but it is also the domain reserved to Demeter: she rules over food and receives into her womb the dead and the seeds, binding life and death between them, as the human condition intertwines life and death, without ever interrupting their embrace.

The Homeric epic closely associated, within the image of the mortal condition, the acts of eating grain and of standing in an upright position upon the earth, thus inviting one to recognize in Demeter the great figure of the cultivated earth. In the very name of this power, ancient exegetes, followed by modern exegetes, have attempted to read the two signs of Mother and Earth (*dā* would become *gē* in Dorian). But beyond Demeter, Gaea designated a less defined power: the force that causes all plant species and human groups to issue from the earth, the mistress of the knowledge that leaps forth with enthusiasm in the space that knows no checkerboard of fields and cultivated crops.

For the Greek warriors stationed before Troy, the valor that they needed to recover Helen was first the energy that bread and wine gave them, because, as a verse of the epic states, flour and grain are the marrow of men (*Odyssey* 20.108). The invention of cereals marked the end of a state of savagery in which men lived like animals, feeding on herbs and fruits gathered in the woods: on acorns, as even in the historical period the Thracians did, clothed in animal skins, or on raw plants that the Earth, Gaea, caused to grow spontaneously. A tradition, which is perhaps Eleusinian, relates that the strength to stand upright came to men on the day that Demeter invented cereals. Previously, the unhappy creatures were condemned to move as babies and the majority of animals do: on all fours. The Eleusinian Games preserved the memory of this: the winner in the race, in the test that verticality had made possible, received barley, gathered in the sacred plain of Rharion, the domain that certain traditions call the "belly," because it was the first to produce the fruits and the grains of barley from which the cakes indispensable to the sacrifice were made (schol. ad Pindar *Olympian* 9.150b).

But the world of foods belonging to Demeter was not limited to cereals. At Mycalessus, in Boeotia, Demeter had a sanctuary, closed every night and opened every morning by Heracles, the Dactyl of Ida: all the fruits gathered when they were ripe were deposited at the foot of the statue and they preserved their freshness all year. Among the ripe fruits, the protection of which she shared with Dionysus and the Charites, Demeter privileged certain species such as the fig, the first food that her sweetness placed in opposition to wild herbs, or the poppy, a half-cultivated, half-wild plant that grows in the midst of corn and barley and that Demeter was supposed to have discovered at Mecone, in ancient Sicyon, where traditions about the first men and mythical accounts about the first blood sacrifice converge. The poppy and the fig indicate the foods around the base of the cereals, and they point in the direction of the Black Demeter, the Demeter of Phigalia, for instance, whom grief impelled to retire to the bottom of a lost grotto where Pan could discover her only accidentally in the course of a hunt. This was precisely the Demeter who, each year, received from the inhabitants of the country who came before her grotto, which was surrounded

Demeter from Cnidos. Ca. 330 B.C. London, British Museum. Photo Giraudon.

by oaks, fruits of the vine and other fruits from cultivated species, beeswax and honeycombs, and pieces of wool still heavy with grease, all nonanimal offerings that are on the boundary between the wild and the cultivated.

In Arcadia, as in other Greek regions, Demeter in mourning for her daughter, Kore or Persephone, threatened to reduce men to famine, even to deprive them of the last wild fruits and to compel them to satisfy themselves with human flesh. For at the side of Demeter with bread, called Sito, there is another who is called the Voracious One, or She-who-eats-to-satiety (Hadephagia), whose ambiguity is revealed through two complementary figures. On one side, Pandareus, the father-in-law of Polytechnus, who received from Demeter the gift of eating as much as he wished, without ever suffering from a stomachache. This is the good hunger, the hunger that satisfies, which has its parallel in the evil hunger, the hunger that devours Erysichthon. Like his father Triopas, he was nevertheless one of Demeter's protégés, and the goddess had no domain more precious than the beautiful dense forest, in which pines, elms, pear trees, and apple trees crowded together for her alone. But Erysichthon had a strange idea: with twenty companions, carrying hatchets and axes, he ran to Demeter's wood; he wanted to cut down the beautiful trees in order to make a covering for the hall in which, day after day, he would offer delicious feasts to his friends, ''to satiety.'' In return, Demeter placed in him an enormous, burning hunger, an evil whose fire consumed him. However much he ate, so much the more did hunger seize him; and Callimachus (*Hymn to Demeter*, 72ff.) relates that his parents were ashamed to let their son go to parties or banquets. All sorts of pretexts were found. There was a wedding. ''Erysichthon hurt himself hurling the discus.'' A dinner was given. ''He fell from his chariot.'' During this time, at a table the whole day in the heart of the palace, he devoured and devoured still more. He was an abyss in which all food was swallowed up without benefit. When he had consumed everything, the mules of the great chariot, the war-horse, and the cat that frightened the mice, and was still famished, his jaw needed other prey. With great bites, Erysichthon began to tear his own limbs to pieces.

This evil hunger, which the Ionians called *boubrōstis*, Hunger-that-grows-to-devour-the-ox, could be exorcised only by offering it a black bull, which had to be consumed in its skin in the midst of the flames. Or as it was done in Boeotia, in Chaeronea, the city of Plutarch: each for himself and the archon for all, in the name of the common hearth, they would expel Hunger, Boulimia, in the form of a slave driven out of the house with blows of rods, to cries of ''Hunger outside, Wealth and Health inside'' (Ploutos and Hygieia). Demeter was present implicitly in this ritual, for Plutus, the god who bestows riches and material well-being, was the product of the love of Iasion and the goddess of food, lying together in a furrow of fallow land that had been plowed three times. The same relationship between the scarcity and abundance of food was inscribed within Athenian space where the ground consecrated to Boulimos, a wild land, faced the field called Bouzugion, the land farmed by men who harnessed the oxen and drove the plow, while protecting agricultural life with a series of curses: against those who slaughter the Plowing Ox, who share neither water nor fire, thus preventing sacrifices, and, finally, against those who do not show the way to those who are lost.

Even in the adventures of Demeter herself, hunger remains profoundly ambiguous, for it is not by chance that at the feast offered by Tantalus, of all the gods who partake in it, Demeter is the only one whom sudden pangs of hunger drive to devour a piece of the child cooked by a father who wanted to test his guests. The power over food borders on death, through the voracious beast enclosed in the belly, this belly always waiting for food, which the myth of Prometheus makes the receptacle for the edible morsels reserved for men; the partners of the gods are in this way condemned never more to be able to live without feeding the odious and always starving belly. But the belly that Demeter feeds is also the belly that begets and gives life by reproducing the human species. In the *Homeric Hymn*, Demeter is an anguished mother, grief-stricken, calling her daughter Persephone everywhere; but for Demophon, the lastborn of the royal House of Eleusis, she becomes the nurse, giving all her care

to the young sprout entrusted to her arms and her body, in order to make him grow. Tradition recounts that in Corinth, she had taken pity on Plemnaeus, all of whose children had given up their soul while uttering their first cry. Demeter had come as one of those women whose age keeps from them the gifts of Aphrodite; she had taken the child and made it grow like the most beautiful of the plants in his father's garden: she was called Orthopolis; thanks to her the city grew straight, rooted anew.

The children that Demeter raises are not bastards: she only takes care of good seeds, those that take root in the soil of the city, children born from a father and mother who themselves belong to the cultivated land and who are a part of the human community that is rooted in a portion of soil removed from savagery. The Demeter of man's good seeds reigned over the Thesmophoria, a festival for women only, to the exclusion of men, but only for married women, legitimate wives of citizens. By entering into a conjugal union, a young girl penetrated into the domain that drew upon the power of cereals. The ritual of marriage marks out her course with a series of symbols and gestures: the requirement to carry a frying pan to roast the barley; the practice of fastening a mortar and pestle in front of the bridal chamber, and of transporting a sieve, entrusted to a young child of the retinue; finally, the formula: ''I have escaped evil, I have found the best,'' pronounced on the day of the wedding ceremony by a young boy carrying on his head a wreath of thorny plants mixed with the fruits of the oak and distributing to all the invited guests the breads contained in a winnowing basket. The woman entered into the life of ground wheat only by renouncing the savagery of a condition dominated by Artemis, the virgin who was devoted to the hunt and who traveled in the space of wild beasts on the horizon of the uncultivated lands. Through the ceremonies of marriage, the woman was assimilated to a field whose plowing and sowing were done by the husband when he fathered legitimate children.

On the ritual plane of the Thesmophoria, Demeter stood opposed to a power that came from the East, Adonis, the effeminate lover of Aphrodite, whose festival exalted the virtues of seduction and the fragrance of aromatics. For the small gardens of the Adonia offered a sort of counterculture to the cereals of Demeter. During the dog days, when erotic seduction culminated, in the burning proximity of the earth and the sun, women, and more precisely concubines and courtesans, transported miniature gardens onto the roofs of houses, using ladders leading to terraces: the plants germinated in eight days but soon passed from green to dry; they withered when they had barely grown green. Instead of knowing the slow maturation of eight months between sowing and harvest, the barley and corn planted in ridiculous little earthen pots were roasted by the solar fire. They were ''gardens of stone,'' infertile and sterile, in which the cereals which men eat could neither ripen nor bear fruit. The seeds of these illusory cultures were deprived of roots and fruits, as were, in the Greek society that so clearly separated the courtesan and the legitimate wife, the women who were devoted to amorous pleasure and were by this excluded even from the company of the Bee-Women, the only servants of Demeter Thesmophoros. For although Demeter's festival, celebrated by legitimate wives, was a ritual of sowing that took place in the autumn, it was directed toward the promise of beautiful children, toward the hope of a good harvest from human seed, as was made explicit by the name that was given to the last day of the Thesmophoria: ''Beautiful Birth,'' Calligeneia.

Demeter and Kore. Stela. Ca. 500–475 B.C. Paris, Musée du Louvre. Photo Chuzeville.

It is here, in the immediate proximity of the image of the city that is reproducing itself under Demeter's surveillance, that one must locate another aspect of the same power, more discrete but no less essential. Formerly in Athens the dead were called "Demeter's people" (dēmētreioi), and we know from Cicero that the Greeks sowed seeds on the grave in which they had just interred a body, setting the womb of the earth within the maternal womb in this way. Demeter receives the dead as she receives the seeds; and that is why a very ancient tradition recalls that sacrifices are addressed to the dead, praying to them "to make good things grow here above," in the conviction that from those that are buried, foods, growth, and seeds come to the living.

Eleusis unfolds its mysteries around this vision of death. But Demeter's mysticism holds fast to the gates of the city, within a space in which the renunciation of the world was never anything but a detour to return to the world with the ballast of strong hope. Eleusis is the counterpart of Athens: the city over which Eumolpus reigned—with his Thracian retinue and the mask of an Orpheus, affiliated with the Muses—confronted the political city of Erechtheus. Eleusis was anyone's ground, external to the politico-religious space, toward which one proceeded in pilgrimage from everywhere and nowhere. For here all differences between men were abolished: sex, status, ethnicity were no longer current; slaves, women, and non-Greeks no longer constituted anything but a single humanity. But the initiation did not imply a decisive rupture with the religious world of the

city. The supreme vision, the epopteia, came at the end of a dramatic spectacle, punctuated by ritual cries, like "Heaven, rain; Earth, conceive," or "Bromius is born"; by contemplating in silence an ear of corn; by representations of the mustai, of death, and perhaps of a hierogamy. But nothing in the initiation seems to draw upon a secret teaching that any indiscretion would have revealed in the course of the centuries. In the life of the initiate, the journey to Eleusis opened a parenthesis and marked a break. Each initiate became the adopted child of Demeter; and the myth from the Homeric Hymn recounts how the mystical experience that passed through the absolute attachment to one divinity, segregated from others, came to be situated in a later stage in the discovery of cereals and the use of ground wheat. Men could not lay claim to the immortality reserved to the Olympians, any more than the small Demophon could, but, on the other hand, bread eaters received from Demeter the rites and mysteries that marked a rupture with the traditional, and thereby profane, image of death as the only measure of life. Through the play of death alternating with life, with the power of food, Demeter opened to the individual the absolute experience of the idea of death or survival. The earth is not only the home of the dead; it is the inexhaustible reserve of seeds and of those who make good things grow here above. Eleusis caused the initiate to participate in the great process of death and rebirth, whose field of extension is phusis, nature that encompasses plants and the living.

M.D./b.f.

155

BIBLIOGRAPHY

N. J. RICHARDSON, ed., *The Homeric Hymn to Demeter* (Oxford 1974). P. BOYANCÉ, "Sur les mystères d'Éleusis," *Revue des Études Grecques* 75 (1962): 460–82. M. DETIENNE, *Les jardins d'Adonis* (Paris 1972). E. HAHN, *Demeter und Baubo* (Leipzig 1897). E. JANSSENS, "Poésie et espérances eschatologiques dans l'Hymne homérique à Déméter," in *Religions de Salut, Annales du Centre d'Étude des Religions* (Brussels 1962), 2:38–57. K. KÉRÉNYI, "Archetypal Image of Mother and Daughter," in *Archetypal Images in Greek Religion*, 4 (New York 1967). K. KÉRÉNYI, "The Divine Maiden," in C. G. Jung and K. Kérényi, *Essays on a Science of Mythology* (rev. ed., New York 1963); original in German. G. E. MYLONAS, *Eleusis and the Eleusinian Mysteries* (Princeton 1961). A. PESCHLOW-BINDOKAT, "Demeter und Persephone in der attischen Kunst der 6. bis 4. Jahrhundert," *Jahrbuch des deutschen archäologischen Instituts* 87 (1972): 60–157. C. ROLLEY, "Le sanctuaire des dieux patrôoi et le Thesmophorion de Thasos," *Bulletin de Correspondance Hellénique* 89 (1965): 441–83. D. SABBATUCCI, *Saggio sul misticismo greco* (Rome 1965). P. SCARPI, *Letture sulla religione classica: L'inno omerico a Demeter* (Florence 1976). R. STIGLITZ, *Die grossen Göttinnen Arkadiens: Die Kultname Megalai theai und seine Grundlagen* (Vienna 1967).

DIONYSUS

1. The Foreigner in the City

In the Greek pantheon, in which each divine power is differentially defined by the totality of his relations with the other powers, Dionysus is without a doubt the sole divinity whose specific character is measured in opposition to the family of the Olympians as a whole. A series of traits seem to assign a marginal position to him: his mother was born a mortal, he brings madness with him, and strange lacerations of living flesh intoxicate him with pleasure. Since ancient tradition loosely attributed to him a foreign origin—Thracian or Lydian—and since the Homeric epic regarded him as of negligible importance, late-nineteenth-century historiography found it easy to believe that Dionysus, as a latecomer to the Greek city, had been imported from the Thracian regions which were known for their orgiastic and barbaric cults. For certain historiographers who wished to keep Greek rationality unsullied by any collusion with madness and its scandals, the worship of Dionysus called for a medical point of view: it was a religious impulse arising from morbid mental states, which attacked the whole social fabric, but only through the chink in the armor—women, in whom the fragility of human nature was most evident.

Since then, the discovery of the Mycenaean archives has provided irrefutable evidence for a Dionysus with a Greek pedigree as solid as that of the other members of the pantheon. Parallel with these discoveries—and countering the opinion that the god had been a foreigner to the Greek city at least until Hellenistic times—more rigorous analyses have demonstrated that Dionysus, who was present in ancient festivals such as the Apaturia (the festival of the phratries) and the Anthesteria (the festival of the new wine and the dead), may have occupied a central place in various politico-religious systems. At Patrai, he is the god who is *Aisumnētes*, a name which designates a referee in the games in the epic and a kind of supreme magistrate on the political level. Elsewhere, in the pantheon of Lesbos in the seventh century, Dionysus reigns next to Zeus and Hera in the sanctuary shared by all citizens, which is also the place in which he clearly bears the title of "eater of raw flesh."

In searching for ways to accredit his reputation as a foreign divinity, the historians of Dionysus yielded to the temptation to transform into historical events the myth of the "coming god," just as others insisted on seeing in the ferocity of the enemies who rose up against him a trace of the resistance met by his cult in the historical course of its invasion. In doing so, they fell into the trap of those they wanted to take by surprise. For Dionysus always took pleasure in playing the role of the foreigner: in several cities—for example at Callatis, a Greek colony on the Black Sea—one of his festivals was called *Xenika*, after the name of the foreigner to whom gifts of hospitality were offered. The Dionysus of the outside is never anything but the other face of the god who lives in the city. And his calendar follows the rhythm of festivals which alternate between his celebration inside and outside the walls of the city. This is a god of the interior, but one whose empire is a limitless space; a space that is crisscrossed and seemingly invested with the multiplicity of forms which his power, his *dunamis*, gives to itself.

One of the signs of Dionysus's presence, in contrast with the Olympian gods who are entitled to temples and sanctuaries that fit into the politico-religious space of the city, is that he has no fixed site. He is honored wherever the thiasos, the group of his devotees, stops: a stake driven into the ground and decorated with a mask. But clothing is added to this mask: this is the peplos, reserved for women, the fawn skin and the belt which join together the different parts of the female clothing, the very same as was worn by the Maenads in the *Bacchae* and by initiates in certain mysteries. The mask facilitates wandering and, in a whole series of traditions constructed on the same schema, the presence of Dionysus is revealed through an effigy, a *xoanon*, a wooden statuette left on the seashore or carried someplace by a hallucinating missionary; and this effigy carries with it the dementia of the god, the black flame of his madness.

It is essentially the mask that reveals the presence of the god, and Walter F. Otto is right to observe that the effectiveness of the symbol lies in its being a "pure full face": thus, on the François vase, on which all the gods are aligned in profile, only Dionysus turns his face with its staring eyes toward the observer. He is not represented so that he may be contemplated, like the other gods. Rising out of the night, his mask suddenly seizes its fascinated prey who becomes entranced by that presence from which none can escape, even if the victim shakes his head in an attempt to evade him. One of the sites specially reserved for the epiphany of Dionysus is the shadowy mouth, the lair, the gaping hole in a cliff. Everywhere in Greece there are grottos in which his thiasoi dwell: their walls are covered with hardy climbing plants such as ivy and vines; in Hellenistic times these were called strewings (*stibadeia*), and they served as sacred sites for the celebration of the ceremonies of the cult.

In the same way as he lends himself poorly to a staff of permanent priests, Dionysus does not accept customary forms of piety. In the city as well as in open space, his devotees constitute the thiasos, the unbounded community of those whom he fills with his presence, the informal group in which women, slaves, and citizens dwell side by side. One

Dionysus at a banquet. Attic hydria. Ca. 510 B.C. London, British Museum. Photo Hirmer.

of the major virtues of the cult of Dionysus is to scramble the images of social order, to question the political and masculine values of the city. Dionysus welcomes both the necessity of individual salvation and the forms of protest that result in ruptures in the social fabric. His marginality runs across the whole of the body politic. We must return to the foreign Dionysus to reveal the profound nature of his marginality: it is his *foreignness* that makes him enroll individuals in a shifting order which goes beyond them, not only by welcoming those who are excluded from political cults (like slaves and women) but also by imposing upon the city and causing to emerge out of it, among the Olympians of whom he is a part, the figure of Otherness.

Dionysus is not one of those gods who are enclosed in an atemporal existence. Conceived by a woman, the mortal Semele, then born miraculously from the thigh of Zeus, his thundering father, he never ceases to consort with those who eat bread, and he teaches them to drink the wine that is "rich in joys" (*polugēthēs*) and the pleasure of mortals. But Dionysus comes to draw men and women out of themselves, rendering them strangers to their own narrowly social condition; he possesses them entirely, body and soul, not in order to teach them how to flee this world, but to help them to discover—through the myths and festivals that tell of his abrupt disappearance and his sudden return out of the depths of the sea and the yawning holes in the earth—that life and death twist together and intersect, that the renewal of spring explodes in the memory of all the dead, and that the Same is necessarily inhabited by the Other. This is why, under the name of the Initiated (*Mustēs*), he has himself introduced into his own mysteries: furthermore, in Dionysopolis, the city of his name, he is his own priest for a full year; while when he is doubled, as on the Hope krater, he attends the initiation of one of his devotees whose appearance makes him yet another Dionysus.

If Dionysus's activities involve him in an often tumultuous human history, his interventions especially bring the feminine element to the fore. This was noted by Louis Gernet, following Henri Jeanmaire. Maenadism is a feminine phenomenon; it is the cultivation of madness in which women play a central part. She who is "delirious," she who is

"demented by the wooded mountains" is a familiar figure in the Homeric epic. And in the Hellenistic period, although men are encountered in the mysteries, sometimes as simple initiates, sometimes fulfilling important functions, it is nearly always women who preside over the thiasos and play the part of mystagogues. More exactly, it is married women, rarely young girls. In the mythic tradition of the childhoods and wanderings of Dionysus, the companions who make up the god's following are wives who have been kidnapped from their looms, torn away from their husbands and homes. But often they carry a child in their arms, a baby at the breast that they breast-feed in alternation with young animals, wolf cubs, fawns, or serpents. There is in this female cortege, which is always suspected of using an overly handsome young man for its debaucheries, something akin to an exaltation of the activity proper to a nurse, a status which in Greece implied the bracketing of sexual relations. But although the nurses—and this was sometimes the name given to those possessed by Dionysus (*Iliad* 6.132)—keep their distance from the pleasures of love, and although they sometimes prove to have great sexual modesty, they must remain outside the closed-in space of the house, as far separated from Hestia as they are divorced from the conjugal sphere that is ruled over by Hera. The dominance of the female element in the Dionysian phenomenon only takes on its true meaning in the sociocultural context of a world where order is expressed in terms of masculine values. In a sense, Greek women prepare the way for Dionysus: they are his best accomplices in a city where their silent presence is already like an internal image of Otherness. In the *Bacchae*, it is Agave whose function it is to reverse such roles; and this at the expense of her son, the king of Thebes, who has risen up against the adolescent who came from Lydia with his magic to explode the contradictions of the political order.

Dionysus also invests the politico-religious world, of which he is an integrating part, with one of its most solid bastions: the blood sacrifice consisting of food, which occupies a central place in the social and religious thought of the Greeks. It is central for two essential reasons; the first is that eating meat coincides exactly with the sacrifice. All meat that is eaten comes from an animal victim whose throat has been ritually cut; and the butcher who makes the animals' blood flow has the same functional name as the sacrificer who stands close to the blood-spattered altar. The first function is reinforced by another: the sacrifice is indispensable to social relationships, at every political level. No power in the city could be employed without sacrifices, whether a magistrate's assumption of his duties, the conclusion of a treaty, the opening of a legislative session, or an engagement with an enemy. At the heart of the sacrifice, and throughout all of the practices, a certain model for the human condition is delimited, by contrast with the realm of the gods and the world of animals. The sacrificial victim, taken from among the domestic animals and put to death without any apparent violence—once it has given its consent—is divided into two parts: the bones and fat, put on the fire, are consumed by the flames along with aromatics for the immortals who know neither hunger nor death and who are fed by odors and perfumes; men, who are fated to death and voracity, divide up the viscera which are cooked on skewers and pieces of red meat cooked in caldrons. Although wild beasts eat each other without ceremony, men, being carnivores and masters of fire, measure, at every sacrifice of this kind, the distance that separates them from the divine powers at the very moment when they establish communication with them. It is this system that Dionysus opens to question by means of various subversive procedures. The tradition of Tenedos offers a good example of this. In honor of Dionysus, "the hammerer of men" (*anthrōporrhaistēs*), a cow about to give birth is given the same care as is given to a woman in childbirth at the moment she begins to deliver her offspring. Then the calf that has just been born is shod with buskins and sacrificed; the person who strikes the calf dead with his ax is in turn chased by stone throwers until he reaches the sea. This unusual ritual must surely be seen in the light of an Argive scenario, in which Dionysus is invoked as the god born from a cow, the *bougenēs,* and is invited to rise from the depths of the waters; he had fled there while being pursued by Perseus, who had inherited this role from Lycurgus, who, in the *Iliad,* chases to the sea the young Dionysus who is terrorized by the deadly goad (*bouplēx*) that torments him and his nurses. We need not take from these two interconnected rituals anything but the distortions made upon the sacrificial model: the victim, oscillating between the animal state of a calf and the human condition of a child that has just been born, but also wearing buskins which are shoes worn only by hunters, is put to death by the double-edged ax which is normally the weapon required to kill the ox led in procession before the altar. At the same time, the blind violence of a shower of rocks is turned against the sacrificer, who becomes in turn the hunted victim. And Dionysus, who is here the terrifying hammerer of men, changes the mask of the killer for that of the nursing baby or the frightened child who has suddenly returned from the waters of the abyss in which he had tried to lose himself.

A more specific Dionysian idiosyncrasy characterizes him as an eater of raw flesh. In his tradition, eating raw flesh is a familiar scenario. To tear apart the body of a wild (rather than domesticated) animal that has been captured after a violent pursuit; to chew its raw flesh instead of eating only certain parts, some grilled and others boiled, is, for those possessed by Dionysus, brutally to throw back the barriers erected

Dionysus and the panther. Mosaic from Delos. Second century A.D. Photo École française d'Athènes.

between the gods, beasts, and men by the politico-religious system. Carried away by the hunt which could, in extreme cases, drive mothers to tear apart newborn children as though they were fawns or kids, the devotees of Dionysus turned into savages and thus followed a path which allowed them to escape from the human condition by escaping to the world of animals and becoming bestial; but they did this following the example of a god born from a cow and called Bull by his followers. Even within the city and with its official complicity, Dionysus imposed his manner of eating and sacrifice. Thus, in Miletus in the third century B.C., on the days of public sacrifices the priestess of Dionysus Bacchius performed a ritual act in the name of the city: she put a "mouthful of raw meat" (*ōmophagion*) in the sacred basket. This was not a substitute for any regular animal sacrifice but a discrete reminder of the great hunts for fresh meat that Dionysus led relentlessly over mountains and valleys.

2. Festival, Theater, and Mysteries

Foreign to Olympus, a stranger coming to the city from the mysterious landscapes of the sea, the mountains, or the east, Dionysus, the god who subverted the traditional structures of the sacrifice, was at the same time the privileged son of Zeus, the first cousin of the king of Thebes—his native city—and the god who offered to man the possibility of establishing the most intimate communication with the sacred by means of enthusiasm and possession. The very being of Dionysus is the focal point of all of the important contradictions which human reason is unable to bear alone: between identity and otherness, presence and absence, imagination and reality, the absolute and nothingness, power and fragility, life and death, eternity and transition. An irruption of the sacred into the world, of the miracle at the heart of day-to-day life, of the irrational in the center of the city, he is the very paroxysm of the tragic tension.

The circumstances of his birth indicate that Dionysus represents an exceptional manifestation of the divine in the course of human history, something very close to the (non-Greek) notions of divine incarnation and avatar. Semele is the only mortal whom the Greeks speak of as having given birth to a god: Zeus had impregnated other mortal women, but always after manifesting himself in a relative and finite form (as a shower of gold for Danaë, a swan for Leda, a bull for Europa) and in an act resulting in the birth of heroes; while here it is a god who is born, precisely, we are told, because Zeus sired him by manifesting himself to Semele in his absolute form of lord of Olympus, of the sky, and of the lightning bolt. As a result, Semele dies immediately: Dionysus is conceived in a burst of fire in which all the glory of being and death are simultaneously manifested. He is perhaps the lightning outcome of this tension, and rumblings of thunder would never cease to accompany Bromius, Dionysus the Thunderer.

Once he has completed his period of gestation in the thigh of Zeus, who had sewn him there after the death of Semele, Dionysus, who thus undergoes two successive births, one human and the other divine, begins his career as a terrestrial god. He is the point where the sacred energy in its absolute density enters into the earth: everywhere he goes, plants proliferate and are resplendent, every vital force is carried to its greatest intensity, ferocious animals bow down, dead wood puts forth new growth, marble is undermined by the growth of ivy, hearts are inflamed. But Dionysus is constantly threatened with death, and his presence inspires as much disorder and disaster as joy and fervor.

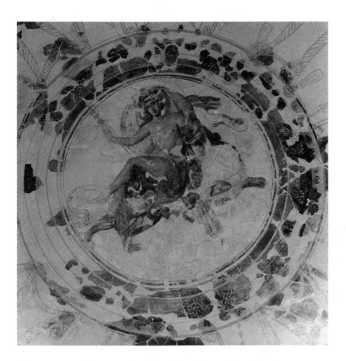

Dionysus and the panther. Painting. Second to third century A.D. Tunis, Bardo Museum. Museum photo.

From his birth, Dionysus is pursued by the jealousy of Hera. Ino, the sister of Semele, raises him, disguised as a girl, in the court of Orchomenus where her husband Athamas reigns. Hera drives Ino and Athamas mad, so that they kill their own children. Ino jumps into the sea with the corpse of the little Melicertes; Dionysus rewards them by changing them into protective marine divinities, thenceforth called Leucothea and Palaemon. The child Dionysus is then brought up by the nymphs, on Mount Nysa (from which, according to the traditional etymology, the god derived his name), in the grottos which his presence covers with ivy and perfume; we see him in the arms of Hermes or the nymphs, or sometimes riding on the backs of lions and panthers.

After surviving a threatened childhood, once Dionysus reached the flower of adolescence—whose hermaphroditic graces would never leave him—he unceasingly strove to make his divine quality recognized by men and his worship definitively installed on earth, following rites which he himself instituted. The order of the sequences of the myth is not immediately clear, as each sequence presents itself as a totality in which the tragic presence of Dionysus is fully manifested.

We see him offering the vine and wine as a gift to Icarius, in Attica. Following the god's advice, Icarius shares the dangerous liquor (*pharmakon*) with some shepherds; the shepherds, drunk with pure wine, believe that they have been poisoned and kill Icarius. His daughter Erigone, with the help of the bitch Maira, finds her father's corpse and hangs herself. Dionysus avenges them: the young girls of Attica are seized with madness and hang themselves, and the god's wrath is appeased only when he obtains from the Athenians the punishment of the shepherds and the institution of rites commemorating the suicide of Erigone.

Elsewhere we see Dionysus appearing "on a jutting promontory, with the features of a young man in early adolescence: his beautiful blue hair floats around him and he wears a dark mantle on his broad shoulders" (*Homeric Hymn I to Dionysus* 3–6). Pirates kidnap him, against the advice of the ship's pilot, who recognizes his divine nature. The ship fills with wine, is covered with bunches of grapes, and "ivy laden with dark flowers curls around the mast" (*ibid.* 40). Dionysus turns into a lion and creates a bear; the captain, who is responsible for this foolish act, is devoured by the lion, while the others jump into the sea where they are turned into dolphins. The pilot, by contrast, is saved and filled with a perfect joy; "*Tharsei*," the god says to him, "Take courage"—using a term characteristic of the mystery religions, which bring the hope of salvation (*ibid.* 55).

In yet another place, we see Dionysus being suddenly attacked by Lycurgus, the king of Thrace, who pursues him to put him to death along with his troop of Bacchae, his nurses who carry his thyrsi; "Wholly lost, Dionysus plunges into the waters of the sea where Thetis, horrified, receives him in her arms" (*Iliad* 6.135–36), and the Bacchae flee, throwing down their thyrsi. In all the versions of this myth, the Bacchae are the victims of Lycurgus and are sometimes put to death. But the god triumphs in the end: either Lycurgus takes his son for the stem of a vine and cuts him into pieces by striking at him viciously with an ax, before being quartered himself (this is the only punishment that can appease Dionysus), or, when he is about to be seized and slain by the blows of an ax, one of the nymphs, Ambrosia, turns herself into the stem of a luxuriant vine that wraps itself around Lycurgus and suffocates him.

In the east, the myth describes Dionysus sometimes as a wanderer driven to madness by Hera and sometimes as a conqueror on his triumphal chariot, followed and preceded by his devotees, satyrs and Bacchae who are seized by enthusiasm. The most detailed accounts of this victorious expedition are also the latest ones (such as the *Dionysiaca* of Nonnus), but the *Bacchae* of Euripides already alludes to this triumphal tour that continues into Persia and Bactria (13–20).

Euripides' play is a particularly rich and ancient illustration of the principal episode in the earthly career of Dionysus, that of his return to Thebes. A rigorous analysis of this work reveals the essential characteristics of Dionysus, above all his relation to the city.

Recognized throughout the world except in Greece, Dionysus finally returns to the city of his birth, still accompanied by his troop of Bacchae; he has taken on the traits of his own priest, appearing as a young Oriental with a long robe and curly hair. The welcome given him by King Pentheus—his cousin—is designed as a nonreception: Pentheus wants his city to be wholly given to virility and clarity, with everything perfectly transparent, rational, and in order. Under no circumstances will he give way to feminine agitation, manifestations of disorder, and the ecstatic dances that the cult of the god inspires. The prophet Tiresias and the venerable Cadmus are wiser; they agree to participate, crowned with ivy, in the follies that the god desires, in which all age-groups become intermingled (209); for they know that the city is not fed on bread alone, but also on wine (274–85). Pentheus scorns them and orders the arrest of Dionysus, who allows himself to be bound in chains. But from this moment on, the city of Thebes enters into an inexorable process of dislocation, which the structure of Euripides' tragedy reveals to its ultimate extent. First of all, inside the city, there is a separation of the sexes: the city is deserted by its women, who go into the mountains to join the Bacchae and the god; next, the palace of the king, the center of power, is dislocated—the marble, a symbol of civil authority, breaks up just as the flame of Zeus reignites on the tomb of Semele.

Dionysus with a gecko. Mosaic. Third to fourth century A.D. Tunis, Bardo Museum. Museum photo.

During this time, the city is assailed from the outside: on the city limits, the Bacchae miraculously cause water, wine, milk, and honey to spring forth (705–11). They then attack the grazing areas, putting the shepherds to flight and cutting the herds into pieces; next they invade the cultivated fields, where they pillage the harvests. They finish by knocking down the houses of the town and confronting the armed men, whom they "attack and rout, they, the women" (748–64). These unhappy events fail to enlighten Pentheus, who remains obstinate and refuses to listen to the warnings of Dionysus. It is now the king himself who falls into the trap: he, virility itself, allows himself to be dressed as a woman; he, the center of the city, permits himself to be led into the mountains to see "what is not allowed," wearing the clothing of one of the Bacchae (912–17). The trap closes in on him: the women take the king for a wild beast, uproot the tree in which he has hidden, and tear him apart—and the drama ends with the triumphal entry of Agave, who brandishes, in the center of the city, the head of her son the king, whom she still takes to be a wild animal; and she invites the city to join in a cannibalistic meal whose victim is the person of the king himself (1242). The dislocation of the city has reached its extreme: the time has finally come for Dionysus to manifest himself in all his glory to impose his worship definitively upon a penitent Thebes.

The greatest insanity (Tiresias and Cadmus never cease, from the beginning of the tragedy, to treat Pentheus as a raving madman) was to have wished for a perfectly reasonable city and to have left no room for the irrational, for the unexpected (1391), for wild forces, for that disquieting part of femininity that must necessarily inhabit the city if it is to maintain its fertility: that is, room for the sacred itself in its unforeseeable manifestation but also in its everyday manifestation. Without Dionysus, the succession of generations and the rebirth of the harvest and of fruits cannot occur; a city that is perfectly governed and in order is in reality a city that is already dead, and Dionysus is that irrepressible greenery at the heart of the city which unceasingly puts its existence in question but which is its very life. As the threat

of death, he is life: the extreme components of his original being are present more than ever in this final episode of the earthly history of the god.

Yet, even as Dionysus animates the city, he goes beyond it. This god who is manifest in the world is at the same time a savior god, the guarantor of a mysterious hope for salvation. Two sequences of the myth, which form a coda to the adventures of the god, are particularly useful in bringing to light these aspects of Dionysus. First there is his *katabasis,* his descent into Hades, from which he succeeds in delivering his mother Semele, who, thanks to her son, is thus granted a dispensation from the fate common to mortals after their death. Then there is the assumption of Ariadne: abandoned by Theseus on the rocks of Naxos, this woman believes that she is completely lost, but Dionysus descends from his celestial home where he has rejoined the immortals to come to her as a husband and share his glory with her.

This is the final sequence of the myth properly so-called. But just as Dionysus himself was an irruption of the divine into the heart of the everyday, his myth overflows myth to become engraved in history. This god, who came once, comes back again. In various ways, he never ceases to haunt the human world.

Ritually, the city welcomes him every year in the course of its great civic festivals. As the master of all verdure and all vital renewal, he manifests himself at Athens at the time of the spring festival of the Anthesteria (February–March), the "flower festival." After a procession in a chariot that has the shape of a ship—undoubtedly an allusion to the return of the god from the foreign regions of the sea in which the Nereids had offered him refuge—the Basilissa, wife of the Archon King, would unite carnally with Dionysus in the Boucoleion, thus ensuring the fertility of the entire city for the coming year. Other celebrations of the coming of Dionysus set the whole collectivity in motion, whenever this master of every manifestation and of every illusion, of every tragic shudder but also of all gaiety (*polugēthēs:* Hesiod *Works and Days* 614), came to bring myths back to life in the theater. In classical Athens, this took place in the countryside during the rural

Dionysia (December–January), and in the city at the time of the Lenaea (January–February), whose name comes from the *Lēnai*, another term for the Bacchae. The greatest theatrical manifestations took place in the urban Dionysia (March–April): the people went to Eleustherae, in the mountains, in the confines of Boeotia, to search for Dionysus Eleuthereus (i.e., of Eleutherae, but also the Liberator) in order to bring him with great pomp into the city and to his temple close to the theater. Then there would be contests in dithyramb, in which members of choruses competed by the hundreds in honor of the god. Finally the days would come that were consecrated to dramatic contests in which, from morning until night, tragedies, comedies, and satiric dramas were performed by hundreds of people, while the remainder of the population came as spectators. The theatrical evocation of the myths was made possible by the magic of the god: around his altar, in the center of the orchestra, the dramatic action unfolded; it was with the sound of his favorite instrument, the *aulos*, the disquieting oboe (the opposite of the soothing lyre of Apollo), that the spectacle opened, and to its rhythm that the drama that followed unfolded; under the supervision of his priest the myths became incarnate, thanks to the genius of the tragic and comic poets who were themselves devotees, inspired by the god. Dionysus thus aroused for the city the resurrection of the gods and heroes, when he made the masks, the favorite symbols of this master of appearances and apparitions, move and speak, thus inspiring in the spectator the shudder of sacred horror or the delirium of the liberating laugh. The city sat in assembly at the theater (the meeting of the *ecclesia* in the theater at the end of the competition is a positive proof of this), but this was a subverted city, whose form recalled that of the Pnyx, but reversed, with barriers abolished, age-groups mixed together, and women, slaves, and children authorized—at least in principle—to attend; resident aliens (metics) and foreigners were numerous. All of the city is thus set in motion, spending money and living for days in an imaginary world that passes for the first level of reality. Finally, the city shares the heroic condition at the moment when the victorious poet, chorus leader, and protagonist are carried in triumph, crowned, and assimilated to the glorious beings whose reincarnation they have successfully brought about on the stage. Ordinarily, Dionysus, the leader of the game, did not appear: we can only guess with what intensity his presence must have been felt when he appeared as the leading character (the only god whose role was entrusted to the protagonist) in plays that, like the *Bacchae*, brought his own myth to life.

The epiphany of the god could take place in completely different forms: his presence, in all its tragic and climactic intensity, could manifest itself individually to his followers through the celebration of the mysteries into which they were initiated. We have little explicit information on the actual performance of the *teletai* (a word meaning "realization") in the classical age. Carried out by the thiasoi of initiates, these were in any case ritual practices whose goal was to provoke states of trance experienced as possession by the god and ecstatic communication with him. As all-powerful lord of the spirits (he could rout the most powerful armies by breathing his madness into them; cf. *Bacchae* 302–5), he can easily possess his followers by imposing on them the mania that makes Maenads of them. Dionysus polarized around himself the orgiastic aspects of Greek religious life, with its possession and ecstasy accompanied by the use of certain rhythms, sounds, and ritual incantations. The god who came into the world is also the one with

whom men can establish a personal and direct relationship; he lives at the heart of all of the places that are the most charged with the sacred and is present at Delphi with Apollo as well as at Eleusis with Demeter. In its external forms, the celebration of the mysteries seems above all to consist of an imitation, on the part of his followers, of the mythological votaries of the god. Through a process of identification, in certain places that are made special by myths, such as the solitudes of mountains or caves, his followers, wearing fawn-skins or carrying thyrsi, became the actors in the Dionysian adventure and reestablished in their midst the personal presence of the god. This identification is clearly suggested by a text such as the *Bacchae*, in which Autonoë, Ino, and Agave (and even Pentheus), forced to become adepts of Dionysus, end up becoming indistinguishable from the Bacchae of the chorus, and in which the priest and Dionysus are one and the same character. This identification is present in thousands of pictorial representations in which the mystic thiasos is led by Dionysus in person, and the devotees are depicted with the traits of their archetypal models—Sileni, satyrs, or Bacchae—and are often accompanied by a mule, a comic figure whose presence remains to be explained (a figure that Aristophanes does not fail to introduce in his *Frogs*, in a disrespectful parody of the *katabasis* of Dionysus). The identification is explicitly described in certain historical texts (e.g., Diodorus 9.3) and is presupposed by the names of the different grades of the initiates, which are known to us in detail through inscriptions (though these are late, second century A.D.). Everywhere, the success of the theater and the mysteries accompanied the progress of Hellenism, thus perpetuating the living presence of Dionysus in the heart of the ancient world. It is not surprising that he did the ancients the favor of returning to them in all his glory to live new earthly adventures: Alexander was a new Dionysus, and his epic cannot be understood without constant reference to the story of the god. After him, Antony and many others were *Neoi Dionusioi* (New Dionysi): the myth died out only with the Dionysian cult itself.

J.-P.D./d.w.

3. Dionysus and the Orphics

In Greek mysticism, Dionysus occupies a central position, first through his own mysteries and second through the major role given him in the theogony and the anthropogonic myth of the disciples of Orpheus. From the fourth century B.C., the killing of Dionysus by the Titans made it possible to explain the state of man, thrown into the world, and was at the origin of the way of life invented by Orpheus for the salvation of the individual soul. The murder committed by the Titans unfolds according to a strange scenario: covered with plaster, the assassins attract the young Dionysus by offering him toys (dolls with moving parts, a top, knuckle bones, and a mirror), and, taking advantage of his astonishment, they strike him down, cut him into pieces, and indulge in a horrible act of cooking. The pieces of his body are tossed into a caldron to boil, after which the Titans skewer them to cook them on a grill. And they have time to swallow all of this boiled and roasted meal except for the heart, which is saved from the destruction reserved by the thunderbolt of Zeus for the killers. Their ashes, mixed with earth, give birth to the human race.

The sacrifice in which Dionysus is the victim is strange both in its procedures and in the place that is given to it by a religious movement whose identifying traits include the absolute refusal to eat meat or to offer blood sacrifices in

Dionysus and Acme with Icarius and the first wine drinkers. Mosaic from Nea-Paphos. Third century A.D. Cyprus Museum. Museum photo.

homage to the immortals. Like the Pythagoreanism which was contemporaneous with it, Orphism is a form of religious protest that challenges the politico-religious system founded upon the distance that separates men from gods. And the chosen route is a regimented diet: Orpheus, the ancient tradition says, came to teach men to abstain from murders (*phonoi*), i.e., not to kill anything animated and alive. Abstinence from meat in the Orphic way of life is an imperative that imposes a rupture with the organized world of the city. It is thus in connection with blood sacrifice that the various details of the killing of Dionysus must be interpreted. Two such details clearly indicate that the murder takes place on the level of sacrifice. First there is the care taken to strike the victim down with a knife, the sacrificial weapon, while avoiding anything that would frighten him or lead him to resist. Next is the use of skewers and of the caldron, which show unambiguously that everything is taking place according to the economy of the regular sacrifice, in which the cooking of the meats is a fundamental operation. But although the Orphic myth refers to the sacrifice, it is not an apology for it. One aspect that seems to indicate this is the inversion between the skewer and the caldron in the cooking which the Titans do. The ritual order is from roasting to boiling: the ritual begins with the grilling of the viscera, which are consumed by the narrow circle of worshipers eating together, and then continues with the cooking of the pieces of meat by boiling them in a caldron. The order which goes from roasting to boiling is simultaneously temporal and cultural; it is that of a humanity committed to a path that leads from the bad to the better, and thus it is a reminder, through ritual gestures, of the fact that man ate grilled food before he learned the art of stewing. By reversing this, i.e., by roasting the boiled food, the Titans deny the positive character of the sacrificial cuisine. The actors themselves, covered with plaster, are not only the ancestors of the human race but are also, by their status as primordial beings and their half-terrestrial, half-igneous nature, the dramatic prefiguration of the first carnivores, men. Their name, formed from *titanos*, ''quicklime,'' particularly qualified them to play the role of ancestors of a race that is deeply rooted in the earth, and perhaps also qualified them to be reduced to ashes by the avenging fire from the sky.

The entire dramatization of the murder of Dionysus is intended to show that the blood sacrifice that is eaten is originally an act of cannibalism, a meal of reciprocal eating in which the Titans, the first living beings to emerge from the earth, acted as the murderers of a child whose carefully cooked parts they gobbled up. The myth of Dionysus comes to illustrate directly the major teaching brought by Orpheus: that one must abstain from murder, in the two senses of not eating meat and of putting an end to the slaughter of human beings. Throughout the account, which parallels the Hesiodic myth of Prometheus, Orpheus teaches men that they must refuse to practice any blood sacrifice, given the fact that the ritual, far from allowing them to establish a relationship with the gods, reproduces a crime in a barely disguised form; that the human race would not cease to participate in that crime as long as it refused to recognize its Titanic descent; and that they must attempt to purify, by means of a new way of life, the divine element that was locked away inside it by the voracity of those who had slaughtered the young Dionysus long ago.

Orphism's choice of Dionysus is not without consequences for the relations between the two movements, since at the heart of the Dionysian cult there is the practice of omophagia—the eating of raw meat—which is the homologue of Orphic vegetarianism, but which employs wholly different means to a similar end. In Dionysian religion, one escapes by becoming beastlike, whereas in Orphic religion, the same process is carried out, but on the side of the gods, by refusing to eat any meat and by eating only perfectly pure foods such as those reserved for the gods. Yet there is more to Dionysus than the orientation toward violence, toward all-devouring, frenetic cannibalism; for the extreme savagery that he carries with him leads, by the same token, to the obliteration of all distance between the divine and the human. The golden age constantly skirts the bestial state, and Dionysus passes without transition from a paradisiacal world to the madness of the wild hunt. In the *Bacchae*, for example, while the maenads nurse young wolves, honey drips from ivy leaves. But suddenly the mountain goes into a trance, along with its wild animals, and the Bacchae descend upon a herd of oxen, tearing them limb from limb and ripping their flesh apart. Drawing on this Dionysian

Indian triumph of Dionysus. Mosaic. Third century A.D. Sousse, Archaeological Museum. Photo Baudot-Lamotte.

Persephone that Zeus finally gives the royal power: Dionysus would be the last sovereign, as the sixth generation marks a return to the first. And Dionysus is none other than another name of Phanes: through Zeus's mediation, the luminous firstborn of the origins is identified with this last-born who would become the new young king of the gods and the world. His rebirth closes the circle of the divine generations, just as his death at the hands of the Titans opened for the human race the cycle of births and generation. Orphism thus bends a part of the Dionysian cult in such a way as to enhance its role as a religion of salvation. But at the same time, the Orphic movement comes to fill in the theological void of the Dionysian cults, which seem to have been richer in initiatory practices than in theoretical discourse.

M.D./d.w.

BIBLIOGRAPHY

H.-C. BALDRY, *Greek Tragic Theater* (London 1971). P. BOYANCÉ, "L'antre dans les mystères de Dionysos," *Rendiconti. Atti della Pontificia Accademia Romana di Archeologia* 33 (1960–61): 107ff. W. BURKERT, *Homo Necans: Interpretationen altgriechischer Opferriten und Mythen* (Berlin and New York 1972). M. DETIENNE, *Dionysos mis à mort* (Paris 1977). EURIPIDES, *Bacchae*. A.-J. FESTUGIÈRE, *Études de religion grecque et hellénistique* (Paris 1972). A. HENRICHS, *Die Phoinika des Lollianos: Fragmente eines neuen griechischen Romans* (Bonn 1972). H. HERTER, *Von dionysischen Tanz zum komischen Spiel* (Iserlohn 1947). H. G. HORN, *Mysteriensymbolik auf dem Kölner Dionysosmosaïk* (Bonn 1972). H. JEANMAIRE, *Dionysos: Histoire du culte de Bacchus* (Paris 1951, 1970). K. J. KAKOURI, *Dionysiaka* (Athens 1965). K. KÉRÉNYI, *Dionysos: Archetypal Image of Indestructible Life* (Princeton 1976). F. NIETZSCHE, *The Birth of Tragedy* (New York 1956), original in German. W. F. OTTO, *Dionysos: Mythos und Kultus* (Frankfurt am Main 1933), also in French. D. M. PIPPIDI, *Scythica Minora* (Amsterdam 1975). E. POCHMARSKI, *Das Bild des Dionysos in der Rundplastik der klassichen Zeit Griechenlands* (Vienna 1974). R. TURCAN, *Les sarcophages romains à représentation dionysiaque: Essai de chronologie et d'histoire religieuse* (Paris 1967).

double movement, Orphism attempted to retain what would allow it to short-circuit the politico-religious system through practices proper to the golden age. In becoming the pitiful victim of a monstrous crime, Dionysus took on a new status in Orphic theology: he became the final term in a series of powers, of which he was also the principle and the initiator.

In the system called *The Theogony of the Rhapsodes*, six divine generations follow in succession: Phanes, also called Metis, was the first to emerge in a flash of light; he then passed on his scepter of sovereignty to Night; Ouranos, then Kronos, succeeded her, and Zeus is the fifth sovereign, whose power was established with the aid of the advice of Night and the complicity of Phanes-Metis, swallowed up by the new king of the gods. It is to the son of his union with

THE DIOSCURI

In the mythology of the Greeks, the Dioscuri are a pair of mediators who are sometimes referred to as "the young boys of Zeus," sometimes as "the two Lords," and sometimes as "the two gods." They are twins, born to Leda and Tyndareos, the king of Sparta, and to his double, Zeus, the lord of the luminous sky, who transformed himself into a swan to unite with the king's wife. Pausanias saw in a temple of Sparta the egg to which Leda gave birth and from which emerged not only the two brothers but also their sister, the beautiful Helen.

The pair of twins concentrates, between its two terms, a whole series of differential traits. Castor is a mortal, since he is the son of Tyndareos, but Pollux, born of Zeus, receives immortality. But this allotment becomes even more intimate in the myth of the theft of the oxen during the war between the Dioscuri and the Apharetids: when Castor loses his life, Pollux, who cannot bear to be separated from his twin,

obtains from Zeus the right to share his immortality with his brother. And from that time on, the Dioscuri have been called *heteromēres;* they live and die from one day to the next, living one day on Mount Olympus and the next day at Therapne, where their tomb is found. There are two possible ways of looking at this: either the two brothers share a day in heaven and a day in their tomb, or else one of the two undergoes death for a day in alternation with the other, who is immortal on that day. On the astronomical level, each of the two viewpoints has its merits: the Dioscuri make up the Gemini, "whose stars rise side by side and sink side by side below the horizon." On the other hand, they are the two aspects of the planet Venus, identified with the Morning Star and the Evening Star, of which one rises when the other sets.

Castor is a warrior, while Pollux's strength is ruled by his intelligence; Castor can run faster, while Pollux wins at boxing, a sport invented by the *kouros* Apollo, who himself beats Ares in pugilism just as he is victorious over Hermes in the footrace. Pollux is often represented with a dog, while his brother is mounted on a horse; Castor invents hunting with horses and Pollux invents hunting with a pack of hounds.

The Dioscuri on horseback. Chalcidian krater. Ca. 520 B.C. Würzburg, Martin von Wagner Museum. Museum photo.

Their duality plays an important role in the double sovereignty of Sparta: one of the kings is associated with the Zeus of the Sky (Ouranios) and the other with the Zeus of mortals, of the Lacedaemonians. When Sparta goes to war against its enemies, the battle is led by only one king at a time. The king who is in charge brings with him one of the Dioscuri, undoubtedly the warrior Castor, as the Spartans fight to the music of the song "of Castor," and Castor is the patron god of the Horsemen, the group of the Hippeis, the Three Hundred, who are chosen to make up the king's guard and are dressed in red like Castor "of the red mantle (chlamus)."

At Rome, as well, the Castors seem to be governed by the same complementarity, whose Indo-European origin is demonstrated by the differences found between the Indian pair of the Nāsatyau, made up of Nakula and Sahadeva.

As the "young boys of Zeus," the Dioscuri are connected not only with sovereignty but also, still at Sparta, with the class of young men, of whom they are the patron gods, presiding over their training for battle, the work in the gymnasium, and the athletic life on the shores of the Eurotas. They were also honored in festivals at which war dances were performed in their honor, of which the most famous—the Pyrrhis—mimed a combat by means of a complex series of geometric figures. A more specific ritual emphasizes their relationship with human society: this is the Theoscenia, a festival of hospitality offered to the gods, performed by a college of priests and directed by a person called "the one who welcomes the gods" (sidektos), who is charged with setting up for the guests a table covered with food of a bygone era (such as cheese, dry cakes, olives, and leeks). The Dioscuri also have a house in Sparta, close to the sanctuary of the armed Aphrodite and to the dwelling in which the egg of Leda is preserved, to which women come each year to weave a garment for the Apollo of Amyclae. It was in this house that the Tyndarids introduced themselves in the guise of handsome foreigners who said they came from Cyrene and asked to be lodged in the room that had pleased them the most when they had lived among men. The owner could not satisfy their desire because that room was occupied by his virgin daughter. But on the next day the daughter had disappeared, along with the strange visitors, and as a souvenir of their passing through they left in that most secret part of the dwelling statues of the Dioscuri and a

table on which was a silphion, the mysterious tuberous plant from the land of Cyrene.

This story highlights the affinities that the Tyndarids had for the inside of human space, affinities that are also emphasized in certain familiar emblems of the Dioscuri: the serpent, the double amphoras, and the double beam (the dokana), that wooden frame that symbolizes both the stabilizing force of the house and the indissoluble brotherhood of which Plutarch speaks. The Dioscuri are saviors, not only because they hold together solidly and steadily what is the foundation of humanity, but also because they can intervene suddenly, with rapid, lightning action. Thus, at sea, for sailors in peril, they appear as the Light Bearers (the Phosphori), shining at the tip of the mast. Navigators in distress offer them sacrifices of white sheep slaughtered in the poop of the ship and ask them to calm the winds of the tempest, to drive away the dark clouds, and in the frightening night to make that light shine which the bright color of their sacrificial victims evokes. This mode of action is defined by Plutarch in specific terms: "They do not navigate with men, nor do they share their dangers, but they appear in the sky and are saviors." At sea as well as in the battles in which they appear as the two horsemen of light, the Dioscuri bring an instantaneous salvation and then disappear into the invisible, where their presence is never invoked in vain.

J.C./d.w.

BIBLIOGRAPHY

E. BETHE, "Dioskuren," in Pauly/Wissowa, Real-Encyclopädie, 1903, cols. 1089–1123. F. CHAPOUTHIER, Les Dioscures au service d'une déesse: Essai d'iconographie religieuse (Paris 1935). R. SCHILLING, "Les Castores romains à la lumière des traditions indo-européennes," Hommage à G. Dumézil (Brussels 1960), 186. G. DUMÉZIL, La religion romaine archaïque (2d ed., Paris 1974), 414–16; English trans., Archaic Roman Religion (Chicago 1970).

EROS

It is in Hesiod that the figure of Eros first appears in ancient Greece. In the Theogony, Eros is, after Chaos and Gaea (the Earth), one of the three primordial divinities:

> Chaos was first of all, but next appeared broad-bosomed Earth, sure-standing place for all . . . , and Eros (Love), most beautiful of all the deathless gods. He makes men weak, he overpowers the clever mind, and tames the spirit in the breasts of men and gods. (Theogony 116–22; trans. Dorothea Wender, Hesiod and Theognis [New York 1981 (1973)], p. 27)

Introduced in this way, the activity of Eros is universal, in that it is extended to all beings, both gods and men. Furthermore, given the primordial position that he enjoyed, the activity is in all likelihood invested with a demiurgical character.

Paradoxically, however, the first generations are made without his assistance:

> From Chaos came black Night and Erebus. And Night in turn gave birth to Day and Space whom she conceived in love to Erebus. And Earth bore starry Heaven (Ouranos), first, to be an equal to herself, to cover her all over, and to

be a resting place, always secure, for all the blessed gods. Then she brought forth long hills, the lovely homes of goddesses, the Nymphs who live among the mountain clefts. Then, without pleasant love, she bore the barren sea with its swollen waves, Pontus. (*Theogony* 123–32)

It is only at this stage that the activity of Eros becomes manifested:

And then she lay with Heaven, and bore deep-whirling Oceanus and Coeus; then Crius, Iapetus, Hyperion, Thea, Themis, Mnemosyne, lovely Tethys, and Phoebe, the golden-crowned. Last, after these, most terrible of sons, the crooked-scheming Kronos came to birth who was his vigorous father's enemy. (*Theogony* 132–38)

Now Hesiod explains the hatred of Kronos for Ouranos in this way:

And these most awful sons of Earth and Heaven were hated by their father from the first. As soon as each was born, Ouranos hid the child in a secret hiding place in Earth and would not let it come to see the light, and he enjoyed his wickedness. But she, vast Earth, being strained and stretched inside her, groaned. (*Theogony* 154–60; trans. Wender, p. 28)

Consequently it is as if Eros, from the time he arises, weaves ties between Gaea and Ouranos that effect a union so strong as to halt, in a sense, the ongoing process of generation and, in so doing, brings on a reverse movement back to Chaos.

In order that the course of the generations may begin again, a good distance between Gaea (the Earth) and Ouranos (the Sky) has to be established, as their extreme proximity constitutes an intolerable state. It is in this sense that one must interpret the act of Kronos when he cuts off the sexual organ of his father, Ouranos—an act which provokes the separation which permits the children to whom Gaea (the Earth) had given birth to emerge into the light:

But the hidden boy stretched forth his left hand; in his right he took the great long jagged sickle; eagerly he harvested his father's genitals and threw them off behind. They did not fall from his hands in vain, for all the bloody drops that leaped out were received by Earth; and when the year's time was accomplished, she gave birth to the Furies, and the Giants, strong and huge, who fought in shining armor, with long spears, and the nymphs called Meliae on the broad earth. The genitals, cut off with adamant and thrown into the stormy sea, were carried for a long time on the waves. White foam surrounded the immortal flesh, and in it grew a girl. At first it touched on holy Cythera, from there it came to Cyprus, circled by the waves. And there the goddess came forth, lovely, much revered, and grass grew up beneath her delicate feet. Her name is Aphrodite among men and gods, because she grew up in the foam, and Cytherea, for she reached that land, and Cyrpogenes from that stormy place where she was born, and Philommedes from the genitals, by which she was conceived. Eros (Love) is her companion; fair Desire (Himeros) followed her from the first, both at her birth and when she joined the company of the gods. From the beginning, both among gods and men, she had this honor and received this power: Fond murmurings of girls, and smiles, and tricks, and sweet delight, and friendliness, and charms. (*Theogony* 178–206; trans. Wender, p. 29)

This act of Kronos thus destroys the extreme proximity of Gaea and Ouranos, whose excessive embraces blocked the ongoing process of generation. Yet even in accomplishing this necessary separation, this same act ensures a complementary union: from the sperm which escaped into the sea from the genitals of Ouranos was born Aphrodite, and she, in a sense, assumes the function of Eros, who, along with Himeros, accompanies her from the beginning. Thus we see established between Gaea and Ouranos, and consequently between all beings, a good distance at which union and separation, proximity and distance, become balanced. After this, all of the other gods and goddesses would be engendered with the help of Aphrodite, and thus of Eros, who is inseparable from her—with some exceptions, of which the most famous are Athena and Hephaestus.

In this perspective then, Eros, a primordial divinity who yields his place to Aphrodite and then accompanies her, is given a demiurgic function by Hesiod, to the extent that he appears as the principle of union that ensures the generation of all beings—when he does not block this process through the effects of an excess of his power. This demiurgic function is also recognized in Pherecydes (DK 7 B 3, A 11), Parmenides (DK 28 B 13), Empedocles (DK 31 B 17, 27, etc.), and Acusilaus of Argos (DK 9, B 2, 3 = FGrH 2 F 6).

But it is Orphism which systematizes and generalizes this aspect of Eros. The god who emerges from the primordial egg is named Eros by Aristophanes:

There was Chaos at first, and Darkness and Night, and Tartarus vasty and dismal; but the Earth was not there, nor the Sky nor the Air, till at length in the bosom abysmal of darkness an egg, from the whirlwind conceived, was laid by the sable-plumed Night. And out of that egg, as the Seasons revolved, sprang Love, the entrancing, the bright, Love brilliant and bold with his pinions of gold, like a whirlwind, refulgent and sparkling! Love hatched us commingling in Tartarus wide with Chaos, the murky, the darkling, and brought us above, as the firstlings of love, and first to the light we ascended. There was never a race of Immortals at all till Love had the universe blended; then all things commingling together in love, there arose the fair Earth and the Sky, and the limitless Sea, and the race of the Gods, the Blessed, who never shall die. (*Birds* 693–702, trans. Benjamin Bickley Rogers, *Aristophanes*, 2, Cambridge, MA (1924), 1961)

As for the twenty-four books of the *Rhapsodies*, which, according to Damascius (OF 60), constitute the customary Orphic theology, these give this god the names of Phanes, Eros, Metis, Protogonos, and Erikepaios. And from this Phanes-Eros come all of the other gods, including Night (who plays the role of his mother, wife, and daughter); Zeus becomes him by swallowing him, before recreating the gods and creating the universe. Finally, Dionysus is identified with this same Phanes-Eros when Zeus restores his power to him even while he is still a child. Drawn into an ambush, the child is killed by the Titans, who dismember and then eat him, after preparing him by a cuisine which reverses that of the traditional sacrifice of the Promethean kind. Only the heart is saved by Athena, who brings it to Zeus so that he can revive Dionysus. And in order to avenge the murder of Dionysus, Zeus reduces the Titans to ashes, from which arise men, who, because of this, are constituted of two parts; one part comes from the Titans and the other from Dionysus, whom they swallowed.

This is why men should seek to purify themselves of the Titanic part that is in them, in such a way as to identify themselves totally with the Dionysian part, in order to escape reincarnation into other men, or even into animals. To

Aphrodite and Eros. Marble. Paris, Musée du Louvre. Photo Giraudon.

Eros, flying, with a lyre. Attic amphora. Ca. 450 B.C. Paris, Musée du Louvre. Photo Giraudon.

he follows, is confined exclusively to the level of the amorous relations between the gods and between men.

It is, moreover, probably this proximity of Eros to Aphrodite that allows him to be made a descendent of Aphrodite. Sappho makes Eros the son of Aphrodite and Ouranos (frag. 198, Lobel-Page PLF); Ibycus, the son of Aphrodite (and of Hephaestus) (frag. 43, Page *PMG*); Simonides, the son of Aphrodite and Ares (frag. 70, Page *PMG*); and Cicero, the son of Aphrodite (the second, the daughter of Zeus and Dione) and Hermes (*De natura deorum* 3.60). Elsewhere, Pindar (frag. 122, 124, 128, Schroeder, Leipzig [Teubner], 1900), Bacchylides (*Epiniceia* 8.72ff.), and Apollonius of Rhodes (*Argonautica* 3.26) makes him the son of Aphrodite without specifying his paternal lineage.

And it is this image of Eros, related to Aphrodite by proximity and/or descent, who appears in the form of a cherub carrying a bow and arrows or a torch and escorting Aphrodite. This image was definitively cast by Alexandrian poetry and was preserved until the present time in part through the medium of Byzantine and Latin poetry and in part through the numerous representations of all sorts that attempted to give it a material form.

But let us leave the field of poetry and iconography and occupy ourselves with the major transformations which the many aspects of the mythical figure of Eros undergo in a philosophical text of the highest importance—Plato's *Symposium*.

In this dialogue, six characters praise Eros, following the rules of the literary mode of the eulogy in ancient Greece (Aristotle *Rhetoric* 1.9.1367b.28–36). Phaedrus, Agathon, Pausanias, Eryximachus, Aristophanes, and Socrates begin by defining the nature of Eros so that they can consider the benefits that should derive from this nature.

The six eulogies of Eros may be regrouped into three pairs, in which an internal opposition may be discerned. For Phaedrus and Agathon, there is but one Eros; but although Phaedrus holds him to be the oldest of the gods, Agathon maintains that he is the youngest. Then Pausanias and Eryximachus state that there are two Eroses who correspond

this end, they must abstain from eating meat, which in this perspective would be the equivalent of a murder and an act of cannibalism. And in becoming Dionysus, those men who abstain from the crime of the Titans would be united with all of the gods, and especially with Phanes-Eros, inasmuch as Dionysus is identified with him.

All in all, Eros, by whatever name he is given, plays a primordial and universal role in Orphism, on the level of theogony as well as cosmogony and anthropogony.

By contrast, throughout the rest of Greek tradition, except in Hesiod, where the role of Eros on the theogonic and cosmogonic levels is sketched without ever being truly developed, Eros appears inseparable from Aphrodite, for whom he plays the role of escort. Furthermore, his role, which is secondary to that of Aphrodite, whose instructions to the two Aphrodites, the Ouranian and the Pandemian; but while Pausanias examines the consequences of this duality only in the case of man, Eryximachus extends his investigation to all living beings. Finally, Aristophanes and Socrates pose the problem at another level. For Aristophanes, Eros is the only god who can let us realize the goal of every human being: the reunion with the half of himself from which he had been separated by Zeus. For Socrates, who reports the words of Diotima, a priestess of Mantinea, Eros is not a god, but a daemon, whose function as intermediary makes it possible to transform the aspiration toward the beautiful and the good (which all men feel) into a perpetual possession, by means of procreation for the body and creation for the soul.

In a still more general sense, while the two first pairs of the discussion—those of Phaedrus and Agathon and of Pausanias and Eryximachus—are based on traditional theology, as transmitted by Hesiod in particular and by the majority of the poets in general, the third pair in the discussion, consisting of Aristophanes (in whom we find a very clear Orphic influence) and Socrates (who reports the words of Diotima), refers to religious movements that are more or less marginal to ancient Greece.

But let us resume our analysis of Plato's *Symposium*. We will begin with the speeches of Phaedrus and of Agathon, for whom there is but one Eros. For Phaedrus (*Symposium* 178a–80b), who bases his assertion on the testimonies of Hesiod (*Theogony* 116ff., *supra*), Parmenides (DK 28 B 13), and Acusilaus of Argos (DK 9 B 2), Eros is the oldest of the gods. And, because of his seniority, he is the god whose benefits are the greatest. He has the greatest dignity and authority in leading men to possess merit and happiness, both when they live and when they are dead, whether they love or are loved, and whether they are men or women.

For Agathon (*Symp.* 194e–97e), by contrast, Eros is the youngest god, the most delicate and the most changeable. And, because he is also just, temperate, and courageous, it is these virtues which he inspires as benefits in those who venerate him. But, in opposition to Phaedrus and Agathon, Pausanias and Eryximachus state that there are two Eroses.

Pausanias (*Symp.* 180c–85c) begins with this postulation: "Everyone knows that Aphrodite and Eros are inseparable" (*Symp.* 180d 3–4). But there are two Aphrodites, the one being the Ouranian Aphrodite born of the sperm which flows from the genitals of Ouranos into the sea (*Theogony* 178–206, *supra*), and the other the Pandemian Aphrodite, who is the daughter of Zeus and Dione (Homer *Iliad* 5.370), and each of them has her temple at Athens (for the Ouranian Aphrodite see Pausanias 1.19.2; for the Pandemian Aphrodite see Pausanias 1.22.3). Similarly, one must distinguish two Eroses. The Eros who is related to the Pandemian Aphrodite, and whose birth involved the participation of a male principle and a female principle, has three characteristics: he works his influence on women as well as men; he is as interested in the body as in the soul, if not more interested; and he is more concerned with the accomplishment of an act than in how it is accomplished.

By contrast, the Eros who is related to the Ouranian Aphrodite, who is the oldest and whose birth only involved the intercession of a male principle, has three characteristics that are opposed to those of the Eros who is related to the Pandemian Aphrodite: he works his influence on men alone; he is interested only in the soul and not in the body; and he is more concerned with how an act is effected than with its effective realization. From this, Pausanias justifies the rule of conduct in force in Attica with regard to the problem of knowing whether it is right for a boy who is loved to bestow

Phanes-Eros. Bas-relief. Second century A.D. Modena Museum. Photo Soprintendenza.

his favors on his lovers. This rule is invested with an absolute character in Elis, as well as in Lacedaemonia and Boeotia, where the phenomenon is considered to be beautiful and good, while in Ionia and among the barbarians the same phenomenon is considered to be ugly and bad. On the other hand, this same rule varies in Attica according to whether the Eros in question is related to the Pandemian Aphrodite or the Ouranian Aphrodite. In the former case, it is ugly and bad for the beloved boy to bestow his favors on his lovers; in the second case, it is beautiful and good.

But while Pausanias applies the distinction that he has made between the two Aphrodites, and consequently between the two Eroses who are indissociable from the two goddesses, only to human beings, Eryximachus (*Symp.* 185e–88e) extends it to all beings. With this generalization he reviews the applications of his distinction in the spheres of medicine, astronomy, and divination.

With Aristophanes and Socrates, the eulogies of Eros take an altogether different turn. Although the four speeches that have just been mentioned take part in a process of interpretation and thus of transformation of the traditional theological teachings about Eros, the two eulogies pronounced by them usher us into quite different religious fields.

More than this, it is not only the theological background

but also the literary composition of Aristophanes' speech (*Symp.* 189a–93d) that are to be distinguished from those of the other speeches of the *Symposium*. Instead of describing the nature of Eros and then showing what benefits derive from such a nature, Aristophanes would rather reveal the power of the god, which alone may heal that ill whose healing constitutes the greatest happiness for the human species. To this end, he will depict the previous state of the human race and indicate the origin of the ill that has afflicted it.

Here then, according to Aristophanes, is what human nature used to be with regard to sex, form, and origin. Formerly, human nature comprised three genera: the male, the androgyne, and the female. Each of these human beings, whose shape was ovoid, was double. It had four hands, four feet, two faces each facing away from the other, and, most importantly, two sexual organs on what now constitutes the posterior part of the human being. In the case of the male, the two sexual organs were masculine; in the case of the female, they were feminine; and in the case of the androgyne, one was masculine and one was feminine. Moreover, the circular aspect of these creatures was indicative of their origins: the male was an offspring of the sun; the female, of the earth; and the androgyne, of the moon—which occupies an intermediate position between the sun (to which it is a sort of earth) and the earth (to which it is a sort of sun).

Unfortunately, these human beings revolt against the gods, like the Giants Ephialtes and Otus, who wished to scale the heavens. Thus, to punish them, Zeus decides to cut them in half, as one cuts an egg with a hair. After doing this, Zeus calls on Apollo to suture the wound, of which the navel

A man and an ephebe. Attic karchesion. Ca. 525 B.C. Boston, Museum of Fine Arts. Museum photo.

now constitutes the final scar. This punishment leads the human race straight to its ruin. Each half attempts to recover its complementary half with such ardor and persistence that it is about to die of starvation. This is why Zeus intervenes a second time, by transposing the sexual organ of each of the halves onto its front side. In this way an intermittent sexual union may be consummated which, even as it allows each human being to find the complementary half, leaves time to attend to other needs, especially those that are absolutely essential: nutrition and reproduction.

In this way, a healthy distance is established between the complementary halves of a human being, which are no longer either conjoined or disjoined permanently, since their intermittent reunion makes bearable a separation that is effective for the rest of the time. As one can see in reading the speech of Aristophanes, this healthy anthropological distance cannot be dissociated from a healthy cosmological distance between the sky and the earth and a healthy theological distance between the gods and men. On this basis, Eros appears to be the only god who can permit men to recover, up to a certain point, their former nature. This is where his power lies, a power that also extends to those opposed pairs that constitute sky and earth, and gods and men.

But since these renewed unions cannot be realized among humans except through sexual union, Aristophanes is led to set up a complete typology of the sexual life of the human being:

> Each of us is but a complementary fraction, a symbol of a man, since everyone shows like a flatfish the traces of having been sliced in two; and each is ever searching for the complementary fraction, the symbol of himself. All the men who are sections of that composite sex that at first was called androgynes are lovers of women; our adulterers are mostly descended from that sex, whence likewise are derived our men-loving women and adulteresses. All women who are sections of the woman pay no attention to men: they are inclined rather to women, and of this stock are the little girlfriends of these women. Men who are sections of the male pursue males, and so long as their boyhood lasts they show that they are miniature slices of the original male by making friends with men and delighting to lie with them and be clasped in men's embraces: these are the finest boys and adolescents, for they have the most manly nature. Some say they are shameless creatures, but falsely: for their behavior is due not to shamelessness but to daring, to having the heart and the demeanor of a male, since they are quick to welcome their like. Sure evidence of this is the fact that on reaching maturity individuals of this type alone prove to be men in a political career. So when they come to man's estate they are lovers of boys and have no natural interest in marrying and having children, but only do these things under the influence of custom; this does not prevent them from living quite contentedly side by side in celibacy all their days. A man of this sort is at any rate born to be a lover of boys or the willing mate of male lovers, for he never ceases to be attached to his own kind. (*Symp.* 191d–92b)

But with Socrates (*Symp.* 199b–212c), the eulogy of love opens a new perspective on the intelligible world.

In the discussion which he has, first with Agathon, Socrates makes three remarks fundamental to his purpose. First, love is always relative to something, because it is always "love of." Second, the object is the beautiful, which cannot be separated from the good. And third, to the extent that love implies the desire that presupposes the absence of

Erotic group. Attic cup. Ca. 480 B.C. Florence, Archaeological Museum. Photo Soprintendenza.

Banquet scene. Campanian krater. Second half of fourth century A.D. Naples, National Museum. Photo Soprintendenza.

its object, love must suffer from a lack of the beautiful and the good.

These three remarks about love indicate, according to Socrates, the nature of Eros (love). This is what Diotima, a priestess of Mantinea, had taught to him. Because he suffers from a lack of the beautiful and the good, Eros is not to be found in the ranks of the gods who are beautiful and good. Because of this, one must consider Eros to be a daemon, that is, a being intermediate between gods and men. This is the origin of this daemon. On the day when Aphrodite—the Pandemian, according to Pausanias, that is, the daughter of Zeus and Dione—was born, the gods were feasting. Expedient, the son of Invention, was at the banquet. Intoxicated with nectar, Expedient entered the garden of Zeus and fell asleep there, dead drunk. Poverty then came there and, "thinking that nothing was ever expedient for her, decided to have a child fathered by Expedient himself" (*Symp.* 203b 7–8). She promptly lay down next to him and became pregnant with Eros.

The origins of Eros explain his character. From his mother, Poverty, Eros inherited that lack of the beautiful and the good from which he suffers. But from his father, Expedient, Eros gets that aspiration toward the beautiful and the good which may only become a perpetual possession through the intermediary of a procreation by the body and a creation by the soul. Procreation by the body, which is accomplished through a union of a man and a woman, allows man to perpetuate himself in the beautiful and the good on the level of the sensory world. On the other hand, creation by the soul, which takes place only through contact between men, allows man to find true immortality, which is located not on the level of the sensory but on the level of the intelligible. The transition from the sensory to the intelligible is made possible by Eros at the end of a process that is related to an initiation. These are the degrees of the initiation. From a single beautiful body, one must pass to the beauty that is in all bodies. Then, from this corporeal beauty, one must rise to the beauty of souls, then to the beauty of knowledge and the productions of the soul in general, so as not to fall back, on the level of the soul, into particularism. Finally, and suddenly, when the other steps have been taken progressively, the initiate will contemplate the beautiful in itself, that is, the beautiful that is intelligible, in which all things that are beautiful participate.

In this, Socrates is radically opposed to Aristophanes. For Aristophanes, the power of Eros is in union, for at the level of the sensory it ensures the realization of union between human beings who seek their complementary half once more. For Socrates, however, Eros allows one to pass from the sensory to the intelligible, which constitutes true reality.

But what conclusions can be drawn from these six speeches, both about the nature and power of Eros and about sexuality—of which these eulogies to Eros allow us not only to draw up a typology but also to explore the boundaries, notably those on which dual sexuality is situated?

As far as the nature of Eros is concerned, we find five different Eroses in the *Symposium*. In the context of traditional mythology, the mythology transmitted by Hesiod in particular and by the majority of the poets in general, three figures of Eros may be distinguished: (1) the primordial Eros who appears after Chaos and Gaea (the Earth), whom Phaedrus mentions; (2) the Eros who accompanies the Ouranian Aphrodite who arose from the sperm that flowed into the sea from the amputated genitals of Ouranos, whom Pausanias and Eryximachus mention; (3) the Eros who is inseparable from the Pandemian Aphrodite, the daughter of Zeus and Dione, whom Pausanias and Eryximachus also mention. Moreover, it seems very likely that the eulogy of Eros by Aristophanes makes allusion to (4) the Orphic Eros, whose birth is described by that comic author in the *Birds* (693–703, *supra*). And Socrates, who relates the words of Diotima, speaks (5) of another Eros, who is not a god, but a daemon, the son of Expedient and Poverty.

Moreover, as far as the power of Eros is concerned, it should be noted that five of the six discourses take up themes that are common to both traditional theology and Orphism. Eros is the god who makes it possible to establish relationships not only between human beings of either sex but also between the sky and earth and thus between the gods and men. This is, moreover, the theme that Socrates takes up and transforms in the service of his philosophical preoccupations. For Socrates, Eros is that daemon—that is, that intermediary being—who permits the sensory to rise up toward the intelligible, where one may contemplate the beautiful and the good in themselves.

In this perspective, that is, to the degree that Eros makes it possible to establish relationships between human beings of

Men and ephebes. Attic amphora. Ca. 540 B.C. London, British Museum. Museum photo.

either sex, these six discourses convey a typology of sexual behavior in ancient Greece which all the mythical elaborations of the figure of Eros come to justify by ricocheting against it. It is Aristophanes who sets up the most complete survey of this typology (*Symp.* 191d–92b, *supra*). But it amounts to what the other five together say on the subject.

The sexual relationship to which all of the participants without exception give the highest value is uncontestedly the sexual relation between masculine partners. This is because this type of sexual relationship, beyond ensuring an effective sexual satisfaction, afterwards orients one either to political activity, as Aristophanes indicates, or toward the initiation of the philosophical type that Socrates describes (reporting the words of Diotima) and that culminates in the contemplation of the beautiful and the good in themselves. Sexual relations between male and female partners come second, in that this type of relationship, beyond allowing for sexual satisfaction, assures the procreation of children. Finally, in last place is the relationship between female partners, of which Aristophanes alone speaks.

This typology is inseparable from a definite ethic and is rooted in an effective social practice. If the masculine element is valorized at the expense of the feminine, this is because public life is reserved for men in ancient Greece, and women are relegated to private life. Because of this, only relationships between men can open up perspectives to political life and to philosophy. Furthermore, the only relationship in which a feminine element participates and which involves anything beyond mere sexual satisfaction is the relationship between a man and a woman for the procreation of children. This should explain why relationships between women are only mentioned incidentally, even if, notably for Sappho, this type of relationship may involve literary creativity.

This is a case of an explanation and a justification through the intermediary of the mythology of a social practice attested by several witnesses. On the other hand, a final characteristic of Eros, dual sexuality, cannot refer to any exact

Bearded men and a hetaera. Attic stamnos. Ca. 430 B.C. Paris, Musée du Louvre. Photo Chuzeville.

case, as Aristophanes himself indicates (*Symp.* 189e 4–5), inasmuch as, like all other infants possessed of any abnormality whatsoever, those who might have been born with both sexual organs would have been eliminated (Phlegon, *Mirabilia* chap. 2). It nevertheless remains true that even if it has no biological or social referent, dual sexuality plays an important role in the mythology of ancient Greece.

Elsewhere, it is in Orphic theology that dual sexuality plays the most important role. If one is to trust the testimony of the *Rhapsodies*, which constitute the usual Orphic theology, the first being to emerge from the primordial egg is Phanes, who is also called Eros, Metis, Protogonos, and Erikepaios. But this Phanes-Eros is of two sexes. Furthermore, it is related to the androgyne described by Aristophanes. It is a double being, since it has "two pairs of eyes that look in all directions"

Sleeping hermaphrodite. Paris, Musée du Louvre. Photo Giraudon.

(*Orphicorum fragmentora* 76) and has "two sex organs placed above the buttocks" (*OF* 80). Since Zeus swallows this Phanes-Eros in the fifth generation in order to identify him with himself by incorporating him, Zeus himself has dual sexuality (*OF* 168). Finally, since this Phanes is also called Dionysus (*OF* 170), Dionysus should also be identified with Phanes-Eros and therefore must also have dual sexuality.

From the Orphic Eros one passes by way of the androgyne that is the offspring of this planet to the moon, which also has two sexes. One may explain this dual sexuality by the ambivalence that characterizes the moon on two levels. On an external level, the moon, as we have seen, is an intermediary between the sun and the earth; for the sun it is a kind of earth, and for the earth it is a kind of sun. And, on an internal level, the moon also appears as an ambivalent being, for on account of its phases it successively governs a whole series of processes which are in opposition: birth and death, the ebb and flow of tides, waxing and waning, etc.

In this perspective, it seems entirely logical that those initiatory practices proper to the Dionysian cult (Corybantes and Bacchae) described by Plato in the *Ion* (533d3–36d5) take place by the light of the moon. Furthermore, the representatives of Orphism—whose role for Plato seems to be to practice initiations destined to deliver individuals and city-states from their past defilements—claim to be the sons of the Muses and of the Moon (*Republic* 2.364e4). But since these initiatory practices imply intersexual disguises, they refer to dual sexuality; and this in itself agrees perfectly with the fact that the initiations have as their ultimate end the fusion of the initiate with Dionysus.

From the practice of initiations, it is easy to pass to divination, which is intimately connected to it, since, like the practice of initiations but in a different way, divination seeks to establish a connection between the world of the gods and that of man. But in ancient Greece, the most important mythic figure of the diviner is Tiresias. And Tiresias assumes this intermediary function not only between gods and men but also between men and women (because he changes sexes), between generations (since his life extends over seven generations), and even between the living and the dead (since he keeps his conscious mind even when he is among the dead). Elsewhere Herodotus mentions the Enareis, Scythian diviners who derive their gift for divination from the Ouranian Aphrodite, a gift which is inseparable

from an androgyny that the goddess imposes on them, as well as on their descendants, to punish them for a sacrilege which they once committed against one of her temples in Syria (Herodotus 1.105; 4.67).

This last testimony brings us to Aphrodite. In his lost book on Attica, Philochorus, according to Macrobius (*Saturnalia* 3.8.3), mentions an Aphrodite who is identical with the moon and whom her followers worshiped after putting on the clothing of persons of the opposite sex. Also on Cyprus, they worshiped a bearded Aphrodite who was named Aphroditus, who had the body and clothing of a woman but the beard and sexual organs of a man, and whom devotees worshiped by engaging in transvestism (Macrobius *Saturnalia* 3.8.1–2; Servius *Commentary on the Aeneid* 2.632). But with Aphroditus one must associate Hermaphroditus, the son of Hermes and Aphrodite, who is none other than the brother of Eros, if we are to believe Cicero (*De natura deorum* 3.60).

Ovid tells the following story on this subject (*Metamorphoses* 4.285ff.). At the age of fifteen, this son of Hermes and Aphrodite leaves the island of Ida where he was born. He arrives at Caria, near a lake whose waters are of a wondrous beauty. The nymph of this lake, Salmacis, who never engages in the strenuous activities of the hunt but spends all of her time in strictly feminine occupations, falls in love with him and makes advances to him. Hermaphroditus, who does not yet know what love is, runs away. But while he bathes in the waters of the lake Salmacis dives in and clings to him, begging the gods to cause their two bodies never to separate. The gods grant her wish in such a way that the two form but a single body which seems "to have no sex, and to have both sexes" (Metamorphoses 4.379). But Hermaphroditus obtains from the gods a wish of his own: that whoever bathes in the waters of the lake will lose his virility. The union of Hermaphroditus and Salmacis cancels out the bisection effected by Zeus on the androgyne in the speech of Aristophanes. Furthermore, it should be noted that on decorated monuments Hermaphroditus is often portrayed among the companions of Dionysus. We may see from this that Hermaphroditus is not as isolated a mythic figure as might at first have appeared.

Finally, let us mention Caenis, whom Poseidon loves and to whom he promises that, in exchange for her favors, he will fulfill any wish that she might ask for; the god transforms her into an invulnerable man, the tyrant Caeneus, who becomes guilty of impiety toward the gods. Zeus then incites the Centaurs against him, and they crush him with tree trunks. And, according to Ovid (*Metamorphoses* 12.522ff.), the buried Caeneus emerges from under the tree trunks piled on him in the form of the phoenix, the mythic bird in which all opposites coincide, including those of masculinity and femininity.

Other mythic personages undergo a change of sex—notably Hypermestra, Leucippe, and Siproïtes (Antonius Liberalis *Metamorphoses* 17)—for different reasons and under different conditions. But the little information that we have about them does not suggest a good explanation for them.

Now that we have examined the nature and power of Eros and the effects of this mythic figure on sexuality in general and on dual sexuality in particular, let us consider the worship of Eros.

Until the end of the classical period, no great cult of Eros exists in Greece. The local cult of Thespiae, in Boeotia (Pausanias 9.27.1), acquires its fame after the time of Plato, thanks to the statue of Eros made by Praxiteles around 370–360. The same seems to have been the case with the cult of Eros at Parion (Pausanias 9.27.1), where there was also a statue of Eros by Praxiteles (Pliny the Elder *Naturalis historia* 36.22) which was represented on the coins of the city-state, starting with Antoninus Pius.

In many other places, the cult of Eros seems to be connected with the gymnasiums, in that Eros is realized to the highest degree in the love of beautiful young boys. This is especially the case in Athens (Pausanias 1.30.1), since for a long time there had been a statue and altar of Eros in the gymnasium where Plato gave his first lessons, before he moved into the garden next door to build a center there and a sanctuary to the Muses (Diogenes Laertius 3.7). The proximity of the academy to the gymnasium in which the cult of Eros was celebrated is all that one needs to see to realize one of the reasons that impelled Plato to write the *Symposium* and the *Phaedrus*. And, following a similar line of reasoning, an attempt has been made to account for the allusions to Eros made by Hesiod in his *Theogony* by the proximity of Ascra, where the poet lived, and Thespiae, where Eros was worshiped.

Finally, the gymnasium was also the place of the particular development of the cult of Anteros, an enigmatic person whose name seems to mean "love in return." At Athens, this son of Aphrodite (the second one, that is, the daughter of Zeus and Dione) and Ares (Cicero *De natura deorum* 3.60) had a statue and a sanctuary erected on the Acropolis in memory of two young men named Meles and Timagoras. Timagoras, a foreigner resident in the city, loved Meles, a citizen, who spurned his love and demanded that he jump from the top of the Acropolis to prove his love. Timagoras did this, and, overcome with remorse, Meles killed himself in the same way (Pausanias 1.30.1).

With Anteros, Eros thus finds the reciprocity that he implies at every level at which he exerts his power, no matter what sort of nature is attributed to him.

L.Br./d.w.

BIBLIOGRAPHY

On the figure of Eros in Greek poetry in general, see F. LASSERRE, *La figure d'Éros dans la poésie grecque* (Lausanne 1946). Concerning Hesiod, the best edition of *Theogony* including a commentary is that of M. L. WEST, Hesiod, *Theogony* (Oxford 1966); this text has been translated into French by P. MAZON, who also published an edition with the Greek text facing the French translation: Hésiode, *Théogonie, Les travaux et les jours, Le bouclier* (Paris 1928; 5th ed., 1960). We borrowed our translations, slightly modified, from P. Mazon [and the English translations in the present edition are based on those modified French versions]. In addition, Orphic fragments have been assembled most recently in O. KERN, *Orphicorum fragmenta* (Berlin 1922; reprint 1972).

L. ROBIN has published an excellent edition, accompanied by a good French translation and preceded by a long introduction, of Plato's *Symposium* (Paris 1929; 9th ed., 1970). We have cited it.

On sexuality in ancient Greece in general, see R. FLACELIÈRE, *L'amour en Grèce* (Paris 1960). On homosexuality in particular, see M. H. E. MEIER and L.-R. DE POGEY-CASTRIES, *Histoire de l'amour grec dans l'antiquité* (Paris 1930); and K. J. DOVER, *Greek Homosexuality* (London 1978). On bisexuality, the books of M. DELCOURT, *Hermaphrodite: Mythes et rites de la bisexualité dans l'antiquité classique* (Paris 1958); and *Hermaphroditea: Recherches sur l'être double promoteur de fertilité dans le monde classique* (Brussels 1966), are excellent introductions. See also L. BRISSON, "Bisexualité et Médiation en Grèce ancienne," *Nouvelle revue de psychanalyse* 7 (1973): 27–48.

In addition, concerning the myths, cults, and illustrated documents relating to Eros, the following works remain indispensable: WASER, "Eros," in Pauly/Wissowa, *Real-Encyclopädie*, vol. 6, 1 (1907), 484–542; and A. FURTWÄNGLER, "Eros," in *Roschers Lexikon*, 1 (1884–90), 1339–72. The same is true for Anteros; see WERNICKE, "Anteros," in Pauly/Wissowa, *Real-Encyclopädie*, vol. 1, 2 (1894), 2354–55. In addition, the book by A. GREIFENHAGEN, *Griechische Eroten* (Berlin 1957), is very useful.

Recent publications on Eros include: A. LESKY, *Vom Eros der Hellenen* (Göttingen 1976); and J. BOARDMAN and E. LA ROCCA, *Eros in Greece* (London 1978).

Abbreviations

Lobel-Page *PLF: Poetarum Lesbiorum Fragmenta*, ed. E. Lobel and D. Page (Oxford 1955).

Page *PMG: Poeta melici Graeci*, ed. D. L. Page (Oxford 1962).

Europa. Attic amphora. Ca. 520 B.C. Würzburg, Martin von Wagner Museum. Museum photo.

EUROPA

The daughter of Telephassa, "who shines in the distance," or of Argiope, "the white faced," the daughter or sister of Phoenix, the Red One but also the Phoenician, Europa was gathering flowers on the edge of the sea near Tyre or Sidon, when Zeus, in the form of a bull, emerged from the water and lifted her onto his back in spite of her cries. He brought her to Crete, where he had three sons by her: Minos, Sarpedon, and Rhadamanthys. He also gave her three gifts: a spear that always hit its mark, a dog that allowed no prey to escape, and a giant made entirely of bronze; this was Talos, the guardian of the island, who could be injured only in one spot. On the images in which she is represented, Europa, sitting upright on the back of the animal, seems less the victim of a kidnapping than a great goddess mounted on a bull.

J.C./d.w.

Gorgon. Plate from Rhodes. Early sixth century, B.C. London, British Museum. Museum photo.

THE GORGONS

The three Gorgons, daughters of Phorcys and Ceto, who were marine deities, lived in the far west, beyond Oceanus and the Hesperides and beyond their sisters, the Graiae, who guarded the entrance to their country. Of these three sister goddesses, Stheno, Euryale, and Medusa, only the last was mortal. The Gorgons had wings of gold and were very beautiful, as is witnessed by the "Sleeping Medusa" of Scopas. But their hands were made of bronze, they had the tusks of boars, and serpents encircled their heads and waists. Above all, their faces had the terrible power to turn anyone who looked at them to stone. They were an object of terror for men and held themselves apart from the gods: only Poseidon dared to mate with Medusa, and when Perseus cut the Gorgon's throat, two of the offspring of the sea god emerged: Pegasus, the horse of Bellerophon, and Chrysaor. After Perseus's victory, Athena wore on her aegis, as a powerful weapon, the Gorgon's mask, the Gorgoneion.

J.C./d.b.

Head of Medusa. Acroterion from the old temple of Athena. Athens. Acropolis Museum. Photo I.A.

THE GRAIAE

The name of the Graiae means "old women"; they were born old. According to Hesiod, Ceto gave Phorcys the Graiae with beautiful cheeks; the Graiae were born with gray hair. The three sisters shared a single eye and a single tooth. Two sisters slept while the possessor of the eye and the tooth stood guard, barring the road that led to the Gorgons. The Graiae lived in the far west, beyond the river Oceanus, in a cavern where the sun never shone.

J.C./d.b.

THE HARPIES

Born of Thaumas, who was the son of Pontus and Gaea and was a god of the sea like Nereus and Phorcys, the Harpies are sisters of Iris, the rainbow messenger. The Harpies are kidnappers, as fast as the wind and as alarming as the tempest. Their rapacity makes them relatives of the turbulent gusts. They steal suddenly. Thus they steal the unfortunate daughters of Pandareos and force them to become the servants of the Erinyes in the netherworld. There are two or three Harpies, according to different sources, and they are "the bitches of the great Zeus." Podarge, "she of rapid feet," by Zephyr, the West Wind, conceived the immortal horses of Achilles' team, Xanthus and Balius. In the *Argonautica* of Apollonius of Rhodes, the Harpies are the guardians of Phineus, the fisher king. Because Phineus talked too much, he was condemned never to touch any food that had not been soiled and covered with excrement by the Harpies, who swooped down from the sky like horrible vultures. Calaïs and Zetes, the sons of Boreas, pursued them until the moment when, on Iris's order, they were allowed to dive into the depths of the earth toward the nocturnal world from which they had emerged.

J.C./d.b.

THE CULT OF HELEN AND THE TRIBAL INITIATION OF WOMEN IN GREECE

Peoples who were not, or are not, acquainted with the institution of tribal initiation are rare, except where there is a Western educational system. The Greeks were no exception, even though they had no specific term for the institution. Since the beginning of the twentieth century, several historians of religion have been able to identify, in certain rituals performed by Hellenic adolescents, rites of an initiatory nature. Far from being simple relics of an earlier time, Greek rites of tribal initiation had the same political and religious weight that they carry in contemporary tribal societies: their decline since the fifth century is due only to the progressive diffusion of the Athenian educational system, which was itself determined by the profound political and economic changes that the Greek city experienced during the classical and then the Hellenistic eras.

The institutional phenomenon of Greek tribal initiation for boys has been thoroughly investigated, and the conclusions reached by religious historians are unambiguous, particularly on the subject of the interpretation of the Spartan rite. For girls, the situation is much more confused: it requires not only certain conceptual definitions but also the delimitation of a general framework which, based on ethnological data, can serve as a basis of comparison for an understanding of Greek life. Within this reality, the case of Sparta, and the cult dedicated to Helen, will be used as an example. This does not mean that other cities did not also have initiation rites for adolescents: one could cite, for example, the festival of the Brauronia at Brauron and that of the Arrephoria at Athens.

The Institutional Framework

In the definition given by ethnologists, rites of tribal initiation represent a particular case of rites of passage. To that degree, their formal structure can be fitted to the schema outlined at the beginning of the twentieth century by A. van Gennep. Generically, they are composed of three essential phases: a moment marking the separation of the initiate from the order to which he formerly belonged, a period of segregation and liminality (of greater or lesser duration), and finally a moment of admission when the initiate is integrated into the new order, the objective of a rite of passage. The moment of separation is generally assimilated to a state of death, while the reintegration into the new order is often conceived as a rebirth.

In the specific case of the tribal initiation rite, the old order is constituted by the world of childhood for the young adolescent who is subjected to the ritual, while the new order is incarnate in the rules and customs that structure and govern adult society. The almost universal institution of tribal initiation thus has the central function of integrating adolescents into adult society and making them members of the community. This institutional structure with its official and public character makes it possible for adolescent girls and boys to assimilate the political, religious, moral, and cultural standards which govern the society on which they depend; the institution prepares them for the role they must play as adult participants in society. Its goal is to reproduce, generation after generation, the social system of the tribe.

With regard to young women, it is also necessary to distinguish between tribal initiation rites proper and puberty rites. The tribal initiation rites are communal and concern a group of adolescent girls as they become adult members of society; the puberty rites, attached to the first menstruation, are individual and private. The tribal rites are often connected with the system that segregates young women according to age categories, while puberty rites generally take place within the framework of the family. Here we are not concerned with puberty rites.

To the extent that tribal initiation must prepare adolescents for their future social roles and that women have within the community a function different from that of men, the rites for girls have different forms and contents from those for boys. In general, the social role of women within the tribal community is mainly motherhood; to this principal function are added all the tasks pertinent to the "internal" survival of the community, in contrast with the function of the "external" maintenance of the tribe, which is assumed by men through activities such as hunting, raising animals, and war.

Thus, for adolescent girls, the first phase of the initiation, the moment of separation and death, is often marked by a violent physical operation: clitoridectomy, removal of the labia minora, or, less cruelly, cutting the hair. During the transitional period, the young woman is generally introduced to the mysteries of sexuality and maternity; also during this period, like her male colleague, she is initiated into certain ethical rules and mythological traditions that are the foundation of the cohesiveness of the adult community. Finally, during the festivities that mark the moment of admission into adult society, dances and songs play an important role for the new initiates. There is nothing surprising in the "spectacular" aspect of the rite, since this third phase signals not only the moment when the adolescent girl emerges from the initiation but also the moment when she is presented to the adult community, which in this way exer-

Chorus of girls. Geometric hydria. Ca. 750 B.C. Paris, Musée du Louvre, Photo Chuzeville.

cises control over the results of the initiation. Note that the third phase of the rite of initiation often means only that the new initiate enters into a period of preparation for the second rite of passage, which will be her marriage. In this way, the female tribal initiation rites are distinct from those of young men, and the various ritual practices marking the progressive integration of a young woman into the adult community, culminating in marriage, may extend over a fairly long time period. This was notably the case in Sparta, where, in the absence of information on the liminal phase of female tribal initiation, which was by definition kept secret, what we know is essentially the ritual process of admitting a young woman into the social body of adults; and this process was characterized by its extension in time.

The Period of Separation and Liminality: Artemis

The existence of an initiatory institution for young women in ancient and classical Sparta can be seen in many cults. For reasons previously indicated, we know very little about the

rites which marked the time of separation and liminality in the tribal initiation. It seems, however, that the cults of Artemis Limnatis and Artemis Caryatis, because of their location at the borders of Laconian territory and because of their typically adolescent purpose, must have served as a framework for the ritual consecration of these two phases of the initiation process. Furthermore, in the myths attached to the cult of the Limnae and the Caryae, there are elements which appear to form the basis of an adolescent rite of passage. In fact, the mythic episode of the suicide of the young Lacedaemonian women who consecrate themselves to the cult of Limnatis after they are raped by the Messenians and the tale of the subsequent vengeance, by means of a feat of *apatē* (ruse) by a troop of Spartan ephebes dressed as young women, inevitably leads one to think of a rite of initiatory death. In the same way, if one takes into account the semiotic transformations in which the meaning of the rite is transposed and explained on the level of mythic narration, the story of how the Messenian hero Aristomenes captured the young Laconian women dancing at Caryae for Artemis and then attempted to rape them, as well as the story of the suicide of the chorus of Caryatids by hanging, seems to indicate that the cult of Artemis Caryatis consecrated the (initiatory) death of the young Lacedaemonian women who were performing their choral dances. In consecrating themselves to Limnatis or Caryatis, at the boundaries of civilized territory, the adolescent girls of Sparta broke with the world of their childhood without being able to assume the patterns of an adult and orderly sexuality. The myths just mentioned, in which the laws of normal and civilized sexual relations are reversed, probably describe the period of chaos and death at the center of the tribal initiation.

Strangely, the cult of Artemis Orthia, who plays a central role in the initiation of Spartan adolescents (cf. the rite of the crypteia and the institution of the *agogē*) does not seem to have served as a framework for any of the phases which constitute female tribal initiation. Only one of the numerous myths attached to Helen sets a feminine exploit in this context: it tells that, before her puberty, the heroine was kidnapped by Theseus as she danced in the choir of Artemis Orthia. No data on rituals correspond to this mythic episode, and if one relies on the various explanations that the ancients gave to the surnames of the goddess, it seems that Artemis Orthia was primarily connected with those aspects of the female side of her cult that dealt with childbirth and early childhood (infancy). To this degree, her cult seems close to the one dedicated to Artemis Corythalia, in whose honor Lacedaemonian nurses celebrated the festival of the Tithenidia on behalf of newborn infants.

The End of the Initiation: Apollo

Although the time of separation and liminality in the tribal initiation falls under the jurisdiction of Artemis, the exit from the initiation in Sparta clearly belongs to Apollo.

In fact, the festival of the Hyacinthia, because it involved the participation of the whole Spartan community, because it had a funeral rite for the hero Hyacinthus alternating with the rejoicing dedicated to the Amyclaean Apollo, because of its pronounced spectacular nature, and because it included several dances and songs (notably a paean) that were performed by the young ephebes of the city, appears to have represented in Sparta the great rite at the end of the initiation of adolescents. The young women participated in the festival in a long procession which took them from Sparta to Amyclae; they rode on floats especially built for the occasion. They then took part in a great nocturnal festival in which dance had an important place. There is little doubt that the procession of young Lacedaemonian women served to present the newly initiated women to the citizens assembled all along their route.

Between Initiation and Marriage: Helen

If one is to believe the chorus in the *Helen* of Euripides, the great Lacedaemonian heroine took part in the festivities of the Hyacinthia in her youth. Thus, if one adds to this information the episode of the abduction of the young woman from the sanctuary of Artemis Orthia, it appears that the myth makes the avatars of the initiatory cursus follow the "divine and splendid leader of the chorus" which Aristophanes mentions in *Lysistrata*.

On the other hand, the twelve members of the chorus in Theocritus's *Bridal Song for Helen* describe the young heroine playing on the banks of the Eurotas in the middle of a troupe of four-times-sixty adolescent girls, all of the same age. These

Abduction of Helen by Theseus. Attic amphora by Euthymides. Ca. 510 B.C. Munich, Antikensammlungen. Photo Koppermann.

young women are taking part in a race (*dromos*), and Helen is distinguished among them not only by her beauty but by the beautiful voice with which she sings to Athena and Aphrodite. But, for the choirs singing Theocritus's poem, this evocation is a part of the past. At the moment when her companions recite the lines, Helen is already the wife of Menelaus celebrated in the myth; she is no longer present in the middle of the crowd of young women of whom she represents the supreme ornament. This is why the young singers of Theocritus demonstrate their intention to perpetuate the memory of Helen's adolescence by offering a crown of lotus blossoms at the foot of a plane tree, which will thereafter be the heroine's sacred tree. In this way, they make the evocation of Helen as a young woman the mythological foundation of the rite that they will perform.

The mythical figure of Helen in Sparta straddles both adolescence and the status of an adult married woman. This ambiguity appears also in the cults dedicated to her in Laconia.

In Sparta, Helen was worshiped in two places with different cults. She was first worshiped at the Platanistas. This place, so called because plane trees were planted there, was at the confluence of the Eurotas and the Magoula, to the southeast of the city of Sparta; surrounded by water, it looked like an island and was in the immediate vicinity of the famous Dromos where young, still celibate citizens of Sparta trained for races. It was for this reason that the young companions of Helen also held their race in this area, probably in a ritual repetition of the mythic race in which the heroine took part on the banks of the Eurotas. However, sources even older than Aristophanes and Euripides associated the figure of Helen and the banks of the Eurotas with choral dances performed by adolescent girls even more than with a race. These two ritual practices may be described together in the poem of Alcman traditionally cited by the incorrect title of *First Virginity*; this poem was probably dedicated to Helen.

Whatever the rites were which constituted the cult of Helen at the Platanistas, the heroine to whom the cult was dedicated was certainly still an adolescent, an adolescent ready to marry. In this respect, her position in relation to adolescence is analogous to the position incarnate in the figure of the Leucippides. The myth of the abduction of the two young Lacedaemonian girls by the Dioscuri and of their marriage to the two great protective heroes of the city of Sparta, as well as their intervention in the ritual race of the eleven Dionysiades, make the Leucippides figures who participate simultaneously in adolescence and adulthood. In Euripides' account of the dances on the banks of the Eurotas, Helen is precisely associated with these two heroines. In addition, Aristophanes compared with mares the young women whom Helen served as leader of the chorus in the execution of the dances. In Greece, the image of the mare and her taming constitutes one of the essential metaphors used to express progressive mastery, through education, of the uncontrolled forces of youth. Both initiation and marriage were conceived as processes of taming in which the yoke played a central symbolic role. Finally, it is necessary to point out that the Platanistas was not only consecrated to Helen but that this aquatic region was also the site of the ritual combats between Spartan ephebes that Lycurgus instituted. Thus the metaphor for the participants in the rite, as well as its general ritual context, marks Helen's cult at the Platanistas as typically adolescent.

With regard to this unusual aspect of the cult figure of a

neoi, are newly initiated citizens, winners at contests in sport and already warriors, but who, as bachelors, are not completely integrated into the adult order of the city.

But as a goddess, Helen is also present on the bank of the Eurotas across from the bank where the Platanistas used to be. The heights of Therapne sheltered a temple to King Menelaus in which the heroine was buried at the side of her husband. In passing from the right bank of the Laconian river to the hill of Therapne, the cult of Helen changes its aspect; it is no longer heroic, but the cult of a goddess; the eminent Lacedaemonian is no longer worshiped as a young girl but as a married woman.

An anecdote told by Herodotus gives us our only glimpse of the meaning of the ritual that was celebrated in the sanctuary of Therapne. The historian tells that the Spartan king Ariston married a woman who had been the ugliest of children. Her nurse, in desperation, took her regularly to the temple of Helen, until one day the goddess appeared to the nurse and caressed the child's head. From that moment, the little girl's appearance changed completely. From the homeliest of little girls, Helen created the most beautiful woman in all of Sparta, and before Ariston carried her off as Paris carried off Helen, this remarkable woman married a Spartan aristocrat. In this story, Helen appears as the goddess who gives beauty to female children. This gift was more important since it was not given for its own sake but for the sake of marriage. For women in Greece, the passage from ugliness to beauty represents, in metaphorical terms, the passage from childhood to nubility.

Thus the Helen venerated in Therapne is not the model of a married woman; she is not the equal or the rival of Hera, who guarantees the bonds of legal marriage; she appears more as the adult woman whose beauty, like that of Aphrodite, expresses sexual attraction and seduction. In the Greek conception of marriage, both of these elements play an essential role. Helen at Therapne incarnates the qualities of an adult woman whose perfect beauty henceforth places her on the threshold of marriage.

The Spartan Initiatory Process

Several gods in ancient Sparta take part in the process that leads the young girl to the status of an adult married woman. As protectress of the growth of young plants as well as of newborn children, Artemis naturally rules over early childhood; but because she also dominates the entire domain outside the closed and civilized space of the city, she is also the one to whom the bordering cults were dedicated. These cults marked the young girl's rupture with the world of childhood and her entrance into the period of liminality, disorder, and death within the tribal initiation process at the heart of nature in its savagery. Though Artemis takes babies under her protection at birth in order to bring them to the rite which signifies the end of their childhood, it is Helen who assumes responsibility for the period between the end of the initiation and the moment of marriage, while Apollo reserves for himself the festivities that mark the end of the tribal initiation. As for marriage itself, an essentially private rite among the Greeks, it may have received an official consecration in Sparta in the sacrifice that the mothers of recently married young women offered to the ancient wooden image (*xoanon*) of Aphrodite-Hera. Thus Helen, in opposition as much to Artemis and Apollo as to Hera, has the role of conducting Lacedaemonian adolescent girls to full sexual maturity; she makes the Lacedaemonian adolescent girls into

Abduction of Helen. London, British Museum. Photo Boudot-Lamotte.

still adolescent Helen, the contact that the heroine had with the Amyclaean Apollo and with Athena Chalcioecos (attested in the texts by Aristophanes and Euripides already cited) is extremely significant. Although the Hyacinthia represents a festival marking the end of the initiation period for Spartan adolescents, both male and female, the presence of Helen at the festival makes the heroine into a young woman just initiated and therefore ready to assume the status of a fully adult woman, a married woman. As for the association with the cult of Athena Chalcioecos, whose function largely escapes us due to insufficient information, it conferred on the figure of Helen the civic qualities of the virgin goddess who was enthroned on the acropolis of the city. Athena is a *parthenos,* a warrior and protectress of the city; she is, like Helen, a young woman who has crossed the threshold of adolescence and is admitted into the community of male and female citizens. Situated at the heart of the cult associations, Helen appears to represent for Spartan adolescent females what her brothers, the Dioscuri, represented for the young men. Helen resembles these heroes who, as true

177

women in her own image. In limiting the exercise of her jurisdiction to a single period in the whole Spartan initiatory process, she is faithful to that fundamental trait of Greek polytheism which dictates that each divinity in the pantheon assumes a function determined within a limited domain of plant, animal, and human reality.

G.C./d.b.

BIBLIOGRAPHY

1. Essential Sources

ALCMAN, frags. 1, 2, 3, 7, and 10, Page. HERODOTUS, 6, 61ff. ARISTOPHANES, *Lysistrata*, 1296ff. EURIPIDES, *Helen*, 1465ff. THEOCRITUS, *Idylls*, 18. PLUTARCH, *Theseus*, 31. PAUSANIAS, 3, 15–20, and 4, 4. ATHENAEUS, 4, 138e ff.

2. Principal Studies

B. BETTELHEIM, *Symbolic Wounds* (2d ed., New York 1962). A. BRELICH, *Paides e Parthenoi* (Rome 1969). C. CALAME, *Les chœurs de jeunes filles en Grèce archaïque*, 1: *Morphologie, fonction religieuse et sociale*; 2: *Alcman* (Rome 1977). Y. A. COHEN, *The Transition from Childhood to Adolescence* (Chicago 1964). M. ELIADE, *Naissances mystiques* (Paris 1959). H. JEANMAIRE, *Couroi et Courètes* (Lille 1939). M. P. NILSSON, *Griechische Feste von religiöser Bedeutung* (Leipzig 1906). A. VAN GENNEP, *The Rites of Passage* (Chicago 1960), originally *Les rites de passage* (Paris 1909). F. W. YOUNG, *Initiation Ceremonies* (Indianapolis and New York 1965).

HELIOS—SELENE—ENDYMION

Helios, according to the *Iliad*, is a god whose indefatigable eye watches over men from the heights of the sky and who is called upon to bear witness to the veracity of oaths. Each evening at sunset, the Sun climbs into the golden cup that carries him while he sleeps over the waves of Oceanus from the country of the Hesperides to the kingdom of the Ethiopians, where Dawn sees him remount his chariot and horses. This is the boat that Heracles borrowed to travel to Geryon to steal his flocks.

Associated with the Horai—the Seasons—the Sun plays a role in several festivals (the Skira, the Pyanopsia, and the Thargelia) and is the generative father of all life. When his flocks were mistreated by the impious companions of Odysseus, he threatened Zeus that he would shine for the dead and deprive the living of his heat and light. Like Selene and Aphrodite Ourania, the Sun accepts no wine with his offerings.

The sister of the Sun, Selene is the star of night, and it is said that she appeared just before the war of the gods against the Giants. The Arcadians were supposed to have been born before the moon shone in the sky, at a time when the violence of men mingled with that of the wolves in the dark of night. The moon had two lovers: Pan and Endymion. The first resorted to subterfuge: by wearing the brilliant skin of a silver ram on his back, he gained the favors of the power of night. As for the second lover, he was a young man, a shepherd or hunter, of great beauty, asleep in a grotto where Selene met him in the night. Endymion's sleep, according to one tradition, was a gift from the god Hypnos (Sleep), who granted him the ability to sleep with his eyes open. Other sources say that this ability was the result of a gift from Zeus, who had granted him the right to decide the manner of his own death.

J.C./d.b.

Helios. Attic amphora. Ca. 490 B.C. Vienna, Antikensammlungen. Photo Sitzenfrey.

HERACLES: THE VALOR AND DESTINY OF THE HERO

"I sing of Heracles, son of Zeus, the greatest by far of the great men on earth (*aristos epichthoniōn*), he who was born to Alcmene in Thebes of the splendid choirs, after her union with Kronos' son, man of the dark clouds. At first he wandered the earth and the immense seas and suffered greatly; but his bravery triumphed, and, alone, he succeeded at many daring tasks (*erga*), beyond compare. Now, on the contrary, he rejoices in living in his beautiful home on snowy Olympus and for a wife has Youth (Hebe) of the beautiful ankles" (*Homeric Hymn to Heracles* 1–8).

With eloquent brevity, the *Homeric Hymn* tells the fate of Heracles: a son of Zeus but nevertheless a man, the greatest, but also the most exposed to suffering; his exploits are solitary but always victorious. And finally he is integrated into the society of the gods and married to Eternal Youth.

In recounting the innumerable exploits which form a heroic career, one could discuss Heracles at length. This has already been done both by the mythographers of the Hellenistic period and by modern mythologists, and I will not follow them on the paths of that story here. If it is nevertheless necessary to sketch the broad outlines of the story of Heracles, I will merely recall how Hera's jealousy delayed Alcmene's delivery of her child, submitting the son of Zeus to Eurystheus, her all too human cousin (*Iliad* 19.98–134); at that moment everything worked against Heracles, caught between the hatred of Hera and the orders of Eurystheus. The terrible goddess never stopped stirring up monstrous adversaries—serpents, whom he strangled in his cradle (Pindar *First Nemean* 33–66); the Nemean lion (Hesiod *Theogony* 327–32), whose defeat is the initiatory act that makes the adolescent Heracles a man; the Hydra of Lerna (ibid. 313–18), and many others. As for the contemptible Eurystheus, who cannot accomplish even the possible himself, he demands the impossible of the hero. Heracles therefore increases his exploits from the twelve labors to great military deeds (wars against Ilion, Pylos, and Sparta), not to mention

Introduction of Heracles onto Olympus: Heracles, Athena, Zeus. Attic cup. Ca. 560 B.C. London, British Museum.

Heracles and the Cretan bull. Metope from Olympia. 470–460 B.C. Paris, Musée du Louvre. Photo Musées nationaux.

Heracles brings Cerberus to Eurystheus, who, terrified, hides in a jar. Hydria from Caere. Ca. 535 B.C. Paris, Musée du Louvre. Photo Chuzeville.

the innumerable acts of prowess (the *parerga,* additional exploits) associated with his name.

I. Man, Hero, or God

Let us confine ourselves to the essential: Heracles is, of all the Greek heroes, the most popular—as is attested by his frequent appearance on the stage—and the only one revered by all the Greeks. He belongs not to one city, but to Greece as a whole, which he traveled in his ceaseless activity, to the point that in more than one city, national heroes yield to him: this extended even to the Athenians, usually so careful to preserve their individuality; they dedicated more sanctuaries to him than to the Athenian Theseus (see Euripides *Heracles* 1324–33 and Plutarch *Theseus* 35.2). What is more, the Athenians bragged that they had preceded other Greeks in honoring Heracles as a god (Diodorus 4.39.1).

Here the reader is surprised: was Heracles a man, a hero,

or a god? From "the most valorous of men" (*aristos andrōn*: Sophocles *Trachiniae* 811; Euripides *Heracles* 183; Aristophanes *Clouds* 1049; see also *Homeric Hymn to Heracles* 1–2) to hero, there is no break in continuity, since the Greeks defined a hero as a man who formerly had lived an exceptional life and whom death had consecrated. Between mortal and god, the gap seems, by contrast, impossible to bridge; it was so at least for the heroes of the Homeric epic, such as Diomedes, who was brutally reminded by Apollo that "there will always be two distinct races: that of the immortal gods and that of the men who walk the earth" (*Iliad* 5.441–42). The paradox of Heracles is that, as the son of Zeus, he is to be a man during his lifetime, while in death he is present both in Hell, a wandering shadow that still terrifies the dead, and at the same time on Olympus, Immortal among the Immortals, enjoying the festivals (*Odyssey* 11.601–8). Heracles is considered a *hērōs theos* (Pindar *Third Nemean* 22)—hero and god, or rather hero-god—not only by the poet but by the cult, both heroic and divine, that was dedicated to him in certain cities (see Herodotus 2.44; Pausanias 2.10.1 for Sicyone; and for Thasos, Pouilloux 1 and 2).

If the Greek hero is truly an "individual apart, exceptional, more than human," who "nonetheless must assume the human condition" in his vicissitudes, tests, and limitations, even to the point of suffering and death; if "what defines the hero, at the very heart of his destiny as a man, are the acts which he dared to undertake and at which he was able to succeed: his exploits" (J.-P. Vernant, pp. 89–90), Heracles is certainly the paradigm of a hero.

But his human history is also written, from the very beginning, in the immobile time of the gods.

This is attested by his difficult but ambiguous relationship with Hera. As protectress of legitimate marriage and the jealous wife of Zeus, the goddess has a dual basis for her hatred for a son of Zeus whom the Athenian theater considers a bastard (Aristophanes *Birds* 1650ff.). Indeed, Zeus, by taking the form of Alcmene's husband Amphitryon in order to seduce her, tried to place this illicit union under the sign of legitimacy (see Diodorus 4.9.3, as well as Hesiod *Shield* 27–56, Apollodorus *Bibliotheca* 2.4.8, and the remarks of M. Delcourt, p. 132). Thus Hera's hatred is from the beginning set in contradiction with itself, a flagrant contradiction proclaimed by the very name of the hero: "glorious through Hera." Delivered by her to the will of Eurystheus and condemned by her to exploits from his cradle, Heracles obtains both his value and his name from Hera—he is "the glory (*kleos*) of Hera" (see Diodorus 4.9.2). At the hour of his death, Sophocles' Heracles will proclaim that he is "named after the most perfect of mothers" (*Trachiniae* 1105, commentary on verse by J. Bollack, *R Ph*, 44, 1970, pp. 46–47), and this mother is no longer the mortal Alcmene, but the wife of Zeus. Hera, the mother of Heracles? As though the goddess did not sufficiently seal her reconciliation with the hero by giving him her daughter Hebe (see *Odyssey* 11.603–4 and *Theogony* 952–53), mythographical tradition keeps trying to make Hera the divine mother of Heracles, by stating that the wife of Zeus had inadvertently suckled the child of Alcmene or had adopted him on Olympus.

But Heracles has more simple and trusting relationships with other gods. Hermes, for example, the god of passage, willingly accompanies the hero in his tribulations between the world of men and the world of the gods, helping him to bring the terrible Cerberus back from Hades or leading the cortege to introduce Heracles on Olympus. A protectress of heroes, Athena especially protects Heracles, whom she aids in many of his exploits, both in the texts (*Iliad* 8.362ff.;

Theogony 318; Euripides *Heracles* 920ff., etc.) and in pictorial representations (such as the famous metopes of Olympia). She is also shown on certain vases presenting the new god to Zeus. Painters occasionally forgot Hermes and reduced the scene to the three principal actors: the father of gods and men, his divine daughter, and his son, finally delivered from a life of sufferings.

Heracles: between man and god, a hero engaged in a ceaseless battle against death. Between the powerful but vanquished Heracles, conquered by the death melancholically described by Achilles in the *Iliad* (18.115–21), and the happy husband of the flourishing Hebe (Hesiod *Theogony* 950–55 and frag. 25 Merkelbach-West; Pindar *First Nemean* 69ff. and 10.17), the heroic life of the son of Alcmene was totally dedicated to breaching boundaries: the boundaries of the inhabited world, where the earth ends and the inaccessible sea begins (Pindar *Third Nemean* 22–26), the boundaries of the human condition.

Heracles simultaneously affirms and surpasses his own humanity when he confronts his various monsters. In the *Theogony* (270–335) there is a monstrous strain—the descendants of Phorcys and Ceto—that heroes must destroy: thus Perseus conquered Medusa the Gorgon, Bellerophon the Chimera, and Oedipus the Phix (or Sphinx). But for the most part, this catalog of deadly monsters proclaims the glory of Heracles, conqueror of the three-headed Geryon and his dog Orthus, conqueror of the Nemean lion and the Hydra of Lerna, conqueror of Cerberus and the terrible serpent who guarded the golden apples (here we recognize the first two and the last three of the labors in the cycle). But of these five exploits, there are three which pit Heracles against the world of the dead. Geryon the herdsman, "in his misty pen, beyond the illustrious Ocean," has often been seen as a double of Hades, and his two-headed dog is the brother of the cruel Cerberus, whom Heracles will also confront in the infernal kingdom of Hades. In order to pick the golden apples, the hero must once again cross the boundaries of the Ocean (Euripides *Hippolytus* 742ff.) and enter the enchanted garden of the singing Hesperides (*Theogony* 215, 275, 517), seductive but frightening creatures who rule over a mysterious Elsewhere (and they are the daughters of Night, sisters of the Moirai and the Keres: see Cl. Ramnoux, *La Nuit et les enfants de la Nuit*, Paris 1959, p. 68). The last exploit in the catalog of labors, the picking of the golden apples, the food of immortality given to Zeus and Hera at the solemn moment of their wedding, was sufficient, in an old version of the legend, to open the road to Olympus for Heracles. Without obstacles. Without other suffering. And perhaps without having to die the death of a mortal.

Thus confronting the Beyond, Heracles conquers death, and the tradition multiplies this victory infinitely, telling how the hero wounded Hades (*Iliad* 5.395ff.) and enchained Thanatos (Euripides *Alcestis* 842–53). To conquer death is also, in the heroic ideal that placed great importance on shining youth (*aglaos hēbē*), to conquer old age, the terrible curse that breaks the arms and legs of the warrior: Heracles the Strong thus will triumph over old age, either by embracing Youth forever or by bringing down the sickly old Gēras (on a pelike from the Louvre G234; ARV² 286, 16).

The fight against death and the quest for immortality: in the interval between the mortal and the divine that forms the career of the hero, Heracles naturally takes his place on the side of the Immortals in the great battle against the Giants. Because the gods need a human auxiliary against the Giants, who as candidates for immortality have become their rivals, he is that auxiliary, whom Athenian ceramists depict

Heracles fighting the triple Geryon. Attic amphora. Ca. 530 B.C. Paris, Musée du Louvre. Photo Chuzeville.

Athens, the grueling tasks give way to harmonious bliss, this choice testifies to the climate of the city, without questioning the meaning of the immortality of Heracles.

After the sufferings, the joy of the festivals of Olympus: thus the history of Heracles avoids the sad ambiguity that is the basis of the human condition. The Homeric heroes are entirely human when they choose undying glory (*kleos aphthiton*), the companion of the good death. As Sarpedon, even though he is the son of Zeus, explains to Glaucus on the field of battle: "If escaping this war would allow us to live eternally without aging or dying, I certainly would not be fighting in the front lines. . . . But no matter what you do, the goddesses of death are there . . . and no mortal can flee or escape them . . . ," and Sarpedon plunges into the thick of the battle (*Iliad* 12.322–28). Man dies, but glory is eternal; the glory of the warrior never dies, but the warrior dies. This terrible ambiguity is expressed by Achilles, king among the dead, in the depths of Hades, as he dreams of being alive again, a servant in the service of a poor farmer (*Odyssey* 11.483–91), but the dead Achilles returns to the choice of the good death that the living Achilles made (*Iliad* 9.410–16; 18.89–93 and 114ff.). From Olympus, his eternal home, Heracles, on the other hand, is ignorant of nostalgia and its contradictions.

But can Heracles understand contradiction? Does he feel the ambiguous density of introspection?

III. The Deviations of Force

Biē Hērakleiē: the "Force of Heracles." This, according to Homer or Hesiod (*Odyssey* 11.601; *Theogony* 289, 314, 332, 943, 982; *Shield* 52, 69, etc.), is the true name of the hero, as if the existence of Heracles was subsumed by his principal characteristic. This is also what the mythographers mean (Diodorus 4.10.1; Apollodorus 2.4.12) when they affirm that before winning the name Heracles, the son of Zeus, "illustrious offspring of the race of Alceus" (Pindar *Sixth Olympian* 68), was called Alcides. For this patronymic plays on the word *alkē*, one of the Greek words for force.

The force of Heracles: completely concentrated in the arm of the hero, this force is the force of the mythical warrior in his youth and courage—the vigor of the Hundred-Handeds who assured the victory of the Olympians over the Titans, or of the bronze men whose invincible arms "were attached to the shoulders of their vigorous bodies" (*Theogony* 150–53, *Works and Days* 148–52), the youth of the Homeric warrior whose arms "flash rapidly, to the right, to the left of his shoulders" (*Iliad* 23.627–28). As the seat of strength, the arm is the surest ally of the warrior (Euripides *Heracles* 740–42), and one day, the eternally young husband of Hebe miraculously restores vigor to the arm of Iolaus, his aged companion (ibid. 858).

But force is mute, and within Heracles silence reigns when, looking for an ally, a witness, or an identity, the hero speaks to his vigorous arm, which he identifies with his very being (Euripides *Alcestis* 837). In the *Trachiniae*, similarly, devoured by an unrelenting disease which is "feeding on his deepest flesh" (1053), the hero lists the parts of his body (1089–90): "O hands! O hands! O loins! O chest! O my arms!" as well as his past exploits (1091–1102). The life of a hero is reduced to his exploits, and more than any other hero, Heracles lives a life in which "each moment is born of the void and returns to it" (M. Delcourt, pp. 118–21). But, by the same token, this life is also constituted from the outside, since "the source and origin of the action . . . are found not within the hero but outside of him" (J.-P. Vernant, p. 91).

mounted on Zeus's chariot or fighting next to Athena: among men he wins fame as the "giant killer" (Pindar *Seventh Nemean* 90; Sophocles *Trachiniae* 1058–59; Euripides *Heracles* 177ff.); he may also have attained apotheosis, in another version of the story (see Pindar *First Nemean* 67–72, and F. Vian, pp. 193–94 and 212).

During the classical era, however, Heracles' career ended on the pyre of Mount Oeta, as if in order to enter Olympus, the hero had to understand death; as if Heracles' death negated his mortality: dying, but dying by purifying fire, on Oeta where Zeus reigned (Sophocles *Trachiniae* 200.436.1191; *Philoctetes* 728–29). It has often been said that the pyre of Oeta was introduced into the legend late, finally taking the step into the many traditions which made immortality the reward for an exploit (see Nilsson, Mingazzini, and M. Delcourt, pp. 127 and 135); there has been much questioning about the meaning of the *Trachiniae*, in which the fire of the pyre cures the hero of life (1208–9), though Sophocles does not indicate whether this was an annihilation or an apotheosis (see Linforth; for an opposing view see Segal). But only the annihilation of the human Heracles permits the apotheosis of the son of Zeus, and perhaps not enough attention has been paid to the tension which constantly sends Heracles between the death of mortals and the death which immortalizes.

II. Beyond the Human

In this tension there is no ambiguity, however: in the tradition of the classical era, Heracles always conquers immortality, no matter what path leads him to it, and the various pictorial representations untiringly detail all the versions of the myth (the apotheosis of the hero, carried off in a chariot pulled by four white horses or playing the lyre among the Immortals, the beatitude finally found in the paradisiacal calm of the garden of the Hesperides, the repose of the victorious warrior, conversing as an equal with Athena on the Olympian metopes). And although, in fourth-century

The dead Sarpedon borne by Thanatos and Hypnos. Attic krater. Ca. 510 B.C. New York, Metropolitan Museum of Art. Museum photo.

Looking within his body for a way to stop the unbearable pain that is destroying it, Heracles addresses himself to what is no longer anything: Heracles is no more. "Deprived of [his] limbs, broken to pieces, destroyed by a blind disaster" (1103–4), the fallen hero has no reserves, no *logos*; only cursing is left to him, and silence falls again. This is the "joy and sorrow of the warrior" who is a prey to the "internal logic of force" (Dumézil, p. 97). But for the hero, this logic is external: external to himself, as in the world of cities where he is never anything but a stranger (just as in the *Trachiniae* of Sophocles and the *Heracles* of Euripides).

Heracles is not tragic, because he is not ambiguous, and in order to make a tragic hero of him, Euripides was forced to invent something like introspection for him.

And yet Heracles has a dimension that allows tragedy to appropriate him as one of its heroes: if the tragic is ambiguity, it is also reversal, and Heracles the Strong can find a place there, since he is entirely subject to the law of reversal. Force is ambivalent, in that it has no norm but excess. Thus Heracles oscillates continuously between the superhuman and the subhuman, violently tossed from one to the other by a force which outdoes him, without ever knowing the human dimension of an Odysseus, who knows how to avoid all the snares of excess. Before being transported by the Immortals, he knew, more than any mortal, humiliation and abjection: seen from either Olympus or Hades, his exploits

were "ignominious labors" and "a miserable fate" (*Iliad* 19.133; *Odyssey* 11.618–19); he experienced servitude, subject to the orders of Eurystheus or the Lydian woman Omphale, and madness: possessed by Lussa (Madness), he killed his children whom he had saved, and the madness abandoned him only to reduce him all the more to the weakness of a child or woman (Euripides *Heracles* 1424; cf. 631–32; 1411–12).

The hero's death is exemplary in this regard; his polarity shows clearly, without interference. We know how Heracles married Deianira, the sister of Meleager, after saving her from a monstrous suitor; how he killed the centaur Nessus, who attempted to rape the young woman (see Sophocles *Trachiniae* 6–26 and 555–79); how he had with Deianira a son, Hyllus. But Heracles is not a hero of marriage: a life without respite, "when he returned home, sent him away again soon, in service to another" (*Trachiniae* 34–35), until, in love with the beautiful Iole, daughter of the king of Oechalia, he conquered her by force, taking her city and killing her father. Heracles left Oechalia in flames. Then, when the hero returned, events happened quickly (see Bacchcylides *Dithyramb* 16.13–35 Snell), in a drama in which it is tempting to see, with Ch. P. Segal, a kind of "inverse Odyssey"— between the return of Odysseus and that of Heracles we find, once again, the opposition between humanity and excess, super- and subhuman. To regain the love of her husband, the too-credulous Deianira sends him a love charm, which turns out to be fatal: the tunic that she has dipped into the blood and sperm of Nessus. The outcome is the devouring fire of the poison, the annihilation of Heracles when he is conquered by savage pain, the suicide of Deianira, and the pyre of Oeta. Sophocles has superbly staged the reversal, which makes the "most noble of all humans" into an object of opprobrium; the killer of monsters is no more than a howling monster, a victim of the savagery that he once conquered and that now rebounds on him. Before finally discovering in himself the crude soul (1295ff.) of the *hērōs theos* and acquiescing to the divine fire, the hero presents to those who are with him the horrible face of the Beast: a beast caught in the net of death and devoured by a bestial disease (1030, 1050–57, 1088–89; see Murray, pp. 113–125, and Segal, pp. 31–32 and 49).

The most significant reversal, however, is still the one that makes Deianira into a man and Heracles into a woman. In Sophocles' version, Deianira stabs herself, like a hero, like Ajax, instead of hanging herself, the feminine death to which tradition condemned her (Sophocles *Trachiniae* 930–31; for an opposing view, see Diodorus 4.38.3 and Apollodorus 2.7.7), while Heracles "cries and weeps like a girl," the strong one, the male who "under such a blow reveals himself to be a simple woman" (*Trachiniae* 1071–75). But among the exploits of Heracles, there are surprising instances of sexual prowess: capable of deflowering fifty virgins in a single night (Pausanias 9.27.6–7; Diodorus 4.29.3; Apollodorus 2.4.10 more generously gave him fifty consecutive nights for this high deed) and having a son by each of them—Heracles, it must be remembered, has only sons: the male cannot father anything but a male (see Apollodorus 2.7.8, which gives a long and edifying list of these sons)—the hero affirms a virility which has no equal but that of the Supermale of Jarry. And "it is a woman, with a woman's body, with nothing of the man about her" who fells him, "without even a knife" (*Trachiniae* 1062–63). The sad Deianira had, it is true, a prophetic name: *Dēianeira*, "killer of men." Our project is certainly not to undertake, like Philip E. Slater, a psychoanalysis of Heracles: perhaps the hero symbolizes a "vigorous denial of weakness in the face of the maternal hostility" of Hera; perhaps Deianira is a figure of the bad mother (Slater, pp. 339 and 352); but the essential point lies elsewhere, in the violent reversal which makes the weakness of a woman the only force capable of bringing death to the hero who has successfully combated it so many times before, and who identifies himself with virile force.

Heracles, or force caught in its own trap. Heracles, or time without memory, conquered by memory and vengeance.

But, just as the story of the hero does not end on the pyre of Oeta, his mythological career does not end there either.

IV. Edifying Figures

The most startling paradox of Heracles is the number of speeches which have been grafted onto his silent strength. Surprising both in the multiplicity of roles he assumes in the philosophical Logos and in the propensity of sages and intellectuals, from the Pythagoreans to the Stoics, as well as the Sophists, to annex to their own use the figure of the hero. As if silence called forth allegory. As if brute force offered a virgin territory to the development of the *exemplar virtutis*. Because the hero-slave became a god, the moralists see his destiny as a symbol of the human condition—the very incarnation of the efficacy of suffering. One step further and, endowed with outstanding deliberative ability, Heracles is deemed to have chosen his life of labors: the choice of a life

is substituted for the coercion of the labors. Another step, and the man of *phusis* (nature) becomes the champion of *nomos* (law).

Heracles of the crossroads, Heracles the musician, Heracles the hero of effort and "the laboring righteous": before the Sophists borrowed these figures, Pythagorean hagiography had already transformed the myth into an edifying paradigm (see M. Detienne, pp. 24, 32–33, and 53).

It remained to the Sophist Prodicus, however, to give this paradigm its most elaborate form, in the famous apology quoted by Xenophon (*Memorabilia* 2.1.21–33). Seated in a solitary place, the adolescent Heracles weighs the respective advantages and disadvantages of the path of virtue (*aretē*) and the path of vice (*kakia*). Two women appear to him, or two goddesses, if great stature is a characteristic of goddesses: they are named Arete and Kakia, and, like the just and unjust discourses in Aristophanes (*Clouds* 889–1114), they plead their causes before the young man. Kakia speaks against the effort that Arete exalts, and although in Xenophon's account the apology concludes with Arete's peroration, Prodicus's listeners all knew that, unheeding of Kakia's seductions and of the name of *Eudaimonia* (Felicity), which her devotees gave her, Heracles chooses the road of pain.

This apology introduced many themes alien to what had been the legend of Heracles until the fifth century. In the allusion to the two paths, one can recognize a reference to Hesiod who, in *Works and Days*, already put the path of the soft life (*kakotēs*) in opposition to the path of merit (*aretē*) and labor (*Works and Days* 287–92); in the contest of eloquence between the two women, it is possible to see a sophistic version of the judgment of Paris (B. Snell, pp. 325–29)—a judgment without Hera, a reversed judgment in which the hero would prefer Arete-Athena to Aphrodite-Kakia: a dilemma evidently unknown to the legendary Heracles, whose virility accommodated itself both to the aid of Athena and to the pleasures of Aphrodite. It is likely that Heracles' choice had much to do with Achilles' choice, a favorite theme of the Athenian schools of the fifth century, which gave *aretē* and *kakia* the traditional meanings of "bravery" and "cowardice" (M. Delcourt, pp. 131–32). The essential remains: Heracles is the center of the apology, a Heracles forever subject to the polarity that, in a continual reversal of more and less, tyrannically rules over his existence. Between the two enemy poles of pain and pleasure, Heracles chooses. He chooses what the myth imposes on him: a life of labors. But in the Pythagorean school, in reinterpreting the exploits of the hero in a moral perspective that placed all value in effort, Prodicus himself made a choice—the choice of an edifying Heracles, against all the amoral images of the hero.

The mythical ambivalence of the son of Zeus was striking. The duality of the two varieties of Heracles remains irreconcilable: the Prodicus type, philosophical, the ancestor of all the virtuous varieties of Heracles, and the comic theater type, profligate, greedy, and somewhat limited (for example, Aristophanes *Birds* 1574–1692).

At the end of this course, Heracles had become wise and chaste: a model of virtue. Olympus has receded, and the hero-god is no more than "the best of men," in a new avatar of the *aristos andrōn*. But Heracles will have been "the best of men" constantly, all through the tradition, from the *Homeric Hymn* to the Stoics: only the meaning of the phrase has changed, while the notion of *aretē* has also changed. Originally designating the valor of the warrior, it became more and more charged with introspection, until it finally meant something like "virtue." The history of the historic destiny of Heracles is partly linked to that of *aretē*, from which the hero

Heracles in the garden of the Hesperides. Attic hydria. Ca. 430 B.C. London, British Museum. Museum photo.

gains good manners that Homer and Hesiod would never have recognized in him.

We will not become involved in such a history, because it would take us too far from the topic, beyond the Heracles of the Stoics toward the Roman Hercules, and from the Roman Hercules to the Christian Hercules, and to the many forms of Hercules in Western civilization; it would take us from Dürer to Annibal Carrache and from Petrarch to Wedekind. Under the circumstances, only the first step counts, and to end, we will emphasize how greatly the hero suffered the counterblow of the evolution which, from the fifth to the fourth century B.C., gradually substituted for the warrior's *aretē* the peaceful virtues at the heart of civic values. "Defender of gods and men against danger" (*Shield* 28–29), Heracles began as a warrior hero in the cities, protector of the gates at Thasos or *promachos* at Thebes (see Pouilloux, 2, and Pausanias 9.11.4), and when, in 510, Milo of Croton led his fellow citizens against Sybaris, he wore the costume of Heracles. But in the fourth century a subtle shift made the warrior hero into a universal helper, invoked by everyone during the vicissitudes of existence. Heracles is still the protector, but the warrior has softened into a benefactor (he is already *euergetēs* in Euripides: *Heracles* 1252). The destroyer of monsters and the "most just of murderers" becomes a civilizing hero who, throughout his wanderings, devotes himself to irrigation works and the founding of cities. The Hellenistic era will even establish him—a surprise—as a legislator and will make him a model of *philanthrōpia* (delivering Prometheus from the shackles which the wrath of Zeus put on him, the hero thereafter acts on his own initiative and not on the orders of his divine father; his goal is no longer glory but philanthropy, which he honors through Prometheus—compare *Theogony* 526–34 and Diodorus 4.15.2).

Many pictorial representations follow this movement, and, on vases as well as on the metopes of temples, the warrior hero gives way to the reconciled hero, and sweat and blood are replaced by the beatitude of the blessed. The armor of the hoplite and the archer's equipment give way to the lion skin and the club, in anticipation of the time when only the heroic nudity and athletic musculature of his body will indicate the identity of the hero. In art, as in thought or religion, the process of interiorization seems irreversible.

It is time for us to leave Heracles. It is not that we feel that everything has been said about the hero. Our choice here was not to tell the story of Heracles, because his "life" cannot be told, at least not without devoting a lifetime to the task. Neither did we hope to isolate in him a "primitive kernel" of truth, because Heracles cannot be reduced to the Dorian hero of Wilamowitz, or to the daemon of vegetation dear to Jane Ellen Harrison, or to the Dumézilian warrior with his "three sins." And we chose to abandon any "totalizing" project about a hero whose vigorous silence resumes its form, intact, beyond all of the discussions it provokes.

But because Heracles, for the Greeks, is *the* hero, we have tried to explore the many configurations in which the heroic force occurs: between men and gods, between god and beast, between overactive virility and the tears of women, and between mute servitude and the silent endurance of thought.

N.L./d.b.

BIBLIOGRAPHY

Because of the extent of the discourse on Heracles, we can only select some major studies.

1. General Studies

M. DELCOURT, *Légendes et cultes de héros en Grèce* (Paris 1942), 118–38 (some pages dense and suggestive). R. FLACELIÈRE and P. DEVAMBEZ, *Héraclès: Images et récits* (Paris 1966). G. MURRAY, "Heracles, the Best of Men," in *Greek Studies* (Oxford 1946), 106–26. A. PUECH, "Héraclès dans la légende et la poésie grecques," *Revue des cours et conférences*, 25 and 26.

To make the list more complete: C. ROBERT, *Die griechische Heldensage*, 422–675, vol. 2 of L. Preller, *Griechische Mythologie* (new ed., Zurich 1967).

2. Some Points of View on Heracles

G. DUMÉZIL, *The Destiny of the Warrior* (Chicago 1970), originally *Heur et malheur du guerrier* (Paris 1969); the whole book elucidates the figure of Heracles better than the pages explicitly devoted to "The Three Sins of Heracles," which, although they seek to prove, carry little conviction. J. HARRISON, *Themis* (2d ed., Cambridge 1927), 364ff. PH. E. SLATER, *The Glory of Hera: Greek Mythology and the Greek Family* (Boston 1968), chap. 12. U. VON WILAMOWITZ-MOELLENDORF, *Euripides Herakles*, vol. 2 (new ed., Darmstadt 1959).

3. The Hero: Heracles in the Cities

L. R. FARNELL, *Greek Hero Cult and Ideas of Immortality* (Oxford 1921), chaps. 5–7.

Heracles in Thasos

M. LAUNEY, *Le sanctuaire et le culte d'Héraclès à Thasos* (Paris 1944), chap. 11. Pouilloux 1: J. POUILLOUX, *Recherches sur l'histoire et les cultes de Thasos*, 1 (Paris 1954). Pouilloux 2: "L'Héraclès thasien," *REA* 76 (1974): 305–16.

Heracles in Athens

S. WOODFORD, "Cults of Heracles in Attica," in *Mélanges G.M.A. Hanfmann* (Mainz 1971), 211–35.

4. The Hero: Life, Death, and Immortality

J.-P. VERNANT, "Aspects de la personne dans la religion grecque," in *Mythe et pensée chez les Grecs* (Paris 1971), 2:79–94.

Heracles in the Battle of the Giants

F. VIAN, *La guerre des géants: Le mythe avant l'époque hellénistique* (Paris 1952).

The Death of Heracles

M. P. NILSSON, "Der Flammentod des Herakles auf dem Oite," *ARW*, 1922, 310–16 (a reference article, but it gives nothing on the death of Heracles, which Nilsson wants to make an etiological myth introduced afterward to explain a rite). F. STOESSL, *Der Tod des Herakles* (Zurich 1945) (presentation of the material).

On the "Trachiniae"; on Heracles, Deianira, and Nessus

CH. DUGAS, "La mort du centaure Nessos," *Recueil Ch. Dugas* (Paris 1960), 85–91. I. M. LINFORTH, "The Pyre on Mount Oeta in Sophocles' *Trachiniae*," *University of California Publications in Classical Philology* 14 (1925): 255–67 (rationalist interpretation: nothing on the apotheosis of Heracles). CH. P. SEGAL, "Mariage et sacrifice dans les *Trachiniennes* de Sophocle," *AC* 44 (1975): 30–53.

Pictorial Representations of the Immortal Heracles

CH. DUGAS, "Héraclès mousicos," *Recueil Ch. Dugas*, 115–21. E. B. HARRISON, "Hesperides and Heroes: A Note on the Three Figure Reliefs," *Hesperia* 33 (1964): 76–82. H. METZGER, *Les représentations dans la céramique attique du IVᵉ siècle* (Paris 1951), chap. 5: "Le cycle d'Héraclès." P. MINGAZZINI, "La rappresentazioni vascolari del mito dell'apoteosi di Herakles," *Atti della Reale Accademia dei Lincei*, 1 (1925): 417–90.

5. The Twelve Labors

F. BROMMER, *Herakles: Die Zwölf Taten des Helden in antiker Kunst und Literatur* (Munster and Cologne 1953) (chiefly on the variations and concordances between pictorial representations and the literary tradition of the Twelve Labors; the author usefully reminds us that

the canonical cycle—the lion of Nemea, the Hydra of Lerna, the boar of Erymanthus, the doe of Cerynia, the birds of Lake Stymphale, stables of Augias, bull of Crete, mares of Thrace, girdle of the Amazons, cattle of Geryon, kidnapping of Cerberus, and golden apples of the Hesperides—does not appear until late; the first appearance, on the metopes of Olympia, surely served as the model but only after a considerable lapse of time).

6. The Civilizing Hero

L. LACROIX, "Héraclès, héros voyageur et civilisateur," *BAB* 60 (1974): 34–59.

7. Heracles at the Crossroads

J. ALPERS, *Hercules in bivio* (Göttingen 1912) (presentation of the material). M. DETIENNE, "Héraclès, héros pythagoricien," *RHR* 158 (1960): 19–53. B. SNELL, "Das Symbol des Weges," in *Die Entdeckung des Geistes* (Hamburg 1955), 320–32.

On the innumerable representations of this theme, from the fifteenth century to the baroque period, see E. PANOFSKY, *Hercules am Scheidewege* (Leipzig 1930).

8. The Destiny of Heracles in Western Civilization

C. K. GALINSKI, *The Herakles Theme* (Oxford 1972) (a complete record with many solid insights).

HERMES

Hermes, the son of Zeus and the nymph Maia, is, of all the gods of Olympus, the only one to reach his full status as an Immortal through contract. The *Homeric Hymn to Hermes* describes the stages of the accession during the adventures of Hermes the child and the end of the accession when the justice of Zeus accords him his share of privilege (of *timē*), while Apollo exchanges his flock for the lyre that Hermes has made. Though in the final analysis the details of these mythical adventures account for all the aspects and functions attributed to the god in the Greek pantheon, their very multiplicity and disparate character may explain why studies on the subject always focus on one of these aspects.

However, in relying on the letter of the myth, one can view the diversity of registers of the god as a whole, where the two chief words of his behavior would be combined: passage and *mētis*. The god of shepherds and travelers, inventor of the pile of stones used to mark roadways, god of trickery and theft, but also master of trade and contract, crafty in his speech and deceitful in his approach, conductor of souls and messenger of Zeus, and finally, lord of sleep, the name of Hermes is inscribed in a space of unexpectedness and mobility qualifying even the ways and means by which he achieves divinity.

I. Hermes the Mediator

Hermes plows the roads. Posted at the crossroads in the form of herms with two or four heads, he marks both directions and distances along the road. *Hodias, hēgemonios, agetōr,* he is the guide for journeys. *Propulaios, strophaios,* he guards the integrity of doors, and at the same time, as god of hinges, he ensures that they can be opened. The god of piles of stone (*herma, hermaion, hermaios lophos*), he is, according to Eustathius (*ad Od.* 16.471), the first to open roads, and after thus blazing the trail, he is the first to mark them with cairns

to show the way. As an adventurer in little-known regions, he is their solitary explorer and civilizing hero. The *Hymn* shows him in this role, driving the herd stolen from Apollo across the *agros, planoia(i):* away from the traveled routes. Alone, he opens his own route.

But he is also blamed for the unfortunate encounters that can befall one at night in the uncertain regions which separate the cities and the surrounding countryside, pasture-lands which are not quite the complete wilderness of the mountains. As the god of travelers, he is also the god of thieves, and though shepherds are included under his aegis (Hermes *nomios, mēlossos, epimēlios, kriophoros*), nothing prevents him from occasionally leading both shepherd and flock astray (*Homeric Hymn to Hermes = HHH* 282ff.). This is one of the principal characteristics of Hermes—he is ambiguous, sly, and deceptive. Of all his powers, trickery is the most significant (Hermes *dolios*), and it organizes each of his functions according to an ambiguity that marks his entire way of life.

Though Hermes is the epitome of one who facilitates trade and acts as a beacon for journeys, at the same time he is also the unsettling figure in these enterprises, the one who at all times threatens to jeopardize their successful outcome. A man of his word, he perjures himself and lies before the tribunal of Zeus (*HHH* 372). He puts into Pandora's heart the ambiguous and chatoyant words full of trickery and deceit (see Hesiod *Works and Days* 67–68 and 77–80, and *Theogony* 58) which make a woman duplicitous and dangerous to the man whom she seduces. Elsewhere, however, together with Aphrodite and Eros, he is among those who whisper the words that reconcile the young married woman with her husband, the whispering that helps them get back together (Plutarch *Praec. conjug.* 138 cd; Souda, s.v. *Psithuristēs*, and H. Usener, "Psithuros," *Rheinisches Museum*, 59, 1904, p. 623). Hermes, with others, makes possible marital union, union that is also spatial, since in his functions of *epithalamitēs*, he enables the young woman to travel the road which separates the *oikos* of her father from the *oikos* of her husband and ensures the integration of the young stranger into the heart of the new family network.

Since he is always in motion, Hermes champions what is involved in putting anything into circulation: goods, words, roles. But these displacements do not take place securely under his influence: there is a primordial uncertainty associated with Hermes, where chance always plays a part. *Hermaion*, the Greeks said: good luck, unexpected good fortune, a lucky throw of the dice. But also bad luck, where every good thing hides its bad side and the hunter is caught in his own trap: "a stroke of Hermes." Giver of goods, *dōtōr heaōn* (*HHH* 2.12), he is as miserly as he is generous, and though he knows how to multiply flocks as well as Hecate, he can also on occasion decrease them (Hesiod *Theogony* 444ff.).

The common trait in all these functions is that Hermes moves in an intermediary space and serves there as an intermediary, whether this involves marriage, travel, or speech, and occurs anywhere between the high and the low, between Olympus, men, and Hades. Hermes is the middle course: the happy spokesman and conductor of souls to the afterworld, the benevolent guide under the orders of Olympus or the carrier of the inexorable decree of death, he has complete mobility between one universe and another and ensures passage where the Greeks had set up strict boundaries.

In this function, the *Iliad* (24.317–30) shows him at Priam's side. Disguised as a *kouros*, he guides the old man across the plain that is surrounded by the river Xanthus and the trenches of the Achaean camp. This intervention is spatially situated between two boundaries, the frontier of the Trojan country and the threshold of Achilles' tent, and is set in the intermediate zone formed by the marine plain, the battlefield which by definition belongs to neither of the two warring opponents. Hermes takes the reins of Priam's chariot, lets the old man pass through the gates of the enemy camp, and protects his passage by putting the guards to sleep. The social impact of Hermes' action doubles its spatial symbolism: for Priam arrives in order to make an exchange. He proposes to Achilles a ransom for the body of his son Hector, which he wants to take back to Troy. Between these two enemies some method of communication must therefore be established that will cut across the state of war that separates their two communities. The total separation that has existed must be replaced by a kind of union carried by the rules of hospitality and social customs. Priam must be able to convince Achilles. Achilles must agree to listen to the stranger.

In an apparently very different context, we can note the common marks that stamp the invocation of Hermes: when Odysseus returns to Ithaca and, keeping away from the banks taken over by the Phaeacians, crosses into the interior of the country, he meets Eumaeus, his old swineherd (*Odyssey* 14.1–22). Disguised as a beggar, he gathers information about his homeland. As a respectful host, Eumaeus hurries to make a sacrifice and offers the firstfruits to Hermes. These meetings occur under the sign of Hermes and in a semiwild space, where blankets are made from animals' skins, wild animals are used for guard dogs, and the swineherd's house is a rude assemblage of stone blocks with a frieze of thorns.

Eumaeus thus invokes Hermes as a welcome to the voyager for whom the god is the *proxenios* (Aeschylus *Suppliants* 920), in that he allows the stranger to enter the *oikos* of transition. He also invokes him because of the geographical location of the return: in the solitude of the *agros*, midway between the city and the mountains, in the middle of the pastureland. But the invocation exceeds the knowledge which Eumaeus believes he has. For although Odysseus is a stranger, he also dissimulates. He keeps his identity a secret

Hermes and Apollo's cattle. Attic hydria. Ca. 490 B.C. New York, Metropolitan Museum of Art. Museum photo.

in order to find out what has become of his power after an absence of twenty years. Hermes is therefore also there for the dissimulation, for the duplicity under the mask of which the return takes place. He is invoked and is there in the midst of a problematic reconnaissance and recognition which Eumaeus himself does not completely understand. Hermes' message is never clear.

Hermes is an outlaw, a trader, one who covers his tracks. He can represent the ordering of a space or its disorganization. He is simultaneously order and disorder. He is misleading and ungraspable. He operates by dissimulation: such was Apollo's experience in the search for his flocks (*HHH*, passim). A child born in the morning, Hermes stole his brother's divine flock with the power of an adult. But when Apollo went to his mother's retreat to call him to account, he found him snug in his swaddling clothes like an infant (*HHH* 245).

The polymorphism of Hermes is also what discourages the bloodhounds of his older brother (Sophocles *Ichneutai* 112ff.; *HHH* 219ff.). Nose to the ground, the Satyrs follow the trail taken by the child and the cattle, but the tracks are blurred, crossed, and doubled back on themselves; a labyrinth without beginning or end. And with reason. The *Hymn* describes how Hermes reversed the signs; he forced the cows to go backwards while he covered his shoes with myrtle branches to erase his own footprints (*HHH* 75ff.).

This is the trickery of Hermes: he is past master of traps and machinations. Using all his artifices, he upsets situations, reverses their order, and confuses his opponents. Armed with the cunning intelligence that the Greeks called *mētis*, he departs in the conquest of his allotted privileges. These bear the indelible mark of the conditions under which they were acquired: admitted through deceit and double-talk, in Olympus Hermes will represent orderly disorder, allowed and recognized by Zeus.

II. Hermes, Disorder, and Exchange

After thus kidnapping half of Apollo's herd, Hermes travels through Greece; from Pieria, the divine pasture where the number of cattle remains fixed, he moves them along the banks and hills toward the valley of the Alpheus. There he stops: the animals find a meadow of clover and aromatic plants in the high valley—normal fodder for domestic animals—as well as stables and a watering place. Separated from their divine land, they become *agrauloi boes* (*HHH* 412), cattle of the *agros*, a herd comparable in every way to those of men, a herd which can therefore reproduce and multiply.

The change in the status of the cattle is a determining factor in Hermes' strategy: humanized, the herd is a divine possession put back into circulation, a possession which its owner Apollo could no longer hoard and contain in its initial divine immobility. Hermes is refused his place on Olympus at the same time as he assumes symbolic responsibility for the new cattle, and Hermes threatens to steal the treasures that Apollo keeps in his sanctuary at Delphi: another way of putting goods back in circulation (*HHH* 174). If he is not to be the god of reciprocal exchanges (*HHH* 516, *epamoibima erga*) and of goods that circulate, he threatens to become the prince of thieves. God of merchants or king of thieves: these are the alternatives, and both sides stem from the ambiguity of his birth away from Olympus. (In Pergamum, money changers made up deficits in their illicit operations with a sort of tithe, "money for Hermes"; see W. Dittenberger, *Or. Gr. Insc. Sel.*, 2, 1905, no. 484, 1.33–34.)

Although Hermes is *athanatos*, immortal, like his mother he receives neither offerings nor sacrifices, and in this sense, he remains excluded from the divine sphere of the *hieros*. Making the herd go toward the side of man is a first step in the determination of his status. The second step is the sacrifice that brings the themes of controlled disorder and transition to their conclusion.

After installing the cattle in their stable and building a fire, Hermes sacrificed two of them. The sacrifice violated the most elementary rules of the ritual. The animals were slain at night, heads turned toward the ground, without shedding blood but by piercing the spinal cord (*HHH* 118ff.). Without distinguishing between the pieces of meat, Hermes roasted at the same time the pieces normally reserved for the gods or priests (*geras, nōta gerasmia, hiera moira*) and those usually eaten by men. From these pieces he made twelve identical portions, absolutely interchangeable, that at the same time he endowed with a *geras*, which clearly marked them as divine portions. Yet he chose them at random (*HHH* 129) as if they were human portions and then refused to consume any of them—for in the end, he affirmed his divinity by contenting himself, as the gods do, with the smoke of the sacrifice (*HHH* 133). Through a clever intermingling of attributes and roles, the initial sacrificer ends up designating himself as the recipient of the sacrifice. Where the representation of separation weighs most heavily for the Greeks, the separation of men from gods, of the *hosios* from the *hieros*, Hermes, after performing an apparently disorganized union of contraries in the mixture of the meats, crosses the uncrossable boundary established between Earth and Olympus: despite his very human hunger for meat, he does not eat the sacrificial and domestic animals. He will be on the side of the gods, satisfied with the honor accorded him.

Hermes thus makes the transition, at the price of scrambling the sacrificial code, which is the equivalent of scrambling his tracks. Yet this momentary disorder challenges a bipartition of the world that the *mētis* and power of Zeus never cease to affirm through the very institution of sacrifice. And from this disorder a new order arises in which Hermes finds his place. The position looks like the exact mirror of his subversive practice.

Using the effectiveness of these ambiguous practices, Zeus recommends an amicable settlement through a division of powers. This agreement, in which the two brothers promise mutual *philotēs*, alliance and friendship (*HHH* 518–26), puts a definite end to the unsettling history of Hermes. But at the same time, it raises to the level of a model of exchange what had been mythical history. Hermes becomes a contractual member of Olympus. Without this contract, however, the destiny of Hermes' herd would remain a dead letter. Let us not forget that when he took fifty of Apollo's hundred cows, Hermes left behind both the bull and the dogs. He could sacrifice all the cows he wanted, stable them, feed them on clover, and look forward to a profit, but there was no possible way to increase the herd. In order for there to be a profit, it was necessary that the two parties, on the one side the cows which Hermes had symbolically given the new status of domestic animals, and on the other side the bull that was indispensable for reproduction, should be reunited. This presupposes an accord between the two parties, and just as the joining of two pieces of a broken potsherd, the *sumbolon*, witnessed the contract between two merchants in classical Athens, so the initial division of the herd presupposed its final reconstitution and at the same time an agreement.

We can therefore clearly understand how Hermes the thief is also the Hermes of exchange. Changing a kidnapping into a convention and at the same time substituting one role for another is the point of his history. His destiny is played along the divide, and all his functions are more or less connected with boundaries. At crossroads, at gates of cities and houses,

Hermes the psychopomp. Attic lecythus. Ca. 525 B.C. Jena, Friedrich-Schiller-Universität. Museum photo.

The child Hermes and Apollo. Hydria from Caere. Ca. 525 B.C. Paris, Musée du Louvre. Photo Chuzeville.

at locks, he is found at the limits of all areas and takes his place wherever change is to be encountered. *Strophaios* (Aristophanes *Plutus* 1154 and scholium), he makes the door pivot on its hinges, but he also aids the man in moving from inside to outside. On the order of the opposition of inside and outside, he opposes Hestia while at the same time completing her: for though the goddess of the hearth represents the immobility of a home attached to the ground, the persistence of the *thalamos* and its treasures, Hermes, on the other hand, will ensure the opening of the *oikos* onto an always problematic and threatening outside. He will guide the members in their encounters with the exterior and will travel at their sides through the uncertainty and mobility of the world. In this way Hermes *agoraios* takes his place at the very meeting place of the citizens (see J.-P. Vernant, "Hestia-Hermes," in *Myth and Thought*, pp. 97–143).

III. Hermes' Lyre

But let us return to the myth: Hermes won his place through exchange, and he gave his lyre to Apollo in exchange for the cows. This lyre was one that he had made himself out of a tortoise shell when he left the cavern. This is a technological object, and Hermes the *polumētis* has all the traits of a clever engineer when he tunes his instrument (*HHH* 24ff.). Lively, watchful, among all the objects which nature offers him he seizes on the one that will best suit his project. *Hermaion*, say the Greeks, a godsend. But this godsend finds its complete meaning only in the context of a specific behavior which is that of the man with *mētis*. His intelligence and skill show him how to use propitious moments and the resources of his environment. He knows how to shape it, to fit into it, and to find his bearings in it.

Hermes' lyre has rightly remained in the mythology not as an attribute of Hermes the musician—because it is really Apollo who has this role—but for the rapidity and technical precision of his touch. In this sense, it is to be compared with

other marvelous technical inventions created by the clever minds of gods like Hephaestus and Zeus. Hephaestus, the blacksmith, knew how to build automatons, servants of gold who seemed to be alive, endowed with life, voice, and strength (*Iliad* 18.376ff.). Zeus conceived the idea of Pandora, in whose creation both Hephaestus and Hermes vied for a part: she too would dazzle with life and seductive charm, even though she was made of clay. In the same way, the paradox of the lyre lies in the fact that the tortoise shell, emptied of its interior, produced an admirable sound which nothing about its exterior would lead one to expect. The lyre tames Apollo with the charm of its song, and though it is a "mechanical" object, it carries the quality of magic which causes the listener to experience a great desire, an *amēchanos erōs* (*HHH* 434). Against this emotion Apollo can do nothing but appropriate the object for himself and propose the exchange to Hermes. The lyre is a *thaumatopoiia*, an object whose use exceeds its appearance and which in the hands of a man of *mētis* causes the reversal of a current situation: Apollo, the elder, the secure, is brutally conquered by the stupor of this charm and sees his preponderance deeply shaken.

The lyre as a product of *technē* is important less as an object than for the place it occupies in a series of other *technai*. *Doliē technē* is the phrase used in the myth to designate the reversal of the tracks of the herd (*HHH* 76); and *aristē technē*, the best of all for getting to Olympus, is used to describe the sacrificial reversal (*HHH* 166).

These *technai* derive from a certain configuration in the behavior of Hermes: he engineers, conjectures, and calculates; he is the *mēchaniōtēs poneumenos* (*HHH* 436). He also sets traps and encircles his adversary with his tricks. He cheats and misleads in discussion (*HHH* 2.17–320). The *technē* of his actions doubles the *technē* of his words. Before the tribunal of Zeus, he uses an ambiguous manipulation of words: he lies and perjures himself. But in the final analysis, Zeus is captivated by Hermes' ability to convince, by his *peithō* as well as his duplicity, and with a great shout of laughter he signals his recognition of his son (*HHH* 389).

Technai are thus sometimes good, straightforward, and just, part of the artisan's skill with which Hermes is occasionally associated (see M. Detienne and J.-P. Vernant, *Les ruses de l'intelligence*, p. 285ff.). More often, however, they brutally raise their masks and show the hidden side of their ambiguity. The charm of the lyre, which at first seems joyful and full of gaiety, becomes fascinating to the point that Apollo feels bound. *Amēchanos erōs*: Hermes was able to create, from what was originally a pleasure, an *amēchania* from which his brother is unable to escape.

Invincible desire echoes another *amēchania*, the one which Apollo used to threaten Hermes as punishment for his theft: he could have tied his brother, too, with inescapable bonds in the bottom of the *amēchanos Tartaros* (*HHH* 156.254–59), thus reducing his revenge to silence. To the threat of this never-ending bondage, Hermes opposed the *mēchanē* of his lyre, which wove in the heart of Apollo a network of bonds equal to the chains of Tartarus. Fascinated, bound by the music as the sailors were bound by the voices of the Sirens, Apollo is paralyzed. The recurrence of the term *phōnē* seems to be important; less the charm of the voice than that of speech, this is the sign that reveals the power of women to seduce: Hermes gives his voice (*phōnē*) to Pandora (Hesiod *Works and Days*), and the deadly charm of the Sirens' song (*Odyssey* 12.40ff.) contrasts with their deceitful promise of new knowledge. And Apollo is finally caught in the net which he himself had threatened. Thus an inversion of roles takes place, which the luxuriant growth of the shoots of the agnus castus (chaste tree) foreshadowed in the myth.

In order to affirm the supremacy of his power over his younger brother, Apollo tries to tie his arms and legs with ropes made from the chaste tree at the very site of the theft, once his herd has been recovered. But through the power of Hermes these soon begin to grow excessively and interlace the cattle in their web. Apollo is stupefied. This moment of suspension, the instant of *thauma* (*HHH* 409–15), marks the reversal in a power relationship, where the weaker reveals himself to be the stronger. Hermes' speed, the oblique and circular nature of the binding, are the master words of a whirlwind, which characterizes his actions throughout the myth. An ungraspable will-o'-the-wisp (*purpalamēs*), gaudy spirit, mime, and magician, he knows the art of knot tying. Whether with real knots, in the case of the plant web which he controls in the end, or the metaphorical knots of the seduction of the song that conquers Apollo, in all cases, Hermes catches unaware an adversary who is sure of his power.

The same power to tie is at work in the stratagems of language used by Hermes the sophist. Master of the arts of persuasion, the roguery of Hermes' speech seduces Zeus. "Father Zeus, I will tell you the truth: I am frank and I do not know how to lie," proclaims Hermes before the tribunal of the son of Kronos (*HHH* 368–69). In doing this, Hermes confers upon himself the virtues of Apollo (*HHH* 311ff.) and he confirms his lie with a false oath (*epiorkos*). Does this mean that the justice and knowledge of Zeus fell into the trap of this deceitful language? No: what convinces and seduces him is the very subversion of the speech, sustained by the art and skill of this child. What he recognizes in his *dikē* is not the false truth of Hermes' defense, but the contrary: the spirit of *kakomētis*. At the very moment when he allows this rogue to make the transition into the ranks of the gods and advises the brothers to come to an understanding, he affirms that on Olympus there will thereafter be a place for cunning language and falsehood. There will also be a place for what this type of language supports at the base of truthfulness: the truth of a transgression, the effectiveness of the practices that underlie it, and finally the consistency of the speech that accompanies them.

At the end of the story of Hermes, his place thus emerges at the axis of his victory. Hermes will be both mediator and trickster: mediator in his field of action, working at the limits, boundaries, and frontiers between worlds, joining what is separated, facilitating communication in all forms. *Aimulomētis* (*HHH* 13) in his method of action: lively, rapid, and transient, a skillful and disconcerting mechanic, a great swindler with words, he takes onto himself the mobility of the world. In the face of this mobility, he will be, for the man who confronts him, helpful or overwhelming.

L.K.-L./d.b.

Hermes and a saytr. Attic amphora. Ca. 500 B.C. Berlin, Antikenmuseum. Museum photo.

BIBLIOGRAPHY

1. Homeric Hymn to Hermes

J. HUMBERT, *Les hymnes homériques* (Paris 1936). ALLEN, HALLIDAY, and SIKSES, *The Homeric Hymns* (Oxford 1936). L. RADERMACHER, *Der homerische Hermeshymnus*, Sitz. Berichte der Akademie der Wissenschaft (Vienna 1931).

2. Books and Articles

E. BENVENISTE, *Le vocabulaire des institutions indoeuropéennes* (Paris 1969), 2:47ff. and 179ff. N. O. BROWN, *Hermes the Thief* (New York 1947). J. CHITTENDEN, "The Master of Animals," *Hesperia* 16 (1947): 69–114; "Diaktoros Argeiphontes," *A.J.A.* 52 (1948): 24–33. L. DEMOULE-LYOTARD, "Sur des épigrammes de l'Anthologie Palatine," *Annales E.S.C.* (May–August 1971). M. DETIENNE and J.-P. VERNANT, *Les ruses de l'intelligence: La métis des Grecs* (Paris 1975). S. EITREM, *Hermes und die Toten* (Christiana 1909); "Hermes," in Pauly/Wissowa, *Real-Encyclopädie*, vol. 8 (1913), cols. 738–92. W. FAUTH, "Hermes," in *Der Kleine Pauly*, 2, cols. 1069–75. H. GOLDMANN, "The Origin of the Greek Herm," *A.J.A.* 16 (1942): 58ff. H. JEANMAIRE, "Le substantif *hosia*," *R.E.G.*, 1947, 66–89. L. KAHN, *Hermès passe ou les ambiguïtés de la communication* (Paris 1978). K. KERENYI, *Hermes der Seelenführer* (Zurich 1944). M. P. NILSSON, *Geschischte der griechischen Religion* (Munich 1955; 3d ed., 1967), 1:501–10. J. ORGOGOZO, "L'Hermès des Achéens," *R.H.R.* 136 (1949): 10–30 and 139–79. P. PERDRIZET, "Hermes Criophore," *B.C.H.* 27 (1903): 300–313. P. RAINGEARD, *Hermes Psychagogue* (Paris 1934). CL. RAMNOUX, *Mythologie ou la famille olympienne* (Paris 1962). W. ROSCHER, *Hermes der Windgott* (1878); "Hermès," in *Ausführliches Lexicon der griechischen und römischen Mythologie*, 1, cols. 2342–2432; *Ausführliches Lexicon . . .* , supplement *Epitheta deorum*, pp. 104–11. J. TOUTAIN, "Hermès, dieu social chez les Grecs," *Revue d'histoire et de philosophie religieuse*, 12 (1932): 289–99. J.-P. VERNANT, "Hestia-Hermes, sur l'expression religieuse de l'espace et du mouvement en Grèce ancienne," in *Mythe et pensée chez les Grecs* (Paris 1965), 97–143. P. ZANKER, *Wandel der Hermesgestalt in der attischen Vasenmalerei* (Bonn 1965).

THE HESPERIDES

Goddesses of the west and daughters of Night, the Hesperides are named Hespere, "of the evening," Aegle, "the brilliant," and Erytheïs, "the blushing." They live in the far west, at the edge of the Other World, beyond the river Oceanus. In the garden of the gods, where the springs of ambrosia (the drink of immortality) flow, they are the guardians of the tree with the golden apples. These fruits are tokens of the eternal life and divine fertility that Earth gave to Hera when the goddess celebrated her wedding to Zeus in the same garden. These clear-voiced goddesses in alliance with the serpent Ladon, the son of the monstrous Echidna, keep watch over the border of the world of the gods and deny men access to the garden of immortality. When Heracles succeeds in securing the golden apples, he obtains a token of the divine condition that is reserved for him.

J.C./d.b.

HESTIA

Hestia is listed as one of the twelve gods in several canonical sources. This Greek divinity bears the name of the domestic hearth and is the oldest daughter and the first child of Kronos and Rhea. Later, however, she became the last of the children of Kronos, since she was swallowed first and regurgitated last. After Zeus's victory over the Titans, when privileges were being distributed which would decide the new order of the world, Hestia received some favors from her brother: she was permitted to remain a virgin always, to receive the first of all sacrifices, and to have her place at the center of the house, where the hearth was located.

As the goddess of the domestic hearth, permanently in the status of a virgin, Hestia defined an entire aspect of marriage in Greece, the same marriage that, paradoxically, she had renounced for all time. In contrast with Hermes, the god of open spaces, of transition and exchanges, Hestia defined the interior space of the female world, which each new bride, after she was installed in the house by her husband, would perpetuate and maintain in its continuity, in a way becoming the daughter of the new house and of the domestic fire which was put in her care. Under the sign of Hestia, the family group conceived its unity as a circle closing in on itself at the center and considered the domestic group to be self-sufficient, refusing to take any food with a stranger. This, it is said, is how one sacrifices to Hestia: by giving no part of the offerings to a person foreign to the house. But at the same time that she is the interior, closed in on herself, the hoarding place where the group can put down its roots, Hestia's association with Hermes opens her to the outside, to passing strangers, to the circulation of wealth, the network of alliances, and the organization of space which was implicit in the patrilocal nature of marriage in Greece.

On the religious and political levels, Hestia plays the same central role. She is the hearth of the city, often associated with the building called the Prytaneum, a place where power was exchanged among equal citizens, as well as a banquet hall where the magistrates in the service of the city were companions at the city's table. A ritual like that of Cos, which centers on the Zeus of the city (Polieus) and on Hestia, shows how a politico-religious system of thought organizes its space according to procedures and gestures. Each of the oxen is presented individually by each of the subdivisions of each tribe and the victim kept for the sacrifice is decided by ordeal. The cattle are then allowed to mingle in a common group. The designated ox, at the end of the test, is brought before Hestia, who has earlier received a sacrifice in homage. At last the offerings are placed on the hearth at the moment of immolation. The division of the victim offered by the social group as a whole takes place at the center of the isonomic circle, which returns individual shares to each of the members of the city through the fellowship that they share in eating together.

J.C./d.b.

BIBLIOGRAPHY

L. GERNET, "Sur le symbolisme politique: Le Foyer commun," in *Anthropologie de la Grèce antique* (Paris 1968), 382–402. J.-P. VERNANT, "Hestia-Hermès" (1963), in *Mythe et pensée chez les Grecs* (3d ed., Paris 1971), 1:124–70.

IO

Io was an Argive princess, priestess of Hera, and beloved of Zeus. In order to keep her from the jealous fury of his wife, Zeus transformed Io into a white heifer. Hera demanded that her rival be brought to her and had Io watched by the hundred-eyed Argos; then, when Hermes killed the guardian at Zeus's request, Hera sent a gadfly to torment Io without respite. Io fled across the Greek lands and seas, giving her name to some of them, such as the Ionian Sea and the Bosphorus ("route of the cow"). When she arrived in Egypt, she gave birth to Epaphus and was worshiped under the name of Isis. Among her descendants is Danaus, who took refuge at Argos with his fifty daughters, the Danaids, who murdered their husbands.

J.C./d.b.

IRIS

Iris was the daughter of Thaumas, an "Old Man of the Sea," and a sister of the Harpies. Her name means "rainbow," and she is the "angel," or messenger, charged with establishing a temporary contact between the Sky and the Earth, gods and men, just as the rainbow does. She is also the one who, at the command of Zeus, plunges to the palace of the goddess Styx in the depths of the netherworld to bring back the icy water on which the gods swear their great oath. The penalty for breaking this oath is the loss of their divine condition for ten years.

J.C./d.b.

IXION

Ixion was the king of the Lapithae, in very ancient Thessaly. A descendant of Ares, impious and a perjurer, he was subjected to an exemplary punishment. When Ixion's father-in-law, Deioneus, came to him to claim the presents promised him in exchange for the hand of his daughter, Ixion prepared a pit of fire for him and thus committed the first murder of a relative. Zeus alone agreed to purify the murderer, and, offering him hospitality, welcomed him into the home of the gods. Ixion, however, coveted the wife of his host. To test him, Zeus sent him a snare: a cloud image of Hera; Ixion had intercourse with her and fathered a monstrous son, Centaur. To punish him, Zeus had Ixion chained to a winged wheel which revolved constantly in the air while the condemned man was forced to repeat: "You should show gratitude to your benefactor."

J.C./d.b.

MARSYAS

Marsyas was a Phrygian satyr who invented the two-piped flute, or rather who incurred the wrath of Athena for picking it up after the goddess threw it down when she became vexed at seeing in a river the reflection of her face, which was distorted by her playing of the instrument. Marsyas was also foolhardy enough to challenge Apollo and his lyre. When the god won the competition, he inflicted a cruel penalty on Marsyas: he was flayed alive and hung from a pine tree, whose red bark retains the color of his blood.

J.C./g.h.

MIDAS

Midas was king of Phrygia. He was cruelly punished for his greed and foolishness. Because he had rendered a service to Dionysus, the god made his imprudent wish come true: everything Midas touched turned to gold; thus he almost died of hunger. Dionysus, feeling compassion for him, showed him how to free himself from his curse by washing in the Pactolus, which since then has contained grains of gold dust. The story goes on to say that Midas preferred Apollo's adversary in a musical contest. The furious god made him grow ass's ears, which the king hid under a headdress. His barber confided the secret to the earth, but according to Ovid, the reeds that grew there rustled in the wind and whispered that King Midas had ass's ears.

J.C./g.h.

THE MOIRAI

The Fates were three sisters whose powers trace the shape of an order older than that of the Olympians. More than destiny, the common noun *moira* designates one's share of booty, food, or inheritance. Moira is the religious power that defines both the share assigned to each person—which accounts for his *timē*, his social status, his place in the hierarchical order—and the limit assigned to each person, the barrier not to be crossed. The emphasis is sometimes on an already established order: allocation, putting things in their proper place; and sometimes on an order in the process of being established: equilibrium, adjustment, reciprocity.

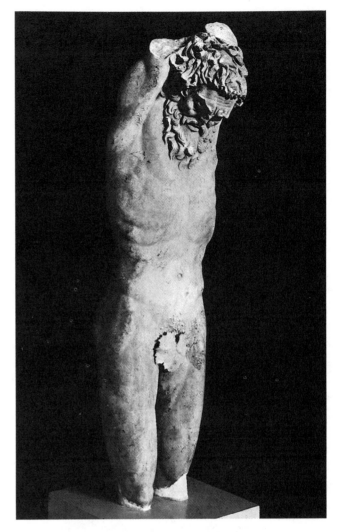

Marsyas hanging from a tree trunk. Istanbul Museum. Photo Sebab and Joaillier.

Any disruption of order—any crime committed within the animal kingdom, the world of men, or the realm of the gods—sets in motion the Fury or Furies (Erinyes), sisters of the Moirai and guardians of the cosmic order, who strike at the fertility of women and of the soil. But in the epic tradition, Moira walks close beside the red death, the brutal hand that deals the sudden blow to the unsuspecting victim, that binds him, subdues him, and does him violence. This brutal, sudden component of death, not the regular component that justifies each person's right to booty and banquet, but death as the inescapable lot of all people, is what the experience of war and combat makes into a figure that is at once familiar and terrifying.

J.C./g.h

BIBLIOGRAPHY

B. C. DIETRICH, *Fate and the Gods: The Development of a Religious Idea in Greek Popular Belief and in Homer* (London 1965).

The Muses and Mnemosyne

From the song of Homer to the decorative friezes on Roman sarcophagi, the presence of the Muses, daughters of Zeus and of Memory (Mnemosyne), has a continuity, whose meaning is inscribed on what the Greeks called "music," and which we call "culture."

The epic poet is powerless to sing without the help of the Muse, who knows how to enumerate the endless names in the catalogs of the best warriors and the exhaustive list of the vessels that sailed to Troy. For she alone possesses memory as it was conceived of in ancient times, memory that is the power to contemplate the past, the present, and the future simultaneously and to know the totality of things in one glance. The Muse bestows this gift of memory on the poet, and she can deprive him of it as well. Thamyris of Thrace boasted that he could conquer the Muses. They became angry and maimed him (undoubtedly by depriving him of his voice) and at the same time caused him to *forget* how to accompany himself on the lyre. On the other hand, the Muses gave Demodocus, the Phaeacian bard who was blind, the gift of singing and of sharing the unfailing memory of the daughters of Memory. The handicap of Demodocus is the visible sign of his quality as a bard beloved of the Muses. And when at the court of Alcinous Odysseus listens to Demodocus recite the episode of the Trojan horse, he does not doubt that Demodocus has seen with his own eyes the adventure that he sings of perfectly ("in the perfect realm of words": Homer *Odyssey* 8.492) and has not merely heard it from someone else's mouth, through the distance of hearsay.

Thanks to the vision of memory, the bard or the poet who deciphers the invisible utters speech whose symbolic efficacy is based on the dominant system of values. In his double register—celebrating the immortals and singing the high deeds of warriors—the poet inspired by the Muses institutes the real: his singing constitutes what is; his activity is ontological by nature. By reciting the myth of the emergence or by enumerating the names of the gods in order, he collaborates directly in the ordering of the world. By confer-ring praise or blame he inscribes within the memorial tradition the words that establish in the daylight and in truth the exploit that he sings about, and he condemns to dark night and silence those exploits which he forgets and does not deem worthy of being celebrated. Master of truth, the poet remains until Pindar's time the keeper of the words in which others are willing to recognize themselves.

Before they became nine and set forth in their names a theology of speech that is sung (starting with the *glory* of Clio and the *festivity* of Thalia, and ending with the *powerful voice* of Calliope), the Muses were three sisters in a very old shrine of the Helicon: Melete, Mneme, and Aoide, three modes of poetic activity. The first designates mental exercise, concentration, and attention. The second bears the name of memory, that psychological function without which there is neither recitation nor improvisation. The third refers to the completed poem, the product of Melete and Mneme.

The cult of the Muses, which the disciples of Pythagoras renewed in Magna Graecia, was based on a recollection in which the soul, the divine principle within the individual, retraces the complete cycle of its former lives and manages to escape the wheel of rebirth, to rise above the flux of becoming, and to attain the immutable existence of the gods. But the Pythagorean Muses add to anamnesis the full knowledge of a doctrine in which the harmony of the spheres leads *music* toward astronomy and mathematics. The Neoplatonists were the heirs to a philosophical circle that placed its activities under the patronage of the Muses. Through this circle, they helped to diffuse within funerary symbolism the representation of these Muses directing scenes of intellectual life; for in that life, the Muses ordered the quality of purification and the function of immortality.

J.C./g.h.

BIBLIOGRAPHY

P. BOYANCÉ, *Le culte des Muses chez les philosophes grecs* (Paris 1936; 2d ed., with additional notes, 1972).

Narcissus

Young, beautiful, loved by boys and girls alike, Narcissus scorned the gifts of Aphrodite and refused to let himself be possessed by anyone who loved him. Despairing of ever attaining the object of his love, his lover Aminias committed suicide; or in another version, it was the nymph Echo who wasted away for love of him. Nemesis (who may perhaps be Aphrodite) or the god Eros avenged the victims of the coldhearted, handsome youth. Narcissus, thirsty, saw his reflection in a pool and fell in love with the image, taking it for someone else. And so then he was the one who failed to possess the one he loved. Consumed with despair, he died of love, or drowned in the pool: from his body or his blood was born the flower that bears his name.

Another metamorphosis made Narcissus the symbol of a deviant behavior known as narcissism. To make this connection, the immediate meaning of the Greek stories had to be overlooked, for in all versions except one, Narcissus does not recognize the one he loves; he is not aware that he is in love with himself. And even when he recognizes his error, he recognizes it for what it is: not a fault, but a punishment. He has sinned, not in loving himself, in which he is merely the victim of divine vengeance, but in scorning the gifts of golden Aphrodite, as did Atalanta and Hippolytus. In this game of amorous exchange under the patronage of the Graces, in which one must let oneself be possessed in order to possess, he refuses to yield. Like them and yet unlike them, he is punished by the inversion of his sin: lack swings to excess. Atalanta offends the goddess by mating in the temple; Hippolytus inspires a fatal love in Phaedra; and Narcissus, who refused to *give* himself, will therefore burn with an excessive love for what he can neither *take* nor possess: a reflection in the water.

He sees his reflection in the water, and the distance between the illusion, which is the image of Narcissus, and the reality of his body opens an ambiguity which makes all the reinterpretations valid.

For illusion is a fundamental given of myth, one that psychoanalytic resemanticization tends to discard too

Poussin, *Echo and Narcissus*. Paris, Musée du Louvre. Photo Flammarion.

Narcissus. Tapestry from the Gothic era, *millefleurs* type. Boston, Museum of Fine Arts (Kling). Museum photo.

quickly. Certainly the mirror is the special instrument of narcissism, but when looking at one's image in a mirror, no one takes it for someone else. Narcissus takes himself for someone else, and this "unlikely" madness (Pausanias) is his punishment. Even in Ovid, where he recognizes his error at the end ("I burn with love for myself"), rather than finding his salvation in this breaking of the illusion, Narcissus considers the radically inaccessible character of this self with which he is in love: *inopem me copia fecit* (possession rendered me without possession). It is because I possess myself that I cannot possess myself, says the one who had once cried, I would rather die than be yours (*emoriar quam sit tibi copia nostri*). Thus Ovid's affected antitheses go further in making the punishment fit the crime, and the curse of a spurned lover takes on added significance: "May he thus love and thus never possess the one he loves." What he loves is inaccessible, not because it is too distant, but because it is too close: "I wish that what I love were far from me." But even in this version, which prepares the way for the analytic interpretation, illusion remains primary and indispensable to the narrative. Narcissus must first believe that he loves another in order to be able to love himself. When the illusion dissipates, it is too late, as it is for Agave when she recognizes—she finally sees—what she holds in her hands: the bloodsoaked head of her son Pentheus. Insight is the ruin of Narcissus, and in Ovid his story is part of a cycle of narratives in which someone is ruined because he has seen or has been unable to see. Tiresias *saw* two snakes mating and thereupon became *blind;* he predicts that Narcissus will live long if he does not know himself—if he does not *see* himself; he tells Pentheus that, to his ruin, he will *see* the sacred rites of Dionysus and that he will perish because the Bacchae *see* him in the guise of a boar. Appropriately, Ovid compares illusion and deceit to narcissistic error by placing both in a Dionysian context.

In the background of the story of Narcissus looms Dionysus the illusionist. Philostratus emphasizes him, describing an ancient painting that we might call "Narcissus beside the Pool," in which the illusion of the mirror is doubled by the painting itself. Nor did the subtle ties with which Narcissus is attached to Dionysus escape Nicolas Poussin, whose painting "The Birth of Bacchus" depicts the metamorphosis of Echo and the death of Narcissus, choosing only these two from all the other "Dionysian" heroes evoked by Philostratus and Ovid, who inspired his painting.

But what about the narcissus? The thirsty Narcissus looks for a cool spring "in the shade of the forests." In this coolness, he finds a burning love that wholly consumes him, and "wanting to quench his thirst, he senses a new thirst growing in him." The narcissus thrives at the water's edge, is mirrored in its springs, and perishes in the excessive heat of summer. It dies young, like the crocus, hyacinth, violet, and anemone, the most beautiful flowers in the garden of Flora, all born of the blood of beautiful children who died in the flower of their youth, all flowers of death, related to the great chthonic goddesses. But the narcissus has one more property. It puts people to sleep, it fascinates; *narkissos* comes from *narkē,* torpor, say the Greeks. The narcissus is the instrument of an illusion, of deceit. Earth made it grow, says the *Homeric Hymn to Demeter,* "as a trick," so that its luster and its fragrance might become a trap in which the fascinated child Persephone would be caught—just as the mirror held by the Titans fascinates and traps the child Dionysus, and the mirror of the waters immobilizes and hypnotizes the adolescent Narcissus. Between the narcissus, the deadly trap whose luster and fragrance open a way into the darkness of the cloven earth that engulfed Persephone, and the mirror of the waters, the frozen surface that inflames passion instead of quenching it, that locks up secure from any capture what it reflects with indifference; between the young man Narcissus, indifferent to all seductions but caught in the fascinating trap set by his own luster, and Dionysus, the master of illusion, also trapped by a mirror, certain threads come and go. They weave a tapestry of relationships that are by no means univocal, but in which one may decipher, more clearly perhaps than "the memory of the primal scene," the interventions of two sovereign powers: Aphrodite, whom one never spurns with impunity, and Dionysus, the master of deadly illusions.

J.C./g.h.

BIBLIOGRAPHY

OVID, *Métamorphoses,* 3.339–510. CONON, *Narrationes,* in Photius *Bibliotheca* 186.24. PHILOSTRATUS *Imagines* 1.23. In addition to a very important bibliography, ancient and modern, there is an illuminating analysis of the utilization of the myth by Plotinus (to which these lines owe much) in the excellent article by P. HADOT, "Le mythe de Narcisse et son interprétation par Plotin," *Nouvelle Revue de psychanalyse* 13 (Spring 1976). A psychoanalytic reinterpretation that is amusing for its very excesses is D. BRAUN-SCHWEIG and M. FAIN, *Éros et Antéros* (Paris 1971), 139–58.

NEMESIS

Nemesis belongs to the children of the Night. When Zeus chases her across the earth and the sea, she becomes alternately fish, goose, and swan before she is finally caught and bears an egg from which Helen is born, and with her the Trojan war. Through the semantic values associated with Nemesis—*nemein*—she is a figure who belongs in the field of distribution and allotment, like the Moirai. She adjudicates through legal authority; more precisely, Nemesis represents just allotment, insofar as she is not respected but is threatened and jeopardized. Associated with Themis, the wife of Zeus who sends the roots of justice down from the gods, Nemesis determines a plan of allotment-retribution in which the accent is not so much on the retribution that reestablishes the order of things as on the belief that a certain attribution is correct and legal while another is not. In ancient Rhamnus, she was worshiped side by side with Themis. In *Works and Days,* Hesiod prophesied that Nemesis, accompanied by Aidos, would ultimately abandon mankind at the end of the Iron Age and return to dwell among the gods.

J.C./g.h.

ODYSSEUS

I. The Man of a Thousand Twists

"Make me sing, Muse, of the man of a thousand twists, who wandered much when he had sacked the sacred citadel of Troy" (Homer *Odyssey* 1.1). Odysseus, the *polutropos.*

Of all the stories of the hero, the only one whose truth is never questioned is the one that he tells at the court of the Phaeacians. Through the effect of a series of infinitely receding nested frames (see F. Frontisi, "Homère ou le temps retrouvé"), the time of this account may be seen as a kind of respite between the lively departure from Calypso and the final test of recognition by his own people, and between the solitude of his voyage and the reunion with Telemachus. During this time of respite, the actual story of Odysseus is spelled out, that is, the story of his wanderings.

Odysseus, the fluent liar, cunning speaker, deceitful thinker, and dazzling wit, speaks the truth before the assembled people of Scheria. He comes before Alcinous and Arete, reveals himself, confesses his identity, and under their very eyes weaves the waning course of his fate. The point that he eventually reaches, however, is not immediately reached by a direct route. His initial behavior is characterized by dissimulation. To the questions that the queen addresses to the stranger, Odysseus the shrewd (*polumētis:* Hom. *Odyssey* 7.240ff.) does not give the right response, the one that would give away the secret of who he is and what he has done. Instead he tells of his skill as a sailor during the terrible storm that Poseidon brought down on him before he was finally washed ashore on the coast of the land of his hosts. And for the question of his origin he substitutes the question of his own skill. About his name, he says not a word; he speaks only of *mētis.*

To show him hospitality, Alcinous calls all the local inhabitants to the celebration and summons Demodocus, the bard, who will delight the gathered throng. Alcinous is unable to name his honored guest: "Hear me, leaders and counselors of the Phaeacians. This guest and stranger whose name I do not know (*ouk oid 'hos tis*) has come to my house after being shipwrecked" (ibid. 8.26ff.). Odysseus refuses to be recognized.

The bard's truth, however, catches the heart and the sealed lips of the hero unawares: "When they had satisfied their thirst and hunger, the Muse inspired the bard. He arose and chose to sing, among the great deeds of men, about an episode whose fame had gone up to the skies, the quarrel between Odysseus and Achilles the son of Peleus . . ." (ibid. 8.72ff.). When he hears this story, Odysseus weeps. But the tears do not betray anything to the Phaeacians, and Odysseus keeps his secret. When the games are about to begin, it takes Euryalus's insolent claim (ibid. 8.158) that the man must be a merchant to make Odysseus stand up and reveal his true rank to all. No, his body is not the body of an accountant "who lists the cargo, or surveys the freights and the profits of thieves" (ibid. 8.161). His body is the body of an athlete. To everyone's surprise, he straightens the frame that has been bent over by pain and suffering and reveals his power. Odysseus removes the mask from his body and displays his valor. What looked like a cheap merchant turns out to be a skilled and powerful discus thrower. Odysseus is slowly recognized, as his body speaks louder than words. But still no name.

Demodocus sings again, Odysseus prepares to leave, and then comes the last supper. Odysseus finally addresses the bard personally so that he can ask him to tell "the story of the wooden horse, and how the godly Odysseus sent this trap into the inner citadel of Troy" (ibid. 8.487ff.). Pure folly from the master of tricks, and yet what fascination: he alone among the gathered throng knows that he is the hero of the episode evoked in the song; he alone knows the truth and the fiction of the bard's words; he alone possesses the key to this past in the present of his return. But Demodocus is skillful in the way he weaves the lines of his poem. It is as if the horse were there, as if the Trojan chiefs were present; and Odysseus is caught in the trap that he thought he could control. He weakens, and tears flood to his eyes; Alcinous notices. The break takes effect in the mirror relationship established between Odysseus and the song that tells of his exploits, between Odysseus and the hymn that spells out the letters of his name. The letters are made of his trickery, his skill, and his intelligence. These are the very claims for his noble rank as well as the means that sustain his silence at the Phaeacian court. Odysseus is told of his trickery even as he is practicing his deception. The same trickery distinguishes him in the minds of the audience: it is the trickery of a hero whom all identify in Demodocus's discourse. But at the very same time, the deceit stands in the way of full recognition. It is simultaneously the symbol and the concealment of an identity. To untie this entanglement requires the power of truth and persuasion in the words of the bard. Odysseus's emotion clings to the way that the song knits events together.

Henceforth, Odysseus himself must recognize his own identity, but not in the signs and indices that can be deciphered like marks and that may function as reminders of a past experience and the promise of future cleverness and caution. Such discoveries are troubling because they exceed the limits that Odysseus had placed on them. They neutralize what Odysseus regards as a decisive separation between his being and his history. The past no longer fits within the brackets of remembrance that he had imposed on it during the unavoidable meanderings of his voyage. He resumes his

Odysseus escaping from the cave of Polyphemus. Attic cup. Ca. 500 B.C. London, British Museum. Museum photo.

function, and the question of his origin inevitably leads to the evocation of his homeland. The past that was cut up into moments in the ten years of wandering has now been suddenly and crudely put back together. From now on it is no longer a question of episodes occurring in different places, nor of successive tests, but indeed of the unbroken thread leading from his past back to his parentage. Until now, Odysseus has kept his own story at bay in his attempts to control the avatars of a difficult return; he is now unable to manipulate his story for the sake of deception. Rather, the story has invaded Odysseus, and he becomes its subject once more. The paradox of the situation is that the change in status of the past—which swings the pendulum of Odysseus from not saying to saying—takes place through the greatest possible separation between the inner and the outer. The words come out of the bard's mouth, at Odysseus's request, but as if Odysseus were not Odysseus. Unity prevails, the listener reintegrates the character, and Odysseus reintegrates his name. But it all had to come after a double separation: a separation in time from a celebrated past to an unknown present, and a separation in space from the mouth that speaks to the ear that hears. The separation operates within a relationship of otherness, in which the inner returns via the outer, the vector of the return being the poet's memory.

Alcinous then says this: "But you should not in turn, my guest, hide with cunning thoughts what I will ask you; it is better to be frank. Tell me the name by which your mother and your father used to call you there, and the others in the town and on the outskirts of the town. For nobody has ever lived who has no name" (ibid. 8.548ff.). Then Odysseus tells his name and begins telling the story of his adventures.

II. Nobody

Nobody is without a name, but one may be named Nobody. This was a painful game for the duplicitous Odysseus, but it did save him from being massacred by Polyphemus, the Cyclops.

We see here the man of *mētis* in action. Trapped with his companions deep inside the monster's cave, terrorized by his thundering voice and the noise of his movements, Odysseus ponders what course to take: "Cyclops, take and drink some wine after you have eaten your meal of human flesh, so that you will know what sort of drink our ship contains" (ibid. 9.347ff.). Overcome by the sweet wine, the Cyclops grows drowsy. "Cyclops, you want to know my most famous name? I will tell it to you. My name is Nobody. Yes, my

father and my mother and all my friends call me Nobody."
"Well, I will eat Nobody last, then, after I eat all his friends,"
replies the Cyclops. Then, under the weight of Hypnos, the
invincible tamer, the Cyclops tumbles. Odysseus's men
hurry and draw the wooden beam out of the red-hot fire;
they drive the sharp end of the beam into the corner of
Polyphemus's eye. Howling with pain, he awakes and calls
for help: "Trickery, my friends! Trickery, and not force! And
who killed me? Nobody." "Nobody? No force used against
you? All alone?" ask his friends. "Then it must be some evil
that great Zeus has sent you, and there is nothing we can do;
call on Poseidon, our king, our father" (ibid. 9.406–11).

Trickery and not force: the field of *mētis* is deployed in the
opposition of these two terms. *Mētis* always resorts to a
process that falsifies the result of the test, a process by which
the one who is considered to be vanquished turns out to be
the victor. In this context, shrewd forecasting and meticulous
planning rely heavily on the deceptive effects of an uncertain
world. As Hera works against Zeus elsewhere, Odysseus
here uses sleep as the indispensable ally of his scheming.
This natural activity, normally unpredictable, is manipulated
by the scheming mind of Odysseus and used against his
adversary. The changing patterns and colors of the world
make a favorable environment for the elusive and mobile
behavior of the man of *mētis*. Because the cosmos is polymorphous, his position will accordingly be polymorphous.
Wherever the outcome is in doubt, his shrewdness will
organize a network of signs and acts that will not only sketch
out the *poros* but will also place his adversary in the initial
state of *aporia*.

Such is the case with Polyphemus, who has force in his
favor. But this force of action and voice is deprived of the
meaning which the ordeal would have established and is
caught in the closed circle of an incomprehensible discourse
that none of the Cyclopes can unravel as they rush to the
rescue: How? Nobody? All alone? This is the encircling
labyrinth of words to which Nobody is the key, and the
prison of the blinding wound that makes it impossible for
him to recognize or name Odysseus.

Odysseus's false identity is here registered in a context
other than that of Phaeacia. It is perfectly in keeping with the
way he acts. Here actions and words are matters of duplicity,
as is Odysseus's parentage. He treats his ancestry and the
name given him by his father and mother like external
objects that he can use against his enemy, like levers
(*mēchanai*) that he uses to his advantage when quickly
premeditating his moves. Even his name, given him at birth,
is an unbroken thread that runs through all his adventures
and is absorbed into the fabric of a fluctuating, doubt-ridden,
and obscure world. It is part of his trickery, like the rest of the
universe, which Odysseus here takes control of: it is mallea-
ble and reversible. It matters little that the price Odysseus
pays is that of his identity by his name, because what sets
him apart at this moment is primarily his mobility and his
actions, that is, his body. As for his words, including saying
his own name, they are treated not for what they are but for
what he can make of them.

III. The Appearance of the World and the
Land of the Forefathers

The world is not what it seems to be, and the gods deceive
us. In the shifting plots that they hatch, how is one to tell the
real from the false? And how is one to respond: with truth or
with falsehood? In this uncertain outer world, what place is
there for the authenticity of the inner world?

Odysseus and his companions who have metamorphosed into pigs.
Attic lecythus. Ca. 500 B.C. Taranto Museum. Photo Soprintendenza.

Odysseus is guided by the Phaeacians and awakens on the
soil of his homeland. But he is the victim of dense clouds
spread by Athena; he recognizes nothing and despairs that
he has not reached his homeland yet. Then a young and
noble shepherd arrives and assures him that he is indeed in
Ithaca. Odysseus, wild with joy, takes care not to tell him
who he is and makes up a story of Crete and Phoenicians for
the benefit of the stranger.

But Athena removes her mask: it is she who is there; it is she who has deceived him. Odysseus is indeed the master of trickery, and Athena, his guide, is very pleased with her protégé. But she reminds him of the law that weighs on all mortals. The *mētis* of Odysseus is immense, but never equal to that of the goddess who inspires him. The gods remain the masters of the play between reality and fiction. *Poikilomētis* though he may be, this time Odysseus is the victim, for just as he sets foot on the land of his forefathers, that is, the only reality after his wandering, he is stuck in the mendacity and the appearance of his deceitful words. Odysseus certainly admits to the appearance. But at the very moment when the goddess tells him that he has returned home, how will he know whether or not she is teasing or deceiving him (ibid. 13.185ff.)?

It is, however, in the confirmation of the reciprocal fraud that both of them find their common bond. Hatch the plot of my vengeance for me, demands Odysseus. Athena answers: "When I have made you unrecognizable, go first to see Eumaeus the swineherd" (ibid. 13.391ff.). Odysseus goes inland disguised as a beggar. The whole problematic of the return is about to be enacted in the game that he will play out between the outer layer of the appearance and the inner layer of his identity. The game depends on a splitting in two that is particularly painful to sustain, because the name of Odysseus is on the lips of every inhabitant of this country mourning its king, and the beggar cannot put an end to the tears of his friends. Powerless, he must accept the notion that he died somewhere, so that, in the final stage of the *Odyssey,* he will be able to recover full rights to his house and his royal power, that is, to start living again.

To this splitting apart of the dead and the living, Odysseus adds yet another level. He is only a beggar, but a beggar whose past is full of adventures. In the course of his travels, he has rediscovered the tracks of the lost master. By means of his false identity, he restores a part of existence to that Odysseus and promises everyone that he will return. Falsifying his origin allows him to evoke his true progression. But there still remains the problem of convincing people, and the moment of the proof.

Eumaeus hears the story of the stranger who has come into his pen, and he believes it by and large: "But there is just one point that seems to me to have been invented. No, no, I don't believe the stories about Odysseus. Why must you, in the state you are in, tell these vain lies?" (ibid. 14.361ff.).

The pattern of reversals here reaches its peak. Below its surface, Odysseus's tale conceals its kernel of truth. But to Eumaeus's ears, the opposite effect takes hold: the core of the story is taken to be its outer crust. We move from implicit to explicit, from true to false, from inner to outer. Uncertainty runs rampant and intuition is threatened. The words with double meanings come out into the open, and the people who hear them fear more than ever that they are the victims of a trick. And it must be understood that there are various levels of discourse within the narrative of the Homeric poem. The first guarantee of truth for the listeners is established by the story within the story of Odysseus's voyage; the nesting of these two time lines comes to a resolution in the liminal and supernatural setting of the land of the Phaeacians. Then the two narrative times of the poem are collapsed into one plane. Up to this point, the *Odyssey* is composed of two superimposed storylines, that of the return of Odysseus and that of the quest of Telemachus for his father. In book 15, this second dimension gives way to the theme of the past that must be retrieved; the two narratives merge into one as the two protagonists meet again. And so

the conflict between the inner and the outer, the true and the false, is debated within the very structure of the poem. So long as the double dimension was maintained, that is, the dimension of past and present, of the bard's speech and Odysseus's speech, the security of an inward truth eclipsed Odysseus's real confrontation with the world as it appears and with the knotty problem of his parentage. With the return to a single time frame, when the plot no longer thickens, all the characters join in the play and in the debate. Odysseus says to Telemachus: "Believe me, I am your father, who has cost you so many tears and such suffering." And Telemachus replies, "No, you are not my father Odysseus, but some god is deluding me in order to redouble my tears and my sufferings" (ibid. 16.188–95). A god deceives, and a god reveals; you cannot judge a book by its cover. Athena had made Odysseus into a beggar; for Telemachus, she makes him into a king. And by reminding his son of the power of the Immortals, he can become his father again.

But what is sufficient between father and son is not sufficient between husband and wife. Penelope asks him his name, and his people, and his city, and his family (ibid. 19.105–7). "For you were not born of the mythical oak or of some stone," she adds (ibid. 19.167). This is a question of parentage, not merely of a mythically autochthonous birth. Odysseus tells of his encounter with Odysseus: "Now all these lies he made appear so truthful" (ibid. 19.204), and Penelope tells of her weeping for the husband that is next to her. We finally move into the labyrinth of problematic evidence: the "brooch made of pure gold with twin tubes for the prongs" (ibid. 19.231) which that Odysseus wore; when it is found here it stamps the seal of truth on the lie told by the now-present Odysseus. "For I have something true to tell you concealing nothing, that I heard but lately: Odysseus is going to return" (ibid. 272ff.).

But signs will be needed: signs to reveal or to conceal, depending on whether the hero is Penelope's husband or the beggar confronting the suitors. Signs of the past or signs of the present, depending on whether memory or trickery is used to achieve recognition. Odysseus vacillates back and forth continuously between one register and the other. For some, he disguises himself, and his skill as an archer and as a speaker ensures his vengeance; for others, he removes his mask, and he must then go back to the time of the Trojan War, the time of his childhood and of his marriage.

In the end, the reunion of Odysseus and his people is articulated as the sharing of a single memory. But this alone does not constitute a proof of the authenticity of the name of Odysseus. The name, which had become Nobody through a cunning trick, must find its final basis in a genealogy by finding evidence right in the hero's body, not the skillful and polymorphous body of the *polutropos*, but the constant body, the body marked by time, the solid body of the craftsman who no longer needs to use tricks but can now construct.

The scar on Odysseus's leg that is recognized by the old nurse Eurycleia has only one real value, that it serves to identify Odysseus by name. Odysseus had once been wounded by a boar when he was following his uncles, the sons of Autolycus, his maternal grandfather. But the complicity of the wound and the name echoes the complicity of the nurse and the grandfather on the occasion of his naming: "Long ago, Autolycus came to the rich land of Ithaca and saw the baby that his daughter had just given birth to. And when he had finished his meal, Eurycleia placed the baby on his knees and spoke to him, calling him by name, 'Autolycus, find a name to give to this son of your own daughter, a child you have so long prayed for' " (ibid. 19.399–404).

Odysseus tied to the mast of his ship. Attic stamnos. Ca. 480 B.C. London. British Museum. Photo Giraudon.

Here is unfolded a genealogy from father to daughter, which makes the sharp-eyed nurse the depository of the secrets of the child's body. Similarly, the secret of the particular construction of the olive tree as the base of the marriage bed allows the couple to authenticate their reunion. "But although the proofs of identity are in the story of an external action, the external action has as its objective the construction of a material interior: tightly fitting beams, a roof that perfectly seals the nuptial bedroom, tightly fitting blocks. Odysseus builds an enclosure inside. The image is that of a concentric structure, of a closed-in circle, and of a protected inner space" (J. Starobinski, "Je hais comme les portes d'Hadès," *N.R.P.* 9, p. 22). A closed-in circle refers back to an inward truth, as did the self-enclosed account of the voyage.

As this inwardness unfolds in time: the time of remembrance and then of the telling of past trials, or in space: the space of the couple's bedroom in the heart of the dwelling, in both dimensions, it rests on the continuity of a memory that in other contexts takes on an altogether different value.

The span of ten years was for Odysseus a time of accumulating expertise and insight into the obstacles that the gods set up to thwart his return from Troy. The space was that of the stormy uncertainty that made him map his way over and over again. Knowing how to speak cleverly, knowing how to act cunningly, tortuous thinking in his view of the world, such was Odysseus's situation as he responded on the outside to his environment, while his judgment all turned inward. The inner meaning of his return was eclipsed by the necessary vigilance constantly demanded by the exterior.

The same time and space are at issue in the staging he has arranged to surprise the suitors, a setting in which word and action are the object of a secret that guarantees their misleading effect and assures the final overthrow of the false rulers of the place.

Elsewhere, however, the value of these categories is transformed, is indeed inverted, as soon as genealogical discourse arises, along with the problem of its roots within a familiar time and space. The time, at one point merely an ephemeral passage, becomes reversible, recollectable, evocable, because it is staked out with a series of signs (*sēmata*) quite different from the flimsy clues picked up by a spy. These markings,

inscribed long before to be rediscovered now, are like the indelible map of an immutable body that substantiates a shared memory. In this sense, Odysseus's activity as a craftsman is the positive side of the activity of the man with *mētis*. He leaves his indelible traces, and however clever he may be, he first moves toward building one of these landmarks.

If the body of Nobody cancels out his past history in the present time of a scheme, the body of the patient carpenter upholds it, so that in the end, the body of Odysseus will bear the name of Odysseus.

L.K.-L./g.h

BIBLIOGRAPHY

1. F. FRONTISI-DUCROUX, "Homère et le temps retrouvé," *Critique*, no. 348 (May 1976), 538–48. J. STAROBINSKI, "Je hais comme les portes d'Hadès," *Nouvelle Revue de Psychanalyse*, no. 9 (1974), 17ff. R. DUPONT-ROC and A. LE BOULLUEC, "Le charme du récit," in *Écriture et poétique, lectures d'Homère, Eschyle, Platon, Aristote* (Paris 1976).

2. On the Homeric world: M. I. FINLEY, *The World of Odysseus* (rev. ed., New York 1965). G. S. KIRK, *The Songs of Homer* (Cambridge 1962).

3. On the Homeric text and its overall structure, see: E. DELEBECQUE, *Télémaque et la structure de l'Odyssée* (Aix-Gap 1958). D. PAGE, *The Homeric Odyssey* (Oxford 1955), opposes to this vision of the text as a whole a course of analysis and internal criticism of the text contesting its unitary character.

4. On Homeric mythology: P. CHANTRAINE, "Le divin et les dieux chez homère," in *La notion du divin depuis Homère jusqu'à Platon, Entretiens sur l'Antiquité classique* (Vandœuvre and Geneva 1952), 1:42–96.

On the symbolic interpretation of certain episodes of the *Odyssey:* C. P. SEGAL, "The Phaeacians and the Symbolism of Odysseus' Return," *Arion* (1962), 4:17–52; "Transition and Ritual in Odysseus' Return," *La Parola del Passato*, 1967, 321–42. P. VIDAL-NAQUET, "Valeurs religieuses et mythiques de la terre et du sacrifice dans l'Odyssée," *Annales E.S.C.*, no. 5 (September–October 1970), 1278–97.

5. Finally, the book of M. DETIENNE and J.-P. VERNANT, *Les ruses de l'intelligence: La métis des Grecs* (Paris 1974), contains many analyses of the narrative and intellectual course of the artful man in relation to the values of the work of the artisan, as does the book of F. FRONTISI-DUCROUX, *Dédale: Mythologie de l'artisan en Grèce ancienne* (Paris 1975).

OEDIPUS

We know the story of Oedipus largely through the version given by the tragedians, especially Sophocles in *Oedipus the King* and *Oedipus at Colonus*. In these works, the hero's character and career are presented in a particular light, in the perspective of tragedy. The "myth of Oedipus" most frequently refers to this tragic Oedipus, to whom Freud's interpretation alludes and from whom he derived the term "Oedipus complex."

The legend, however, goes back to a period before the Attic tragedy of the fifth century. Homer was already aware of it: in the *Odyssey* 11.271–80, a passage in the *Nekuia* refers to it briefly. The mother of Oedipus was called, not Iocasta, but Epicasta. Unaware that he was her son, she married Oedipus, who had killed his own father and seized his weapons. When the gods revealed the truth to men, Epicasta hanged herself, leaving Oedipus on the throne of Thebes and cursing him with the vengeance of the maternal Erinyes. In this tradition, Oedipus did not gouge out his own eyes and was driven neither from power nor from his native city.

Before it was poured into the tragic mold, the Oedipus legend was part of a vast body of myths known as the Theban cycle, which focused on the origins of Thebes. The narrative told of the heroic deeds of Cadmus, his quest for Europa, his victory over the dragon, the birth of the Spartans, the founding of Thebes, the hero's marriage to Harmonia (who was born of the illegitimate union of Ares and Aphrodite), the descendants of Cadmus and Harmonia (the first legendary kings of the city), and the conflicts over succession. In this sense, it is inappropriate to talk of an "Oedipus myth." We should rather speak of a Theban mythology in which the story of Oedipus constitutes one link in the thematic chain of an epic poem, known as the *Oedipodia* (Pausanias 11.5.11), of which nothing remains.

In dealing with Oedipus, we must distinguish between two rather different ways of interpreting the myth. The first is the reading of the tragedies, that is, separate but related works, taking into account their dates, their contexts, and their authors. In this area, decipherment tries to shed light on various levels of meaning and to show how these levels of meaning can be understood as a function of the requirements and motivations peculiar to the dramatic genre. To apply the second method of interpretation, mythological analysis, two conditions must first be met. First, the interpreters must take into account all versions of the myth, even the most marginal ones, in order to attempt to isolate a common framework that will bring order to the play of the variants, using their differences as well as their similarities. Then they must analyze the Oedipus episode within the broader context to which it belongs.

The ancients saw the Oedipus of Sophocles as the model for the tragic hero: master of Thebes, pride and salvation of the city, but also the scum of the earth, defiled and cast out of the city; the all-powerful *turannos,* supplicated by the people, and the vile *pharmakos,* driven from the territory like a scapegoat; lucid and blind, innocent and yet guilty, the decipherer of enigmas is for himself an enigma he cannot decipher. His exceptional fate and the exploit that brought him victory over the Sphinx placed him above other citizens, beyond the human condition, equal to a god. But because he rose to power through parricide and incest, his deeds excluded him from civilized life and the community of men and reduced him to nothing. The two crimes that he unwittingly and unwillingly committed made him, although an adult man standing firmly on his *two feet,* resemble his father, a "three-legged" old man leaning on his walking stick, the man whose place next to Iocasta was taken by Oedipus; but the same acts also made him resemble the old man's grandchildren still crawling on all *four feet,* grandchildren to whom he was a brother as well as father. His inexpiable fault was to mix within himself three generations that should have followed one another without ever intermingling or overlapping at the heart of a family line. Without any clear distinction and regular succession between the generations, there can be no stable conditions, no sustained continuity in rank and function, no order in the city.

Oedipus, the hero of knowledge and power, himself turned into that creature of chaos that the Sphinx evoked when she described man by propounding a riddle, defining him as one who simultaneously walks on two, three, and four legs. When he found the correct answer, Oedipus entered Thebes and took the place of the King, and he entered Iocasta's bed and took the place of her husband, thus making himself an example of the very question that he thought he had answered.

The analysis of the myth of Oedipus has taken two directions. Marie Delcourt has sought to identify a small number of themes that have to do with rituals, archaic institutions, or beliefs. In combination, these give rise to a legend of conquest and power that dramatizes the struggle and the victory of the young king over the old king. Thus the motif of Oedipus exposed on Cithaeron is closely tied to the ritual of expulsion of evil creatures at birth—creatures who are all the more powerful if they manage to survive—and to the initiation trials of young men. The fight with the monstrous Sphinx is situated at the crossroads of two beliefs: that the souls of the dead survive in the form of winged creatures, and that nightmares are demons who oppress the sleeper. The murder of the father bespeaks the victory of the young over the old. The union with the mother symbolizes taking possession of a territory, gaining sovereignty over the land of a city.

Altogether different is the reading of Claude Lévi-Strauss, who chose the example of Oedipus to illustrate his structural method of analysis. The focus is no longer on the great general themes; rather, he seeks to determine the basic elements of the narrative and to delineate each of the actions that constitutes one of the essential sequences of the narrative within the plot of the text. The next problem is to isolate the relationships of opposition and homology among the elementary narrative units or mythemes. To that end, the units are sorted and then listed in columns according to their thematic affinities, regardless of their place in the narrative. At the same time, the field of analysis is enlarged to encompass, over and beyond the strictly Oedipal sequences, the greater mythical whole within which the accounts are fitted, whether it concerns Cadmus; Laius, father of Oedipus; Labdacus, his grandfather; or his sons and daughters. The mythemes are divided into four groups that combine in various pairs: those which reflect the overestimation or underestimation of kinship relationships; those which deny the autochthony of man or which, on the contrary, assert his original roots in Mother Earth, a deep-rootedness attested by the malformations of the foot (Oedipus means "swollen foot"), or a limping and shuffling walk (Labdacus means "lame man"; Laius means "clumsy man"). Within this frame of reference, "the myth of Oedipus expresses the inability, for a culture that holds the belief that mankind is autochthonous, to find a transition from this theory to the recognition that each of us is actually born from the union of a man and a woman. Although the problem obviously cannot be solved, the myth of Oedipus provides a kind of logical tool which makes it possible to build a bridge between the original problem and the derivative problem that might be formulated: is the self born from the same self or from someone else? By this means, a correlation emerges: the overvaluation of blood relations is to their undervaluation as the attempt to escape autochthony is to the impossibility of succeeding in it." (Claude Lévi-Strauss, *Structural Anthropology,* New York 1963.)

In keeping with this analysis by Lévi-Strauss, Clémence Ramnoux has proposed another reading, which ties the adventures of Oedipus closely to the mythology of the origins of Thebes. This mythology is dominated in the divine world by the amours of Aphrodite (the mistress of unions) and of Ares (the master of warring discords). According to this view, all the narratives gravitate around the problem of the dangers of an excessive separation or union among "closely related" individuals, such as parents or allies, on the

Oedipus and the sphinx. Attic cup. Ca. 470 B.C. Rome, Vatican Museum. Photo Alinari.

can read the mythology of Oedipus, then, in terms of communication over the full extent of the social framework—sometimes direct and straightforward, sometimes deviant and awkward because of an excess of openness or the blockage of channels.

J.-P.V./g.h.

BIBLIOGRAPHY

I. Texts

Oedipe Roi and *Oedipe à Colone,* in SOPHOCLE, *Tragédies,* preface by Pierre Vidal-Naquet, trans. by Paul Mazon, notes by René Langumier (Paris 1973).

The most recent critical edition of *Oedipus the King* is that of J. C. KAMERBEEK, *The Plays of Sophocles, Commentaries,* 4: *The Oedipus Tyrannus* (Leiden 1967).

For interpretations of *Oedipus the King,* see B. KNOX, *Oedipus at Thebes: Sophokles Tragic Hero and His Time* (New Haven and London 1957; 2d ed., 1966).

II. Studies

J.-P. VERNANT and P. VIDAL-NAQUET, *Mythe et tragédie* (Paris 1972; 3d ed., 1977), 75–132. B. VICKERS, *Towards Greek Tragedy* (Bristol 1973), 495–525. R. GIRARD, *La violence et le sacré* (Paris 1972), 102–29.

The psychoanalytic perspective is presented in A. GREEN, *Un oeil en trop: Le complexe d'Oedipe dans la tragédie* (Paris 1969). D. ANZIEU, "Oedipe avant le complexe ou de l'interprétation psychanalytique des mythes," *Temps Modernes,* no. 245 (October 1966), 675–715; "Freud et la mythologie: Incidences de la Psychanalyse," *Nouvelle Revue de Psychanalyse* 1 (1970): 114–45. R. S. CALDWELL, "The Misogyny of Eteokles," *Arethusa* 6 (1973): 197–231.

On the "mythology of Oedipus," in its relations with drama or in itself, see: C. ROBERT, *Oidipus* (Berlin 1915). M. DELCOURT, *Oedipe ou la légende du conquérant* (Liège and Paris 1944). F. VIAN, *Les origines de Thèbes: Cadmos et les Spartes* (Paris 1963). C. LÉVI-STRAUSS, *Anthropologie structurale* (Paris 1958), 1:227–55, and *Anthropologie structurale* (Paris 1973), 2:31–35 (both volumes are translated into English); *Annuaire du Collège de France,* 1961–62, pp. 200–203. C. RAMNOUX, "Pourquoi des Présocratiques?" *Revue Philosophique de Louvain* 66 (1968): 397–419. T. S. TURNER, "Oedipus: Time and Structure in Narrative Form," *Forms of Symbolic Action, Proceedings of 1969 Annual Spring Meeting of the American Ethnological Society* (Seattle and London 1969), 26–68.

one hand; and "distantly related" individuals, separated as gods and men are separated, on the other.

Using Lévi-Strauss as a starting point, the anthropologist Terence S. Turner also undertook to reexamine the whole issue. His study stands today as the most enlightening effort to apply the rules of mythological analysis to the various versions of the myth about the line of descendancy of Labdacus, Laius, and Oedipus. The whole field of inquiry is organized around two axes, the first focusing on the relationships, normal or otherwise, between relatives and nonrelatives; and the second dealing with the relationships, correct or deviant, between the successive generations within the limits of the same line of descent. This reading gives an account of a series of deviations and diversions: in the inappropriate transfer of power after the throne has been usurped by nonrelatives, as in the case of Labdacus and Laius alike; in sexual relationships, for example in Laius's perverse relationships with both the young Chrysippus, whom he rapes, and his wife, from whom he wants no children; in relationships between parents and children, as in the case of Laius who very early in life is "fatherless" as the result of the premature death of Labdacus and, like Oedipus, finds himself swerving away from his line of descent, just as he is thrust aside from the throne and banished from the city.

These various deviations illustrate the importance of the problem underlying the narrative as a whole. Under what conditions is it possible for the sons in each new generation to follow a straight path so as to attain without violence the position held by their fathers, in such a way as to occupy their fathers' exact positions without either ousting them from those positions or identifying with their fathers? In other words, how can order in its various configurations be transmitted and still remain the same and permanent? We

ORION

A hero of Greek mythology, Orion was transformed into a constellation next to the Pleiades, the young women pursued by the wild hunter who was a companion of Artemis. He is most familiar as the giant who crosses the sea: the brute who comes to Chios, where he gets drunk on the pure wine served to him by his host Oenopion. When Orion attempts to rape his host's daughter, Oenopion puts out his eyes and forces him to leave. He heads in the direction of the sun, bearing on his shoulders the smith Cedalion, his guide to the Orient, where the solar fire restores the fierce giant's eyesight. In the course of the same mishap, Orion draws attention to himself once again by an excessive hunt, in which he destroys all the wild beasts borne and nurtured by Earth, and thus boasts of being a better hunter than Artemis, who, according to another tradition, feels threatened by his acts of sexual violence. As a result, Earth's outrage and the anger of Artemis arouse a new monster that will be Orion's undoing: the scorpion born from the entrails of Earth like a poison, a solar venom whose bite condemns Orion to death.

By contrast with the Orion of the potent and destructive force, Greek tradition knows another Orion, situated in Boeotia, but this time he is a wise king and soothsayer, the incumbent of a famous oracle at Tanagra; his unusual metamorphosis is a bird nesting in a honey tree, the bird Orion, whose song rises at dawn like a hymn intoned in honor of the young bridegroom about to be married.

J.C./g.h.

ORPHEUS AND EURYDICE

A singer with a marvelous voice, king of Thrace, son of a Muse, Orpheus charmed all who heard him: men, the most ferocious of animals, trees, and stones, all were captivated by his singing. When he accompanied the Argonauts on their adventures, his voice appeased the storms; more powerful than the bonds of Odysseus, his voice alone protected men against the song of the sirens, seducers of sailors. But his excessive charm was his downfall. When his young wife, the Dryad Eurydice, died of a snakebite while fleeing the pursuing Aristaeus, Orpheus was unable to bear his separation from her and set out to look for her, even in the netherworld. His singing silenced the dog Cerberus and moved the infernal deities to such pity that they granted him permission to take Eurydice home, provided he did not look back at her until he had reached the light of day. But Orpheus did not know how to maintain the necessary distance between himself and his wife. He turned around. Eurydice was

Orpheus leading the Muses. Paris, Musée du Louvre. Photo Giraudon.

immediately surrounded by deep darkness and disappeared "like an intangible smoke," lost forever. Inconsolable, the musician retired into the icy solitudes of Thrace. But the local women, feeling scorned during a nocturnal orgy in honor of Bacchus, tore his body to pieces and scattered his limbs. As the waters of the Hebrus carried away his head, his voice continued to call for Eurydice: "Eurydice! echoed the banks all along the river" (Virgil *Georgics* 4).

J.C./g.h.

Orpheus. Apulian amphora. Ca. 375–50 B.C. Bari, Museo archeologico. Photo Soprintendenza.

PAN

I. Pan and Pastoral Space

Pastoral space may be considered as a whole, as a more or less homogeneous entity, whether it is envisaged in contrast with the city or in specifically rural contexts. When examined for its own sake, however, it shows, in addition to the precise features that characterize it unmistakably, other features far less distinct, ambiguities that often blur the dividing line that sets it off from other spaces. The mountain (*oros*), with its peaks, valleys, high plateaus, wooded slopes, thickets, and brush, unequivocally enters into the pastoral space. The word *eschatia* (extremity, frontier, confines of a territory) very frequently evokes a natural setting good for herds to graze in. But the same does not hold true for other words in the pastoral vocabulary. Even a word like *agros*, with its particularly pastoral resonance, designating an open terrain far away in the country where herds and shepherds wander, can also apply to fields, and this leaning toward the sense of "land tilled by man" began to break into the word as early as the Homeric epic. Semantic oscillations appeared, even more accentuated in certain words such as *pedion* (plain), *leimōn* (meadow), or *helos* (damp or swampy place), which, while pertaining directly to pastoral space, go substantially beyond it and also express aspects alien to the world of animals and herdsmen.

This space, which in terms of physical relief encompasses mountainous regions, flatlands, riverbanks, and coastal zones, is often represented as an isolated world, set far apart and without communication with the life of the city or cultivated fields. But it is not necessary to give an absolute value to this image, which is exploited especially by bucolic poetry, which situates shepherds almost exclusively in the solitary setting of remote mountains, on the border between myth and reality. Certainly the universe of shepherds and herds leans more toward *phusis* and to that extent is antithetical to the world of farming, which is closer to the city and its life governed by civic laws. But it is not a wild universe. It is populated by domestic animals who live in the open air most of the time but according to a rhythm imposed by man. When the herds graze at high elevations, they often stumble into areas frequented by wild animals. But there is a clear distinction between wild animals (*agria zōa*) and domesticated animals (*hēmeros*, an adjective also applied to cultivated land or plants, as well as to "civilized" man). The one is the other's worst enemy. Wild animals lurk in dens and lairs that nature supplies. Domesticated animals, when outside their natural but temporary shelters, find security in pens and stables of more or less elaborate construction.

Herdsmen guard, protect, and accompany domesticated herds. Characterized as rough, vulgar, and uncultivated people, as country bumpkins, they are considered inferior to farmers, simpleminded and inarticulate people, since they "do not go to the city" but instead spend most of their time in solitary places, *en erēmia*, surrounded only by a nature that is disquieting and even dangerous for the city dweller. But they are not referred to as *agrioi* (wild). They are intermediaries linking the town and the countryside, playing the role of messenger between cities (because of their frequent presence on the edges of the city), functioning as guides and sentries in time of war. According to Aristotle, their lives in the open air make them suitable for warfare and qualify them to defend a threatened territory. The Greek herdsman is clearly distinguished from the city dweller and even from the plowman; but he is never identified with a barbarous nomad, an impious Cyclops (even though a Cyclops may be a shepherd), or a man left in the wilderness, like Philoctetes, abandoned on a desert island.

This world of herds and herdsmen is dominated by the figure of Pan, the preeminent pastoral deity, unknown to Homer or Hesiod but very much present in the religious life of the Greeks by at least the sixth century. In the Greek polytheistic system, in which each divine power, even a lesser one, takes on several functions that often affect different areas, Pan remains faithfully tied to the pastoral universe and reflects its ambiguous character. According to the best-known version, Pan is the son of the Hermes of Mount Cyllene in Arcadia and a nymph. He is represented as a mixed being of dual form (*dizōs*), half human, half goat, with human arms and hands, hairy legs, and goat's feet (*tragopous*); his face is often bearded and on certain images closely resembles a goat's head, when he is not completely zoomorphous. Pan never loses his animal features, and even his idealized representations copied from Doryphorus by Polycletus, wholly anthropomorphic and devoid of the usual expression of bestial cunning, preserve the two horns that always adorn the god's forehead.

His "dual nature" (*diphuēs*) makes him all smooth (*leios*) on top, but "down below he is bristly and looks like a billy goat" (*trachus kai tragoeidēs*), which reinforces his ambiguous character and allows Plato to compare Pan to language that is "double, true and false," since "all that is truth in him is all smooth, divine, and resides above among the gods, whereas his falseness is below, among the multitudes of men, a thing bristling with inequalities, where there is *tragos*, the billy goat" (Plato *Cratylus* 408 cd).

Not being altogether "divine," Pan oscillates between the status of a god (*theos*)—sometimes even called *megalos* (great) or *kratistos* (very powerful), he who can "in the manner of the mightiest gods grant men's wishes and punish the wicked" (Pausanias 8.37.11)—and that of a demigod (*hēmitheos*), or, in any case, of an earthly god (*epigeios*), as opposed to the Olympians (Artemidorus 2.34). In fact, only once did Pan ever cross the threshold of Olympus, when as a newborn child he was carried there in the arms of his father, Hermes. But his brief visit had no effect other than the pleasure of the Immortals who "rejoiced heartily" on seeing this monstrous-looking being (*teratōpos*), this "noisy and smiling" child (*Homeric Hymn to Pan* 35ff.).

On earth, Pan takes possession of the mountains, a natural setting which is "appropriate," *oikeion*, to him. "The mountains and the valleys are Pan's," asserts Dionysius of Halicarnassus (*Antiquitates Romanae* 1.38.1), while the shores and islands belong to the deities of the sea. Pan the "mountaineer" (*oureios, oreiōtēs*) "lives in the mountains" (*ouresioikos*), "walks in the mountains" (*oressibatēs*), "loves the mountains" (*philōreitēs*), is "master or king of the mountains" (*oreiarchēs*), and has for his lot all the crests and snowy heights, as well as the hills (*bounitēs, lophiētēs*). While he wanders through these areas, crossing the forests (*hulobatēs*), following the rocky paths, and staying in caves, of which he is particularly fond (*androcharēs*), the "pastoral god" (*nomios theos*) meets shepherds and their flocks during their seasonal migrations. Scaling steep mountainsides (*krēmnobatēs*), he climbs to the top of the highest peak "from which the sheep are watched," and he observes the surroundings (*skopiētēs*), like the Homeric goatherd who "from the height of his watch" sees the menacing cloud and hastens to "drive his flock to the shelter of a cave" (Homer *Iliad* 4.275ff.). A bronze

Three nymphs, Hermes, Pan, and three dedicants. Votive relief. Ca. 360 B.C. Athens, National Museum. Museum photo.

statuette (fifth century B.C.) represents Pan with the torso of a man and the head of a goat, scrutinizing the horizon, ears pricked, and raising his right arm above his eyes as if to intensify the sharpness of his gaze. It is not surprising that this figure was found in Arcadia, Pan's native country, the "mother of small livestock," where the mountains (Lycaeus, Cyllene, Maenalus, Parthenium, Cotilium, Lampeia, etc.) bear signs of the omnipresence of "the oldest and most honored among the gods of the Arcadians" (Dion. Hal. *Ant. Rom.* 1.32), of the "master of Arcadia," according to Pindar (*Partheneia* 3: *Arkadias medeōn*).

A pastoral deity cannot be dissociated from the *agros*. Pan is unmistakably a "country dweller" (*agronomos*), a "country god" (*agrotēs daimōn*), who "sleeps outdoors" (*agraulos*), a "protector of the countryside" (*agrōn tamias*: Euripides *Electra* 704). Pan's *agros* is clearly pastureland, for the god is a total stranger to the works of Demeter. And if a plowman ever wanted to thank him, he gave him "unsown land" (*aspora temenē*) so Pan could let his flocks graze there (*Anthologia Palatina* 6.79).

But how does this god of shepherds and flocks intervene in their universe? Pan apparently does not intervene but rather occupies this space wholly. Unlike Hermes, he is only rarely invoked to increase the size of herds or to care for them. It is true, according to Claudius Aelianus (*On the Nature of Animals* 11.6), that the god "saves" animals who are pursued by wolves and take refuge in a certain sanctuary of Pan in Arcadia. But this refers to animals in general, not domestic animals in particular, and probably refers to the common theme of the sacred site that functions as an asylum and protects all living creatures who enter it "as suppliants." Again unlike Hermes, Pan is almost never seen

herding flocks (although he owns some) or carrying an animal, as his illustrious father does. A single statuette showing Pan with an animal on his shoulders is considered to be a faithful transposition of the theme of Hermes Criophorus.

Pan's pastoral function is chiefly to be present in the places frequented by herdsmen and their flocks. He moves around like the migrant shepherds but is not a nomad, as he was according to an old, now outdated conception that equated seasonal migrations with nomadism. Shepherds and country people offer him chiefly milk, cheese, or kids; they dedicate to him crude figurines representing peasants wearing warm clothes and hats, like their Hesiodic brethren during the freezing days of winter. Among the offerings is the crook habitually carried by Pan himself, often resembling the curved sticks still seen in the hands of modern Greek goatherds. But the feature that more than any other gives Pan the look of a shepherd is his "melodious" (*eukelados*) pipes or syrinx, its reeds joined with wax (*kērodetos*), which Pan himself was the first to play, in Arcadia (Pausanias 8.38.11).

It was generally believed in antiquity that music had a beneficial effect on animals and, in particular, that it functioned as an aphrodisiac that aided their mating. Apollo—so sings the chorus of Euripides' *Alcestis* 569ff.—kept Admetus's flocks while playing "pastoral wedding songs" (*poimnitas humenaious*) on his pipes, songs, the scholiast tells us, that stimulated the animals to mate; and Plutarch later cited a particular air (*hippothoros nomos*) that excited the ardor of stallions as they covered mares (Plutarch *Moralia* 138b). Undoubtedly one function of Pan's pipe, especially of its tone, was to promote good pasturage and consequently

Pan with pipes in a grotto with Hermes and nymphs. Votive relief. Late fourth century B.C. Athens, National Museum. Museum photo.

abundant milk (*Anthologia Planudea* 17.231). One could conjecture that the flagellation of Pan by the Arcadians whenever "the portions of meat were small"—according to an equivocal passage from Theocritus, *Idylls* 7.106ff.—had something to do with not fulfilling this fertilizing function through the intercession of music, rather than with a fruitless hunt, for which Pan was supposedly held responsible.

Pan was sometimes supposed to be involved in the hunt; indeed, he received offerings from hunters. But he was not a functional god of the hunt. Rather, his relation to hunting stemmed from his home and presence in places that were the crossroads of pasturelands and hunting grounds. Hunters addressed Pan by calling him a mountain god or a god of the countryside rather than a hunting god; and if they wanted to be sure of a good hunt, they were more inclined to turn to Artemis, with whom Pan had little connection. Furthermore, as an inhabitant of mountains and remote places, Pan was also venerated by travelers and frontier guards. The name *lagōbolon* (a stick to kill hares), often given to the instrument carried by the god, is ambiguous, since it also designates the shepherd's crook, as bucolic poetry, among other sources, clearly shows.

We can better understand Pan's indirect effect on the sexual life of the herd when we compare it with the considerable sexual activity that characterizes the god himself. An ithyphallic god, Pan is debauched (*lagnos*), given to lovemaking (*erōtikos*), as lewd as a donkey stallion (*kēlōn*), with abundant semen (*polusporos*), and constantly in pursuit of the nymphs, whose cries echo in the caves during the furtive sexual activities of the god (*Panos gamoi*: Euripides *Helen* 190). He also pursues young shepherds ("pederast" Pan), or seeks satisfaction by himself when he is without a partner. Onanism, which Pan taught to the shepherds, according to Diogenes the Cynic (after Dio Chrysostomus 6.203 frag.), was particularly characteristic of goatherds, whose general lewdness became proverbial and was sharply contrasted with the continence of the cowherds (schol. ad Theocritas *Idylls* 1.86a). Pan, moreover, is closely connected with female goats, animals said to be "inclined to pleasure" (*katōpherēs*). Not only does he look like a goat, but he is born, according to one tradition, of a perverse union between Penelope and Hermes transformed into a billy goat. He himself, as a billy goat, has sexual relations with the females of the species: he is *aigibatēs*, "he who mates with goats," a *caprarum maritus*. Finally, on the level of sacrifice, "he does not rejoice in bovine victims," but quite naturally prefers the uncastrated billy goat (*tragos enorchis*) that he so strikingly resembles.

As a deity of the mountain regions or of the *agros*, Pan stands in opposition to the city. If Pan should show up in your dreams—advises Artemidorus 4.72—seated in the agora in city attire, rest assured that he will tell you deceitful lies, as happens when the gods "do not have their own features or . . . are not in the place where they belong or in their proper attitudes." For Pan, who loves solitary places (*philerēmos*), does not concern himself with the affairs of the city (*apragmōn*). He himself asserts that as a mountaineer and simple goatherd, he has not studied the elegant expressions used in the city (Lucian *Double acc.* 11).

We must not, however, think of Pan and the city as being diametrically opposed and confine the god to caves and dens. Certain cities, especially in the Peloponnesus, dedicated shrines, altars, or images to Pan within the space of the city, sometimes giving him a major role, as is witnessed by coins bearing his likeness: at Megalopolis, Pan is ranked "among the first gods"; in Tegea, he is called "conductor, guide" (*prokathēgetēs*); in Troezen, Pan "who unbinds" (*lutērios*) has a genuine temple near the Acropolis for having saved the city from a plague (Pausanias 8.31.3–4, 2.32.6). His presence is also marked in shrines of great renown, side by side with the great gods; this may be why he earned the title of "guardian of venerable shrines" (Pindar op. cit.): he holds an important place among the deities honored in the sanctuary of Despoina near Lycosura (Pausanias 8.37.11); he has three altars at Olympia, one of which is in the Prytaneum where the sacred hearth of the Eleians burns (Paus. 5.15.8–9). In the temple of Asclepius at Epidaurus, an influential Pan has been recovered: several statuettes of the god, four altars, and a hymn composed in his honor testify to his importance.

Because the Athenians attributed to him a role in the victory of Marathon (490 B.C.), Pan was introduced into the city of Athens, and from there his cult spread throughout Greece. In Athens and generally in Attica, Pan occupied his usual pastoral habitat, the cave. Besides his cave on the northwest slope of the Acropolis, made famous by Euripides as the site of the union of Apollo and Creusa (*Ion* 925ff.) and qualified in Aristophanes by the important word *aulion* (a term from the pastoral vocabulary designating a stable or pen), archaeologists have explored in Attica and elsewhere in Greece a series of caves where the worship of Pan is closely associated with that of the nymphs. For Pan is not only the insistent lover in hot pursuit of the nymphs. He is also their faithful companion (*opados*), their guide (*hēgētōr*) who leads them in dance on the flowery or wooded meadows, and who accompanies their rounds with his pipes. Several reliefs that come from his retreats portray a languid scene in which three women dance, sometimes around an altar, to the sound of the pipes of the god, surrounded by his grazing goats. Often it is Hermes who leads the dance, while Acheloüs, the river god, looks on from a nearby corner.

Pan maintains especially close ties with the nymphs who inhabit the countryside near and far: with the Oreiads, the mountain nymphs; the Naiads and Hydriads, water deities; the Dryads, whose lives are connected to the lives of trees; the Crenides, nymphs of springs; and the Epimelides, protectors of herds. He shares the same caves with them; he wanders through the same canyons and valleys; he loves the same trees (plane trees, oaks, elms, pines, poplars); he often receives the same offerings from shepherds and country people; and he is honored in the same hymns and epigrams.

Of course, neither Pan nor the nymphs—whose varying functions touch several aspects of human life—are limited to the few areas of activity that we have attempted to sketch. From the fourth century, Pan in particular entered into the Dionysian cycle and played yet another role as "servant" (*propolos*) of Dionysus. Further philosophical speculation came to see this god as an incarnation of the Universe, the Whole (*pan*). But no transformation of his person has managed to erase the dominant element of his character that

Pan accompanying on his pipes the dance of the three seasons. Votive relief. Second half of the fourth century B.C. Athens, National Museum. Museum photo.

unites Pan with the rural and pastoral world as a whole, and that has unquestionably contributed to the survival of his myths right up to modern times.

S.G./g.h.

II. Pan and Panic

The beginning of the *Rhesus* attributed to Euripides constitutes the oldest evidence we have about panic. The scene takes place at night in the Trojan camp. There is some noise; the sentinels have left their posts and spread rumors. Hector wonders if the agitation might not be coming from Pan. Could the god have aroused terror by cracking his whip of madness?

The whip is a shepherd's instrument. Pan's function in war is not unlike his function of raising cattle: Homer compares the army to a herd, and for his part, the shepherd Pan readily turns into a warrior to protect his sheep from a raid (cf. Longus *Pastorales* 2.20ff.). For the Greeks, however, panic is first experienced as a military matter. Starting with Aeneas the Tactician (*Poliorceticus* 27), several authors became interested in this particular mental state, which is referred to as fear, accompanied by noise and disorder, that unexpectedly overcomes a military camp, mostly at night. Panic is bound up with illusion, delivering its victim to conjectures, to imagining the worst. In order to spread panic, Aeneas the Tactician suggests that a herd of cows wearing bells be sent into the enemy camp at night. Others advise echoing shrieks. On the other hand, to cut down the process at its root, certain strategists reduce panic to laughable proportions: they promise a generous reward to anyone who will denounce the soldier guilty of having let the donkey or horse escape, this being the alleged source of the initial noise. Panic spreads. Soldiers break ranks. If a severe injunction does not succeed in immobilizing them, they may experience what happened to the Gauls after their defeat before Delphi: "Only a few, at first, lost their minds. They thought they heard the sound of horses let loose against them, or of enemies making an assault. In no time the delusion spread everywhere. Taking up their arms and splitting into two groups, they started to fight among themselves, unable to understand their own language, incapable of recognizing each other's faces or shields. . . . The madness sent down by the god brought about a terrible mutual carnage among the Gauls'' (Pausanias 10.23.6–8).

That panic can be artificially provoked does not exclude the possibility that it may be Pan's doing. Being the son of Hermes, Pan is certainly not a stranger to trickery. The ancients never doubted the connection between the god and panic, although this connection, barely evident at first, poses a problem. Recall that all the panics whose memory has been preserved in Greek history have taken place in close proximity to a cave dedicated to Pan. Similarly, the ancient interpretations of panic refer to the god. Some underscore the analogy between panic (a phenomenon of noise) and the rituals performed to the god: he is not approached in silence, but is celebrated with music and shouts; he loves noise. Others make Pan the deity of the inexplicable and assert that what has no known cause is attributable to him. Some seek the primary and exemplary source of panic in the phenomenon of the echo, a disembodied voice, deformed but originating from within the space inhabited by Pan and the nymphs. Sometimes, especially in Arcadia, men hear Pan's music in the vicinity of a mountain dedicated to the god. The echo itself reverberates a peculiar version of this experience, one that describes the jealousy and hatred involved in the impossible passion of Pan for the nymph Echo. Jealous of the nymph's musical talents and vexed that he cannot touch her beauty, the god becomes angry. He drives shepherds and goatherds mad. Behaving like wolves and wild dogs, they tear the young girl apart and scatter her limbs, which still vibrate with song. The echo, as Echo, signifies this aborted effort, the elusive sound that is always in motion and cannot be pinned down to one place. Consequently, although the echo seems to establish a communication between a region of the divine (Pan and the nymphs) and the human world, the mediation that it performs is immediately accompanied by a transformation: what was music, on the one hand, is perceived as inarticulate sound, on the other hand. The fruitless communication set up by the echo leads to the illusory: the god does not appear, but what remains is the disquieting, unexpected sudden opening into the unknown.

For Aeschylus (*Agamemnon* 56), Pan acts as the equal of Apollo or even Zeus. He is a great god; the object of his role of watchman on top of a boulder or on the peak of a hill is justice and moderation. An episode in the mythology of the establishment of the celestial kingship of Zeus relates that Pan, the foster brother and ally of Zeus, participated in the struggle of the gods against the Titans. He routed the latter thanks to the invention of a seashell whose noise spread panic. This myth, in which Pan's action puts the finishing touches on the victory of the Olympians over the regressive powers of disorder, can serve as an exemplary model for historical manifestations of panic. The instances when Pan intervenes in military history show that panic either made battle impossible or, when it occurred after the battle, crushed the already conquered enemy. The second case concerns barbarians. When the Greeks themselves are victims of panic, they retreat back into their city, as if the fight they were about to wage were not appropriate to the order of things (cf. Polybius 5.96.3, 20.6.12). Panic, which has as its victim a reduced and special image of the city (the army on the field of battle), indicates the possibility of a regression toward what falls short of the cultural balance guaranteed by Zeus. It dissolves the ties of a small society, and the soldier no longer recognizes his own kind.

Pan. Bronze by Lousoi. Berlin, Staatliche Museen Preussischer Kulturbesitz, Antikenmuseum. Photo Tietz-Glagow.

In the *Homeric Hymn to Pan*, the monstrous appearance of the god at his birth causes his nurse to flee. But there is a double flight. Corresponding to the flight of the human nurse (Pan was born of a mortal), who takes to her heels, there is another departure: Hermes immediately picks up the baby, wraps it in the fur of a mountain hare, and goes with the infant toward Olympus, where the gods are charmed by the new arrival. But Pan is not an Olympian. On the outer peripheries of human space, hunting, sheep breeding, and even war (the army in the field, defending the frontiers) are also activities that pervade the territory where the god prowls. The dual movement of withdrawal (the human terror and the removal of the god to Olympus) that characterizes the first appearance of Pan in the Homeric hymn sheds light on the meaning of panic: the disorder triggered by panic answers to an exaggerated withdrawal of the divine from mankind.

A collective disorder, panic is defined by a breakdown in communication. It stands in sharp contrast to the kind of possession that the Greeks call theolepsy (seizure by a god). Contrary to panic, theolepsy involves individuals, whom it may make sacred, and is characterized by an immediate proximity of the divine. Pan's powers in the realm of disorder move from one pole to the other. In panic, Pan refuses to be apprehended. In possession, Pan makes himself known: he reveals himself. The person possessed by Pan, the panoleptic, takes on the behavior of the god who invades him. Thus, possession, although resulting from Pan's action, can take different forms. According to Aristophanes in *Lysistrata* (998), one form would be ithyphallicism: the possessed man in this case is the object of a sexual strike and participates directly in the agonies of the god Pan, who lives among the nymphs but is unhappy in love. According to the women surrounding her, it is because Phaedra did not honor a deity of the wilderness as she should have that she lives in a state of prostration even while she is attracted in spirit to the realm of Pan (Euripides *Hippolytus* 175ff.). Phaedra too is unhappy in love. Her wandering matches the wandering of Pan (Hippolytus in reality, though those around him are not aware of it), when his hunting carries him away over mountains and valleys. She is "absent." Iamblichus (*De Mysteriis* 122) mentions the panoleptics and nympholeptics who sometimes appear chained and at other times wander around the mountains. When Jason's young wife, again in Euripides (*Medea* 1167–77), suddenly changes color, starts to tremble, falls, and foams at the mouth, a servant woman thinks that the poor wretch may be a victim of Pan. A whole series of links woven between the goat (the animal of Pan, himself a billy goat) and epilepsy shows the logic of this attribution at the level of popular belief. Finally, the fit of laughter—excessive, mad laughter—as a symptom of panolepsy (*Oxyrhynchus Papyri* 3, p. 50) is yet another mode of manifestation of this god. The importance of laughter in the Greeks' understanding of Pan is well attested: people laugh at his festival; he himself laughs; the gods are charmed by his laughter. Pan's laughter, among the gods or at the festival, expresses joy, pleasure, and fertility. Outside of its context, it understandably becomes senseless and disquieting.

Any oversight, any error in the ritual, can be a cause for possession. At noon, one must avoid attracting Pan's attention while tending sheep. Theocritus (*Idylls* 1.15–18) puts the following words into the mouth of a goatherd: "It is not permitted to play the pipes at the noon hour. We are afraid of Pan. He is tired after the hunt, and he rests at that time. He is nervous and tense, and a sour bile flows from his nostrils." Silence and immobility characterize noon, the stationary hour. To rouse the attention of Pan, the god of noise and movement, at that hour would be equivalent to inviting him to move in on that silence and immobility. In his wrath, Pan would be liable to turn the shepherd, the protector of the flock, into its worst enemy, the wolf. The goat-god himself in his rage and the flocks over which he watches could acquire the violence of carnivorous animals (see Apuleius *Metamorphoses* 6.12).

Possession by Pan is only one of several possible forms of theolepsy. Besides the panoleptics, there are people possessed by Apollo (phoiboleptics or pytholeptics), by the mother goddess, by the Muses, by Eros, and especially by

Pan pursuing the goatherd. Attic krater. Ca. 480 B.C. Boston Museum of Fine Arts (James). Museum photo.

nymphs. Nympholepsy, the best-known of these phenomena, appears in the sources side by side with possession by Pan, who is himself inseparable from the nymphs. They share the same type of countryside and the same cult sites: the banks of the Ilissus (where the inspired Socrates feared he would become nympholeptic) and the caves of Vari and of Cithaeron (where cases of nympholepsy are attested) seem to be dedicated to Pan as well as to the nymphs. Noon, the hour threatened by the wrath of Pan, is also the hour when the nymphs prefer to carry away their chosen ones. This closeness between Pan and the nymphs does not mean, however, that panolepsy and nympholepsy should be confused. The descriptions of panolepsy stress an abnormal physiological behavior ranging from prostration to animal rage. No such condition is known with regard to nympholeptics; what is stressed for them is something outside the natural world.

Nympholepsy is first of all a form of inspiration. Aristotle (*Ethica Eudemia* 1214a) lists several hypothetical origins of happiness: happiness can be natural (like the color of one's skin); it can be learned or practiced, unless one is happy "in the manner of nympholeptics or theoleptics, who are as though filled with an inspiration coming from some god." In this case, happiness would be a gift, analogous to what is said about the knowledge of Melesagoras, who "not because he learned the trade, but because he was possessed by the nymphs, had the gift of wisdom and of divination." Maximus of Tyre (*Diss.* 38) compared Melesagoras to the famed Epimenides, the son of a nymph, who drew his knowledge from dreams. Tiresias was also the son of a nymph, and in the archaic period there was a class of soothsayers, the Bacis, whom tradition regarded as nympholeptics.

Nympholepsy does not always appear to be a form of inspiration bound up with possession and enthusiasm. It also manifests itself more literally as kidnapping. One group of myths relates the stories of young men kidnapped by nymphs. The most famous is Hylas. This young lover of Heracles saw a choir of nymphs when he went to fetch water at a spring. They pulled him down to the bottom of the water and he disappeared, never to be seen again. Although it resembles death, kidnapping by nymphs should not be reduced to death. Nymphs carry their victims away into a space that looks like death only to those who stay here. The person who has disappeared enters into a new mode of existence. "Astacides the Cretan goatherd was carried off from the mountain by a nymph, and now Astacides is holy" (Callimachus *Epigrammata* 22). The epitaph for a five-year-old girl makes the following distinction: "The Naiads, charmed by her beauty, have taken the child away, not death" (*Inscriptiones Graecae* 14.2040).

Theocritus called the nymphs "terrible divinities" (*Idylls* 13.44). A scholiast adds: "Terrible because of the fear that seizes those who encounter them; that fear makes one nympholeptic." In this sense, nympholeptic means neither inspired nor kidnapped. The term designates one who is taken not *by* but *with* the nymphs, as one is "taken with" an impressive spectacle. The nympholeptic in this case remains out of contact with the nymphs, but is stupefied and torn away from all other preoccupations. His fear at the individual level meets and goes beyond the experience of panic. Communication is denied even in the presence of its object.

P.Bo./g.h.

BIBLIOGRAPHY

A. MICHELIS, "Il dio Pan colle Ore e con Ninfe su rilievi votivi greci," *Annali dell'Istit. di Corrisp. Archeol.* 35 (1863): 292–336. W. H. ROSCHER, "Pan," in *Ausführliches Lexicon der griechischen und römischen Mythologie,* W. H. Roscher, ed., vol. 3 (1897–1902); "Über den gegenwärtigen Stand der Forschung auf dem Gebiete der griechischen Mythologie und die Bedeutung des Pan," *Archiv für Religionswissenschaft* (1898), 1:43–90. A. SKIAS, "The cave of Pan in Phyle" (in Greek), *Archaeologiki Ephemeris,* 1918, 1–28. I. TRAVLOS, "The grotto of Pan near Daphnis" (in Greek), *Archaeologiki Ephemeris* 1 (1937): 391–408. F. HEICHELHEIM, "Nymphai," in Pauly/Wissowa, *Real-Encyclopädie,* 1937, cols. 1527–99. R. CAILLOIS, "Les démons de Midi," *Revue de l'Histoire des Religions* 115 (1937): 142–73 and 116 (1937): 54–83, 143–86. F. BROMMER, "Pan im 5. und 4. Jahrhundert v. Chr.," *Marburger Jahrbuch für Kunstwissenschaft* 15 (1949–50): 5–42. R. HERBIG, *Pan, der Griechische Bocksgott* (Frankfurt am Main 1949). M. LAUNEY, *Recherches sur les armées hellénistiques* (Paris 1950), 2:931–36. F. BROMMER, "Pan," in Pauly-Wissowa, *Real-Encyclopädie,* spl. 8 (1956), cols. 949ff. N. HIMMELMANN-WILDSCHÜTZ, *Theoleptos* (Marburg-Lahn 1957). A. D. NOCK, "Nymphs and Nereids," *Mél. Univ. Saint-Joseph* (Beirut), 37 (1961), reprinted in A. D. Nock, *Essays on Religion and the Ancient World* (1972), 2:919–27. C. GALLINI, "La follia panica," *Studi e Materiali di Storia delle Religioni* 32 (1961): 205–36. P. MERIVALE, *Pan the Goat-God: His Myth in Modern Times* (Cambridge, MA, 1969). C. MEILLIER, "L'épiphanie du dieu Pan au livre II de Daphnis et Chloé," *Revue des Études Grecques* 88 (1975): 121–30. F. CASSOLA, *Inni Omerici,* Fondazione Lorenzo Valla (1975), 361–65. PH. BORGEAUD, *Recherches sur le dieu Pan* (Rome 1979).

PELOPS

Pelops the Lydian (as Pindar calls him), the son of Tantalus, was above all the hero of Olympia, the founder of the games. While still young, he was, it is said, dismembered by his father, who served him to the gods because he wanted to test their clairvoyance. At least one deity tasted the human flesh, the famished Demeter, or Ares, but the other gods recognized what they were being served, punished the blasphemer cruelly, and brought Pelops back to life, fitting him with a shoulder of polished ivory to replace the one that Demeter had swallowed.

Pelops was beloved by Poseidon, and had sought the god's help to obtain the beautiful princess that he coveted.

> He drew near the foaming sea, and, alone in the darkness, called aloud on the loudly roaring god of the fair trident; who appeared to him, even close beside him, at his very feet; and to the god he said:—"If the kindly gifts of Cypris count in any wise in one's favor, then stay thou, Poseidon, the brazen spear of Oenomaus, and speed me in the swiftest of all chariots to Elis, and cause me to draw nigh unto power" (Pindar *Olympian Odes* 1.70–78, trans. Sir John Sandys, *The Odes of Pindar,* Cambridge: Harvard University Press, 1937, p. 11).

The god supplied him with a golden chariot drawn by winged horses, for the princess of Elis, Hippodamia, was the most beloved daughter of Oenomaus, the king of Pisa, who challenged each of her suitors to a chariot race, which the king always won. When he overtook the contestant, he cut his head off and hung the trophy on his door to discourage the next suitors. But Hippodamia fell in love with Pelops and wanted him to win. Betraying her father, she talked the coachman Myrtilus into replacing the wooden pegs on her father's chariot with pegs of wax. The resulting accident cost Oenomaus his life. Badly paid for his services, Myrtilus was soon killed by Pelops, either because he attempted to seduce Hippodamia, or because she was offended by his refusal and falsely accused him of seducing her. The curses that he pronounced before he died are one of the origins of the misfortunes that befell the descendants of Pelops: his sons Atreus and Thyestes, and later Agamemnon and Orestes.

Hippodamia was expelled, or killed, by Pelops after she plotted, or perpetrated, the murder of her son-in-law Chrysippus.

Despite the indignation of Pindar, who refuses to accuse a god of cannibalism, the theme of the scandalous meal offered to the Immortals permeates the entire tradition. It inaugurates the strange cuisine of the descendants of Tantalus, who love, kill, dismember, and eat one another—all in the family circle.

J.C./g.h.

Pelops's chariot with Eros flying above. Hydria. Potenza, Archaeological Museum. Photo Soprintendenza.

BIBLIOGRAPHY

L. LACROIX, "La légende de Pélops et son iconographie," *Bulletin de correspondance hellénique*, 1976, 327–41. C. PRÉAUX, "La légende de Pélops et la royauté sacrée," *Annales du Centre d'études des religions* 1 (1962): 83ff. G. DEVEREUX, "The Abduction of Hippodameia as 'Aition' of a Greek Animal Husbandry Rite: A Structural Analysis," *Studi e Materiali di Storia delle Religioni*, no. 36, fasc. 1.

PERSEUS

Acrisius, the king of Argos, had a daughter named Danaë. An oracle foretold that she would have a son, and that this son would kill his grandfather. Acrisius therefore locked Danaë in an underground bronze chamber and put her under heavy guard. But Zeus united with the young woman in the form of a shower of gold; gold will open all doors, the ancients remarked. So Danaë gave birth to a son, Perseus, and she nursed him in secret. But Acrisius overheard the crying of the infant; he locked mother and child in a chest and cast it into the sea. Zeus made the chest land on the island of Seriphus, where a fisherman, a brother of the tyrant who ruled the island, picked up the castaways and raised the child. When Perseus had grown into a valiant young man, he fulfilled the promise he had made to the tyrant to get the head of the Gorgon. The exploits of Perseus in its acquisition constitute his story.

On the advice of Athena and Hermes, who protected him, Perseus first went to the Old Women, the Graiae, the guardians of the land of the Gorgons, and he succeeded in stealing their single, common eye at the moment when they passed it from one to another; thus they could not see anything. To recover their precious possession, they agreed to show him the way to the nymphs; or according to another version, he did not return their eye to them, but on the contrary took advantage of their sleep (since without their eye all they could do was sleep) to cross the passage that they guarded. The nymphs gave the hero the three talismans that would bring him success: winged sandals, a sack, and the helmet of Hades, which made the wearer invisible. Hermes added to these gifts a very sharp billhook.

Thus armed, Perseus confronted the Gorgons. Lifted up in the air on his winged sandals, he cut off the head of the Gorgon Medusa, using the billhook that Hermes had given him. He guarded against looking at her face, but was able to see her reflection mirrored on his polished brass shield; thus he could see her without looking at her and without being seen by her, for he had surprised her in her sleep. He put into his sack the head, which had the power to turn to stone those who looked at it. Then he escaped from the pursuit of the other two Gorgons by putting on the helmet of invisibility.

While passing through Ethiopia on his return, Perseus found a young girl named Andromeda tied to a rock. To appease the wrath of Poseidon, her parents had been forced to give her to a sea monster who was about to devour her. Perseus made them promise him the young girl's hand in marriage, killed the monster with his magical weapons, and married her. To rid himself of any rival, he merely had to take Medusa's head out of the sack. When he returned to Seri-

Perseus after beheading the Medusa, and Athena. Attic hydria. Ca. 480 B.C. London, British Museum. Museum photo.

phus, he took vengeance in the same way on the tyrant who had attempted to rape his mother. His mission accomplished, Perseus returned the three talismans to Hermes, who in turn gave them back to the nymphs.

Perseus, however, wished to return to his homeland, Argos. When he learned this, remembering the oracle, Acrisius fled far away, to Larissa. But one day when he was attending the games, a discus carried astray by the wind wounded him in the foot and he died. The discus was thrown by Perseus, who had come to Larissa to participate in the games. In despair, the hero buried his grandfather outside the town. No longer wanting to rule in Argos, he exchanged his kingdom for Tiryns, the kingdom of his cousin, where he reigned from then on.

As Jean-Pierre Vernant (*Mythe et Pensée*, vol. 2, p. 91, no. 33) remarks, the same initiation scheme organizes all of the exploits of Perseus: in each test, one must "see without being seen, make oneself invisible to the vigilant adversary."

J.C./g.h.

PHAETHON

When his mother told him that he was the son of Helios, the sun god, Phaethon asked his father for permission to drive the solar chariot. Helios consented; or according to another version, Phaethon took possession of the chariot with the help of his sisters, the Heliades. But the young man was unable to manage the horses and keep them on their proper course. Frightened by the animals of the Zodiac, they drew closer to the earth, drying up the rivers and burning the fields. In order to avoid a universal conflagration, Zeus killed Phaethon with a thunderbolt, and he fell into the Eridanus River. As his sisters, the Heliades, mourned him, the tears which fell from their eyes turned into amber.

J.C./g.h.

THE PLEIADES

A group of timorous virgins condemned to flee from the hunter Orion, who pursues them, the Pleiades are closely connected with the birds of the same name, rock doves (*peleiades*), that are the symbols of such feminine virtues as marital fidelity and the refusal to commit adultery. As figures of continence and virginity, they define a whole dimension of femininity as it applies to the young woman, whom the Greeks called a *numphē*, and whom it is particularly impious to pursue and to violate. One of the main functions of the Pleiades is to bring to the infant Zeus the ambrosia which increases and renews indefinitely the vitality of the gods.

J.C./g.h.

RHADAMANTHYS

Tradition has it that Rhadamanthys, the son of Zeus and Europa, gave Crete its laws. His wisdom earned him the right to sit in judgment in the netherworld, along with Minos and Aeacus.

J.C./g.h.

THETIS

Thetis was a sea deity, a daughter of Nereus. According to the oracle, she was fated to bear a son mightier than his father. The gods therefore gave her to a mortal, Peleus. Their son was Achilles. A mere Nereid in Hesiod's *Theogony,* Thetis appears in Alcman's cosmogony as a great primordial power. She should not be confused with Tethys, the wife of Oceanus and the grandmother of all living creatures in the cosmogony of which there are traces in the *Iliad.*

J.C./g.h.

THE WINDS

The winds play an essential role in the way that space is depicted in Greek mythology. Hesiod's *Theogony* (868ff.) compares the winds born of the gods for the benefit of mortals to the furious blasts born from the body of Typhon for the misfortune and distress of men. The former are the children of Dawn (Eos), the eternally new light of the dawning day, and Astraeus, the luminous radiance of the night sky. There are four of them: Zephyrus, the west wind; Boreas, the north wind; Notus, the south wind; and the fourth, the east wind, called Euros or Argestes. Posted in the four corners of a luminous sky where all the stars are visible

Thetis and Peleus. Attic cup from Peithinos. Ca. 490 B.C. Berlin, Staatliche Museen. Photo Tietz-Glagow.

by day as well as by night, the regular winds help to organize human labor and to orient the routes of navigation. Each of them has its function, blowing at particular times of the year or at particular times of each day. Several trace sea lanes and are even specialized for certain crossings. Associated with the cycle of work and the cycle of the seasons, they open the seasons of sailing and trading; they help to ripen fruit and to fertilize herds. Others that are life-giving, psychotrophic, sow the seeds of souls when that season comes.

Conversely, the winds of rout have no name, nothing that might contradict their confusing nature. Born wild from the monstrous corpse of Typhon, they are the allies of disorder, the powers of chaos. Blowing haphazardly, heedlessly, they behave like the Bacchae: they become frenzied together and dance wildly. And when the Pleiades sink into the mist-covered sea, all navigation is suspended, for all sorts of airy blasts converge on one another. Winds of storm, they are also destructive winds that wreck crops and fruit and carry diseases. Strange sacrifices are required to counter their effects: open pits in the ground, nighttime bloodletting, incantations to Medea.

J.C./g.h.

BIBLIOGRAPHY

K. NIELSEN, "Remarques sur les noms grecs et latins des vents et des régions du ciel," *Classica et mediaevalia* 7 (1945): 1–113. R. HAMPE, "Kult der Winde in Athen und Kreta," *Sitzungsberichte der Heidelberger Akad. d. Wissenschaften, Philol. Hist. Kl.* (Heidelberg 1967).

ZEUS, THE OTHER: A PROBLEM OF MAIEUTICS

How nice to be first among the gods in the Greek pantheon and to find oneself bringing up the rear in the alphabetical scheme of a dictionary of mythologies. [Editor's note: This article was commissioned for the French edition at the last moment, when it was realized that there was no article on Zeus in the dictionary (which, unlike this English edition, ended with Z), nor, indeed, any listing at all under Z. It was thus last in more than one sense.] But was it not because he was the last of Rhea's newborn children that Zeus was allowed to become foremost among the Immortals (Hesiod *Theogony* 435–91) and to experience the irresistible ascension of him who is the earth, the sky, and everything in between, and "that which lies above everything" (Aeschylus frag. 105 Mette)?

In that inconspicuous place, on the other side of the world from the Thundering Father whose somber eyebrows sent shivers up and down Olympus, it was fitting to evoke the unusual and the least Olympian: the Cretan blood of birth and two of the uncanny pregnancies that occur unexpectedly in a career so obstinately patriarchal. According to Antoninus Liberalis (*Metamorphoses* 19), there was a cave which no one was allowed to enter, a sacred cavern in which nurturing bees garnered a fiery honey, and from which each year a dazzling flame burst out, commemorating the gushing blood shed when Zeus came into the world. "Nothing is as imperfect, needy, naked, shapeless, and soiled as a human being at the moment of birth . . . All covered with blood, full of filth, he looks more like a slaughtered creature than a newborn child" (Plutarch *Moralia* 496b). In the cave on Mount Dicte in Crete, during a mysterious sacrifice, a sow roaming around the altar of Zeus imitated with her snorting the newborn baby's cries, so well that none would have dared to touch the flesh of so venerable a victim (Agathocles of Cyzicus in *Fragmente der griechischen Historiker*, 472 frag. 1a, ed. Jacoby).

What secret path leads from the bloody swaddling clothes of the maternal cave to the desire to become pregnant and to be the male who goes into labor and delivers? The accounts do not use the same language, even when it concerns the preservation of the sovereign power yet to be gained. In the Orphic theogony, as told by the rhapsodes, when sexual union and generalized conjugality brought the world to a state of extreme differentiation, Zeus turned to Night and her prophetic knowledge to learn how he could bring about the fusion of the whole and the distinction of the parts. By swallowing Phanes-Metis, Firstborn and First Begetter, male and female, Zeus gathered in the pit of his stomach all things that were created anew, the Ocean and the Abyss of Tartarus. And all that existed then and that would exist later, all was there, blending like the waters of the rivers within the god's body. A full stomach, closed in its rounded fullness like the primeval Egg made by Kronos in the first generation (*Orphicorum fragmenta*, ed. Kern, pp. 165–67).

The perfection of the beginning lies in masculine pregnancy. But in the narration of the adventures of Olympian sovereignty by Hesiod and others, the swallowing of Metis at the moment when she was to deliver Athena (Hesiod *Theogony* 886–900) transformed Zeus into a woman in labor and compelled him to summon the Eileithyiae, the goddesses of childbirth, and also to seek the help of Hephaestus, whose double ax came to deliver him of the "shining [power] of his weapons" (*Orphicorum fragmenta*, ed. Kern, p. 174), this smith's masterpiece fashioned by Metis. A dazzling bronze virgin to whom Zeus all alone gives birth from his forehead (Hesiod *Theogony* 924), the "motherless" daughter spares her father the vivid agony of seeing a son born "more powerful than the thunder" and eager to dethrone him (Chrysippus in *Stoicorum veterum fragmenta*, vol. 2, 256, by Achim von Arnim).

M.D./g.h.

BIBLIOGRAPHY

Zeus has found an encyclopedist in the person of A. B. COOK, *Zeus: A Study in Ancient Religion*, 3 vols. (Cambridge 1914–40).

Egypt

EGYPT: FOREWORD

This contribution does not claim to present a complete survey of Egyptian religion. It attempts to describe as theoretically as possible some areas of Egyptian religious thought in order to determine basic, underlying principles. No attempt was made to catalog phenomena, which is why entries such as "sacred animals," "kingship," "Ma'at," "motherhood," "temple architecture," and the like, which the reader may have expected to find, do not appear; this material can however be found in the body of the text.

Ph.D./d.b.

BIBLIOGRAPHY

In addition to the bibliographic references given after each article, readers wishing to learn more about various aspects of Egyptian religion may refer to the following works:

H. BONNET, *Reallexikon der ägyptischen Religionsgeschichte* (Berlin 1952). W. HELCK, E. OTTO, and W. WESTENDORF, *Lexikon der Ägyptologie* (Wiesbaden 1972). F. DAUMAS, *La civilisation de l'Égypte pharaonique* (Paris 1965), 247–380, with bibliography, sometimes out of date. P. DERCHAIN, "Religion égyptienne," in *Encyclopédie de la Pléiade: Histoire des religions* (Paris 1970), 1:63–140. W. HELCK, "Die Mythologie der Ägypter," in *Wörterbuch der Mythologie* (Stuttgart 1965), 1:313–406. E. HORNUNG, *Der Eine und die Vielen* (Darmstadt 1971). H. KEES, *Der Götterglaube im alten Ägypten* (Berlin 1956); *Totenglauben und jenseitsvorstellungen der alten Ägypter* (Berlin 1956). S. MORENZ, *Ägyptische Religion* (Stuttgart 1960), also in French. W. WESTENDORF, *Das alte Ägypten* (Baden-Baden 1968).

EGYPTIAN COSMOGONY

There is an excellent collection of sources on Egyptian cosmology, the volume by Sauneron and Yoyotte, "The Birth of the World," in the series *Sources orientales*.[1] In it we learn how at Heliopolis the world was born from the masturbation of Atum—a god whose name means simultaneously "not to be and to be perfect"—from whose seed the first couple was formed, Shu and Tefnut, who in turn gave birth to Geb and Nut, themselves the parents of Osiris, Isis, Seth, and Nephthys. In Memphis, on the other hand, the artisan god Ptah began by representing the world in thought, in his heart, before making it real by pronouncing its names.

At Esna, by contrast, the ram Khnum molds living beings on his potter's wheel, while the primordial celestial goddess Nut is charged with producing the physical universe. At Hermopolis the first sun bursts forth from the calyx of a lotus that has just grown from the first mound that emerged from the ocean, and its light immediately draws to it four pairs of serpents and of frogs. Finally, at Edfu, the creator develops the world as an increasingly refined system of defense against the ever-changing attacks of Evil.

Cosmogonic thought is basic to Egyptian religion,[2] following a general conception of a universe whose creation must be constantly begun again every time a cycle is repeated—whether it is the cycle of day and night, of the month, of the flooding of the Nile, or of a reign. Each new beginning is the equivalent of "the first time," according to a very frequently used expression, and this gives rise to the necessity to represent the first time that accounts for all those that follow.

Because of the multiplicity of the systems that have just been evoked, it is useful to attempt to classify them and to isolate the lines of Egyptian cosmogonic thought. In doing so, we will not attempt to establish a chronological classification, since most of the sources are late ones that have nevertheless incontestably preserved much older traditions whose real age is impossible to specify. The most striking case is that of Memphitic theology, preserved by a stela of the Ethiopian period (eighth century B.C.), which claims to be based upon a very early text and which Egyptologists had placed back in the Old Kingdom; but a recent analysis has in fact dated it from the period in which it was engraved on the stone.[3] On the other hand, the cosmogony of Edfu, recently reconstituted by J. C. Goyon and attested exclusively by texts of the Hellenistic period, appears to have had its origins in the New Kingdom.[4]

The problem of cosmogony naturally presupposes the problem of the world before creation.[5] Most of the sources assume that in the beginning there was a kind of chaos which is represented as a dark, frozen, and formless primordial ocean, which seems always to have been there, and

The deities of Heliopolis. In Davie, *The Temple of Hibis.*

whose limits are never indicated. In any case, it is not regarded as a void but as a material mass containing the potential for all of the creation that would follow, a mass which can be defined only negatively, as the time in which "there still did not yet exist. . . ."[6] Yet here and there one finds some allusion to attempts at a precreation which were abandoned to bring about finally the system of the world in which we live, which is definitive. These abortive efforts, moreover, appear to be nothing but imprecise reflections of our universe.

What is interesting about these observations is that they show to what level the Egyptians had pushed their reflections on origins, a level that modern astronomy has not surpassed, since except for the big bang theory we have only invented the theory of the pulsating universe, which is only a more complicated formulation of the same aporia. This is also connected with the equally insoluble problem of spatial or temporal infinity,[7] which some Egyptians seem to have posed as well. But the historical inscriptions generally use such expressions as "until the limits of time," "up to the orbit of the sun," and "millions and millions of years," which suggest that an abstract notion of infinity did not exist. However, in chapter 175 of the *Book of the Dead*, the subject is taken up in a dialogue that from the beginning contrasts the creator, Atum, to Osiris, who symbolizes the power of renewal wherever it may manifest itself. The anguish of Osiris in the face of death in this text clears the way for two solutions: the first, in which Atum promises him that his son will succeed him, eludes the idea of the end, as it imagines a succession of generations that repeat the same acts and thus insure a cyclic infinity, whose precarious nature is left obscure. The second solution goes more directly to the heart of the problem: as a creator who is identical with the primal matter that he has organized, Atum will return to this matter, bringing Osiris with him, and Osiris, uniting with him in a single point, will escape the eternal return and belong definitively to the past, to a stability without duration. This return to the primordial uncreated is foreseen for a very distant future and seems to be necessarily definitive, since the powers of renewal (Osiris)[8] or of organization (Ma'at)[9] would be enclosed in it and by their conservative character would prohibit any change.[10]

This end of the world is inspired by the spectacle of the islands of the Nile that sometimes appear for a few years and, after they have borne aquatic birds and vegetation for some time, and sometimes even after they have been cultivated, are again washed by the river that carries them off until no trace of them remains.

With a cyclic conception like that of the Egyptians—a kind of permanent creation—coupled with the perpetual spectacle of nature destroying itself as it is created, it is not surprising

that the Egyptians never lost their fear of annihilation. Even the best organized of worlds contained its reserves of chaos that could never be totally reduced; the best one could do was to keep the destructive forces within tolerable limits by fighting against them every day, every year, and with every flood that one rejoiced to see return; and one rejoiced all the more because it was one's own rites that set the cycles in motion and one's own personal attitude of respect toward the laws of nature and society that helped to contain the destructive forces.[11]

The central problem in classical Egyptian cosmogony results from the difficulty of reconciling in one coherent image a physical universe in which all the great phenomena appear as an eternal new beginning regulated by invariable periodic cycles, combined with a necessarily linear vision of the fate of living beings.[12]

But the creative process and its motive were rarely the objects of long explanations. According to the Hermopolitan system, for example, chaos is wholly differentiated and the world is there.[13]

In other systems, an attempt was made to distinguish the prime mover, inherent in the creator and compelling him to create, from the actual realization of his creative work. At Heliopolis, an erotic excitation that Atum carries within himself suddenly moves him to draw out of his sexual organ the first divine couple, from which the rest of the cosmos is born through the normal biological process of generation. At Memphis, the will to create arises from the imagination of Ptah—from his heart, according to the Egyptian text—whereas the realization of this creation is the work of the speech commanded by this imagination.

These two theses may be viewed as very close to one another, since the motive power of creation is in both cases inherent in the creator and is then hypostasized in order to give it a mythological existence. The erotic impulse of Atum thus becomes his daughter who excites him, though she does not become his sexual partner and the nature of their father-daughter relationship is never explained;[14] Ptah's imagination is presented in the form of the god Sia, knowledge.

In order to move from the conception, from desire to reality, Atum uses his hand, often hypostasized under the name of Iwsa'as, that provokes his ejaculation,[15] while the tongue, which would pronounce the names of the creatures and thus give them their existence, is identified as Hu, the personification of the apodictic word.[16]

On the other hand, the theology of Esna sees no need for any decision by the creator and is content to present the speech of the primordial goddess Neith as the source of the material world and the art of the potter Khnum, who molds them on his wheel, as the source of living beings.[17]

The distinction between the creation of a physical universe and the creation of a living world appears in the Heliopolitan system, in which the first two generations of Shu, Tefnut, Geb, and Nut represent the atmosphere, earth, and sky, while the last generation includes the opposed couples Osiris and Isis, and Seth and Nephthys, and thus introduces the universal dynamic by representing the conflicts of life and introducing its component periods.

The absence, at Esna, of the first, purely internal, stage of creation does not automatically mean that its doctrine was purely materialistic.

The conception of an internal constraint as the prime mover of creation, conceived as an act of will on the part of the creator who cannot avoid it, marks the extreme limit of Egyptian cosmogonic thought, which no other system has since surpassed. More preoccupied with knowing why the creator created than with fixing the time in which he acted, the Egyptians conceived their cosmogonies more as explanations for a universal dynamic than as the search for origins at some given time (with the possible exception of some royal lists, whose character would have been more historical than cosmogonic in any case). As has already been mentioned, the universe is constantly on the brink of being dislocated, and its integrity depends on the performance of rites, that is, on the intensity with which man represents the universe for himself.[18] Cosmogony thus becomes an element of political and social life that belongs especially to the present moment.[19] The belief in the present nature of creative activity is translated, in the teachings of Memphis, Heliopolis, and Esna, into the transmission of the creative power to all living beings, who are thus charged with continuing what has already been set in motion. The great natural phenomena remain the province of the gods, whose rites maintain their activities; but representation, the conception of the world, and biological production are the affairs of men,[20] who continue the creative work once it has begun. The genetic process also served as a model for some cosmogonies, particularly those of Heliopolis,[21] in which the world is created from three successive generations that arose from the creator Atum, who is none other than the Void capable of becoming the Whole—if we are to trust the possible etymologies of his name.[22]

The genetic model thus furnishes a series of oppositions that are manifested everywhere and that give Egyptian thought its characteristic structure. The universe functions through the contradictory activity of two gods: Seth, who strives constantly to destroy and manifests himself as the storm or as sterility, but also as a killer; and Osiris, who maintains the power of renewal in nature wherever it may be recognized: in vegetation, in the Nile, the moon, the sun, and in the theoretically uninterrupted succession of sovereigns. Each of the two gods has as a double a female figure who, conforming to the character of her male counterpart, symbolizes sterility (Nephthys) or maternity (Isis).

Typical among Egyptian myths, which are presented as theses rather than narrations, is the following. The generation of four divinities is succeeded only by a single god, Horus, the son of Osiris and Isis, who succeeds his father, thus demonstrating the functioning of the genetic process and also furnishing a pattern for social order. Creation is thus at its end, and history may begin: every pharaoh to the end of Egyptian history, whether Persian, Macedonian, or a Roman emperor, would be Horus himself, "on the throne of the living," in contrast to the Horus-idea who lives in temples and in the sky.

The antagonism between creative and destructive forces in the world is the leitmotiv of Egyptian cosmology. At Esna, for example, the sun, Ra, and his eternal enemy, Apophis, who tries to prevent him from rising in the morning by placing himself across his path (as may be seen in Egypt, where black stratus clouds often stripe the horizon at sunrise), are both born of the great primordial goddess Neith. But although Ra is brought into the world in a normal fashion, Apophis is vomited and thus comes out of the mouth, by which, according to contemporary tradition, the sky in the evening conceives the sun of the following day.[23] This unnatural birth may well be the mythic expression of the rebellion represented by Apophis.

In the cosmogonies of Edfu and of Athribis, recently reconstituted by J. C. Goyon, conflict is itself the principle of creation.[24] It may even be seen as its source, since the creator

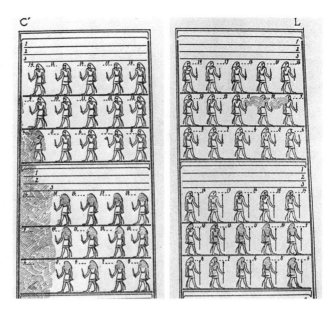

Differentiation of the protectors of the universe, represented as four companies of guardian daemons. In Chassinat, *Le Temple d'Edfou*, 9.

apparently develops the companies of guards who surround him and insure the proper functioning of his temple and thus of the world, only in response to the attacks that he must fend off more and more specifically as Evil varies its plan of action more and more. To infer from this the preexistence of Evil is nonetheless risky, since destruction is inherent in the cosmos, and the nonorganized from which the organized arose continues to exist everywhere and threatens to reconquer everything at the slightest sign of weakness,[25] as one senses in the trivial experiences of everyday life.

Starting from these premises, the Egyptians do not define the relationship between chaos and cosmos historically. The resulting difficulty in explaining creation may be removed only at the price of identifying chaos and the creator from the beginning and interpreting genesis as the simple inversion of one into the other—which was easy to express verbally because of the homophony between Atum's name and two verbal roots that meant "to be complete," and "not to be." This principle is, moreover, not limited to Heliopolitan theology, since it is found elsewhere in the myth of the "Great Swimmer," the primordial cow who is identified with the primordial ocean until she emerges from it.[26] It thus follows that creation may be nothing more than an internal performance by the creator, as already seen in the systems that tried to describe the mechanism of creation.

The identity of the creator and chaos also carries with it the logical necessity of partially preserving chaos as evidence for the difference between the two. The difference thus becomes the explanatory principle of the cosmogony, and consciousness and refinements develop more and more in the differentiation as its human components take on increasing detail.

The Hermopolitan system is the one in which this principle is most perfectly expressed to show the genesis of light. The eight primordial gods, who surround the first sun as it is born from a lotus and who are represented as men and women with the heads of frogs and serpents, have a series of names which are merely the differentiation of the notion of obscurity and invisibility; that is, of chaos beginning to organize itself by a kind of dawning awareness of its own

The ordering of the world: above the serpent (the symbol of chaos) and behind Osiris, who assures the return of spring, the sun rises in a vessel that crosses the sky and from which the sun directs creation. In Piankoff-Rambora, *Mythological Papyri*. Bollingen Foundation. Paris, Bibliothèque d'Eygptologie. Photo Flammarion.

nature, in contrast with the luminous being that has just sprung forth from its heart.

A text from a Middle Kingdom sarcophagus interprets the Heliopolitan myth in an analogous way by making not Atum alone but Atum and the couple Shu-Tefnut that arose from his seed the source of the organized world, which gets its first momentum when "the One is changed into Three."[27]

After this time, the organization of space is possible; the organization of time follows later, after the last generation of the Ennead becomes operative, as we have seen. The biological model is then developed with all of its consequences, the most important being the construction of a systematic dualism, both cosmological and political, which permits an organization of the world on the basis of the association of opposites. The opposites include light and darkness, order and disorder, male and female, life and death, being and nothingness, and Upper and Lower Egypt (along with the double symbolism of crowns, of tutelary divinities, etc.) to the extent of constituting pairs such as black and red (the Egyptians did not consider black and white to be opposites, as seems natural to us), and infinite duration and extratemporal eternity (which corresponds to the opposition between movement and the cessation of movement), as well as an opposition between this world and the beyond, which leads to the opposition between matter and spirit, and between reality and myth, whose indispensable connection the Egyptians always felt deeply.

It might be possible to describe in this way the mental schema by which the Egyptians built their cosmogonies. The schema has been described here as independent of the particular forms of the cosmogonic myth that are related to local conditions and to the individual fantasies of those who invented them.

We should indicate one curious exception. In a passage in the Bremmer-Rhind Papyrus, the god Khepri, the rising sun, whose name is derived from the root that means "being and becoming," undertakes a series of subtle ratiocinations on his own name.[28] This may be a particularly clever development

Child crouching on a lotus surrounded by eight gods. In Davies, *The Temple of Hibis*. Paris, Bibliothèque d'Egyptologie. Photo Flammarion.

in the theory of creation by words (the theory of the *logos*)[29] based on a succession of plays on words, which the Egyptians used whenever they had to explain the inexplicable.[30] This text may belong to a long Egyptian tradition, or it may result from the influence of Hellenistic rhetoric, since this document dates precisely from the time of Alexander's conquest.[31] It is certain that the Egyptians of this period were open to foreign influences.[32] But since the expression "he who is sprung from himself" (*hpr-ds.f*) is attested from the time of the Pyramid Texts of the Old Kingdom, a reciprocal influence is perhaps the most likely solution.

Ph.D./d.w.

NOTES

The substance of this article is basically borrowed from the one I wrote for the *Lexikon der Ägyptologie*, 3 (1979).

1. SAUNERON-YOYOTTE, "La naissance du monde selon l'Égypte ancienne," *Sources orientales* 1 (1959): 17–91.

2. This has been particularly illumined by S. MORENZ, *Ägyptische Religion: Die Religionen der Menschheit*, 8 (1960), chap. 8: "Weltschöpfung und Weltwerden." English and French translations of this book exist, from which the reader may get only a very approximate impression of the author's thought.

3. F. JUNGE, "Zur Fehldatierung des sog: Denkmals memphitischer Theologie," *Mitteilungen des Deutschen archäologischen Institutes in Kairo* 29 (1973): 195–204. Although the theory manifest here may have been elaborated much earlier, it did not find definitive expression. On this subject see the dialogue of Osiris and Atum in chap. 175 of the *Book of the Dead*, part 3, in H. KEES, "Göttinger Totenbuchstudien," *Zeitschrift für ägyptische Sprache* 65 (1930): 7ff.

4. J. C. GOYON, "Les Dieux-gardiens des temples égyptiens à l'époque gréco-romaine" (diss., Lyon 1976).

5. H. GRAPOW, "Die Welt vor der Schöpfung," *Zeitschrift für ägyptische Sprache* 67 (1937): 34–38. L. KAKOSY, "Schöpfung und Weltuntergang in der ägyptischen Religion," *Acta Antiqui Academiae Scientiarum Hungaricae* 11 (1963): 17–30.

6. E. A. E. REYMOND, *The Mythical Origin of the Egyptian Temple* (Manchester 1969).

7. J. ASSMANN, "Zeit und Ewigkeit im alten Ägypten," *Abhandlung der Akademie Heidelberg*, 1975.

8. Osiris remains the only being in creation after the end of the world decreed by Atum, according to chapter 175 of the *Book of the Dead*.

9. Maat, the daughter of the primordial serpent and symbol of cosmic and social order, is also the only being saved at the time of the final submersion, according to the "Shipwreck Story." See M.-T. DERCHAIN-URTEL, "Die Schlange des Schiffbrüchigen," *Studien zur altägyptischen Kultur* 1 (1974): 83–104.

10. The subtlety of this conception, which results in making the end of the world final, that is, the state of rest which nothing can stir, has come to light in a still unpublished dissertation by G. WIRZ, *Tod und Vergänglichkeit*. On the end of the world in Egypt, see S. SCHOTT, "Altägyptische Vorstellungen von Weltende," *Analecta Biblica* 12 (1959): 319–30.

11. E. HORNUNG, "Chaotische Bereiche in der geordneten Welt," *Zeitschrift für ägyptische Sprache* 81 (1956): 28–32; "Licht und Finster-nis in der Vorstellungswert Altägyptens," *Studium Generale* 18 (1965): 72–83. Note also my observations on this subject in "Le rôle du roi d'Égypte dans le maintien de l'ordre cosmique," *Le Pouvoir et le Sacré* (Brussels 1962), 72–73.

12. P. DERCHAIN, "Perpetuum Mobile," *Orientalia Lovaniensia Periodica* 6/7 (1975–76): 153–54.

13. In this system, as will be explained later, it is the creation of light that begins with the differentiation of the darkness.

14. P. DERCHAIN, "Hathor Quadrifrons: Recherches sur la syntaxe d'un mythe égyptien," *Publications de l'Institut historique et archéologique de Stamboul* 27 (1972): 47–48.

15. J. VANDIER, *Iousaâs et Nebethetepet*, 1964–66.

16. H. RINGGREN, *Word and Wisdom* (Lund 1947), 9ff.

17. S. SAUNERON, *Les Fêtes d'Esna: Esna V* (1962), 273ff.

18. DERCHAIN, "Perpetuum Mobile," 153–54.

19. MORENZ, *Ägyptische Religion*.

20. DERCHAIN, "Perpetuum Mobile," 153–54.

21. It is thus that the Ennead was realized, composed of three generations that reproduced by normal genetic methods after the second generation.

22. DERCHAIN, "Hathor Quadrifrons." The double meaning of the name Atum was well known long ago. See *Lexikon der Ägyptologie*, 1, s.v. "Atum."

23. SAUNERON, *Les Fêtes d'Esna: Esna V* (1962), 265ff.

24. See note 4.

25. See note 11.

26. H. BONNET, *Reallexikon der ägyptischen Religionsgeschichte*, s.v. "Methyer."

27. A. DE BUCK, *The Egyptian Coffin Texts* (Chicago 1938), 2:39.

28. *Papyrus Bremner-Rhind*, 26, 21–27, 5 and 28, 20–29, 6.

29. J. ZANDEE, "Das Schöpferwort im alten Ägypten," *Verbum: Essays . . . Dedicated to Dr. H. W. Obbink* (1964), 33–66.

30. On the word play explanation of the world, see S. MORENZ, "Wortspiele in Ägypten," *Festschrift Joh. Jahn* (1957), 23–32.

31. The text of Khakheperraseneb has been republished in G. E. KADISH, "The Complaint of Kha-Kheper-Re'-Senebu," *Journal of Egyptian Archeology* 59 (1973): 77–90.

32. Some examples of the Egyptian reception of foreign thought appear in the following cases, among others: the tomb of Petosiris at Touna el Gebel (publication by G. LEFÈBVRE, 1923–24). R. A. PARKER, "A Vienna Demotic Papyrus on Eclipse- and Lunar-Omina," *Brown Egyptological Studies* 2 (1959). J. YOYOTTE, "Bakhthis," *Religions en Égypte hellénistique et romaine* (1969), 129–41. P. DERCHAIN, "Miettes," § 4: "Homère à Edfou," *Revue d'égyptologie* 26 (1974): 15–19.

EGYPTIAN ANTHROPOLOGY

This article will describe the means by which the Egyptian defined himself in relation to the cosmos. For the Egyptian, the creation of man is not distinct from that of other living beings. He is molded on the wheel of the potter god Khnum, who says in a myth that he has transmitted the action of his machine to the bellies of all female beings;[1] or he is pronounced by Ptah in the same way as the rest of creation.[2] The tradition that has him born from the tears of a god depends merely on a play on words between *rmj*, "cry," and *rmt*, "man," and no attempt seems to have been made to draw any moral or metaphysical conclusions from this assonance. By the same token, the myth of molding apparently did not lead to any particular association between man and the clod of earth.

Man's place in the universe is that of a creature who is exceptional not because of his origins but because as a thinking creature he is capable of conceiving of things, and of giving them a coherent reality into which he seeks to integrate himself.[3]

Some of the traits that define his personality are held in common with the gods and with beasts. All are manifestations of life; man is special in that he has represented life to himself and in that he has made of life a "power" to which he is not willing to submit himself, but which he imagines he can control by rites whose regular performance makes him feel a continuity beyond the death and destruction that overtake individuals every day.[4]

It is necessary first to establish a relationship between the visible, material, and individual world and the world as represented; that is, the world of gods and of myths. The action of man who thinks about nature is materialized in rites that, located on a representational level, can logically be performed only by a man who is also a "sign." The sign is the Pharaoh, who is in theory the sole officiating priest and who is divine because he can deal with the gods; he defines the place of man as a species in the cosmos and in the presence of other natural forces. On the other hand, the real or imaginary involvements of each individual in his environ-

Presentation to Amon of Amenophis III (in his capacity as son of god and future sovereign) at his birth. The king and his *ka* are represented separately. From *Lepsius Denkmäler*, III. Photo Flammarion.

ment presuppose means of communication that are so many aspects of his personality. The Egyptians knew a great number of such aspects, of which some are difficult to understand, since they are without equivalents in our languages or concepts. The body-soul polarity that is so familiar to us, in spite of its surface similarities (the Egyptians conceived of the world in terms of polarities), cannot in every case be applied to the Egyptian schema.[5] For the diverse aspects of that scheme could not be so simply divided, since they took account of physical, social, religious, and magical relationships. Indeed, it is quite impossible to trace clear boundaries between these different fields.

Over the past few years, careful studies of several ideas have nevertheless made it possible to substitute acceptable definitions for the translations, such as "soul" or "double," that were current in older Egyptology, but that hardly covered the ancient concepts, whose names, *ba* and *ka*, we will keep. Though these concepts are the best known, Egyptian anthropology makes use of many others that attempt to encompass the human personality, such as the name, the shadow, the heart, the character, the god who resides in everyone, the body—which becomes the mummy after death—and the *akh*, which might be translated literally as "luminous one" or "illumined, transfigured one," but which in practice corresponds more to what we would call a ghost. As may be deduced from this enumeration, all of these aspects, with the exception of the last one, are connected with the living man and are not dissociated from him except by death. The goal of the funerary rite is to "reunite" once again what was one, so that it is essentially through funerary texts that we may learn about the nature of man, since the salvation of the individual consisted in the restitution of his integrity on the level of the imaginary.

The first determinant of personality evidently consists of the name, which at the same time indicates a social integration, for the simple and wholly material reason that the name that allows one to be called provides the environment with a means of acting upon the person. The fundamental importance of the name is demonstrated by the Egyptians' insistence on writing it in tombs and on stelae, specifying the genealogy whenever possible, and by the often-repeated wish to hear it pronounced in order to give some semblance of existence to the deceased. Since the name was an aspect of the personality common to men, gods, and animals, we may, by dwelling briefly on it, trace the practical limits between these three categories of beings. And we will discover that in the end the difference is one of degree rather than of kind.

An animal rarely has an individual name. An animal comes to have one only through a personal relationship with its master, since the names of family dogs are the only ones we know.[6] Men, by contrast, always have names, sometimes two, the second being a surname or a nickname.[7] The importance of the name is further stressed by the phenomenon of the *damnatio memoriae*, in which, long before the Roman emperors, the victims were usurping sovereigns or criminals whose names were transformed to make them agree with their personalities.[8] The gods, by contrast, have an infinite number of names. There are prayers in which the god is invoked "by all of his names," so that he is sure to be reached. On the other hand, one myth relates that the supreme god Ra had a secret name that symbolized his supremacy, a name that the goddess Isis did her utmost, through trickery, to have revealed to her in order to get the means of dominating him and thus of gaining power over the whole world.[9]

But although the narrative implies that she realized her goal and that she was even able to transmit the secret to her son Horus—the prototype of all the kings of Egypt[10]—the papyrus took care not to transcribe it, because the power of men, even of the greatest magicians, could not extend to command the creator and master of space and time, at least in the periods in which Egyptian mythology still belonged to the Egyptians.[11]

But although the name gives power to its bearer when he is enclosed in the tomb, the calling of his name is one of the rare circumstances in which he feels called back to life and in which he may send his *ba* (see below) to collect the libations and the announcement of the offerings that his visitor would have made along with his evocation.[12] We must nevertheless understand that the Egyptian was well aware that this evocation restored his life only as a memory, because a true evocation of the deceased that could make him appear was a complicated undertaking whose success depended on the intervention of all the gods through a solemn invocation. This is related in the story of Khonsuemheb[13] and is taught in some formidable divinatory formulas found in magic Demotic or Greco-Egyptian papyruses from about the first century A.D.

We may easily pass from the name to a second aspect of the personality, the ka,[14] for at the end of their theological history the Egyptians had practically given up the ka in their funerary conceptions, because it had become confused with the name. Indeed, this confusion sometimes led them to write a hybrid word, composed of the two hieroglyphs which denoted them: ⏁ and ⏁ . The connection between the two concepts was ancient in any case, since among the diverse possibilities for representing the ka, one sometimes finds the hieroglyph of two arms folded at right angles turned toward the sky, holding between them the facade of a palace topped by the royal falcon, on which the names of the kings were written.[15] Another way to represent the ka was to make a copy of the person walking behind it; because of this, Egyptology for a long time designated the ka as the "double." Finally, the ka is sometimes a statue carrying on its head the hieroglyph of its name, following a frequently used iconographic procedure.[16] Aside from royal iconography in certain birth scenes or scenes of the Jubilee festival (ḥb sd),[17] the ka is never represented.

In the analysis of human functions, as they appear in funerary texts, the ka is what makes possible the enjoyment of offerings. It is to the ka that offerings are explicitly sent in the formula of the evocation of the name that is our subject.

A formula such as "to be reunited with one's ka" as a means of saying "to die" led Egyptologists to false interpretations that we will not repeat here. This expression simply means that this vital function of the individual was interrupted by the accident of death and that it is now a matter of returning it to its owner through rites. Death is the separation of the ka and the man; that is, the loss of the life force. "Life force" is very appropriate for a definition of the ka from the Egyptian viewpoint: it is the vitality of a being, his faculty to perform the activities of life. The plural of the word for "life force" is frequently used to designate foods, through which life is maintained in the body.

Once we accept this definition of the ka, it is no longer surprising that the gods also have it, since vitality is one of their essential qualities. For the gods, however, the Egyptians are careful to differentiate the manifestations of vitality and attribute to the gods as many as fourteen ka, including strength, power, domination, nourishment, honor, brilliance, renown, influence, authority, vision, hearing, and knowledge, insofar as these translations approximate the Egyptian notions.[18] The absence of sexuality among these manifestations of vitality may appear strange, but can easily be explained, since its function does not concern the individual so much as the entire species. This is probably why the Egyptians gave sexuality a particular place when they represented it by a shadow, if the proposed interpretation of the shadow is correct.[19]

Over against these fourteen divine ka, the Egyptians knew of a group of four ka that expressed the limits of terrestrial well-being: abundant goods, a long life, a beautiful burial, and a worthy posterity.[20]

The ka thus has a double nature, sometimes active, sometimes passive. It expresses life itself as an exchange of actions for food. This explains how during life the ka can never be

distinct from its owner. After death its importance becomes central, as it must express a vitality of which no sign is to be found in the corpse. The assertion that the dead have a ka is in a way the negation of death, a negation that makes no sense unless the living continue to attend to their ancestors through remembrance and offerings (the visible manifestation of remembrance).

Another aspect of personality is the heart, which men as well as gods possess. According to the stela of Shabaka, which preserves a curious cosmogony, the heart is the seat of creative power—the imagination, in a sense—which becomes reality through the mediation of language, as language transforms thought into word and thus into action. But the heart also functions as memory and in this way serves to characterize the person even in the hereafter, where hearts are weighed against Ma'at, the notion of social and cosmic order in which an equilibrium must be maintained. The heart thus occupies a central place in the conception of the judgment of the dead, where the integration of the man is measured against a series of prescriptions ranging from respect for social conventions to ethics and from local taboos to deontological rules for civil servants.[21] But the heart does not play the role of conscience in this confrontation, as has sometimes been said, but simply plays the role of a witness, which assures us that its function was indeed that of being the seat of memory. If we now attempt to find a connection between these two functions of the heart—creative imagination and memory—I believe it will suffice to recall that the heart is the seat of the god Sia, whose name simply means "knowledge." Knowledge of the past is obviously "memory," while the creative imagination is necessarily related to the future.[22]

Beyond this, the heart may also be the seat of courage[23] and perhaps also of the affective life, since the Egyptians used expressions such as "the stopping of the heart" to describe a deep emotion. It is nevertheless difficult to know whether the heart does anything more than manifest the movements of the soul, without being their source.[24]

It is also in the heart that "the god who lives in man" is established.[25] This formula seems to express an idea of the dependence of the individual on a divinity who in some way possesses him and determines his behavior, either temporarily or permanently. Despite the possibility of being possessed by any god, the only concrete case attested is of a possession by Seth, the god of disorder and confusion, which seems to constitute an attempt to exculpate a person from his reprehensible actions.

Another approach to the personality is the "character," which does not seem to carry any religious connotation, so perhaps this term covers more or less the same notion as the heart, expressed sometimes through myth and sometimes abstractly. The character is responsible for the social behavior of an individual and in certain cases may even serve as an excuse for him, as we will see.[26] Unlike the god who lives in man, the character has permanence and constitutes what differentiates one man from another and dictates his personal line of conduct. The character, innate by nature, is the subject of the curious discussion between the sage Ani and his son, which raises for the first time in history the question of the limits of education and responsibility. For the master, every being is educable and thus responsible; for the disciple, the innateness of character is sufficient grounds to exculpate anyone.[27]

A complete man also possesses a shadow.[28] Strangely, the shadow does not seem to play any role until after death. It thus often seems to be interchangeable with the ba (see below), which it replaced in popular understanding at the end of Egyptian history.[29] Victory over death permits the return of the shadow, along with the rest of the elements of the personality, which leads to the deduction that the shadow by nature never leaves its owner as long as he is alive, except at night, which is a period similar to death.[30]

As for the shadow itself, the shadow that a tree or a wall projects is a sign of coolness and protection and may be used in a figurative sense, like the shadow of a god or a king who shelters his subjects. All of this is obviously inspired by everyday life, since under the implacable Egyptian sun the shadow is always a desirable thing, associated with a feeling of well-being.

The silent mobility of the shadow is also a quality that one would wish to retain in the hereafter, which was thought to be totally bereft of movement.

The confusion of the shadow and the *ba*, which took place in a late period, parallel to the confusion of the name and the *ka* that was previously discussed, implies a simplification and an impoverishment of the anthropological analysis for reasons that are unknown to us. This runs in opposition to the evolution of cosmology, theology, temple architecture, and their symbolic system, all of which, by contrast, became more and more refined and differentiated.

We thus come to the *ba*, represented in ancient times as a wading bird and later, beginning in the Eighteenth Dynasty, as a bird with a human head, which is difficult to define.[31] Like all the other elements reviewed up to this point, the *ba* is not unique to man. From an examination of all the manifestations that we know, we may deduce that it is more a function than an aspect. This function may be defined as what joins the two faces of being, the real and the imaginary, the past and the future, the night and the day, the gods and men, and the hereafter and this world, and thus gives a person his continuity.

It is in this way that the divine statue is made capable of receiving worship and is made the effective seat of the divinity who becomes immanent in it when the *ba* is made to descend into it. The sacred animal who incarnates a god in the enclosure reserved for him near the temple is also called the *ba* of the god. *Ba* is further used to describe the powers that make the sun pass each day from the subterranean world of night to the sky in order to illuminate the earth.

It is quite understandable that this liaison between the real and the imaginary—this continuity—would be essential to man, who, once dead, must have a means to maintain a contact with the living who will assure his worship. A famous representation, which is reproduced here, depicts in a telling fashion a *ba* bird descending into a tomb shaft to bring to the mummy the pitcher of fresh water and the bread that had been left for it in the chapel to which it evidently was unable to go to get them. As an anthropological notion, this tie with the personality that exists beyond death is taken up in summation by the memory, in the two senses of the word, as G. Wirz has shown (in a thesis prepared at Cologne, now in press; cited in note 22). The permanence of memory is the only guarantee one has of not dying to posterity definitively; the memory that one preserves within oneself is the sum of one's past, and losing it or forgetting it signifies a diminution of the personality, as sometimes happens to the aged. The *ba* memory will always return to the places that it knew; it is also the *ba* who will show to a despairing man,[32] who feels excluded from the world by the events that he witnesses, the contact that he may still have with those around him.

The nuances that separate the various conscious aspects of the personality are not always easy to grasp. In the preceding

The four elements of personality carried in procession. From G. Lefevre, *Tombeau de Pétosiris* (Cairo 1923).

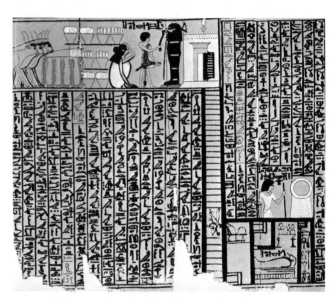

The *ba* going to rejoin the mummy. Detail from the papyrus of Neb Qed. Paris, Musée du Louvre.

rapid review, it will surely have been recognized that the name gives power to the person, that the *ka* keeps him alive and allows him to be fed in the hereafter, that the heart is the seat of memory and imagination, and that the character and the god that live in a man mark the limits of freedom and responsibility. The shadow seems to stand for mobility and, for unknown reasons, in some cases, for sexual potency. As for the *ba*, it insures continuity and in some way constitutes a man's identity.

In every case, the elements described up to this point, supported by the body, define the individual in life and after death, death appearing as a rupture in the personality that the rites strive to reestablish by joining back together the dispersed constituents.

After death, however, man undergoes a change in nature that is expressed by the notion of the *akh*, a word that is apparently related to a root that means "luminous" and that also designates all kinds of supernatural beings such as phantoms and demons; the *akh* thus belongs exclusively to the imaginary world that populates the unknown. The *akh* is the form of the deceased that possesses a superior power, which one may invoke in times of need but which is also capable of manifesting itself simultaneously in a way that may be disagreeable to the living.[33] It is, in short, the expression of the fear felt in the presence of the dead, a fear which would have left no traces in Egypt if one had to rely only on the traditional expressions of the funerary cult.

The reader who is perplexed by the complexity of the Egyptian analysis of man might like a classification, though I am aware of its provisional and artificial nature. Going back to the distribution of data on the basis of their relation to the concrete and the imaginary, which I have used elsewhere (see "The Problem of the Divine and the Gods in Ancient Egypt," below), we may arrange along two axes all the terms that have been discussed, ordering them from the most perceptible to the most private, while taking note of a "displacement" between the two series, which are not synonymous; for the terms of the "concrete" series themselves bear meaning. We thus obtain:

CONCRETE	IMAGINARY
body	*akh*
name	*ka*
shadow	*ba*
heart	*god in man, character*

The late reduction which I mentioned earlier caused the terms of the "imaginary" series to disappear, transferring to the organs themselves the functions that they expressed and that had always been manifested through those organs.

All the elements mentioned up to this point may be easily integrated into a system of personification that modern psychology would not repudiate.[34] But the Egyptians apparently did not stop there, and the limits of the person are not reached by the limits of the body and its faculties. I will cite, to complete this survey, an Eighteenth Dynasty text that enumerates in a single passage the *ka*, the stela and the tomb in the necropolis, destiny, the duration of life, the birthing stool, the wet nurse, and the creator of the embryo (the goddesses Meskhenet and Renenut and the god Khnum, respectively), the *ba*, the *akh*, the body, the shadow, and all of the forms of beings capable of benefiting from offerings.[35]

In this way the Egyptian integrated into the personality the elements whose external properties were indispensable to the continuation of one's existence and one's memory, in a way that reminds us of the conceptions of some modern African people.[36]

Since we have placed man at the center of our article, the diverse elements that we have enumerated appear as the constituents of his personality; but since they also belong to other categories of beings, it is impossible to establish an ontological distinction between man and the others. The difference is only a quantitative one, depending upon the relative participation in the two facets of the world, the imaginary and the perceptible. The imaginary world is essentially composed of the gods, who are connected to the perceptible world through their statues, temples, and diverse manifestations. Man, by contrast, located essentially in the perceptible world, passes into the imaginary through the intermediary of the Pharaoh, who is the incarnation of the idea of man and is in this way on an equal footing with the gods on the level of artistic representation.

Beyond this aspect, death also provided the means to pass from the perceptible to the imaginary, even though every effort of thought was made to bring the two facets together.

It thus follows that the hierarchy of the diverse categories of beings that populate the universe is not clear, because, if we recognize in the gods a sovereign power over all and in the dead faculties not possessed by the living, the existence of both depends fundamentally upon ritual activity, which is itself completely anchored in the perceptible. We thus find again in Egyptian anthropology the same dilemma as that which marked its cosmogony.

Ph.D/d.w.

NOTES

1. S. SAUNERON, *Esna V* (Cairo 1962), 235.

2. H. JUNKER, "Die Götterlehre von Memphis," *Abhandl. Preuss. Akad. Wiss.* (1940).

3. H. BRUNNER, "Anthropologie," in *Lexikon der Ägyptologie* (Wiesbaden 1975), 303ff. See also P. DERCHAIN, "Le rôle du roi d'Égypte dans le maintien de l'ordre cosmique," in *Le pouvoir et le sacré* (Brussels 1962), 72–73.

4. On the role of ritual, see P. DERCHAIN, "Religion égyptienne," in *Encyclopédie de la Pléiade: Histoire des religions*, 1 (Paris 1970): 95ff.

5. J. SAINTE-FARE GARNOT, "L'anthropologie de l'Égypte ancienne," in *Studies in the History of Religions*, supplement to *Numen II*, *L'Anthropologie religieuse* (Leiden 1955), 14–27, and the critique of this thesis, B. GEORGE, *Zu den altägyptischen Vorstellungen vom Schatten als Seele* (Bonn 1970), 16ff.

6. J. M. A. JANSSEN, "Über Hundenamen im pharaonischen Ägypten," *Mitteil. Deutsch. Archäol. Inst. Kairo* 16 (1958): 176–82.

7. H. DE MEULENAERE, *Le surnom égyptien à la basse époque* (Istanbul 1966).

8. G. POSENER, "Les criminels débaptisés et les morts sans noms," *Rev. d'Égyptol.* 5 (1946): 51–56.

9. E. BRUNNER-TRAUT, *Altägyptische Märchen* (Düsseldorf and Cologne 1963), 115–20.

10. On the transmission of the father into the offspring, see J. ASSMANN, "Das Bild des Vaters im alten Ägypten," in TELLENBACH, ed., *Das Vaterbild in Mythos und Geschichte* (Stuttgart 1976), 12–49.

11. Greco-Egyptian magical papyruses (H. D. BETZ, *The Greek Magical Papyri, in Translation*, Chicago 1985–), provide, on the other hand, a quantity of mysterious names that give power over the gods.

12. J. SAINTE-FARE GARNOT, *L'appel aux vivants dans les textes funéraires égyptiens* (Cairo 1938).

13. G. LEFÈBVRE, *Romans et contes égyptiens* (Paris 1949), 173.

14. L. GREVEN, "Der Ka in Theologie und Königskult der Ägypter des alten Reichs," *Ägyptol. Forsch.* 17 (1952). U. SCHWEITZER, "Das Wesen des Ka," *Ägyptol. Forsch.* 19 (1956). See also the articles "Ka," in H. BONNET, *Reallexikon der ägypt. Rel.-gesch.* (1952), and *Lexikon der Ägyptologie*.

15. See the illustration.

16. The famous *ka* of King Hor, from the Cairo Museum, often reproduced.

17. On this festival see E. HORNUNG et al., "Studien zum Sedfest," *Aegyptiaca Helvetica* 1 (Basel and Geneva 1974).

18. D. MEEKS, "Génies, anges et démons en Égypte," in *Génies, anges et démons: Sources orientales*, 8 (1971), 40.

19. B. GEORGE, *Zu den altägyptischen Vorstellungen vom Schatten als Seele*, 112ff.

20. D. MEEKS, as in note 18.

21. It is not, in any case, a matter of a conscience (German *Gewissen*) as has sometimes been believed. On the meaning of the judgment of the dead, see J. YOYOTTE, "Le jugement des morts dans l'Égypte ancienne," *Sources orientales*, 4 (1961), and R. GRIESHAMMER, "Das Jenseitsgericht in den Sargtexten," *Äg. Abhandl.*, 20 (1970).

22. All that I have said here on the function of memory is borrowed from the thesis of G. WIRZ, *Tod und Vergänglichkeit: Ein Beitrag zur Geisteshaltung der Ägypter von Ptahhetep bis Antef*, in press.

23. In the "Shipwreck Tale," for example, G. LEFÈBVRE, *Romans et contes égyptiens*.

24. A. HERMANN, *Altägypstische Liebesdichtung* (Wiesbaden 1959), 95–97.

25. H. BONNET, *Reallex. äg. Rel.-gesch.* (Berlin 1950), 225.

26. E. GRAEFE, *Untersuchungen zur Wortfamilie Bj3-* (Cologne 1971), Dok. 106–8.

27. Ibid., Dok. 108.

28. On the shadow, see B. GEORGE, *Zu den altägyptischen Vorstellungen vom Schatten als Seele.*

29. F. VON BISSING, "Tombeaux d'époque romaine à Akhmim," *Annales du Service des Antiquités* 50 (1950): 570ff.

30. For example, in the hymns of Amarna, M. SANDMAN, "Texts from the Time of Akhenaton," *Bibliotheca Aegyptiaca*, 8 (1938), 13, 1; 93, 17–18. See also A. DE BUCK, *De godsdienstige opvatting van de slaap* (Leiden 1939).

31. KLEBS, "Der ägyptische Seelenvogel," *Zeitschr. äg. Spr.* 61 (1926): 104–8. E. OTTO, "Die beiden vogelgestaltigen Seelenvorstellungen der Ägypter," *Zeitschr. äg. Spr.* 77 (1942): 78–91.

32. H. GOEDICKE, *The Report about the Dispute of a Man with His Ba* (Baltimore 1970). W. BARTA, *Das Gespräch eines Mannes mit seinem Ba* (Berlin 1969).

33. See *Lexikon der Ägyptologie,* 1 (Wiesbaden 1975), "Akh."

34. On the application of modern psychological theories to the analysis of Egyptian concepts, see especially B. GEORGE, *Zu den altägyptischen Vorstellungen vom Schatten als Seele.*

35. N. DE GARIS DAVIES and A. H. GARDINER, *The Tomb of Amenemhet* (London 1915), 21 and 23. J. QUAEGEBEUR, *Le dieu égyptien Shaï* (Louvain 1975), 133.

36. P. TEMPELS, *Philosophie bantoue* (Paris 1949).

For general bibliography, see the various articles of the *Lexicon der Ägyptologie.*

The Divine and the Gods in Ancient Egypt

In our study of Egyptian anthropology, it became apparent that there is no ontological difference between man and god, since it is possible to define both of them in connection with the same components, such as the *ba,* the *ka,* the name, the heart, the body, etc. The distinction must be sought elsewhere, essentially in the relative proportion of the real and the imaginary, but there is no clear boundary between the two, since the Pharaoh, who is quite real, belongs to the divine world by virtue of certain aspects of his function, while the gods are identified with their statues or their sacred animals.

Of course, the Egyptians had a word that we usually translate as "god," indicating the existence of a concept that could be recognized in each divine person and as a common denominator for all the gods; but this does not imply that we should look in Egypt for any sort of primitive monotheism or for any tendency toward monotheism, as has been done all too often.[1]

In order to understand how this interpretation could have been introduced, we must consider the structure of Egyptian religion, which is on the one hand organized in a unitary way—the gods of every region are found in every temple and come every year to Memphis, for example, for the royal jubilee—and on the other hand entirely realized on the local level in each sanctuary. For the myths and theology of each locality, the indigenous god is the synthesis of all the gods of the country, whose functions he fulfills to the extent that they are differentiated; and his person is recognized in each foreign god who would, in his own locality, perform his specific function.

A particularly eloquent example that illustrates this principle is found in the Jumilhac Papyrus, a document that comes from a very recent period but has preserved venerable traditions about the Anubis of Hordai, a locality of Middle Egypt.[2]

Two successive lists enumerate all of the gods of the myth of Osiris that Anubis incarnates at the time of the celebration at Hordai of ceremonies ordinarily referred to as "mysteries," and all of the sanctuaries of Egypt where Anubis is worshiped because his specific function of embalming must be practiced on certain ritual occasions. The system is so lucid that it was even possible in one case to affirm that Shu, the son of Ra of the temple of Per Hapy, was none other than Anubis, because on some occasion he must have fulfilled the function of the latter. It is possible that this interpretation, as seen from the perspective of Hordai, was not even known at Per Hapy.[3]

The Egyptian gods are thus representations of the energies that are diffused throughout nature, living in the sky—i.e., in the realm of the imaginary—but manifesting themselves everywhere in the real where those energies are sufficiently concentrated to act or to be visible, as in a tree, an animal, the Nile, a heavenly body, or even an image.

We thus arrive at a diagram by which it is possible to describe the divinity and its implications, by contrasting personality and function, and locality and potentiality, two by two, in the two fields of the real and the imaginary:

REAL		IMAGINARY
	personality	
temple		sky
locality		potentiality
natural phenomenon	function	myth

In what follows, we shall see how this schema may be applied to reality. It must nevertheless be recognized that the Egyptian gods are manifested and not revealed gods,[4] if Egyptian religion is to be integrated into a system that contrasts revelation with natural religion. But it is difficult to draw the line, since the gods sometimes speak for themselves, beginning in the earliest period.[5] They did this usually in the style of aretologies, since there was never any idea of exclusiveness (with the possible exception of the Amarna period, when there appeared intolerant movements like those that characterize revealed religions). Apart from this, the conflicts that sometimes opposed neighbors on the religious level were concerned with worship and practice but never with questions of dogma.[6] Even the progressive abolition of the cult of Seth, beginning at the end of the second millennium, corresponds for the most part to the development of a historical situation which had become more and more confused and disastrous, against which was set the persecution of a god (who signified in his very essence disorder and confusion in nature and society),[7] which was almost the last battle that the Egyptians would fight. This was not religious fanaticism; it was simply the logical consequence, on the level of the imaginary, of the exhaustion of the forces of order.

A few examples will help to bring this greatly oversimplified diagram to life, and will introduce at the same time some Egyptian divinities chosen to give an idea of the often considerable complexity of the interactions of the various components.

Thoth is the god of Hermopolis. Like all the gods of Egypt, he enjoyed a daily worship in his temple which essentially consisted of the care of his body, meals, and adoration, as befitted an Egyptian god. This daily ritual is known from diverse sources from the New Kingdom and the Late Period.[8]

But apart from this, Thoth is the object of a specific offering, a writing case (and we know that many other offerings belonged to different gods). Thoth is the model bureaucrat: he knows how to write and perform calculations, is invested with the highest functions in governing the world beside the sovereign Sun, and is conscious of his duties of justice and precision. Thus he regulates the course of the moon, checks the balance of the scale at the court of judgment of the dead, inscribes the name of the Pharaoh on the fruits of the tree of history in the temple of Heliopolis, and surveys the precinct of projected temples, except in those cases in which he assigns this function to one of his companions. For all of this, he must know how to write, like any scribe; and the palette, which holds the ink holders and the brushes and is also used for quick notes, is the instrument of his function.[9]

Ithyphallic god. Edfu. From Chassinat, *Le Temple d'Edfou.* X.

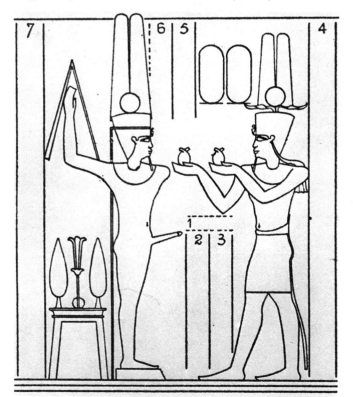

The internal logic of mythic thought makes further expansions possible. It is known, for example, as I noted in trying to define Egyptian anthropology, that the heart was considered the seat of memory and imagination. It may thus be said of Thoth that he is "the heart of Ra," since he decrees laws, names places, and composes the procedures of medicine and magic through which men hope to alleviate their ills. Thoth thus becomes a doctor and a magician—he is assigned the healing of the lunar eye, as well as the calculation of the lunar course—and the great killer of adversaries of every sort, because he knows the words that can reduce them to powerlessness. As a scholar, he is obviously also a priest, and in the myths it is he who fulfills the functions of the ritual expert beside Osiris. All of these activities of the god, whose sacred animal is sometimes the ibis and sometimes the dogfaced baboon, are universal and thus justify his frequent presence in all parts of Egypt, wherever the local god needed his knowledge and his support.

Thoth also provides the confirmation of the ontological identity of man and deity, which only differ quantitatively: it sometimes happens that he may cheat or steal.[10] Thoth is thus an excellent illustration of the diagram in which I attempt to capture the notion of god. The arbitrary nature of the relationship between a god, his place of origin, and his animal manifestations is only apparent and is probably the result of our own ignorance; it is possible to show with the help of examples that the function is determined by the locality, and the animal is determined by the function.

Min, the ithyphallic god of Coptos, is the last god to whom it is possible to address oneself before venturing into the eastern desert by way of the famous Hammamat Wadi that leads to the Red Sea and the wealth of Arabia. Since he was the all-powerful local god there, it is evident that alongside his primitive fertilizing function he must also have insured the protection of all those who had business in the mountains and beyond: quarry workers and those who sought gold, incense, or perfumes. This is the function that would be essential to him outside of his city, since it would signify his person for all those who did not otherwise know him. This is notable in the rites in which he is implicated, rites connected with the supply of powdered antimony and malachite that were sought in the sterile wastelands. These substances played an important role in Egyptian ophthalmology and in the cult of the moon in its aspect of the celestial eye that must be healed each time it grows weak.[11] Min is a classical case: those I am about to evoke are certainly less well known.

To the east of Lower Egypt, in a valley that opens wide to the desert zone of the isthmus, lived the god Sopdu, whose name means something like "the pointed One," apparently an allusion to the teeth of the ferocious beast that he might originally have been. When he is known, however, Sopdu has become a falcon god, like so many others, all of whom are warrior gods.[12] Whether he is a ferocious beast or a falcon, Sopdu occupies the most dangerous place in the whole country, the one through which the Bedouins who moved across the sands always tried to penetrate into the productive Nile Valley, which had to be defended against them. It is only natural that the god of this place was a warrior and that this function, the local implications of which were very strong, became specific to him and was given a universal value.

At the other end of Egypt, at the point where the Nile enters the country after it has worn down the granite wall that blocks all passage, another border guard lives. This is the ram god Khnum of Elephantine, the island that is the

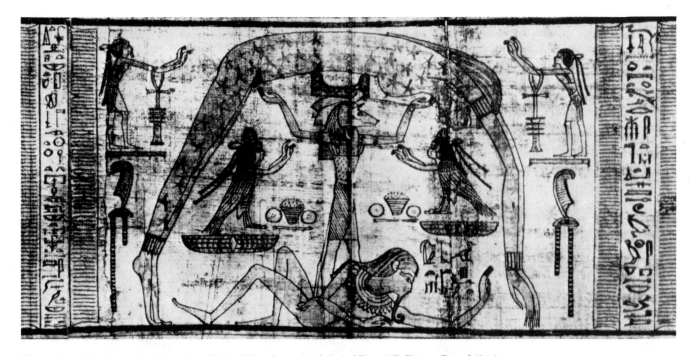

Sky and earth kept apart by Shu. From Piankoff-Rambova, *Mythological Papyri* (Bollingen Foundation).

first inhabitable place north of the cataracts, where the Pharaonic governors of the region were established.

If the system is to be logical, it is difficult to understand why, when it is a predator that watches over the eastern marches of the country, it is a peaceful herbivore—who becomes aggressive only when females are concerned—who is entrusted with the post over the cataracts. Although the Bedouins of the Sinai were a constant menace, the Nubians, who populated the Nile Valley to the south of Aswan, had always been, by contrast, quite peaceful. Their country, before it was destroyed by the various dams constructed in the twentieth century, was rich. It could be cultivated and therefore lived in. Moreover, the meaning of this frontier was very different from that of the other. Although nothing but pillaging came from the northeast, nothing but wealth came from the south: first the wealth of the rising of the Nile itself, which entered Egypt from there, and then the wealth of all of the products that could be peacefully imported and even taxed upon their entry. Nubia was a region into which Egypt always tried to extend itself, as long as this did not pose problems other than the technical ones of getting through the rapids.

Everything that comes from the south is therefore a blessing, which a ram god, a sign of fertilizing virility, clearly symbolizes. An archaeological detail confirms this thesis to some extent. From the time of the Middle Kingdom, the eastern frontier was walled in by a line of fortresses that were not easy to pass through. On the contrary, when the Egyptians decorated the secondary door of the pylon of Philae, which looks to the south and leads northwards to the mammisi—the chapel where the mother goddess brings the god, her son, into the world, as a sign of the perpetuity of life—they decided to engrave bearers of offerings representing the Nubian districts, moving towards the interior.[13] This did not hinder Khnum from being an effective protector of

Horus and Seth tie up seedlings of sacred plants. Throne of a statue of King Sesostris I. Cairo Museum. Photo Hirmer.

the African border, where he also carefully controlled the rising of the Nile.

It should be noted that many examples support the thesis of a geographical determination of the divine bestiary of Egypt. Thus, in the amphibious zones of Fayum and Mareotis, the divine is freely manifest as a crocodile, the animal that best represents the strength of water in its dreadful aspect.[14] The substitution of falcons for an aquatic monster in the northwestern part of the Delta is nevertheless a difficult problem; a thorough investigation of the symbolism of the falcon might help to solve it. This bird of prey is well known for its high flight (it is the manifestation of Horus, "he who is on high") and for its aggression (fighting gods, like Horus, Sopdu, and Montu, are often falcons), but this is not enough.

According to the principles applied so far, a complete inventory of the Egyptian pantheon should be a total representation of the world. For example, the eyes of cosmic gods like the one of Letopolis are the sun and the moon.[15] According to whether these heavenly bodies shine or are not visible, the god sees or is blind. At Heliopolis they even developed a system of several generations, which we have discussed in the context of Egyptian cosmology, to describe the fundamental functions of the universe.[16] Geb is the earth in all of its aspects. Plants grow out of his back, but it is also he who holds prisoner the dead who are buried.[17] Nut, his consort and a goddess of the sky, is at the same time the mother goddess responsible for the permanent rebirth of the heavenly bodies, which she is able to bring into the world every morning and evening, even though she has had no more relations with her husband since the very first time, when she conceived the dynamic gods by him.[18] Impossible unions are a frequent iconographic theme, in which the god

Shu plays an essential role. He is the image of the air that holds up the sky and keeps it from collapsing onto the earth. But the Egyptians did not think of Shu as a simple myth of the air. At a deeper level, he is the sign of all that is found in between. As the intermediary between sky and earth, he can separate them as well as unite them, by transmitting the prayers of men up to the gods or by transmitting the light and the orders of the gods downward.[19]

Mythic analysis was at times carried very far. So it is that the two goddesses Hathor and Isis--so close to one another in certain regards that they share equally certain rooms of the Temple of Dendera—in the final systemization of Egyptian religion represent two clearly distinctive aspects of maternity. These are the biological function, which extends from conception to birth and naturally also implies love, pleasure, and intoxication, and the social function, which begins with birth and includes education and the stability of the family.[20]

On the other hand, the Theban goddess Mut, though her name means "mother," is a strictly local personality who resists any attempt to establish a profound connection between her name and the function that it indicates.

A final aspect of maternity may be represented by Nekhbet, the goddess of El-Kab whom the Greeks called Ilithyia, whose name means "childbirth" and whose characteristic animal, the vulture, is the sign used in hieroglyphics to write the word "mother," for reasons that were explained by Horapollo.[21] But the sole universal function of Nekhbet is to confer royalty, for reasons that are difficult to discern but that probably derive from the role that the mother plays in the transmission of power in Egypt, rather than from a geographical determinism,[22] even if the implantation of Nekhbet's cult at El-Kab may be explained by local topography.

Seth killing Apophis at the bow of the bark of the sun. From Pinkoff-Rabova, *Mythological Papyri,* plate 2.

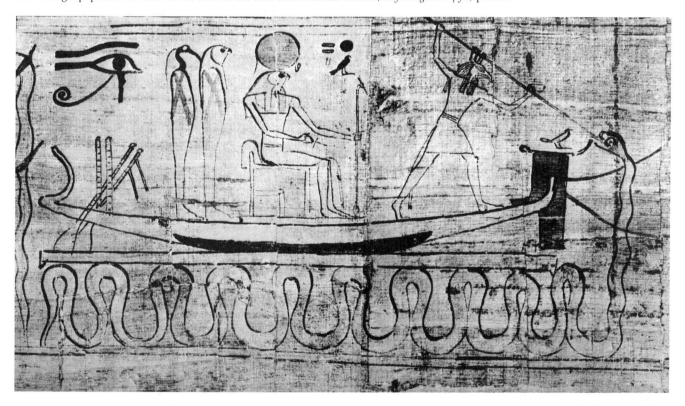

The opposition between person and function may resolve a great many of the questions posed by Egyptian religion, questions that historical methods have been unable to answer satisfactorily. In particular, much has been said about Egyptian syncretism, because the gods may have double names, or two gods may apparently combine into a single individual. There have been attempts to see in this the effects of the political or ideological domination of certain sanctuaries or other historical causes, which have generally had to be consigned to an inaccessible past.[23] If such combinations are related to exchanges of structures, the difficulties fall away of themselves. Every time two divinities combine into one and every time a god has a double name, it may be said that one of the names designates the person—i.e., a local presence—while the other designates the function that this person fulfills at a given time. The combination of two names is thus necessarily local and may be best understood by comparison with what takes place in a play, when the actor identifies himself with his role for the duration of the performance.[24] Combinations such as Amon-Re, Khnum-Re, Montu-Re, or Sobek-Re, all of which are strictly local, have no purpose other than to represent the local god in his function as master of the world and dispenser of universal energy. The name of Khonsu-Thoth, for example, simply emphasizes the idea that the moon god Khonsu is capable of maintaining the nocturnal star on the proper path. Examples of this sort may be multiplied and accompanied by all those in which compound names are replaced by chains of epithets, each of which specifies a temporary function.[25]

The relationship between the gods in a syncretic combination in Egypt is always vertical, i.e., one which establishes a relationship of dependence between the members of the association, and has never been horizontal, i.e., one which founds a relationship of identity between gods who are equivalent but have distinct origins. An individual is so much identified by his locality that one cannot name a god without also indicating his domicile or residence. This is necessary because in the end the Egyptians used very few names; many names are not proper nouns at all but rather simple nouns or adjectives found in everyday speech, such as Mut (mother), Sekhmet (powerful), Meskhenet (birthing stool), Renenut (wet nurse). But gods are like madonnas in this; the local epiphany acquires the personality. By contrast, in the great hymns of theological or cosmological import and in myths, the function is most important, and it is to this other side of the diagram that the rest of this article will be devoted.

Leaving aside what have been called "concept gods" (*Begriffsgötter*), such as Commandment and Thought, Sight and Hearing, Order-Justice—which were never anything more than theological abstractions with no cult—we may recognize some divinities in Egypt who are also the mythical expression of highly abstract notions, like Shu, discussed above and defined as "the Mediator."[26]

Now the most illustrious god of the Nile Valley is also certainly the expression of an abstract idea. Osiris is the god whose myth and cult most contradict any historical analysis.[27] His story may be summarized in a very few words. Osiris is the dead king who cedes the throne to his son and withdraws from the world to reign only in the hereafter. He was assassinated by his brother Seth, who later brought an interminable case before the tribunal of the gods against his nephew, whom Isis had conceived by her reanimated husband. One may see this simply as a myth of the rights of succession and as historical evidence for the transition from a matrilineal succession (the brother assuming his

Statue combining a cow, a serpent, and two women, one of whom has the head of a lion. Paris, Musée du Louvre. Photo Musées nationaux.

right to succeed his brother) to a dominating patrilineal succession (the son inheriting from the father). But Osiris is also invested with so many terrestrial and celestial functions that it is impossible not to look further than this. He is a god of vegetation, which was often taken to be his primary function: the floodwaters of the Nile rise out of his body, he is the moon, and he helps the sun to return to its path each night. It is a vain pursuit to try to discover which of these was the first of his aspects, even for those which are semantically derivable. A structural analysis, however, solves the question easily. In relation to all of the phenomena enumerated, the position of Osiris is always identical. He is the mythical expression of recurrence. Everything that repeats itself is Osiris—the king, the moon, the sun, the plants, the floods of the Nile—and by extension he becomes the great god of the dead whom he allows to return to life. This abstraction had already evolved sufficiently when the cult of Osiris developed that it was possible to recognize the identity of a single phenomenon in many spheres: cosmic, physical, biological, and social.

Seth, who is found at the crossroads of many myths in which he plays the role of disorder, is equally abstract.[28] As a fratricide and a pederast, he disturbs the social order; as a rapist who is sterile, he disturbs the biological order. As the sun, he dries up the harvests; when he is water, he is the roaring flood that ravages villages. In the desert, he is solitude, thirst, and death. The only positive aspect that remains to him is that it is sometimes possible to use his chaotic power against others. Thus, at the prow of the boat of the sun he impales the adversaries who try to impede its progress. Nevertheless, his negative aspects gradually gain the upper hand because of the growing success of the cult of Osiris; and the cult of Seth is eliminated, as we have already noted.

It is now easy to understand how natural phenomena may correspond to several gods, according to the aspect under which they are envisaged.

As we have seen, maternity was represented by several goddesses, according to the angle taken in speaking about them. The moon is another clear example. In Egypt, a great number of gods who never combined into a single god correspond to the moon, for each god was connected with the moon only through his function, and that function elsewhere connected him with other phenomena.

If one wished to express the periodicity of the moon, one would call it Osiris; to emphasize the complexity of the calculations that regulate its course, one would call it Thoth. If one thought of the moon's instability, it was the sick eye of the god of the sky, which must be healed. But to express the social function of the moon, so important in Egypt where its light allows the evening festivities to last longer and invites one to celebrate at night the feast that the crushing heat of the sun made impossible by day, one would turn to Hathor, the goddess who is a traveler—like the moon—and whom we have already discussed above.

This "diversity of approaches," as H. Frankfort defined it, is in the final analysis nothing but a very common form of human behavior. What object exists that we do not approach diversely? The Egyptians simply developed a very complicated mythology in the hope of lending more dimensions to their perception of the universe, so that we may compare the sum of the myths about a given fact with a hologram. Inversely, each myth draws part of its nature from a god who is the expression of a physical or social law.

A final problem is the polymorphy of the Egyptian gods: they are humans to the extent that they think and order the world, and animals to the extent that animals are signs in a mythical language, susceptible to ambiguity.

Thus, the jackals that course over the desert may be dangerous demons who devour the corpses of drowned men washed up on the shore,[29] but also—because they never get lost in the arid wastelands—they may be the friends of the dead who search for the path to the Western lands of the blessed ones. The meanings of the Egyptian bestiary nevertheless still remain poorly known, and we do no more here than indicate the problem.

One case, however, merits an explanation. This again concerns Hathor, of whom the Louvre has a curious statue that brings together a cow, a serpent, and two women, one of whom has the head of a lioness.[30] This astonishing association surely must be explained as an attempt to grasp the theoretical and topographic aspects of the goddess in one image. Hathor is, as we have seen, a goddess of love and of the sky, connected with the moon and with the sanctuaries that are often found at the entrances of valleys leading into the desert over which she comes and goes. Now if the woman directly evokes Hathor's erotic function, the three animals surely allude to a place of worship. At the bottoms of the wadis that run into the desert, ponds form, which constitute the last sources of water available as one leaves the valley. These are the realms in which bovines—relegated as far as possible from agricultural lands, to places where they can still find the pasturage and water that they need—come into contact with serpents and wild animals of the desert in search of easy prey. The statue is thus a synthesis of the functions of the goddess and alludes explicitly to her biological environment.

Ph.D./d.w.

NOTES

1. A bibliography on "Egyptian monotheism" has been assembled by E. HORNUNG, *Einführung in die Ägyptologie* (Darmstadt 1967), 31.

2. J. VANDIER, *Le Papyrus Jumilhac* (Paris 1962).

3. *Pap. Jumilhac*, 5, 1ff.; 5, 17 and 6, 2 for the passages mentioned.

4. SIEGFRIED MORENZ, *Ägyptische Religion* (Stuttgart 1960), 32, 43.

5. E. OTTO, "Zur Komposition von Coffin Texts Spell 1130," in *Fragen an die Literatur* (Wiesbaden 1977), 1–18.

6. JUVENAL, *Satire* 15.

7. H. TE VELDE, *Seth: The God Confusion* (Leiden 1967).

8. ALEXANDRE MORET, *Le rituel du culte divin journalier* (Paris 1902). MAURICE ALLIOT, *Le culte d'Horus à Edfou* (Cairo 1949, 1954). H. W. FAIRMAN, "Worship and Festival in an Egyptian Temple," *Bull. John Rylands Library* 37 (1954): 165–203.

9. On Thoth, PATRICK BOYLAND, *Thoth, the Hermes of Egypt* (London 1922).

10. S. SCHOTT, "Le dieu qui vole les offrandes et qui trouble le cours du temps," *C.R. Acad. Inscr.* (Paris 1970), 547–56.

11. H. GAUTHIER, *Les fêtes du dieu Min* (Cairo 1931); *Le personnel du dieu Min* (Cairo 1931). C. J. BLEEKER, *Die Geburt eines Gottes* (Leiden 1956).

12. On Sopdu: H. BONNET, *Reallexikon der ägyptischen Religionsgeschichte*, s.v.

13. See my review of H. JUNKER, "Der grosse Pylon der Tempels in Philae" (Vienna 1958), in *Bibliotheca Orientalis* 18 (1961): 47–49.

14. H. KEES, "Zu den Krokodil- und Nilpferdkulte im Nordwestdelta," in *Studi in Onore Ippolito Rosellini* (Pisa 1955), 141–52. J. YOYOTTE, "Le Soukhos de la Maréotide . . . ," *Bull. Inst. fr. archéol. orientale* (1956–57), 81–95.

15. H. JUNKER, *Der Sehende und blinde Gott* (Munich 1942).

16. W. BARTA, *Untersuchungen zum Götterkreis der Neunheit* (Munich 1973).

17. *Lexikon der Ägyptologie*, 2, s.v. "Geb."

18. A. RUSCH, *Die Entwicklung der Himmelsgöttin Nut zu einer Totengottheit* (Leipzig 1922).

19. P. DERCHAIN, "Sur le nom de Chou et sa fonction," *Rev. d'Égyptol.* 27 (1975): 110–16.

20. See my review of M. MÜNSTER, "Untersuchungen zur Göttin Isis," in *Bibliotheca Orientalis* 27 (1970): 22.

21. HORAPOLLON, *Hieroglyphica*, 1, 11.

22. On Nekhbet, H. BONNET, *Reallex. äg. Rel.-gesch.*, s.v.

23. The limits of the historical method have been reached by K. SETHE, *Urgeschichte und älteste Religion der Ägypter* (Leipzig 1930), who has used in this book a genial rigor and imagination.

24. P. DERCHAIN, *Elkab*, 1 (Brussels 1971); *Hathor Quadrifrons* (Istanbul 1972), 25.

25. D. KURTH, "Götter determinieren Götter," *Studien z. altägypt. Kultur* 5 (1977): 175ff. W. SCHENKEL, "Amun-Re," ibid., 1 (1974): 275ff.

26. See *Lex. d. Ägyptol.*, 2, s.v. "Götter (Begriffs-)."

27. The essay by G. GRIFFITHS, *The Origins of Osiris* (Berlin 1966), demonstrates the impossibility of the undertaking. See my review in *Rev. d'Égyptol.* 21 (1969): 166–70.

28. H. TE VELDE, *Seth*.

29. *Book of the Dead* 17: GRAPOW, *Religiöse Urkunden*, 5, 67.

30. J. VANDIER, "Nouvelles acquisitions," *La revue du Louvre* 19 (1969): 49ff. and fig. 14.

EGYPTIAN RITUALS

I

It is impossible to describe Egyptian rituals within the limits of this brief article. My purpose is rather to show that ritual in its various forms imparts movement to the static diagram with which I have portrayed the nature of divinity (in the article "Egyptian Cosmogony," above); one might even say that ritual dynamizes divinity. Just as divinity oscillates on two axes between the poles of person/function and locality-/potentiality, so we can say that rituals are divided into classes corresponding to these polarities.

Some rituals, which address the *person* of the god, are intended to satisfy the god's needs. One is the everyday ritual, consisting of a fixed series of offerings of food, libations, and incense, and of dressing and anointing the image of the god, all of which hardly differ from the care one takes in looking after a living person;[1] the only difference is in the symbolic character of these rituals (the statue that is the object of these rites naturally does not consume the food that it is offered). The solemnity of the act evoked the service of a person of high rank, a sovereign, and prevailed in courtly ceremonies until very late, for instance, at the court of Louis XIV. This ritual was intimate and took place deep inside the shrine, sheltered from profane eyes, where it attempted to capture the imaginary reality of the god whose *ba* had been brought down into the statue.[2] But the statue was also carried in a procession around the sanctuary and was thus offered for the joyful veneration of the people to whom it could, merely by passing by them, give all kinds of blessings, such as answering questions that were asked of it or causing flowers to bloom under its feet.

On the other hand, the great liturgical performances that, depending on their nature, took place either in the strict privacy of the chapels or out in the open, had the role of

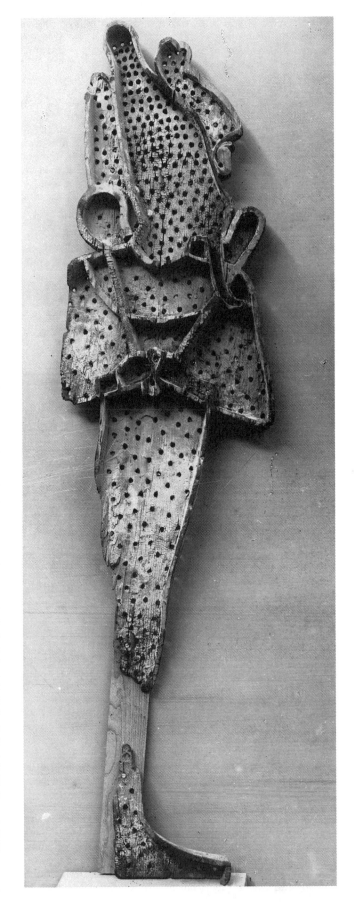

Vegetating Osiris. Cairo Museum. Museum photo.

animating the myths, that is, of representing the god's *function*, whether cosmic or political. When the function was cosmic, whether the intent of the liturgical action was to ensure the daily return of the sun, the reappearance of the moon, or the periodicity of agrarian life, the ceremonies were always secret.[3] When the function was political and the intent was to establish the sovereignty of the local god, at least some of the episodes would take place in public, such as the presentation of the falcon-king at Edfu and Philae.[4]

Along the two basic axes, the above-mentioned rituals are situated as follows, maintaining their fundamental connection with the two fields of the real and the imaginary, the connecting of which constitutes the essence of religion:

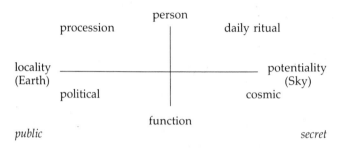

The position of the god in relation to the various aspects of the liturgy is thus easily definable, if it is understood that we are for the moment excluding from our study the funerary rites that fall into other categories (see the article "Death in Egyptian Religion," below).

Less simple is the structure of ritual in relation to its components, the whole being more than the sum of its parts. Its primary significance is that it manifests the coherence of the real and the imaginary, and that it indicates their reciprocal influence upon one another. By offering an object to the statue of the god, one called upon the whole spectrum of his activities, the ultimate goal of which was to produce whatever the object symbolized. Thus, by offering Khnum a potter's wheel, the instrument on which he molded living beings and gave them their vital force, one promoted the growth of embryos.[5] If he was given a vessel of water from the Nile, he responded by causing the flood waters to rise.[6] The culmination of the ritual was logically the offering of the symbol of Ma'at, the guarantor of both cosmic and social order in her capacity as guiding force of the universe. This ritual was usually performed deep inside the shrine as the final act of the celebrant in his progress toward the meeting with the god. In this rite the interdependence of a represented order (a physical and moral force all in one) and the existence of a society appears very clearly. For if Ma'at were abstractly guaranteed by the gods whom she nourished, it was necessary for men, led by their king, to *act* daily in accordance with this order, each one himself and according to his rank, so that the gods could draw from this well-ordered reality the energy needed to sustain the process of creation.[7]

The problem of the meeting of the two planes of the imaginary and the real was obviously resolved, as far as the gods were concerned, in the way I have stated, by endowing the statue with a *ba* of heavenly origin. The necessary consequence was naturally that the celebrant was also able to move around on the plane of the representation at the cost of remaining totally alien to the world of the gods. This problem was resolved by creating the notion of a single celebrant, in some cases the Pharaoh, who by virtue of his

function as ruler was the visible sign of the maintenance of the political and social order and of the ability to conceive the abstract expression of this order through his laws and decrees. Egyptians clearly expressed the Pharaoh's presence on the imaginary plane by making him a god.[8]

Moreover, corresponding to the ambiguity of the god and the Pharaoh was the ambiguity of the temple, the meeting place of the two, conceived entirely as a *representation* of the world and called "the sky" because it was the divine dwelling place.

However, in order to be distinguishable from an ordinary action,[9] the ritual also had to be supported by a myth, whether the myth was introduced secondarily (as in the daily ritual, by assimilating the offering to the eye of Horus,[10] or in the case of the ritual of the opening of the mouth, originally a simple sculptural operation[11]), or the myth was the very argument in support of the ritual, as in the solemn rituals and specific rites.[12] The following diagram sets out the synthetic and converging relationships of the two sides of the universe:

REAL		IMAGE		IMAGINARY
Earth	→	temple	←	Sky
men	→	Pharaoh	←	gods
phenomena	→	ritual	←	myths

We will now make a simple, almost algebraic, transformation of this last diagram in order to arrive once more at the diagram that, in an earlier article, helped us to define the notion of divinity and thereby to demonstrate the nature of Egyptian ritual, taking into consideration the universal dynamic that results from representation:

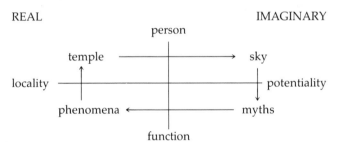

The direction of the arrows indicates the direction of the movement, whose circular character corresponds to what we already know about the cosmological conceptions of the Egyptians. In fact, through the liturgy addressed to the statue inside the temple, the celebrant reaches the person of the god who begins to act according to the mechanism described in his myth in order to effect on earth the phenomena that the ritual will in turn use and represent to the god. The circle is thus formed in a reassuring fashion that proves the indissolubility of the relation between signifier and signified on which the Egyptian system is implicitly founded.

II

Some papyruses dating back to the end of the New Kingdom and even earlier, but especially the inscriptions in temples from the Ptolemaic and Roman periods, tell us, apparently precisely, about the performance of Egyptian rituals. Thus, the columns of the huge porch of the temple of Esna have preserved a copy engraved in stone of books

Offering of Ma'at. Relief from the temple of King Sethi I at Abydos. Photo The Egypt Exploration Society, London.

Khnum receiving the potter's wheel on which he fashions man.
From Sauneron, *Le Temple d'Esna*, vol. 3, p. 227. Photo Flammarion.

containing a full account of the liturgy of certain festivals and of the texts chanted during the festivals. At Edfu and Dendera, long inscriptions, often with pictures, allow us to reconstruct the performance of the festival of the victory of Horus and his enthronement and the festival of the resurrection of Osiris. The pictures are so exact and the texts so literal that one of the rites was recently actually performed in a theater, with apparent success.[13]

But these examples are the exception, for Egyptians generally preferred a far more allusive method, indicating by means of a small number of typical scenes the nature of the sets of liturgies that they knew, so that they merely needed to refer to their existence. Such is certainly the case for all temples prior to the Macedonian period. Moreover, we must remember that the temple and its decoration were conceived not to transmit knowledge but to actualize certain ideas[14]— not to communicate a signifier, but to realize a signified. Indeed, the signified could have been entirely contained in the slightest allusion, provided that the reader *understood*.[15] The result was a type of representation that isolated things within entirely discrete rectangles, each of which could be read individually. However, they are only apparently complete sets of figures and texts; in fact, they are the tips of icebergs all drifting in a common current toward the same destination. This destination is subtly suggested by complex processes such as unusual exchanges of signs, repetitions, and parallelisms, which we are still far from understanding. This may explain why the attempts to reconstitute rituals by making assumptions about the liturgical realism of the decoration of the temples differ so markedly from one another.[16]

The rituals whose object is the *person* of the divinity naturally have a stereotyped character common to all parts of Egypt, since in the final analysis the needs of all gods are the same, whether they be in Thebes, Edfu, Dendera, Abydos, or anywhere else. On the other hand, the rites appropriate to the *function* of the divinity have a character specific to that function and to the mythical expression it has received.

We will now consider the *specific rite,* tied to a particular shrine because the god in this shrine, in addition to his role as a local manifestation of the divine and his universal cosmic or political function, also practiced there an activity strictly related to the locality or expressed by a myth created in that place and popular only within that limited district. We have such an example in the temple of Esna, where the local god Khnum frequently received the offering of a potter's wheel because the local myth expressed his creative activity with the help of that instrument. The offering that is connected to a cosmic activity is not, however, attested in the temple of Edfu, for instance, where the idea of creation found other forms of expression. On the level of the grammar of myth, we may consider this offering as a single transformation, or perhaps better still as a simple dialectal variant, of other myths that attempted to represent the genesis of living beings.

On the other hand, when Khnum receives the ewer, although he appears on a painting at Edfu, it is a reference to his cult on the Elephantine island, where he presides over the two caves from which the floods of the Nile are thought to originate.[17] However, at Semen-Hor, located not far from the entrance to the Fayum, a crocodile was sacrificed to him.[18] This ceremony can obviously only signify the victory of the forces of fertility over the forces of useless water. The nearby Fayum was the domain of the crocodile god Sebek and was regarded as a more or less amphibious territory that several times in the course of Egyptian history was the object of concerted royal attempts to push back its limits in favor of agriculture. Thus, the two rites that connect Khnum with the aquatic element have opposite values conditioned by the place where water and the god of fertility intersect. The flood that reaches Egypt via the Elephantine island allows Khnum to exercise his fertile function, which is otherwise expressed by his aspect as a ram. He must therefore be incited to come forth, which is within his power since he rules over the ground where springs are located, whereas the vast watery stretches of the Fayum are—except for a few fishing grounds and hunting expeditions for waterfowl—an obstacle to the appearance of life useful for man, life of which Khnum is the guarantor. The crocodile is precisely the mythic sign of the hostility of water toward farming.

The two rites that I have just described make sense only with reference to the particular land on the one hand and the function of the god on the other.

My intention was to show through a description of the three rites connected with the god Khnum that the specific ceremonies of a god are in the final analysis only various ways of expressing his universal function, means adapted to

real circumstances. When the rites—aside from the daily ritual that is addressed to the person of the god—manifested a function, they could take a form closely tied to the local reality, because they originated in a natural phenomenon that they transposed to the level of myth. The rushes and reeds offered to Amon of Tell Balamun had an analogous nature; his territory in the Delta was supposed to yield these plants.[19] On the other hand, there were specific rites that seemed to have functions of a personal nature. A closer look shows, however, that they dramatically actualized the function of the god. For example, when Thoth was offered a writing table, it is quite clear that the writer was the functionary in mind.[20] Similarly, when the god of Letopolis was offered eyes, the reference was to the myth in which he is alternately sighted and blind, depending on whether the sun and the moon shine or remain hidden from view.[21]

III

As we stated above, seasonal rituals were of two kinds, cosmic and political. The cosmic rituals aimed to represent the functioning of the great universal cycles and were usually performed deep inside the shrine. The best known are the ones commonly referred to as "the Mysteries of Osiris," which simulated the return of vegetation and the perpetuity of life, and which were known to have been performed in many temples. But the same idea could be manifested to the people by means of processions, such as the one that carried Khnum of Esna to his temple in the countryside, during which flowers would bloom at the feet of his companion, the "lady of the land,"[22] or the procession in Thebes during which the sacred bull and the image of the virile god Min moved across the countryside.[23] Ceremonies also took place at night; the secret representation was intended to guarantee the movement of the sun from west to east so that it would reappear the following morning.[24]

Among the political rites, as I have called them, those that are connected with kingship and thereby take on a public character are the most important. Foremost among those we would rank the rite of enthronement of the falcon-king celebrated at Edfu and Philae. The episodes included the presentation of the chosen animal to the people from a high balcony that crowned the main gate of the temple between the solid masses of the pylon. This episode was transposed from the ceremony of the enthronement of a king, as is shown by certain scenes from the temple of Hatshepsut at Deir el-Bahari, for example.[25] The political meaning of the ceremony is demonstrated by the undeniably propagandistic character of the engravings of the temple of Deir el-Bahari and by the fact that at Philae the presentation of the falcon-king took place facing south, in the direction of Nubia, which Ptolemy Philometor had just reconquered when this ritual was introduced into the decoration of the temple. The principal deity of this temple, Isis, has an altogether different relationship with kingship.[26]

There are still other rituals that are less easily classified because they seem to fall within several types simultaneously. The most striking example, which also reveals the processes of Egyptian thought, is the ritual known as "the myth of Horus," which has been the object of many studies.[27]

This was a way of representing in a dramatic form, which called for an audience, the victorious expedition of Horus of Edfu across Egypt to defeat his enemies, who were crocodiles and hippopotamuses. The extermination of monsters is surely one of the primary duties of the lord, who is responsible for the survival of his tribe, constantly threatened by these voracious animals.

The struggle against crocodiles and hippopotamuses, the preeminent royal task (the protection of the people), also takes on a historical character in the sense that the drama localizes it in places where it appears that the cult of the falcon was eventually substituted for the cult of other animals that were worshiped because of the terror they inspired. But on this double aspect of the ritual a third aspect was superimposed. This one is cosmic, by virtue of the assimilation of the reign of Horus into the solar cycle and the assimilation of the aquatic monsters into forces that might imperil the beginning of the new year, as is clearly indicated by other myths.[28]

The myth of Horus, which has an extremely clever composition, garnished with etymological glosses and commentaries, is a splendid example of the complexity that Egyptian thought could attain. It could connote the same fact on different planes and sustain the connotation with implacable logic throughout an entire ritual. This was the culmination of Egyptian genius.

Naturally there were innumerable elementary rituals, like all those that were designed to reduce to impotence all hostile powers, cosmic or political. In the first category, rituals warded off the heavenly dragon Apophis,[29] who threatened to stop the sun in its course, chained up Evil,[30] and trampled the fish that were symbols of impurity, etc.[31] In the second category, they broke vessels and figurines on which were inscribed the names of peoples or individuals whose existence might be dangerous.[32]

IV

Up to this point we have viewed ritual as an activity appropriate to the temple and intended to actualize the functioning of the universe. By returning to the definition that we adopted at the beginning of this study, we may be justified in viewing the courtly ceremonial as a ritual, because it was often supported by myth. When King Snefru, for instance, organized a boating party on the pond that adjoined his residence and had twenty scantily clad beauties row, a close analysis of the account reveals that this was an imitation of the navigation of the creator sun, of whom the king is the incarnation on earth.[33] Similarly, when the exiled

Sinuhe returned from Asia to the court of Sesostris I, his reception appeared to take the form of a ritual of resurrection in the presence of Atum, the creator god, who was incarnate in the king, and of Hathor, the queen, the dispenser of life.[34]

Generally speaking, one may conclude that all royal activity took on a ritual character, since the ruler was at the point of contact between the real and the imaginary, as we have already seen.

This is the source of the conception of history as a "festival"—that is, as a liturgy—which Hornung demonstrated, so that the exercise of power was in itself already a liturgical act.[35] A detailed analysis of this concept would take us beyond the scope of a study of Egyptian ritual, whose connections with the basic forms of thought are what I have attempted to show.

Ph.D./g.h.

NOTES

1. A. MORET, *Le rituel du culte divin journalier* (Paris 1902).

2. S. SAUNERON, *Les fêtes d'Esna (Esna V)* (Cairo 1962), 125–26.

3. As, for example, the "mysteries of Osiris." See E. CHASSINAT, *Les mystères d'Osiris au mois de Khoiak* (Cairo 1966); P. DERCHAIN, *Le Papyrus Salt 825, rituel pour la conservation de la vie en Égypte* (Brussels 1965).

4. M. ALLIOT, *Le culte d'Horus à Edfou* (Cairo 1954), 561ff. H. W. FAIRMAN, "Worship and Festival in an Egyptian Temple," *Bull. John Rylands Library* 37 (1954): 165–203. H. JUNKER, "Der Bericht Strabos über die heiligen Falken von Philae," *Wiener Zeitschr. Kunde des Morgenlandes* 26 (1912): 42–62.

5. S. SAUNERON, *Fêtes d'Esna,* 71ff.

6. S. SAUNERON, *Esna VI,* 491.

7. Numerous examples of the offering of Ma'at since the New Empire.

8. On this point, see P. DERCHAIN, "Le rôle du roi d'Égypte dans le maintien de l'order cosmique," in *Le pouvoir et le sacré* (Brussels 1962).

9. On the connections between rite and myth, see E. OTTO, "Das Verhältnis von Rite und Mythus im Ägyptischen," *Abhandl. Akad. Wiss.* (1958).

10. G. RUDNITZKY, "Die Aussage über das Auge des Horus," *Analecta Aegyptiaca,* 5 (1956).

11. E. OTTO, "Das Mundöffnungsritual," *Ägyptol. Abhandl.* 3 (1960): 1–5.

12. On the notion of the specific rite, see P. DERCHAIN, "Un manuel de géographie liturgique à Edfou," *Chronique d'Égypte,* 1962, 37.

13. H. W. FAIRMAN, *The Triumph of Horus* (London 1974). This contains the English adaptation of the Egyptian text and the stage directions which made it possible for a theatrical group to "perform" the ritual.

14. On the function of the temple, see the basic study of M. DE ROCHEMONTEIX, "Le temple égyptien," in *Œuvres diverses* (Paris 1894), 1–38.

15. On the role of knowledge in the sacerdotal function, see J. ASSMANN, *Der König als Sonnenpriester, Abhandl. Deutsch. archäol. Inst. Kairo, Ägyptol. Reihe* 7 (Glückstadt 1970), and my review of this book in *Chronique d'Égypte* 48 (1973): 291.

16. For example, those of MORET, ALLIOT, and FAIRMAN, cited above.

17. E. CHASSINAT, *Le temple d'Edfou,* 5, 198–99.

18. Ibid., 3, 287.

19. Ibid., 5, 99–100.

20. G. POSENER, "Un dieu écrivain, le Thot égyptien," *Annuaire du Collège de France* 62 (1962): 287–90; 63, 299–303; 64, 301–5; 65, 339–42.

21. H. JUNKER, "Der sehende und blinde Gott," *Sitzungsber. Bayer. Akad. Wiss.,* 1942, Abhandl., 7.

22. S. SAUNERON, *Les fêtes d'Esna,* 31–32.

23. J. BLEEKER, *Egyptian Festivals,* supplements to *Numen* 13 (Leiden 1967).

24. For example, H. JUNKER, "Die Stundenwachen in den Osirismysterien," *Denkschr. Akad. Wiss Wien,* 54 (1910).

25. H. BRUNNER, "Die Geburt des Gottkönigs," *Ägyptol. Abhandl.* 10 (1964), pl. 17.

Enthronement of the sacred falcon. From Chassinat, *Le Temple d'Edfu*, vol. 14, plate 553. Photo Flammarion.

26. P. DERCHAIN, "Remarques sur la décoration des pylônes ptolé-maïques," *Bibliotheca Orientalis* 18 (1961): 47–49.

27. See above, notes 4 and 13, and W. SCHENKEL, "Kultmythos und Märtyrerlegende," *Göttinger Orientforschung* 4: *Reihe: Ägypten, Band 5* (1977).

28. P. DERCHAIN, "En l'an 363 de Sa Majesté Râ Harakhty," *Chronique d'Égypte*, forthcoming.

29. *Papyrus Bremner-Rhind*.

30. S. SCHOTT, *Urkunden mythologischen Inhalts* (Leipzig 1929–39).

31. P. DERCHAIN and J. HUBAUX, "L'affaire du marché d'Hypata dans la 'Métamorphose' d'Apulée," *L'Antiquité classique* 27 (1958): 100–104.

32. K. SETHE, "Ächtungstexte," *Abhandl. Preuss. Akad. Wiss.* (1926). G. POSENER, *Princes et pays d'Asie et de Nubie* (Brussels 1940); "Les textes d'envoûtement de Mirgissa," *Syria* 43 (1966): 277–87.

33. P. DERCHAIN, "Snéfrou et les rameuses," *Rev. d'Égyptol.* 21 (1969): 19–25.

34. P. DERCHAIN, "La réception de Sinouhé . . . ," *Rev. d'Égyptol.* 22 (1970):79–83. W. WESTENDORF, "Die Wiedergeburt des Heimgekehrten Sinuhe," *Stud. altäg. Kultur* 5 (1977): 293–304.

35. E. HORNUNG, *Geschichte als Fest* (Darmstadt 1966).

DEATH IN EGYPTIAN RELIGION

The confrontation with death is certainly one of the moments that most powerfully motivates the religious behavior of human beings. Similarly, it can be asserted that the primordial anxiety about death increases with the development of culture. The more refined and civilized a culture, the more the end of life preoccupies the individual. This may be because civilization gradually isolates him, as the complexity of abstract relationships works to dissolve the affective unity of society, and as a person's existence is defined more and more by himself and no longer as a function of the social group. Civilization and especially urbanization have generally brought about the religions of salvation that have spread throughout the world; but they have also produced such grotesque creations as some American cemeteries, where a theatrical production is designed to camouflage the very fact of death. Egypt never attained the stage of urbanization; Memphis must have been the only authentic city in Egypt until very recently. Yet the Egyptians knew all the methods, from burial in tombs that they tried to camouflage as houses to attempts to integrate into the very order of the universe the person who had stopped living.[1]

In the course of centuries an extremely complex system of funeral rites evolved, supported by a considerable apparatus of increasingly elaborate myths. From the beginning to the end of the Old Empire, cosmic integration remained the privilege of the ruler, who by virtue of his divine nature already belonged to the world in its aspect of representation. Later, a "democratization" of this system evolved.

But survival has always been closely tied to the existence of a tomb, which is simultaneously the dwelling place of the dead person, a support for the memory of his existence, and a meeting place for his world and the world of the living.

In his tomb, the dead person leads an existence analogous to the life that he had on earth, experiencing the same needs, which must be satisfied by the offerings and libations that he receives. Being a ghost, he receives these in the form of emanations, through the symbolic gate that permits passage from the real world to the imaginary world; on this gate, commonly known as the stela, is an embrasure on which a portrait of the dead person was sometimes carved. In addition, the inscriptions around the stela identify the dead person precisely, by enumerating the titles that he had received and by citing his name and sometimes his genealogy.

The world beyond is not, however, limited to the tomb. It naturally extends to the entire necropolis, which is the projection of the world of the living on the scale of the village or of the royal court, where all those who had known each other on earth again meet those who had been their relations during their lifetimes. Many of the formulas that have been transmitted by large collections of funeral texts such as the *Coffin Texts*[2] or *The Book of the Dead*[3] are intended to allow the deceased to find his family and friends again, to obtain fresh water to breathe, to clean off the dust that covers him, to keep his virility, and so forth. But the necropolis is not exactly the village. In a very real sense, it is also the desert, for tombs are relegated to the area that is of no practical use, and the world of the dead is also the world of the horrors of solitude and drought. All the disadvantages of the desert threaten the dead: innumerable harmful beings lie in wait for them, ready to rob, capture, dismember, roast, and devour them. That is how the inhabitants of the valley of the Nile depicted the afterlife. For the inhabitants of the Delta, the image of the retreat of the dead was the amphibious, inhospitable landscape of the far north—where a boat is always needed to cross the innumerable channels, and where only a few rare bird catchers find their way through the thickets of papyrus that surround the low-lying islands where waterfowl nest—as can be deduced from certain of the *Pyramid Texts*.[4] These birds, moreover, are merely apparitions of the dead from neighboring villages, who have transformed themselves into birds. Indeed, from this identification of birds with the dead, we may perhaps deduce an early attempt to situate the resting place of the dead in the sky, just as some beliefs have assimilated them to the stars.

Nonetheless, this very realistic representation of the resting place of the dead probably became idealized relatively early. During the New Empire the territories in which the dead spent eternity, depicted as fields always blessed with exceptional harvests, can only be situated in the realm of the imagination.

Whatever the chosen resting place may be, the dead must not be cut off from the world of the living who provide them with offerings and libations, and they also need a means of communication. The means of communication is the *ba*, which hovers around the tomb in the form of a bird and brings back to the mummy whatever it has been able to observe or to scavenge in the countryside. Numerous texts show that the *ba*'s power of communication stems from the fact that he *remembers*. He is the sum total of what has been lived, and he knows the places that were frequented by the person he represents; he can therefore go back to those places and return with news and food. In this way the deceased can receive goods from the land of the living, but he can no longer appear there himself. The Egyptians, however, were no different from other people when it came to knowledge (or lack of knowledge) about the return of the dead. When a dead person needed to enter into an active relationship with the living, he would use another aspect of his personality, his *akh*. For all intents and purposes, the *akh* is the ghost; he is the one who appears in ghost stories and is invoked in letters that are addressed to ancestors and set down in funeral chapels, or written on the rim of a bowl full of food; such letters were sent in order to enlist the help of the powerful spirit that could still reunite in the afterlife all the friends he ever had on earth in order to play a trick on an adversary of one of his descendants. According to these letters, the deceased continues to be part of the family; although he is no longer its leader, as he had been in the past, at least he maintains the duty of defending it in a universe where lawsuits are the rule, and his assistance is depended upon.[5] All that is expected of him is that he assemble the friends, relatives, and ancestors whom he sees every day and call in his scribes. But the effect is felt here below.

In the world of the dead, there is no time. The imagination is unaware of change. The Egyptians used the expression "coming ashore" for dying. Death is the end of the voyage. To come ashore is to attain immobility, invariability, and stability; it is to be put in a space that has only three dimensions. But although the mind can thus choose, man's heart remains the prisoner of emotional facts and accepts with difficulty an ataraxia, or stoic indifference, so complete, both subjective and objective. If the funeral cult ever had to stop because of a lack of descendants or the destruction of the tomb, the statues, or the mummy, or if no one was there to read the name or recite the formula for the offering, there would be total annihilation.[6] Survival is nothing but the remembrance of the dead, which rituals strive to prolong. Myth is excluded from this conception, and this entails a persistent dilemma: the duration of survival is limited to personal memory or rather to the duration of the foundation that provides offerings to the priests. Everyone knows that this is not forever. Egyptian literature addressed this subject often. Myth, by contrast, integrates the individual into the universe rather than into the single small group of which he is a part, and thus guarantees him the possibility of an unlimited existence.

We shall now examine the various types of myths to which the Egyptians had recourse, which are divisible into two basic categories, depending on whether the model was based on biological phenomena or cosmic facts. Of course, there were many contaminations between the two types.

Of all the Egyptian myths, the myth of Osiris is undoubtedly the most famous, because it spread outside of Egypt and in classical antiquity became the vehicle of a very popular religion of salvation, and because many writers spoke of it, notably Plutarch and Apuleius.

Whoever identified himself with Osiris identified himself with the forces of renewal in the universe, as we have seen elsewhere. The dead man survives not because he has a son alive on earth but because he has been integrated into the generalized scheme of father-son relationships.[7] Nevertheless, each dead man keeps his personality. By becoming such and such an Osiris, he is a particular case of recurrence. Human destiny, linear as it is, is projected as a cyclical phenomenon at the level of the species, in which the individual finds his salvation.

Moreover, every periodic phenomenon could serve as the model of a myth of the negation of death, such as the daily course of the sun. To reach the boat of the sun and sail with it was originally the privilege of the king alone, who also had

to win his place by taking the sky by storm and by uttering terrible threats against the gods.[8] Later the sun would take everybody on board, so that people would commonly refer to the boat as the "boat of millions." This is one of the doctrines that formed the basis of *The Book of the Dead*.

The Egyptians of the New Empire rethought the myth of the solar circuit, first on behalf of the kings, by placing special emphasis on the nocturnal half, in which energies are mysteriously restored. The various versions of the story that appeared during that period are essentially uniform in outline. The evening sun penetrates into a cave to the west, and over a period of twelve hours (or units) it passes through an antiworld from which it emerges again the next morning, regenerated. Lining his path are the dead, whom he awakens as he passes by, and the demons who torture the damned. At midcourse the sun meets Osiris, from whom he draws the energy of renewal.[9] In this view a dead man is integrated into a perpetual movement that is the very negation of his fixed state in the tomb and that consequently expresses his salvation.

But the biological model reacted on the astral model. The evening sun is depicted as an old man who is rejuvenated and put back into the world every morning by the goddess of heaven in the guise of a nursling or a calf.

The result was a new possibility of the mythical identification of death and birth, the nightly sojourn of the sun being its passage through the body of its mother, the tomb being the symbol of this voyage. A considerable body of embryological literature followed, rather obscure and strictly funerary in function.[10] In this context the coffin could become the equivalent of the heavenly matrix, and the cadaver, the equivalent of the embryo. Typical of the rigor of Egyptian mythical thought are certain preoccupations that this doctrine inspired; although it was desirable to be born again like the young sun, in no case was the coffin to eject its contents. Myth and reality came into a conflict that the theologians knew how to sidestep elegantly.[11]

Since the Egyptians treated death as a birth into an idealized life, some tombs contain pictures of deities assisting women in labor or scenes of unmistakably erotic significance.[12] Even an innocent fishing line becomes a symbol of birth when it hooks two tilapias at the same time, for this fish appears constantly to be producing young fish that it shelters between its jaws in case of danger.[13]

The perpetual regeneration of life was also represented by the blue lotus with a yellow heart; this flower, which opens and closes with the rhythm of the sun, imitates the colors of the sun set against the blue sky. Regeneration is also expressed by the fruit of the persea tree, which ripens precisely when the floods of the Nile reach their highest level in promise of future harvests.[14] Peasant images thus came to complete the more grandiose imaginings, placing within the reach of everyone the idea of the eternal return, which was the exact opposite of the stagnation and immobility expressed in other doctrines of death.

In fact, the Egyptians gradually added various beliefs, myths, and symbols, which made the tomb—from which there was no exit and to which the corpse belonged—the very sign of the rebirth that concerns other aspects of the person. Certain rites naturally marked the moment of passage: those connected with embalming, those in which the body was identified with the various deities, especially the "ritual of the opening of the mouth," which was originally only a transposition of the acts that the sculptor performs when he carves the eyes, nose, and mouth of a statue. As

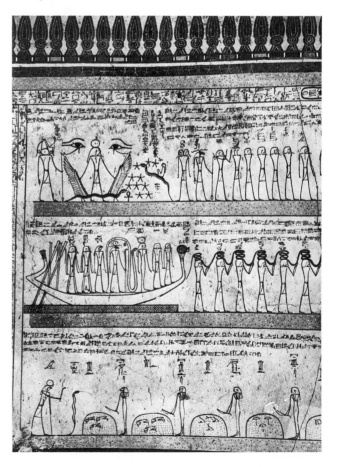

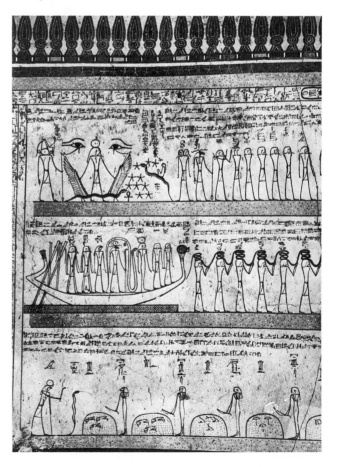

DEATH IN EGYPTIAN RELIGION

time passed, however, complex ceremonies were added, such as lamentations, purifications, and the presentation of various objects, including the thigh of a calf, cut off while the calf was alive so that its strength would pass directly to the beneficiary of the ritual.

The funerary ritual with its navigations centered around the idea of "passage" from one world to the other, for which one of the best known expressions is the famous judgment of the dead before the tribunal of Osiris, a judgment that bestows on the person who passes it the privilege of entering the world beyond. Other ways of expressing the passage are also known, such as the game of draughts played without an opponent, at the conclusion of which the player is regarded as being "justified," as after the verdict of Osiris.[15] The notion of passage and judgment brings us back to the individual.

Sometimes Egyptian literature allows us to hear a personal voice. I will cite two examples in conclusion. The first goes back to the end of the third millennium. It is the song of Antef, in which the poet expresses all his irony and skepticism about the great pains that people go to in order to meet the idea of death and to hide the tragedy of the end. None is effective, so it is better to enjoy life and to spend as much of the time as one can in feasting and merrymaking.[16] The same advice is found two thousand years later on a Memphis stela, which clearly indicates the existence of a current, probably minor, but sustained throughout Egyptian history.

Stela, false door of the tomb of Iteti at Saqqara. Cairo Museum. Photo Hirmer.

Armrest of a chair from the tomb of Yusa and Thuin. Cairo Musuem. Museum photo.

The eleventh hour. From P. Bucher, *Tombs of Thoutmosis III and Amenophis II.*

237

Above: Fishing scene. From Davies, *Seven Private Tombs at Thebes.*

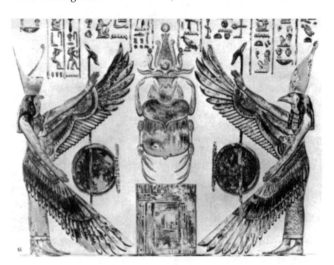

Central panel from the chapel of the tomb of Petosiris. From Lefèvre, *Tombeaux de Petosiris III*, plate 53.

Painted mummy cloth. Third century A.D. Paris, Musée du Louvre. Museum photo.

The other example is borrowed from the inscriptions on the tomb that Petosiris, the great priest of Thoth, had built in the necropolis of Hermopolis for several members of his family and himself, at the time of the Macedonian conquest. Petosiris was a pious and conservative man for whom success was the proof of the gods' blessing. His attitude sometimes evokes stoicism. On the occasion of the death of a child, he had engraved on the tomb a lamentation which expresses with much reserve a feeling of the injustice of death, doubt about the legitimacy of a judgment in the afterlife, worry about the solidarity of the generations, and the vanity of the hopes of a young life: "I am a child carried off to the city of eternity, toward the realm of the 'blessed.' I have thus arrived before the Master of gods, while I had not yet received my share [on earth]. Though I had many friends, none was in a position to protect me. Everyone in town, men and women alike, is in mourning after what happened to me because everyone was attached to me. All my friends moaned, my father and my mother raised questions about death, my brothers prostrated themselves when I was taken away toward this province of misfortune, where one must present one's reckoning before the Master of gods. . . . O you who endure in life . . . each time you enter this necropolis, recite the formula: 'All good things for your *ka*, little child whose life passed by so quickly that you were not able to do what your heart might have desired on earth!'"[17]

The exceptional tone, the time and place, and the seemingly philhellenic attitude of Petosiris, do not allow us to exclude a foreign influence on this work, because by its tone it calls to mind many Greek epitaphs composed for the young—epitaphs of which Egypt, and particularly the necropolis of Hermopolis, provided examples, but only in a later period.[18]

For himself, however, Petosiris had adopted the theme of solar rebirth as it is expressed in the very axis of his chapel by what seems to be a specially composed painting.[19]

Thus, from the naive trust of Prince Harjedef, the son of Kheops, author of a rule of life in which he advises the "founding of a home to have children and the building of a tomb for oneself," to the doubts raised about rituals and myths that we just mentioned, Egypt knew several attitudes, the most common of which was to combine a funeral cult linked to the tomb with the idea of an integration into the universal force of renewal embodied in Osiris, the most telling manifestation of which is obviously the rebirth of the sun.

Ph.D./g.h.

NOTES

1. All the works devoted to Egyptian religion in general contain a chapter on funerary beliefs. Specifically on this topic are H. KEES, *Totenglauben und Jenseitsvorstellungen der alten Ägypter* (2d ed., Berlin 1956); G. WIRZ, *Tod und Vergänglichkeit: Ein Beitrag zur Geisteshaltung der Ägypter von Ptahhetep bis Antef* (in press); similarly, C. E. SANDER-HANSEN, *Der Begriff des Todes bei den Ägyptern* (Copenhagen 1942). Particular questions have been treated by E. HORNUNG, *Altägyptische Höllenvorstellungen* (Berlin 1968), and J. ZANDEE, *Death as an Enemy* (Leiden 1960).

2. A. DE BUCK, *The Egyptian Coffin Texts*, 7 vols. (Chicago 1935–61); the only extant translation: R. O. FAULKNER, *The Ancient Egyptian Coffin Texts* (Warminster 1973–78).

3. Innumerable editions. For the French reader, there is only one trustworthy translation: P. BARGUET, *Le livre des morts des anciens Égyptiens* (Paris 1967).

4. In particular, the chapters known as "texts of the ferryman," 516ff.

5. A. GARDINER and K. SETHE, *Letters to the Dead* (London 1928). Since then, some new discoveries have enriched the series.

6. S. SCHOTT, "Zur Unvergänglichkeit des Namens," *Mitt. D. Arch. Inst. Kairo* 25 (1969): 131–35.

7. J. ASSMANN, "Das Bild des Vaters im alten Ägypten," in *Das Vaterbild in Mythos und Geschichte*," H. Tellenbach, ed. (Stuttgart 1976).

8. In particular, the formulas of the "Pyramid texts," 273–74.

9. Translation of the whole of these texts by E. HORNUNG, *Ägyptische Unterweltsbücher* (Zurich 1972).

10. B. STRICKER, *De Geboorte van Horus*, 3 vols. (Leiden 1963–75), in which so many foreign sources have been cited that the force of the argument about the New Empire of Egypt is weakened.

11. S. SCHOTT, "Nut spricht als Mutter und Sarg," *Revue d'égyptologie* 17 (1965): 81–87. J. ASSMANN, "Nut spricht als Mutter und Sarg," *Mitt. D. Arch. Inst. Kairo* 28 (1973): 115–39.

12. For example, on a Cella of Tut-Ankh-Amon: W. WESTENDORF, "Bemerkungen zur Kammer der Wiedergeburt im Tutanchamunsgrab," *Zeitschr. ägypt. Sprache* 94 (1967): 139–50.

13. C. DESROCHES-NOBLECOURT, "Poissons, tabous et transformations du mort," *Kêmi* 13 (1954): 39ff.

14. P. DERCHAIN, "Le lotus, la mandragore et le perséa," *Chronique d'Égypte* 50 (1975): 85–86.

15. As has been demonstrated by E. Pusch in a Bonn dissertation.

16. French translation: S. SCHOTT, *Les chants d'amour de l'Égypte ancienne*, P. Kriéger, trans. (Paris 1956), 75, 140ff.

17. G. LEFÈBVRE, *Le tombeau de Pétosiris*, 2 (Cairo 1923), Inscr. 56; the translation given is shortened and sometimes paraphrased.

18. E. BERNAND, *Inscriptions métriques de l'Égypte gréco-romaine* (Paris 1969), texts 62–100.

19. G. LEFÈBVRE, *Le tombeau de Pétosiris*, pl. 52–53. For the commentary, F. DAUMAS, "La scène de la résurrection au tombeau de Pétosiris," *Bull. Inst. fr. Archéol. orient.* 59 (Cairo 1960): 63–80.

MEROITIC RELIGION

I. Meroe

In recent years research has brought to light all along the middle Nile in upstream Egypt the remains of cultures worthy of attention. Beyond Nubia, the zone that one must pass through to go between Egypt and the deeper parts of Africa, there were prehistoric cultures that influenced the development of ancient Egyptian civilization. During the Egyptian Middle Kingdom, ca. 2000 B.C., south of the Second Cataract of the Nile and protected by a network of fortresses, the kingdom of Kerma, afterwards known as Cush, was a formidable threat to the Pharaohs. And in the Dongola basin between the Third and Fourth Cataracts, a dynasty arose ca. 750 B.C., with Piye (Piankhi), that quickly became strong enough to conquer Egypt and that took Pharaonic power with the succession of the rulers Shabaka, Shebitka, Taharqa, and Tanwetamun: this is the twenty-fifth dynasty in Egyptian historiography (715–663 B.C.). After the Assyrians under Ashurbanipal triumphed over the Cushites in a fierce battle, an echo of which was preserved in the Bible (the Book of Kings), the Cushites withdrew to the south. Their capital was first Napata, downstream from the Fourth Cataract. Then, farther upstream, it was Meroe, in an area of steppe that comes before the swampy region of the Nile on the border with Chad; there the Meroitic Empire developed.

During the brilliant period of the twenty-fifth dynasty, the Cushites borrowed forms of expression from the ancient Egyptian tradition. As the rulers of Egypt and of the Sudan (this double base of power was undoubtedly expressed in the double uraeus which adorned their heads), they seem to have adopted the essential elements of the Egyptian heritage: their gods, their clothing, and their symbols resemble those of the preceding dynasties. They even affected a tendency toward archaism, often taking their models from Memphis; it was the same during the first dynasty of Napata. The Cushite rulers had themselves buried under the pyramids. They continued to use the language and the hieroglyphs of classical Egypt, even though their texts have something artificial about them. Their willing efforts to achieve a systematic acculturation tended to mask their original character. But little by little, the submerged roots became manifest. Despite phases of reversion to Egyptianization, Meroitic culture developed its own particularities. With Shanakdakhete (around 180 B.C.), texts in the original Meroitic language appeared with their own unique script that borrowed its hieroglyphics and most of the notations of its cursive from the repertory of signs of Pharaonic Egypt, although it used them in a new way.

The first travelers who, at the beginning of the nineteenth century, noticed Meroitic inscriptions throughout Nubia did not identify them as such. The Egyptian trimmings masked their originality, as they did in Meroitic culture as a whole. But once this originality was revealed, it was still necessary to penetrate the meaning of the new messages. The meaning of the Meroitic signs was discovered in 1911 by the English scholar F. L. Griffith, who was then able to identify the anthroponyms, the toponyms, and the names of certain deities, and to analyze some pronunciations of the funeral texts, without going any further. Though additional details have since then made his decipherment more precise, little progress has been made in the absence of a bilingual text. The nature of the language remains a mystery to us. The Meroitic Empire continues to provide us with a large album of images without legible captions. Many pages still remain hidden, as the archaeological exploration of the Sudan is still in its pioneer phase.

This long preamble was necessary to explain why there is still so little that can be said about the religion of this empire, which reached from the Egyptian frontier in Lower Nubia to a considerable distance south on the Blue Nile, the White Nile, and the Nilotic swamp of Chad, and which flourished from the eighth century B.C. until the fourth century A.D., when Meroe collapsed under the destructive force of the young Kingdom of Axum. Nevertheless, because of its presence in the heart of Africa, a deeper knowledge of Meroe would seem to be of major importance today, not only to Western scholars but also to many Africans.

Given the current state of archaeological knowledge, there seems to be a real disparity between the information collected in the northern part of the empire, in lower Nubia, and that collected in the central part of the empire, which is still called the "island of Meroe," as the ancient authors called it. The successive rebuildings of the Aswan Dam, together with the threat of total submersion under the waters of Lake Nasser, have spurred a relatively thorough study of Nubia. But in fact Nubia was always a neglected area. In the intense tropical heat, the obstacles posed by the Cataracts made it a difficult, albeit unavoidable, route of contact between the countries of the south and Egypt. There are indeed buffer principalities there in a kind of no-man's-land;

but it was especially the necropolises that the surveys of the region made known. The imagery and the texts engraved on stelae and on offering tables are essentially those of the funeral service for important people. Somewhat exceptionally, the area of Napata, which is dominated by the high plateau of Gebel Barkal located far upstream in Nubia, has royal monuments and great temples, the remains of a traditional metropolis and a "holy mountain." On the other hand, there are huge shrines and royal documents in the Meroe zone, where we find the great complexes of Meroe itself, of Naga, of Wad-Ban-Naga, and of Musawwarat Es-Sufra. Of course, further research will bring a more detailed understanding to enhance this general view. It will probably also make it possible to distinguish among more sharply contrasted periods over a span of more than one thousand years of history.

II. Gods from Egypt

Documentation in an Egyptian style gives Amon an important role as the dynastic god of the Pharaohs. The Cushite rulers of the twenty-fifth dynasty had already shown their devotion to him by beautifying his shrines. Taharqa built a roofed gateway with colonnades extending in the four cardinal directions for the Temple of Amon at Karnak. Several royal daughters of the dynasty—Amenirdis the Elder, Shepenwepet II, and Amenirdis the Younger—were "divine votaresses," that is, the earthly wives of Theban Amon. South of Nubia, the metropolis of Napata at the foot of the Gebel Barkal (the "holy mountain") had become the Cushite counterpart of Egyptian Thebes. The Egyptian Pharaohs of the New Kingdom had built great temples there; the Pharaohs of the twenty-fifth dynasty, Piye (Piankhi) and Taharqa among others, continued to build shrines and to erect stelae there. They were imitated by their successors of the Meroitic period; the discovery of numerous Meroitic stelae and royal statues on this site shows quite well the veneration that pervaded this great Nubian center of the worship of Amon.

Although during the Napatan period the Cushite religion seems to be a faithful copy of that of Egypt, we can nevertheless discern slight peculiarities that were to become increasingly accentuated. The Meroitic Empire had a predilection for representing Amon in his criocephalic, ram-headed form, which is more typically African, whereas the Egyptian Amon is generally anthropomorphic. This poses the problem of the kinship between this criocephalic Amon and the ram, the god of the water, whose presence is manifest on the vast periphery of the Sahara.

Besides Napata, Amon was worshiped in several great shrines of the empire: Tore (probably Sanam), Gempaton (Kawa), and Pnoubs (Tabo on the island of Argo). After the empire's center of gravity moved southward and settled at Meroe itself, Amon occupied a choice place. He could be found at Musawwarat Es-Sufra on a relief of King Arnekhamani (235–218 B.C.). Later he remained the master of shrines typically Egyptian in their structures and embellishments, built at Naga and at Amara by Natakamani and Queen Amanitere in about the first century A.D.

The Meroitic texts show that Amon received various epithets, depending on the site of worship. They mention a particularly important clergy. Two inscriptions seem to associate one form of Amon with the sun god Mesh, an aspect that may evoke the Egyptian Amon-Ra.

The iconography of the ram is obviously tied to the Cushite Amon. Rams carved in stone decorated the approaches to the temples at Meroe, Naga, and Soba. At

Ram's head framed by Sebiumeker and Onuris. Temple of Musawwarat es-Sufra. Photo Menil Foundation/Mario Carrieri, Milan.

Musawwarat Es-Sufra, two groups of statues of a relatively late period, which were apparently encased in a wall, represent a beautiful ram's head flanked by two leonine deities and adorned with a double uraeus topped with two plumes and a flat disk. One can recognize Amon, Shu, and Tefnut here. Another triad found at the same site features a similar ram's head framed by two deities with human heads: one may be the indigenous god Sebiumeker; the other may be Onuris, adorned with the high four-plumed crown, well known among the Egyptians and particularly in favor among the Cushite rulers.

Also of Egyptian origin are Osiris and Isis, particularly present in the funeral concepts of the Meroites. According to Herodotus (2.29), Osiris was supposed to be the great god of the "Ethiopians," on an equal footing with Amon. He does not, however, seem to have held a place in the first rank in the Meroitic Empire. As in Egypt itself and especially in the Isiac cults which spread all around the Mediterranean, Isis prevailed over her consort, Osiris. Thus, inscriptions on Meroitic offering tables and stelae consistently open with the double invocation, "O Isis, O Osiris." The role of the god is not, however, insignificant. In the stela of Harsiyotef (ca. 400 B.C.), ten of the thirteen sites mentioned between Meroe and the Third Cataract have a local Osiris for their god. The god also appears on reliefs of chapels and royal tombs, and again side by side with Isis on royal stelae such as that of Taqideamani. The Osirian cult is one of the elements that made up the funeral practices of the late necropolises of Nubia. For example, various statuettes of Osiris have been found in the tombs of Sedeinga. On the two splendid glass vessels, gilded and polychrome, found on the tomb WT8 of Sedeinga, figures bearing gifts converge on the god superbly represented in the Egyptian style with his flesh evenly painted blue-green and his torso covered with a kind of net; he holds a flagellum in his right hand and the *heqa* or sceptre in his left hand, along with a second object, a small whip, and he wears a crown (*atef*) on his head.

Isis occupies an important place in Meroitic religion, in royal cult and funeral cult alike. This vogue can be compared to the growing success that the goddess enjoyed in Egypt and later in the Mediterranean basin. In the texts, the Meroitic rulers often bear the title of "son of Isis" or "beloved of Isis." The stela of Harsiyotef mentions a temple of Isis, Horus, and Osiris. An ornate head of Isis wearing the skin of a vulture on her head adorns an aegis of Temple A at Kawa, which bears the cartouches of Arnekhamani. Isis appears in several groupings of deities on the reliefs of Meroitic temples, often wearing a garment made of interlocking wings, her head topped with the solar disk and the horns of a cow. At the Lion Temple in Naga, she leads a procession of goddesses approaching the king. On the south wall of the Lion Temple at Musawwarat Es-Sufra, she stands as a sign of protection behind King Arnekhamani, while Prince Yerkie is designated "the priest of Isis, of Ibrp (Musawwarat), and of

241

Irbiklb." (In this last toponym, some have wanted to recognize Wad-Ban-Naga, where a temple attributed to Isis was formerly described, though it has unfortunately disappeared.)

It would certainly be imprudent to refer to one of the only shrines that exist today in Meroe as a temple of Isis, without any additional proof. However, the epithets of the goddess found in the Meroitic texts show that she was worshiped at Atiye (Sedeinga) and also at Abaton and on the island of Philae. Although it is located on Egyptian territory, the Temple of Isis on Philae received many pilgrims who came from the south. A Meroitic priesthood is attested by several documents in this major place of the worship of Isis. Toward A.D. 254, King Teqerideamani sent to Philae an embassy with money for the priests and their families. The statue of the goddess was paraded every year throughout Lower Nubia, then occupied by the tribes of Nobatae and Blemmyes. The worship of Isis of Philae was not abolished until the reign of Justinian between 535 and 537.

Isis plays an important role in Meroitic funeral religion. As we have seen, she is invoked together with Osiris at the beginning of inscriptions engraved on funeral stelae and on offering tables. It was thought that the goddess was represented (on offering tables) in the act of making a libation, using a *situla,* facing Anubis, the god of the dead in ancient Egypt; but when (as rarely occurs) a sign is depicted on the head, it is a symbol that evokes the name of Nephthys or even the sign of Nut rather than the throne of Isis.

Another divinity with an Egyptian look is a hawk-headed (hieracocephalic) figure that appears in the divine processions, particularly on the south wall of the Lion Temple at Musawwarat Es-Sufra. The head of the hawk also decorates jewelry and small objects. It could be Horus. The name of Ar can be identified, in the company of Isis and Apedemak, on a stela of Meroe. Inscriptions make it possible to localize him on Philae or at the Abaton, as well as at Atiye (Sedeinga). One Cushite ruler bears the Egyptian name of Harsiyotef: "Horus, son of his father." But to date not a single Meroitic shrine can be unmistakably attributed to Horus, and the texts do not attest any priesthood of the god.

III. Local Gods

The gods Apedemak and Sebiumeker orient us toward an altogether different universe of ideology and images, more properly African in nature. The lion Apedemak seems to have been the great Meroitic dynastic god. Numerous temples were dedicated to him in the empire, except in the northern province of Nubia. The first to have been studied was dedicated to him at Musawwarat Es-Sufra by King Arnekhamani. Built between 235 and 218 B.C., it was to remain one of the principal sites of the worship of Apedemak throughout Meroitic history, together with the Lion Temple at Naga of a later date, the work of the royal couple Natakamani and Amanitere (20 B.C. to ca. A.D. 15). The reliefs of these two shrines are particularly valuable for our understanding of the Meroitic pantheon. Apedemak, depicted in the form of a human with a lion's head, appears there under several aspects. As a god of war, he stands equipped with a long bow and arrows, holding by the hair a cluster of bound prisoners; his lion's snout is topped with the Egyptian crown called the *hmhm.* At Naga, the lion, who flings himself at a group of enemies or ferociously swallows a prisoner at the feet of the royal couple, confirms the warrior role of Apedemak, the protector of the Meroitic dynasty. On other representations, the king welcomes the divine procession led by

Isis and other deities. Lion temple at Naqa. Photo Menil Foundation/Mario Carrieri, Milan.

Apedemak. Temple of Musawwarat es-Sufra. Photo Menil Foundation/Mario Carrieri, Milan.

Glasswork decorated in gold and polychrome from tomb WT8 of Sedeinga. Photo Menil Foundation/Mario Carrieri, Milan.

Glasswork decorated in gold and polychrome from tomb WT8 of Sedeinga. Photo Menil Foundation/Mario Carrieri, Milan.

Apedemak, who abandons his warrior's gear in order to carry the Egyptian scepter or *uas* and the sign of life or *ankh*. Elsewhere he has a sheaf of wheat which makes him a god of fertility. Solar symbols may be attributed to him, which may be evidence of a kinship with the Hellenistic Serapis. He has as a consort Isis or the mysterious "black goddess," whose role is still difficult to define. At Musawwarat Es-Sufra, Apedemak has wings. Certain figure drawings at Naga are particularly unusual: the snout of the Apedemak lion rests on a serpentine body which is emerging from a flower; at the base of the temple the god is depicted as a lion with three

heads and four arms. This may be an attempt simultaneously to show the successive phases of the god's movement and to multiply the effect of his presence. In this respect, some would rather evoke Hindu religious iconography: Meroe may have been exposed to influences resulting from its commercial relations with the Red Sea, where there was considerable traffic of merchandise from India and the Far East.

Although the lion was the preeminent animal of Apedemak, the elephant was apparently also associated with him, at least at the Musawwarat Es-Sufra site. Since the cult of the lion was typically African, and the leonine deities of the Egyptian pantheon are tied to the countries to the south by a sort of predilection, Apedemak appears to be a local African element within the Meroitic pantheon.

The excavations of the Lion Temple at Musawwarat Es-Sufra revealed the importance of Sebiumeker, who was also unknown in Egypt. On the back wall, symmetrically opposed to Apedemak, he is represented anthropomorphically with a double Egyptian crown, holding in front of him a scepter (*uas*) and a curious attribute. The presence of numerous signs of life (*ankh*) around him would lead one to see in Sebiumeker a god of creation. In the captions written in Egyptian hieroglyphs that accompany him, one can discern the elements of a hymn to Osiris. The god adds—and this does not seem to have any parallel in Egypt—"I give you all that comes out of the night, all that emerges during the day. I give you the years of the sun, the months of the moon, in joy." Like Apedemak, Sebiumeker is described as the "master of Naga and of Musawwarat," but his representations are much more Egyptian than those of the lion god. It is surely correct to recognize Sebiumeker as the figure in a beautiful bronze statuette in Temple T at Kawa (Khartoum 2715), which was previously identified as Atum or a king, and also perhaps in a statue in the Lion Temple at Musawwarat.

Numerous priestly titles as well as Meroitic toponyms are formed on the noun Mesh (*Mš*). Since "mash" means sun in modern Nubian, one is tempted to recognize in Mesh the star that, according to classical authors, was one of the great Meroitic deities. Furthermore, the famous "table of the sun" described by Herodotus (3.18) is thought to have been found among the vast ruins to the east of the city of Meroe; but although these ruins still have left among them a few reliefs, badly damaged and illustrating cruel scenes of victory, this temple has not given any evidence of a cult of the sun, with the exception of a block that is decorated with a solar disk. Of a more recent date, the beginning of the first century A.D., a rock drawing in the Gebel Qeili, south of the steppe of the Butana, shows King Sherkaror trampling underfoot those he has vanquished, and facing the solar god, of whom only the head and shoulders are depicted: the head, viewed from the front, is surrounded by a halo and rays. On one arm the god holds a cluster of bound prisoners, and with his other arm he extends a sheaf of grain to the king. This solar god with his militant and agrarian characteristics evokes Apedemak. Finally, one could speculate that the same deity is represented in a head depicted from the front and surrounded by rays, found on the walls of the Temple of Naga and on the stones set in seal rings found in Meroitic tombs.

Although Egyptologists have long known the god Arensnuphis because of the evidence of him on the island of Philae, for us he nevertheless remains no more than a name. One might have thought that he was a local deity of Lower Nubia, as is Mandulis, the god made famous by the vision of Maximus and the poem engraved in Greek on the Temple of Kalabsha. Indeed, the name of Arensnuphis can be found beneath Arnekhamani in Egyptian hieroglyphs in faraway Musawwarat Es-Sufra, where he is called "the lord of Abaton, at the head of Bigeh." He is depicted wearing a long robe, holding a gazelle in his left hand and a kind of bouquet in his right hand. He could also be the god represented in a statue from the fifth century B.C. erected parallel to the statue of Sebiumeker. Other statues at Tabo and at Meroe may also represent him. There is also evidence of Arensnuphis under Ptolemy IV and Ergamenes (218–200 B.C.) at Philae and Dakka. But although he had a certain vogue at Philae and in Lower Nubia, Arensnuphis is probably not an Egyptian god.

The etymological spelling of his name, which makes him appear as the "good traveler," is probably only secondary. He is a god of the south, as is indicated by his connections with the lion and by his epithets: "the beautiful Medjay, come from Punt." In certain respects he seems close to the gods Shu and Onuris.

These few remarks, which may appear rather disparate, reflect the poverty of the documentation. It is not possible to catch a glimpse of Meroitic theology. The shrines have been empty since that period. The texts, which still resist decipherment, provide only the titles of priesthoods. In this new area of archaeology, we can only hope for progress in the excavations and discoveries in the Sudan.

J.Le./g.h.

BIBLIOGRAPHY

General Studies, Bibliographies

W. Y. ADAMS, "Meroitic North and South," in *Meroitica* (East Berlin 1976), vol. 2. A. J. ARKELL, *A History of the Sudan from the Earliest Times to 1821* (2d ed., London 1961). F. F. GADALLAH, "A Comprehensive Meroitic Bibliography," *Kush* 11 (1963): 207–16. J. LECLANT, "Les études méroïtiques, état des questions," *Bulletin de la Société française d'Égyptologie* 50 (December 1967): 6–15; in *Problèmes et méthodes d'histoire des religions*, École pratique des Hautes Études, 5th section, 1968, 88–92; "La religion méroïtique," in *Encyclopédie de la Pléiade, Histoire des Religions* (Paris 1970), 1:141–53; "Les recherches archéologiques dans le domaine méroïtique," in *Meroitica* (East Berlin 1973), 1:19–64; "Le panthéon méroïtique," in *Exposés présentés aux Journées internationales d'études méroïtiques*, 10–13 July 1973, Paris. P. L. SHINNIE, *Meroe: A Civilization of the Sudan* (New York 1967).

Documents and Studies

D. DUNHAM, *Royal Cemeteries of Kush* (Boston 1950–62); "From Tumulus to Pyramid and Back," *Archaeology* 6 (1953): 87–94. F. L. GRIFFITH, *Karanòg* (Philadelphia 1909); ECKLEY B. COXE, JR., "Expedition to Nubia," vol. 6; *Meroitic Inscriptions* 1–2 (London 1911–12). A. HEYLER, "L'invocation solennelle des épitaphes méroïtiques," *Revue d'Égyptologie* 16 (1964): 25–36. FR. HINTZE, *Die Inschriften des Löwentempels von Musawwarat es-Sufra* (Berlin 1962). J. LECLANT, "Usages funéraires méroïtiques d'après les fouilles récentes de Sedeinga," *Revue de l'histoire des religions* 171, no. 457 (1967): 120–25; "Aspects du syncrétisme méroïtique," in *Le syncrétisme dans la religion grecque et romaine*, Travaux du Centre d'études supérieures spécialisé d'histoire des religions de Strasbourg (1973), 135–45, pl. VII–VIII. B. G. TRIGGER, *The Meroitic Funerary Inscriptions from Arminna West* (with comments and indexes by A. Heyler) (New York 1970).

Studies of Divinities

A. BERNAND and E. BERNAND, *Les inscriptions grecques de Philae*, 2 vols. (Paris 1969). I. CAZZANIGA, "Proskynema al dio Mandulis," *Parola del Passato*, 1964, pp. 69–72. I. HOFMANN, "Arensnuphis, ein meroitischer Gott?" *MNL* 14 (February 1974): 52–55; "Nochmals zur Herkunft des Arensnuphis," *Göttinger Miszellen* 22 (1976): 31–37; "Satis in der meroitischen religiösen Vorstellung," ibid. 10 (1974): 21–24; "Zur Darstellung von Schu und Tefnut im meroitischen Reich," ibid. 23 (1977): 45–47. H. LEWY, "A Dream of Mandulis," *Annales du Service des antiquités de l'Égypte* 44 (1944): 227–34. E. MINKOWSKAJA, "Über den Gott Arensnuphis," in *Studia Aegyptiaca* (Budapest 1976), 2:79–87. U. MONNERET DE VILLARD, "Il culto del Sole a Meroe," *Rassegna di studi Etiopici* 2 (1942): 107–42. A. D. NOCK, "A Vision of Mandulis Aion," *Harvard Theological Review* 26 (1933): 53–104. J. SCIEGIENNY-DUDA, "A propos d'une étude sur Apedemak," *MNL* 15 (October 1974): 7–9. ST. WENIG, "Arensnuphis und Sebiumeker, Bemerkungen zu zwei in Meroe verehrten Göttern," *MNL* 13 (July 1973): 71–72; "Arensnuphis und Sebiumeker," *Zeitschrift für ägyptische Sprache* 101 (1974): 130–50. E. WINTER, "Arensnuphis, sein Name und seine Herkunft," *Revue d'Égyptologie* 25 (1973): 235–50; "Arensnuphis," *Lexikon der Ägyptologie*, 1, 3 (1973), cols. 424–25. L. V. ŽABKAR, *Apedemak, Lion God of Meroe, a Study in Egyptian-Meroitic Syncretism* (Warminster 1975).

The Cults of Isis among the Greeks and in the Roman Empire

If ever a religion seemed totally connected to its geographical and social frame of reference, it is the religion of Egypt during the time of the Pharaohs. And yet, by a surprising paradox, certain gods of the valley of the Nile were known across the Greco-Roman Mediterranean, far from the sun of the tropics and the river and far from the Pharaoh. Knowledge of these gods reached as far as Pannonia, the banks of the Rhine, and the boundaries of England.

This was not an exportation of Egyptian religion as such. Only Isis and some divinities associated with her seem to have passed through the "customhouses" of Alexandria to the Greek islands and from there to the Roman world. Earlier, some Egyptian forms and themes were circulated throughout the western Mediterranean countries by Phoenician trade, and, by way of Carthage, even reached Spain. Then the Greeks were able to give an *interpretatio graeca* to the Pharaonic pantheon; Herodotus provides an example of this. It was not until the Ptolemies, however, that Isis blossomed fully. In favor under the final indigenous dynasty of the Nectanebos, she took on a Grecian air in Alexandria, with a large shawl and a new hairstyle. Her consort is Serapis, a composite god created by the Ptolemies. Next to this couple were both the jackal-headed god Anubis, conductor of souls to the afterworld, and the child Harpocrates, sometimes equipped with the wings of Eros. To these traditional aspects of ancient Egypt were added traces of Greek iconography.

The first work to be devoted to the cults of Isis was written by G. Lafaye in 1883, *Histoire du culte des divinités d'Alexandrie hors d'Égypte.* Except for the sometimes disorganized curios of scholars such as E. Guimet, the most brilliant report was written by Franz Cumont, *Les religions orientales dans le paganisme romain* (lectures given at the Collège de France in 1905 and published in 1906; these took final form in the fourth edition of 1929 and were reprinted in 1963). So great was the impact of this book that this area of study seemed exhausted, even though this synthesis was not yet a true analysis: it was enough simply to call attention briefly to certain Egyptian or Egyptianized objects that kept coming to light throughout the Mediterranean world. In 1922–24, the collection of Greek and Roman texts about ancient Egypt published by Th. Hopfner does not appear to have aroused any particular interest. Aside from the monograph of Father W. von Bissing (1936) and the exemplary study by A. Alfoldi, *A Festival of Isis* (1937), it was not until the 1950s that there was a relatively sudden enthusiasm for research on the cults of Isis. Discoveries of *aegyptica* throughout the Roman world were then rapidly reported. Systematic surveys by region were published, particularly in the format of the excellent series edited by M. J. Vermaseren, *Études préliminaires aux religions orientales dans l'Empire romain.* Work proceeded from the curiosities of historians of religion, Egyptologists (more rarely), philologists, and archaeologists. The bibliography that we prepared on the Isiac publications that appeared during the last quarter–century shows how these studies were pursued on different levels and using diverse methods. In spite of the scholars' general ignorance of one another, these studies were nonetheless convergent: thus the analyses of R. Merkelbach (*Roman und Mysterium in der Antike*) agree, for the most part, with the conclusions of K. Schefold (*Vergessenes Pompeji*); the two essays appeared in the same year, 1962.

Statue of Isis. Alexandria. Greco-Roman Museum. Museum photo.

I. Isis

The principal figure in the Isiac pantheon is of course Isis. In the Late Period (first millennium B.C.), Isis became a major god of the Pharaonic pantheon; the goddess who was the consort of Osiris benefited from the great popularity of the Osirian myth and the funeral doctrines that were attached to him. Worshiped at the sanctuary of the Iseum, the present-day Behbeit el Hagar, in the Delta, the goddess had the favor of the Nectanebos, the last indigenous rulers of this region; thanks to them, she ruled as mistress all the way to the island of Philae. She was identified with several other divinities, particularly with Hathor, which reinforced her aspect as a mother goddess and protectress of love and childhood; she thus became a goddess with a universalist tendency, which contributed to the extension of her cult outside the valley of the Nile. From the seventh century B.C., the Greek mercenaries and colonists who had settled in Lower Egypt identified Isis with Demeter, also a mother goddess and a dispenser of fertility. Herodotus (2.156) echoed this rapprochement between Greek and Pharaonic divinities.

This *interpretatio graeca* perfectly suited the Ptolemaic rulers, the new masters of Egypt after the conquest by Alexander, in their desire to create a combined Greco-Egyptian religion that might be adopted by both the Hellenic and the native elements of the population. At Alexandria, the iconography of Isis took form. She abandoned her long narrow tunic for a chiton, a himation, and a fringed shawl tied between her breasts; she no longer wore an Egyptian wig, but long coiled curls, a style of Libyan origin; yet her head was usually adorned with the ancient Pharaonic symbols—the horns of Hathor holding the solar disc, topped with two high plumes. The cult of Isis was thus closely connected with royal politics; several Ptolemaic queens dressed themselves in imitation of Isis and identified themselves with her. Her favor reached the popular level.

The character of Isis as a mother goddess, her role in the Osirian myth, and her connection with Demeter and the Eleusinian doctrines explain her popularity in the Greek world; she was introduced there mostly by merchants and seamen, from the fourth century B.C., bringing with her the other divinities of the Isiac circle, especially Serapis, whom she supplanted fairly rapidly. Moving into Italy at the end of the second century B.C., she quickly became very popular. Her qualities as mother and protectress of love were pleasing. She became popular with the women of the demimonde who were celebrated by the elegaic poets.

Another aspect of the goddess, Isis-Fortuna, was also popular; in her honor many dedications and statuettes were made. From the period of Sulla, Isis had been assimilated to the Fortuna of Praeneste; both were goddesses of agriculture, fertility, and love. What occurred was essentially an evolution corresponding to a profound change in the religious mentality: all-powerful Destiny, so feared by the Greeks and Romans, and before whom even the deities were powerless, was from then on subjugated to Isis. "I have conquered Destiny," the goddess boasts in Kyme's Isiac aretalogy; in Apuleius's *Metamorphoses,* Isis is the Providence who supplants blind Fortune; and it is in this spirit that the dedications and references to Isis Victrix, Invicta, and the like should be understood. Not only was Isis victorious over fate, but she herself assumed the role of Destiny. Through initiation into the Isiac mysteries, the initiate was saved; he began a new existence that would save him from the void after death and would allow him to share the fate of his goddess. Isis tended more and more to become a universal goddess; her assimilation to still more varied divinities made her the goddess "of a thousand names" ("Myrionyma").

The consort god beside Isis was sometimes the traditional Osiris and sometimes Serapis, the creation of the Ptolemies.

II. Osiris

The best-known version of the Osirian myth is the one recounted by Plutarch (*De Iside et Osiride,* 12–19). Seth, jealous of his brother Osiris, kills him, cuts his body into pieces, and throws them into the Nile; Isis, the faithful wife, aided by her sister Nephthys and by Anubis, undertakes the reassembly of the pieces of the body; she succeeds in restoring life to him so that he is able to unite with her. Horus, the fruit of the union, had to avenge his father. Osiris is not one of the Hellenized gods of the Isiac circle. Though

Bust of Serapis. Alexandria. Greco-Roman Museum. Museum photo.

he retained his role as a funeral god among the local population in Ptolemaic Egypt, his cult did not spread outside the valley of the Nile; Serapis was substituted for him and replaced him beside Isis. However, during the Roman period, with the clear Egyptianization of the Isiac religion and the popularity of the Isiac mysteries and initiation that promised the initiate life in the afterworld, there was a renewed interest in Osiris. Osiris was associated with the holy water of the Nile, a symbol of fertility and resurrection, which played a great part in the ritual of the Isiac temples of the Roman Empire. These temples all had reservoirs and cisterns of sacred water, while *hydreia* and *situlae* were used for aspersions. One particular depiction of the god Osiris-Canopus shows him in the form of just such a vessel topped with a human head.

The important festival of the Isia in November, celebrated even in the Roman capital, retraced the passion, death, and resurrection of the god; the Iseum of Pompei was decorated with, among other things, two paintings of the passion of Osiris. As a god of vegetation continuously reborn, he was sometimes associated with Dionysus. Although we know of the existence of the mysteries of Osiris in Rome, few inscriptions mention him. On the other hand, quite a number of statuettes, generally of bronze, have been found in various locations throughout the Roman Empire, often in tombs: there the god is represented as in ancient Egypt, mummiform, holding the curved scepter (*heqa*) and the flail, and wearing the high *atef* crown flanked with plumes.

General view of the Serapeum at Ephesus (Turkey). Photo Salditt-Trappmann.

III. Serapis

The usual companion of Isis in Ptolemaic Alexandria and during the early years of the spread of the Isiac cults was, however, not Osiris but Serapis. The elaboration of this cult has given rise to an abundant literature, but nonetheless remains very controversial. Though we may agree that Serapis was derived from Osor-Hapi, a Memphite combination of Osiris and Apis, the sacred bull, there is still no unanimous agreement as to who gave this god the Hellenistic qualities that made him a Greco-Egyptian god. According to the accounts of several classical authors, the foundation of the cult of Serapis is most often attributed to Ptolemy I Soter, at the beginning of the third century B.C. But according to another theory, which is currently regaining favor, Alexander himself was responsible for the creation of the Hellenized cult of Serapis. Although the famous Serapeum of Alexandria was built in the reign of Ptolemy III Euergetes, various dedications unearthed on the hill of Rhacotis indicate the official existence of the god in Alexandria from the reign of Ptolemy II Philadelphus.

There is also uncertainty regarding the origin of the iconography of the god and of the famous cultic statue at the Serapeum of Alexandria. Deriving from Osiris, who was the god of the dead but also of vegetation and resurrection in ancient Egypt, Serapis had a dual personality as both a chthonic god and a fertility god. So his iconography, totally Hellenicized, borrowed from Hades, the Greek god of the

netherworld, its severe expression, abundant hair and beard, and garb of a chiton and a himation. The monster that often accompanies the god, who at first glance could be taken for Cerberus, the three-headed dog, guardian of Hell, was actually the symbol of Aion, the god of time, who has three heads: the heads of a dog, a wolf, and a lion. This makes Serapis the master of time and eternity. The headdress (*calathos* or *modius*) that he wears, a sign of agricultural fertility, reminds us that Serapis is also a dispenser of fertility.

Following ancient literary testimony, we are tempted to attribute the cult statue at the Serapeum of Alexandria to Bryaxis: it shows Serapis enthroned, holding his scepter in one hand and placing the other hand on the head of the three-headed monster; this model is confirmed by numerous copies and interpretations throughout antiquity. It is likely, however, that the famous Carian sculptor from the second half of the fourth century B.C. was the creator of this work. We can therefore no longer accept the legend attributing the iconography of Serapis to a statue of Pluto sent from Sinope.

Like Isis, Serapis was, because of his hybrid nature, destined to facilitate the religious symbiosis between the Greek and Egyptian elements of the Ptolemaic Egyptian population. Unlike Isis, however, he never achieved popular appeal during the Ptolemaic period. Although he had been the great dynastic Ptolemaic god with much official recognition during the third century B.C., he fell into partial disfavor, from which he would not emerge until the Roman period.

Gold pendant found in Mesopotamia. Serapis is represented on a reclining seat; in his right hand he holds a cup from which a serpent is drinking as it writhes on the back of the seat. Isis, nursing Horus, is shown to the left of Serapis; to the right of Serapis is Isis-Thermuthis, whose body ends in the form of a serpent. Paris, Musée du Louvre.

Isis Pelagia. Relief from Delos. From Ph. Bruneau, *Bulletin de correspondance hellénique*, 85, 1961.

Certainly knowledge of Serapis spread throughout the Greek world during the Hellenistic period; the Isiac temples of the island of Delos are dedicated to him, and many Isiac inscriptions in Rhodes attest to his presence. But when he was incorporated into the Isiac triad he was first relegated to a secondary position by his consort goddess.

During the imperial era Serapis was successful, as evidenced by dedications and numerous statues. His chthonic character seems to have yielded to his role as fertility god. Like Asclepius, he became a healing god. He had the special protection of some emperors, such as Commodus, Caracalla, and Septimius Severus; he became for them a dynastic god, protector of the fertility of the reign, reminiscent of the Ptolemaic dynastic cult. When the Eastern sun cults came into vogue toward the end of the second century B.C., Serapis was assimilated to Helios, as is attested by various dedications and representations of the god with his head surrounded by rays of sunlight. But Serapis was soon to capitulate before triumphant Christianity; the destruction of the Serapeum of Alexandria in 391 on the order of the Emperor Theodosius dealt him a fatal blow.

IV. Harpocrates

Egyptian tradition required the presence of a young god beside Isis and her consort. In fact Harpocrates often occupied fourth place, yielding to Anubis. However, many statuettes show him on the goddess's lap, in the charming figurines where Isis is preparing to nurse her son; but he may also appear alone.

The Greco-Roman iconography of Harpocrates follows that of Horus, the child of ancient Egypt. Born of a primordial lotus, sometimes assimilated to the rising sun, he is a naked baby, his head shaved except for the "lock of childhood" that falls over his right temple, and he raises his right index finger to his mouth in a childish gesture. Hellenized, he comes to resemble Eros; Harpocrates exchanges his lock of childhood for the curly hair of a little god of love, who is then decorated with some characteristic symbol, a lotus bud or flower, or sometimes the double Pharaonic crown (*pschent*). He holds in his left arm a horn of plenty, a symbol of fertility, which evokes his relationship with Osiris, god of vegetation and fertility. He often has the wings of Eros on his back; he may also hold the quiver of the god. Sometimes he borrows attributes from Dionysus: the fawn skin, the crown of moss, or the vinestalk that he leans against. But he is always depicted holding his index finger to his lips, a very characteristic gesture interpreted by the Romans as a warning not to divulge the secrets of the initiation into the Isiac mysteries. Although inscriptions that mention Harpocrates are quite rare, the many statuettes, lamps, intaglios, and jewels attest to the popularity of the little god during the Roman Empire.

V. Anubis

The popularity of Anubis in the Isiac circle of the Greco-Roman world may at first seem curious. It is not clear how the god of the dead from ancient Egypt, represented as a jackal or in human form with the head of a dog, could be tolerated in the classical world that scornfully rejected zoolatry. At the beginning of the second century B.C., Anubis even had his statue in the Sarapieion A of Delos. This acceptance is difficult to explain. Anubis had helped Isis in her search for the pieces of Osiris's body and watched over the body so that the goddess was able to revive him. According to a late Egyptian tradition recalled by Plutarch,

Anubis was the son born of the adultery of Osiris and Nephthys and had been adopted by Isis as her own child. In the Isiac cult, Anubis served primarily as a psychopomp god, an intermediary and messenger between the netherworld and the world of the living. His chthonic and funereal aspects explain quite naturally his close association with Hermes. Their identification gave rise to a new word, "Hermanubis," and to a specific iconography. The Greco-Roman Anubis, while retaining his jackal head, borrowed from Hermes his short tunic and his mantle pinned to one shoulder, as well as his attributes: the caduceus and the palm. Anubis may also hold the *sistrum* and *situla,* both instruments used in the Isiac cult.

VI. Rites and Doctrine

In order to understand the Isiac rites, the organization of the clergy, and even the various aspects of its doctrine, it is appropriate to follow the gods in their wanderings across the eastern Mediterranean and then through the provinces of the Roman Empire. The rites were comparable to those of the Greek cults, though always with Egyptian influence. This is true of the rituals of caring for the divine statue, the rites of purification and lustration; the importance attached to water in the Isiac cult naturally evokes the holy water of the Nile, symbol of regeneration and immortality; the role of lamps and the popularity of ritual meals are well documented in Ptolemaic Egypt. The Isiac temples had a great number of ponds and waterways. An exotic note is lent by a dromos bordered with sphinxes, as at the Serapieion C of Delos, or a rounded pediment as at the Iseum of the Field of Mars in Rome. Egyptian statues or statues in the Egyptian style add to the Nilotic atmosphere. This tendency was confirmed in Italy during the imperial period, where it corresponded to a clear Egyptianization of the Isiac cult; Egyptian temples at Rome and Benevento were decorated with obelisks, statues of pharaohs, dog-headed figures, and lions.

Annexations permitted the combination of various confraternities. Under the growing influence of eschatological preoccupations, Isis became a goddess of mysteries. The faithful were no longer content to ask her for earthly happiness; they wished to ensure their survival in the afterworld and their eternal happiness. It is not known whether the mysteries originated in Egypt proper. Probably sacred dramas were enacted there, such as the passion of Osiris. But there was nonetheless an essential difference: in ancient Egypt, the deceased alone was consecrated and deified; in the Hellenicized mysteries, it was the living person who was initiated, and thereby liberated from present and earthly misery. The existence of Isiac mysteries during the Hellenistic era has long been contested. However, in several aretalogies Isis declares that she has "shown the initiation to men"; in the new aretalogy discovered in Maroneus, dating from the end of the second century B.C., the goddess confirms that she has given the sacred writings to the initiates.

The aretalogies constitute the best proof of the *interpretatio graeca.* Isis affirms her universality, her supremacy over fate, and her role as the goddess of the mysteries. It is not known whether the mysteries are versions of an Egyptian original or are Greek works; it has been much debated. R. P. J. Festugière argued for a Greek origin. R. Harder and J. Bergman defended the Egyptian point of view. The recent study of the Maroneus document seems to show that the basic text was felt by the Greeks to be of foreign origin; various verses inspired by the Egyptian religious tradition were poorly understood and reinterpreted according to the Greek men-tality; the wish to Hellenize the basic text as much as possible is obvious.

VII. The Vicissitudes of the Isiac Cults

It is important to follow the destiny of Isis and her companions in southern Italy, Sicily, and Rome. As we have noted, the first and most important *interpretatio romana* of Isis was apparently her identification with the Fortuna Primigenia of Praeneste. The Isiac cult developed under Sulla, who began the restoration of the temple of Fortune. Alongside Isis Fortuna, Isis Pelagia or Pharia, protectress of navigation, became popular; her popularity is attested by inscriptions and especially by reports about the festival of the Navigium Isidis, celebrated on 5 March, which marked the opening of the navigational season in the spring.

The Isiac cult in Italy became rapidly Egyptianized; this tendency could be seen from the end of the first century A.D., and it would continue and increase. During the imperial era there was an Osirianization of the Isiac religion. As we have already seen, numerous statuettes of Osiris in the Egyptian fashion were found in the provinces of the empire. Another influence of Egypt was felt—the liaison between the Isiac cult and the imperial cult; the Caesars, as Pharaohs, tended to become divine kings. Caligula, an avowed Egyptophile, gave a new dimension to the imperial cult in claiming to be a god on earth. This example was followed by a number of his successors.

Despite a clear regression of the Isiac religion during the third century A.D., while the sun cults and Mithraism were coming into vogue, the Isiac cult remained solidly implanted in the Roman Empire. During the fourth century, the last burst of paganism, that of Vettius Agorius Praetextatus and Q. Aurelius Symmachus, was particularly affirmed by the Isiacs. Victorious Christianity would have difficulty extirpating the worship of Isis; in addition to destroying her statues and building churches over her temples, there was also an attempt to integrate her subtly: the Madonna with child evokes Isis holding the young Horus on her lap.

VIII. Ammon

In this evocation of the gods of ancient Egypt throughout the Greco-Roman world, it is perhaps surprising not to have encountered the name of Ammon, the god with ram's horns, made famous by the devotion of Alexander and the many statues of the Roman period. However, the spread of the cult of Ammon was very different from that of the Isiac cults themselves.

The Greek Ammon was derived from the Egyptian Amon. The two gods have in common not only similar names, but also close ties with the ram. The horns wound around the ear are the only attribute that is truly characteristic of the Greek Ammon; the Amon of Egypt was worshiped either as a ram or as a god in human form with a ram's head. More generally, however, he was totally anthropomorphic and wore a cap topped with two high plumes; yet throughout his history he retains the ram as his sacred animal. Both the Greek Ammon and the Egyptian Amon are also oracular divinities. The famous oracle of Siwa in the sands of Libya seems to be related to the oracle of Thebes, the Egyptian capital of the New Kingdom; the Libyans may have worshiped on this site a local ram god, who was assimilated to the Pharaonic Amon after the conquest of the oasis by the Egyptians.

The first Greeks to have a relationship with the god of Siwa were the Dorians from Thera. Soon after 640 B.C. they had founded the colony of Cyrene; they quickly adopted the god of their Libyan neighbors, who then occupied an important place in their pantheon: effigies of Ammon were preponderant on the coins of the colony from 570 B.C. to the Roman period. The adoption of Ammon by the Cyreneans may have been facilitated by the ancient worship of the ram god Carneus by the Dorians, and descriptions of Carneus are sometimes difficult to distinguish from those of Ammon.

It is presumably at Cyrene that the metamorphosis of Ammon took place. The colonials adapted him to Greek tastes; they assimilated him to their Hellenic Zeus and created a new iconographic type. Of his bestial origins, the god retained only the ram horns curling at his temples; he borrowed from Zeus his Olympian and severe expression, his beard, and his draped mantle; next to him was a young man, sometimes called Parammon. In the first half of the fifth century B.C., the first Greek literary accounts that mention Ammon consider him a hypostasis of Zeus. Up to the Roman period, Ammon was taken to be a Hellenic god to whom some cities devoted a public cult, and not an exotic god.

Through the commercial relations that they maintained with Sparta and Thebes, the Cyreneans propagated the cult and the image of Ammon in Greece. Beginning in the sixth century B.C., Ammon seems to have penetrated the Peloponnesus. He had temples at Gythion and Sparta; the Spartans, who particularly worshiped him, consulted the oracle of the Oasis about important problems. Ammon also had a temple at Thebes in Boeotia; Pindar consecrated a statue of the god there, a work of Calamis; the poet was also the author of a hymn to Ammon that was engraved in the sanctuary of Siwa. The oracle of the Oasis and his god enjoyed great popularity with the Athenians, who consulted him frequently; they established an official cult during the fourth century B.C.; a temple to the god is attested in Piraeus. Ammon was the object of very special worship in Aphytis, in Chalcidice, in the northeast of the peninsula of Pallene; in this village (which he had saved, it was said, during the siege of Lysander), the god had an oracle, the only one outside the oracle of Siwa. It was at Aphytis that the Macedonian dynasts, close cousins of the Chalcidice, came in contact with Ammon; it seems that Ammon then gained the favor of the court; in 348 the conquest of the Chalcidice delivered the Ammoneion of Pallene into the hands of the Macedonians.

Such were the antecedents of the famous pilgrimage undertaken by Alexander in 331 to the sanctuary of the Oasis, where the priests greeted the conqueror with the title, "Son of Zeus." Alexander came to Siwa to find in the solitude of the Libyan desert not only confirmation of his divine origin but also Ammon's recognition of his aspirations for universal domination. The name of Ammon would thereafter be associated with that of Alexander; the conqueror often reminded others of his divine ancestry.

With the death of Alexander, the worship of Ammon was neglected during the Hellenistic period. The oracle of Siwa was deserted during the second century B.C. Only the Ptolemies maintained their worship of Ammon. The cult of the god does not seem to have been widespread in the Greek world during the Hellenistic and Roman periods, despite his presence on the coins of many cities.

During the Empire, probably under the influence of the cult of the Ptolemaic sovereigns, Ammon seems sometimes to have been connected with the imperial Roman cult; he shared this quality with Serapis, with whom he may have been associated as a composite personality: Serapis-Ammon. Ammon was also a protector god for the Roman armies; he

Bronze medallion (probably a decorative boss) from Vetera-Xanten, ornamented with a mask of Jupiter-Ammon. Bonn. Rheinisches Landesmuseum. Museum photo.

Image of the month of November from a mosaic from El Djem (Tunisia) representing the seasons and the months of the year. From H. Stern, *Journal des Savants*, 1965, p. 119, fig. 3.

appears on medallions of phalerae and breastplates; and he was the patron of certain military units.

Ammon is well attested in the Roman Empire through inscriptions and theophoric names. He became Jupiter-Hammon, surely through the influence of Ba'al-Hamman, who had been worshiped in Carthage. His bearded mask with its curling horns appeared on many artifacts (for example, lamps, medallions, architectural elements, funeral monuments, etc.). His role was not only decorative but also apotropaic and eschatological. He remains outside the circle of Isiac divinities, except for his fairly rare association with Serapis; he is, however, present in the same regions where the Isiac cults flourished. Doubtless he is therefore a tributary of a certain Egyptizing or exotic climate. After having been regarded by the Greeks as a Hellenic god, Ammon seems to have rallied the camp of Eastern gods during the imperial era. The triumph of Christianity led naturally to his downfall; Procopius reports that Justinian had his temples of the Oasis closed during the sixth century. However, after a thousand years of neglect, the Renaissance, attracted to the strangeness of the gods of ancient Egypt, would again popularize the motif of the mask of the horned god.

J.Le./d.b.

BIBLIOGRAPHY

1. General Works

G. LAFAYE, *Histoire du culte des divinités d'Alexandrie hors d'Égypte* (Paris 1883). W. DREXLER, in Roscher, *Ausführliches Lexikon der griechischen und römischen Mythologie*, 2 (Leipzig 1890–97), article "Isis," cols. 360–548. H. P. WEITZ, in Roscher, *Ausführliches Lexikon . . .* , 4 (Leipzig 1900–1915), article "Sarapis," cols. 338–82. J. TOUTAIN, *Les cultes païens dans l'Empire romain*, 1, 2: *Les cultes orientaux* (1911). F. CUMONT, *Les religions orientales dans le paganisme romain* (4th ed., 1929; new edition 1963). F. W. VON BISSING, "Ägyptische Kultbilder der Ptolemaier und Römerzeit," *Der Alte Orient* 34 (1936). J. LECLANT, "Notes sur la propagation des cultes et monuments égyptiens en Occident à l'époque impériale," *Bulletin de l'Institut Français d'Archéologie Orientale* 55 (1956): 173–79; "Histoire de la diffusion des cultes égyptiens," *Problèmes et méthodes d'histoire des religions*, École pratique des hautes études, section 5, Sciences religieuses (Paris 1968), 92–96; various articles in *Annuaire de l'École pratique des hautes études*, section 5, Sciences religieuses: 73 (1965): 85–87; 74 (1966): 89–92; 75 (1967): 112–15; 76 (1968): 122–26; 77 (1969): 173–79; 79 (1971): 197–200; 80–81, fasc. 3, 159–63 and 165–66; 82 (1974): 115; 83 (1975): 131–33; 84 (1976): 215–16. J. LECLANT and G. CLERC, *IBIS* (= *Inventaire Bibliographique des Isiaca, 1940–1969*), vol. 1: *A–D* (Leiden 1972), and vol. 2: *E–K* (1975). L. VIDMAN, *Isis und Sarapis bei den Griechen und Römern*, Religionsgeschichtliche Versuche und Vorarbeiten, Bd. 29 (Berlin 1970). R. E. WITT, *Isis in the Graeco-Roman World* (1971).

2. Monographs and Specific Studies

A. ALFÖLDI, *A Festival of Isis in Rome under the Christian Emperors of the 4th Century*, Dissertationes Pannonicae (Budapest 1937); "Die alexandrinischen Götter und die Vota Publica am Jahresbeginn," *Jahrbuch für Antike und Christentum*, 8–9 (1965–66): 53–87. PH. BRUNEAU, "Existe-t-il des statues d'Isis Pelagia?" *Bulletin de Correspondance Hellénique* 98 (1974): 339–81, 23 figs. F. DUNAND, "Le syncrétisme isiaque à la fin de l'époque hellénistique," in *Les syncrétismes dans les religions grecque et romaine*, Colloque de Strasbourg, 9–11 June 1971 (Paris 1973), 79ff. F. DUNAND, "Les mystères égyptiens aux époques hellénistique et romaine," in *Mystères et syncrétismes*, Études d'histoire des religions de l'Université de Strasbourg, 2 (1976): 11–62. J. GWYN GRIFFITHS, *Plutarch's De Iside et Osiride* (Cardiff 1970). TH. HOPFNER, *Fontes Historiae Religionis Aegyptiacae*, 5 fasc. (Bonn 1922–25). G. J. F. KATER-SIBBES, *Preliminary Catalogue of Sarapis Monuments* (Leiden 1973); *Apis*, 3 vols. (Leiden 1975–77). R. MERKELBACH, *Roman und Mysterium in der Antike* (1962); *Isisfeste in griechisch-römischer Zeit,*

Daten und Riten, Beiträge zur Klassischen Philologie, Heft 5 (Meisenheim am Glan 1963). K. SCHEFOLD, *Vergessenes Pompeji* (Bern 1962). J. E. STAMBAUGH, *Sarapis under the Early Ptolemies* (Leiden 1972). V. TRAN TAM TINH, "Isis et Sérapis se regardant," *Revue Archéologique* (1970): 55–80, 26 figs. L. VIDMAN, *Sylloge Inscriptionum Religionis Isiacae et Sarapiacae* (Berlin 1969).

3. Regional Studies

F. DUNAND, *Le culte d'Isis dans le bassin oriental de la Méditerranée* (Leiden 1973), 1: *Le culte d'Isis et les Ptolémées*; 2: *Le culte d'Isis en Grèce*; 3: *Le culte d'Isis en Asie Mineure*. T. A. BRADY, *The Reception of the Egyptian Cults by the Greeks, 330–30 B.C.*, University of Missouri Studies 10 (1935). P. M. FRASER, "Two Studies on the Cult of Sarapis in the Hellenistic World," *Opuscula Atheniensia*, 7 (1967). SALDITT-TRAPPMANN, *Tempel der ägyptischen Götter in Griechenland und an der Westküste Kleinasiens* (Leiden 1970). PH. BRUNEAU, *Recherches sur les cultes de Délos à l'époque hellénistique* (Paris 1971). M. F. BASLEZ, *Recherches sur les conditions de pénétration et de diffusion des religions orientales à Délos* (Paris 1977). M. CALVET and P. ROESCH, "Les Sarapieia de Tanagra," *Revue Archéologique*, 1966, 297–332. V. WESSETZKY, *Die ägyptischen Kulte zur Römerzeit in Ungarn* (Leiden 1961). A. DOBROVITS, "Az Egyiptomi Kultuszok Emlékei Aquincumban (Remains of Egyptian Cults at Aquincum)," *Budapest Régiségei* 13 (1943): 47–75, summarized and critiqued by J. Leclant in *Revue des Études Anciennes* 53 (1951): 383–86. J. LECLANT, "Un relief pannonien d'inspiration égyptisante," *Revue Archéologique*, 1950, 147–49. B. PERC, *Beiträge zur Verbreitung ägyptischer Kulte auf dem Balkan und in den Donauländern zur Römerzeit* (Munich 1968). P. SELEM, "Divinités égyptiennes dans l'Illyricum romain," *Godisnjak* 9 (1972): 5–104, includes summary in French, 95–104. M. MALAISE, *Les conditions de pénétration et de diffusion des cultes égyptiens en Italie* (Leiden 1972); *Inventaire préliminaire des documents égyptiens découverts en Italie* (Leiden 1972). A. ROULLET, *The Egyptian and Egyptianizing Monuments of Imperial Rome* (Leiden 1972). M. FLORIANI-SQUARCIAPINO, *I culti orientali ad Ostia* (Leiden 1962). V. TRAN TAM TINH, *Essai sur le culte d'Isis à Pompéi* (Paris 1964); *Le culte des divinités orientales à Herculanum* (Leiden 1971); *Le culte des divinités orientales en Campanie en dehors de Pompéi, de Stabies et d'Herculanum* (Leiden 1972). H. W. MÜLLER, *Der Isiskult im antiken Benevent*, Münchner ägyptologische Studien 16 (Berlin 1969). G. SFAMENI-GASPARRO, *I culti orientali in Sicilia* (Leiden 1973). G. GRIMM, *Die Zeugnisse ägyptischer Religion und Kunstelemente im römischen Deutschland* (Leiden 1969). J. LECLANT, "Du Nil au Rhin, de l'antique Égypte au cœur de l'Europe," in *Mélanges offerts à Polys Modinos* (Paris 1968), 71–84; "Osiris en Gaule," in *Studia Aegyptiaca*, 1 (Budapest 1974), 263–85, 2 pl.; "Iconographie des petits bronzes d'Isis allaitant Horus exhumés en France," in *Actes du IVe Colloque International sur les bronzes antiques* (Lyons, May 1976). L. RICHARD, "Aegyptiaca d'Armorique," *Latomus* 31 (January–March 1972): 88–104, 3 pl. E. HARRIS and J. R. HARRIS, *The Oriental Cults in Roman Britain* (Leiden 1965). A. GARCIA Y BELLIDO, *Les religions orientales dans l'Espagne romaine* (Leiden 1967). G. PESCE, *Il tempio d'Iside in Sabratha* (Rome 1953). G. PICARD, *Les religions de l'Afrique antique* (1954), 223ff.

4. Studies of the Aretalogies

D. MÜLLER, *Ägypten und die griechischen Isis-Aretalogien*, Abhandlungen der Sächsischen Akademie der Wissenschaften, Phil.-Hist. Kl. 53, 1 (Leipzig 1961). H. ENGELMANN, *Die delische Sarapis-Aretalogie*, Beiträge zur klassischen Philologie, Heft 15 (Meisenheim am Glan 1964). J. BERGMAN, "Ich bin Isis: Studien zum memphitischen Hintergrund der griechischen Isisaretalogien," *Acta Universitatis Upsaliensis, Historia Religionum*, 3 (Uppsala 1968). V. F. VANDERLIP, "The Four Greek Hymns of Isidorus and the Cult of Isis," *American Studies in Papyrology* 12 (1972). Y. GRANDJEAN, *Une nouvelle arétalogie d'Isis à Maronée* (Leiden 1975).

5. Studies of "Egyptophilia"

S. MORENZ, *Die Begegnung Europas mit Aegypten*, Sitzungsberichte der sächsischen Akademie der Wissenschaften zu Leipzig, Phil.-Hist. Kl., Bd. 113, Heft 5 (1968). J. BALTRUŠAITIS, *Essai sur la légende d'un mythe, la guête d'Isis, introduction à l'égyptomanie* (Paris 1967); cf. *Revue de l'Art* 5 (1969): 82–88. E. IVERSEN, *Obelisks in Exile*, 2 vols. (Copenhagen 1968, 1972).

Isis the Magician, in Greek and Coptic Papyruses

The magical power of Isis "of a thousand names" ("Myrionymos" PGM 57.13) derives mainly from the power that belongs to the god of the word, Hermes, her teacher. In a formula that asks for a vision in a dream, taken from the great bilingual scroll of Leiden, Osiris and Isis are invoked as the father and mother of Hermes: "I entreat you, by your father Osiris and by Isis, your mother: show me a form of yourself and make known your oracle on what I desire" (PGM 12.148–50). As in the aretalogy where she is proclaimed to be both the mother and the daughter of the same god, Isis the magician, mother of Hermes in the Leiden Scroll, is also said to be his daughter in the Paris codex: "Yes it is indeed you (the moon) whom I know, I, the Archegetes of all magicians, I, Hermes the Elder, I, the father of Isis" (4.2288–90), as in the writings of Plutarch (*Moralia* 352A; 355F). This Hermes the Elder, that is, Thoth the Great (4.95–97), father of Isis, stands in opposition to the young Hermes, her son, that is, Horus-Harpocrates. Searching for her brother and husband Osiris, Isis finds him with the help of a magical formula of twenty-nine letters, taken from a "sacred book" of the "archives of Hermes" (PGM 24.1–10). A scarab and an Isis must be engraved one above the other on the emerald of a ring of Hermes, which serves to know all things (PGM 5.239–42). Hermes remains the constant protector and benefactor of Isis. In the love charm of Astrampsouchos, in the form of a bond (*philtrokatadesmos*) (P. Lond. 122 = PGM 8.1–63), the magician entreats Hermes by enumerating the multiple figures of his manifestations and the titles to which he has a right; among these, the supplicant reminds him that he had been of help to Isis: "Since it is true that Isis, the greatest of all the divinities, invoked you amidst all dangers, in all places, against the gods, men, demons, animals of the waters and of the land, and since she obtained your favor and victory over the gods, men, and all the animals who live beneath the earth, therefore I, a mere mortal, invoke you in the same way! Favor me also with good appearance, beauty. Answer my prayers, Hermes, benefactor, inventor" (22–28). A charm of success and invocation contained in the great magical papyrus of Paris (PGM 4.2373–2440) is said to have been composed by Hermes himself, in honor of wandering Isis (2376). This charm is called "little beggar" (*ēpaitētarion*), because it consists of modeling in beeswax a beggar with a bag, a stick, and an apron, who "must stand, like Isis, on a globe around which a serpent is coiled." Each part of his anatomy corresponds to a series of incantations, breathing magical power into the figurine. In the final formula of the performance (2434–37), Isis is called the widow and Horus the orphan: it is by their names that the magician summons this talisman to himself. Placed in an attic or in any other room of a house, this figurine of Hermes will bring luck, success, and wealth (2437–40).

But the "multiple names and forms" (*polyōnumos, polymorphos*, PGM 7.503) of Isis the magician also derive from her ability to assimilate the forms and functions of the two goddesses of the moon and the earth. In an amulet (P. Lond. 121 = PGM 7.490–504), Isis is invoked during a sacrifice (consisting of sulfur and the seeds of reeds from the Nile) to the moon as "She who permitted the Good Daemon (Agathos Daimon) to rule over the entire black land" (*teleion melan*), that is, the land of Egypt fertilized by the floodwa-

ters. She thus assimilates herself to the lunar Artemis, and her name is associated in a series of magic words to the star Sothis (= Sirius; also in 36.364), to Bastet, the goddess of Bubastis, who according to Herodotus corresponds to Artemis (*Hist.* 11. 59), to the goddess of Buto, who for the Greeks was Leto (Latona), the mother of Artemis, and finally to Nemesis Adrastea, another name for Artemis (Suidas, I.54.524), whom a Hermetic treatise calls "the one who watches over the universe with piercing eyes" (*Kore Kosmou*, 48). In the great tablet of conjuration addressed to the moon (Selene-Mene-Hecate), of the Greek codex of Paris, the magician enumerates the names and titles of the goddess of night, and then, to force her to comply, he tells her of the impiety of the one for whom the evil spell is destined: "Unleash your rage, virgin, against him, the enemy of the gods of the sky, of Helios-Osiris and of his wife Isis" (PGM 4.2340–42). In the first of the magic papyruses of Oslo, to make his love charm (*agōgē*) efficacious and to constrain the goddess, the supplicant attributes a sacrilegious act to the girl he desires, in this case an offering of eggs that do not conform to the ritual, at which "Isis cries out aloud and the world is stricken by shock; she tosses on her holy bed and her bonds are broken, as are those of the demonic tribe"; Isis and Osiris are thus invoked along with all earthly and subterranean demons, "who come from the abyss," so that the girl in question "will lose sleep, fly through the air, and, starving, thirsty, no longer able to sleep . . . come to fit her vulva around the organ" of the supplicant (PGM 36.140–50). But it is primarily in the tablet of conjuration of the Paris codex that the reciprocity of power between Isis and Selene is affirmed. The magician declares to the moon, in an invocation in a text that is rather uncertain but that can be translated as follows: "Fix your eyes on yourself; it is the beauty of Isis that you will admire in the mirror, if you watch yourself, before your eyes begin to spit out a black light" (PGM 4.2297–99). The prayer of consecration of the sacrifice of perfumes to the moon, which serves as the love charm of Claudianus (PGM 7.862–918), calls Isis by the "great magical names" of the goddess "who embraces all," "who conducts the workings of the world," that is, the celestial and lunar Aphrodite.

It is very significant that in the same charm one finds associated, next to Isis, the names of three infernal divinities—Ortho, Baubo, and Ereškigal (7.894–97). Henceforth, because of her lunar conjunction, Isis becomes a chthonic power. In a magic hymn inserted by some ancient editors into the Homeric invocation of the dead in the *Odyssey* (11.34–50, itself already an interpolation), the chthonic power of Isis, among other divinities and demons of the "people of the dead," was invoked by Odysseus when he visited hell; the rhetor Julius Africanus recorded these pseudo-Homeric verses in his *Kestoi*, from which they were taken by the transcriber (P. Oxy. 412 = PGM 23.1–3): "Listen to me, you who are kind and protective, Anubis of generous seed! Listen also, astute and secret wife, you who saved Osiris! Here, greedy Hermes! Here, subterranean Zeus of the beautiful curls!" Isis protects the tombs; whoever violates them risks incurring her punishment (PGM 59.14–15). A love charm to bring someone to oneself (*agōgē*), contained in the Greek magical book of Paris (= PGM 4.1390), works through the intervention of heroes and gladiators killed in combat, or anyone else who died a violent death. The prayer recited during the sacrifice of perfumes invokes the chthonic aspect of Hermes and of Hecate, the demons of the dead, the goddesses of destiny (Moirai) and of revenge (Poinai), and then one reads the following formula (1471–76): "Isis went

The Farnese Isis. Statue in beige marble. Naples Museum. Photo Boudot-Lamotte.

away, carrying on her shoulders her bedmate—her brother. But Zeus came down from Olympus and stayed to wait for the spirits of the dead who were going to a woman's house to accomplish the task in question," that is, the submission of the girl to her lover. The goal of the spell is to cause the woman to be as much in love as Isis was.

Celestial and subterranean, above and below, Isis also occupies the intermediary space as a goddess of fertility. This terrestrial Isis appears in the formula of consecration of a magic ring, contained in the bilingual scroll of Leiden (= PGM 12.202). On the jasper intaglio an uroboros snake is engraved; in the middle of the snake is a moon with two stars on the ends of its points, surmounted by a sun named Abraxas (203–5). In the formula of consecration that accompanies the ritual, the magician begins by invoking in the second person the celestial and infernal gods (216–27); then in the first person he evokes the power and the magical virtues of the ring: "I am the plant called the palm branch. I am the flow of blood from the palm branches, which comes

from the tomb of the great Osiris. . . . I am the god that no one can see or name thoughtlessly. I am the sacred phoenix. I am Crates the saint, also called Marmarayoth. I am Helios who makes the light appear. I am Aphrodite, also called Typhi. I am the saint of blowing winds. I am Kronos who makes the light appear. I am the mother of the gods, called Sky. I am Osiris, who is called Water. I am Isis, who is called Dew. I am Esenephrys (= Isis-Nephthys), who is called Spring. I am Eidolos, who resembles true images. I am Souchos who resembles the crocodile" (227–36). According to the formula of a magic hymn of the Paris codex, Isis is "the earth that drinks the dew and is fertilized" (PGM 4.2345–46). Associated with water, dew, and the spring sap, the goddess of the Nile (4.2297), with the cornucopia and the oar (cf. the intaglio no. 109 Delatte-Derchain), thus represents the earth mother, fertilizing the lands of Egypt with the waters of the flood. The same statue of Isis is embossed with a formula to be used in gathering plants (PGM 4.2967–3006). For each plant he digs up, the magician who specializes in herbs carries out a purification ritual in which he sprinkles natron, uses kyphi and pine resin as incense, and uses milk as a libation. The ritual is accompanied by a prayer, which invokes the diverse titles of the demon to whom the plant is consecrated: "You were planted by Kronos, conceived in the womb of Hera, preserved from all evil by Amon, born of Isis, nourished by rainy Zeus, and raised to maturity by Helios (= Osiris) and the dew (= Isis). You are the dew of all the gods, you are the heart of Hermes, you are the seed of the ancestral gods, you are the eye of Helios, you are the light of Selene, you are the ashes of Osiris, you are the beauty and the glory of Ouranos, you are the soul of the demon of Osiris, which dances everywhere, and you are the breath of Amon" (2978–89).

The pancosmic position of Isis, mistress of life and protector of the dead, determines her curative ability to grasp the sympathies and antipathies that calm or trouble people. Her curative power is invoked in a recipe against stomachache contained in a Coptic magical papyrus of Berlin (BKU I, pp. 2–3). Horus hunts down a falcon that "he cuts up without a knife, cooks without a fire, and eats without salt." Sick and unable to sleep, he sends a demon to tell his mother in Heliopolis; the demon finds her wearing her helmet and busily lighting a fire on a copper stove. Isis then gives the messenger the recipe: incant either her "true name that carries the sun to the west, the moon to the east, and the six propitiatory stars subject to the sun," or "the three hundred blood vessels surrounding the navel" (II, pp. 9–12 Kropp). Isis at the oven, regulator of the stars and of the microcosm and thus the ruler of the culinary, cosmic, and somatic orders, is entirely capable of giving anyone who has strayed from the norm the power to return to it. To protect oneself from the bad demon who can cause the failure of a request for a vision in a state of vigil (*autoptos*), a recipe from the magical Greek book of Paris recommends the use, as an amulet, of a piece of veil from a stone Harpocrates (PGM 4.1071–84). On the piece of cloth, the theurgist, who identifies himself with Horus, writes with ink made of myrrh the name of the son of Isis and Osiris, Orsoronophris; then he rolls some of the plant called sempervivum in the cloth and ties up the bundle with seven threads of the linen of Anubis; the amulet is worn around the neck for the duration of the magical procedure (*poiēsis*).

Whether she is invoked as "ruler" ("Kyria") in oracular requests (PGM 24.a.1), in imprecations (59.14–15), or in phylacteric formulas (7.492.503), Isis the doctor remains above all the consoler and patron of lovers. In a Coptic charm from the Carl Schmidt collection, it is while encircled by her seven young girls and from the interior of her temple of Habin where she gives her oracles, that she carries the potion and the amulet of healing to her tearful adept, who is identified with Horus (I A Kropp). In the following charm on parchment, the adept evokes the seven young girls of the goddess, who are seated next to a fountain, and complains of his beloved who "did not want to receive his kiss" (I B Kropp). Again to bring a little rest and relief to the suffering of the lover, a Coptic magical papyrus (BKV I, p. 21) invokes the celestial Isis, who rules over the sun, the moon, and the Pleiades, and the infernal Isis, descended into the Noun with her sister Nephthys to look for Osiris (= II, pp. 12–14 Kropp). The true object of the charm is to bring drowsiness and sleep to whoever burns with love, that is, to satisfy his immediate sexual desire so that his health can be restored. In Greek papyruses, the love spell would not attempt primarily to heal the sufferer but to punish the woman who is causing his illness, by transmitting to her the same illness from which he is suffering—insomnia (PGM 4.2943; 7.374.652; 12.16.376; 52.20). The myth of Isis and Osiris furnishes the material for two invocatory formulas from the cryptogram that is preserved in the library of the University of Michigan (= PGM 57). The first formula of constraint (2–13) is addressed in all likelihood to Isis-Pronoia; in the form of a veiled threat, it attempts to force the divinity to accomplish the goal of the recipe. If his wish is granted, the reciter, an adept of Isis who knows "the secrets" (krupta), that is, the multiple magic names of the goddess, commits himself—a promise that in fact hides a constraining threat—to "let the sun (= Helios-Osiris) rise and set as it wishes," to "save the body of Osiris," to "not break the ties" that bind Typheus, to "not kill Amon" (= Osiris), to "not scatter the limbs of Osiris," and to "hide Osiris and allow him to escape from the Giants." The second formula of constraint (16–18) is also directed to Isis, so that the goddess is forced to tell her adept that his request has been granted: "Isis, pure virgin, give me a sign that will let me know that the task has been accomplished; uncover your sacred peplos, shake off the black Tyche that clothes you, put the constellation of the Bear into motion." Thus constrained, Isis sends a sign of her celestial and astral nature. For the sake of the adept, the magician describes it as follows: "The goddess will detach from her bosom the end of one of her hands. You will see a star shoot toward you. Look at it without fear: it will shoot out of itself and aim at you, like an arrow, a magical sign (charaktēr), which will erupt inside you, in such a way that you will be possessed by the goddess. Keep this sign as an amulet. Since it comes from the goddess, it is the sign of Kronos and will fill you with courage" (22–28). The procedure ends with the standard directions: to thank the goddess, magic words to address to the stars "to avoid any rebellion or any change in their good intentions," and a last invocation to Isis-Pronoia to call on her to act right away (29–37).

Under the tutelage of her instructor Hermes, Isis is the inventor of philters. A potion with a base of olive oil, beet juice, and leaves of the olive tree, whose use is recommended by the first of the two love charms of the bilingual papyrus of the British Museum (= PGM 61), is called "mucus of Isis:" "You are olive oil and you are not olive oil, but rather the sweat of the Good Daemon, the mucus of Isis, the maxim of Helios, the power of Osiris, the grace of the gods! I unleash you to descend upon a certain woman, the daughter of a certain woman. Make her blind so that she no longer knows where she is. Set her loins on fire so that she will come to me, so that she will love me always, and so that

Coptic magical papyrus (MSS Schmidt 1 and 2). Isis and the seven young women. From Kropp, *Ausgewählte koptische Zaubertexte* (Brussels 1931).

she is unable to drink or eat, so that she will come to me, so that she will love me always" (7–9, 15–19). The name of Isis-Sothis (Sisisoth), written on the skin of a donkey with blood from the womb of a catfish mixed with juice from the plant of Serapis, constitutes an efficacious and infallible love charm that works the very same day (PGM 36.361–71). In another spell from the same Oslo papyrus (= PGM 36.283–94) entitled "little key to the vulva" (phusikleidion), it is recommended that the one in love smear his organ with a mixture of honey, a crow's egg, plantain juice, and the bile of a ray, while reciting the following prayer: "I declare to you, womb of my woman, spread yourself and receive the sperm of this man! . . . May this woman love me for all of her life as Isis loved Osiris, and may she stay as chaste for me as Penelope was for Odysseus!"

To provoke discord between a man and a woman, the enmity between Typhon and Isis is cited, as in this malevolent spell from the bilingual scroll of Leiden, which is suitable to be written on an earthenware fragment of a vessel for curing food (PGM 12.372–74). Opposed to the "godless" (atheos) Typhon, Horus is also invoked in love charms, as in this recipe for opening a door using the umbilical cord of a firstborn ram that has not yet touched the earth: after having burnt myrrh and purified the cord with the smoke emitted from it, the suppliant, who speaks in the name of Horus, inserts the cord into the lock, while reciting the formula for opening first in Coptic and then in Greek (PGM 36.312–20). Myrrh is particularly effective in magic for love. A recipe used to attract someone, from the same papyrus of Oslo (= PGM 36.333–60), advises the lover to make use of myrrh by throwing it on the flat part of an oven and, while it is being consumed, to recite a prayer enumerating the titles of nobility of the personified fruit of the balsam: "Myrrha, Myrrha, you who are at the service of gods and who move rivers and mountains, you who set fire to the swamp of the Achalda and burn the godless Typhon, you who are the battle companion of Horus, the protector of Anubis, and the leader of Isis, just as I throw you, Myrrha, on the turning platform of this oven so that you are consumed, so you too consume my woman, because I entreat you out of powerful and inexorable necessity. . . . Rouse yourself, Myrrha, set out for all places and begin your search for my woman, open her right thigh, penetrate her like thunder, like lightning, like a burning flame, and make her weak, pale, sickly, anemic, her whole body disarmed, so that to escape from her plight she will come to me, this man, son of a certain woman, right away, right away, quickly, quickly!"

Because she is the one who loves most, Isis is above all the goddess of love charms. She too has known the dramas of separation and adultery. A charm preserved in Coptic in the Greek magical codex of Paris (PGM 4.94–144) evokes the infidelity of Osiris. "Isis is the one who comes from the mountains, at noon, in the summer, a dusty young girl with tears in her eyes, while her heart is filled with sobs." Her father, Thoth the Great (= Hermes the Elder in the Greek interpretation), rushes to her, and Isis tells him that Osiris is deceiving her with her sister Nephthys. Thoth advises her to go to the south of Thebes, to see Belf the blacksmith, so that he can make her a key that she must soak in the blood of Osiris. At first meant to be used by women, this charm was adapted so it could be used by men, with this sham curse: "Let her drink, eat, sleep with another—I will put a spell on her heart, on her breath, on her three holes, but above all I will put a spell on her vulva into which I want to penetrate until she comes to me and I know what is in her heart, what she has done and what she is thinking of, now, now, right away, right away" (147–53).

Isis, who heals bodies and consoles hearts, can also reactivate a defective magic tool or rid a place of nuisances. To restore oracular power to a skull that has become mute, a recipe from the Greek magic book of Paris (= PGM 4.2125–39) advises sealing its opening with scum from the doors of a temple of Osiris and with dirt from a barrow, then to cold hammer a hobble to make a signet ring from it, on which will be engraved a female cat grasping the head of a Gorgon and a headless lion who wears a crown of Isis instead of a head and whose right foot rests on the skull of a skeleton. To obtain the blessing of a Good Daemon on a place, a recipe from the same magic book advises using Tyrrhenian wax to form a statuette of a three-headed god: in the middle is the head of a sparrow hawk wearing a crown of Horus; to the right, the head of a dog-headed god wearing a crown of Hermanubis; and to the left, the head of an ibis wearing a crown of Isis. The statuette must have the clothing of Osiris and must be placed in a little temple made of juniper, at the place that one wants to bless. Then comes the ritual (the sacrifice of an onager and a libation of milk) and the incantory prayer to the "angel" of the place, who is assimilated to the Good Daemon and to the Aion, "bestower of riches" (= PGM 4.3125–71).

What Isis has bound together by her magic powers is indivisible and forever indissoluble. A Coptic recipe for tying up a dog (British Museum Ms. Or. 1013A) invokes her for this purpose: "I bind the sky, I bind the earth. I bind the sun to the east [so that it can no longer rise], I bind the moon to the west so that it can no longer rise, I bind the [rain] so that it no longer falls to the ground, I bind the cultivated earth so that it no longer [produces]. I change the sky into bronze, I change the earth into iron. . . . No human lineage belonging to the race of Adam and to the complete creation of Zoe (= Eve) can undo the bonds that I have tied or the charm that I have written" (= 2, pp. 14–15 Kropp). The effectiveness of a formula of constraint directed at the "daemon of the dead," and cited in a love charm (P. Lond. 121), comes from the fact that it was written and recited by Isis when she was bringing back Osiris and restoring his dismembered limbs—which Asclepius himself, aided by Hebe, was unable to do (PGM 7.1000–1009). Similarly, the amulet from the Coptic magical papyrus of London cited above, used to tie up a dog, is said to have been written by Isis herself (= 2 p. 14 Kropp). She alone, the inventor of philters, has the power to put an end to the effects of her spells. Binding and unbinding according to the wishes of her adepts, Isis is the ruler of magic, because she is the universal ruler, the mistress of the three worlds, celestial, terrestrial, and subterranean, and thus is herself able to control the elements that attract or combat one another. But, set in place by her myths and her rituals, she traverses papyruses without being the object of a particular esoteric overevaluation. This point distinguishes her from her Greek neighbor, Hecate. For Isis, magic remains one function among others; for Hecate it is a state of being.

M.T./t.l.f.

BIBLIOGRAPHY

TH. HOPFNER, *Griechisch-ägyptischer Offenbarungszauber,* SPP 21 (Leipzig 1922), particularly §§ 727–28, 788–90; "Orientalisch-Religions geschichtliches aus den griechischen Zauberpapyri Aegyptens," *Archiv Orientální* 3 (1931): 121–27. H. D. BETZ, *The Greek Magical Papyri in Translation,* 2 vols. (Chicago 1985–). A.-M. KROPP, *Ausgewählte koptische Zaubertexte,* 3 vols. (Brussels 1930–31), especially 3:7–9. F. SBORDONE, "Iside maga," *Aegyptus* 26 (1946): 130–48. J. GWYN GRIFFITHS, *Apuleius of Madauros: The Isis-Book* (Leiden 1975), 47–51.

Abbreviation

PGM: K. PREISENDANZ, *Papyri Graecae Magicae: Die griechischen Zauberpapyri,* 2 vols. (Leipzig and Berlin 1928–31). Translated into English by H.D. Betz—see above.

THE FATE OF THE EGYPTIAN GODS FROM THE MIDDLE AGES TO THE EIGHTEENTH CENTURY

For their ideas about Egyptian mythology, Renaissance scholars used not only material left to them by their Greek and Roman predecessors but also theories about the nature of Egyptian religion advanced by mythologists of antiquity and of the Middle Ages. Insofar as mythology was concerned, the Egyptian Renaissance of the fifteenth century was not so much the inauguration of a new tradition as the revival of a flagging but not altogether abandoned argument whose historical background determined in advance the developments to come.

To understand these new developments, it is therefore necessary to analyze the mythological ideas and to show how they were handed down through the centuries and what theories they produced.

Two types of material can be distinguished which are distinct but closely related and mutually complementary. On the one hand, information about the gods of the Egyptian myths can be gleaned from the accounts of Greek and Roman writers. On the other hand, theosophical speculations are contained in the works of the late Neoplatonists and the "Corpus Hermeticum," a collection of theosophical and philosophical treatises composed about the third century A.D., which humanist scholars regarded as a reflection of the work of the Neoplatonists as much as the concepts of Egyptian thought and its legendary wisdom. Transmitted through an authentic literary tradition, these diverse texts presented no difficulties other than those of translation and interpretation.

But unfortunately such was not the case for the strictly mythological data, which suffered profound alterations on their way from Egypt to Greece. For the Greeks and Romans subsequent to Plato and Aristotle, whose religious and philosophical concepts were founded on the abstractions of Plato perceived in the light of the logic of Aristotle, the paths of Egyptian thought and its manner of speaking about myth seemed no less strange than they do now to us. Representing in its highest degree of systematic development that which is commonly called the mythic mentality, the speculative theosophy of the Egyptians was based on the laws of a complex logic and its rigorous point of view, which saw in the concrete representations characteristic of these myths the highest manifestation of all phenomena, of all ideas. For the Greeks, however, as for us, the idea of myth as *ultima ratio* and *ultima veritas* was incomprehensible, and as the concrete Egyptian idea passed into the abstraction of the Greek philosopher, this *translatio graeca* changed the original character of the myths under consideration and blurred the defining characteristics of specific divine figures so as to facilitate their assimilation to the gods of the Greek pantheon.

And this assimilation was enhanced by the theory of the universality of religion and the common origin of all the gods that Herodotus had already advanced. According to this doctrine, Egypt was the primordial home of religion, of all true piety, and of the gods themselves. At some time before the dawn of history, religion knew a new era of expansion; the Egyptian gods had spread throughout the world, including Greece, and they were worshiped in these diverse places under new names and different forms and incorporated into myths adapted to their new environments. But at a deeper level they always represented the same ideas and the same principles. With the exception of such gods as Osiris, Isis, and Serapis, who were known to the Western world through their own regional cults, the Egyptian gods were thus most often called by their Greek and Roman names and consequently appeared under those names in the classical literature, as well as in the mythologies of the Renaissance. Amon, for example, was in general identified with Zeus or Jupiter, Thoth with Hermes or Mercury, Ptah with Hephaestus or Vulcan, Re with Helios, Nut with Hera, and Seth with Typhon. Even Osiris was frequently called Dionysus or Bacchus, and Isis, Demeter or Ceres.

This theory of the Egyptian origin of the gods was not, however, universally accepted throughout the ancient world. Some haughty Roman intellectuals found it incompatible with the disdain for Egypt and her religion straightforwardly publicized by Cicero in his book on the nature of the gods (3.19). And for the mythological tradition accepted by the Renaissance, it was clearly of great importance that a source as influential as the *Metamorphoses* of Ovid gave Greek genealogies to such important Egyptian gods as Isis and Thoth and considered their appearance in the Egyptian pantheon as a secondary development of minor interest. No less important for the Renaissance tradition was the revival of a radical theory proposed in the fourth century B.C. by the Greek scholar Euhemerus, who rejected the fundamental dogma of the divinity of the gods and substituted for it the

Alexandrine Isis. Detail from the ambo of Henry II at Aix-la-Chapelle. Photo Marburg.

rationalist principle that the gods were all of human origin and our images of them developed from that beginning. According to Euhemerus, the gods were in the beginning either great seers or sages who were respected for their great virtues or wisdom or they were ambitious tyrants who during their lifetimes had usurped the honors owed to the gods and ended up passing for divine persons.

I. The Middle Ages

When taken up by the Christian apologists, the theory of Euhemerus proved to be an effective weapon in their struggles against the pagan cults. When applied to the figure of Thoth, the Egyptian god of wisdom and writing, it must have exercised a profound influence on the only genuine debate that took place in the Middle Ages directly in regard to a problem in Egyptian mythology, a controversy over the relative age of Thoth, "the Egyptian Hermes," and of Moses, and over their importance in the invention of letters and the establishment of a literary tradition. In the *Philebus* (8) and the *Phaedo* (59), Plato had called attention to an Egyptian tradition that Thoth had been the first to notice that the "infinity of sounds" could be divided into distinct elements such as consonants and vowels, a discovery that led decisively to the invention of hieroglyphs, giving rise to all future developments in the field of graphic symbols. The problem of knowing whether Thoth was a god or only a sage remained unanswered, but on Plato's word he was recognized for all antiquity as the inventor of letters and as the author of the Hermetic writings.

After the triumph of Christianity and the decline of Neoplatonism as an independent religious and philosophical movement, this conception of the role of Thoth necessarily appeared incompatible with the biblical texts on Moses. But as a theory supported by Plato, it could not be dismissed with a mere wave of the hand, and the problem of a reciprocal correlation between the two figures provoked heated theological discussions between the Aristotelians, most of whom supported the cause of Moses, and the Platonists, who defended Thoth. The controversy continued, never stopping completely and never completely settled. But the solution accepted by most of the scholars of the Middle Ages and the Renaissance was formulated by Lactantius as early as the fourth century A.D. Lactantius, a zealous Christian convert, naturally enough rejected any idea of the divinity of Thoth, and, like the Romans, even gave him a Greek origin, identifying him with the "historic" Mercury who killed Argus and fled after the murder to Egypt, where he was ultimately deified. Nevertheless, he considered him to be a seer and a visionary, comparable in this respect to the Sibyls, and he acknowledged him to be the author of the Hermetic texts, in which he anticipated certain Christian doctrines, such as that of the Unity of God, the immortality of the soul, and even the coming of Christ. These explanations of Lactantius were of little importance as a contribution to the debate on mythology, it is true; yet in a larger perspective they had far-reaching consequences, since they determined the attitude of the Renaissance Neoplatonists toward the Hermetic literature and their concept of the relationship between Platonism and Egyptian philosophy.

From all other points of view, the Egyptian pantheon played only an insignificant role in the essentially theological problematics of the Middle Ages. The Church did not favor the study of mythology in general and had inherited the Roman contempt for things Egyptian, an attitude that Eusebius expressed clearly in his prayer that "this thrice unhappy race be delivered of its long and continual blindness," which he interpreted as vile superstition. Gregory of Tours admonished the Christian scholars further: in direct reference to the mythologists, he asked that they "leave the gods where they are and return to the Gospels."

In the scholastic literature, like the *Mythologies* of Fulgentius or *The Marriage of Philosophy and Mercury* of Martianus Capella, the Egyptian myths, when alluded to, were always regarded in the light of Greek mythology and transformed into pious parables or moralizing fables after the manner of the *Physiologus*. In the centuries that followed, a number of references to Egypt and her gods appeared in scholarly encyclopedias and grammatical anthologies. But it was only toward the end of the fourteenth century that the first signs of a new approach to the problem began to appear, secular this time, freed from the constraints and prejudices of theology and nurtured by the study of the classics for their own sake. It was in Boccaccio's *Genealogy of the Gods*.

This book preceded the Neoplatonism of the Renaissance by nearly half a century, and it therefore belongs, in spite of its secular appearance, to the scholasticism of the past rather than to the humanism to come. The myths are completely secularized and transformed into pseudohistoric accounts of characters completely devoid of life, actors for a parade or a triumphant entrance. As far as the Egyptian gods were concerned, Boccaccio had in fact only a very superficial

interest. He, too, completely Hellenized Isis, Apis, and Thoth-Mercury; he considered them only on the basis of their assumed Greek origin and provided them all with Greek genealogies. Isis, for example, is regarded as the daughter of Prometheus, which is characteristic of the scholastic point of view, based in this case on the identification of the goddess with Io, who was generally considered the daughter of Iacchus, but in one obscure passage cited by Clement of Alexandria is called the daughter of Prometheus. Apis was similarly identified with Argus, the son of Zeus and Niobe, and Mercury was called the son of Milus, who was the son of Oceanus and Gaea. Boccaccio clearly considered their status as Egyptian gods to be inferior, if not a debased condition, compared with their Greek origins. Since the author had some authority and this was the first "modern" mythology, the work was referred to with great respect in subsequent literature, although it was often criticized for its lack of erudition. And based on its historical approach to the myth of Osiris, it had an influence on the pseudohistorical tradition of the following century. But as a contribution to scholarship, it was almost immediately overshadowed by the mythological studies of the fifteenth and sixteenth centuries, whose approach toward the primary source material was completely different.

II. The Renaissance

As far as the Egyptian heritage is concerned, the new attitude appeared as one of the by-products of the Neoplatonist revival inaugurated by Marsilio Ficino in his commentaries on the works of Plato and Plotinus; his book on the

Head of Serapis in imperial porphyry. Oxford, Ashmolean Museum of Art and Archaeology. Museum photo.

Pinturicchio, *Death of Osiris*. Vatican, Borgia apartments. Photo Anderson-Giraudon.

Christian religion (1478); his *Platonist Theology,* which dealt with the immortality of the soul (1482); and his translations and editions of Iamblichus and the Hermetic texts. Ficino based his idea of the historical and spiritual ties that connected Egyptian, Christian, and Platonic positions on the belief that at the highest level philosophy and religion are one, and that Platonic and Hebraic traditions prior to Christianity thus represented parallel approaches toward the same ultimate goal: the knowledge and the manifestation of God as truth and love. He believed that the Platonic tradition, which ultimately culminated in the works of Pythagorus, Plato, Plotinus, and Iamblichus, had been established by Hermes-Thoth, the greatest of the Egyptian sages, and that it was therefore inspired by his wisdom, which we also know from the authentic work of Thoth, the *Corpus Hermeticum.*

Through divine will, the Hebrews were favored with the revelation of Christ and the Gospels, a revelation that was in turn refused to the Platonists, whose teaching nevertheless represented the highest pre-Christian manifestation of inspired truth, emanating from the same divine essence that was later incarnate in Jesus. For this reason, Platonic and Hermetic traditions must be regarded as anticipations of the message of Christianity, imperfect and premature but fundamentally truthful. As Lactantius had noted, Thoth had already anticipated the essential point of this doctrine and in his *Asclepius* had even had a vague idea of the dogma of the Holy Trinity.

These principles held for Egyptian religion as well; its greatest manifestation was the myth of Osiris, as it was transmitted through Herodotus, Diodorus, Plutarch, and Apuleius. This myth tells of the treacherous murder of a benevolent god, his resurrection, and his enthronement as a savior-king and judge of the dead, all of which contributed a number of elements to the anticipation of the Passion of Christ. The gods of the myth, especially Osiris himself, Isis, his sister-spouse, Horus, their son, Anubis, his younger brother, Seth, the murderer of Osiris, and Thoth, the wise counselor of Isis, were therefore all considered manifestations of the dead Osiris, as were Apis and Serapis, completely dissociated for the first time from Greek mythology, freed from the soulless images of earlier tradition, and charged with a new spiritual significance.

As the founder of the tradition and author of the Hermetic treatises, Thoth occupied a preeminent position among the Platonists of this period. Generally known by the name of Hermes Trismegistus, the thrice-great, he was frequently called the Egyptian Moses and compared to the prophets, just as the Hermetic texts were compared to the Gospels, and one of them, the *Poimandres,* was considered the Egyptian Genesis. It was therefore only natural that Thoth's new position in the spiritual hierarchy would lead to a critical revision of the problem of his relationship to Moses. The official Platonic solution to the problem found its monumental expression in the decorated pavement tiles of the Cathedral of Sienna, completed about 1498 by Giovanni di Maestro Stefano.

Thoth is dressed in a flowing caftan, and he wears a miter on his head. He appears on the central panel in the middle of the floor in the western part of the church. The words *Hermis Mercurius Trismegistus Contemporaneus Moysi* are written near him. His left hand rests on a marble plaque carried by sphinxes and engraved with a Latin paraphrase of the passage from the *Asclepius* that was presumed to refer to the Trinity. With his right hand he holds out the Tablets of the Law toward two figures, who represent the Greeks and the Egyptians, the two populations of Egypt. On the tablets are written the words: "Receive, O Egyptians, the letters and the laws." This schema is obviously polemic and reflects the Platonist definition of Thoth in its most minute details. The fact that in a Christian church an artist was able to substitute Thoth for Moses, the oldest and the most venerable of the prophets of his religion, clearly illustrates the rivalry between the Hermetic and Hebraic traditions and the importance that the Platonists attached to the problem.

The argument continued into the next century with an ever-greater violence, and in his preface to Turnebus's edition of the *Poimandres* in 1554, Vergicius affirmed that Thoth had lived before Pharaoh, and consequently before Moses, while Flussas, going still further, indicated that Thoth "had attained an understanding of things divine that surpassed that accorded to the Hebrew prophets and equaled that of the Apostles and the Evangelists." These debates took place at the highest philosophical level, as did those on Osiris in the lectures given by Poliziano, a student of Marsilio Ficino, in Venice.

At the same time, however, a no less ardent interest in Egyptian mythology was spreading into other spheres as well, among authors who had only skimmed the surface of the Neoplatonist doctrines. Among these the most noteworthy was Giovanni Nanni de Viterbus (Annius), who in 1498 published with his own commentary an edition of what he claimed were rediscovered works of several ancient writers, among whom were the Chaldean Berosus and the Egyptian Manetho. The texts were false, probably fabricated by Annius himself, because they showed evidence of a point of view clearly influenced by Boccaccio, with the difference that the principal concern of Annius was chronology, here introduced for the first time into the problem of mythology. In the fifth book of his *Babylonian Antiquities*, Annius's Pseudo-Berosus gives a list of seventeen Babylonian sovereigns, accompanying each with a brief outline of the principal events of his reign. The most surprising thing is that all the principal episodes of the myth of Osiris have been included. Thus one learns that Osiris was born of Rhea in the twentieth year of Nino, the third king of Babylon. In the forty-third year of the reign of this same prince, Osiris was adopted by Dionysus, the son of Ammon, and made king of Egypt. Isis was born of Rhea in Egypt, in the first year of the reign of Queen Semiramis, and she invented the art of gardening and the cultivation of oats and wheat during the reign of Zamea, the fifth king. Osiris invented the plow under the reign of Berosus and shortly afterward went abroad to teach the barbarians agriculture and the cultivation of grapes. During his stay in Italy, the people of the country asked him to help them in their war against the Giants, whom he conquered. He ruled Italy for ten years after his victory and then returned to Egypt. Soon after his return, he was assassinated by Seth-Typhon, who usurped the throne with the assistance of the Giants, but who was deposed in turn by the Egyptian Hercules, son of Osiris and Isis, according to Thoth and Anubis.

In this version of the myth, which is based essentially on the account of Diodorus, the process of demythologization and reduction to history was carried to its farthest extreme, since the gods have become historical personages, and all the episodes are treated as past events. The Greek genealogies were taken from Boccaccio with one notable exception: Annius in his commentary insisted on the Egyptian ancestry of Isis and rejected her identification with Io, even though most of the mythographers had accepted this equivalence blindly on the authority of Ovid's *Metamorphoses*. There, as elsewhere, this identification rested on the association of each with the cow. In the case of Isis, this connection, which is referred to in Plutarch, goes back to an authentic Egyptian source that reflects the gradual assimilation of Isis to Hathor, the primordial cow-goddess of Egypt: a process recorded on the mythic level in the account that tells how Horus, her son, in a burst of anger cut off his mother's head, which was later

replaced with the head of a heifer. In Ovid's account, the myth of Io tells how she was carried off by Jupiter, who then changed her into a white cow to protect her from Juno's wrath. But Juno persuaded her husband to make her a gift of the cow, which she placed under the watchful eye of Argus Panoples, "He who sees all." There was nothing for Jupiter to do but suggest to Mercury that he kill Argus, which he did, and Io was chased around the world by a gadfly sent after her by Juno. She finally arrived on the banks of the Nile where she was restored to her human form and was worshiped as Isis by the Egyptians.

Annius's book was much studied before it was unmasked as a fraud, and there is no doubt that his insistence on the Egyptian ancestry of Isis helped to liberate the Egyptian gods from their Greek chains. As a more immediate consequence, the distinction between the myths of Io and Isis was clearly illustrated by Pintorrichio in his ceiling decoration in the Borgia apartments in the Vatican. On one side the principal episodes of the myth of Osiris are shown in six panels, representing (1) the marriage of Isis and Osiris; (2) Osiris and Isis teaching horticulture and farming; (3) the murder of Osiris by Typhon and the Giants; (4) Isis with the dismembered body of Osiris and his funeral ensemble; (5) the miraculous appearance of Apis at the tomb of Osiris; and (6) the triumph of Apis, an episode which had been completely invented by Annius, whose direct influence on the iconographic design is evident. The influence involves a substitution of Apis for Isis, an unusual development, the reasons for which we shall consider later. The figures are painted in an affected style, extremely stylized, and their exotic nature is indicated solely by their clothing and sophisticated headdresses. Except for Apis, they all appear in human form with nothing indicating their divinity, which agrees perfectly with the Euhemerism of the historical connections made by Boccaccio and Annius. The Egyptian background of the entire account, however, is discretely indicated by the sepulcher of Osiris, in the shape of a pyramid.

But accompanying the main theme there are five smaller panels that illustrate five episodes of Ovid's version of the myth of Io. These are (1) Io courted by Jupiter, (2) the metamorphosis he effects to protect her from Juno's wrath, (3) Argus lured to sleep by Mercury's flute, (4) the murder of Argus, and (5) Io in human form consecrated anew as the Queen of Egypt. Since it illustrated the *Metamorphoses*, this cycle of Io had to include the representation of Io deified, but for the rest, the distinction between the two myths is maintained even in the very style used to represent them, because the completely Arcadian simplicity of the series dedicated to Io contrasts sharply with the mannered style of the Osirian cycle.

The reason behind this nonetheless rather surprising choice of the myth of Osiris to decorate one of the private apartments of the sovereign pontiff becomes evident in the panel where the bull replaces Isis as the central figure in the triumphal procession which, according to Apuleius, always ended the goddess's annual festival. To flatter Alexander VI, Annius had followed the practice of Roman genealogists, who were great inventors of heroic ancestries for their noble patrons. He identified the bull Apis with the bull on the coat of arms of the Borgia family, thus establishing a direct line between Osiris and the pope, whose first ancestor was none other than Osiris-Apis himself through the intermediary of his son, the Egyptian Hercules. It was very much in the spirit of Annius, pseudohistoric and secular, that Osiris was reduced in the Vatican to such common ends as genealogical vanity.

This was not, however, an isolated case. Olivier de la Marche, in his *Memoires*, which covered the period from 1435 to 1488, retraced the ancestry of the dukes of Burgundy as far back as Hercules the Egyptian, who supposedly visited Flanders in his voyages around the world; and Johannes Turmair (Aventinus, 1470–1534), founder of German historiography, wrote in his *Chronicle* of Bavaria that the Emperor Maximilian was descended from King Osiris. He based this connection on the existence of an ancient German cult of Isis mentioned by Tacitus and on the ancient folk tradition that identified Apis with the Golden Calf of the book of Exodus, a motif also used by Filippo Lippi in 1490 in the famous painting now hanging in the National Gallery. The Egyptian fashion in the field of genealogy proved remarkably durable, since even in 1600 the anonymous author of the *Royal Labyrinth of the Gallic Hercules Triumphant* could flatter Maria de Medici by having her royal spouse descend from Hispalus, the Spanish son of the Egyptian Hercules.

III. Reformation and Counter-Reformation

In Catholic countries as well as Protestant countries, the Reformation and Counter-Reformation in the following century led to a new attitude toward mythology. In the midst of debates on erudition and theology, Neoplatonism retreated into the background; it was replaced by a return to the orthodoxy of the Old Testament, and apparently, in mythological studies, the center of gravity changed from the subtle metaphysics of the heirs of Plato to pure and solid science, as is demonstrated by the *Mythology* of Lilio Gregorio Giraldi, published in 1548 under the title *De deis gentium varia et multiplex historia*.

Although it amounted to an enormous compilation of raw data rather than a systematic study, this book represented the first serious attempt to consider mythology according to its own laws and as an autonomous object of study. It made a clear distinction between Greek and Egyptian mythologies; Egyptian gods are no longer considered simple reflections of their Greek counterparts in an exotic mirror, but are considered independent figures with an independent existence in myth. From the point of view of methodology, it is also of the greatest importance that the facts in this case are treated in an entirely objective style and no longer merely as support for preconceived ideas or personal or partisan opinions. The author borrowed from all accessible sources, that is to say, not only those that were well known and basically traditional, but from innumerable obscure authors and publications and from unpublished manuscripts as well. The work still places the gods of the Osirian cycle in the foreground, but it also adds mythological figures that had been left out until then, like Ibis, correctly identified as "lunae avis et tutela Toth," and Canopus, whose obscure origins would make him a figure of great controversy.

It is, moreover, a very curious fact that no divinity by the name of Canopus ever appears in even the most insignificant Egyptian text, and that all relevant information regarding him comes from later classical sources or archaeological artifacts of the Greek and Roman periods. The literary texts of later antiquity refer occasionally to a god of the waters sometimes associated with Poseidon or Neptune but called also Serapis Hydreius or Serapis Canopites, who had a cult in the village of Canopus, about twenty kilometers from Alexandria on an estuary of the Nile. It seems that the Egyptians of the region considered him a manifestation of the drowned Osiris whose corpse had reached the sea by way of a branch of the river that passes by Canopus. They worshiped him in the form of a potbellied jar topped with a human head, which supposedly represented Osiris, and they sometimes added a female figure to represent Isis. The jar stands on a garland of roses (this is well known from the description of the cult of Isis and Osiris by Apuleius), and was probably a hollow vessel that served as a receptacle for fresh river water, purified by its contact with the corpse of the god and consequently believed to be capable of overpowering the impure waters of the sea. Representations of this divinity were discovered on Roman coins from the times of Hadrian and Antoninus Pius, as well as in high-relief sculptures, both in full figure in limestone or terra-cotta and on decorative vessels.

But this simple and reasonable interpretation of the cultural nature of the god was obscured by the Hellenistic speculations of Greek and Roman mythologists, who tried to identify him with the Greek Canopus (Kanobus), the helmsman of Menelaus. On his return from Troy, this Canopus was bitten by a snake in Egypt and died there. He was then deified by the Egyptians, who placed him with the ship Argo among the stars. The association of Canopus with the constellations Argo and Eridanus (the latter sometimes associated with the Nile) led Petrarch to identify this deified Greek with the mythical navigator of the boat of Osiris, and his Egyptian wife Menuthis with Isis, thus deifying the protagonists of a Greek legend by integrating them with Egyptian mythology.

Last is the story that more than any other came to intrigue and fascinate mythologists of the Renaissance. It is found in the *Historia ecclesiastica* of Rufinus (2.11.26) and was evidently borrowed from a folktale. Rufinus tells how a group of itinerant Chaldean priests once carried their god of fire around the world, challenging other gods to rival him, in the hope that their god would consume those images and prove himself superior. But the priests of Canopus made holes in the face of their god, which then took on the form of a jar, and stopped up the holes again with wax. They filled the jar with water so that when the Chaldeans lit their fire all around, the wax melted and the water ran out. When the flames were extinguished, Canopus was proclaimed champion and the most powerful of all the gods.

It was very difficult for the mythologists of the sixteenth and seventeenth centuries to synthesize these confusing and contradictory data, and the problem was further complicated when archaeology entered the debate. Archaeologists wrongly identified Canopus, first with the "block statues" of Egyptian art and then with the stone jars with human or zoomorphic heads that the ancient Egyptians used as receptacles for the viscera of the dead. These assimilations gave rise to still more speculations and new theories, and although the problem of his origin and nature was never resolved, Canopus resurfaced often (although always with some controversy) in the debate that followed the publication of Giraldi's *Mythology*—to the point that (and there is something curiously reminiscent in this) the Egyptologists of our time continue to refer to these viscera jars from ancient Egypt quite improperly as canopic jars.

In 1551, the great work of Giraldi was followed by Natale Conti's *Mythologiae sive explicationum fabularum libri X*, a less scholarly but more accessible book that has been published in more than twenty editions since its publication in 1627. The author was less ambitious; he sought to amuse as much as to instruct. Clearly influenced by the propensity to allegory that Alciati had made into a literary genre in his *Emblemata* (1531), Natale Conti revived the allegorical interpretation of myth, explaining, for example, the myth of Isis

Left: Pinturicchio, *Meeting of Isis and Osiris.* Vatican, Borgia apartments. Photo Anderson-Giraudon.

Below: Pinturicchio, *Osiris teaching men how to grow fruit trees.* Vatican, Borgia apartments. Photo by Anderson-Giraudon.

Filippo Lippi. *The Golden Calf.* London, National Gallery. Museum photo.

and Io as a subtle allegory of the human spirit, tortured by sexual desire, then pursued by the gadfly of reproach, and finally redeemed and deified through remorse. For each of the gods, taking them one by one, he followed a similar idea. Seth-Typhon, who is identified with Python on the basis of the inversion of the letters *t* and *p*, was regarded as the untamed strength of underground volcanic fire, as well as the atmospheric disturbances of the highest reaches of the sky, provoking storms and cyclones. The murder of Osiris by his hand and the punishment that was later inflicted on him by Horus was, in Conti's view, an allegory warning against unbridled ambition.

Conti's taste for the bizarre and enigmatic led him to attach great importance to the appearances of the gods, their emblems, and their attributes. His portrait of Seth-Typhon is characteristic; he borrows heavily from the horrifying description in Macrobius, who depicts Seth-Typhon as a fire-breathing monster with multiple heads, covered with feathers and surrounded by snakes.

Directly inspired by Conti, Vincenzo Cantari published *Le imagini colla sposizione degli dei degli antichi* in 1556. This was the first mythology ever written in the vernacular, and it had even more success than Conti's work. In its 1571 edition, with illustrations by Bolognino Zaltieri, it was also the first illustrated mythology of its time, although the representations of the gods were still fantastic inventions based on the descriptions of the ancients and not on authentic archaeological data. Of the Egyptian gods, Jupiter-Ammon is shown in human form but with horns on his head and cloaked in an animal skin to recall his mythic association with the Ram. Thoth appears as Mercury, according to convention, and Isis, identified with Io, appears in human form, carrying the boat that recalls her ties to the constellation Argo and her journeys in Egypt. Although an Egyptian goddess, she also conforms to Apuleius's description, which makes her into a Ceres in her star-studded dress. This reminds us that she is also identified with Sirius and that she is the queen of the night sky. She carries her usual symbol, the *sistrum*, which Zaltieri made into a tambourine, and her head is decorated with stalks of wheat.

A divinity with the head of a falcon, who was, the text states explicitly, worshiped by the Egyptians, is later identified as the male Hecate, or Apollo. This appears to be the first modern representation of Horus, the god with the head of a falcon, who is compared to Apollo in other texts as well. As for Seth-Typhon, his description is entirely based on Macrobius and Natale Conti. Serapis is compared to Osiris and Pluto as god of the netherworld, an elderly man wearing a wheat measure, or *modius*, on his head and carrying in his right hand a measuring stick. In accordance with Macrobius's description, his *signum triceps* appears nearby, a monster with three heads: of a lion, a dog, and a wolf. They join to form the body of a serpent who turns toward the god. The real meaning behind this representation remains obscure, but it should probably be compared to the man-eating monster of the Egyptian *Book of the Dead*, in which it is shown facing Osiris. In classical mythological literature, this monster was frequently identified with the infernal dog Cerberus. This enigmatic creature had fascinated and intrigued ancient mythologists as much as modern mythologists, and Petrarch (*Africa*, 3.158) had already agreed with Macrobius in interpreting it as a symbol of "fleeting time," the head of the wolf representing the past, the lion, the present, and the dog, the future, while the serpent signified time itself in its continuous, unending path. Understood in this way the monster became one of the recurrent motifs of art and

literature, and inspired Giordano Bruno, who would sign in his own blood his faith in the Hermetic gospel, in an extremely moving sonnet. In Cesare Ripa's *Iconology* (1611) and elsewhere, the sign meant "Good Counsel" and was even used occasionally as an allegory for "Prudence," the heads in this case becoming those of a man in youth, maturity, and old age.

Canopus also appeared in the work, with the features that would become conventional in later iconography: a pitcher with a man's head, spouting water from its rounded pot-belly, and with tiny legs, as described by Rufinus. Harpocrates also appeared, another false idea that was also destined to recur regularly in the mythic literature. This name is the Hellenized version of the Egyptian *Har-pe-hered*, meaning the child Horus, in contrast with Haroeris, the older Horus. To indicate childhood, Egyptian art depicted the god sucking his thumb. The Greeks and Romans, however, took this to be an exhortation to silence, more particularly to silence about secrets of the cult and esoteric beliefs. In the mythologies of the classical era as well as those of the sixteenth century, Harpocrates became the god of silence, a child pressing a finger to his lips.

During the second half of the sixteenth century, interest in Egyptian mythology spread to other circles, because fashion had turned toward hieroglyphs. This was the time when more or less fantastic references to Egyptian letters, symbols, and hieroglyphs made their way into the rapidly growing allegorical and iconographical literature, culminating in the publication of the huge encyclopedia of allegorical hieroglyphs by Piero Valeriano, the *Hieroglyphica* of 1556. It would seem that the scholarly tradition, philological at the beginning of the century, reached its peak with Giraldi and then gave way to the literary and esoteric use of mythological data largely reinforced with allegorical interpretations.

IV. The Tablet of Isis and the Beginnings of Comparatism

But the literary and esoteric use of mythology did not last long. The century was hardly over when the old taste for Egyptian mythology as such was suddenly and feverishly revived by the discovery of what was called the Tablet of Isis. In fact, the place of origin of this rectangular bronze plaque, with engraved mythological figures inlaid in gold and silver, is unknown. We know only that it was first found in Rome in 1525 under obscure circumstances, and that a little later, in 1527, it was acquired by Cardinal Bembo and was subsequently known as the "Tabula Bembina." Today it is preserved in the Museum of Turin. It is an object from the late Roman Empire, probably made in Italy at a time when both the artistic and the hieroglyphic traditions of ancient Egypt were dying out, but its decoration undoubtedly follows authentic Egyptian models from much earlier times, used here simply for ornamental purposes and no longer for religious purposes.

The "hieroglyphic" inscriptions that appear on it, composed of symbols that the artist had for the most part completely invented, had clearly lost all scriptural significance and were used only to mark boundaries between the panels. The center panel shows Isis on her throne. There are no less than thirty-five mythological figures around the goddess; among them Thoth with the head of an ibis, Ptah of Memphis, Horus with the head of a falcon, Anubis with the head of a dog, Sekhmet with the head of a lion, and the bulls of Apis and Mnevis can be clearly recognized. Surrounding this is a whole collection of secondary figures in the form of crocodiles, sphinxes, dogfaced baboons, canopic vases, scarabs, scorpions, and various mummies amid a profusion of cultic objects and symbols, such as crowns, headpieces and diadems, staffs, scepters, and vases, intermixed with mysterious emblems and hieroglyphs that mystified scholars took for authentic Egyptian artifacts.

All of this was engraved by Eneas Vico in 1559, and his prints were reprinted and sold by Giacomo Franco in Venice; but the publication subsequently referred to was an annotated edition published in 1605 by Lorenzo Pignoria, entitled *Vetustissimae Tabulae aeneae . . . explicatio.*

From the point of view of the results obtained, the purely speculative efforts of Pignoria to resolve the enigma of the tablet did not differ substantially from those that his predecessors had obtained from other sources, and his importance to the study of mythology rests not on his contribution to the solution to the problems of Egyptian religion but on his introduction of a new method. Through his study of the mythological details of the tablet, he discovered the possibilities for understanding, unsuspected until then, that could be opened by comparing objects with other objects of a similar or related nature. He began to illustrate his theories and interpretations not only with reproductions of the figures on the tablet but also with a wealth of material borrowed from other sources, coins, for example, or amulets, seals, bronzes, and statues, all of which he had found in his own excavations or tracked down in collections of antique objects.

His interpretations were often fantastic and misleading, but the new method stimulated interest among collectors of Egyptian objects and other enthusiasts. It also encouraged mythologists to pay more attention to these objects, making them gradually more critical and independent in regard to the classics. Pignoria went still further, however. In close connection with his study of the tablet, he published *Le vere e nove imagini de gli dei de gli antichi* (1615), a revised edition of Cartari's book, in which he used reproductions of the gods from the tablet in a comparison with the gods of India, advancing the theory that the Indian gods were actually of Egyptian origin. He supported this with Diodorus's account of the voyages of Osiris. As Pignoria formulated it the theory was obviously untenable, but once introduced, it entrenched itself to such an extent that, placed in conjunction with the old theory of India's colonization in the time of Sesostris, it was still taken seriously by Newton in his chronological studies. It is not necessary to judge a new method by its short-term results, and Pignoria's method may very well have opened up the entire fields of comparative mythology and comparative religions, as well as comparative archaeology.

At approximately the same time, around 1610, Herwart von Hohenburg published his *Thesaurus Hieroglyphicorum*, the greatest collection of documents on Egyptian mythology ever published until that time. Another book by him was published by his son in 1623 after his death; in it he defended the thesis that all Egyptian gods represented natural phenomena. Among the objects used to illustrate the *Thesaurus* were a false Roman votive stela with the figure of Anubis, a "block statue" that he wrongly identified with Canopus, and a magnificent authentic Canopus, among a profusion of gems, amulets, and other objects supposedly charged with esoteric meanings. The etched engravings, by Nicolaus van Aelst, were often copied in later publications on the subject.

Toward the middle of the century Pignoria's theory of the Egyptian origin of the Indian gods was revived by Athanasius Kircher and was amplified so as to include the gods of China, Japan, and even the Americas. Kircher's *Oedipus Aegyptiacus*, published in 1652, could be considered the apex

Isis enthroned. Detail of the Tablet of Isis. Turin, Soprintendenza archeologica. Photo Rosso.

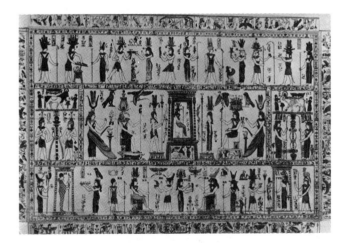

The Tablet of Isis. Turin, Soprintendenza archeologica. Photo Rosso.

not only of all the studies on Egyptology of the century but of the whole Neoplatonist tradition in this area. Kircher himself acknowledged that he had set out to give a complete idea of the religion, theosophy, and philosophy of Egypt, which he held to be inseparable and even identical in theory. His method was based on decoding the hieroglyphs, each of which, he believed, concealed one concept or one cosmological idea, identical with those described by the treatises of

Frontispiece from *Pignorii mensa isiaca*. 1669. Oxford, Ashmolean Museum of Art and Archaeology. Museum photo.

late Neoplatonism or Hermeticism, along with each religious symbol, representation, and figure. The Egyptian gods were the elemental forces of the cosmos in the midst of a universe that emanated from an invisible divine center by crossing four spheres in succession: the idea, the intellect, the sidereal regions, and the elemental world, each of which represents a spiritual level and is also united with all the others by the endless play of forces that rise or fall. Kircher compared these forces to the gods, who had different forms and functions according to the level at which they were sought.

At the highest level, Amon, for example, represented "divine will," or "that which brings to light the hidden causes or secret forces." But at a lower level, he was "cosmic heat and humidity," which "assured the perpetual generation of matter through elevation and descent." At the elemental level, he was Agathodaemon, as he was present in the ibis. Typhon or Seth represented the confused combination of elements and evil forces which are present everywhere in the universe and which on the elemental level signified a confused mind, or the faults, such as hate, envy, and hypocrisy, that are allegorically expressed in the monstrous appearance of the god described by Macrobius and illustrated by Zaltieri. Isis was the "natura panmorpha," the "mater universae naturae," but also the moon, the queen of the earth, the sea, and the stars. She incarnated the force of

fertile and fruitful nature, the passive principle that could be seen as complementary to the active, penetrating force signified by Osiris. And the combination of the two forces was Horus, their son, the third term of the highest triad, the right-angled triangle of geometry.

Thus, by associating each god or goddess, each hieroglyph, and each sculpture or bas-relief with a Neoplatonist idea or concept and by revealing their esoteric and cosmic meaning through what he called the *lectio idealis*, Kircher was soon in a position to make a grandiose harmony within his dynamic unity at the heart of an ideally reordered cosmos. His axioms were false and his conclusions untenable in our eyes, but one should give credit to an accomplishment that is rigorously appropriate to the premises and logic of the method. Yet it was "ein End und kein Beginn," an end and not a beginning, because in the astounding fireworks of his erudition, mental agility, and phantasmagoria, the whole of Neoplatonist Egyptology was consumed. It would only be revived, as we will soon see, in very different form in other sectors of society.

V. The Eighteenth Century

After efforts as extensive as those of Giraldi and Kircher, it was very difficult to draw the slightest new information out of this overworked data. As far as Egypt was concerned, the debates on mythology in the second half of the seventeenth century were no more than resifted discussions and sterile polemics. Books for the general public, like Pomey's *Pantheum mythicum* (1688), simply fell into the didacticism of reducing myths to moralizing fables, and though the divinities and hieroglyphs were still very much present in allegorical and emblematic literature, there was hardly any serious study of Egyptian mythology except by antiquarians and other enthusiasts of ancient things. The antiquarians went excavating and developed collections—it had become a fashion among the rich and the idle, much as it is today. Montfaucon tells us that at the beginning of the eighteenth century, Greek, Roman, and Egyptian artifacts were being found daily in Rome. This same Montfaucon published accounts of almost everything found from 1719 to 1724 in an enormous fifteen-volume encyclopedia, *Antiquity Explained and Represented in Pictures*, which covered all the known aspects of classical and Egyptian civilizations.

Montfaucon was a friend of Greece and a true son of the rationalism of his day, and therefore he admired neither the art nor the wisdom of Egypt. He considered the religion "monstrous"; he rejected all the interpretations that Neoplatonism had given it and substituted his own. According to Montfaucon, the entire Egyptian pantheon reflected nothing more than a simple dualistic belief in the eternal conflict between good and evil. The principle of good was represented by the gods of the Osirian triad and evil by Seth and his acolytes. Even if in theory good was stronger than evil, in reality it could not triumph, and that was all that the Osirian myth had to say. The art wasn't worth much more. Montfaucon considered the statuary "horrible" or at least "bizarre," and while he felt it his duty to reproduce the gods and mythological figures of Egypt, he took care to indicate that this was only for historical reasons.

This was approximately the point of view of de Caylus, his successor, who published his *Collection of Egyptian, Etruscan, Greek, Roman, and Gallic Antiquities* between 1752 and 1767. But in spite of this lack of sympathy for Egypt, the two publications were invaluable sources of iconographic material, and they greatly increased the interest of artists and artisans of the time in Egyptian motifs. The German goldsmith Melchior Dinglinger, for example, built an altar of Apis around 1730. The works of Piranesi date from shortly thereafter. It is also curious to observe that even while Montfaucon complained of the futility and the tedious nature of the mythological discussion and mocked the philologists who were enslaved by the classical authors, reeling off endless wearisome citations to explain the slightest critical significance, the ancient scholarly tradition was flourishing again, for better or for worse, in the *Pantheon Aegyptiorum* (1750–52) of Paul Ernst Jablonski, a work that was to become for the eighteenth century what the *Mythology* of Giraldi was for the seventeenth. Within the scholarly milieu of the times, Jablonski's scholarship was considered a salutary reaction to the extravagances of Neoplatonism, even though his own approach to religious, historical, and chronological problems seems to us hardly less speculative.

The three volumes of his work form a series of monographs devoted to the principal divinities of Egypt: Ptah, Osiris, Amon, Horus, Serapis, Apis, Harpocrates, Isis, and Hathor, a much wider field than that of earlier mythologies. The analysis was based completely, or almost completely, on literary sources known at the time. Like Kircher, Jablonski resorted to his knowledge of Coptic for his etymologies, which were unfortunately dubious more often than not, and he took pleasure in emphasizing the autonomous nature of the Egyptian gods with respect to the Greeks. But his efforts as a theoretician to put this enormous mass of facts into a single homogenous system of dogma and doctrine was doomed to failure. His fundamental theory was that the Egyptians had adored the God of the Pentateuch and the patriarchs until about three hundred years after the Flood. It was only then that they succumbed to idolatry and superstition. Their new gods had spread not only to Greece and Rome but to India and all the other countries of the Orient. In Egypt, the vestiges of the ancient faith survived in the cult of the god of Thebes, Kneph-Ammon, in whom Jablonski saw the supreme manifestation of *nous*, the active principle in the universe. He saw him as uncreated and immortal, in contrast to the secondary zoomorphic deities who were created and perishable. In its Osirian form, the Egyptian religion was in Jablonski's view essentially a type of physics, since Osiris, Serapis, Isis, and all the other protagonists of the myth directly incarnated celestial phenomena, such as the sun, the sky, and the earth's interior, the moon in its different phases, the constellations, the planets, and the stars.

Strongly supported by references, citations, and fantastic etymologies, his theories gained favor, and although he was as modest as he was benevolent, Jablonski's erudition forced the scholars of subsequent generations into timid acceptance, a situation that is not without its parallels in more recent Egyptology. There was, meanwhile, one very refreshing exception to this rule, the little book by President De Brosse which appeared in 1760, *On the Cult of the Fetish Gods, or Parallels between the Ancient Religion of Egypt and the Present-day Religion of Nigritia*. In a totally unorthodox and original way, the author essentially rejects all the presuppositions of previous studies in favor of a direct attempt at comparison between Egyptian religion and the practices of the tribes of West and Central Africa. But De Brosse's ideas were almost completely suppressed during his lifetime, and until Champollion and his great decipherment the problem of Egyptian mythology withered in Jablonski's shadow.

VI. Osiriomania, from Terrasson to Mozart

Just as when a wave is stopped in one place it creates new outlets and interests somewhere else, for the rest of the century the Egyptian mirage continued to perpetuate itself very well, but this time in a literary form, through its influence on the imitators of Fénelon's didactic and moralizing novel, *Telemachus* (1699). Fénelon's immediate successor, Michael Andrew Ramsey, included a description, certainly fantastic, of the mysteries of Isis in his didactic novel, *The Voyages of Cyrus with a Discourse on Mythology* (1728). However, the book that was to spread the Osiriomania so characteristic of the end of the century more than any other was *Sethos, a Life Drawn from the Monuments of Ancient Egypt*, published in 1731 by the Abbot of Terrasson, the translator of Diodorus. Within a pseudohistorical framework, it describes the education and spiritual growth of the young prince Sethos, the "Egyptian Telemachus," whose vicissitudes and ultimate rise to perfection are meant to assert certain moral, social, and political principles; it was a fusion of a vague social and cosmopolitan idealism with the ethics of a Christianity rationalized in the spirit of Freemasonry. Strangely, this very secular message was presented as a highly ritualized and abstract metaphysics, culminating in the hero's solemn accession to the sacred mysteries of Isis and Osiris after long trials of initiation "by fire and water," in which he tested and proved his courage, physical as well as moral.

Panorama of Egypt. Frontispiece to the first edition of the *Description of Egypt*. Oxford, Queen's College. Photo Bodleian Library.

Thanks to Tannevot, in 1739 *Sethos* presided over the appearance of Isis and Osiris on the theatrical scene. Then Cahusac and Rameau wrote an opera-ballet in 1749 entitled *The Celebration of Hymen and Love, or The Gods of Egypt*, in which three acts took place successively under the symbols of Osiris, Canopus, and Haroeris, before the finale that evoked the celebration of Isis. Lenoir depicted the same celebration in his 1814 painting. Cahusac and Rameau produced a sequel to their first Egyptian success in 1754, another ballet on an analogous subject, this one entitled *The Birth of Osiris*.

Meanwhile, and because of translations of Ramsey and Terrasson, the Osirian fashion spread to Germany, inspiring von Koppen's *Crata Repoa, or Initiation into the Ancient Society of the Egyptian Priests* (1770), Gebler's drama *Thamis* (1771), and Wieland's *Dschinnistan* (1786–89), as well as the attacks by Goethe and Schiller against the excesses of the Egyptian mania. Spiess wrote *Mysteries of the Ancient Egyptians* from a sense of "irresistible nostalgia for Egypt," and J. G. Naumann wrote his opera *Osiride*, performed in Dresden in 1781 for the Duke's wedding. The apex of this long succession of dreams and works was Mozart's *Magic Flute*, written to a text by Schikaneder in which whole passages were taken directly from *Sethos*. Before being admitted into the Osirian world of light and truth, Mozart's hero Tamino must undergo various ordeals and purifications by fire and water, under the guidance of the high priest Sarastro, who embodies all of the Osirian virtues. The character of Sarastro, according to local tradition, owed much to Ignaz von Born, a geologist from Vienna, who had opened his *Journal for Freemasons* with a long study of the mysteries of Egypt, and who was master of the masonic lodge *For True Harmony* to which Mozart and Schikaneder both belonged.

It is possible that the so-called Egyptian ritual introduced to the Freemasons by the French reformers of the eighteenth century was based more or less directly on the descriptions that Terrasson had given of the initiation of Sethos. It is very striking, for example, that among all the devotees and prophets in this strange neo-Osirian religion, there is hardly one who was not a high-ranking Freemason. It is not surprising then, if the ideals, virtues, and principles of this humanitarian and enlightened masonry can be recognized in their works. But nothing else provides a clearer proof of the vigor and power of fascination of occult Egyptian wisdom, since this was the cloak that these convinced rationalists used to shelter their own rituals and doctrines.

E.I./d.b.

BIBLIOGRAPHY

J. BALTŠAITIS, *Essai sur la légende d'un mythe: La quête d'Isis* (Paris 1967). R. H. H. CUST, *The Pavement Masters of Siena* (London 1901). F. EHRLE and E. STEVENSON, *Gli affreschi del Pinturicchio nell'appartamento Borgia del Palazzo Apostolico Vaticano* (Rome 1897). R. ENKING, "Der Apis-Altar Johs. Melchior Dinglingers: Ein Beitrag zur Auseinandersetzung des Abenlandes mit den alten Aegypten," *Leipziger aegyptologischen Studien* 11 (Glückstadt 1939). A. J. FESTUGIÉRE, *La révélation d'Hermes Trismégiste*, 1–5 (Paris 1950–54). K. GIEHLOW, "Die Hieroglyphenkunde des Humanismus in der Allegorie der Renaissance," *Jahrbuch der Kunsthistorischen Sammlungen des Allerhöchsten Kaiserhauses* (Vienna 1915). E. IVERSEN, *The Myth of Egypt and Its Hieroglyphs* (Copenhagen 1961). S. MORENZ, *Die Zauberflöthe: Eine Studie zum Lebenszusammenhang Aegypten- Antike- Abendland* (Münster and Cologne 1952); *Aegyptische Religion* (Stuttgart 1960); *Die Begegnung Europas mit Aegypten* (Zurich 1969). G. D. NOCK and A. J. FESTUGIÉRE, *Corpus Hermeticum*, 1–4 (Paris 1945–54). E. PANOFSKY and F. SAXL, "A Late Antique Religious Symbol in Works by Holbein and Titian," *Burlington Magazine* 49 (1926). E. PANOFSKY, "Hercules am Scheidewege und andere antike Bildstoffe," in *Der neueren Kunst*, Studien der Bibliothek Warburg, 18 (Leipzig and Berlin 1930), 1–35; "Titian's Allegory on Prudence: A Postscript," *Meaning in the Visual Arts* 4 (New York 1955); "Canopus Deus: The Iconography of a Nonexisting God," *Gazette des Beaux-Arts*, April 1961. F. SAXL, "The appartamento Borgia," in *Lectures*, Warburg Institute (London 1957), 174–88. E. SCAMUZZI, *Egyptian Art in the Egyptian Museum of Turin* (Turin 1964). W. SCOTT, *Hermetica*, 1–4 (Oxford 1924–36). J. SEZNEC, *The Survival of the Pagan Gods* (New York 1953). L. VOLKMANN, *Bilderschriften der Renaissance*, 1962. E. WIND, *Pagan Mysteries of the Renaissance* (London 1968). F. YATES, *Giordano Bruno and the Hermetic Tradition* (London 1964).

Index

Italicized numbers denote pages containing illustrations